THE BATMAN WHO LAUGHS

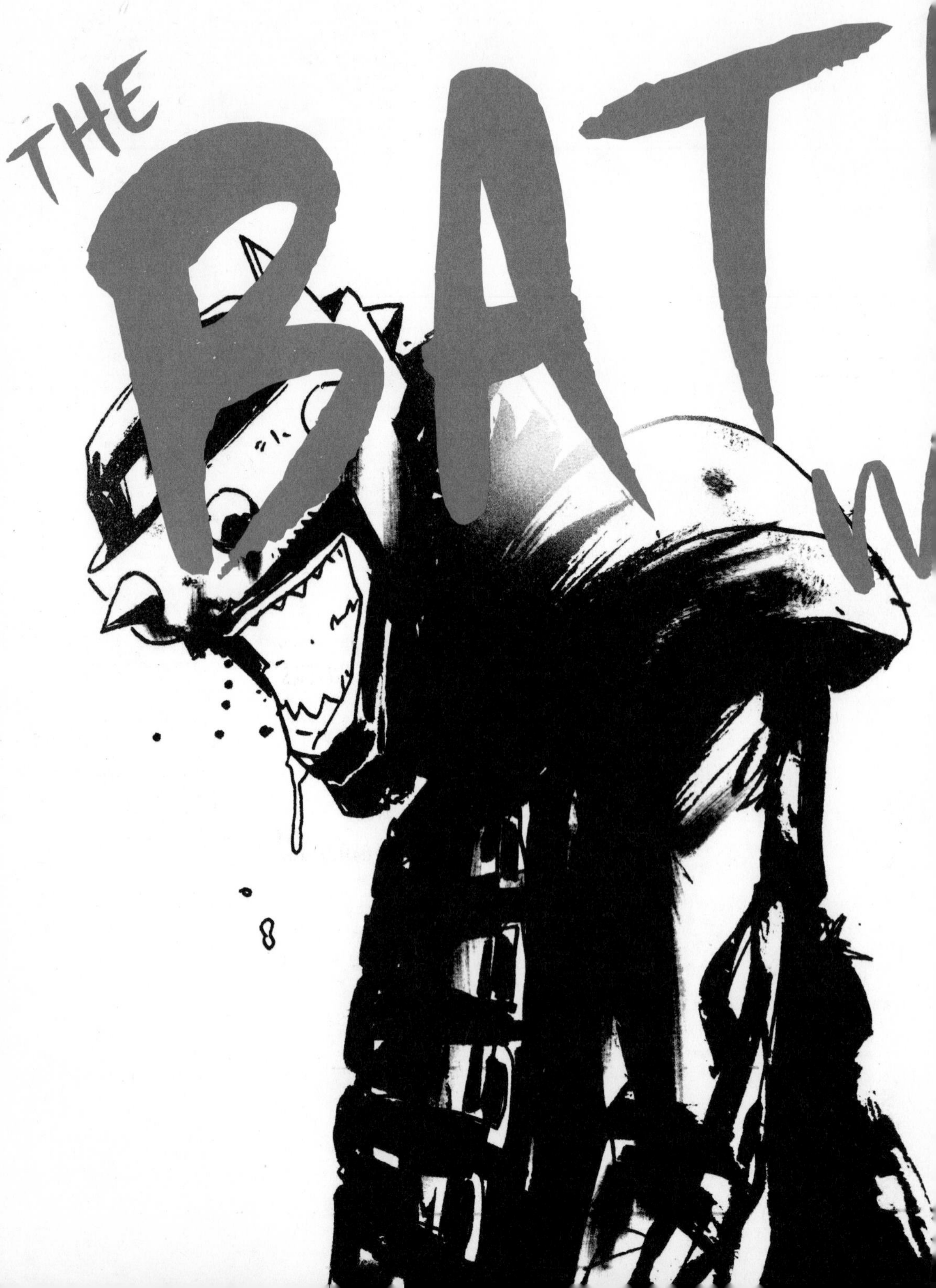
THE
BAT

SCOTT SNYDER JAMES TYNION IV **WRITERS**

JOCK EDUARDO RISSO **ARTISTS**

DAVID BARON DAVE STEWART **COLORISTS**

SAL CIPRIANO **LETTERER**

JOCK **COLLECTION COVER ARTIST**

BATMAN CREATED BY BOB KANE WITH BILL FINGER

KATIE KUBERT Editor – Original Series
DAVE WIELGOSZ Assistant Editor – Original Series
ROBIN WILDMAN Editor – Collected Edition
STEVE COOK Design Director – Books
MONIQUE NARBONETA Publication Design
KATE DURRÉ Publication Production

MARIE JAVINS Editor-in-Chief, DC Comics

DANIEL CHERRY III Senior VP – General Manager
JIM LEE Publisher & Chief Creative Officer
DON FALLETTI VP – Manufacturing Operations & Workflow Management
LAWRENCE GANEM VP – Talent Services
ALISON GILL Senior VP – Manufacturing & Operations
NICK J. NAPOLITANO VP – Manufacturing Administration & Design
NANCY SPEARS VP – Revenue
MICHELE R. WELLS VP & Executive Editor, Young Reader

THE BATMAN WHO LAUGHS

DC Comics, 2900 West Alameda Ave., Burbank, CA 91505
Printed by Transcontinental Interglobe, Beauceville, QC, Canada. 2/26/21. First Printing.
ISBN: 978-1-77950-446-3

Library of Congress Cataloging-in-Publication Data is available.

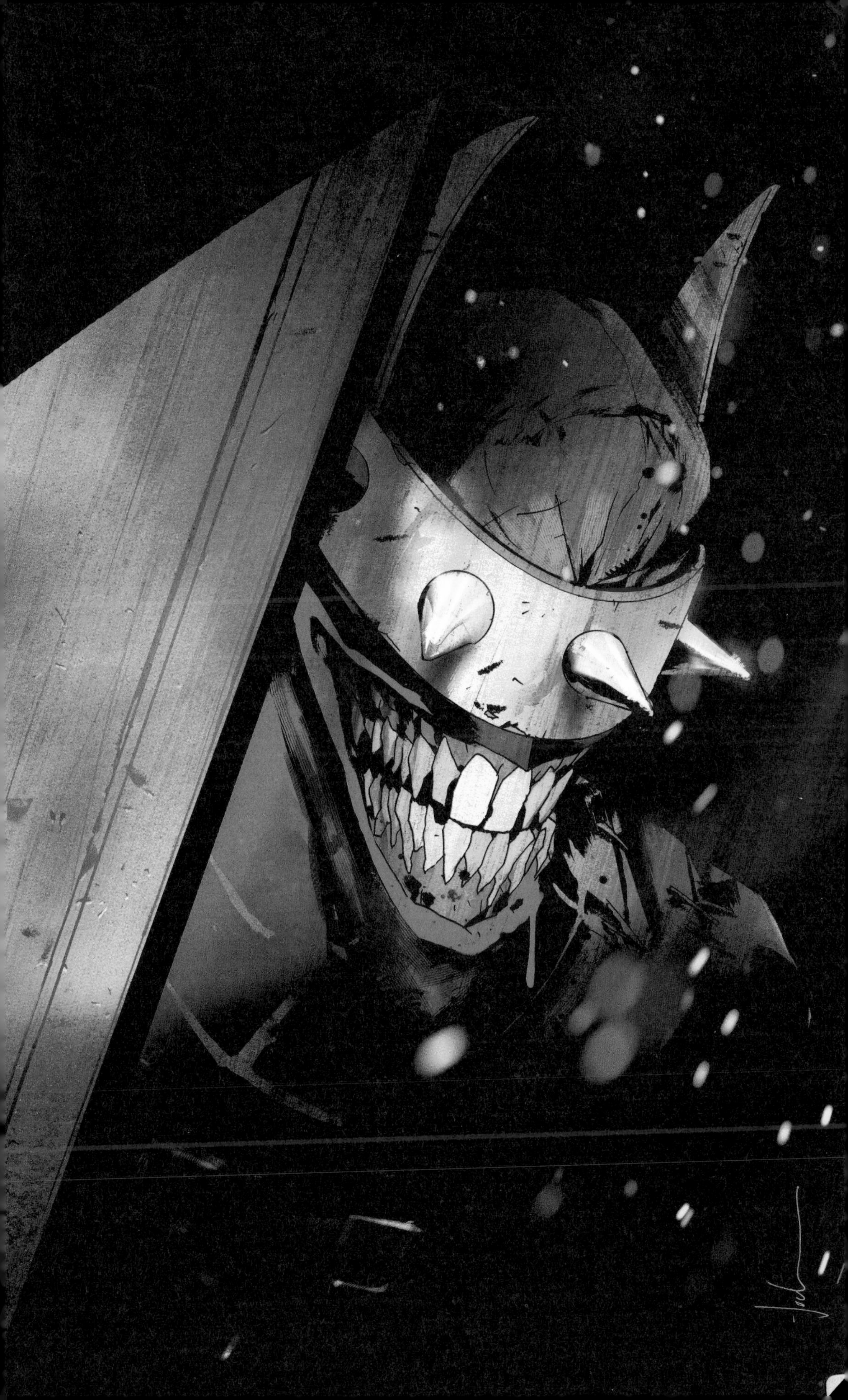

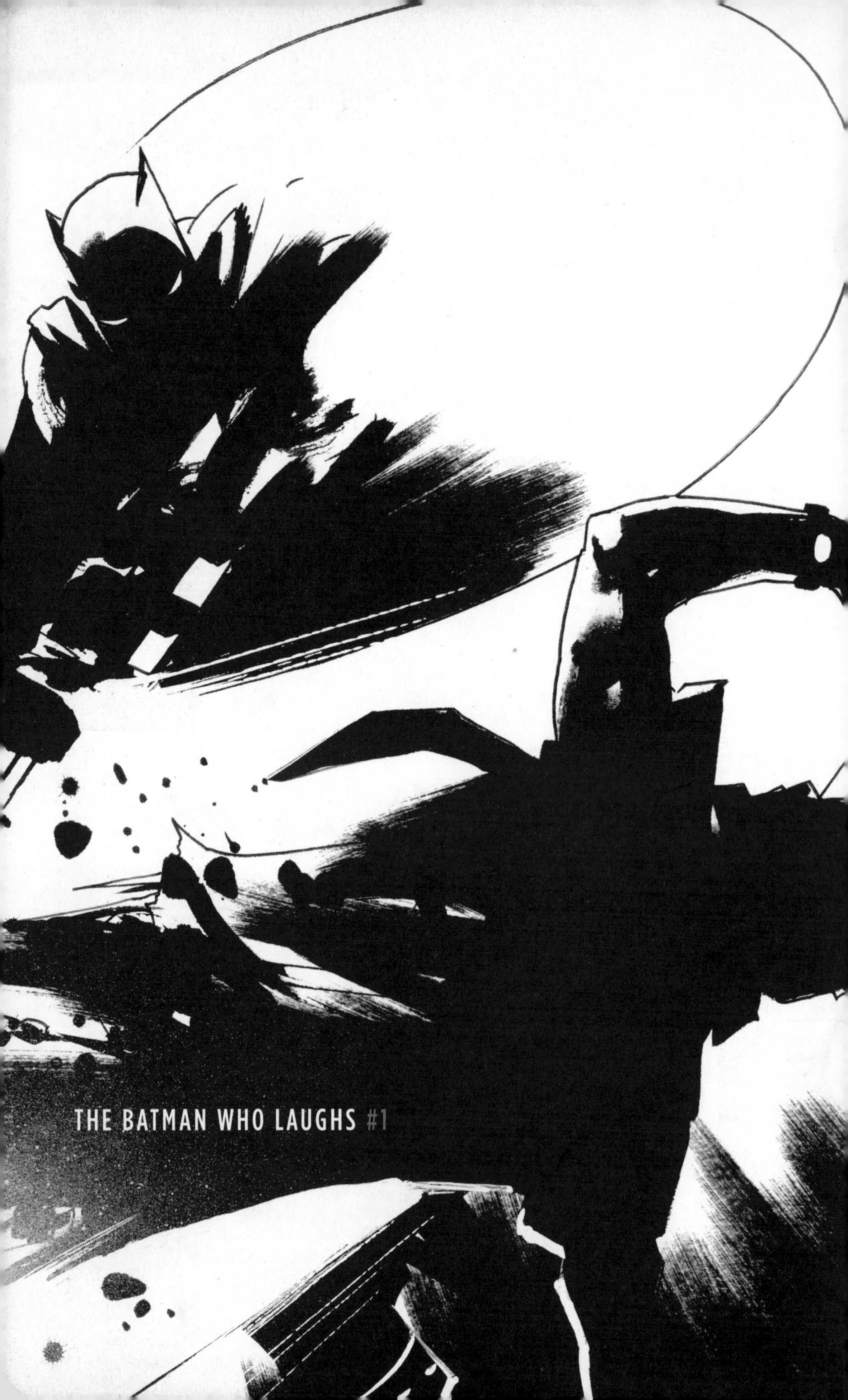

THE BATMAN WHO LAUGHS #1

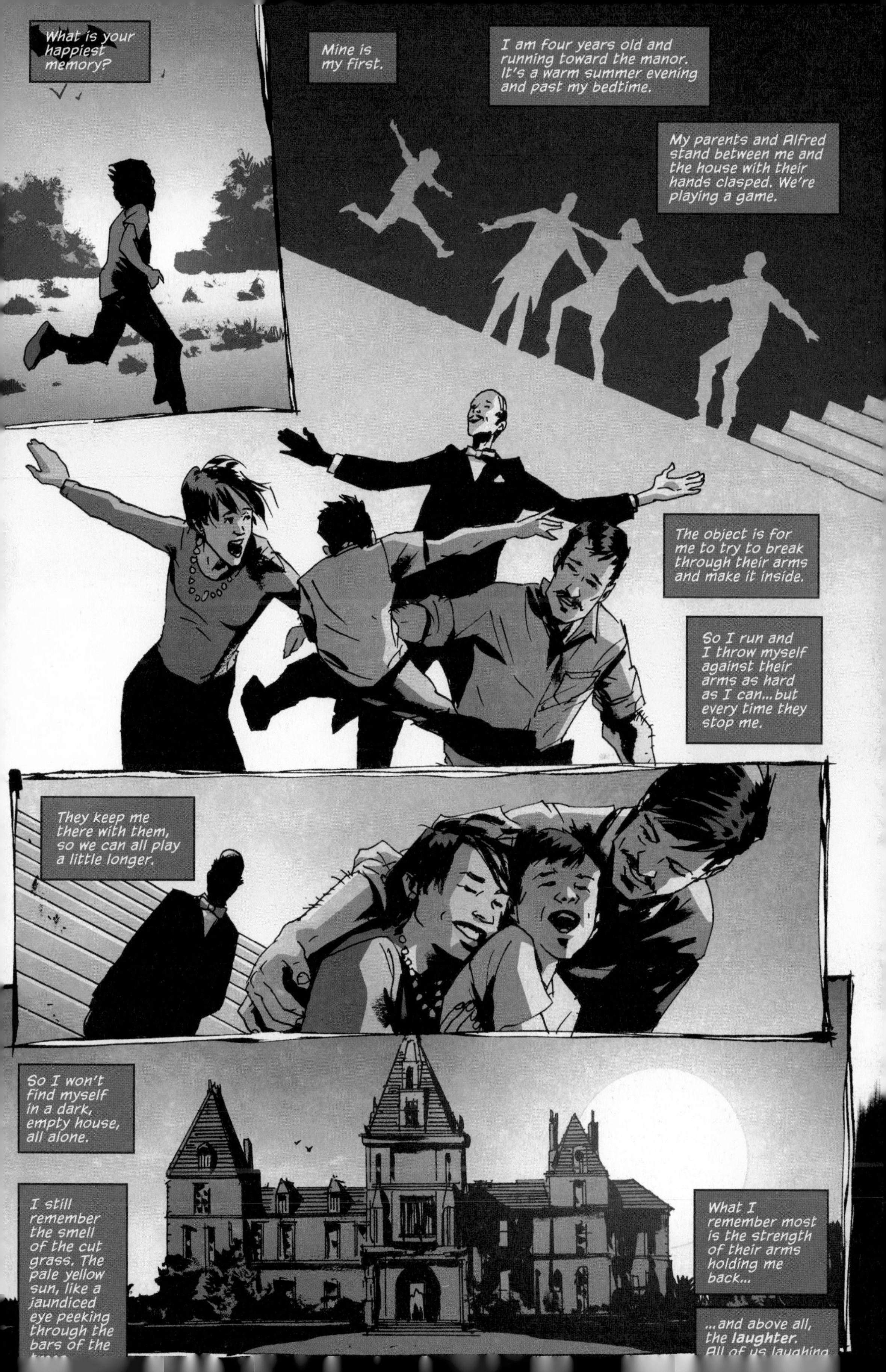
What is your happiest memory?
Mine is my first.
I am four years old and running toward the manor. It's a warm summer evening and past my bedtime.
My parents and Alfred stand between me and the house with their hands clasped. We're playing a game.
The object is for me to try to break through their arms and make it inside.
So I run and I throw myself against their arms as hard as I can...but every time they stop me.
They keep me there with them, so we can all play a little longer.
So I won't find myself in a dark, empty house, all alone.
I still remember the smell of the cut grass. The pale yellow sun, like a jaundiced eye peeking through the bars of the
What I remember most is the strength of their arms holding me back...
...and above all, the **laughter**.

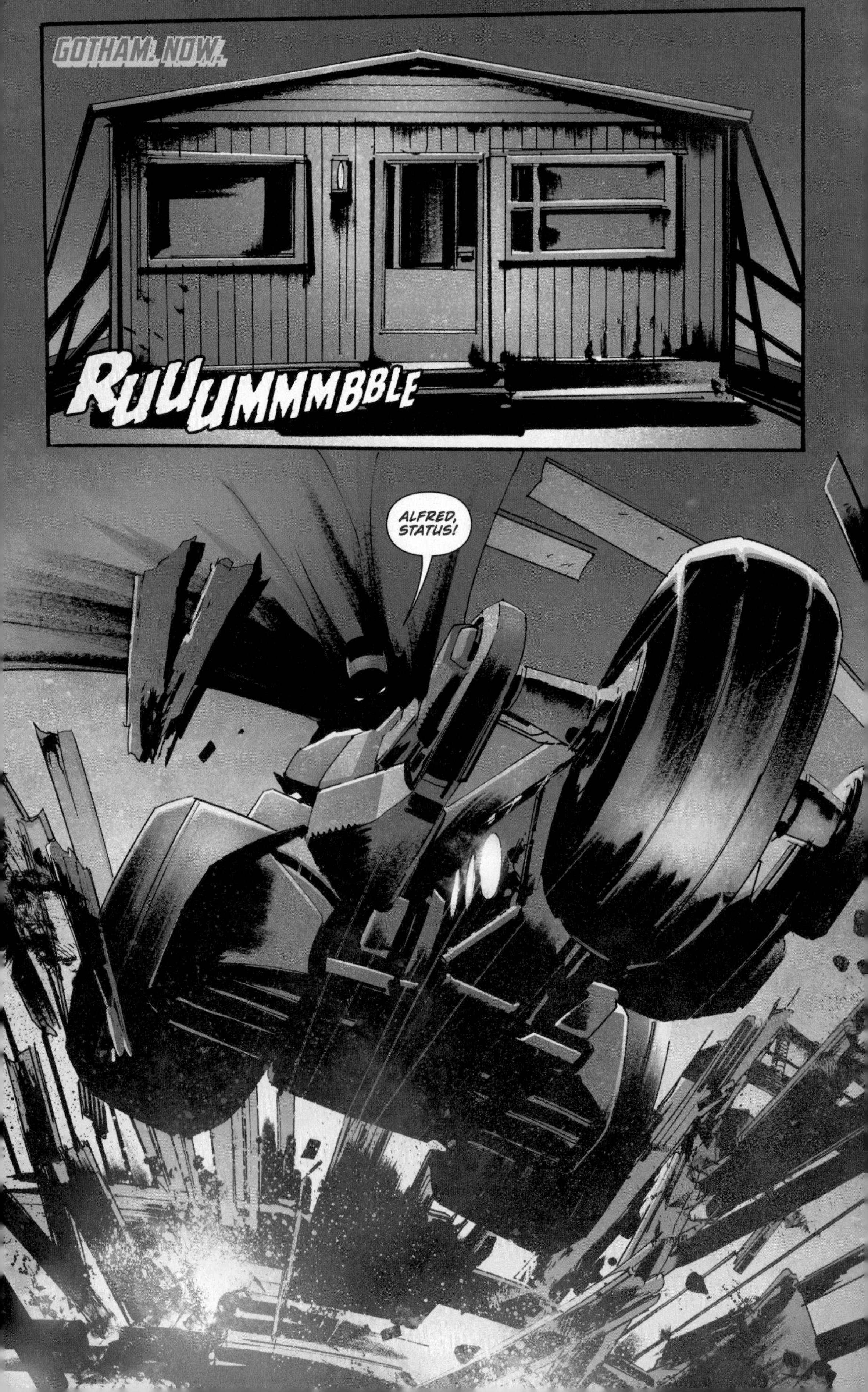
GOTHAM. NOW.
RUUUMMMMBBLE
ALFRED, STATUS!

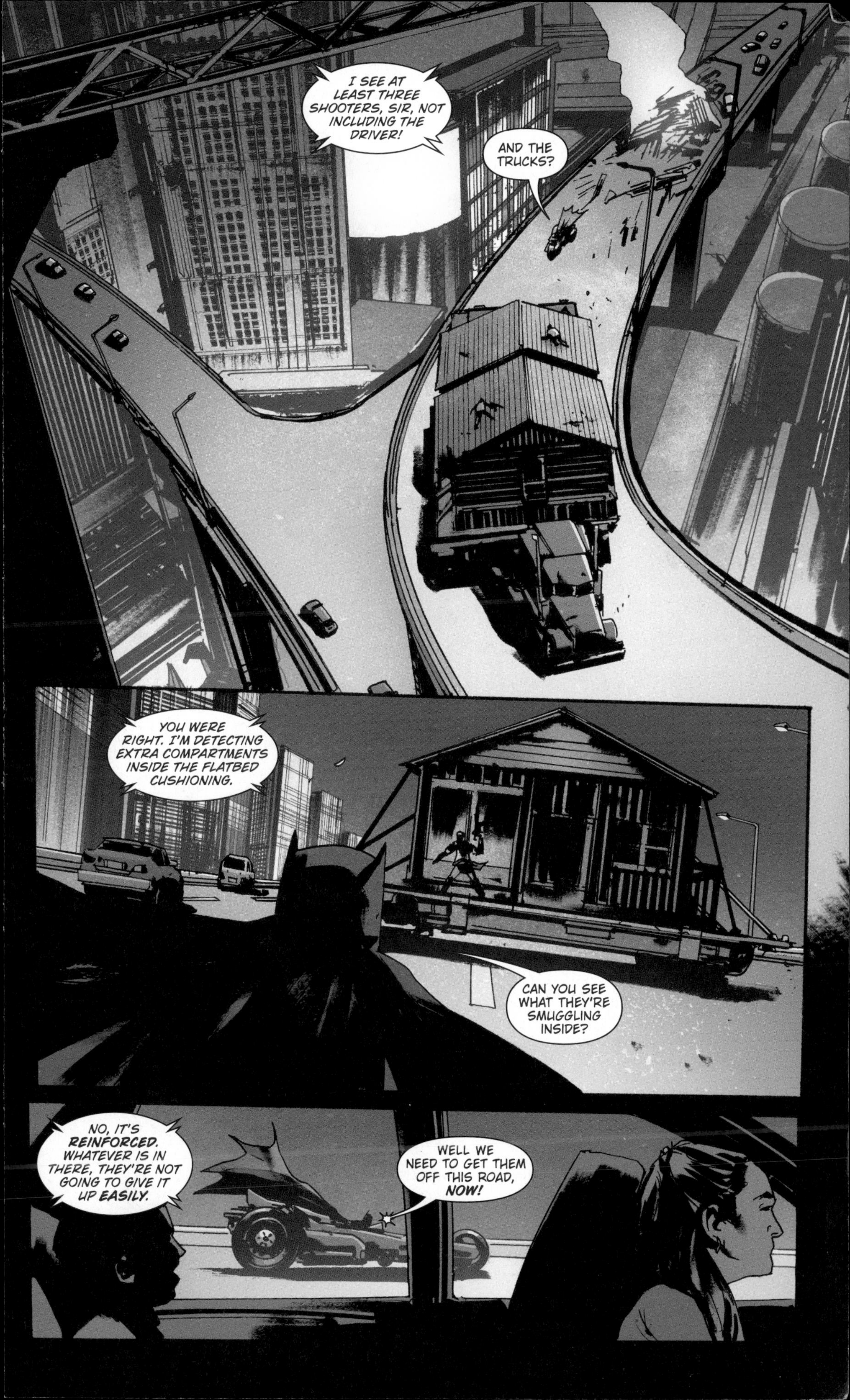
I SEE AT LEAST THREE SHOOTERS, SIR, NOT INCLUDING THE DRIVER!
AND THE TRUCKS?
YOU WERE RIGHT. I'M DETECTING EXTRA COMPARTMENTS INSIDE THE FLATBED CUSHIONING.
CAN YOU SEE WHAT THEY'RE SMUGGLING INSIDE?
NO, IT'S **REINFORCED.** WHATEVER IS IN THERE, THEY'RE NOT GOING TO GIVE IT UP **EASILY.**
WELL WE NEED TO GET THEM OFF THIS ROAD, **NOW!**

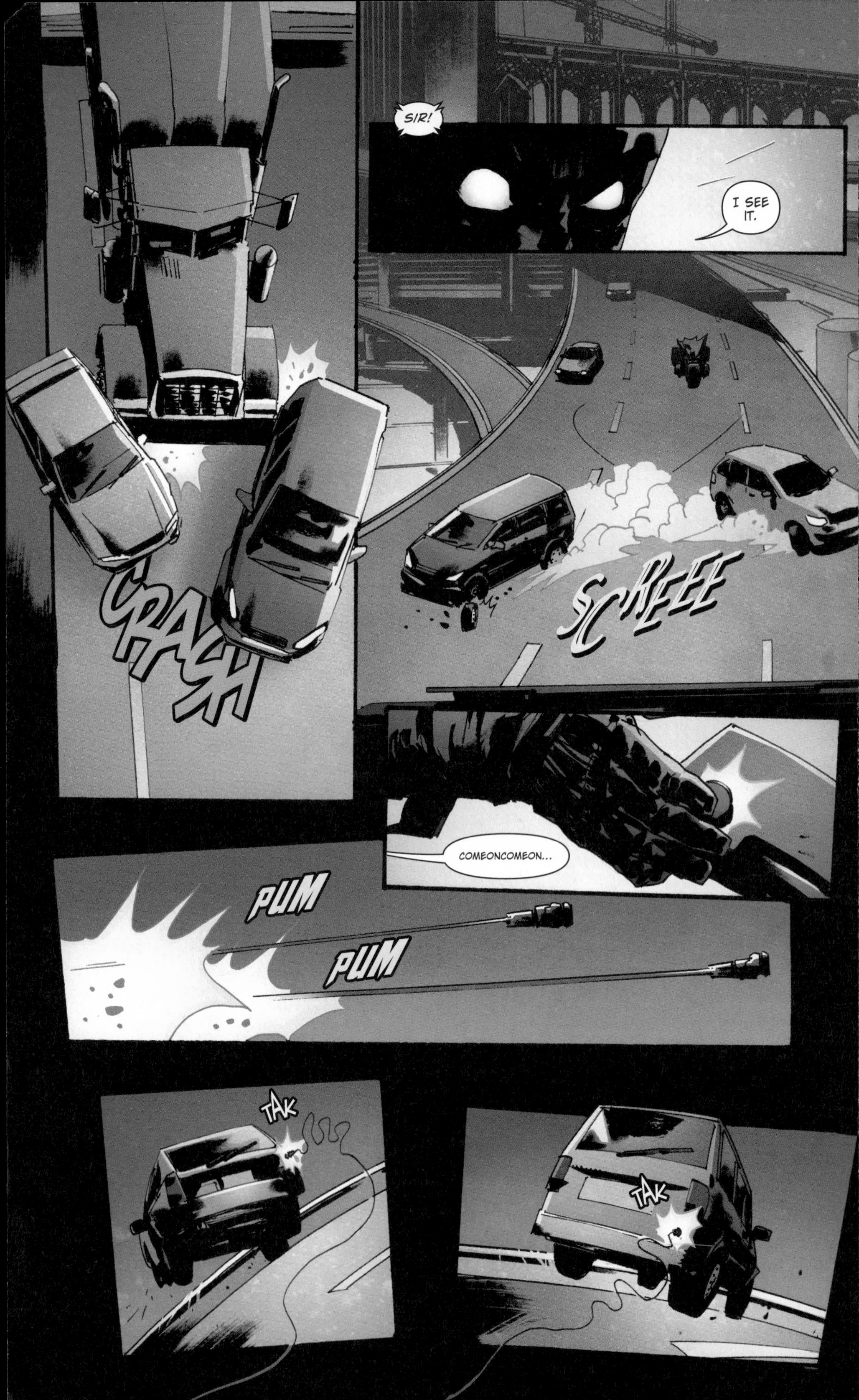

CRASH
SIR!
I SEE IT.
SCREEE
COMEONCOMEON...
PUM
PUM
TAK
TAK

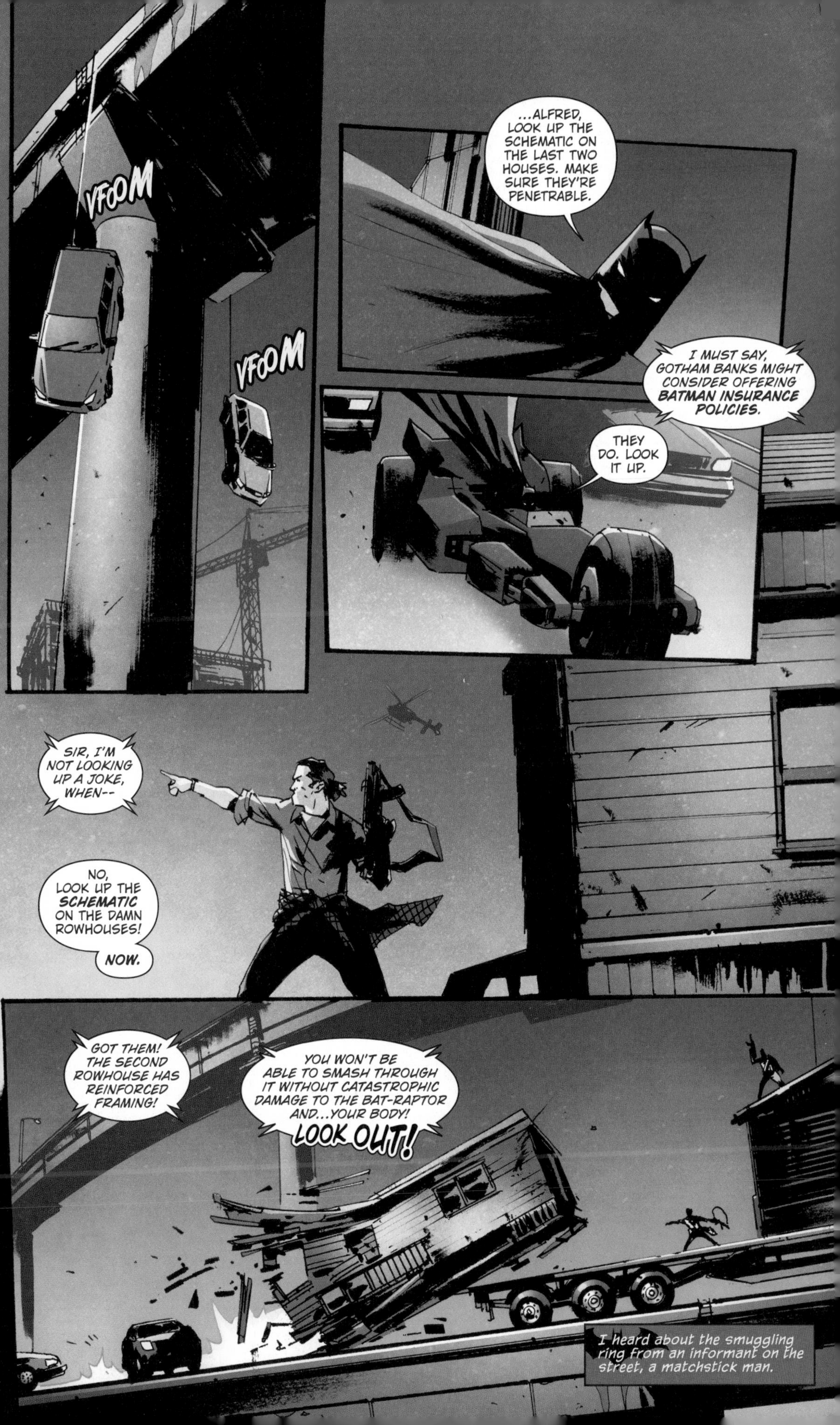
VFOOM
VFOOM
...ALFRED, LOOK UP THE SCHEMATIC ON THE LAST TWO HOUSES. MAKE SURE THEY'RE PENETRABLE.
I MUST SAY, GOTHAM BANKS MIGHT CONSIDER OFFERING BATMAN INSURANCE POLICIES.
THEY DO. LOOK IT UP.
SIR, I'M NOT LOOKING UP A JOKE, WHEN--
NO, LOOK UP THE SCHEMATIC ON THE DAMN ROWHOUSES!
NOW.
GOT THEM! THE SECOND ROWHOUSE HAS REINFORCED FRAMING!
YOU WON'T BE ABLE TO SMASH THROUGH IT WITHOUT CATASTROPHIC DAMAGE TO THE BAT-RAPTOR AND...YOUR BODY!
LOOK OUT!
I heard about the smuggling ring from an informant on the street, a matchstick man.

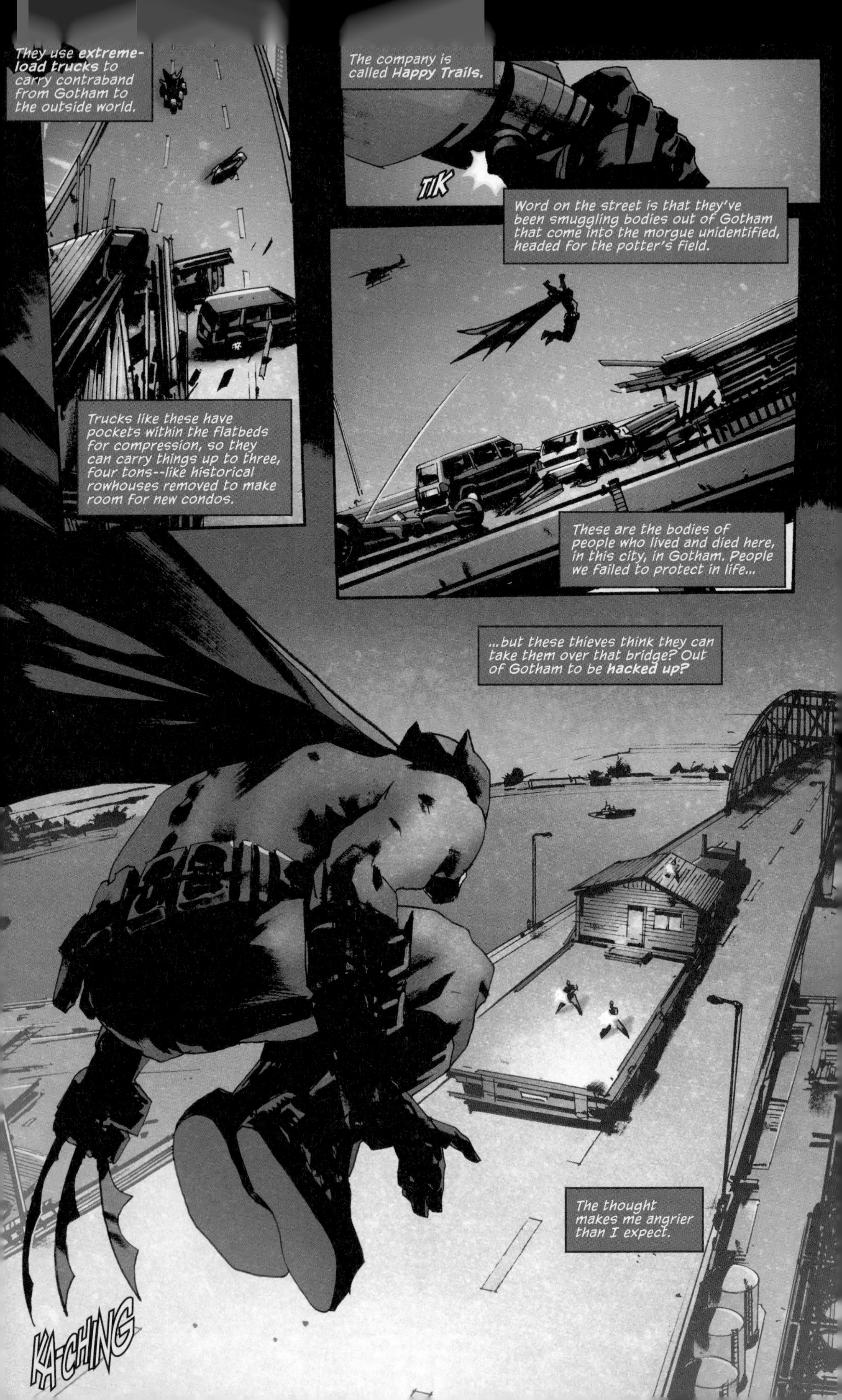
They use **extreme-load trucks** to carry contraband from Gotham to the outside world.
The company is called **Happy Trails.**
TIK
Word on the street is that they've been smuggling bodies out of Gotham that come into the morgue unidentified, headed for the potter's field.
Trucks like these have pockets within the flatbeds for compression, so they can carry things up to three, four tons--like historical rowhouses removed to make room for new condos.
These are the bodies of people who lived and died here, in this city, in Gotham. People we failed to protect in life...
...but these thieves think they can take them over that bridge? Out of Gotham to be **hacked up?**
The thought makes me angrier than I expect.
KA-CHING

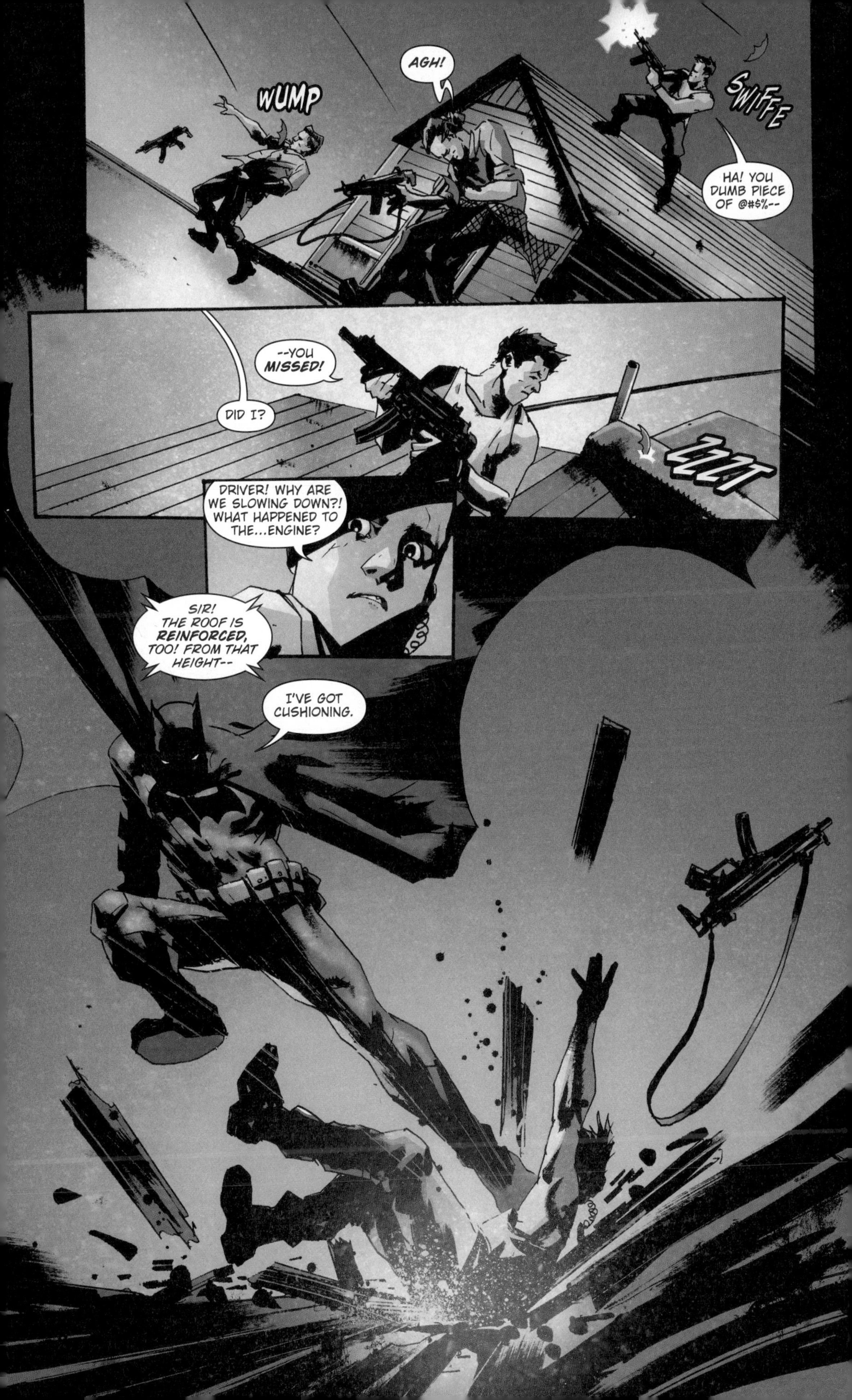
WUMP
AGH!
SWIFFE
HA! YOU DUMB PIECE OF @#$%--
--YOU MISSED!
DID I?
ZZZT
DRIVER! WHY ARE WE SLOWING DOWN?! WHAT HAPPENED TO THE...ENGINE?
SIR! THE ROOF IS REINFORCED, TOO! FROM THAT HEIGHT--
I'VE GOT CUSHIONING.

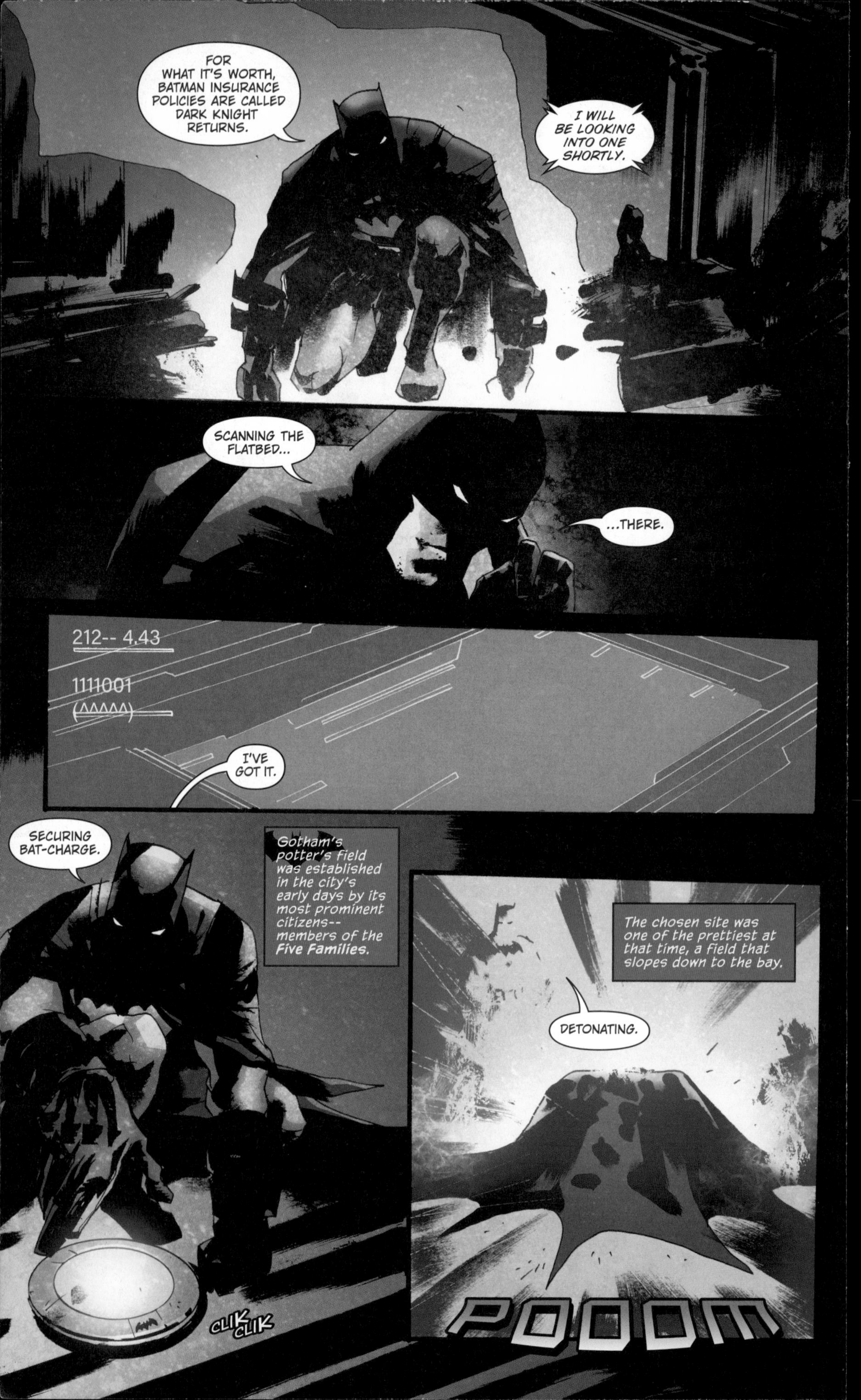

FOR WHAT IT'S WORTH, BATMAN INSURANCE POLICIES ARE CALLED DARK KNIGHT RETURNS.
I WILL BE LOOKING INTO ONE SHORTLY.
SCANNING THE FLATBED...
...THERE.
212-- 4.43
1111001
I'VE GOT IT.
SECURING BAT-CHARGE.
Gotham's potter's field was established in the city's early days by its most prominent citizens--members of the Five Families.
CLIK CLIK
The chosen site was one of the prettiest at that time, a field that slopes down to the bay.
DETONATING.
POOOM

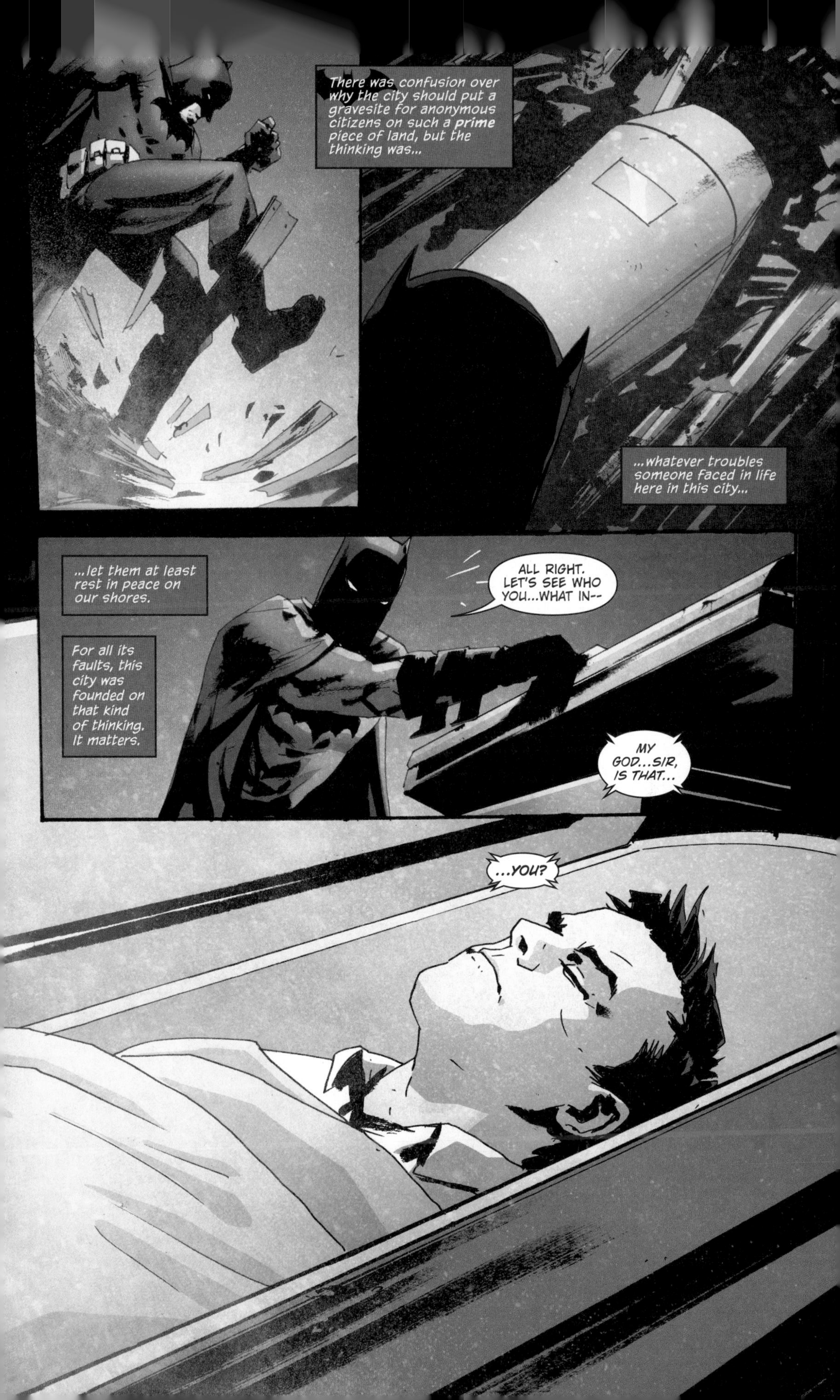

There was confusion over why the city should put a gravesite for anonymous citizens on such a **prime** piece of land, but the thinking was...
...whatever troubles someone faced in life here in this city...
...let them at least rest in peace on our shores.
For all its faults, this city was founded on that kind of thinking. It matters.
ALL RIGHT. LET'S SEE WHO YOU...WHAT IN--
MY GOD...SIR, IS THAT...
...YOU?

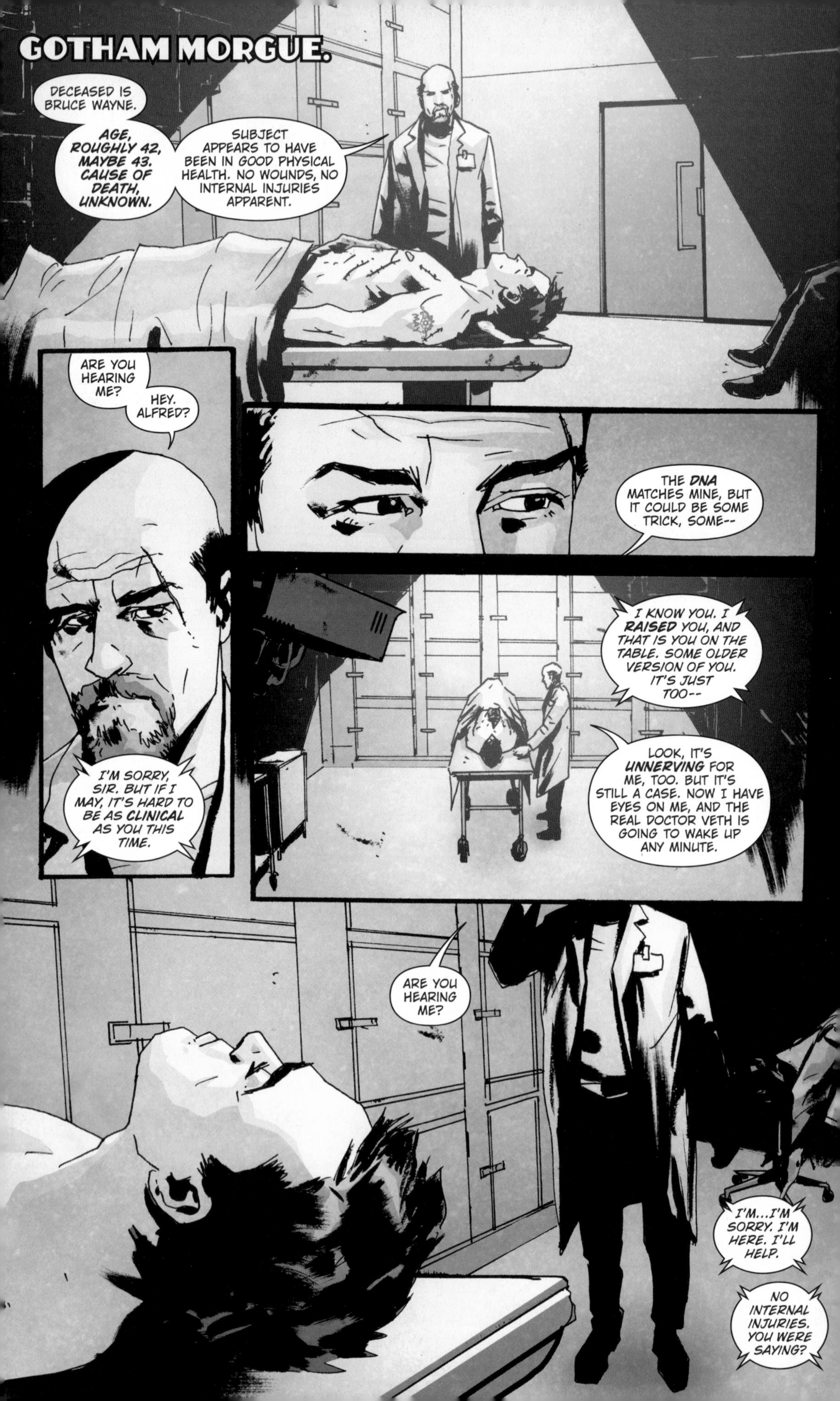
GOTHAM MORGUE.
DECEASED IS BRUCE WAYNE.
AGE, ROUGHLY 42, MAYBE 43. CAUSE OF DEATH, UNKNOWN.
SUBJECT APPEARS TO HAVE BEEN IN GOOD PHYSICAL HEALTH. NO WOUNDS, NO INTERNAL INJURIES APPARENT.
ARE YOU HEARING ME?
HEY. ALFRED?
THE DNA MATCHES MINE, BUT IT COULD BE SOME TRICK, SOME--
I'M SORRY, SIR. BUT IF I MAY, IT'S HARD TO BE AS CLINICAL AS YOU THIS TIME.
I KNOW YOU. I RAISED YOU, AND THAT IS YOU ON THE TABLE. SOME OLDER VERSION OF YOU. IT'S JUST TOO--
LOOK, IT'S UNNERVING FOR ME, TOO. BUT IT'S STILL A CASE. NOW I HAVE EYES ON ME, AND THE REAL DOCTOR VETH IS GOING TO WAKE UP ANY MINUTE.
ARE YOU HEARING ME?
I'M...I'M SORRY. I'M HERE. I'LL HELP.
NO INTERNAL INJURIES. YOU WERE SAYING?

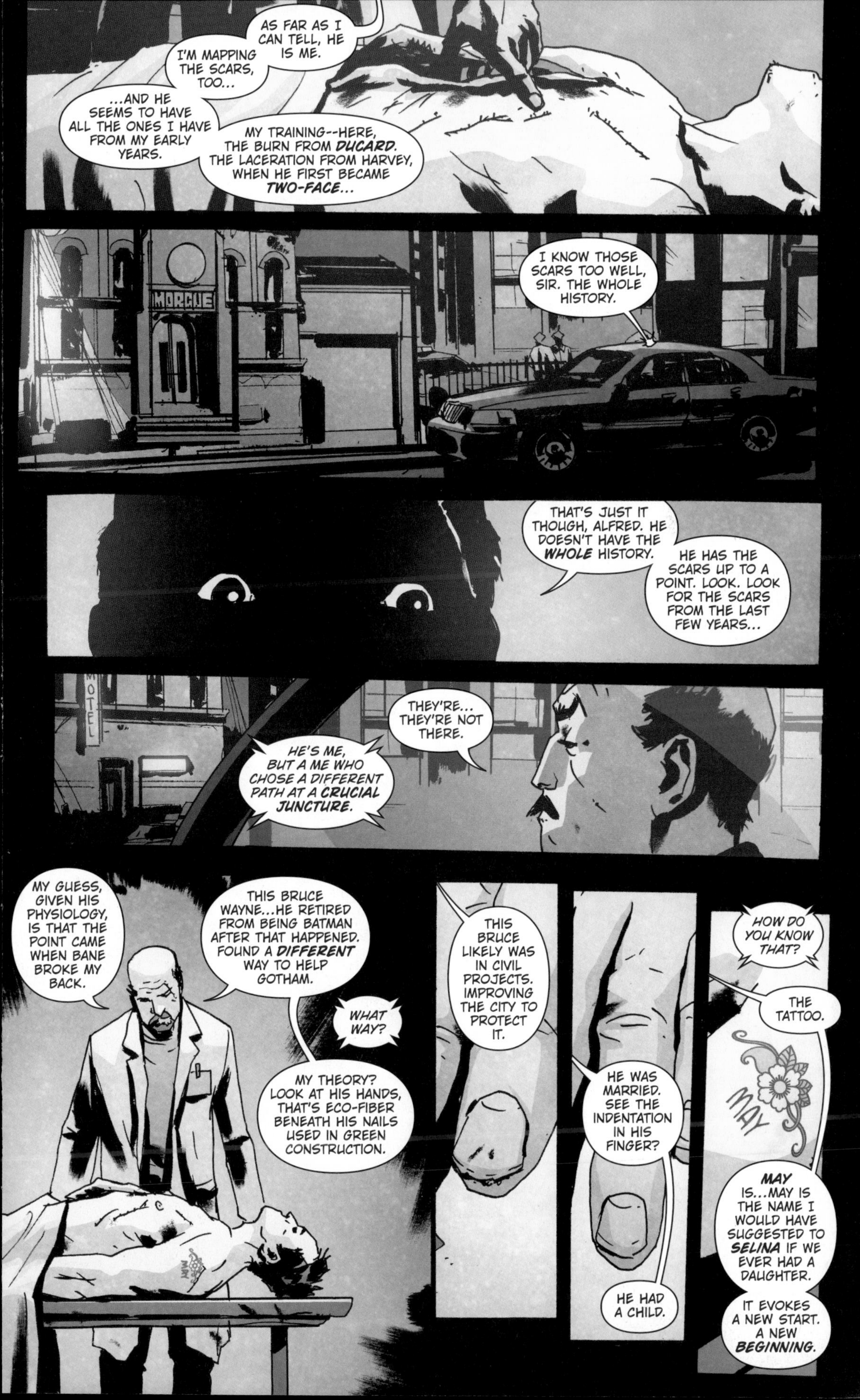
AS FAR AS I CAN TELL, HE IS ME.
I'M MAPPING THE SCARS, TOO...
...AND HE SEEMS TO HAVE ALL THE ONES I HAVE FROM MY EARLY YEARS.
MY TRAINING--HERE, THE BURN FROM DUCARD. THE LACERATION FROM HARVEY, WHEN HE FIRST BECAME TWO-FACE...
MORGUE
I KNOW THOSE SCARS TOO WELL, SIR. THE WHOLE HISTORY.
THAT'S JUST IT THOUGH, ALFRED. HE DOESN'T HAVE THE WHOLE HISTORY.
HE HAS THE SCARS UP TO A POINT. LOOK. LOOK FOR THE SCARS FROM THE LAST FEW YEARS...
MOTEL
THEY'RE... THEY'RE NOT THERE.
HE'S ME, BUT A ME WHO CHOSE A DIFFERENT PATH AT A CRUCIAL JUNCTURE.
MY GUESS, GIVEN HIS PHYSIOLOGY, IS THAT THE POINT CAME WHEN BANE BROKE MY BACK.
THIS BRUCE WAYNE...HE RETIRED FROM BEING BATMAN AFTER THAT HAPPENED. FOUND A DIFFERENT WAY TO HELP GOTHAM.
WHAT WAY?
MY THEORY? LOOK AT HIS HANDS, THAT'S ECO-FIBER BENEATH HIS NAILS USED IN GREEN CONSTRUCTION.
THIS BRUCE LIKELY WAS IN CIVIL PROJECTS. IMPROVING THE CITY TO PROTECT IT.
HE WAS MARRIED. SEE THE INDENTATION IN HIS FINGER?
HE HAD A CHILD.
HOW DO YOU KNOW THAT?
THE TATTOO.
MAY
MAY IS...MAY IS THE NAME I WOULD HAVE SUGGESTED TO SELINA IF WE EVER HAD A DAUGHTER.
IT EVOKES A NEW START. A NEW BEGINNING.

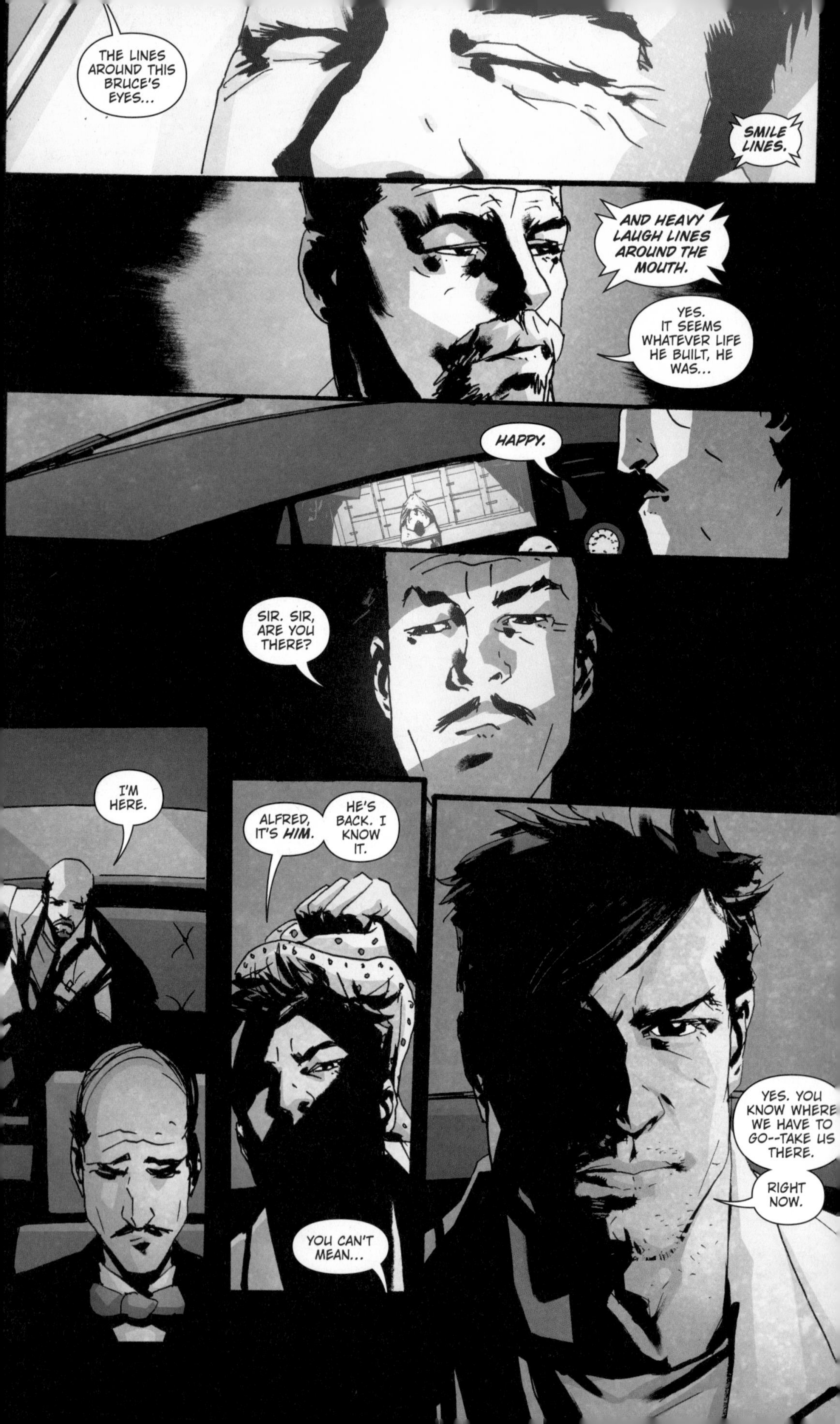
THE LINES AROUND THIS BRUCE'S EYES...
SMILE LINES.
AND HEAVY LAUGH LINES AROUND THE MOUTH.
YES. IT SEEMS WHATEVER LIFE HE BUILT, HE WAS...
HAPPY.
SIR. SIR, ARE YOU THERE?
I'M HERE.
ALFRED, IT'S HIM.
HE'S BACK. I KNOW IT.
YOU CAN'T MEAN...
YES. YOU KNOW WHERE WE HAVE TO GO--TAKE US THERE.
RIGHT NOW.

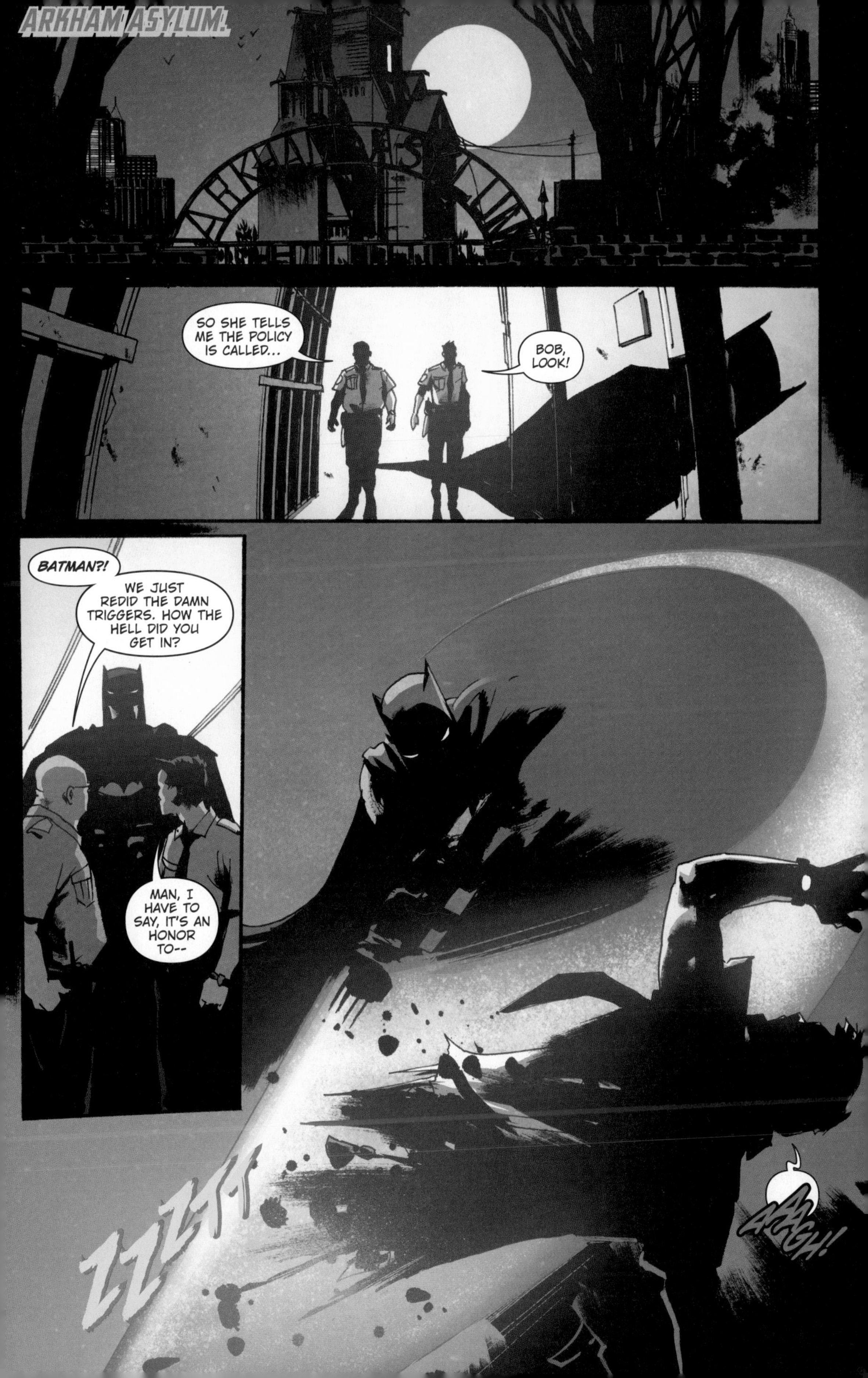
ARKHAM ASYLUM.
SO SHE TELLS ME THE POLICY IS CALLED...
BOB, LOOK!
BATMAN?!
WE JUST REDID THE DAMN TRIGGERS. HOW THE HELL DID YOU GET IN?
MAN, I HAVE TO SAY, IT'S AN HONOR TO--
ZZZZT-T-
AAAGH!

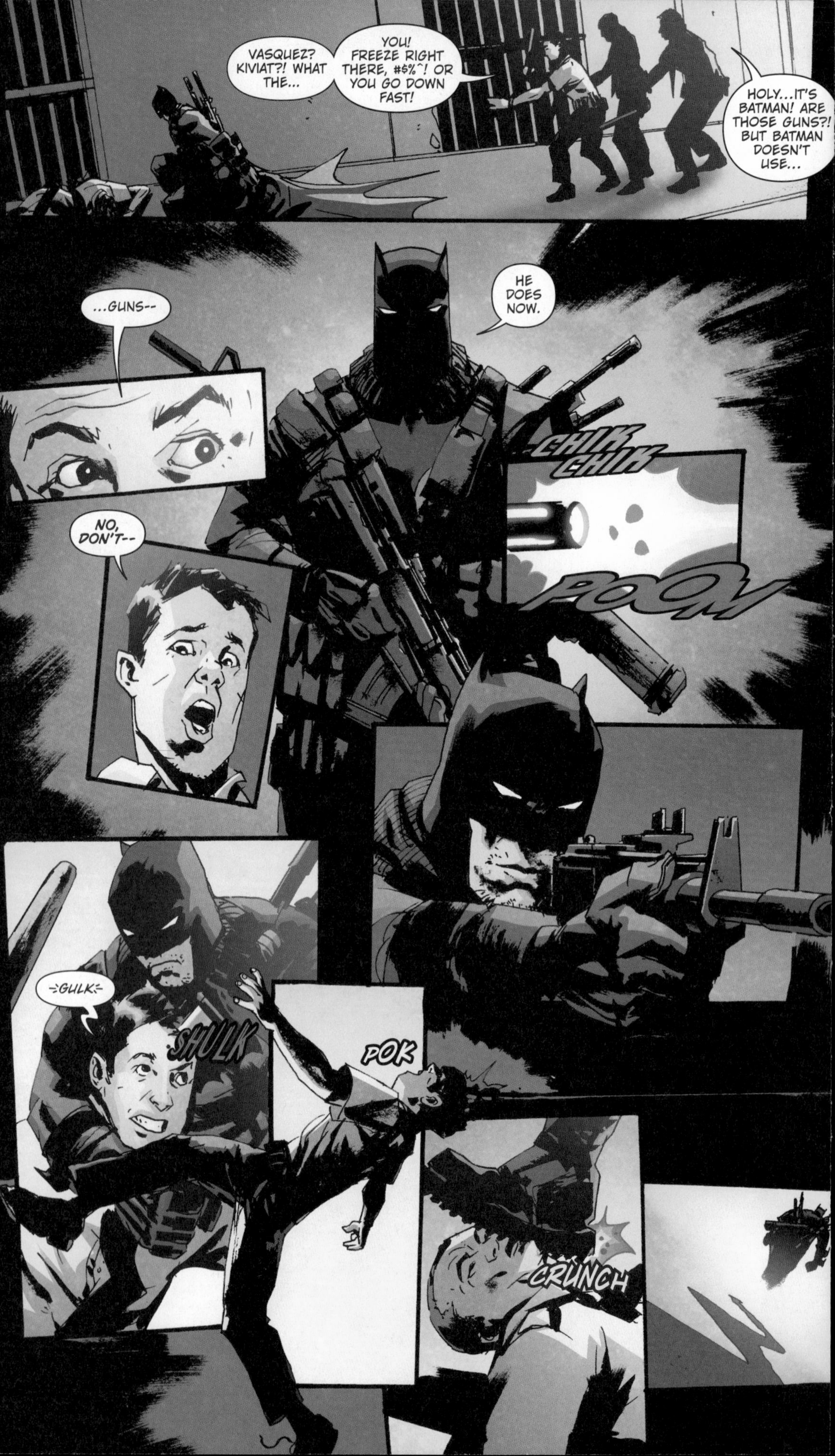
VASQUEZ? KIVIAT?! WHAT THE...
YOU! FREEZE RIGHT THERE, #$%^! OR YOU GO DOWN FAST!
HOLY...IT'S BATMAN! ARE THOSE GUNS?! BUT BATMAN DOESN'T USE...
...GUNS--
HE DOES NOW.
NO, DON'T--
CHIK CHIK
POOM
=GULK=
SHULK
POK
CRUNCH

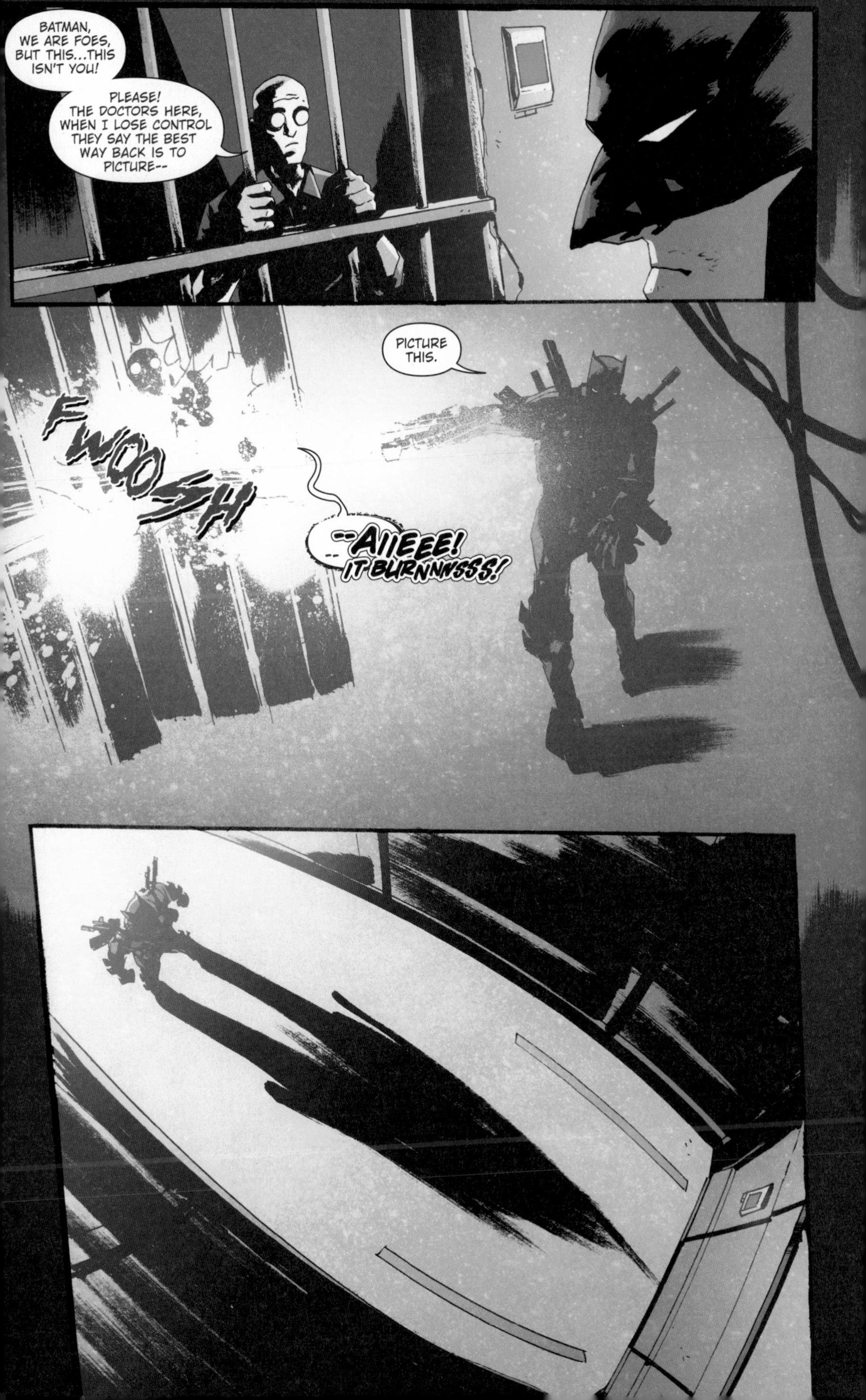
BATMAN, WE ARE FOES, BUT THIS...THIS ISN'T YOU!
PLEASE! THE DOCTORS HERE, WHEN I LOSE CONTROL THEY SAY THE BEST WAY BACK IS TO PICTURE--
PICTURE THIS.
FWOOSH
--AIIEEE! --IT BURNNNSSS!

I'M HERE.
KOFF
COME IN... ANYONE...BATMAN, HE'S LOST HIS MIND!
HE'S ABOUT TO OPEN THE CELL FOR--
SHUNK
HELLO, OLD FRIEND.

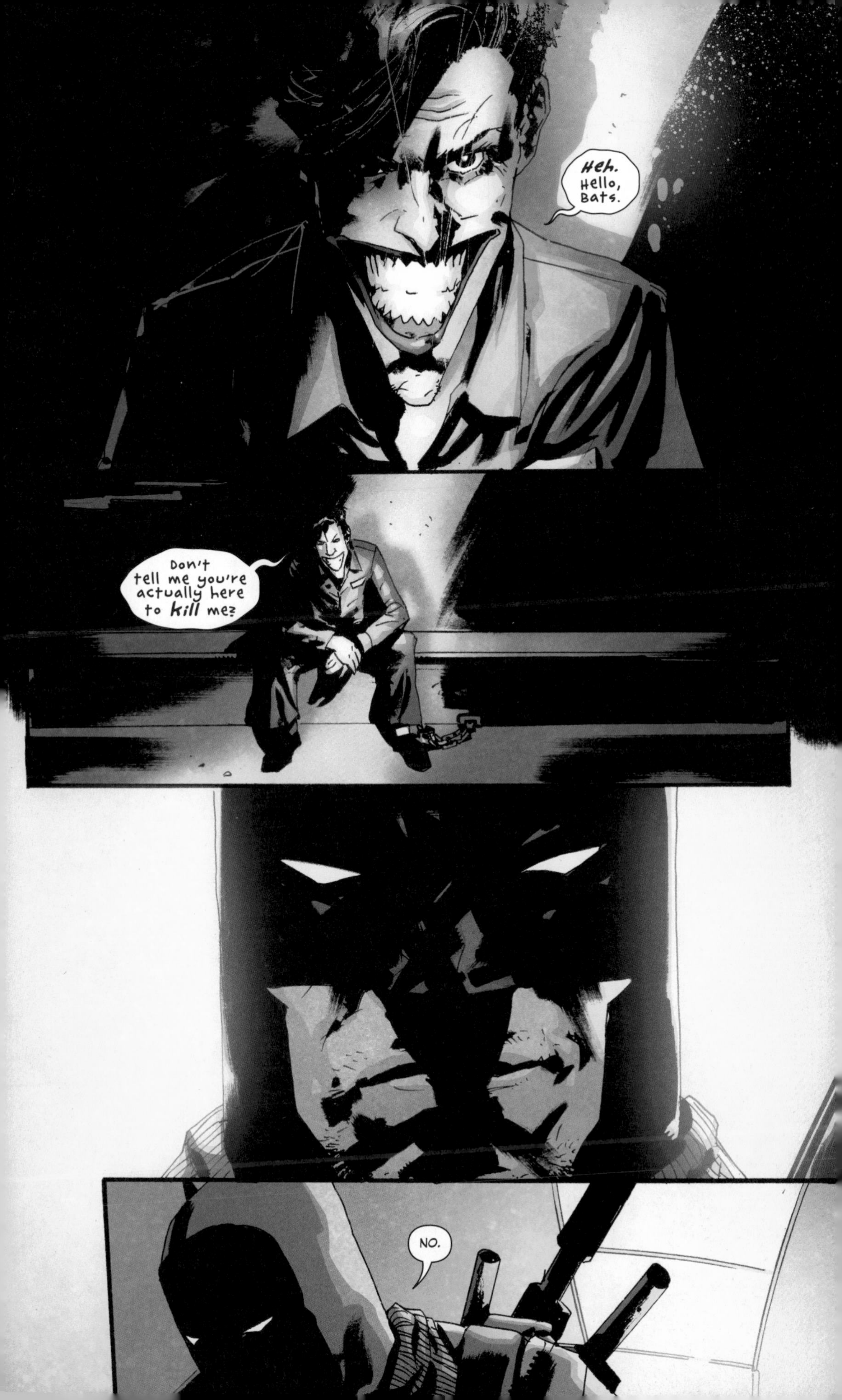
Heh. Hello, Bats.
Don't tell me you're actually here to kill me?
NO.

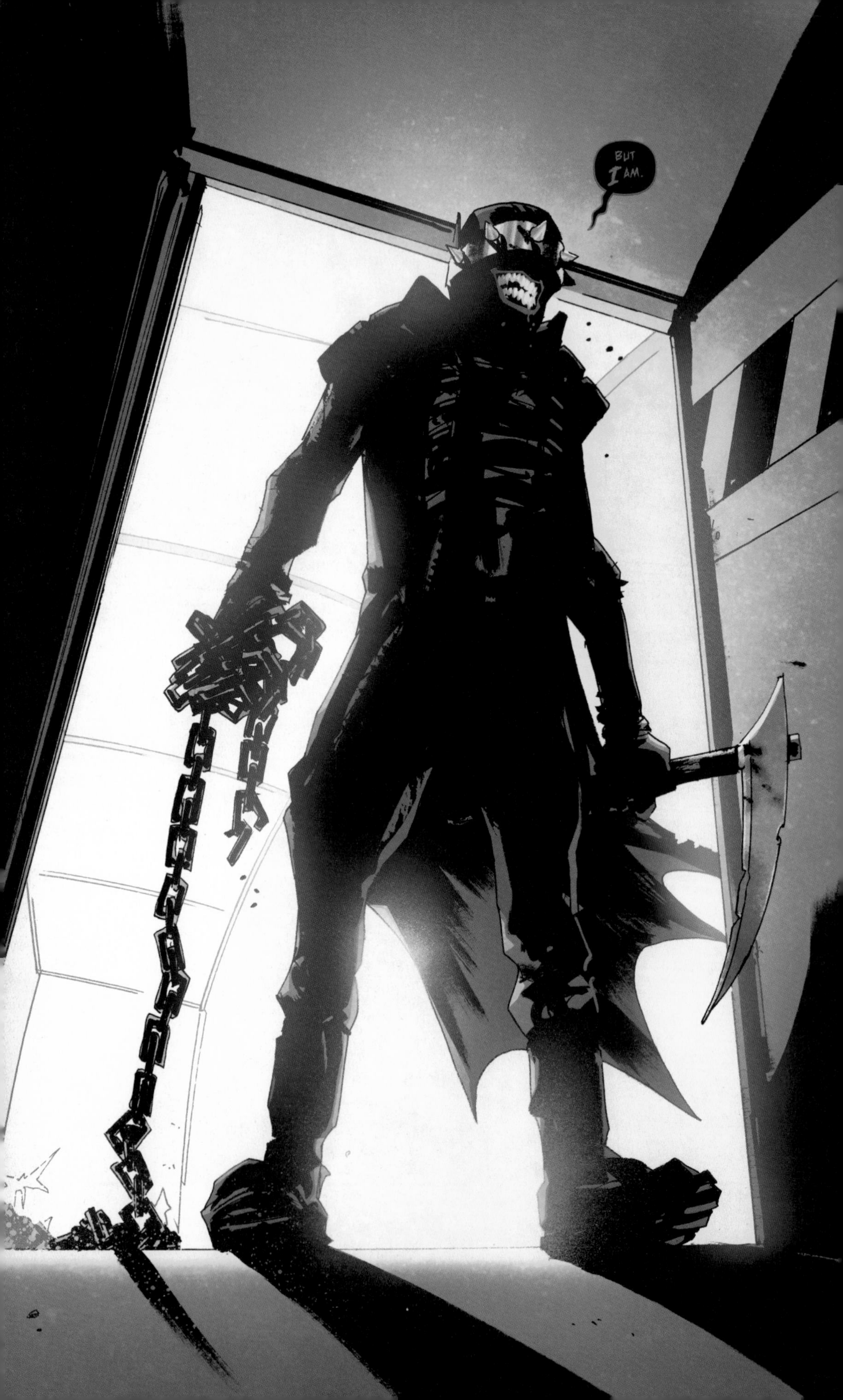
BUT I AM.

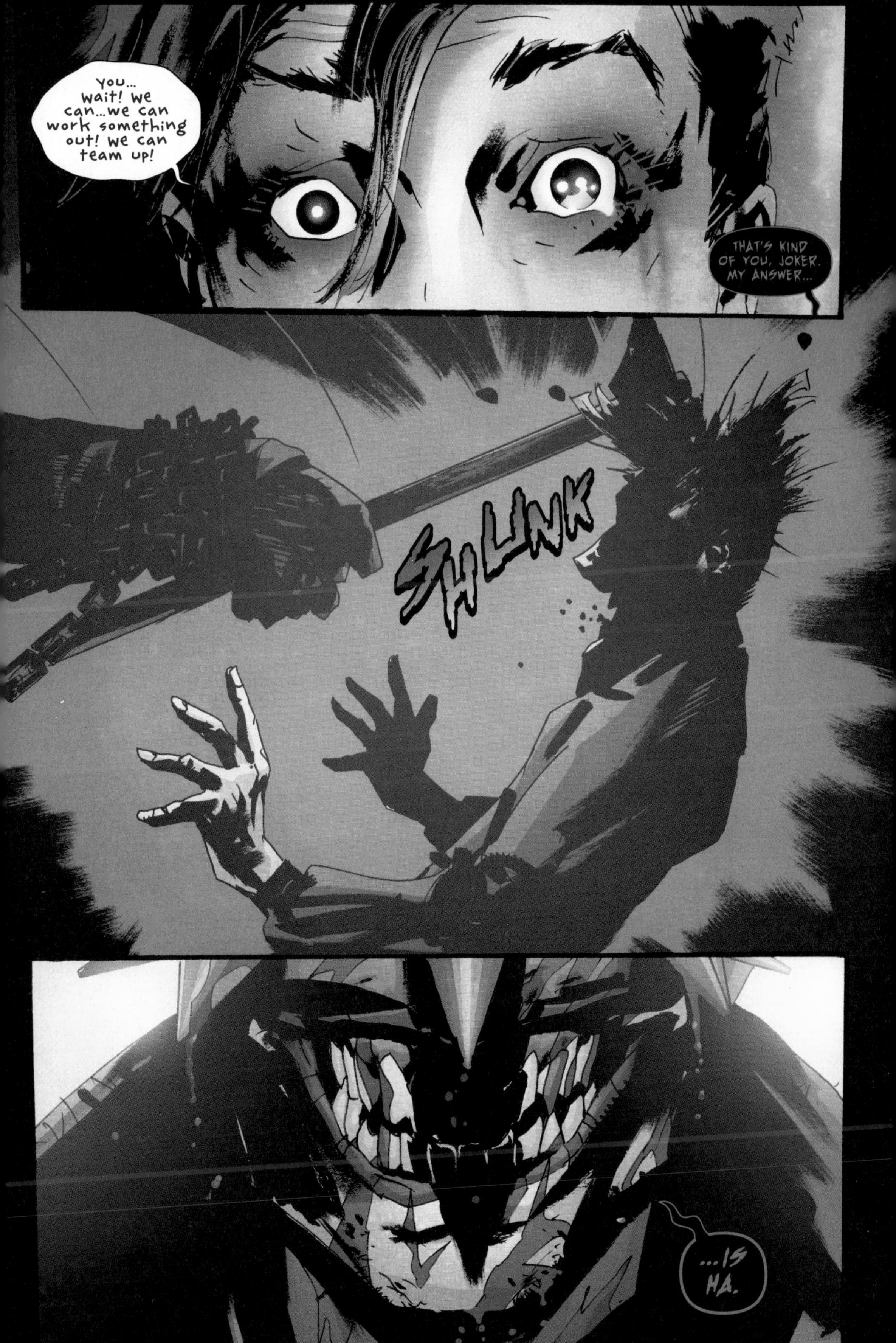
You... wait! We can...we can work something out! We can team up!
THAT'S KIND OF YOU, JOKER. MY ANSWER...
SHLINK
...IS HA.

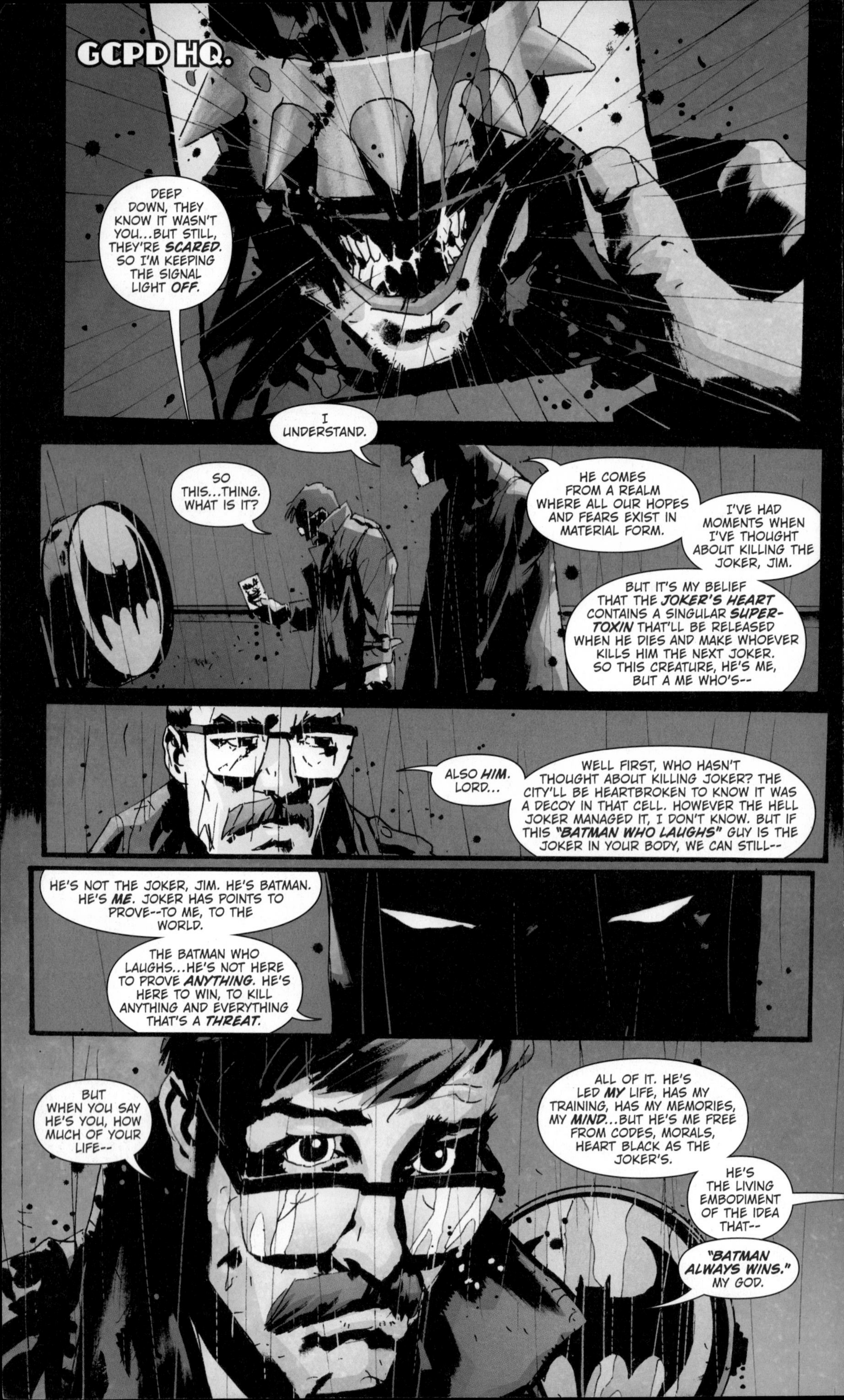
GCPD HQ.
DEEP DOWN, THEY KNOW IT WASN'T YOU...BUT STILL, THEY'RE SCARED. SO I'M KEEPING THE SIGNAL LIGHT OFF.
I UNDERSTAND.
SO THIS...THING. WHAT IS IT?
HE COMES FROM A REALM WHERE ALL OUR HOPES AND FEARS EXIST IN MATERIAL FORM.
I'VE HAD MOMENTS WHEN I'VE THOUGHT ABOUT KILLING THE JOKER, JIM.
BUT IT'S MY BELIEF THAT THE JOKER'S HEART CONTAINS A SINGULAR SUPER-TOXIN THAT'LL BE RELEASED WHEN HE DIES AND MAKE WHOEVER KILLS HIM THE NEXT JOKER. SO THIS CREATURE, HE'S ME, BUT A ME WHO'S--
ALSO HIM. LORD...
WELL FIRST, WHO HASN'T THOUGHT ABOUT KILLING JOKER? THE CITY'LL BE HEARTBROKEN TO KNOW IT WAS A DECOY IN THAT CELL. HOWEVER THE HELL JOKER MANAGED IT, I DON'T KNOW. BUT IF THIS "BATMAN WHO LAUGHS" GUY IS THE JOKER IN YOUR BODY, WE CAN STILL--
HE'S NOT THE JOKER, JIM. HE'S BATMAN. HE'S ME. JOKER HAS POINTS TO PROVE--TO ME, TO THE WORLD.
THE BATMAN WHO LAUGHS...HE'S NOT HERE TO PROVE ANYTHING. HE'S HERE TO WIN, TO KILL ANYTHING AND EVERYTHING THAT'S A THREAT.
BUT WHEN YOU SAY HE'S YOU, HOW MUCH OF YOUR LIFE--
ALL OF IT. HE'S LED MY LIFE, HAS MY TRAINING, HAS MY MEMORIES, MY MIND...BUT HE'S ME FREE FROM CODES, MORALS, HEART BLACK AS THE JOKER'S.
HE'S THE LIVING EMBODIMENT OF THE IDEA THAT--
"BATMAN ALWAYS WINS." MY GOD.

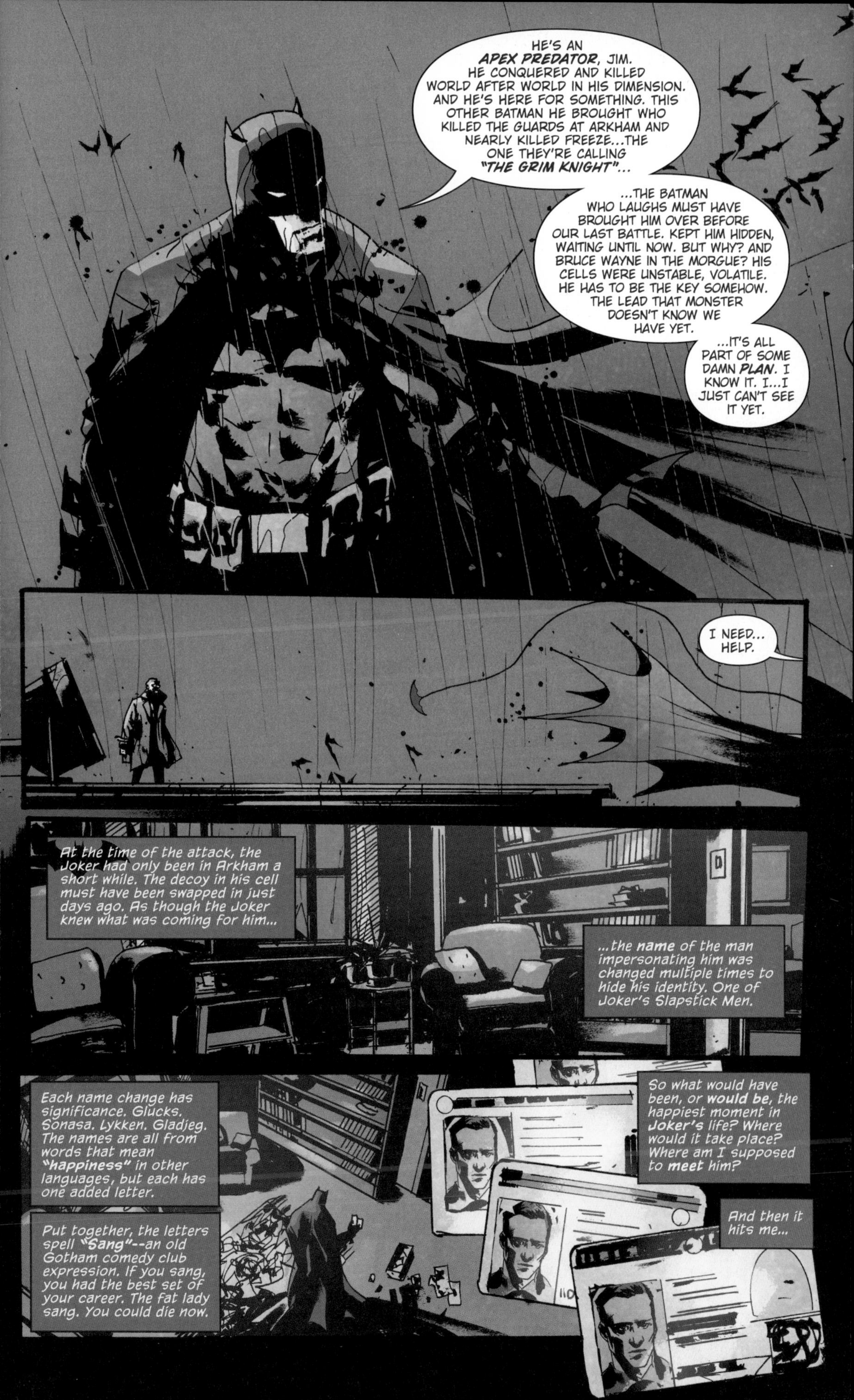
HE'S AN APEX PREDATOR, JIM. HE CONQUERED AND KILLED WORLD AFTER WORLD IN HIS DIMENSION. AND HE'S HERE FOR SOMETHING. THIS OTHER BATMAN HE BROUGHT WHO KILLED THE GUARDS AT ARKHAM AND NEARLY KILLED FREEZE...THE ONE THEY'RE CALLING "THE GRIM KNIGHT"...
...THE BATMAN WHO LAUGHS MUST HAVE BROUGHT HIM OVER BEFORE OUR LAST BATTLE. KEPT HIM HIDDEN, WAITING UNTIL NOW. BUT WHY? AND BRUCE WAYNE IN THE MORGUE? HIS CELLS WERE UNSTABLE, VOLATILE. HE HAS TO BE THE KEY SOMEHOW. THE LEAD THAT MONSTER DOESN'T KNOW WE HAVE YET.
...IT'S ALL PART OF SOME DAMN PLAN. I KNOW IT. I...I JUST CAN'T SEE IT YET.
I NEED... HELP.
At the time of the attack, the Joker had only been in Arkham a short while. The decoy in his cell must have been swapped in just days ago. As though the Joker knew what was coming for him...
...the name of the man impersonating him was changed multiple times to hide his identity. One of Joker's Slapstick Men.
Each name change has significance. Glucks. Sonasa. Lykken. Gladjeg. The names are all from words that mean "happiness" in other languages, but each has one added letter.
Put together, the letters spell "Sang"--an old Gotham comedy club expression. If you sang, you had the best set of your career. The fat lady sang. You could die now.
So what would have been, or would be, the happiest moment in Joker's life? Where would it take place? Where am I supposed to meet him?
And then it hits me...

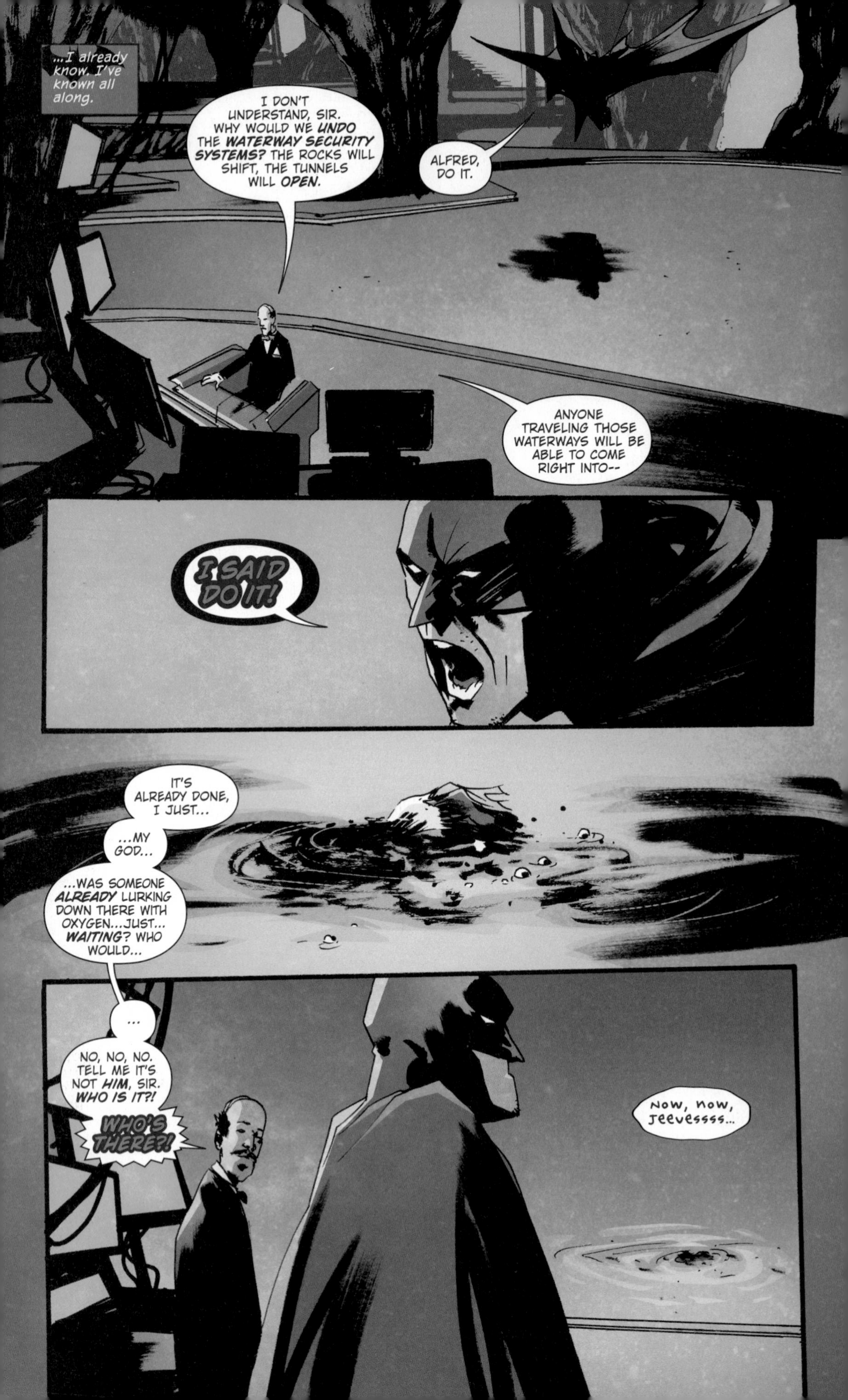
...I already know. I've known all along.
I DON'T UNDERSTAND, SIR. WHY WOULD WE UNDO THE WATERWAY SECURITY SYSTEMS? THE ROCKS WILL SHIFT, THE TUNNELS WILL OPEN.
ALFRED, DO IT.
ANYONE TRAVELING THOSE WATERWAYS WILL BE ABLE TO COME RIGHT INTO--
I SAID DO IT!
IT'S ALREADY DONE, I JUST...
...MY GOD...
...WAS SOMEONE ALREADY LURKING DOWN THERE WITH OXYGEN...JUST... WAITING? WHO WOULD...
...
NO, NO, NO. TELL ME IT'S NOT HIM, SIR. WHO IS IT?!
WHO'S THERE?!
Now, now, Jeevessss...

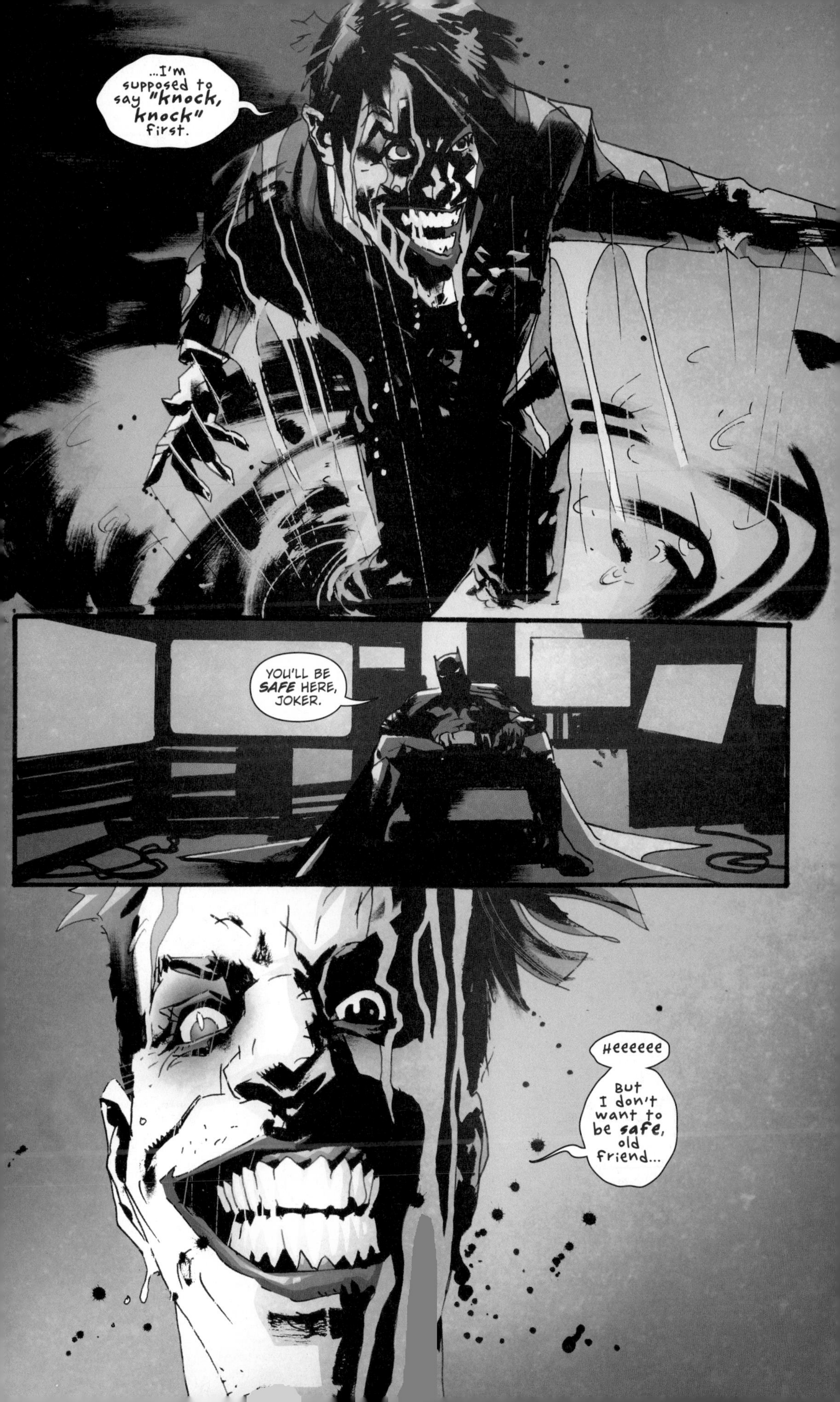
...I'm supposed to say "knock, knock" first.
YOU'LL BE SAFE HERE, JOKER.
Heeeeee
But I don't want to be safe, old friend...

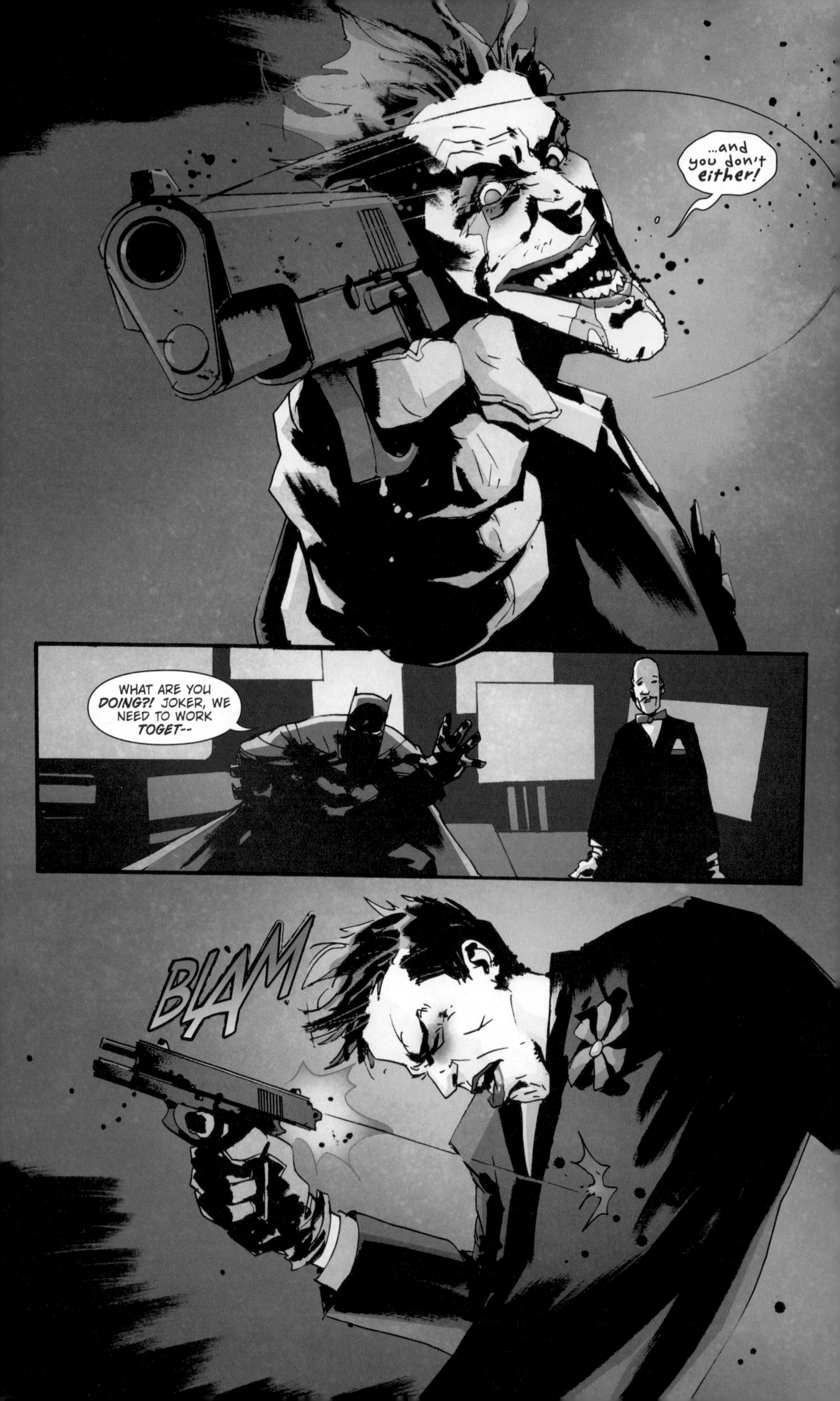
...and you don't either!
WHAT ARE YOU DOING?! JOKER, WE NEED TO WORK TOGET--
BLAM

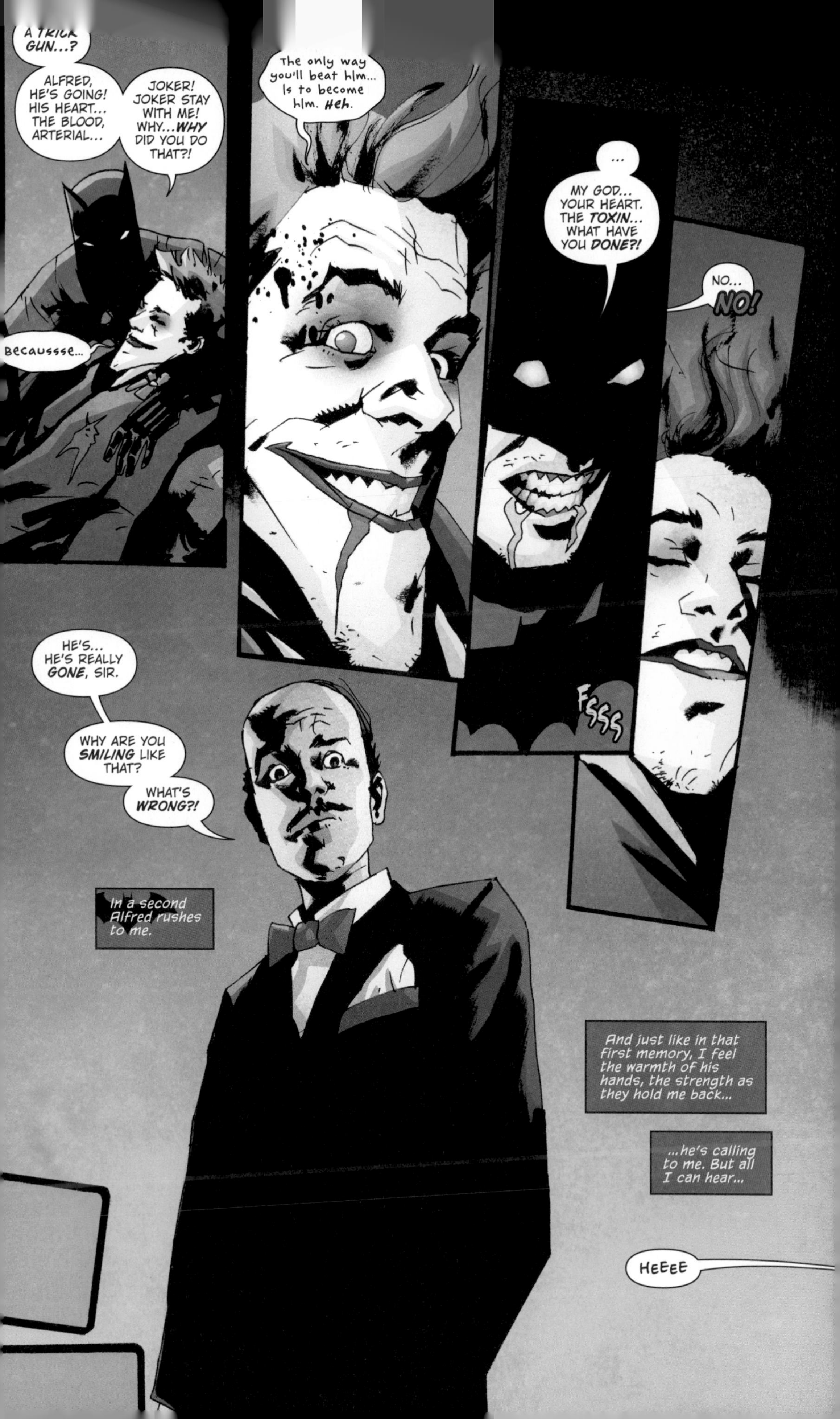

A TRICK GUN...?
ALFRED, HE'S GOING! HIS HEART... THE BLOOD, ARTERIAL...
JOKER! JOKER STAY WITH ME! WHY...WHY DID YOU DO THAT?!
Becaussse...
The only way you'll beat him... Is to become him. Heh.
...
MY GOD... YOUR HEART. THE TOXIN... WHAT HAVE YOU DONE?!
NO... NO!
FSSS
HE'S... HE'S REALLY GONE, SIR.
WHY ARE YOU SMILING LIKE THAT?
WHAT'S WRONG?!
In a second Alfred rushes to me.
And just like in that first memory, I feel the warmth of his hands, the strength as they hold me back...
...he's calling to me. But all I can hear...
HEEEE

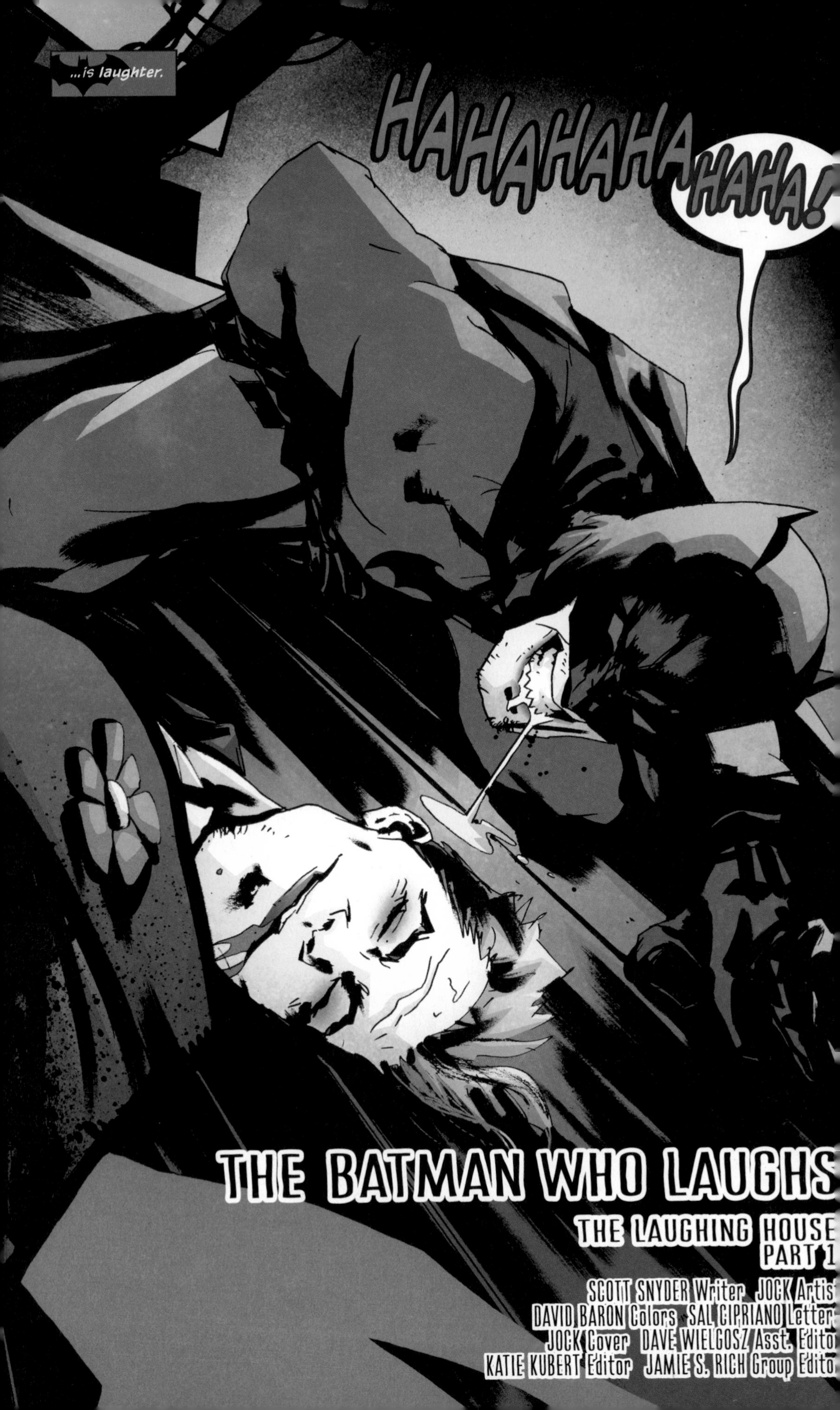
...is laughter.
HAHAHAHAHAHAHA!
THE BATMAN WHO LAUGHS
THE LAUGHING HOUSE
PART 1
SCOTT SNYDER Writer JOCK Artist
DAVID BARON Colors SAL CIPRIANO Letters
JOCK Cover DAVE WIELGOSZ Asst. Editor
KATIE KUBERT Editor JAMIE S. RICH Group Editor

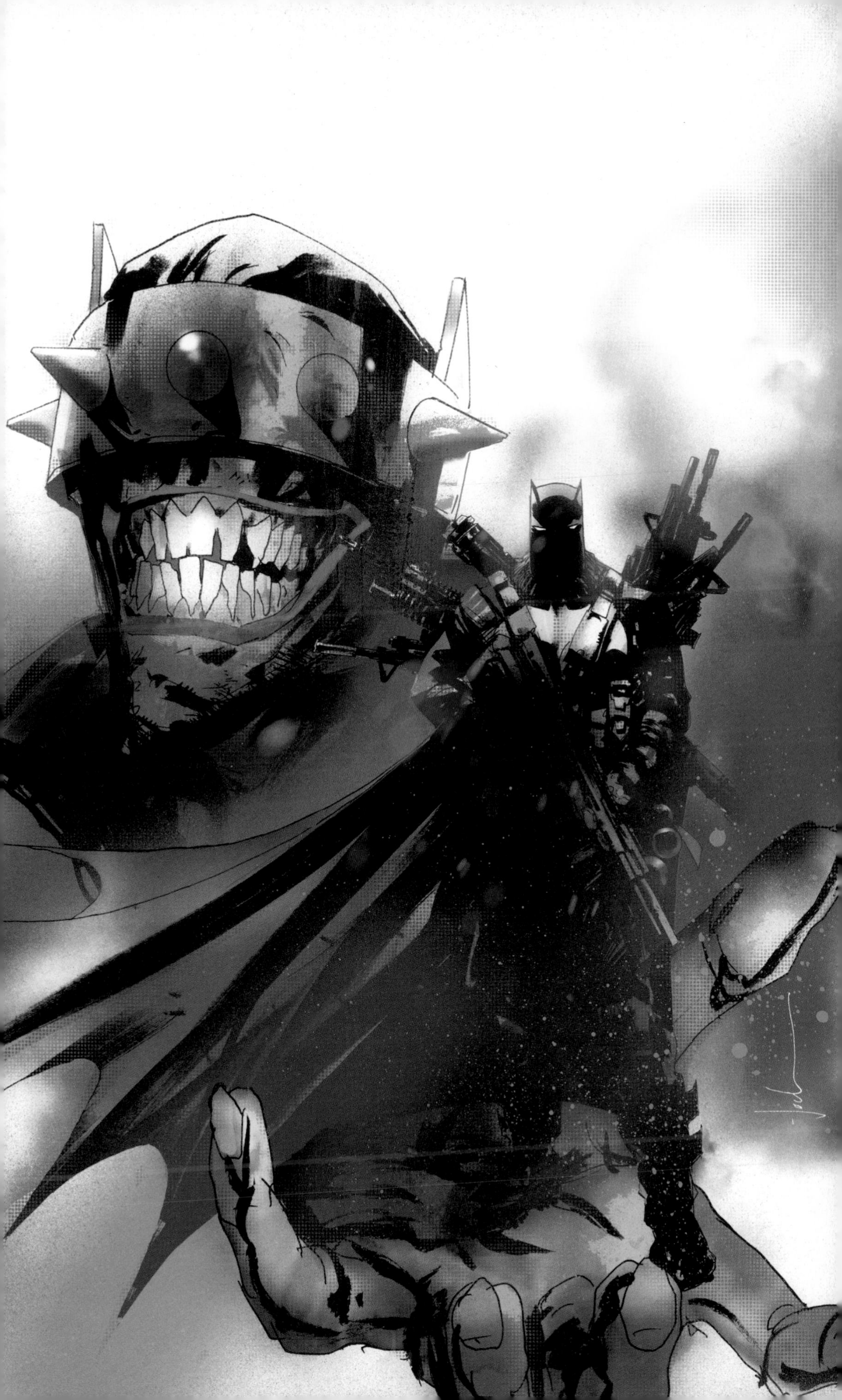

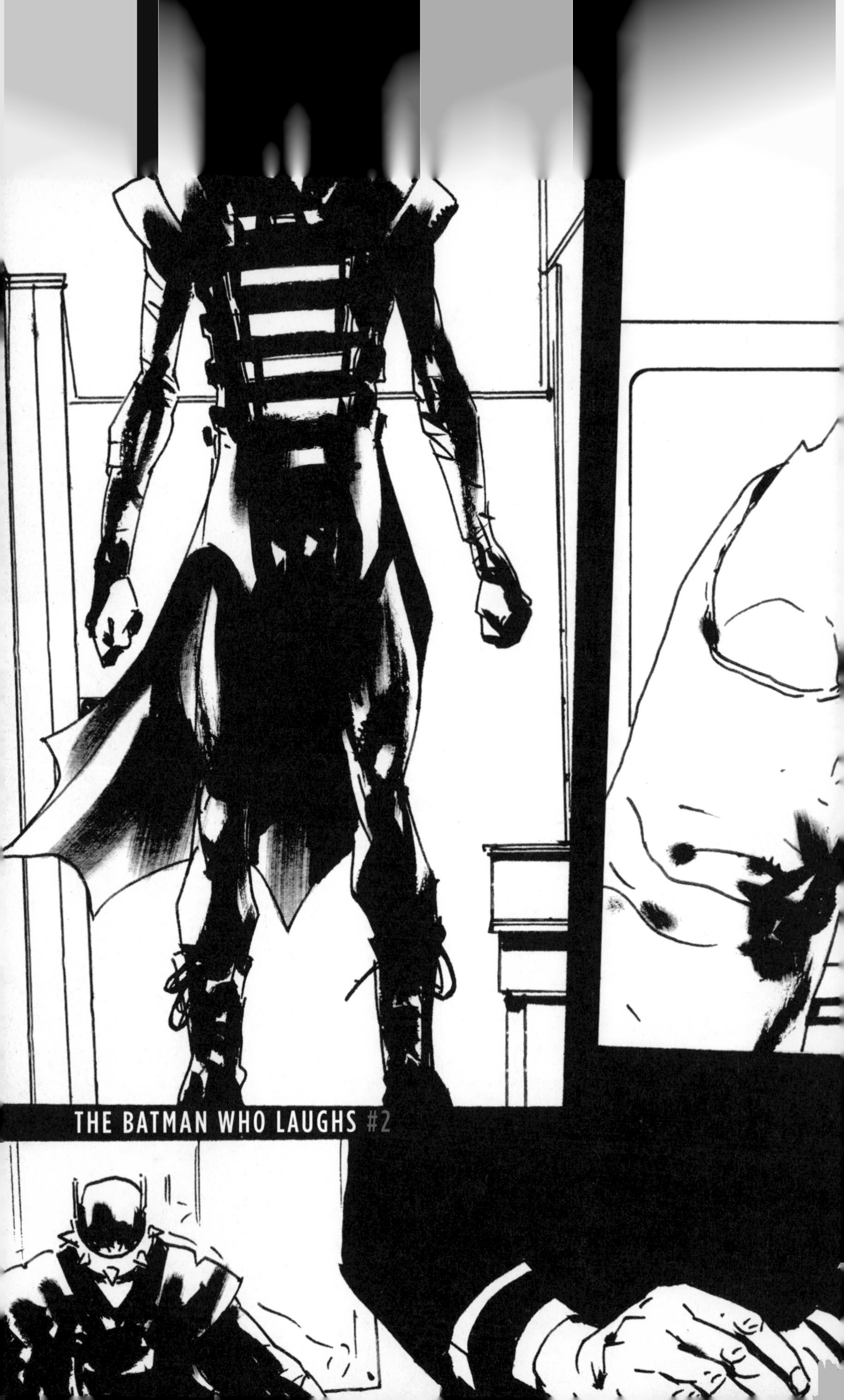
THE BATMAN WHO LAUGHS #2

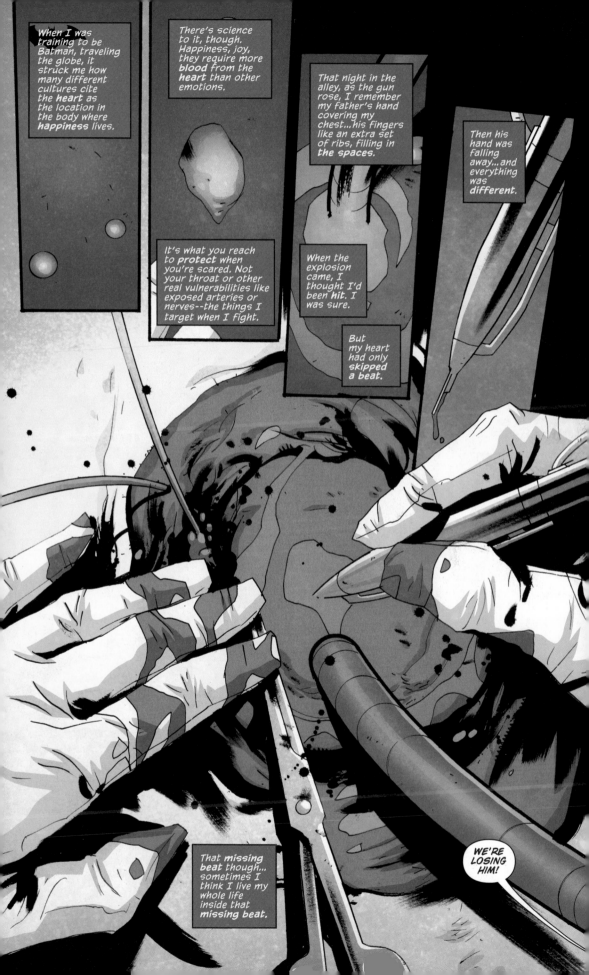

When I was training to be Batman, traveling the globe, it struck me how many different cultures cite the **heart** as the location in the body where **happiness** lives.

There's science to it, though. Happiness, joy, they require more **blood** from the **heart** than other emotions.

It's what you reach to **protect** when you're scared. Not your throat or other real vulnerabilities like exposed arteries or nerves--the things I target when I fight.

That night in the alley, as the gun rose, I remember my father's hand covering my chest...his fingers like an extra set of ribs, filling in **the spaces.**

When the explosion came, I thought I'd been **hit.** I was sure.

But my heart had only skipped a beat.

Then his hand was falling away...and everything was different.

That missing beat though... sometimes I think I live my whole life inside that **missing beat.**

WE'RE LOSING HIM!

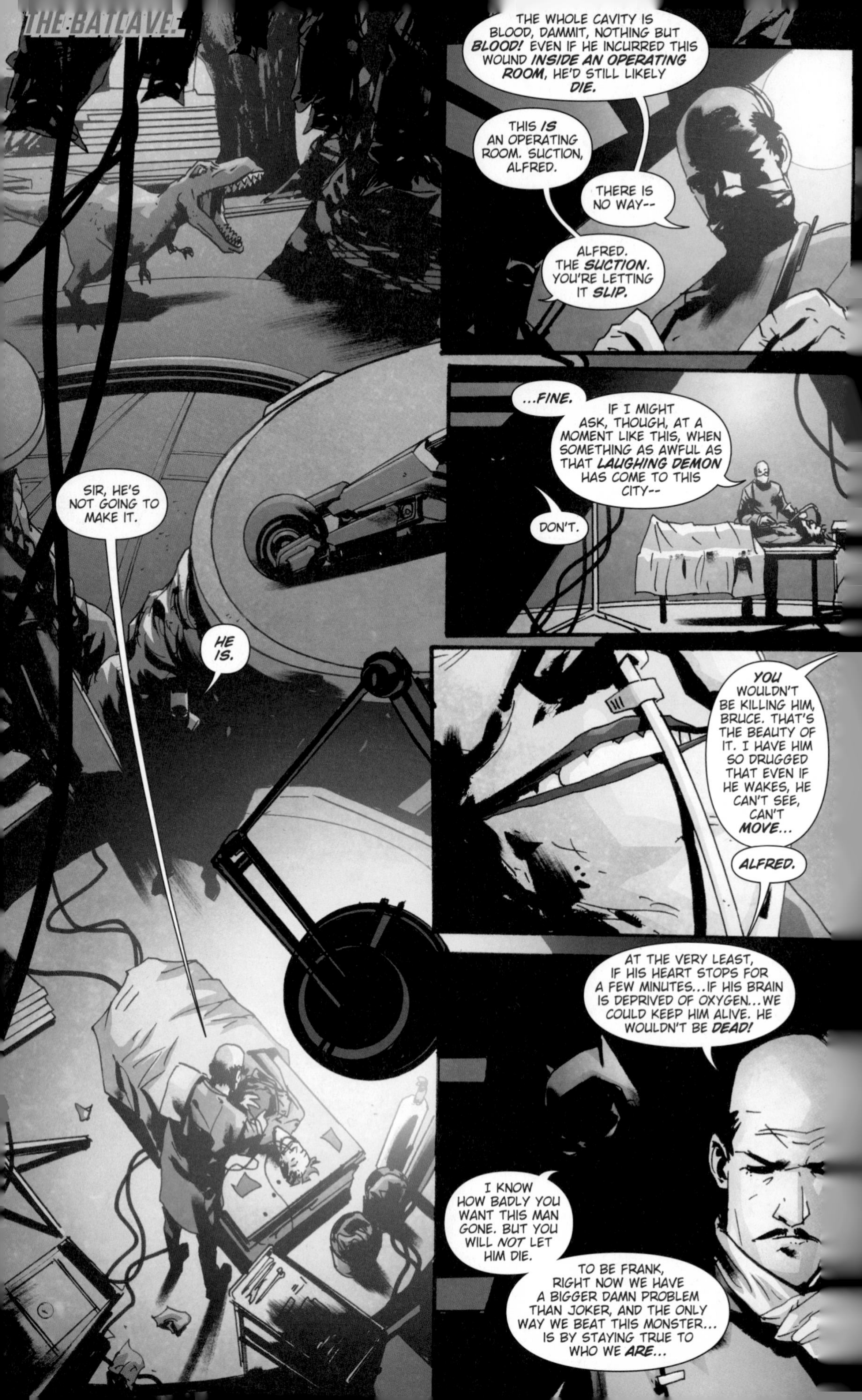
THE BATCAVE.
THE WHOLE CAVITY IS BLOOD, DAMMIT, NOTHING BUT BLOOD! EVEN IF HE INCURRED THIS WOUND INSIDE AN OPERATING ROOM, HE'D STILL LIKELY DIE.
THIS IS AN OPERATING ROOM. SUCTION, ALFRED.
THERE IS NO WAY--
ALFRED. THE SUCTION. YOU'RE LETTING IT SLIP.
...FINE.
IF I MIGHT ASK, THOUGH, AT A MOMENT LIKE THIS, WHEN SOMETHING AS AWFUL AS THAT LAUGHING DEMON HAS COME TO THIS CITY--
DON'T.
SIR, HE'S NOT GOING TO MAKE IT.
HE IS.
YOU WOULDN'T BE KILLING HIM, BRUCE. THAT'S THE BEAUTY OF IT. I HAVE HIM SO DRUGGED THAT EVEN IF HE WAKES, HE CAN'T SEE, CAN'T MOVE...
ALFRED.
AT THE VERY LEAST, IF HIS HEART STOPS FOR A FEW MINUTES...IF HIS BRAIN IS DEPRIVED OF OXYGEN...WE COULD KEEP HIM ALIVE. HE WOULDN'T BE DEAD!
I KNOW HOW BADLY YOU WANT THIS MAN GONE. BUT YOU WILL NOT LET HIM DIE.
TO BE FRANK, RIGHT NOW WE HAVE A BIGGER DAMN PROBLEM THAN JOKER, AND THE ONLY WAY WE BEAT THIS MONSTER... IS BY STAYING TRUE TO WHO WE ARE...

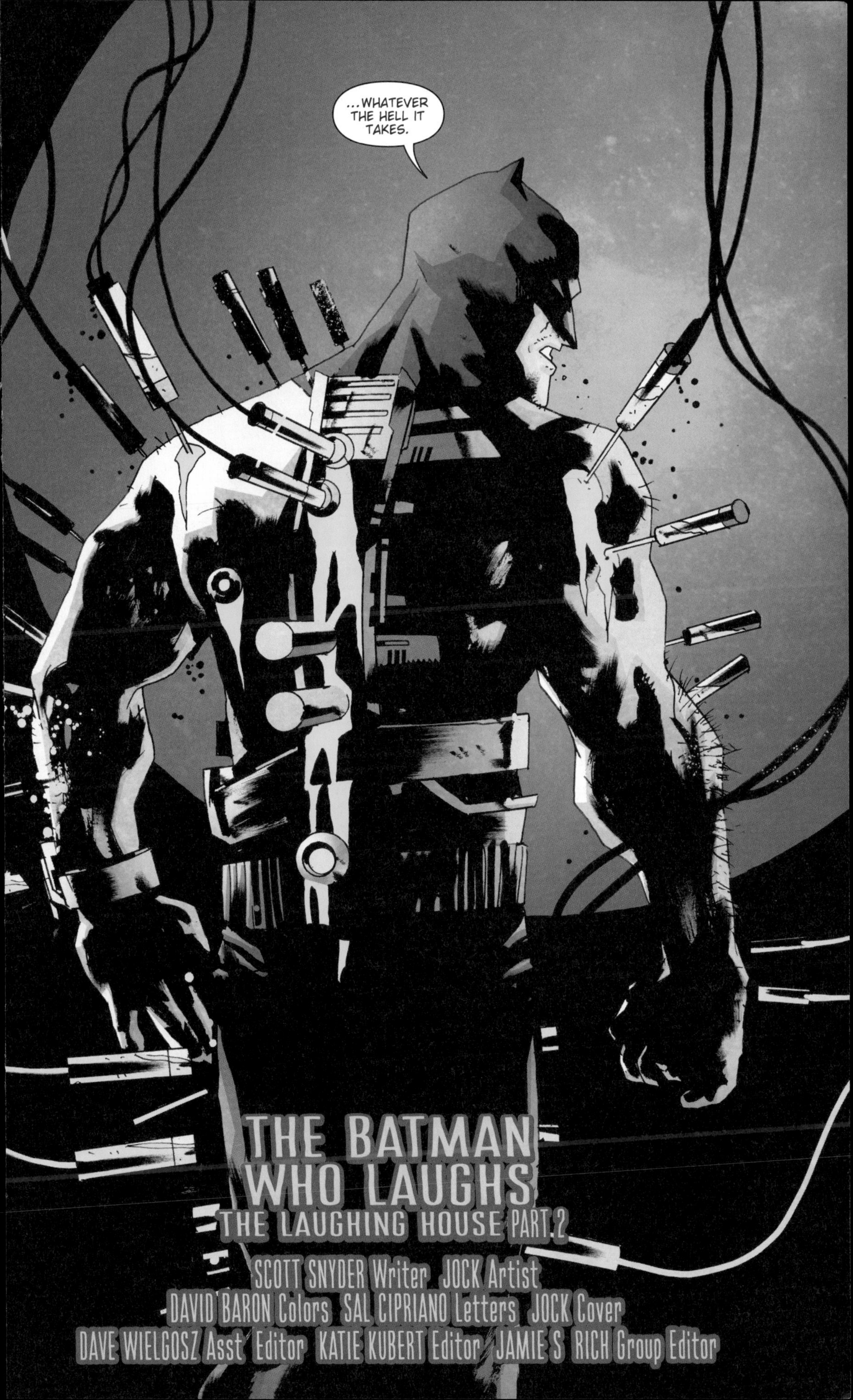
...WHATEVER THE HELL IT TAKES.
THE BATMAN WHO LAUGHS
THE LAUGHING HOUSE PART 2
SCOTT SNYDER Writer JOCK Artist
DAVID BARON Colors SAL CIPRIANO Letters JOCK Cover
DAVE WIELGOSZ Asst Editor KATIE KUBERT Editor JAMIE S RICH Group Editor

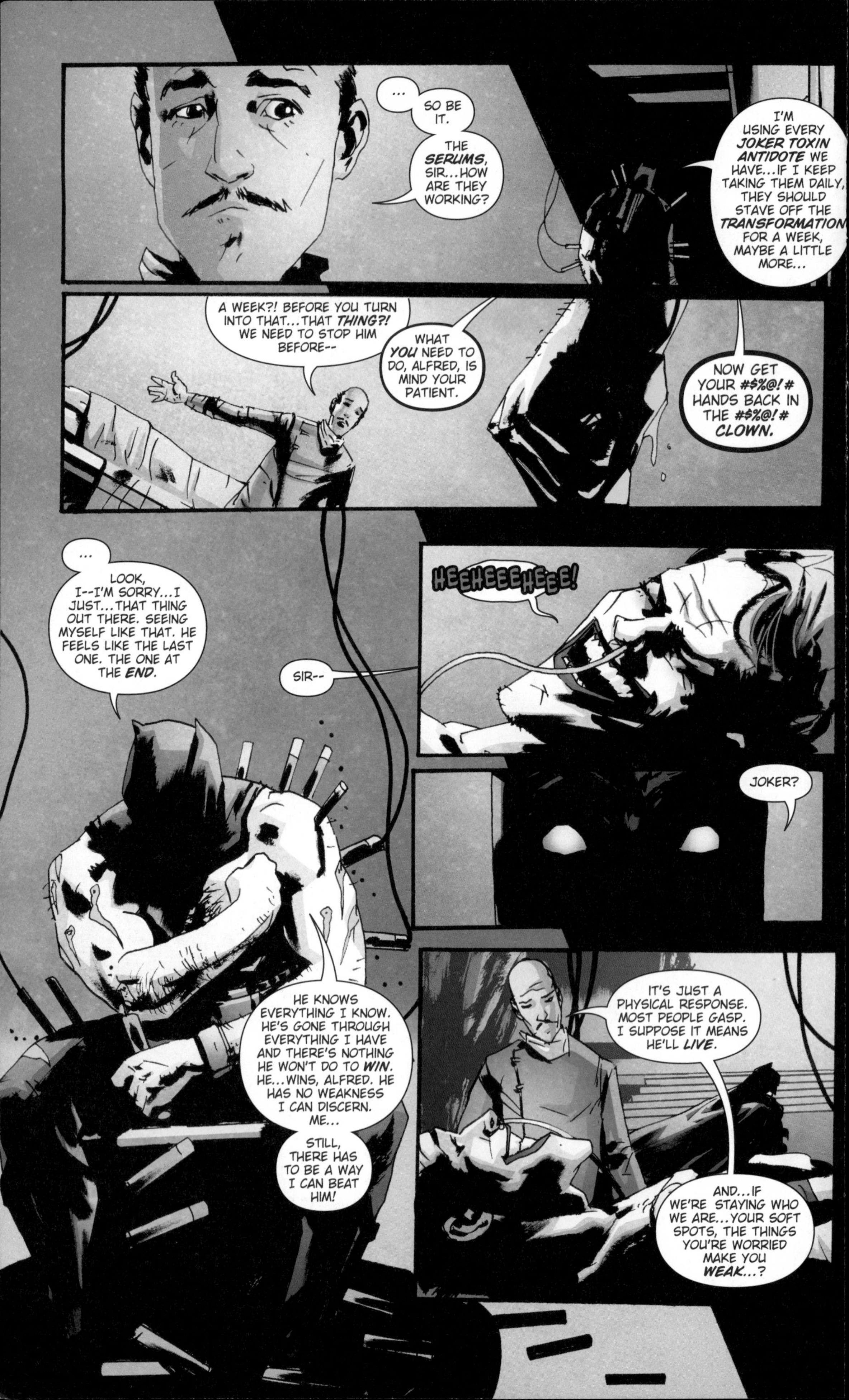
...
SO BE IT.
THE SERUMS, SIR...HOW ARE THEY WORKING?
I'M USING EVERY JOKER TOXIN ANTIDOTE WE HAVE...IF I KEEP TAKING THEM DAILY, THEY SHOULD STAVE OFF THE TRANSFORMATION FOR A WEEK, MAYBE A LITTLE MORE...
A WEEK?! BEFORE YOU TURN INTO THAT...THAT THING?! WE NEED TO STOP HIM BEFORE--
WHAT YOU NEED TO DO, ALFRED, IS MIND YOUR PATIENT.
NOW GET YOUR #$%@!# HANDS BACK IN THE #$%@!# CLOWN.
...
LOOK, I--I'M SORRY...I JUST...THAT THING OUT THERE. SEEING MYSELF LIKE THAT. HE FEELS LIKE THE LAST ONE. THE ONE AT THE END.
HEEHEEEEHEEEE!
SIR--
JOKER?
HE KNOWS EVERYTHING I KNOW. HE'S GONE THROUGH EVERYTHING I HAVE AND THERE'S NOTHING HE WON'T DO TO WIN. HE...WINS, ALFRED. HE HAS NO WEAKNESS I CAN DISCERN. ME...
STILL, THERE HAS TO BE A WAY I CAN BEAT HIM!
IT'S JUST A PHYSICAL RESPONSE. MOST PEOPLE GASP. I SUPPOSE IT MEANS HE'LL LIVE.
AND...IF WE'RE STAYING WHO WE ARE...YOUR SOFT SPOTS, THE THINGS YOU'RE WORRIED MAKE YOU WEAK...?

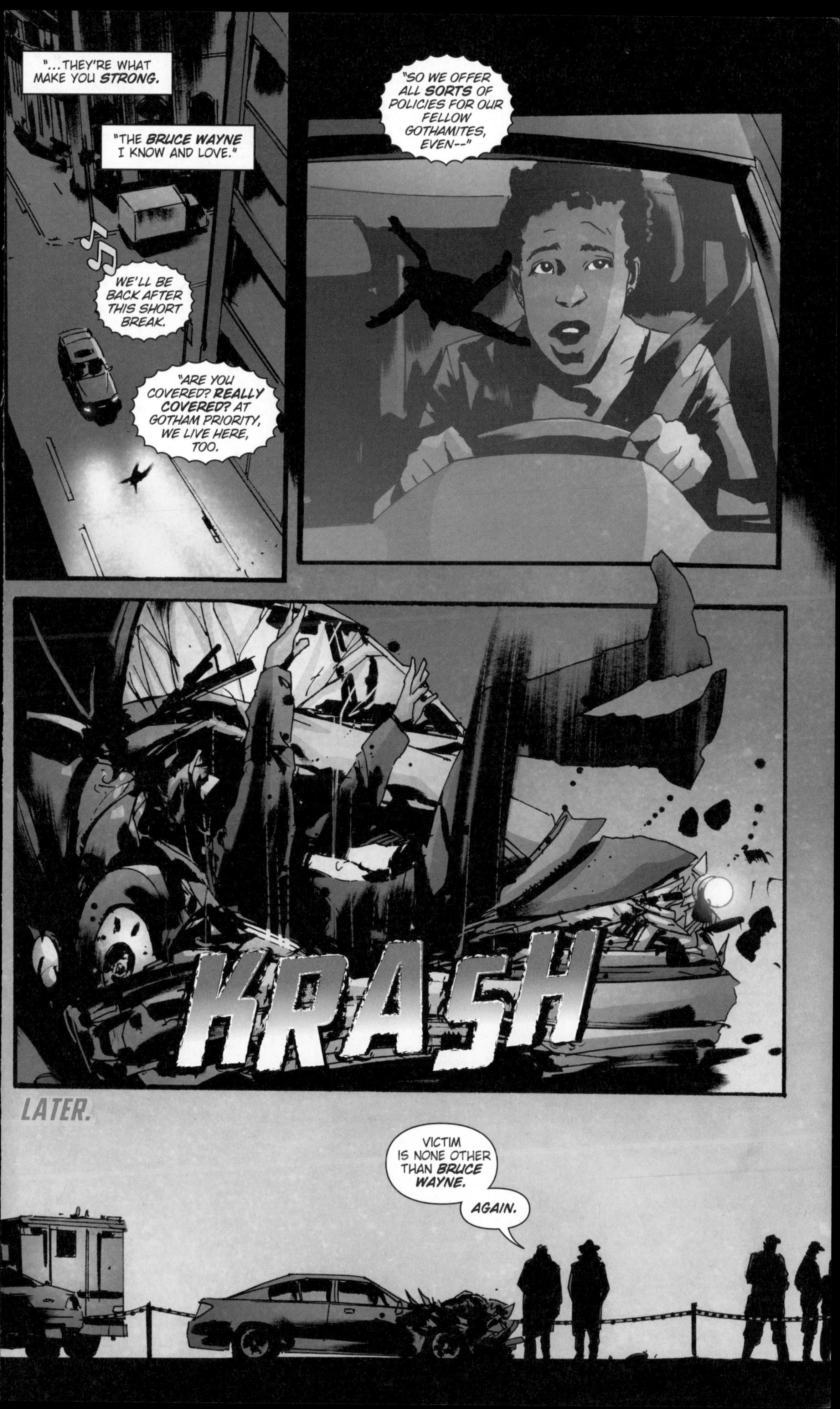
"...THEY'RE WHAT MAKE YOU STRONG.
"THE BRUCE WAYNE I KNOW AND LOVE."
WE'LL BE BACK AFTER THIS SHORT BREAK.
"ARE YOU COVERED? REALLY COVERED? AT GOTHAM PRIORITY, WE LIVE HERE, TOO.
"SO WE OFFER ALL SORTS OF POLICIES FOR OUR FELLOW GOTHAMITES, EVEN--"
KRASH
LATER.
VICTIM IS NONE OTHER THAN BRUCE WAYNE.
AGAIN.

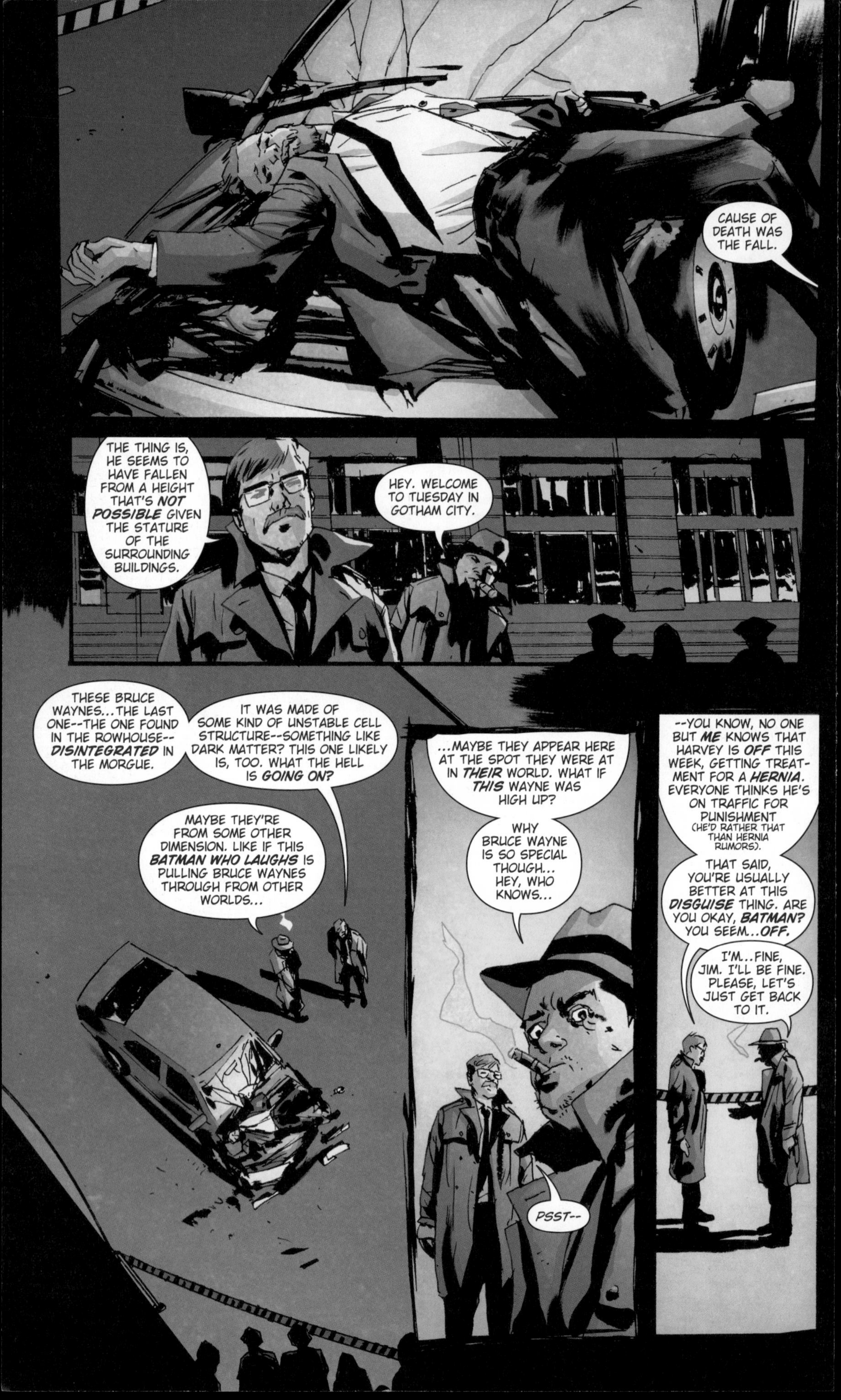
CAUSE OF DEATH WAS THE FALL.
THE THING IS, HE SEEMS TO HAVE FALLEN FROM A HEIGHT THAT'S NOT POSSIBLE GIVEN THE STATURE OF THE SURROUNDING BUILDINGS.
HEY. WELCOME TO TUESDAY IN GOTHAM CITY.
THESE BRUCE WAYNES...THE LAST ONE--THE ONE FOUND IN THE ROWHOUSE--DISINTEGRATED IN THE MORGUE.
IT WAS MADE OF SOME KIND OF UNSTABLE CELL STRUCTURE--SOMETHING LIKE DARK MATTER? THIS ONE LIKELY IS, TOO. WHAT THE HELL IS GOING ON?
MAYBE THEY'RE FROM SOME OTHER DIMENSION. LIKE IF THIS BATMAN WHO LAUGHS IS PULLING BRUCE WAYNES THROUGH FROM OTHER WORLDS...
...MAYBE THEY APPEAR HERE AT THE SPOT THEY WERE AT IN THEIR WORLD. WHAT IF THIS WAYNE WAS HIGH UP?
WHY BRUCE WAYNE IS SO SPECIAL THOUGH... HEY, WHO KNOWS...
PSST--
--YOU KNOW, NO ONE BUT ME KNOWS THAT HARVEY IS OFF THIS WEEK, GETTING TREATMENT FOR A HERNIA. EVERYONE THINKS HE'S ON TRAFFIC FOR PUNISHMENT (HE'D RATHER THAT THAN HERNIA RUMORS).
THAT SAID, YOU'RE USUALLY BETTER AT THIS DISGUISE THING. ARE YOU OKAY, BATMAN? YOU SEEM...OFF.
I'M...FINE, JIM. I'LL BE FINE. PLEASE, LET'S JUST GET BACK TO IT.

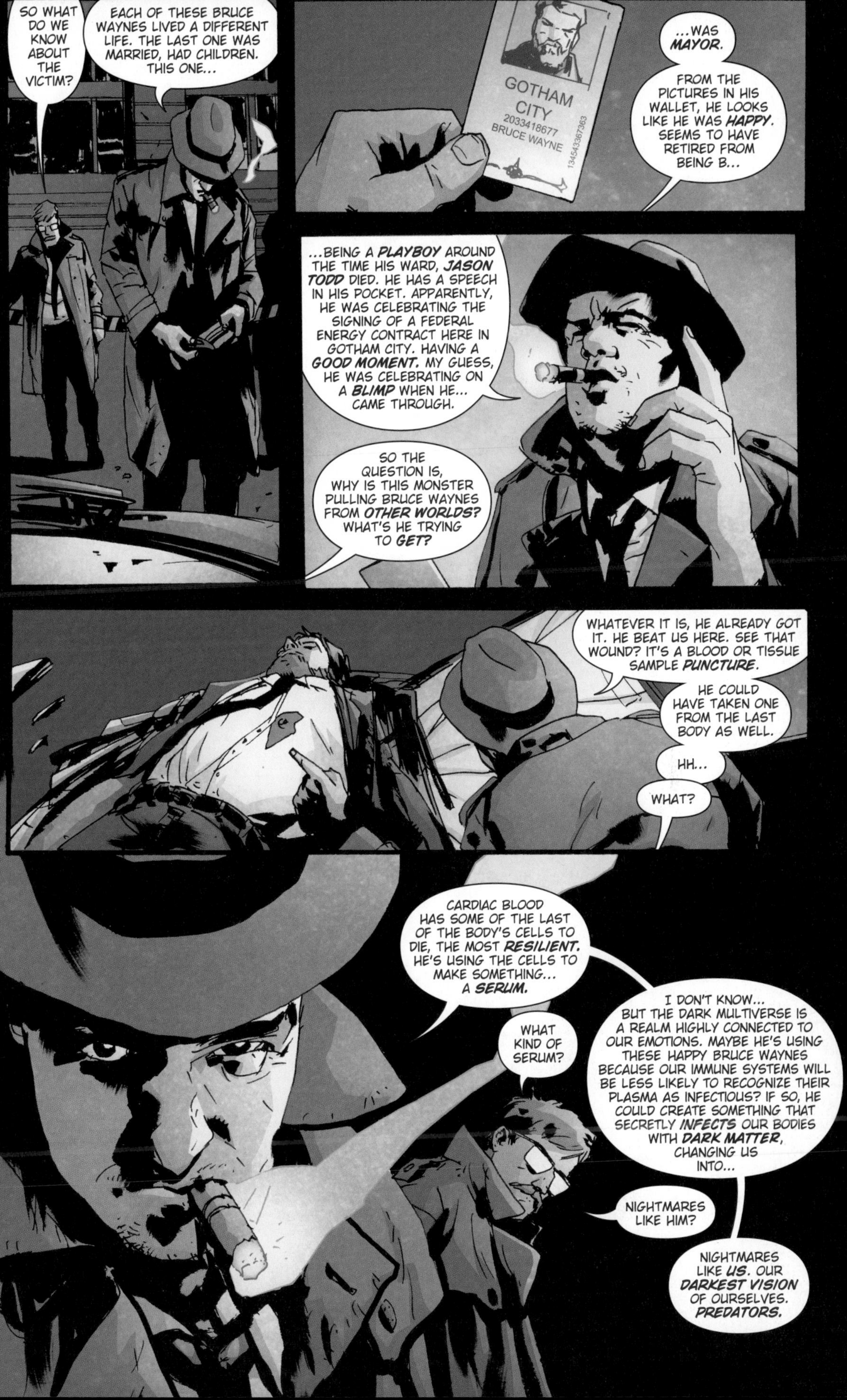
SO WHAT DO WE KNOW ABOUT THE VICTIM?
EACH OF THESE BRUCE WAYNES LIVED A DIFFERENT LIFE. THE LAST ONE WAS MARRIED, HAD CHILDREN. THIS ONE...
GOTHAM CITY 2033418677 BRUCE WAYNE 1345433367363
...WAS MAYOR.
FROM THE PICTURES IN HIS WALLET, HE LOOKS LIKE HE WAS HAPPY. SEEMS TO HAVE RETIRED FROM BEING B...
...BEING A PLAYBOY AROUND THE TIME HIS WARD, JASON TODD DIED. HE HAS A SPEECH IN HIS POCKET. APPARENTLY, HE WAS CELEBRATING THE SIGNING OF A FEDERAL ENERGY CONTRACT HERE IN GOTHAM CITY. HAVING A GOOD MOMENT. MY GUESS, HE WAS CELEBRATING ON A BLIMP WHEN HE... CAME THROUGH.
SO THE QUESTION IS, WHY IS THIS MONSTER PULLING BRUCE WAYNES FROM OTHER WORLDS? WHAT'S HE TRYING TO GET?
WHATEVER IT IS, HE ALREADY GOT IT. HE BEAT US HERE. SEE THAT WOUND? IT'S A BLOOD OR TISSUE SAMPLE PUNCTURE.
HE COULD HAVE TAKEN ONE FROM THE LAST BODY AS WELL.
HH...
WHAT?
CARDIAC BLOOD HAS SOME OF THE LAST OF THE BODY'S CELLS TO DIE, THE MOST RESILIENT. HE'S USING THE CELLS TO MAKE SOMETHING... A SERUM.
WHAT KIND OF SERUM?
I DON'T KNOW... BUT THE DARK MULTIVERSE IS A REALM HIGHLY CONNECTED TO OUR EMOTIONS. MAYBE HE'S USING THESE HAPPY BRUCE WAYNES BECAUSE OUR IMMUNE SYSTEMS WILL BE LESS LIKELY TO RECOGNIZE THEIR PLASMA AS INFECTIOUS? IF SO, HE COULD CREATE SOMETHING THAT SECRETLY INFECTS OUR BODIES WITH DARK MATTER, CHANGING US INTO...
NIGHTMARES LIKE HIM?
NIGHTMARES LIKE US. OUR DARKEST VISION OF OURSELVES. PREDATORS.

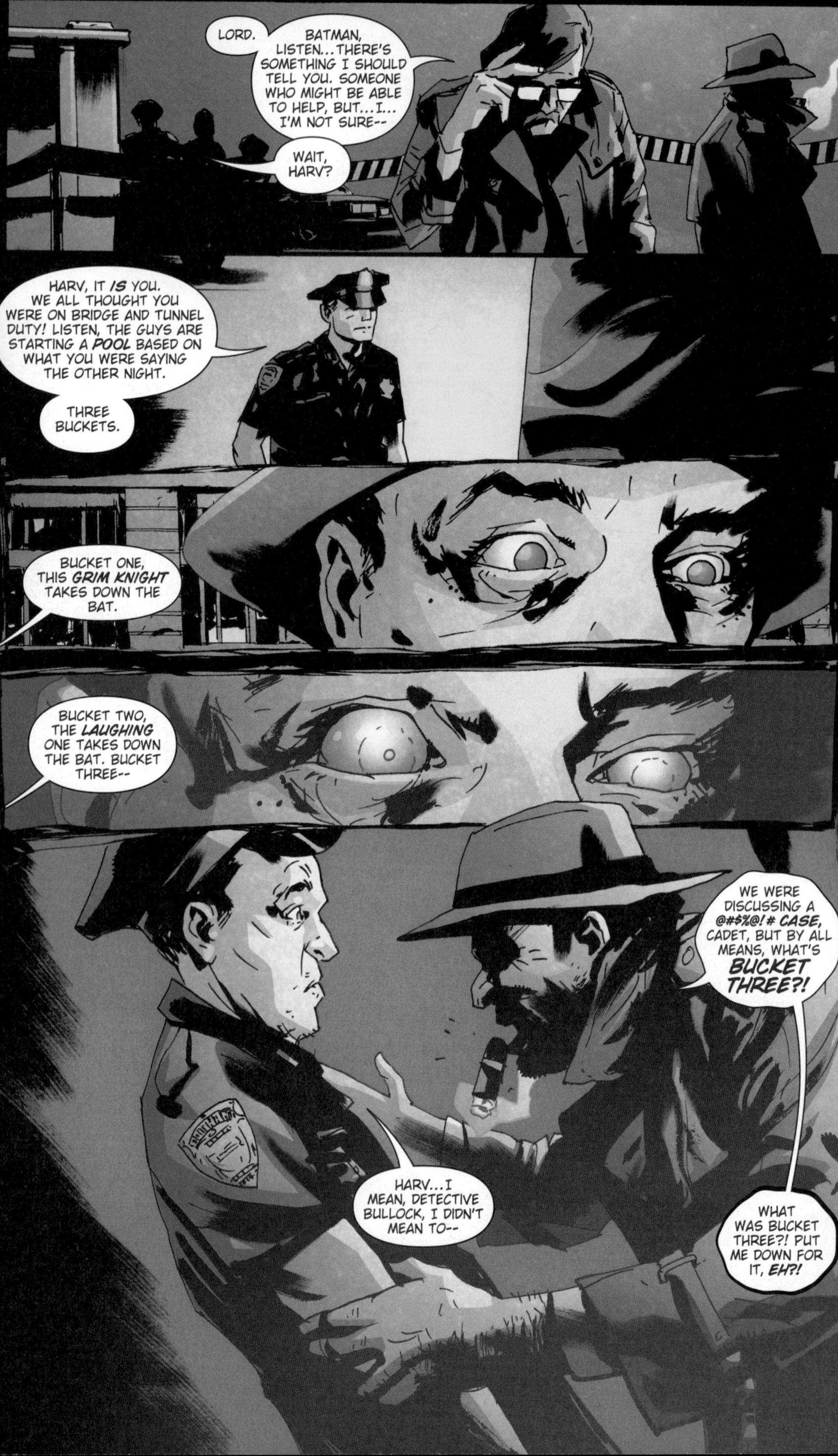
LORD.
BATMAN, LISTEN...THERE'S SOMETHING I SHOULD TELL YOU. SOMEONE WHO MIGHT BE ABLE TO HELP, BUT...I... I'M NOT SURE--
WAIT, HARV?
HARV, IT *IS* YOU. WE ALL THOUGHT YOU WERE ON BRIDGE AND TUNNEL DUTY! LISTEN, THE GUYS ARE STARTING A **POOL** BASED ON WHAT YOU WERE SAYING THE OTHER NIGHT.
THREE BUCKETS.
BUCKET ONE, THIS **GRIM KNIGHT** TAKES DOWN THE BAT.
BUCKET TWO, THE **LAUGHING** ONE TAKES DOWN THE BAT. BUCKET THREE--
WE WERE DISCUSSING A @#$%@!# **CASE**, CADET, BUT BY ALL MEANS, WHAT'S **BUCKET THREE?!**
HARV...I MEAN, DETECTIVE BULLOCK, I DIDN'T MEAN TO--
WHAT WAS BUCKET THREE?! PUT ME DOWN FOR IT, **EH?!**

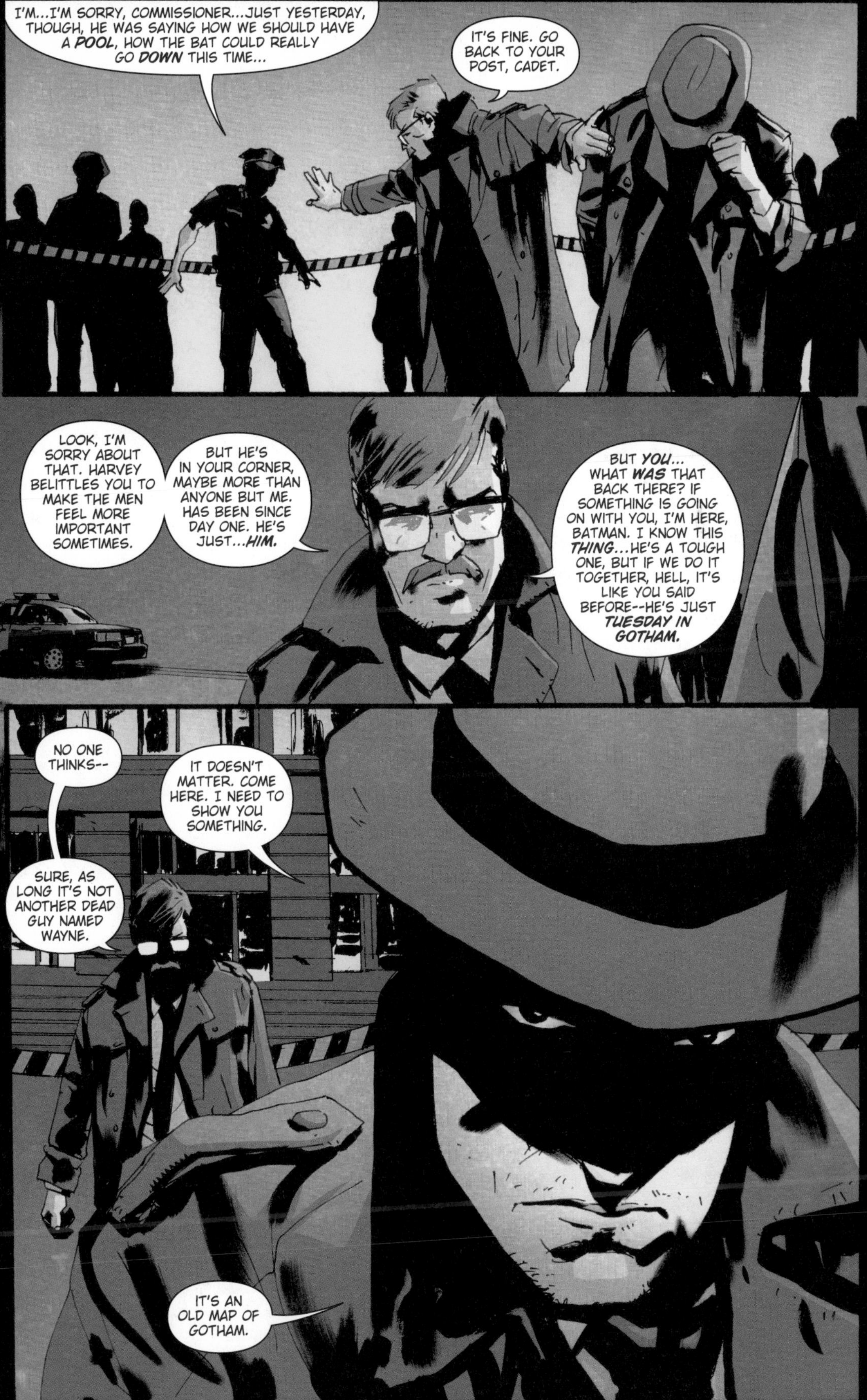
I'M...I'M SORRY, COMMISSIONER...JUST YESTERDAY, THOUGH, HE WAS SAYING HOW WE SHOULD HAVE A POOL, HOW THE BAT COULD REALLY GO DOWN THIS TIME...
IT'S FINE. GO BACK TO YOUR POST, CADET.
LOOK, I'M SORRY ABOUT THAT. HARVEY BELITTLES YOU TO MAKE THE MEN FEEL MORE IMPORTANT SOMETIMES.
BUT HE'S IN YOUR CORNER, MAYBE MORE THAN ANYONE BUT ME. HAS BEEN SINCE DAY ONE. HE'S JUST...HIM.
BUT YOU... WHAT WAS THAT BACK THERE? IF SOMETHING IS GOING ON WITH YOU, I'M HERE, BATMAN. I KNOW THIS THING...HE'S A TOUGH ONE, BUT IF WE DO IT TOGETHER, HELL, IT'S LIKE YOU SAID BEFORE--HE'S JUST TUESDAY IN GOTHAM.
NO ONE THINKS--
IT DOESN'T MATTER. COME HERE. I NEED TO SHOW YOU SOMETHING.
SURE, AS LONG IT'S NOT ANOTHER DEAD GUY NAMED WAYNE.
IT'S AN OLD MAP OF GOTHAM.

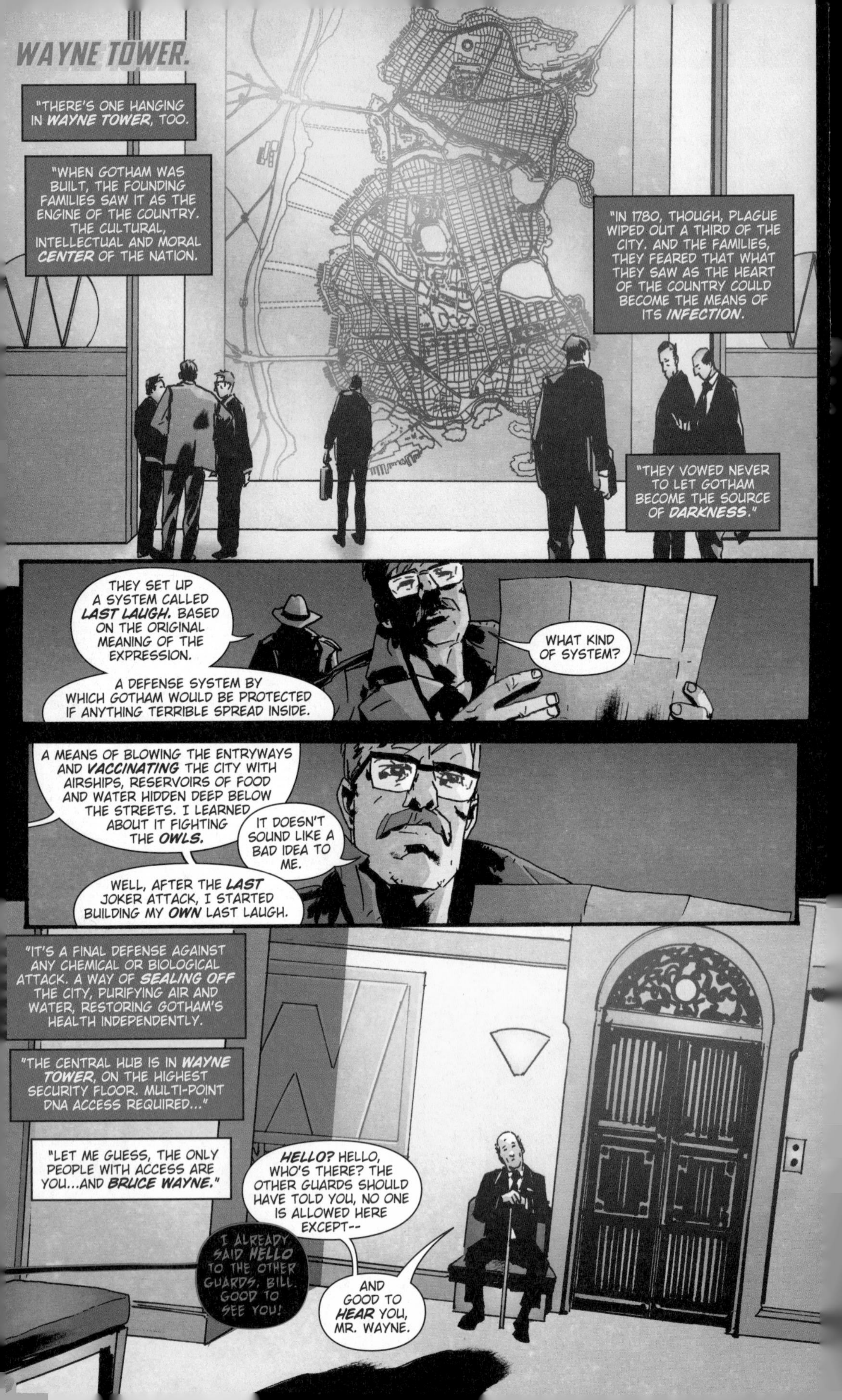
WAYNE TOWER.
"THERE'S ONE HANGING IN WAYNE TOWER, TOO.
"WHEN GOTHAM WAS BUILT, THE FOUNDING FAMILIES SAW IT AS THE ENGINE OF THE COUNTRY. THE CULTURAL, INTELLECTUAL AND MORAL CENTER OF THE NATION.
"IN 1780, THOUGH, PLAGUE WIPED OUT A THIRD OF THE CITY. AND THE FAMILIES, THEY FEARED THAT WHAT THEY SAW AS THE HEART OF THE COUNTRY COULD BECOME THE MEANS OF ITS INFECTION.
"THEY VOWED NEVER TO LET GOTHAM BECOME THE SOURCE OF DARKNESS."
THEY SET UP A SYSTEM CALLED LAST LAUGH. BASED ON THE ORIGINAL MEANING OF THE EXPRESSION.
WHAT KIND OF SYSTEM?
A DEFENSE SYSTEM BY WHICH GOTHAM WOULD BE PROTECTED IF ANYTHING TERRIBLE SPREAD INSIDE.
A MEANS OF BLOWING THE ENTRYWAYS AND VACCINATING THE CITY WITH AIRSHIPS, RESERVOIRS OF FOOD AND WATER HIDDEN DEEP BELOW THE STREETS. I LEARNED ABOUT IT FIGHTING THE OWLS.
IT DOESN'T SOUND LIKE A BAD IDEA TO ME.
WELL, AFTER THE LAST JOKER ATTACK, I STARTED BUILDING MY OWN LAST LAUGH.
"IT'S A FINAL DEFENSE AGAINST ANY CHEMICAL OR BIOLOGICAL ATTACK. A WAY OF SEALING OFF THE CITY, PURIFYING AIR AND WATER, RESTORING GOTHAM'S HEALTH INDEPENDENTLY.
"THE CENTRAL HUB IS IN WAYNE TOWER, ON THE HIGHEST SECURITY FLOOR. MULTI-POINT DNA ACCESS REQUIRED..."
"LET ME GUESS, THE ONLY PEOPLE WITH ACCESS ARE YOU...AND BRUCE WAYNE."
HELLO? HELLO, WHO'S THERE? THE OTHER GUARDS SHOULD HAVE TOLD YOU, NO ONE IS ALLOWED HERE EXCEPT--
I ALREADY SAID HELLO TO THE OTHER GUARDS, BILL. GOOD TO SEE YOU!
AND GOOD TO HEAR YOU, MR. WAYNE.

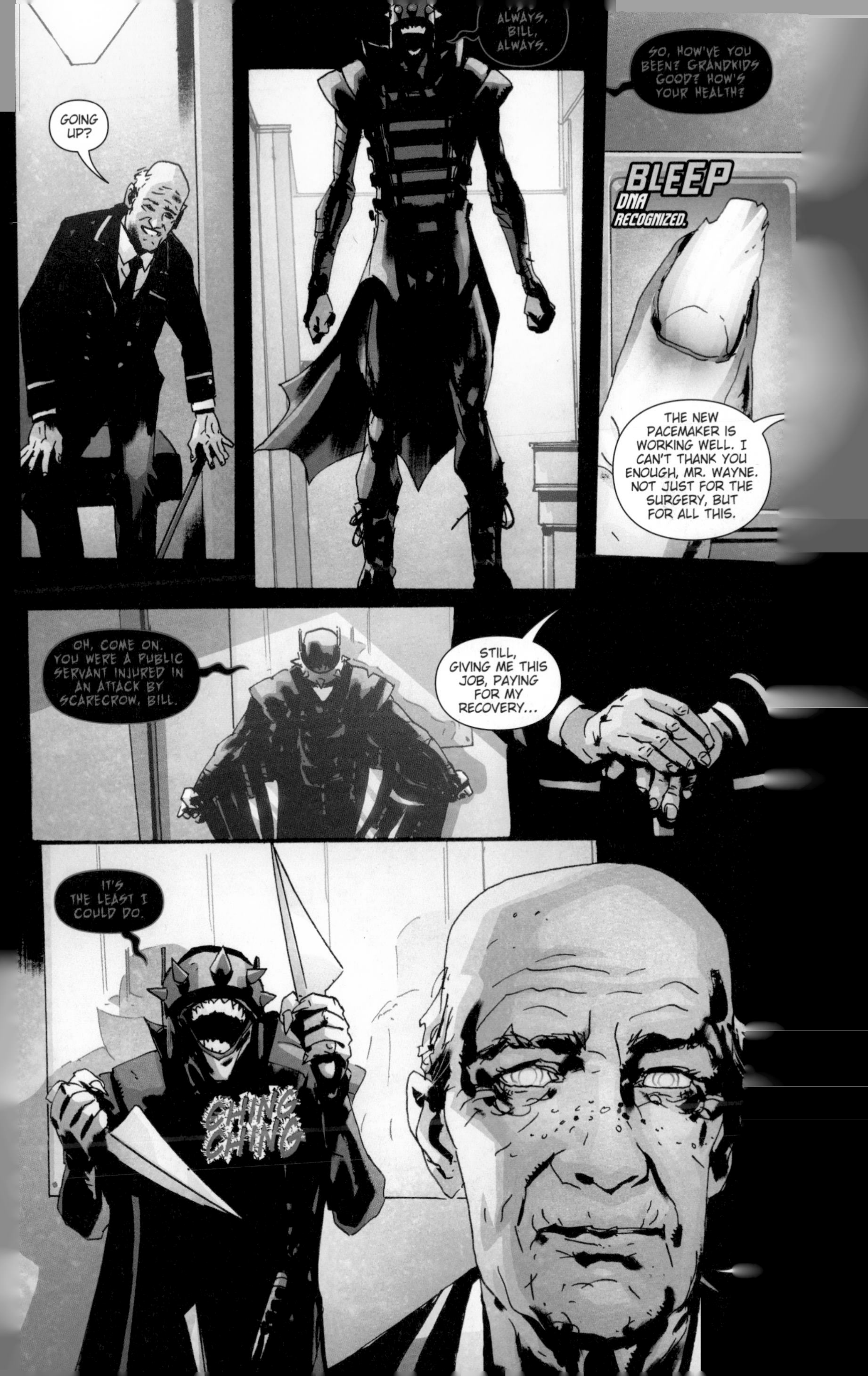
GOING UP?
ALWAYS, BILL, ALWAYS.
SO, HOW'VE YOU BEEN? GRANDKIDS GOOD? HOW'S YOUR HEALTH?
BLEEP
DNA RECOGNIZED.
THE NEW PACEMAKER IS WORKING WELL. I CAN'T THANK YOU ENOUGH, MR. WAYNE. NOT JUST FOR THE SURGERY, BUT FOR ALL THIS.
STILL, GIVING ME THIS JOB, PAYING FOR MY RECOVERY...
OH, COME ON. YOU WERE A PUBLIC SERVANT INJURED IN AN ATTACK BY SCARECROW, BILL.
IT'S THE LEAST I COULD DO.
CHING CHING

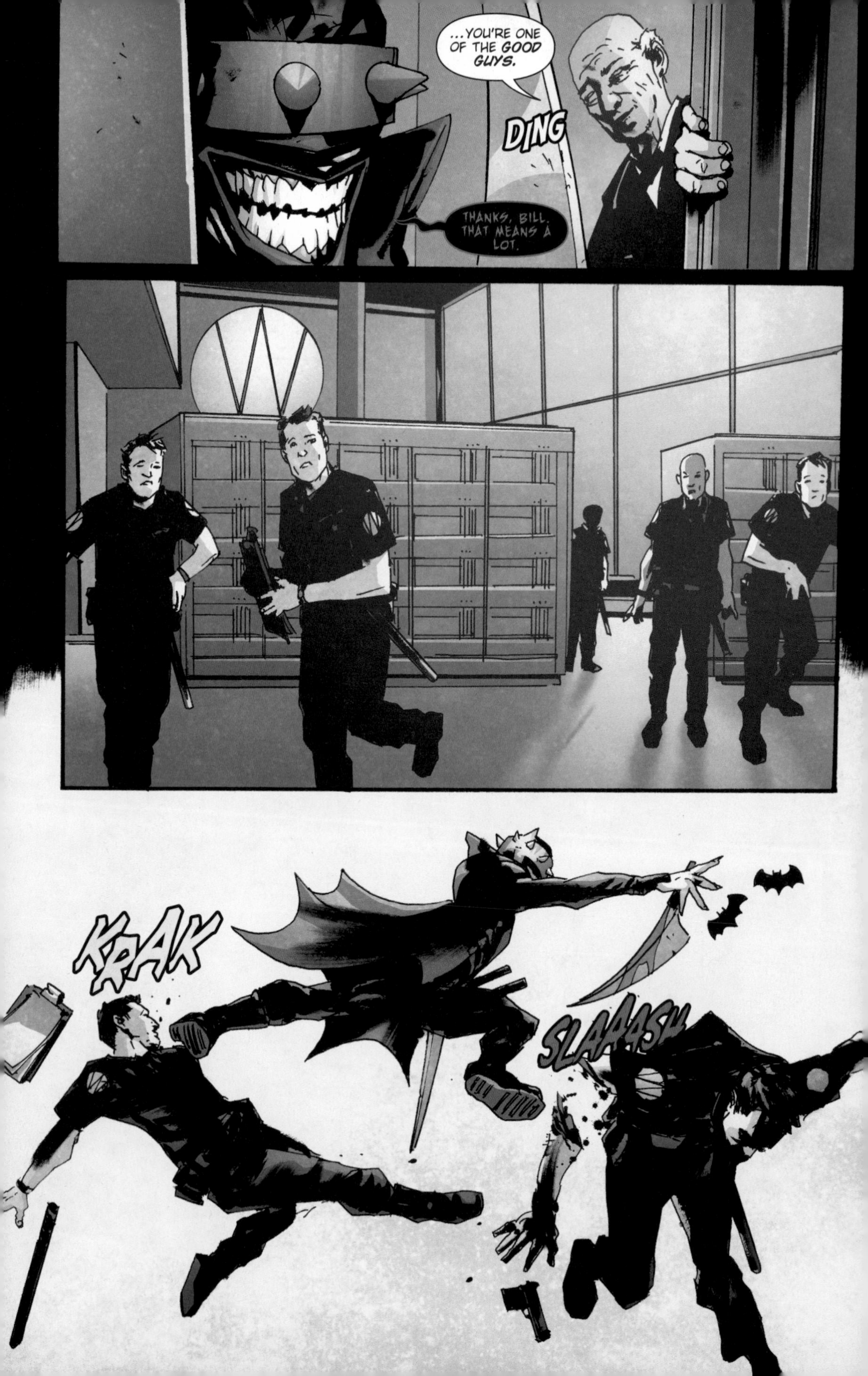

...YOU'RE ONE OF THE GOOD GUYS.
DING
THANKS, BILL. THAT MEANS A LOT.
KRAK
SLAAASH

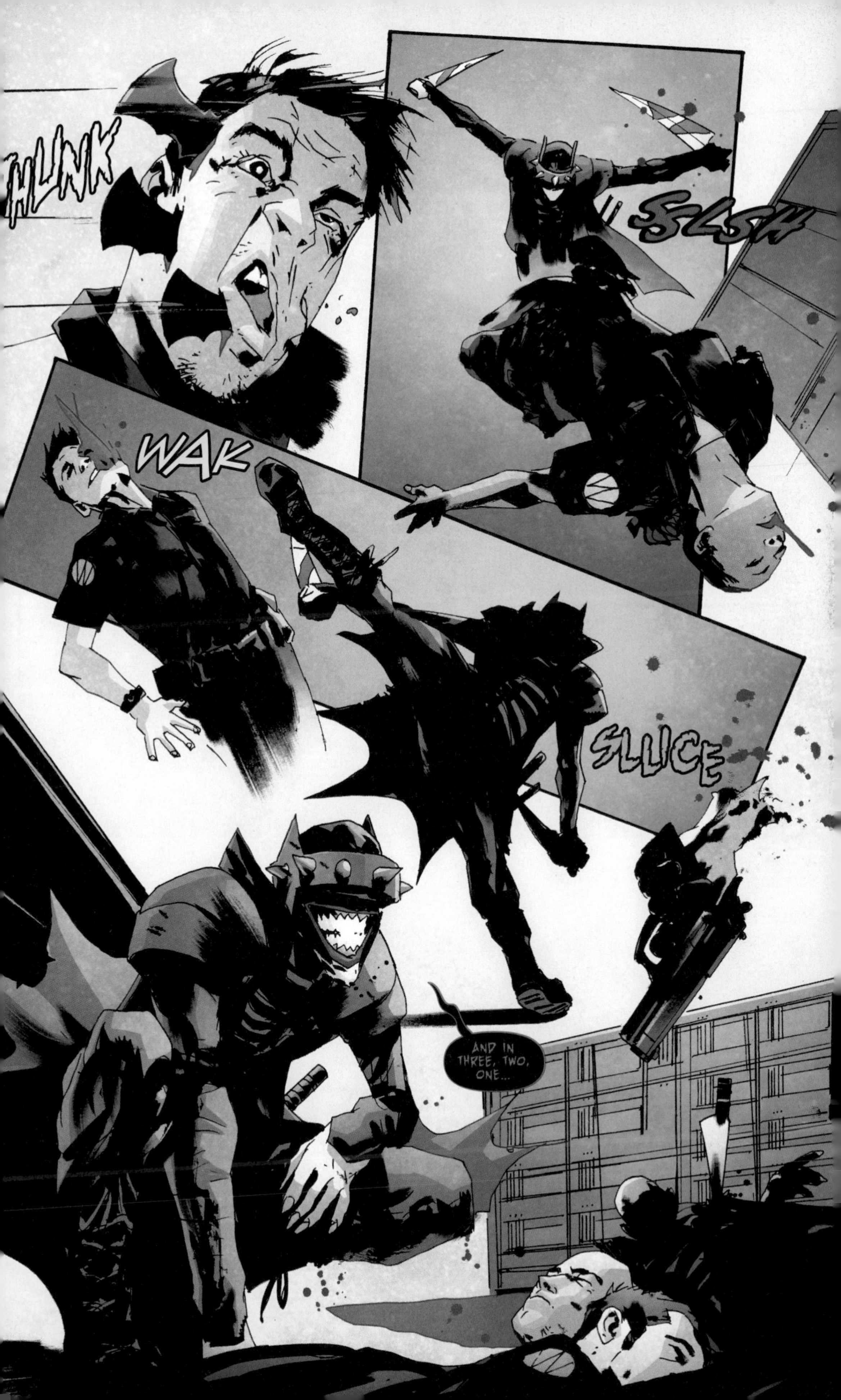
HUNK
SLSH
WAK
SLLICE
AND IN THREE, TWO, ONE...

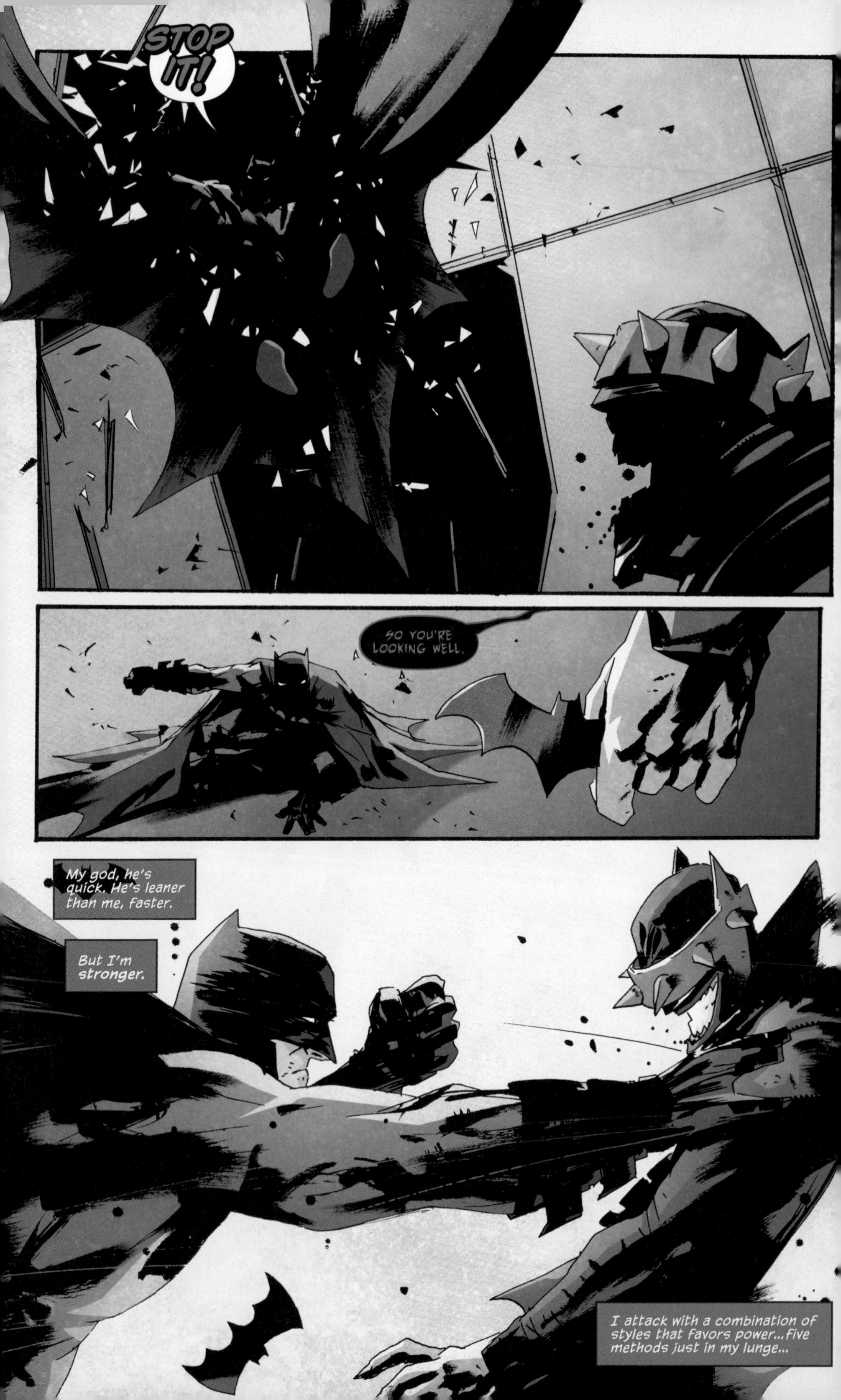
STOP IT!
SO YOU'RE LOOKING WELL.
My god, he's quick. He's leaner than me, faster.
But I'm stronger.
I attack with a combination of styles that favors power...five methods just in my lunge...

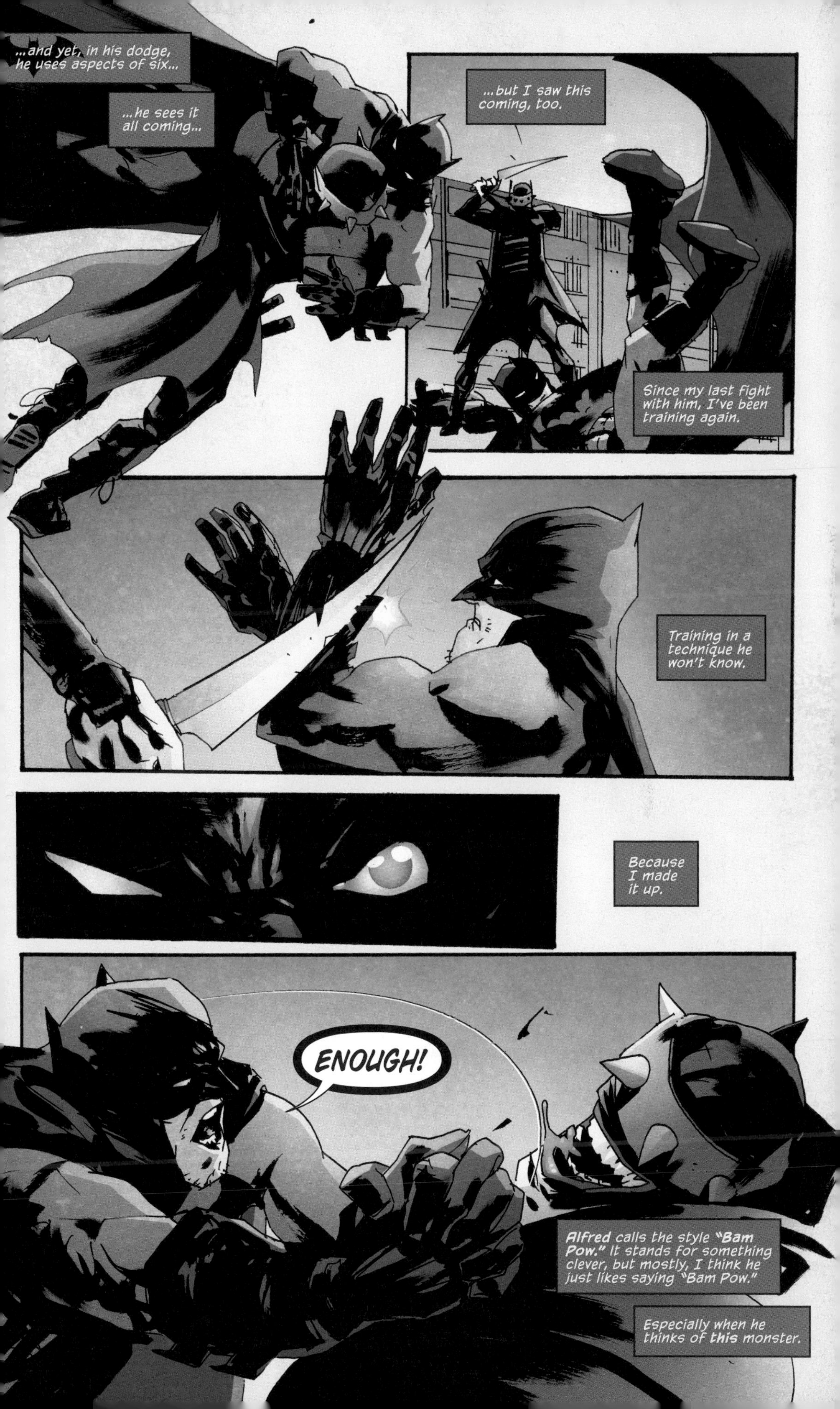
...and yet, in his dodge, he uses aspects of six...
...he sees it all coming...
...but I saw this coming, too.
Since my last fight with him, I've been training again.
Training in a technique he won't know.
Because I made it up.
ENOUGH!
Alfred calls the style "Bam Pow." It stands for something clever, but mostly, I think he just likes saying "Bam Pow."
Especially when he thinks of this monster.

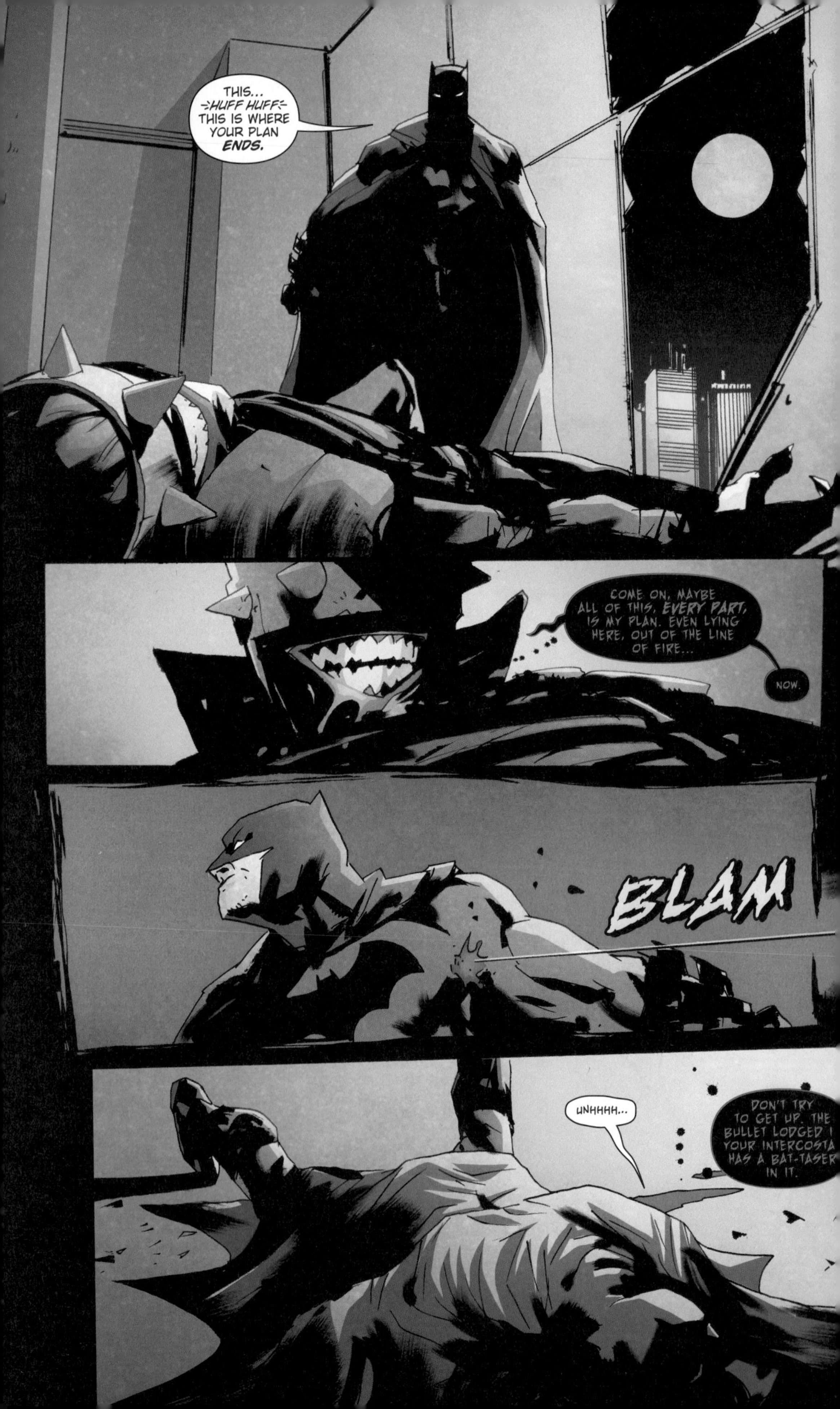
THIS... -HUFF HUFF- THIS IS WHERE YOUR PLAN ENDS.
COME ON, MAYBE ALL OF THIS, EVERY PART, IS MY PLAN. EVEN LYING HERE, OUT OF THE LINE OF FIRE...
NOW.
BLAM
UNHHHH...
DON'T TRY TO GET UP. THE BULLET LODGED I YOUR INTERCOSTA HAS A BAT-TASER IN IT.

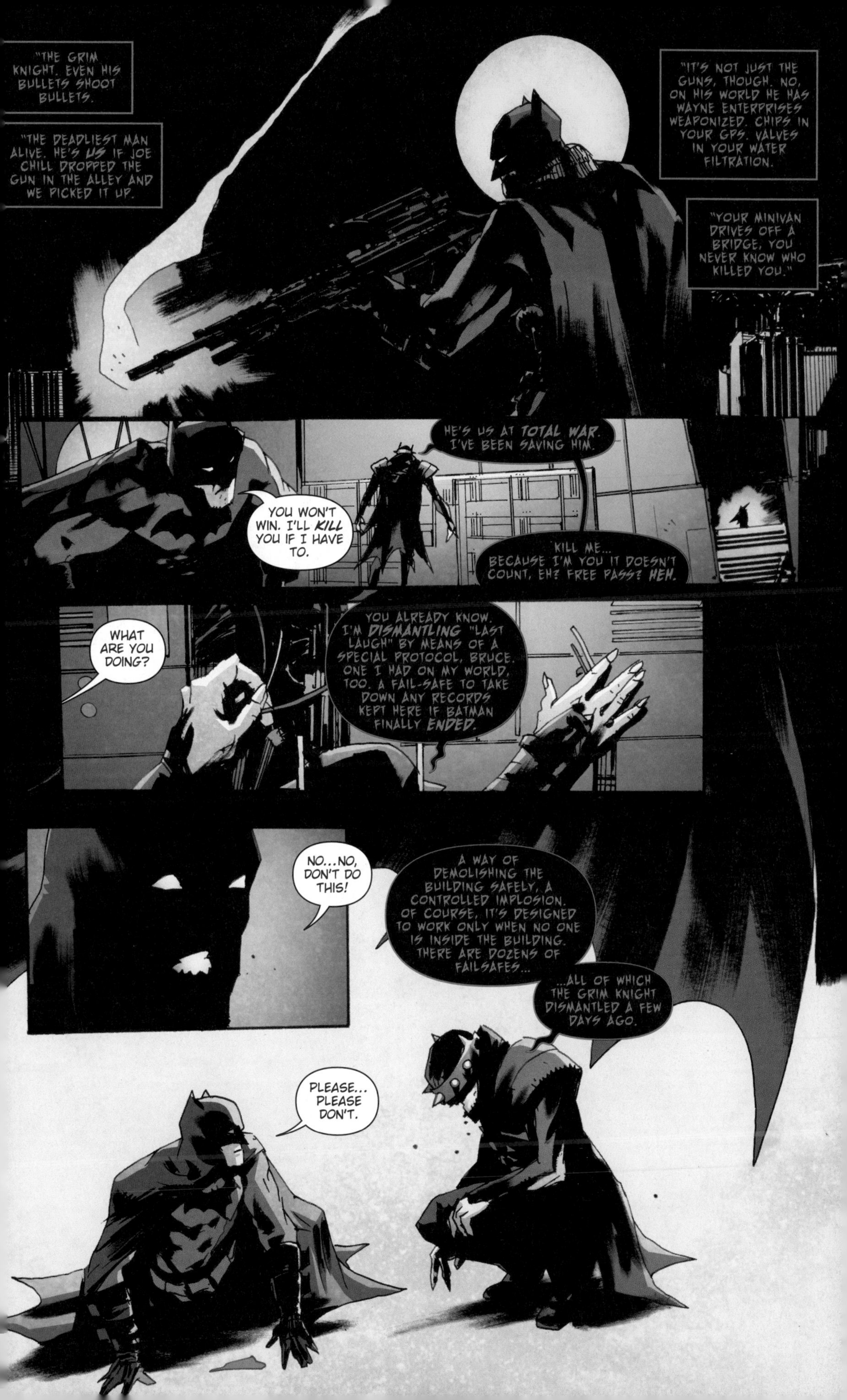
"THE GRIM KNIGHT. EVEN HIS BULLETS SHOOT BULLETS.
"THE DEADLIEST MAN ALIVE. HE'S US IF JOE CHILL DROPPED THE GUN IN THE ALLEY AND WE PICKED IT UP.
"IT'S NOT JUST THE GUNS, THOUGH. NO, ON HIS WORLD HE HAS WAYNE ENTERPRISES WEAPONIZED. CHIPS IN YOUR GPS. VALVES IN YOUR WATER FILTRATION.
"YOUR MINIVAN DRIVES OFF A BRIDGE, YOU NEVER KNOW WHO KILLED YOU."
HE'S US AT TOTAL WAR. I'VE BEEN SAVING HIM.
YOU WON'T WIN. I'LL KILL YOU IF I HAVE TO.
KILL ME... BECAUSE I'M YOU IT DOESN'T COUNT, EH? FREE PASS? HEH.
WHAT ARE YOU DOING?
YOU ALREADY KNOW. I'M DISMANTLING "LAST LAUGH" BY MEANS OF A SPECIAL PROTOCOL, BRUCE. ONE I HAD ON MY WORLD, TOO. A FAIL-SAFE TO TAKE DOWN ANY RECORDS KEPT HERE IF BATMAN FINALLY ENDED.
NO...NO, DON'T DO THIS!
A WAY OF DEMOLISHING THE BUILDING SAFELY, A CONTROLLED IMPLOSION. OF COURSE, IT'S DESIGNED TO WORK ONLY WHEN NO ONE IS INSIDE THE BUILDING. THERE ARE DOZENS OF FAILSAFES...
...ALL OF WHICH THE GRIM KNIGHT DISMANTLED A FEW DAYS AGO.
PLEASE... PLEASE DON'T.

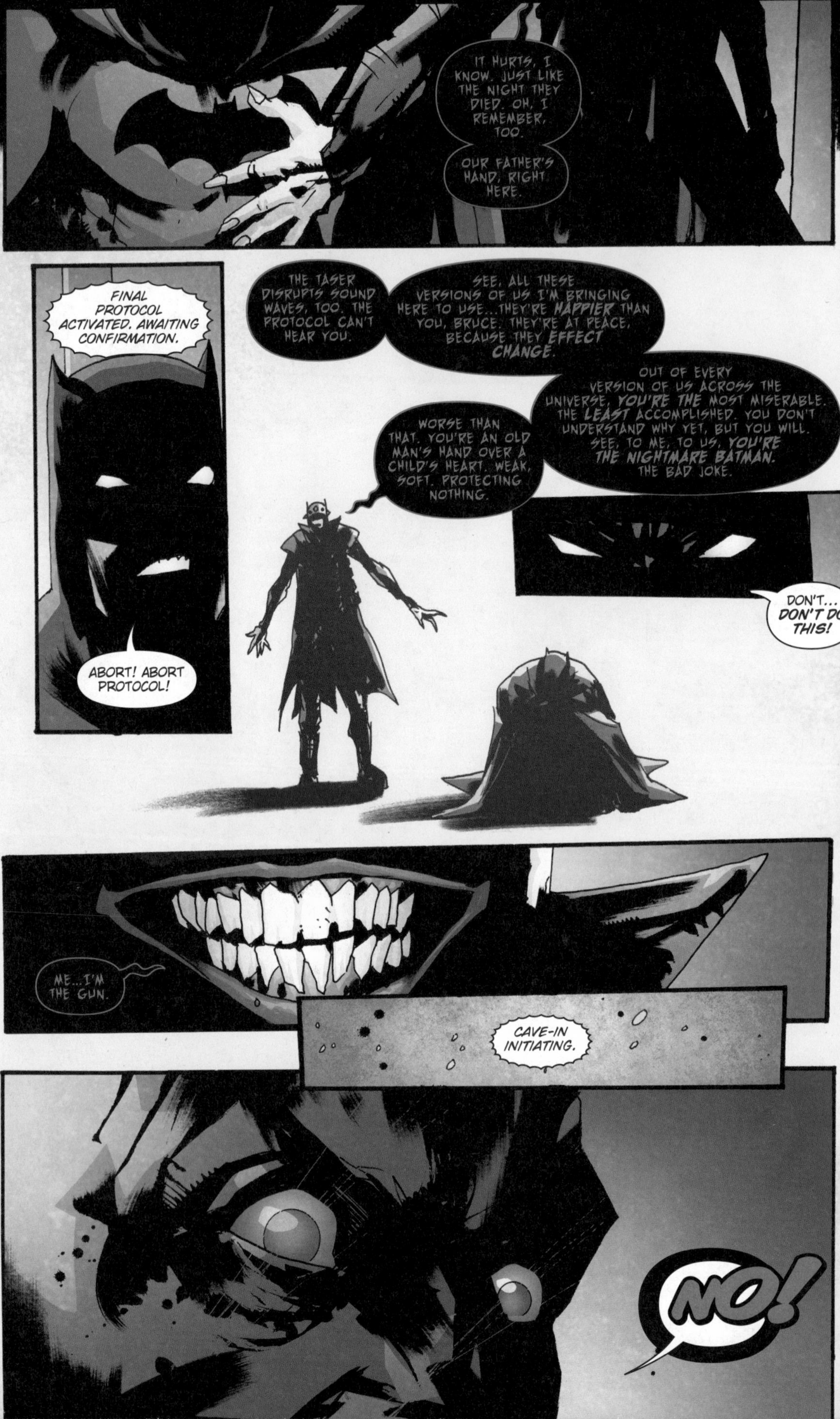
IT HURTS, I KNOW. JUST LIKE THE NIGHT THEY DIED. OH, I REMEMBER, TOO.
OUR FATHER'S HAND, RIGHT HERE.
FINAL PROTOCOL ACTIVATED. AWAITING CONFIRMATION.
THE TASER DISRUPTS SOUND WAVES, TOO. THE PROTOCOL CAN'T HEAR YOU.
SEE, ALL THESE VERSIONS OF US I'M BRINGING HERE TO USE...THEY'RE HAPPIER THAN YOU, BRUCE. THEY'RE AT PEACE, BECAUSE THEY EFFECT CHANGE.
OUT OF EVERY VERSION OF US ACROSS THE UNIVERSE, YOU'RE THE MOST MISERABLE. THE LEAST ACCOMPLISHED. YOU DON'T UNDERSTAND WHY YET, BUT YOU WILL. SEE, TO ME, TO US, YOU'RE THE NIGHTMARE BATMAN. THE BAD JOKE.
WORSE THAN THAT. YOU'RE AN OLD MAN'S HAND OVER A CHILD'S HEART. WEAK, SOFT. PROTECTING NOTHING.
ABORT! ABORT PROTOCOL!
DON'T... DON'T DO THIS!
ME...I'M THE GUN.
CAVE-IN INITIATING.
NO!

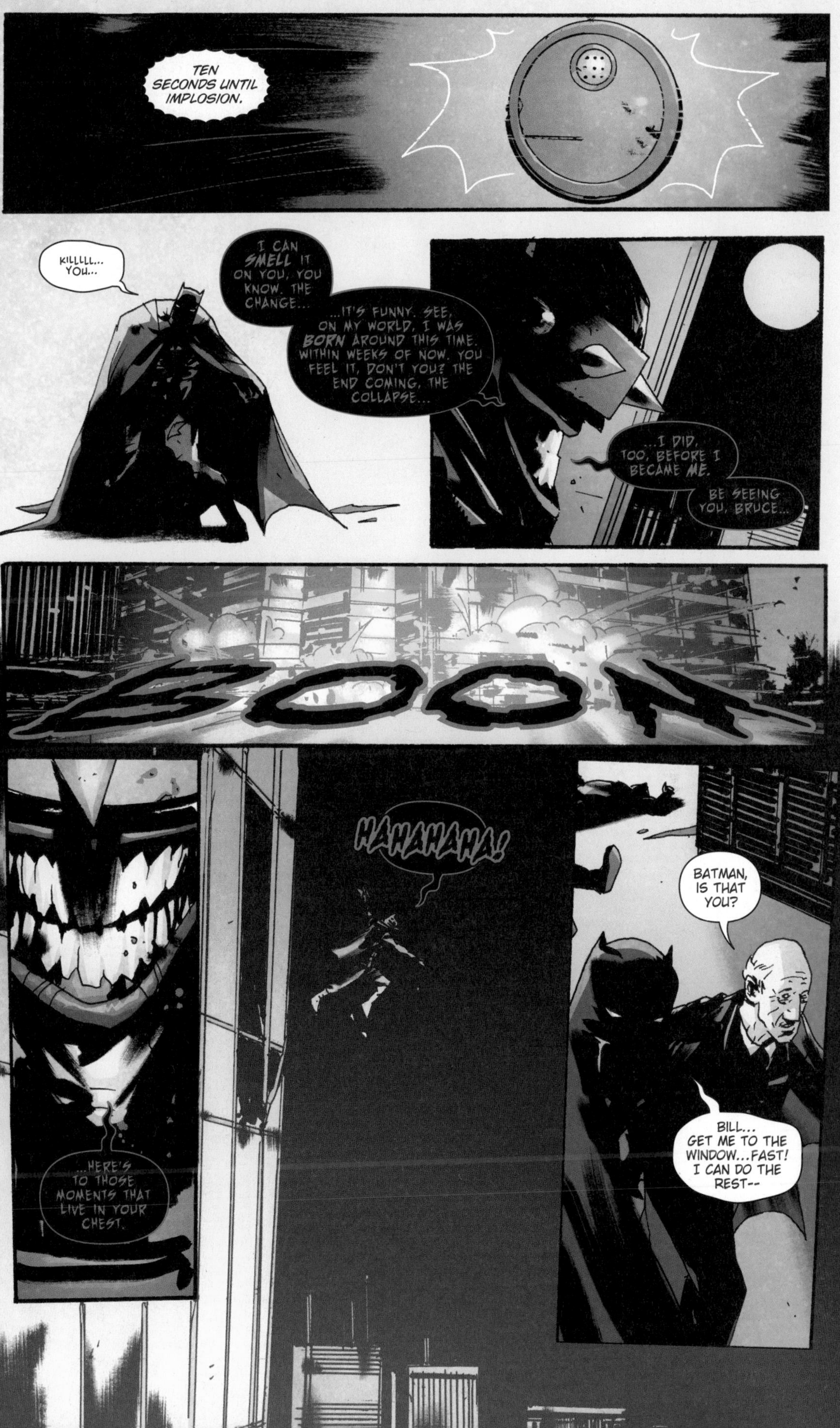
TEN SECONDS UNTIL IMPLOSION.
KILLLLL... YOU...
I CAN SMELL IT ON YOU, YOU KNOW. THE CHANGE...
...IT'S FUNNY. SEE, ON MY WORLD, I WAS BORN AROUND THIS TIME. WITHIN WEEKS OF NOW. YOU FEEL IT, DON'T YOU? THE END COMING, THE COLLAPSE...
...I DID, TOO, BEFORE I BECAME ME.
BE SEEING YOU, BRUCE...
BOOM
...HERE'S TO THOSE MOMENTS THAT LIVE IN YOUR CHEST.
HAHAHAHAHA!
BATMAN, IS THAT YOU?
BILL... GET ME TO THE WINDOW...FAST! I CAN DO THE REST--

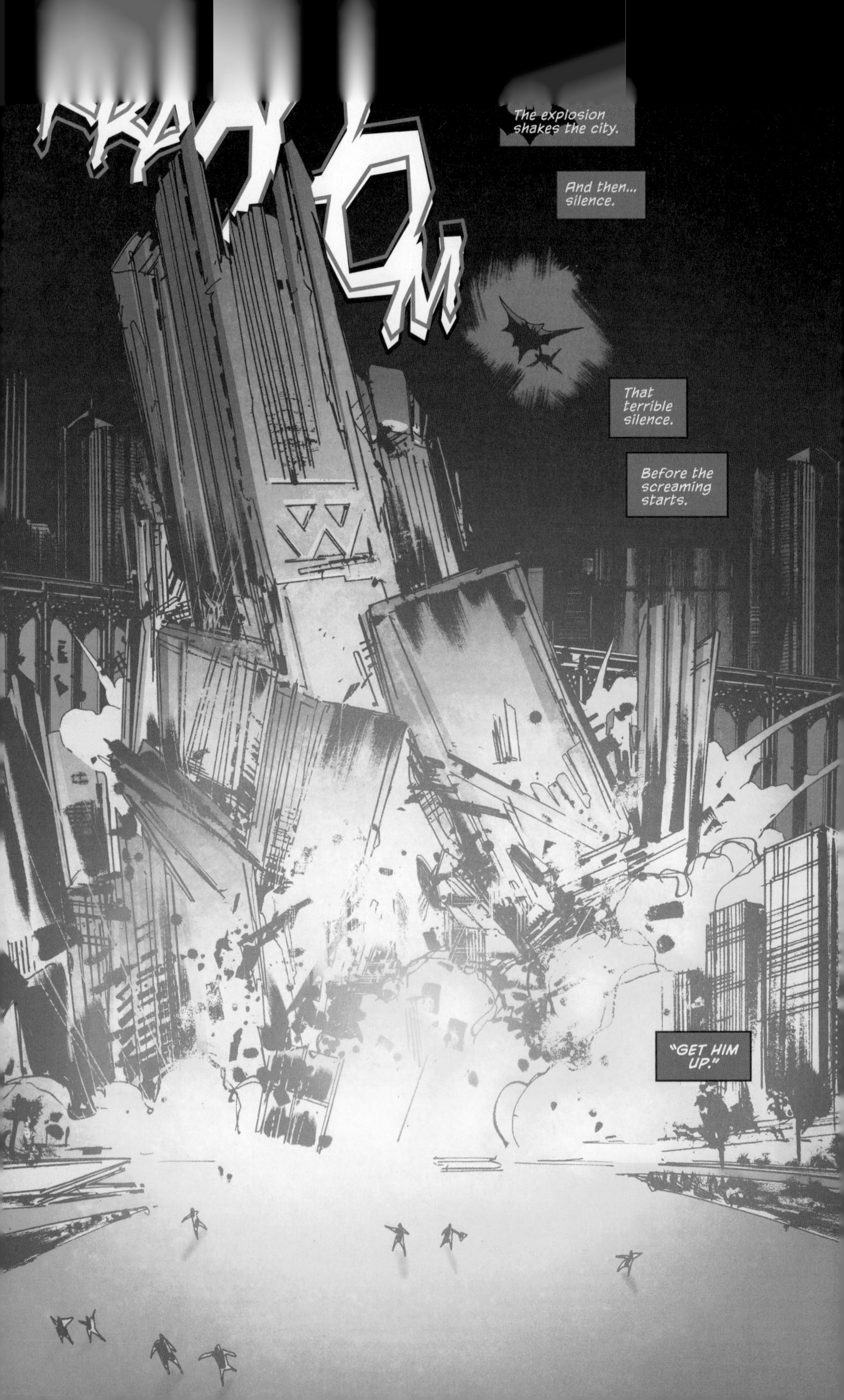
The explosion shakes the city.
And then... silence.
That terrible silence.
Before the screaming starts.
"GET HIM UP."

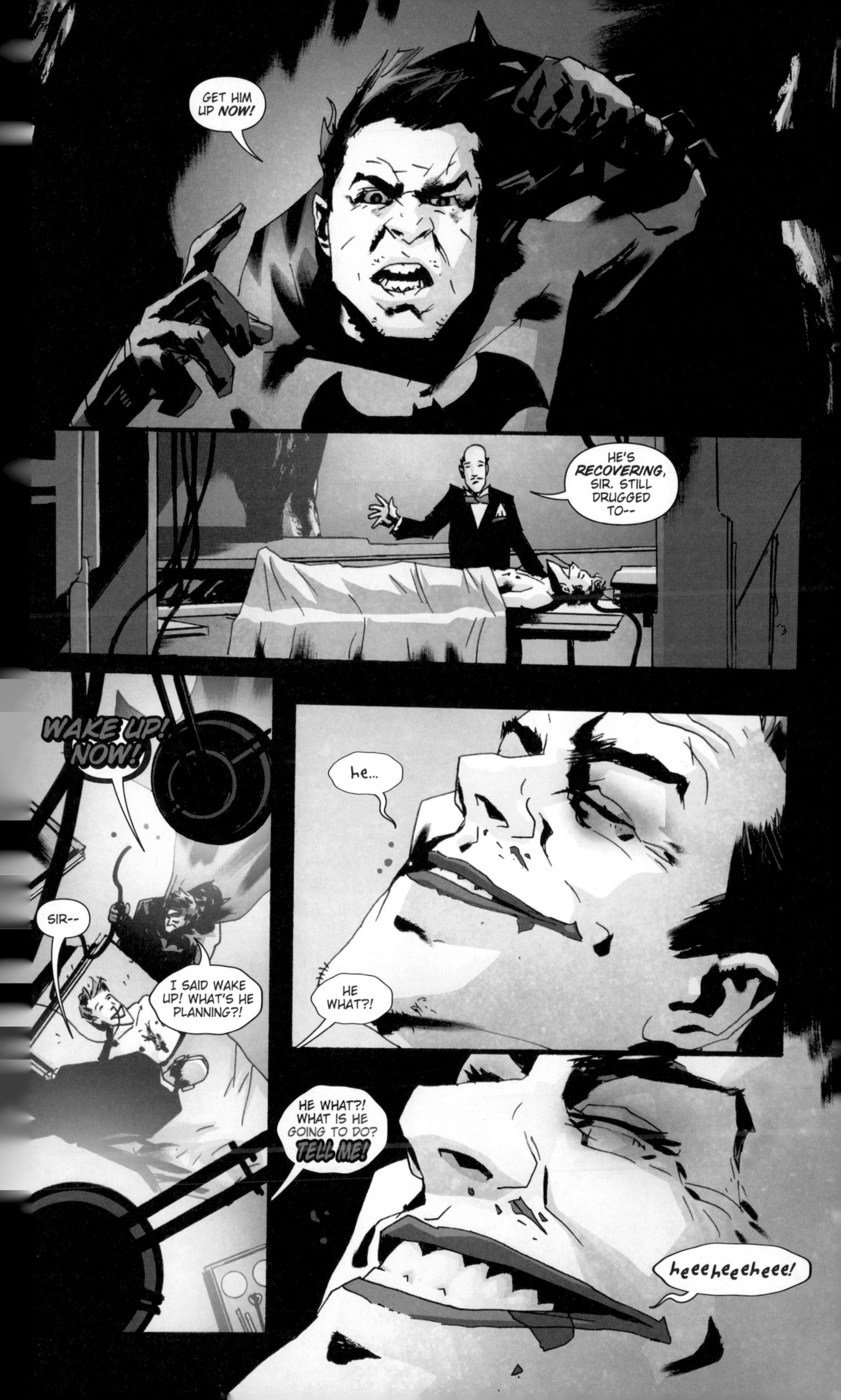
GET HIM UP **NOW!**
HE'S **RECOVERING,** SIR. STILL DRUGGED TO--
WAKE UP! NOW!
SIR--
I SAID WAKE UP! WHAT'S HE PLANNING?!
he...
HE WHAT?!
HE WHAT?! WHAT IS HE GOING TO DO? TELL ME!
heeeheeeheee!

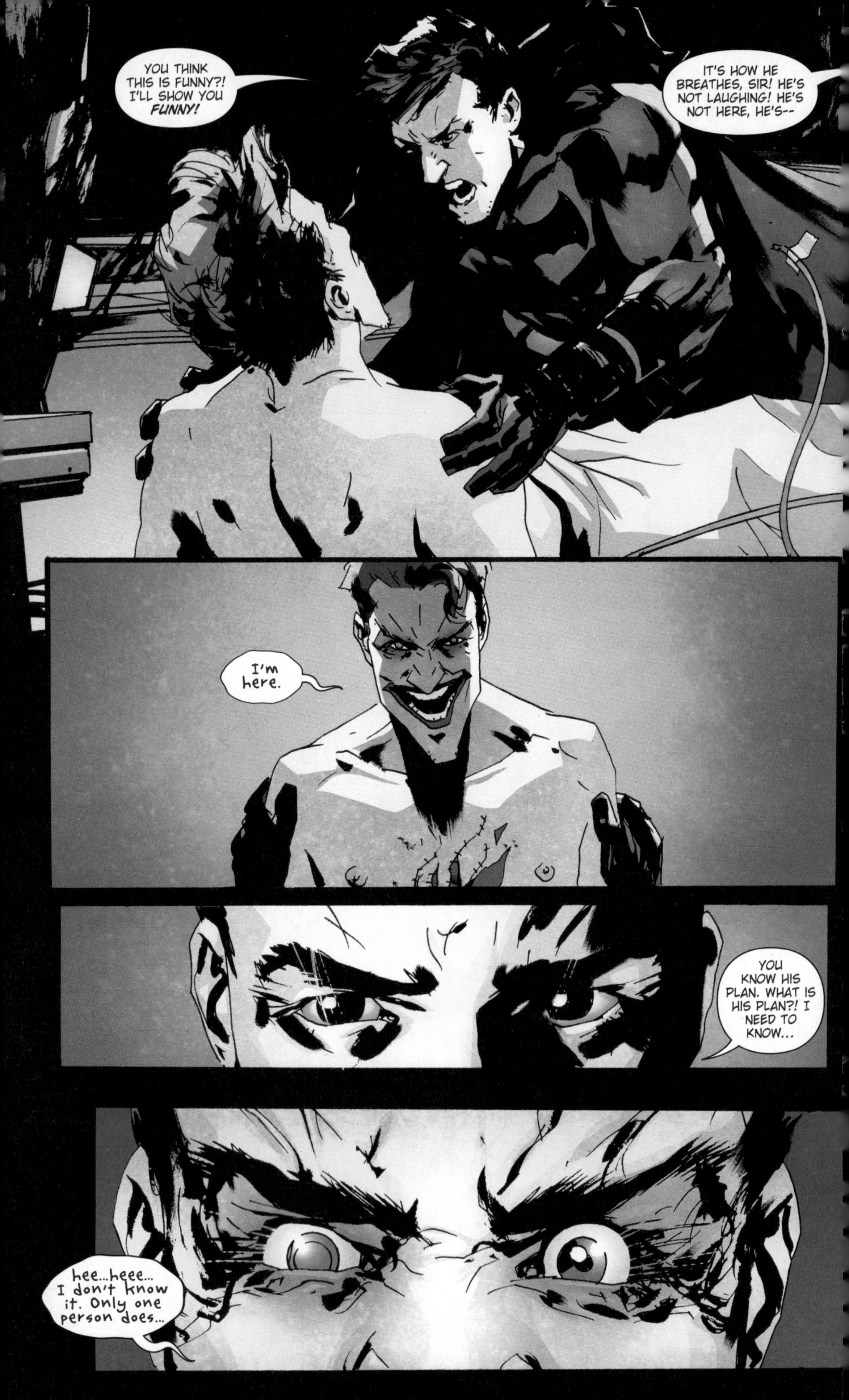
YOU THINK THIS IS FUNNY?! I'LL SHOW YOU *FUNNY!*
IT'S HOW HE BREATHES, SIR! HE'S NOT LAUGHING! HE'S NOT HERE, HE'S--
I'm here.
YOU KNOW HIS PLAN. WHAT IS HIS PLAN?! I NEED TO KNOW...
hee...heee... I don't know it. Only one person does...

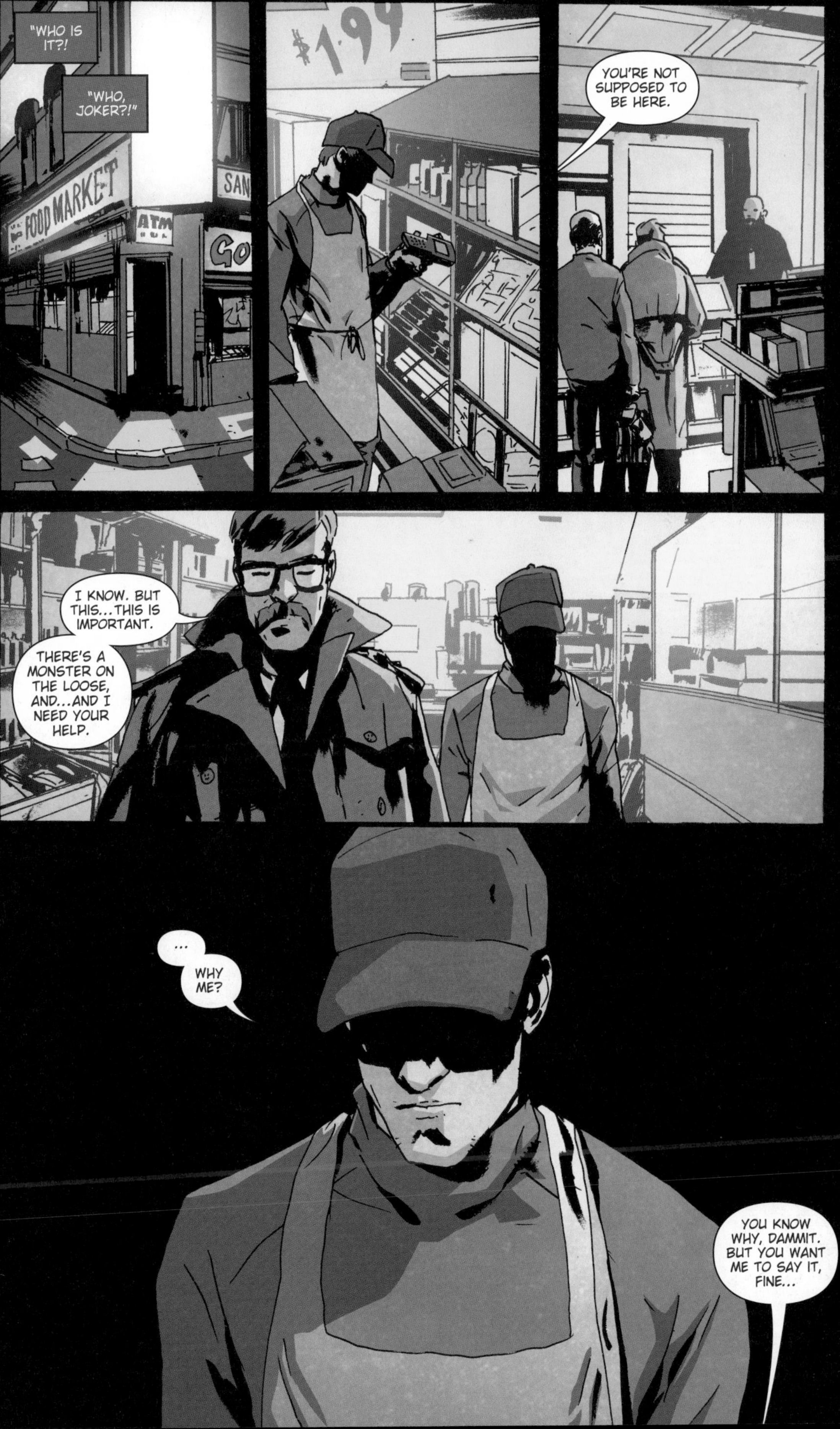
"WHO IS IT?!
"WHO, JOKER?!"
$1.99
FOOD MARKET
ATM
YOU'RE NOT SUPPOSED TO BE HERE.
I KNOW. BUT THIS...THIS IS IMPORTANT.
THERE'S A MONSTER ON THE LOOSE, AND...AND I NEED YOUR HELP.
...
WHY ME?
YOU KNOW WHY, DAMMIT. BUT YOU WANT ME TO SAY IT, FINE...

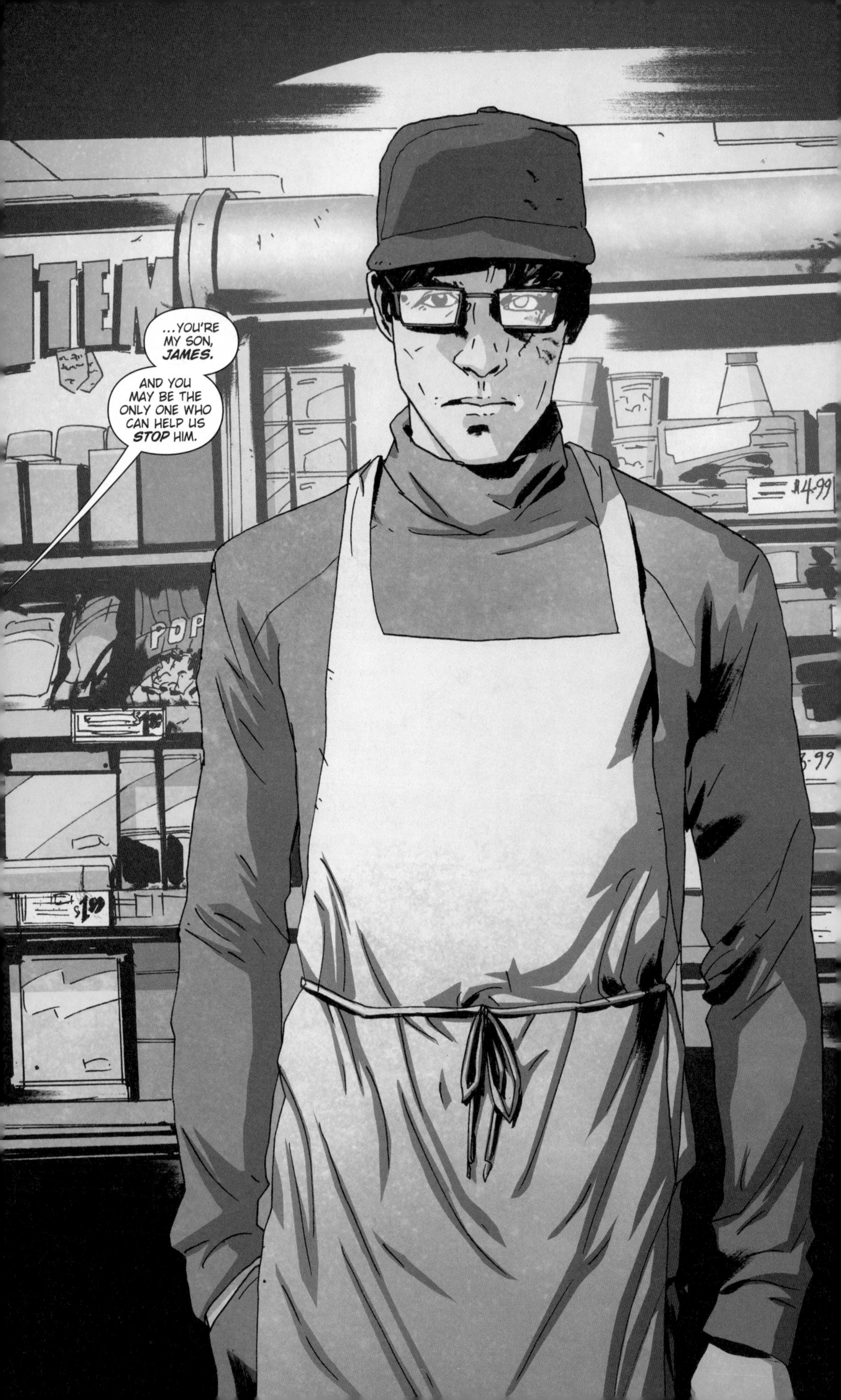
...YOU'RE MY SON, JAMES.
AND YOU MAY BE THE ONLY ONE WHO CAN HELP US STOP HIM.

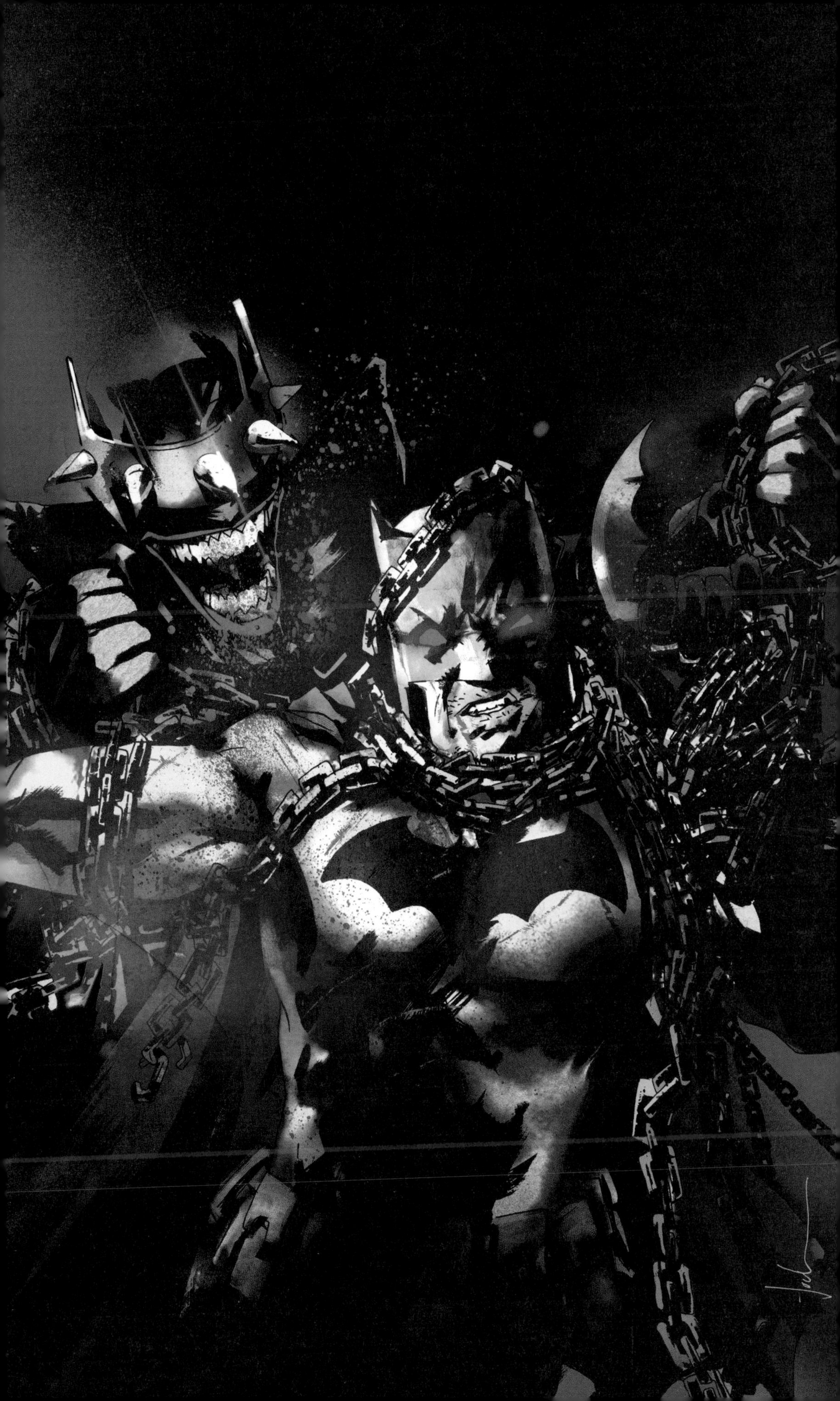

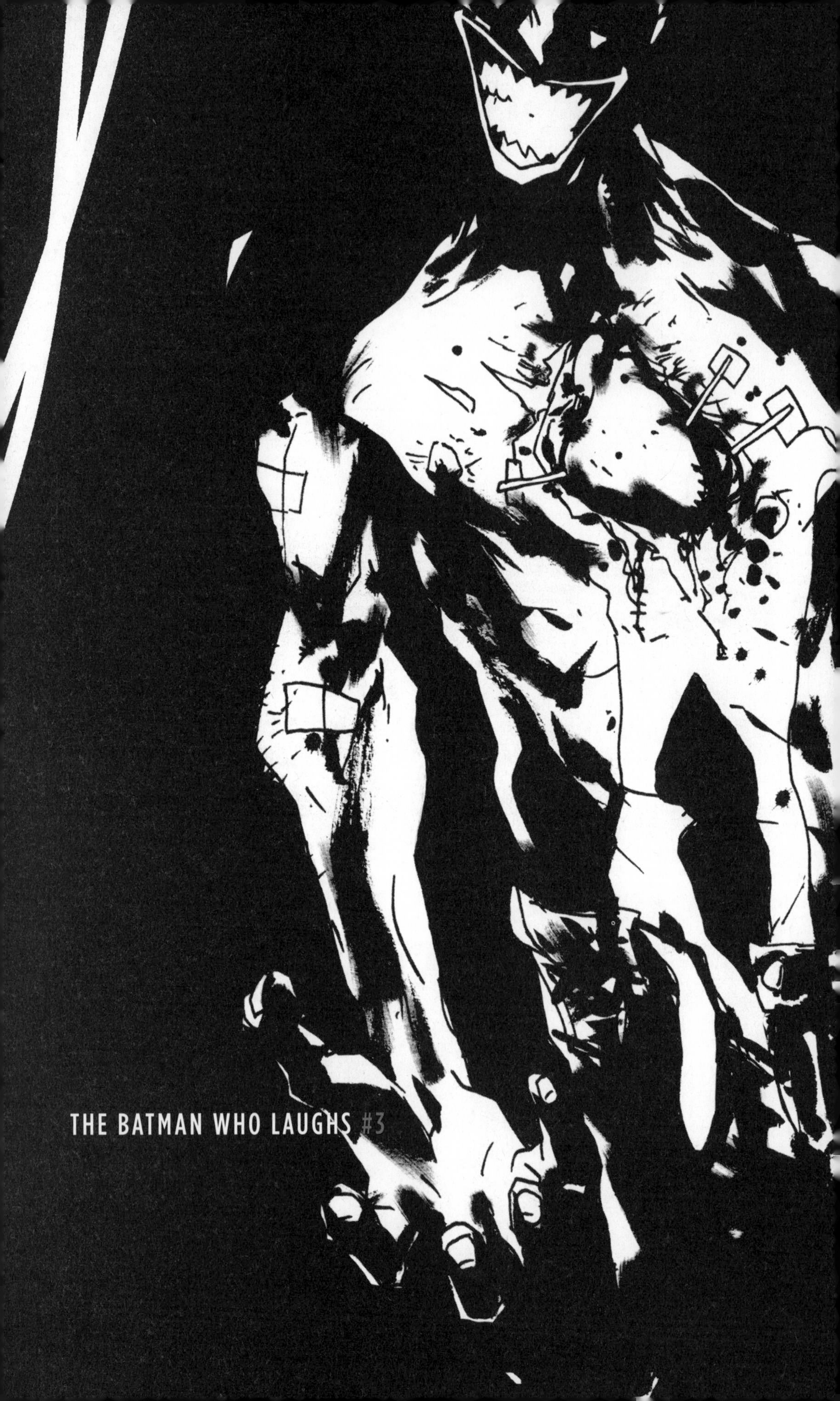

THE BATMAN WHO LAUGHS #3

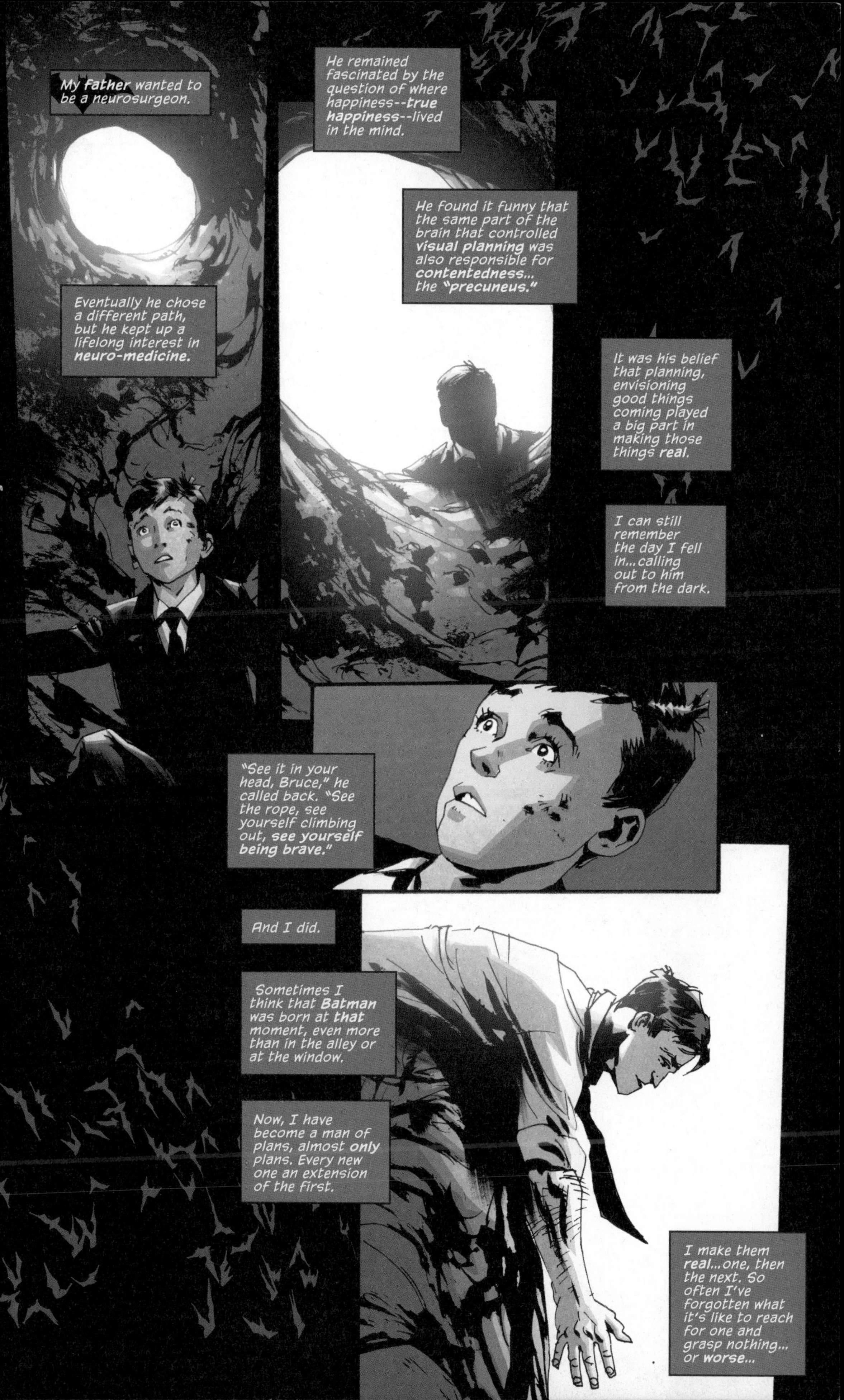
My father wanted to be a neurosurgeon.
He remained fascinated by the question of where happiness--true happiness--lived in the mind.
He found it funny that the same part of the brain that controlled visual planning was also responsible for contentedness... the "precuneus."
Eventually he chose a different path, but he kept up a lifelong interest in neuro-medicine.
It was his belief that planning, envisioning good things coming played a big part in making those things real.
I can still remember the day I fell in...calling out to him from the dark.
"See it in your head, Bruce," he called back. "See the rope, see yourself climbing out, see yourself being brave."
And I did.
Sometimes I think that Batman was born at that moment, even more than in the alley or at the window.
Now, I have become a man of plans, almost only plans. Every new one an extension of the first.
I make them real...one, then the next. So often I've forgotten what it's like to reach for one and grasp nothing... or worse...

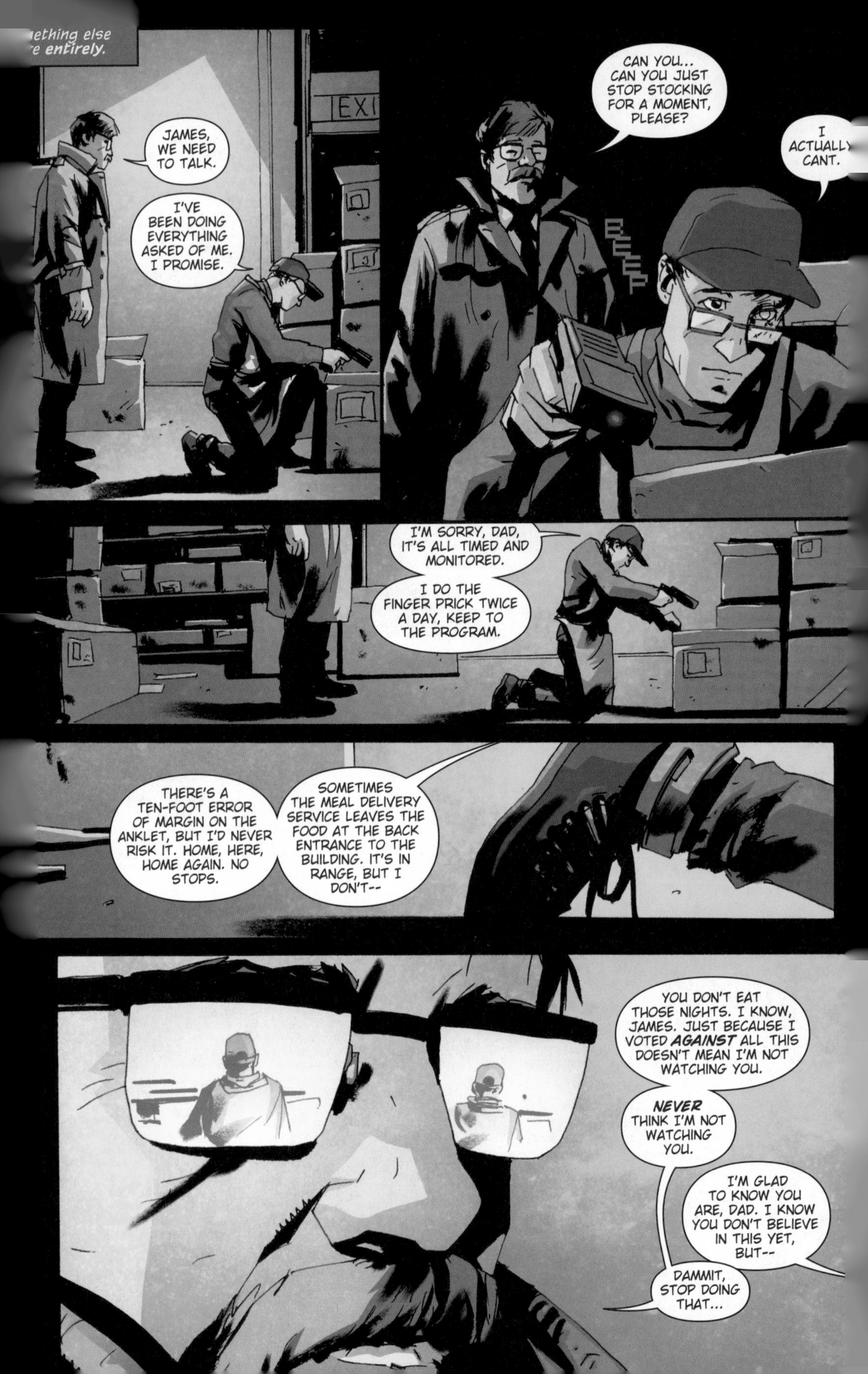

...ething else
...e entirely.
JAMES, WE NEED TO TALK.
I'VE BEEN DOING EVERYTHING ASKED OF ME. I PROMISE.
EXI
CAN YOU... CAN YOU JUST STOP STOCKING FOR A MOMENT, PLEASE?
BEEP
I ACTUALLY CANT.
I'M SORRY, DAD, IT'S ALL TIMED AND MONITORED.
I DO THE FINGER PRICK TWICE A DAY, KEEP TO THE PROGRAM.
THERE'S A TEN-FOOT ERROR OF MARGIN ON THE ANKLET, BUT I'D NEVER RISK IT. HOME, HERE, HOME AGAIN. NO STOPS.
SOMETIMES THE MEAL DELIVERY SERVICE LEAVES THE FOOD AT THE BACK ENTRANCE TO THE BUILDING. IT'S IN RANGE, BUT I DON'T--
YOU DON'T EAT THOSE NIGHTS. I KNOW, JAMES. JUST BECAUSE I VOTED ***AGAINST*** ALL THIS DOESN'T MEAN I'M NOT WATCHING YOU.
NEVER THINK I'M NOT WATCHING YOU.
I'M GLAD TO KNOW YOU ARE, DAD. I KNOW YOU DON'T BELIEVE IN THIS YET, BUT--
DAMMIT, STOP DOING THAT...

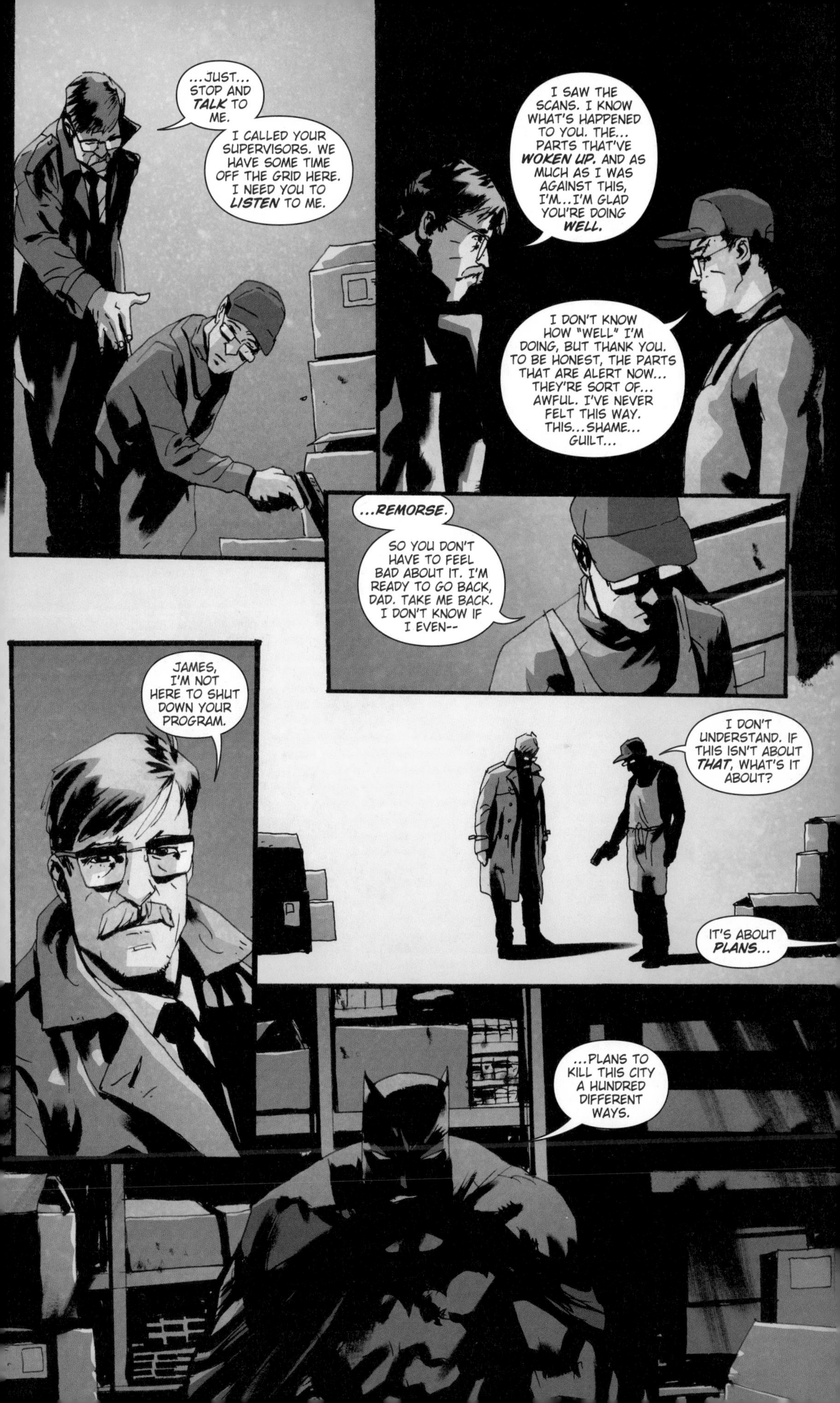
...JUST... STOP AND TALK TO ME.
I CALLED YOUR SUPERVISORS. WE HAVE SOME TIME OFF THE GRID HERE. I NEED YOU TO LISTEN TO ME.
I SAW THE SCANS. I KNOW WHAT'S HAPPENED TO YOU. THE... PARTS THAT'VE WOKEN UP. AND AS MUCH AS I WAS AGAINST THIS, I'M...I'M GLAD YOU'RE DOING WELL.
I DON'T KNOW HOW "WELL" I'M DOING, BUT THANK YOU. TO BE HONEST, THE PARTS THAT ARE ALERT NOW... THEY'RE SORT OF... AWFUL. I'VE NEVER FELT THIS WAY. THIS...SHAME... GUILT...
...REMORSE.
SO YOU DON'T HAVE TO FEEL BAD ABOUT IT. I'M READY TO GO BACK, DAD. TAKE ME BACK. I DON'T KNOW IF I EVEN--
JAMES, I'M NOT HERE TO SHUT DOWN YOUR PROGRAM.
I DON'T UNDERSTAND. IF THIS ISN'T ABOUT THAT, WHAT'S IT ABOUT?
IT'S ABOUT PLANS...
...PLANS TO KILL THIS CITY A HUNDRED DIFFERENT WAYS.

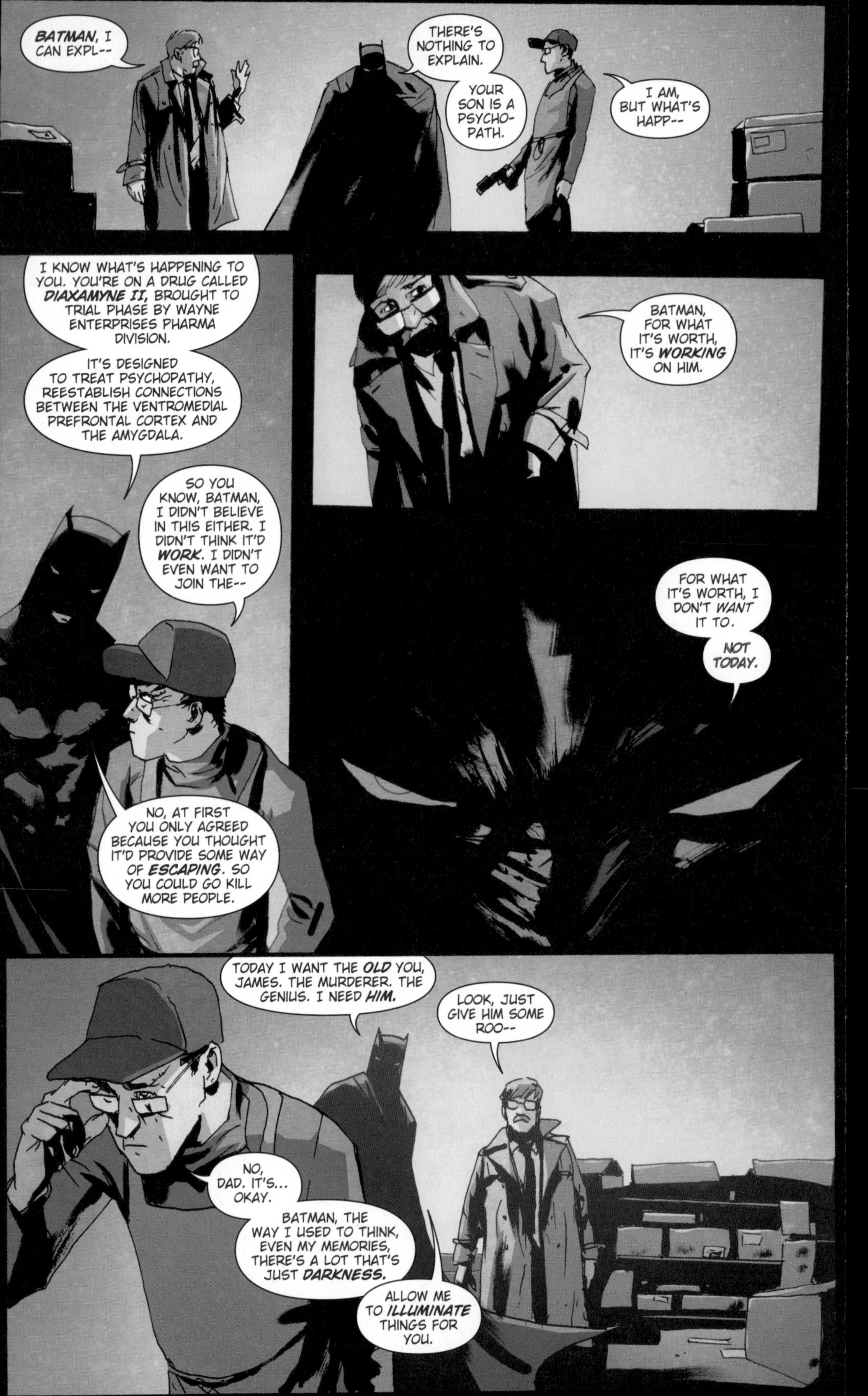
BATMAN, I CAN EXPL--
THERE'S NOTHING TO EXPLAIN.
YOUR SON IS A PSYCHOPATH.
I AM, BUT WHAT'S HAPP--
I KNOW WHAT'S HAPPENING TO YOU. YOU'RE ON A DRUG CALLED DIAXAMYNE II, BROUGHT TO TRIAL PHASE BY WAYNE ENTERPRISES PHARMA DIVISION.
IT'S DESIGNED TO TREAT PSYCHOPATHY, REESTABLISH CONNECTIONS BETWEEN THE VENTROMEDIAL PREFRONTAL CORTEX AND THE AMYGDALA.
BATMAN, FOR WHAT IT'S WORTH, IT'S WORKING ON HIM.
SO YOU KNOW, BATMAN, I DIDN'T BELIEVE IN THIS EITHER. I DIDN'T THINK IT'D WORK. I DIDN'T EVEN WANT TO JOIN THE--
NO, AT FIRST YOU ONLY AGREED BECAUSE YOU THOUGHT IT'D PROVIDE SOME WAY OF ESCAPING. SO YOU COULD GO KILL MORE PEOPLE.
FOR WHAT IT'S WORTH, I DON'T WANT IT TO.
NOT TODAY.
TODAY I WANT THE OLD YOU, JAMES. THE MURDERER. THE GENIUS. I NEED HIM.
LOOK, JUST GIVE HIM SOME ROO--
NO, DAD. IT'S... OKAY.
BATMAN, THE WAY I USED TO THINK, EVEN MY MEMORIES, THERE'S A LOT THAT'S JUST DARKNESS.
ALLOW ME TO ILLUMINATE THINGS FOR YOU.

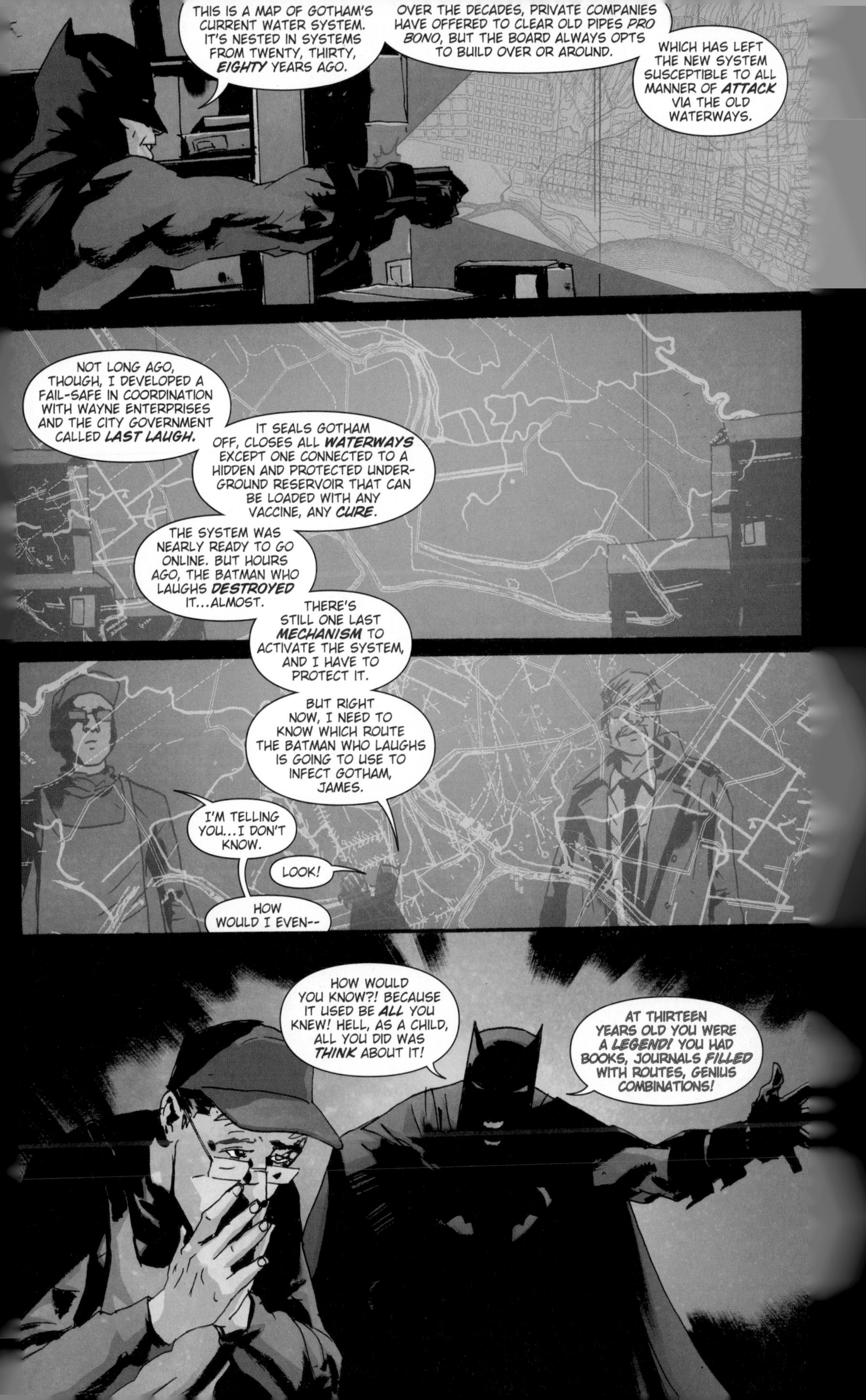

THIS IS A MAP OF GOTHAM'S CURRENT WATER SYSTEM. IT'S NESTED IN SYSTEMS FROM TWENTY, THIRTY, EIGHTY YEARS AGO.
OVER THE DECADES, PRIVATE COMPANIES HAVE OFFERED TO CLEAR OLD PIPES PRO BONO, BUT THE BOARD ALWAYS OPTS TO BUILD OVER OR AROUND.
WHICH HAS LEFT THE NEW SYSTEM SUSCEPTIBLE TO ALL MANNER OF ATTACK VIA THE OLD WATERWAYS.
NOT LONG AGO, THOUGH, I DEVELOPED A FAIL-SAFE IN COORDINATION WITH WAYNE ENTERPRISES AND THE CITY GOVERNMENT CALLED LAST LAUGH.
IT SEALS GOTHAM OFF, CLOSES ALL WATERWAYS EXCEPT ONE CONNECTED TO A HIDDEN AND PROTECTED UNDERGROUND RESERVOIR THAT CAN BE LOADED WITH ANY VACCINE, ANY CURE.
THE SYSTEM WAS NEARLY READY TO GO ONLINE. BUT HOURS AGO, THE BATMAN WHO LAUGHS DESTROYED IT...ALMOST.
THERE'S STILL ONE LAST MECHANISM TO ACTIVATE THE SYSTEM, AND I HAVE TO PROTECT IT.
BUT RIGHT NOW, I NEED TO KNOW WHICH ROUTE THE BATMAN WHO LAUGHS IS GOING TO USE TO INFECT GOTHAM, JAMES.
I'M TELLING YOU...I DON'T KNOW.
LOOK!
HOW WOULD I EVEN--
HOW WOULD YOU KNOW?! BECAUSE IT USED BE ALL YOU KNEW! HELL, AS A CHILD, ALL YOU DID WAS THINK ABOUT IT!
AT THIRTEEN YEARS OLD YOU WERE A LEGEND! YOU HAD BOOKS, JOURNALS FILLED WITH ROUTES, GENIUS COMBINATIONS!

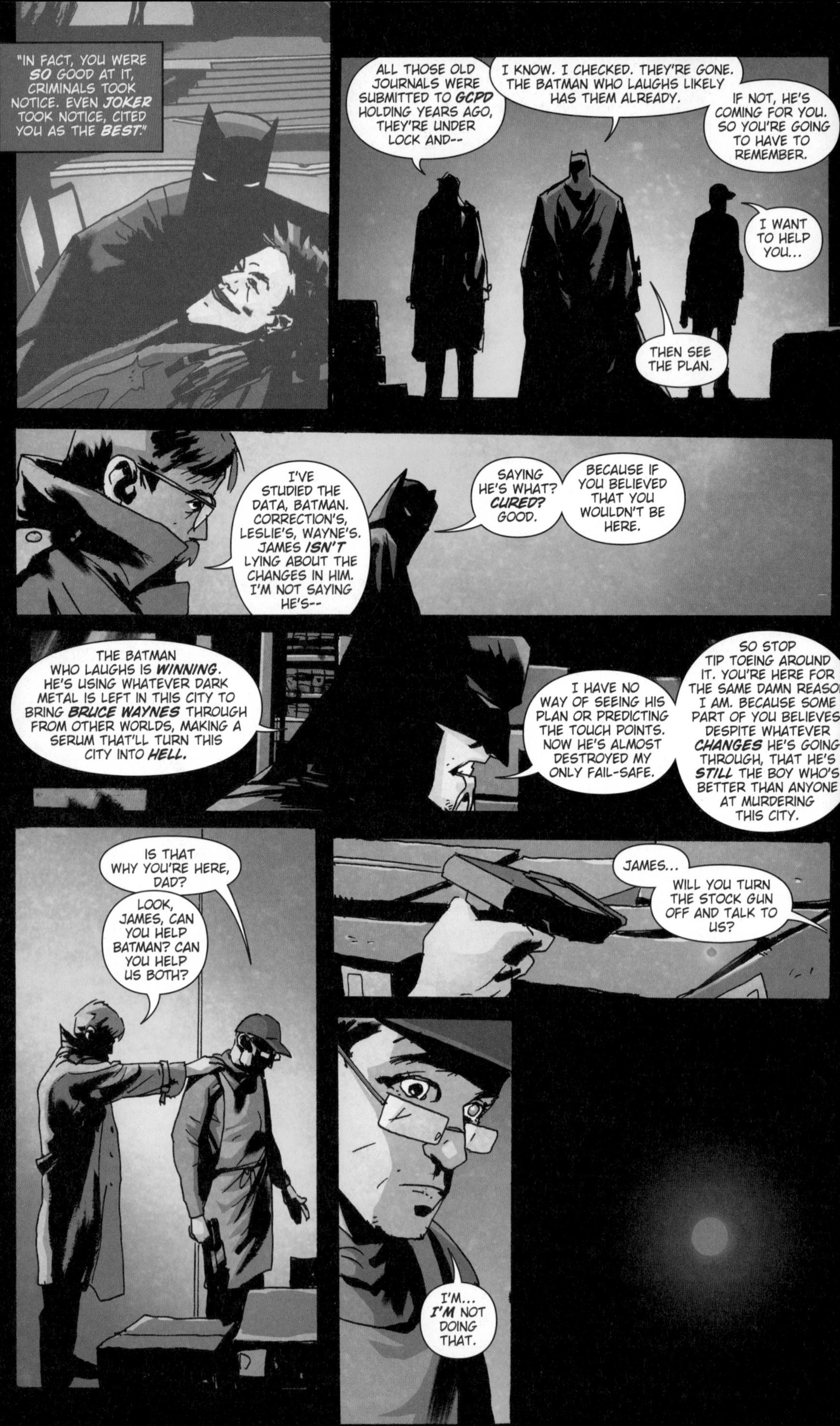
"IN FACT, YOU WERE SO GOOD AT IT, CRIMINALS TOOK NOTICE. EVEN JOKER TOOK NOTICE, CITED YOU AS THE BEST."
ALL THOSE OLD JOURNALS WERE SUBMITTED TO GCPD HOLDING YEARS AGO, THEY'RE UNDER LOCK AND--
I KNOW. I CHECKED. THEY'RE GONE. THE BATMAN WHO LAUGHS LIKELY HAS THEM ALREADY.
IF NOT, HE'S COMING FOR YOU. SO YOU'RE GOING TO HAVE TO REMEMBER.
I WANT TO HELP YOU...
THEN SEE THE PLAN.
I'VE STUDIED THE DATA, BATMAN. CORRECTION'S, LESLIE'S, WAYNE'S. JAMES ISN'T LYING ABOUT THE CHANGES IN HIM. I'M NOT SAYING HE'S--
SAYING HE'S WHAT? CURED? GOOD.
BECAUSE IF YOU BELIEVED THAT YOU WOULDN'T BE HERE.
THE BATMAN WHO LAUGHS IS WINNING. HE'S USING WHATEVER DARK METAL IS LEFT IN THIS CITY TO BRING BRUCE WAYNES THROUGH FROM OTHER WORLDS, MAKING A SERUM THAT'LL TURN THIS CITY INTO HELL.
I HAVE NO WAY OF SEEING HIS PLAN OR PREDICTING THE TOUCH POINTS. NOW HE'S ALMOST DESTROYED MY ONLY FAIL-SAFE.
SO STOP TIP TOEING AROUND IT. YOU'RE HERE FOR THE SAME DAMN REASO I AM. BECAUSE SOME PART OF YOU BELIEVES DESPITE WHATEVER CHANGES HE'S GOING THROUGH, THAT HE'S STILL THE BOY WHO'S BETTER THAN ANYONE AT MURDERING THIS CITY.
IS THAT WHY YOU'RE HERE, DAD?
LOOK, JAMES, CAN YOU HELP BATMAN? CAN YOU HELP US BOTH?
JAMES...
WILL YOU TURN THE STOCK GUN OFF AND TALK TO US?
I'M... I'M NOT DOING THAT.

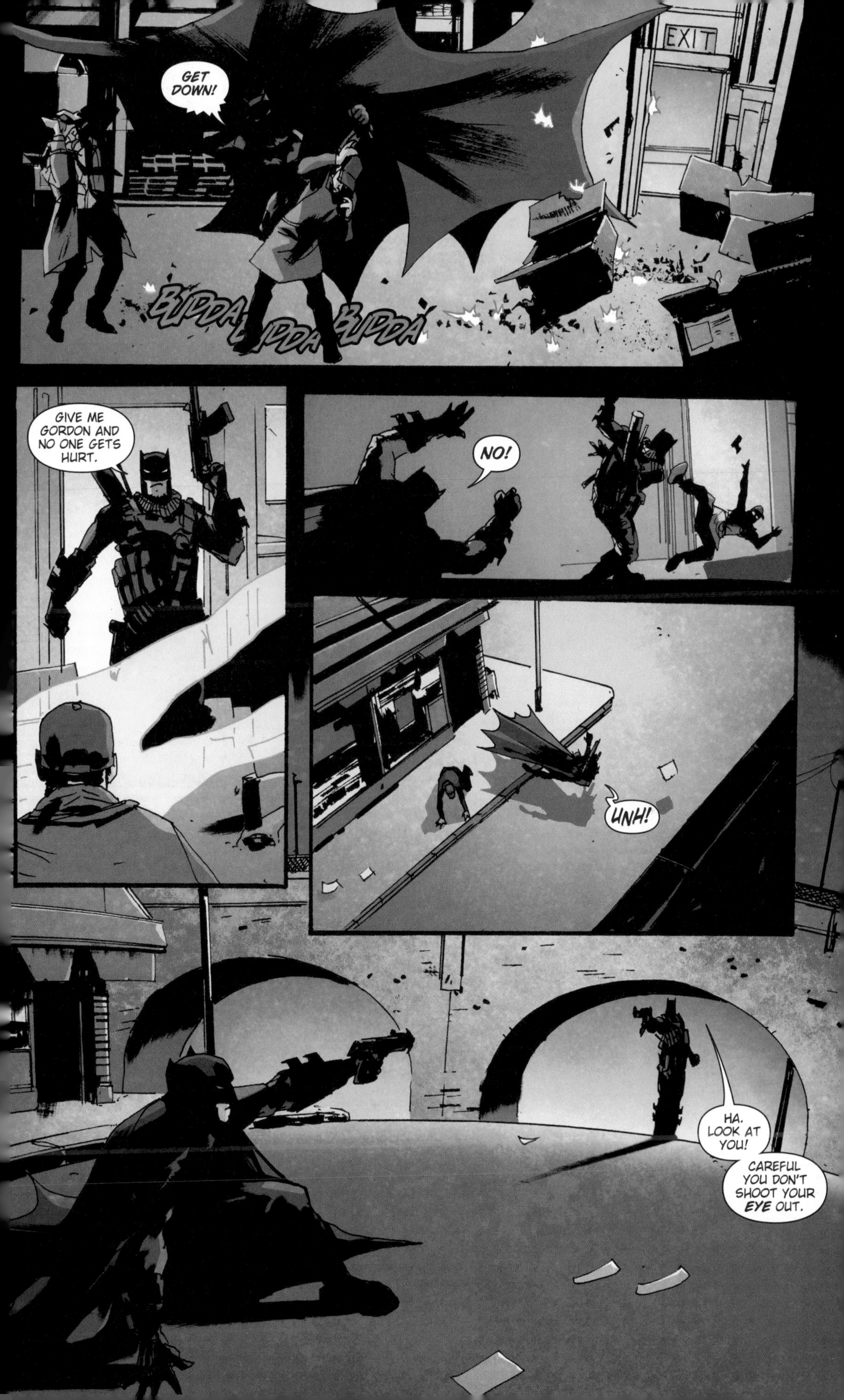
GET DOWN!
BUDDA BUDDA BUDDA
GIVE ME GORDON AND NO ONE GETS HURT.
NO!
UNH!
HA. LOOK AT YOU!
CAREFUL YOU DON'T SHOOT YOUR EYE OUT.

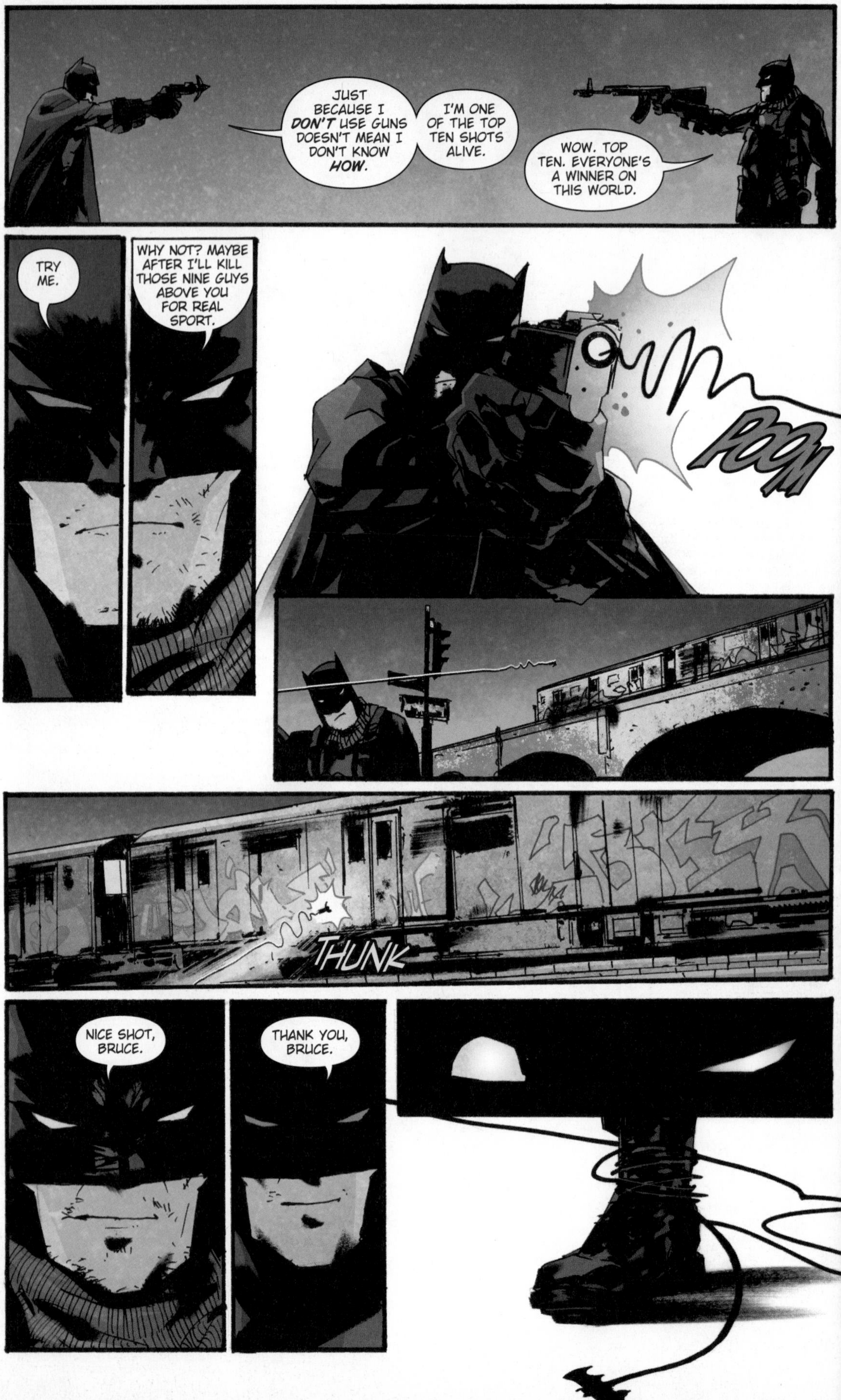
JUST BECAUSE I DON'T USE GUNS DOESN'T MEAN I DON'T KNOW HOW.
I'M ONE OF THE TOP TEN SHOTS ALIVE.
WOW. TOP TEN. EVERYONE'S A WINNER ON THIS WORLD.
TRY ME.
WHY NOT? MAYBE AFTER I'LL KILL THOSE NINE GUYS ABOVE YOU FOR REAL SPORT.
POOM
THUNK
NICE SHOT, BRUCE.
THANK YOU, BRUCE.

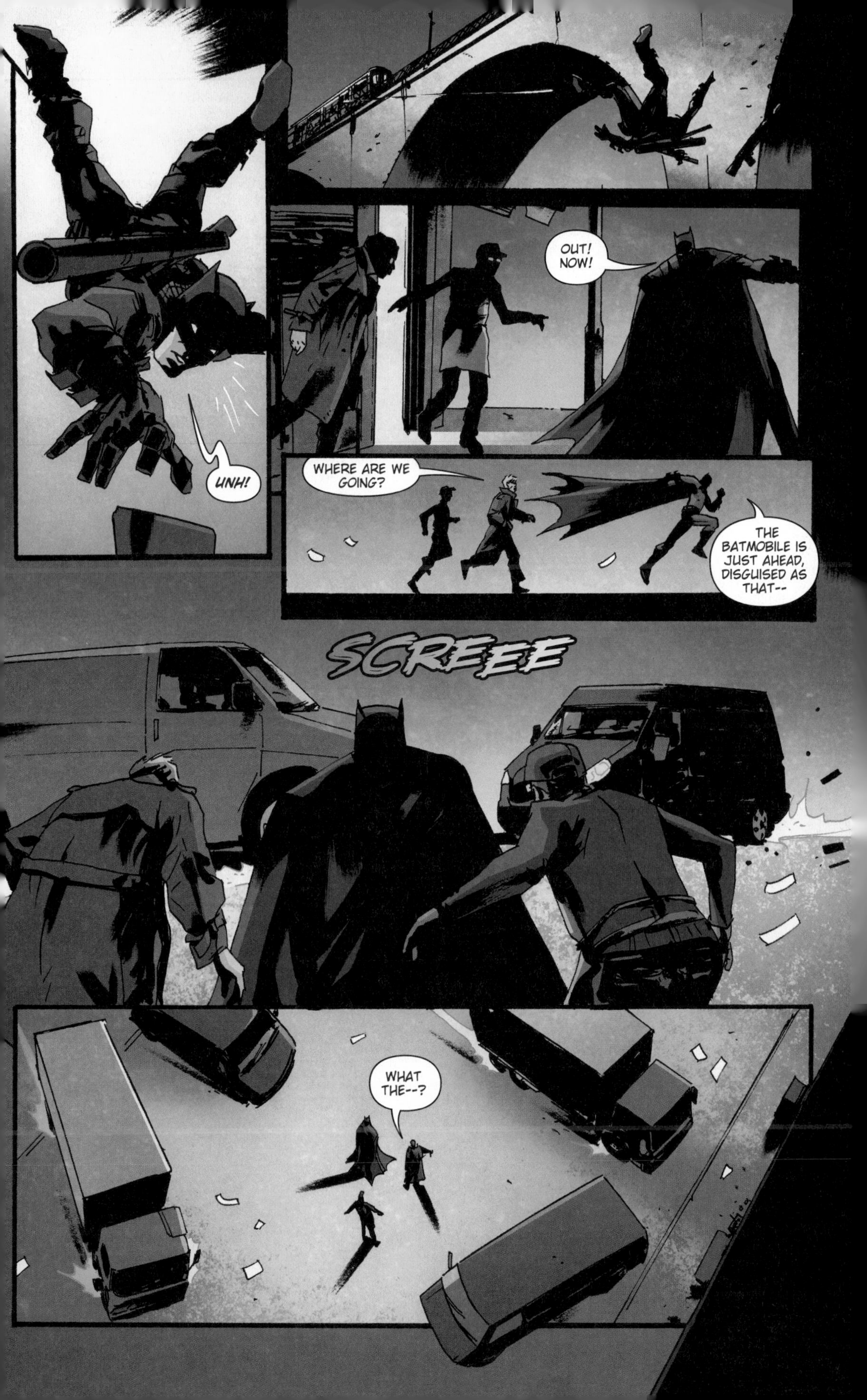
UNH!
OUT! NOW!
WHERE ARE WE GOING?
THE BATMOBILE IS JUST AHEAD, DISGUISED AS THAT--
SCREEE
WHAT THE--?

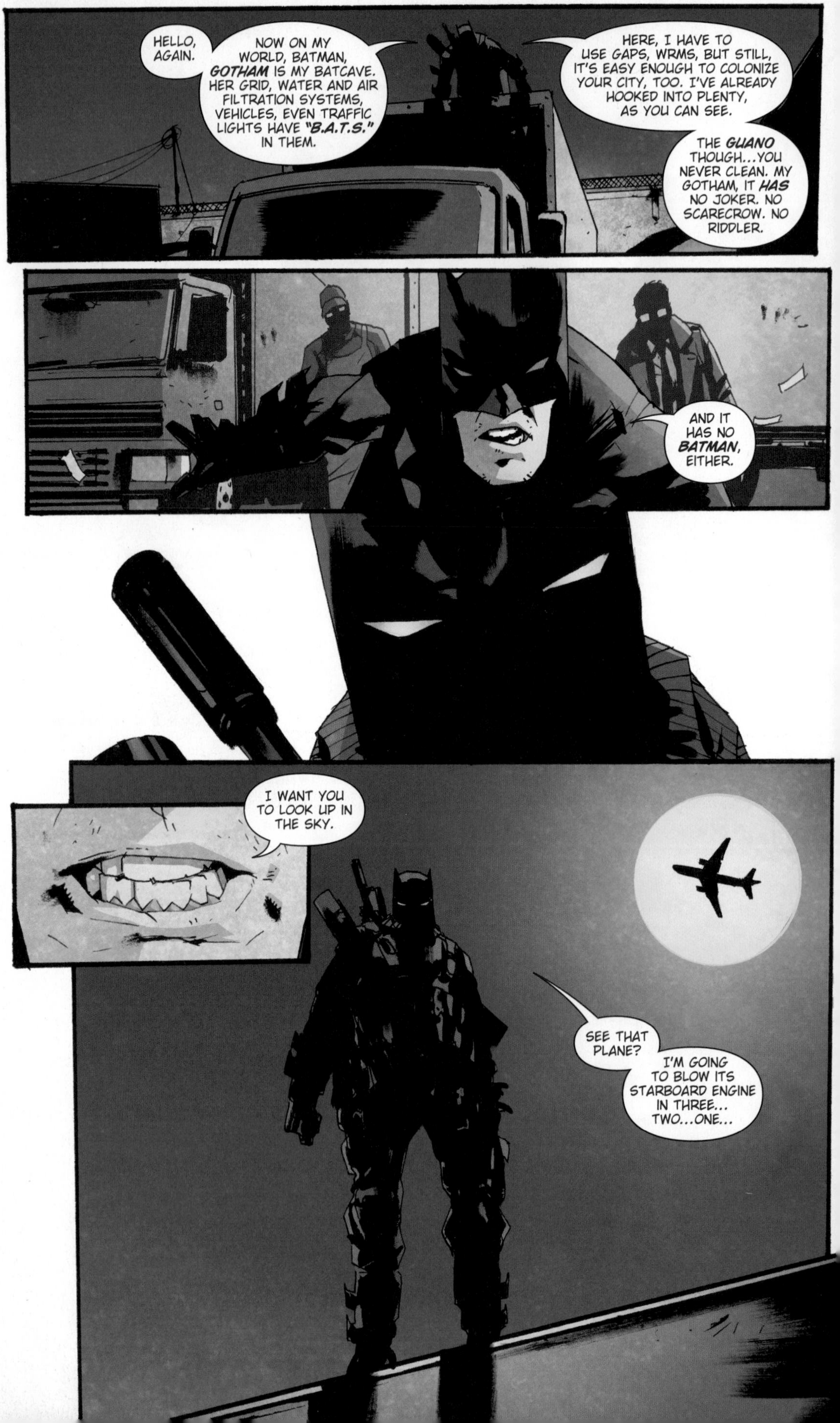
HELLO, AGAIN.
NOW ON MY WORLD, BATMAN, GOTHAM IS MY BATCAVE. HER GRID, WATER AND AIR FILTRATION SYSTEMS, VEHICLES, EVEN TRAFFIC LIGHTS HAVE "B.A.T.S." IN THEM.
HERE, I HAVE TO USE GAPS, WRMS, BUT STILL, IT'S EASY ENOUGH TO COLONIZE YOUR CITY, TOO. I'VE ALREADY HOOKED INTO PLENTY, AS YOU CAN SEE.
THE GUANO THOUGH...YOU NEVER CLEAN. MY GOTHAM, IT HAS NO JOKER. NO SCARECROW. NO RIDDLER.
AND IT HAS NO BATMAN, EITHER.
I WANT YOU TO LOOK UP IN THE SKY.
SEE THAT PLANE?
I'M GOING TO BLOW ITS STARBOARD ENGINE IN THREE... TWO...ONE...

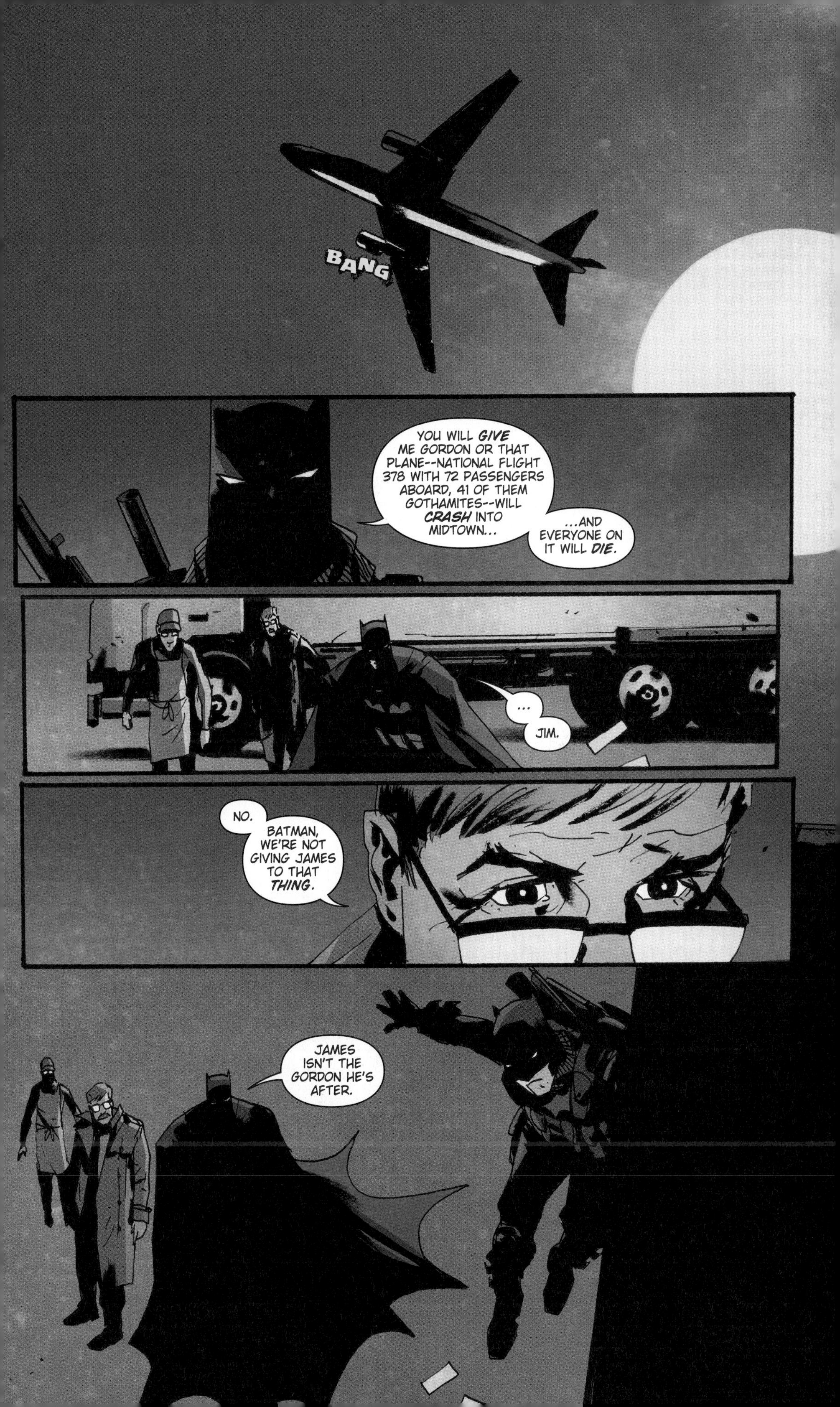
BANG
YOU WILL GIVE ME GORDON OR THAT PLANE--NATIONAL FLIGHT 378 WITH 72 PASSENGERS ABOARD, 41 OF THEM GOTHAMITES--WILL CRASH INTO MIDTOWN...
...AND EVERYONE ON IT WILL DIE.
... JIM.
NO.
BATMAN, WE'RE NOT GIVING JAMES TO THAT THING.
JAMES ISN'T THE GORDON HE'S AFTER.

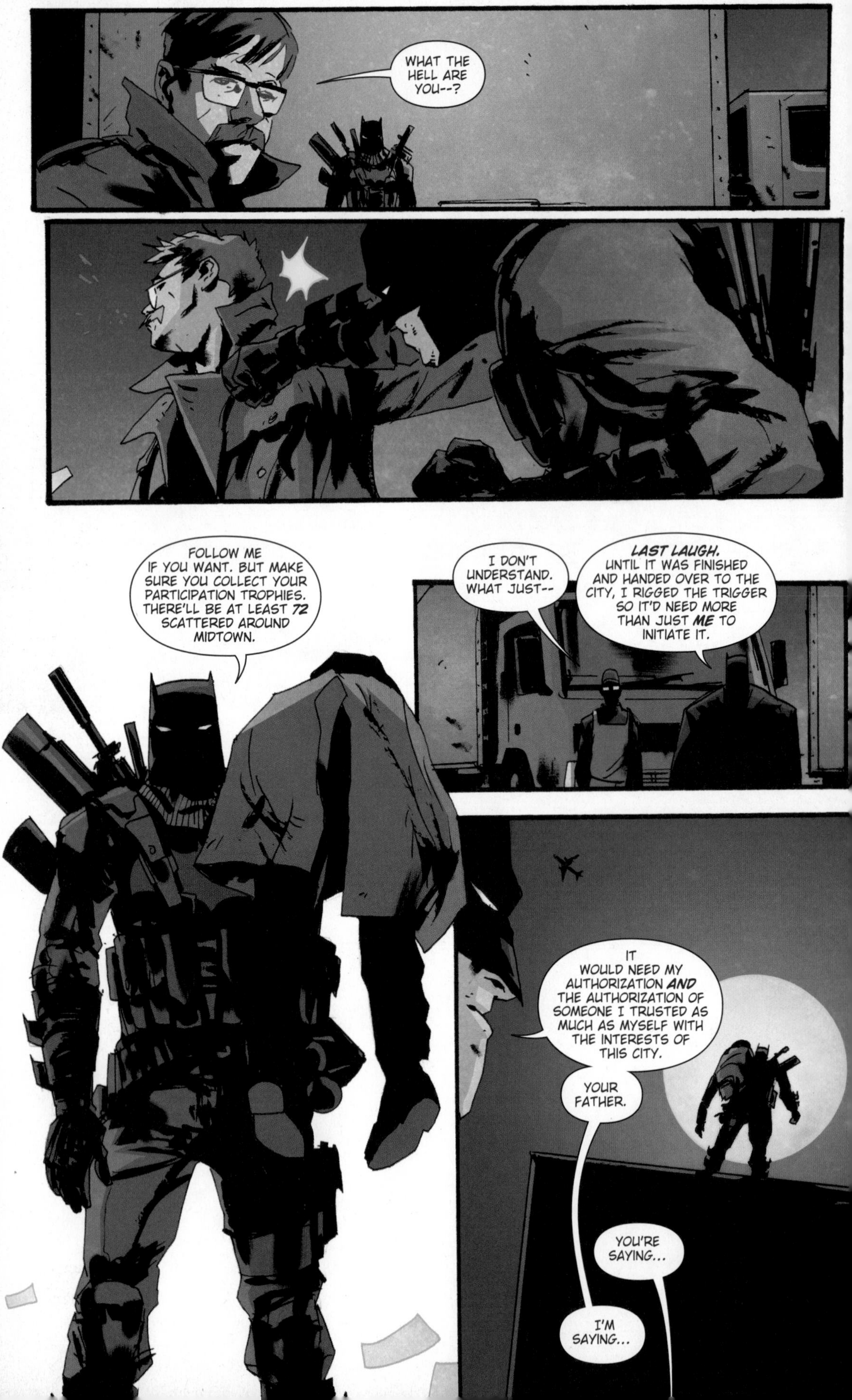
WHAT THE HELL ARE YOU--?
FOLLOW ME IF YOU WANT. BUT MAKE SURE YOU COLLECT YOUR PARTICIPATION TROPHIES. THERE'LL BE AT LEAST 72 SCATTERED AROUND MIDTOWN.
I DON'T UNDERSTAND. WHAT JUST--
LAST LAUGH. UNTIL IT WAS FINISHED AND HANDED OVER TO THE CITY, I RIGGED THE TRIGGER SO IT'D NEED MORE THAN JUST ME TO INITIATE IT.
IT WOULD NEED MY AUTHORIZATION AND THE AUTHORIZATION OF SOMEONE I TRUSTED AS MUCH AS MYSELF WITH THE INTERESTS OF THIS CITY.
YOUR FATHER.
YOU'RE SAYING...
I'M SAYING...

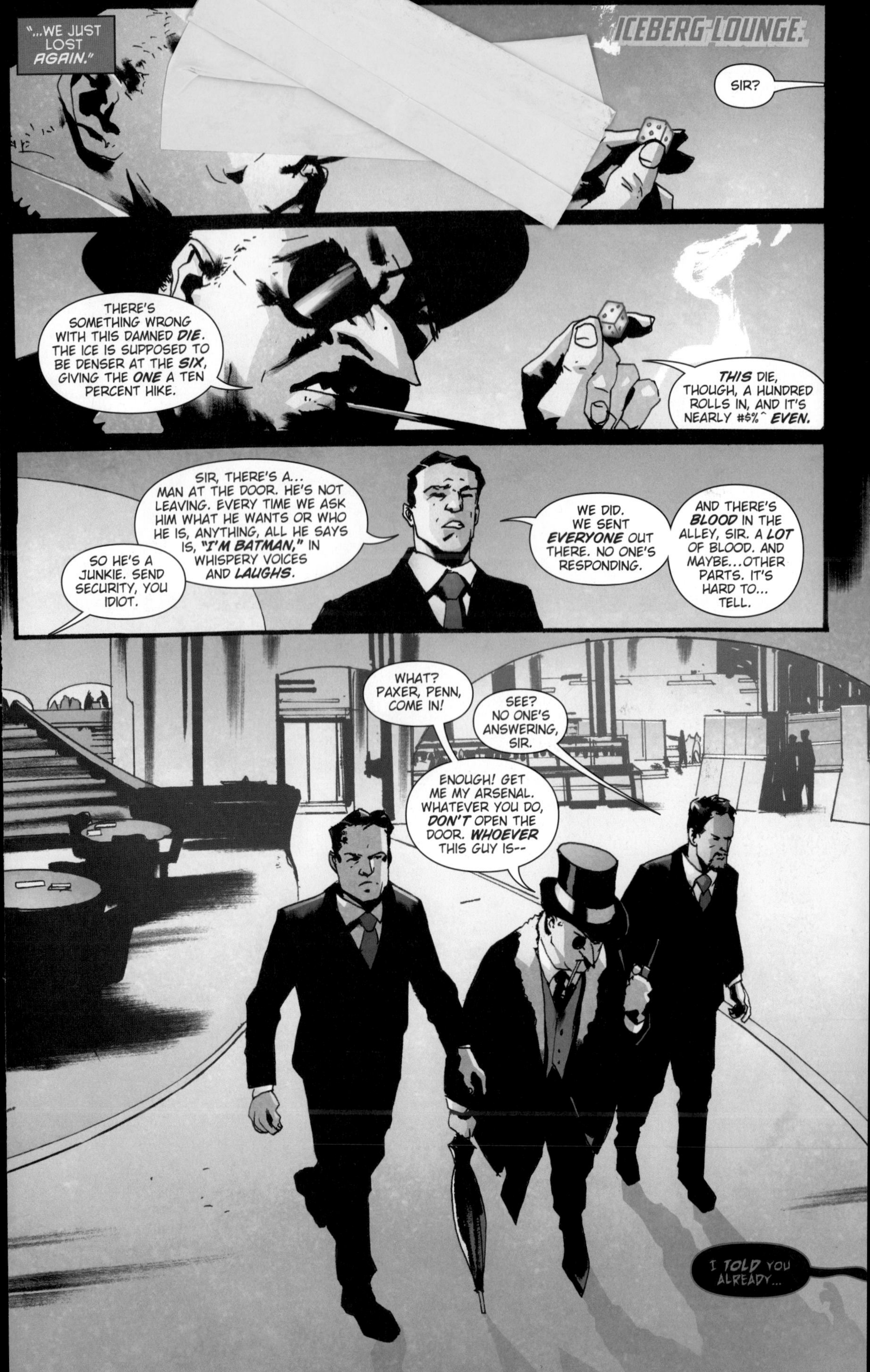
"...WE JUST LOST AGAIN."
ICEBERG LOUNGE.
SIR?
THERE'S SOMETHING WRONG WITH THIS DAMNED DIE. THE ICE IS SUPPOSED TO BE DENSER AT THE SIX, GIVING THE ONE A TEN PERCENT HIKE.
THIS DIE, THOUGH, A HUNDRED ROLLS IN, AND IT'S NEARLY #$%^ EVEN.
SIR, THERE'S A... MAN AT THE DOOR. HE'S NOT LEAVING. EVERY TIME WE ASK HIM WHAT HE WANTS OR WHO HE IS, ANYTHING, ALL HE SAYS IS, "I'M BATMAN," IN WHISPERY VOICES AND LAUGHS.
SO HE'S A JUNKIE. SEND SECURITY, YOU IDIOT.
WE DID. WE SENT EVERYONE OUT THERE. NO ONE'S RESPONDING.
AND THERE'S BLOOD IN THE ALLEY, SIR. A LOT OF BLOOD. AND MAYBE...OTHER PARTS. IT'S HARD TO... TELL.
WHAT? PAXER, PENN, COME IN!
SEE? NO ONE'S ANSWERING, SIR.
ENOUGH! GET ME MY ARSENAL. WHATEVER YOU DO, DON'T OPEN THE DOOR. WHOEVER THIS GUY IS--
I TOLD YOU ALREADY...

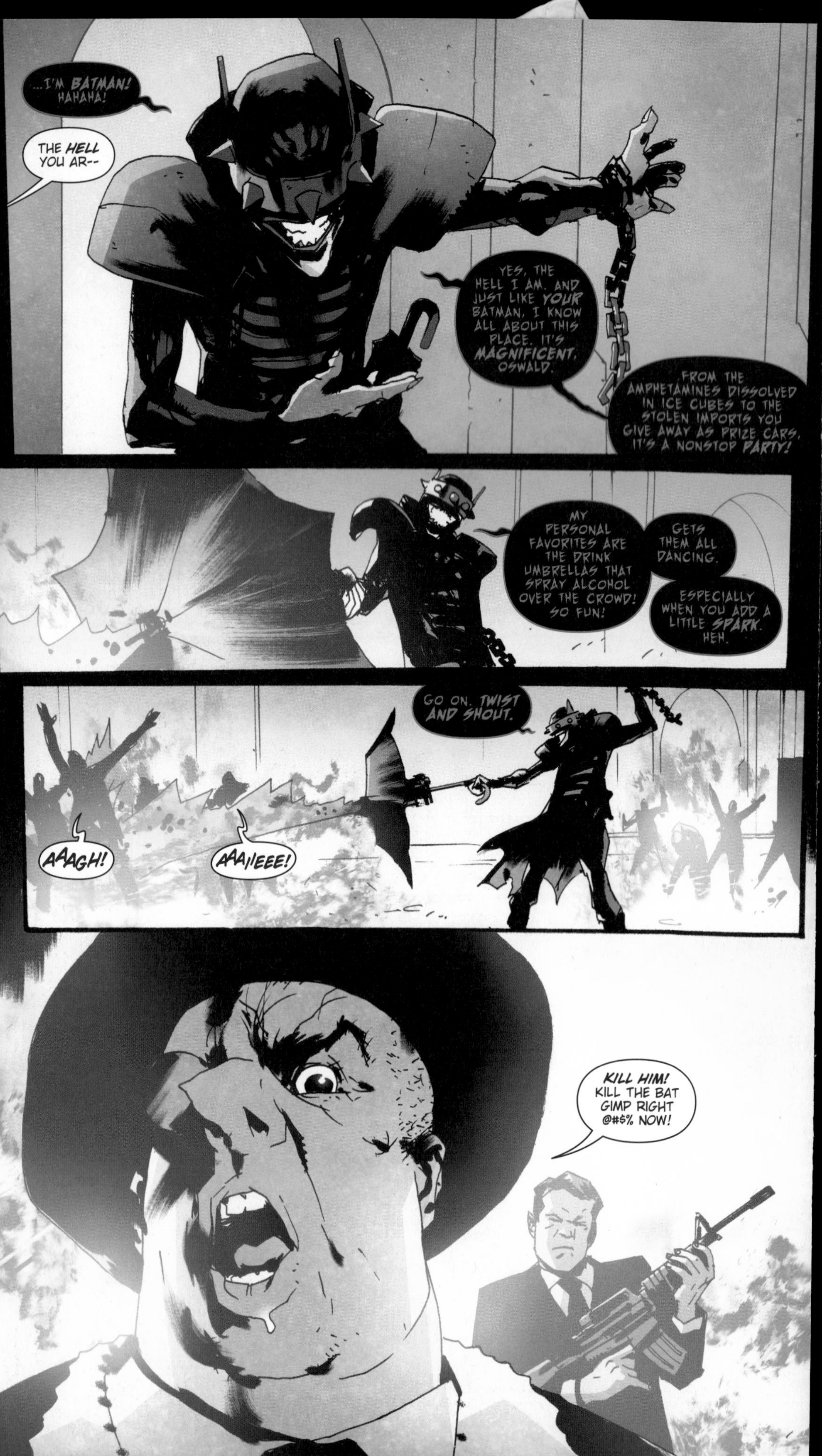

...I'M BATMAN! HAHAHA!
THE HELL YOU AR--
YES, THE HELL I AM. AND JUST LIKE YOUR BATMAN, I KNOW ALL ABOUT THIS PLACE. IT'S MAGNIFICENT, OSWALD.
FROM THE AMPHETAMINES DISSOLVED IN ICE CUBES TO THE STOLEN IMPORTS YOU GIVE AWAY AS PRIZE CARS, IT'S A NONSTOP PARTY!
MY PERSONAL FAVORITES ARE THE DRINK UMBRELLAS THAT SPRAY ALCOHOL OVER THE CROWD! SO FUN!
GETS THEM ALL DANCING.
ESPECIALLY WHEN YOU ADD A LITTLE SPARK. HEH.
GO ON. TWIST AND SHOUT.
AAAGH!
AAAIEEE!
KILL HIM! KILL THE BAT GIMP RIGHT @#$% NOW!

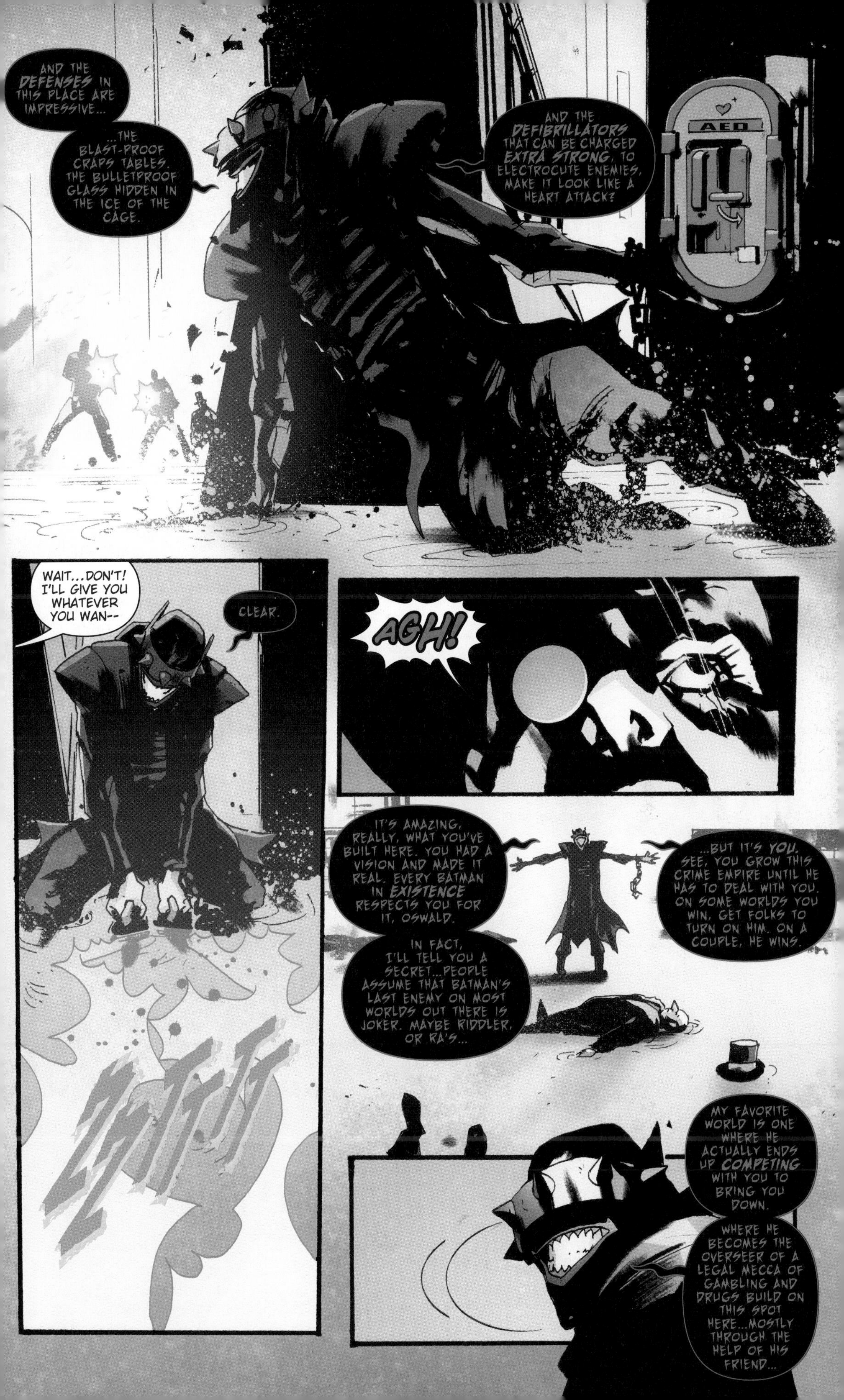
AND THE DEFENSES IN THIS PLACE ARE IMPRESSIVE...
...THE BLAST-PROOF CRAPS TABLES. THE BULLETPROOF GLASS HIDDEN IN THE ICE OF THE CAGE.
AND THE DEFIBRILLATORS THAT CAN BE CHARGED EXTRA STRONG, TO ELECTROCUTE ENEMIES, MAKE IT LOOK LIKE A HEART ATTACK?
AED
WAIT...DON'T! I'LL GIVE YOU WHATEVER YOU WAN--
CLEAR.
ZZTTTT
AGH!
IT'S AMAZING, REALLY, WHAT YOU'VE BUILT HERE. YOU HAD A VISION AND MADE IT REAL. EVERY BATMAN IN EXISTENCE RESPECTS YOU FOR IT, OSWALD.
IN FACT, I'LL TELL YOU A SECRET...PEOPLE ASSUME THAT BATMAN'S LAST ENEMY ON MOST WORLDS OUT THERE IS JOKER. MAYBE RIDDLER, OR RA'S...
...BUT IT'S YOU. SEE, YOU GROW THIS CRIME EMPIRE UNTIL HE HAS TO DEAL WITH YOU. ON SOME WORLDS YOU WIN, GET FOLKS TO TURN ON HIM. ON A COUPLE, HE WINS.
MY FAVORITE WORLD IS ONE WHERE HE ACTUALLY ENDS UP COMPETING WITH YOU TO BRING YOU DOWN.
WHERE HE BECOMES THE OVERSEER OF A LEGAL MECCA OF GAMBLING AND DRUGS BUILD ON THIS SPOT HERE...MOSTLY THROUGH THE HELP OF HIS FRIEND...

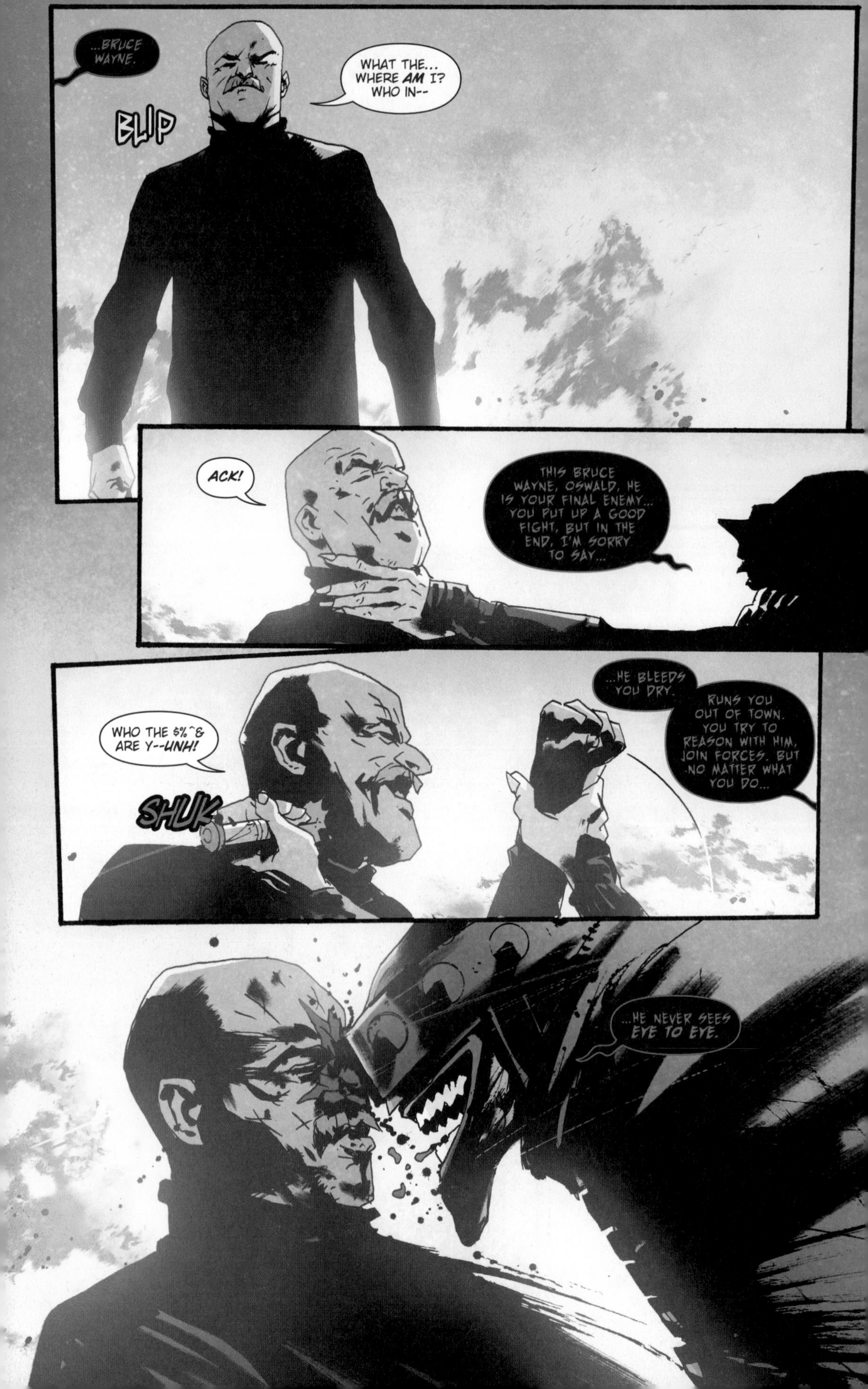
...BRUCE WAYNE.
WHAT THE... WHERE AM I? WHO IN--
BLIP
ACK!
THIS BRUCE WAYNE, OSWALD, HE IS YOUR FINAL ENEMY... YOU PUT UP A GOOD FIGHT, BUT IN THE END, I'M SORRY TO SAY...
WHO THE $%^& ARE Y--UNH!
SHUK
...HE BLEEDS YOU DRY.
RUNS YOU OUT OF TOWN. YOU TRY TO REASON WITH HIM, JOIN FORCES. BUT NO MATTER WHAT YOU DO...
...HE NEVER SEES EYE TO EYE.

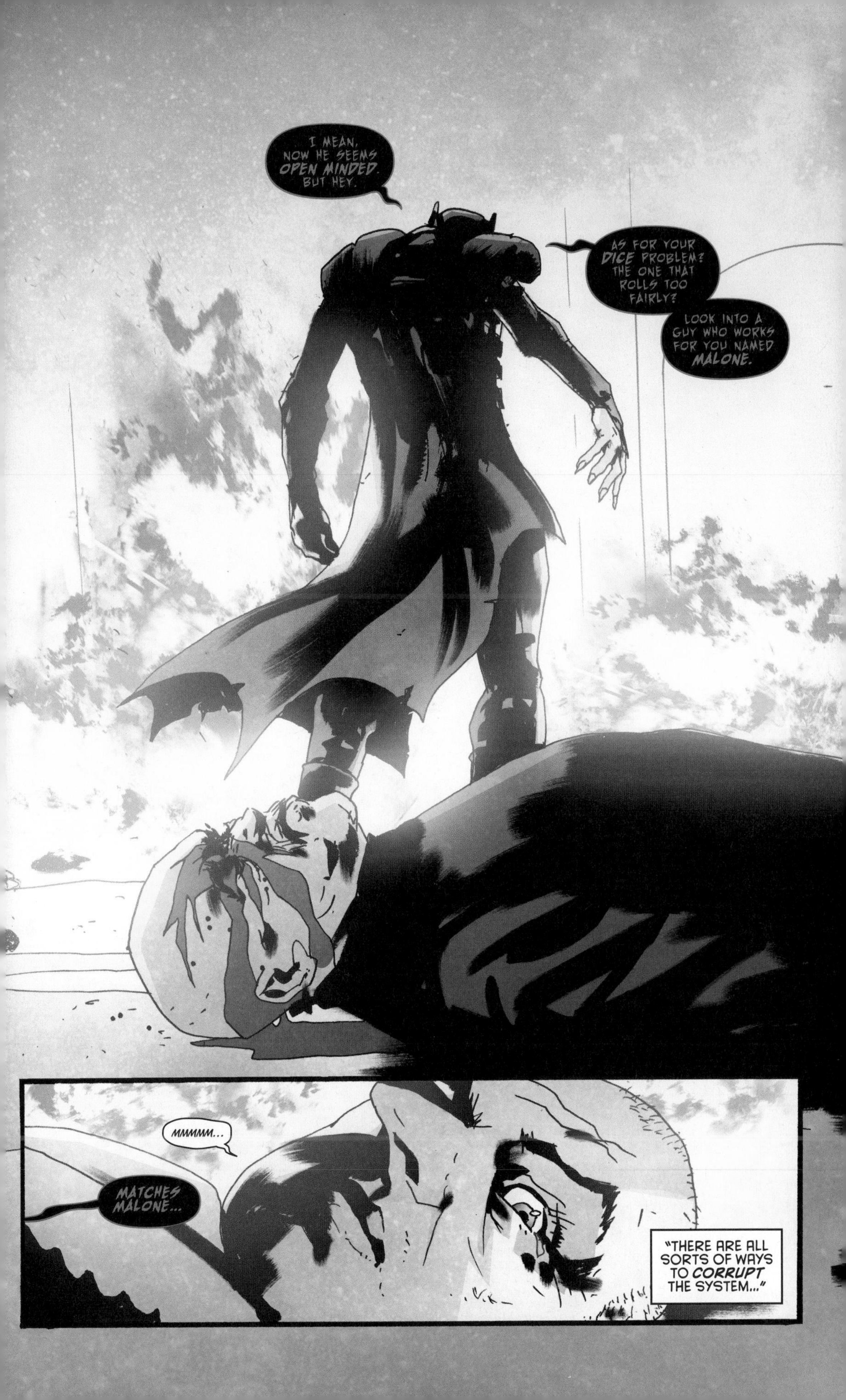

I MEAN, NOW HE SEEMS OPEN MINDED. BUT HEY.
AS FOR YOUR DICE PROBLEM? THE ONE THAT ROLLS TOO FAIRLY?
LOOK INTO A GUY WHO WORKS FOR YOU NAMED MALONE.
MMMMM...
MATCHES MALONE...
"THERE ARE ALL SORTS OF WAYS TO CORRUPT THE SYSTEM..."

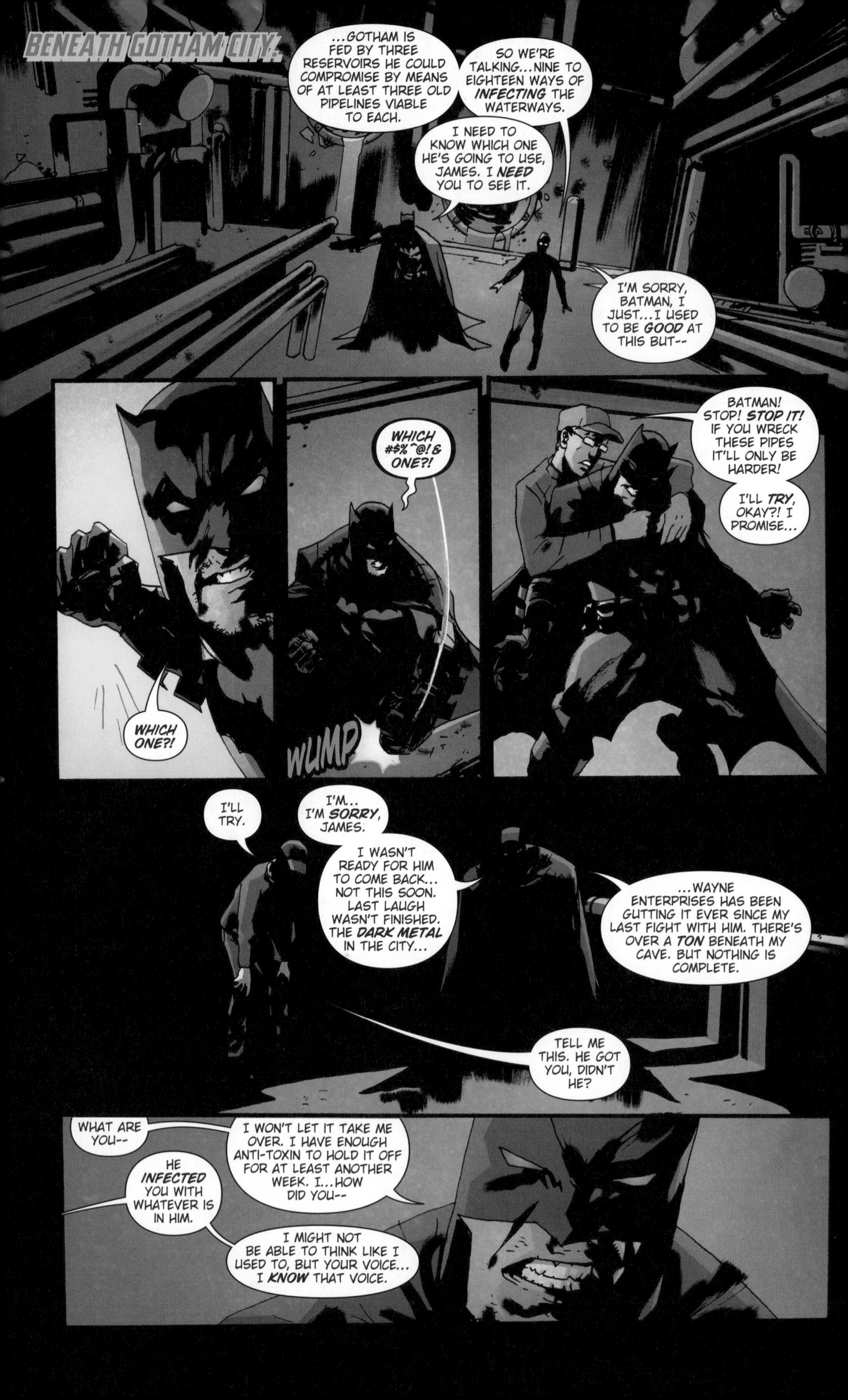
BENEATH GOTHAM CITY.
...GOTHAM IS FED BY THREE RESERVOIRS HE COULD COMPROMISE BY MEANS OF AT LEAST THREE OLD PIPELINES VIABLE TO EACH.
SO WE'RE TALKING...NINE TO EIGHTEEN WAYS OF INFECTING THE WATERWAYS.
I NEED TO KNOW WHICH ONE HE'S GOING TO USE, JAMES. I NEED YOU TO SEE IT.
I'M SORRY, BATMAN, I JUST...I USED TO BE GOOD AT THIS BUT--
WHICH ONE?!
WHICH #$%^@!& ONE?!
WUMP
BATMAN! STOP! STOP IT! IF YOU WRECK THESE PIPES IT'LL ONLY BE HARDER!
I'LL TRY, OKAY?! I PROMISE...
I'LL TRY.
I'M... I'M SORRY, JAMES.
I WASN'T READY FOR HIM TO COME BACK... NOT THIS SOON. LAST LAUGH WASN'T FINISHED. THE DARK METAL IN THE CITY...
...WAYNE ENTERPRISES HAS BEEN GUTTING IT EVER SINCE MY LAST FIGHT WITH HIM. THERE'S OVER A TON BENEATH MY CAVE. BUT NOTHING IS COMPLETE.
TELL ME THIS. HE GOT YOU, DIDN'T HE?
WHAT ARE YOU--
I WON'T LET IT TAKE ME OVER. I HAVE ENOUGH ANTI-TOXIN TO HOLD IT OFF FOR AT LEAST ANOTHER WEEK. I...HOW DID YOU--
HE INFECTED YOU WITH WHATEVER IS IN HIM.
I MIGHT NOT BE ABLE TO THINK LIKE I USED TO, BUT YOUR VOICE... I KNOW THAT VOICE.

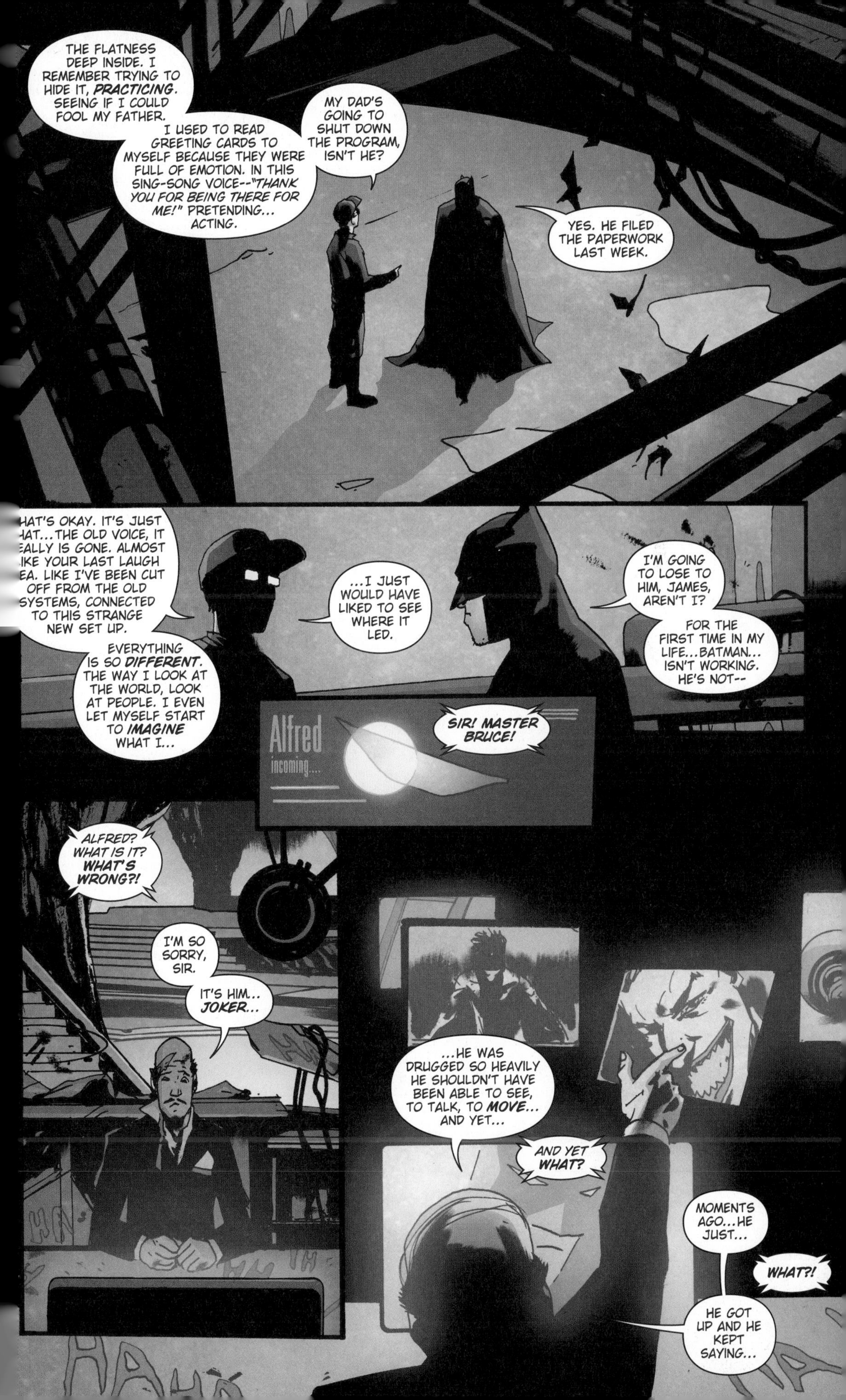
THE FLATNESS DEEP INSIDE. I REMEMBER TRYING TO HIDE IT, PRACTICING. SEEING IF I COULD FOOL MY FATHER.
I USED TO READ GREETING CARDS TO MYSELF BECAUSE THEY WERE FULL OF EMOTION. IN THIS SING-SONG VOICE--"THANK YOU FOR BEING THERE FOR ME!" PRETENDING... ACTING.
MY DAD'S GOING TO SHUT DOWN THE PROGRAM, ISN'T HE?
YES. HE FILED THE PAPERWORK LAST WEEK.
HAT'S OKAY. IT'S JUST HAT... THE OLD VOICE, IT EALLY IS GONE. ALMOST IKE YOUR LAST LAUGH EA. LIKE I'VE BEEN CUT OFF FROM THE OLD SYSTEMS, CONNECTED TO THIS STRANGE NEW SET UP.
EVERYTHING IS SO DIFFERENT. THE WAY I LOOK AT THE WORLD, LOOK AT PEOPLE. I EVEN LET MYSELF START TO IMAGINE WHAT I...
...I JUST WOULD HAVE LIKED TO SEE WHERE IT LED.
I'M GOING TO LOSE TO HIM, JAMES, AREN'T I?
FOR THE FIRST TIME IN MY LIFE... BATMAN... ISN'T WORKING. HE'S NOT--
Alfred
incoming....
SIR! MASTER BRUCE!
ALFRED? WHAT IS IT? WHAT'S WRONG?!
I'M SO SORRY, SIR.
IT'S HIM... JOKER...
...HE WAS DRUGGED SO HEAVILY HE SHOULDN'T HAVE BEEN ABLE TO SEE, TO TALK, TO MOVE... AND YET...
AND YET WHAT?
MOMENTS AGO... HE JUST...
WHAT?!
HE GOT UP AND HE KEPT SAYING...

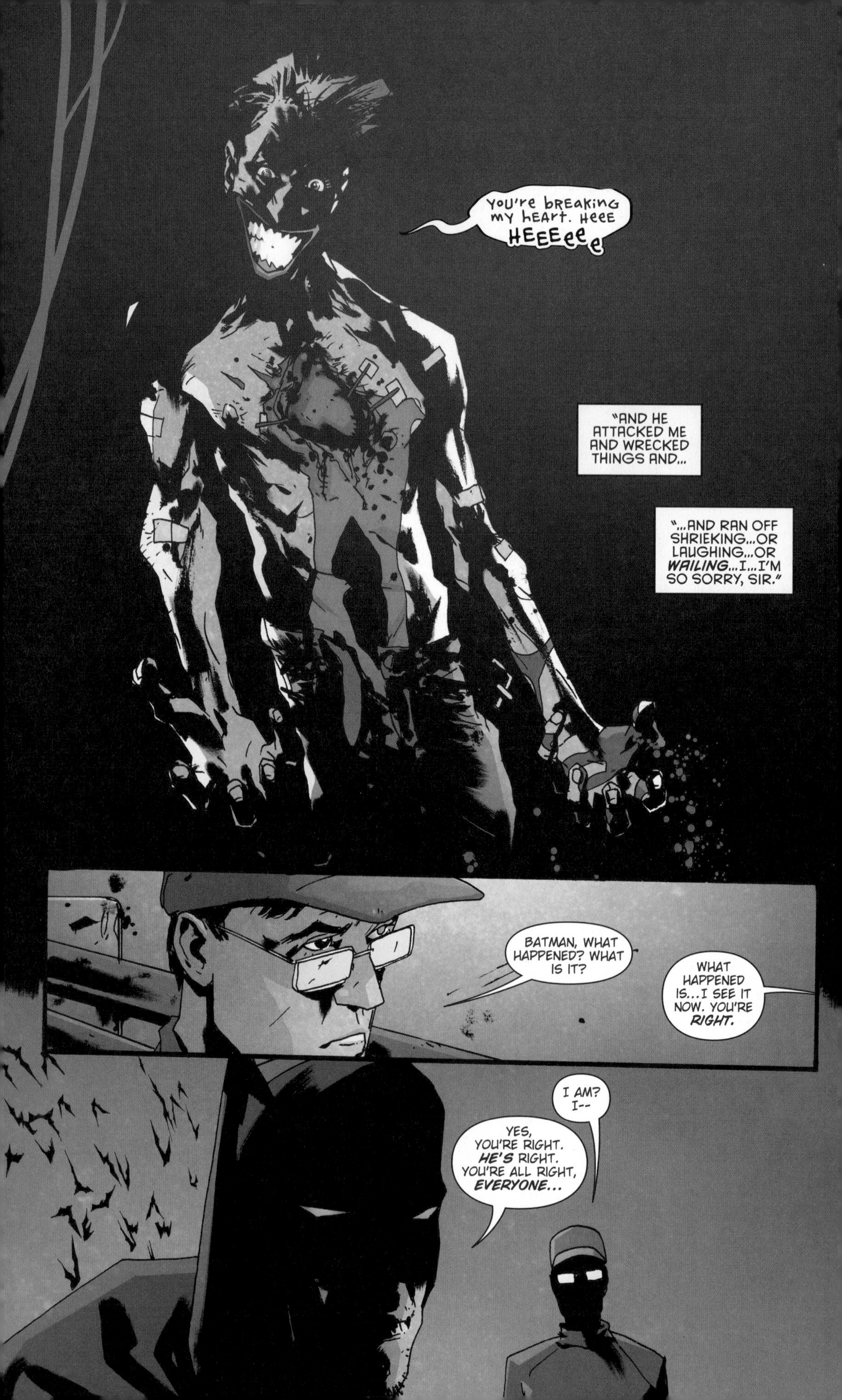
You're breaking my heart. Heee HEEEeee
"AND HE ATTACKED ME AND WRECKED THINGS AND...
"...AND RAN OFF SHRIEKING...OR LAUGHING...OR WAILING...I...I'M SO SORRY, SIR."
BATMAN, WHAT HAPPENED? WHAT IS IT?
WHAT HAPPENED IS...I SEE IT NOW. YOU'RE RIGHT.
I AM? I--
YES, YOU'RE RIGHT. HE'S RIGHT. YOU'RE ALL RIGHT, EVERYONE...

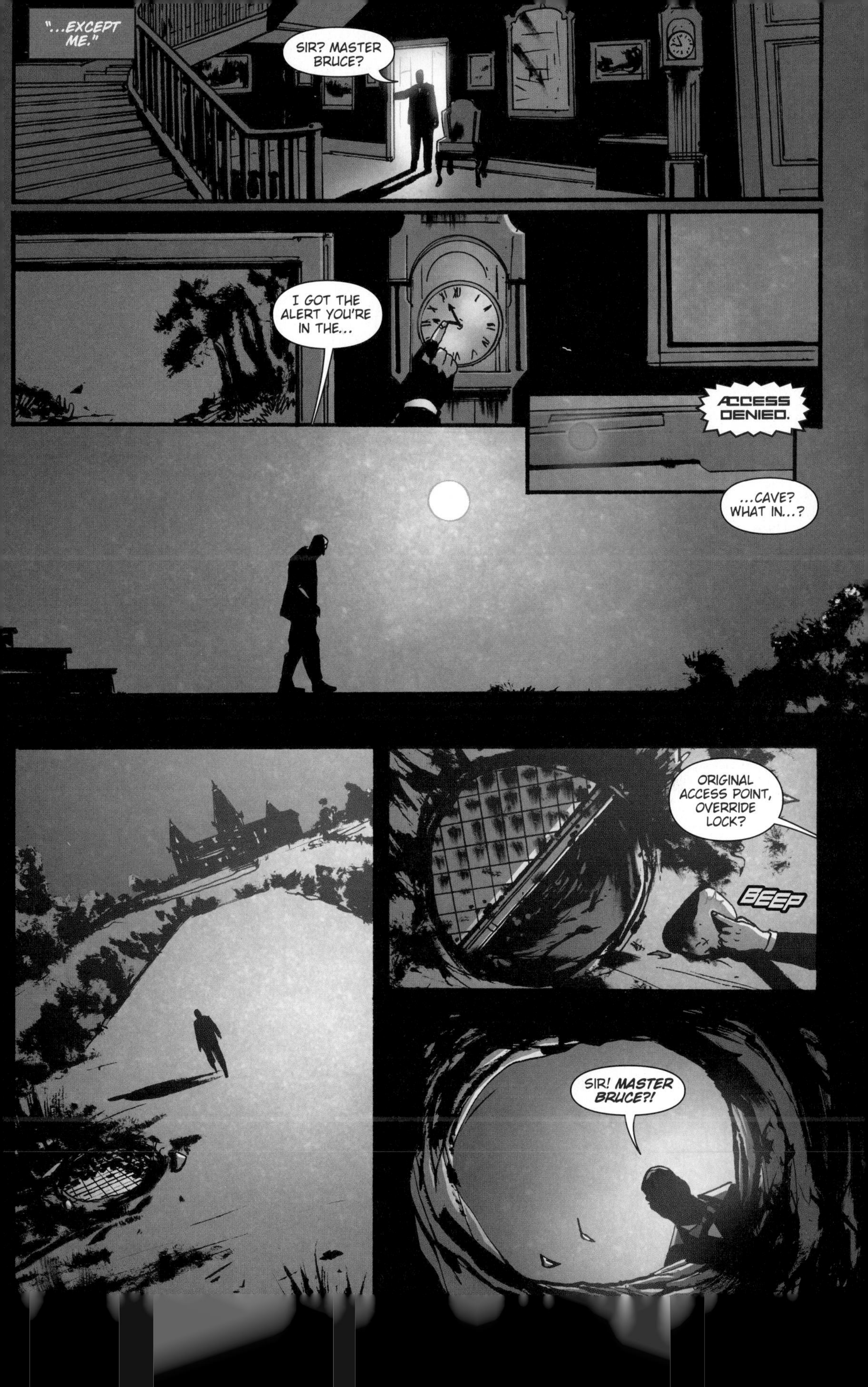
"...EXCEPT ME."
SIR? MASTER BRUCE?
I GOT THE ALERT YOU'RE IN THE...
ACCESS DENIED.
...CAVE? WHAT IN...?
ORIGINAL ACCESS POINT, OVERRIDE LOCK?
BEEP
SIR! MASTER BRUCE?!

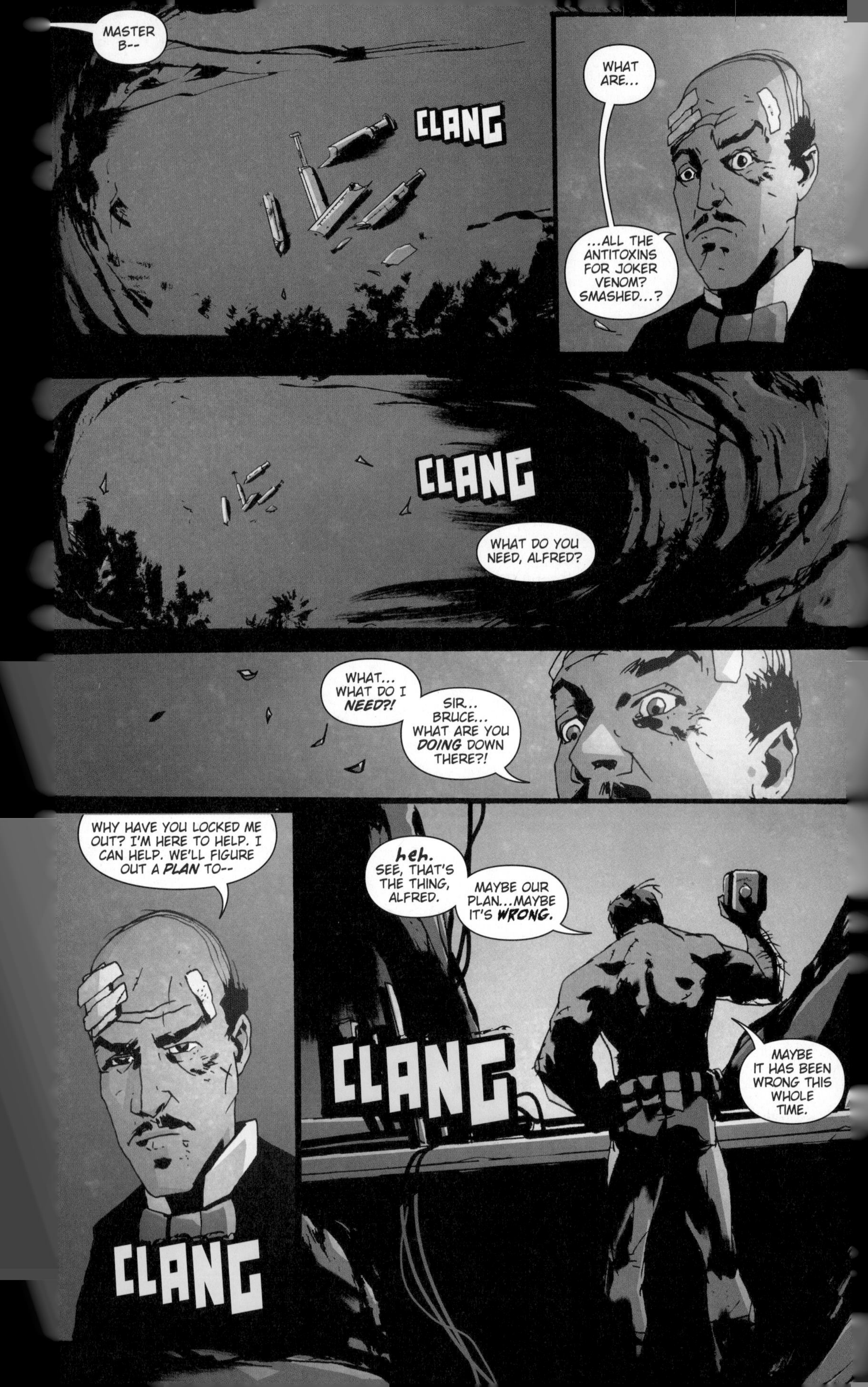
MASTER B--
CLANG
WHAT ARE...
...ALL THE ANTITOXINS FOR JOKER VENOM? SMASHED...?
CLANG
WHAT DO YOU NEED, ALFRED?
WHAT... WHAT DO I NEED?!
SIR... BRUCE... WHAT ARE YOU DOING DOWN THERE?!
WHY HAVE YOU LOCKED ME OUT? I'M HERE TO HELP. I CAN HELP. WE'LL FIGURE OUT A PLAN TO--
CLANG
heh. SEE, THAT'S THE THING, ALFRED.
MAYBE OUR PLAN...MAYBE IT'S WRONG.
MAYBE IT HAS BEEN WRONG THIS WHOLE TIME.
CLANG

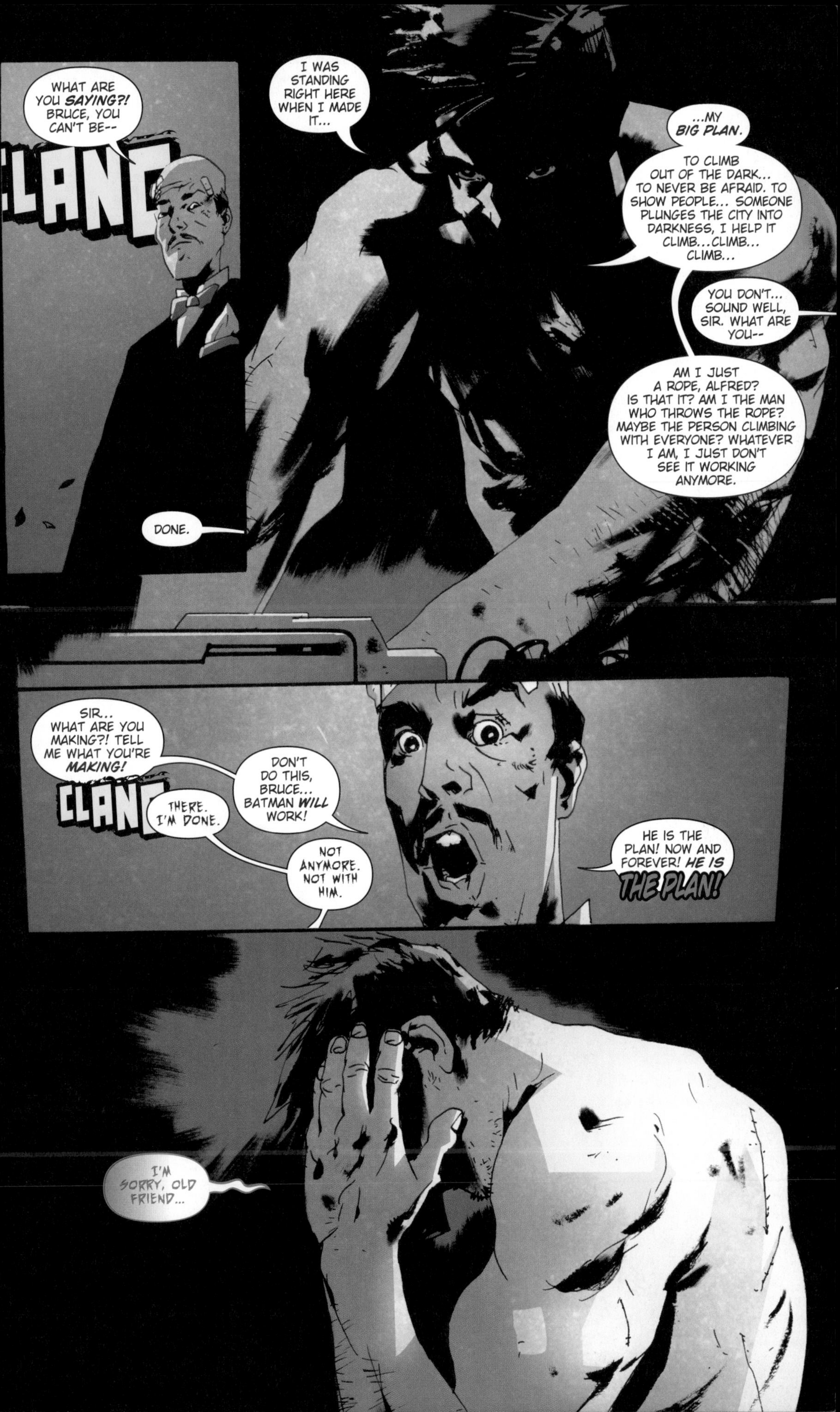
WHAT ARE YOU SAYING?! BRUCE, YOU CAN'T BE--
CLANG
I WAS STANDING RIGHT HERE WHEN I MADE IT...
...MY BIG PLAN.
TO CLIMB OUT OF THE DARK... TO NEVER BE AFRAID. TO SHOW PEOPLE... SOMEONE PLUNGES THE CITY INTO DARKNESS, I HELP IT CLIMB...CLIMB... CLIMB...
YOU DON'T... SOUND WELL, SIR. WHAT ARE YOU--
AM I JUST A ROPE, ALFRED? IS THAT IT? AM I THE MAN WHO THROWS THE ROPE? MAYBE THE PERSON CLIMBING WITH EVERYONE? WHATEVER I AM, I JUST DON'T SEE IT WORKING ANYMORE.
DONE.
SIR... WHAT ARE YOU MAKING?! TELL ME WHAT YOU'RE MAKING!
CLANG
DON'T DO THIS, BRUCE... BATMAN WILL WORK!
THERE. I'M DONE.
NOT ANYMORE. NOT WITH HIM.
HE IS THE PLAN! NOW AND FOREVER! HE IS THE PLAN!
I'M SORRY, OLD FRIEND...

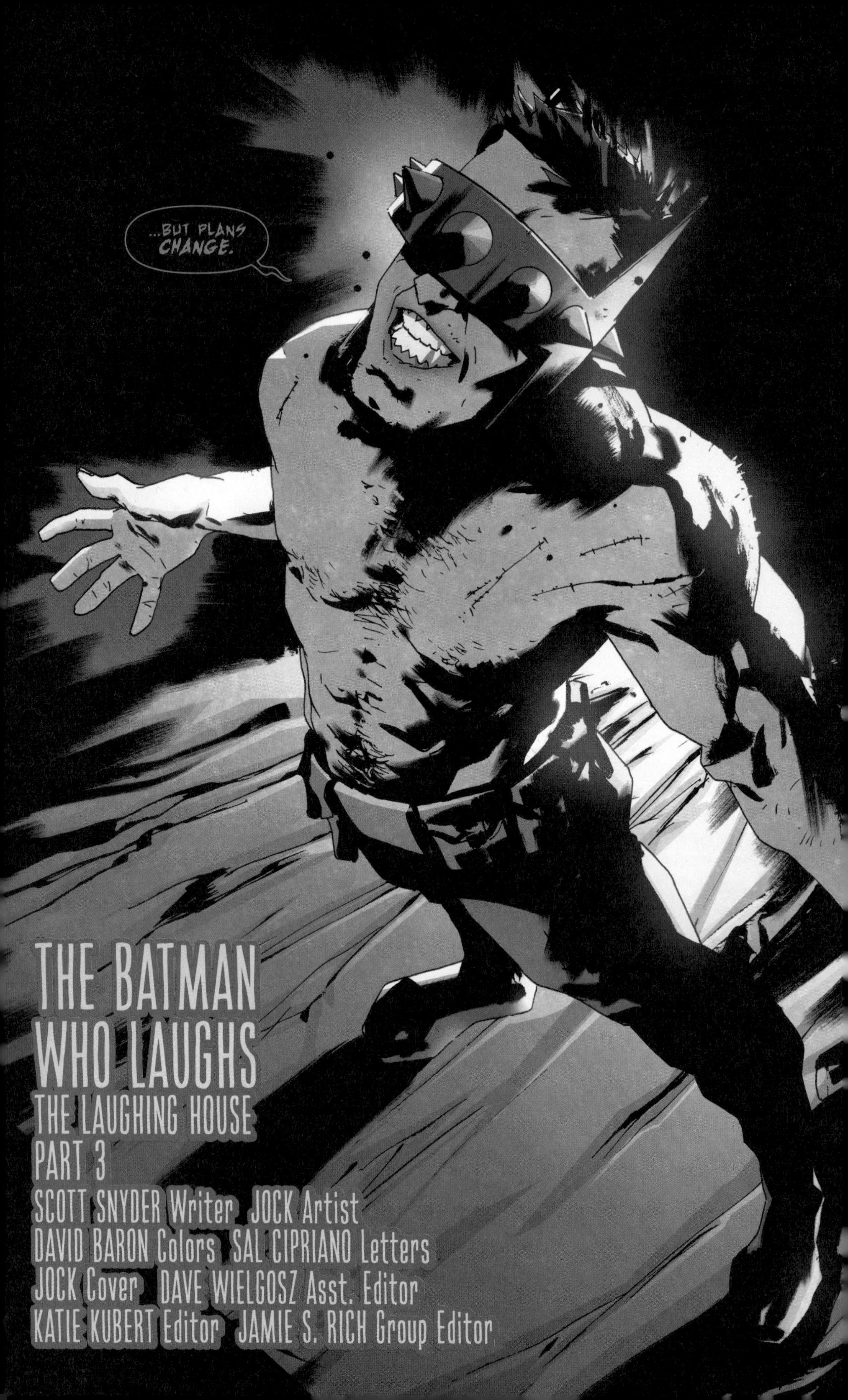
...BUT PLANS CHANGE.
THE BATMAN WHO LAUGHS
THE LAUGHING HOUSE
PART 3
SCOTT SNYDER Writer JOCK Artist
DAVID BARON Colors SAL CIPRIANO Letters
JOCK Cover DAVE WIELGOSZ Asst. Editor
KATIE KUBERT Editor JAMIE S. RICH Group Editor

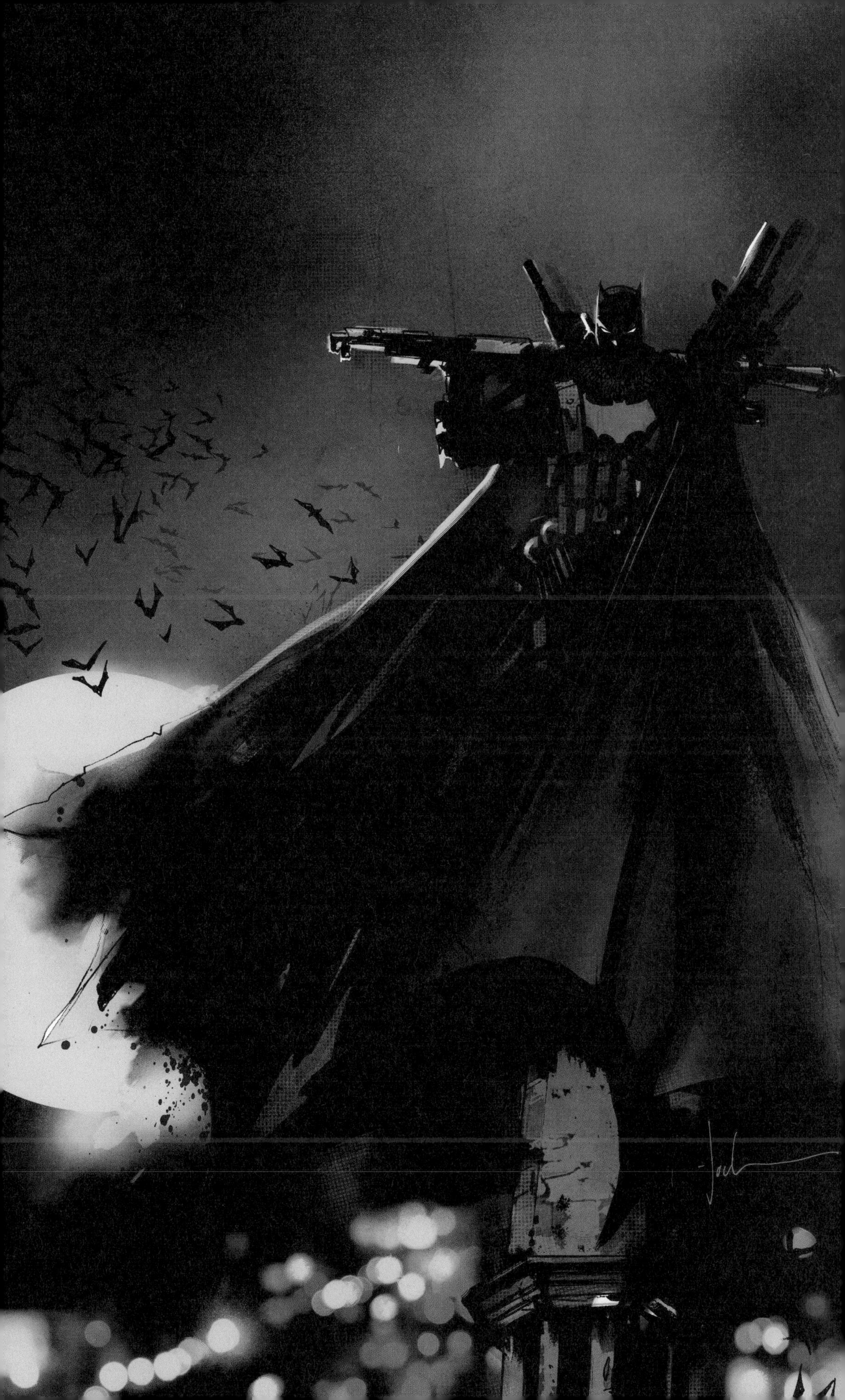

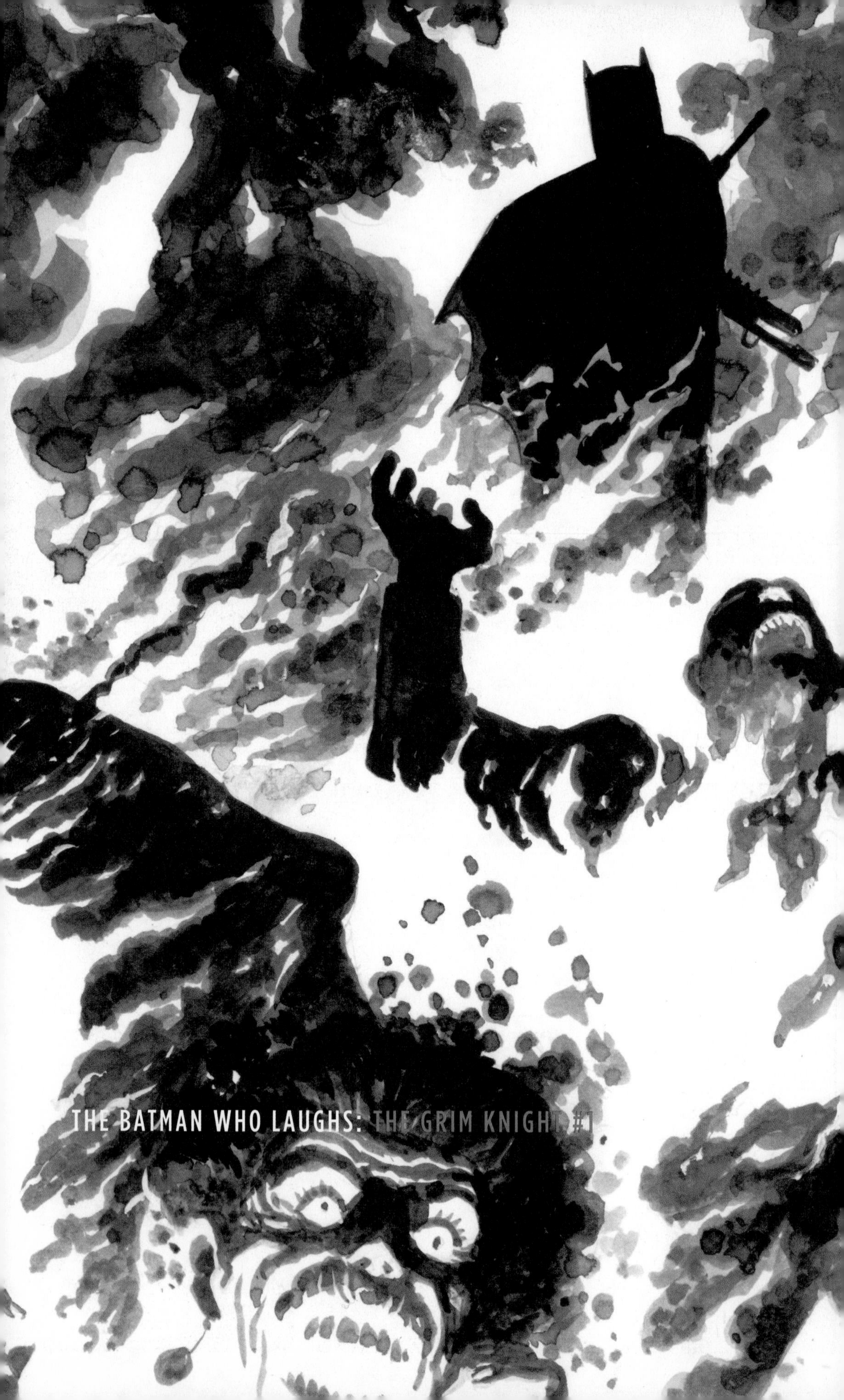

THE BATMAN WHO LAUGHS: THE GRIM KNIGHT #1

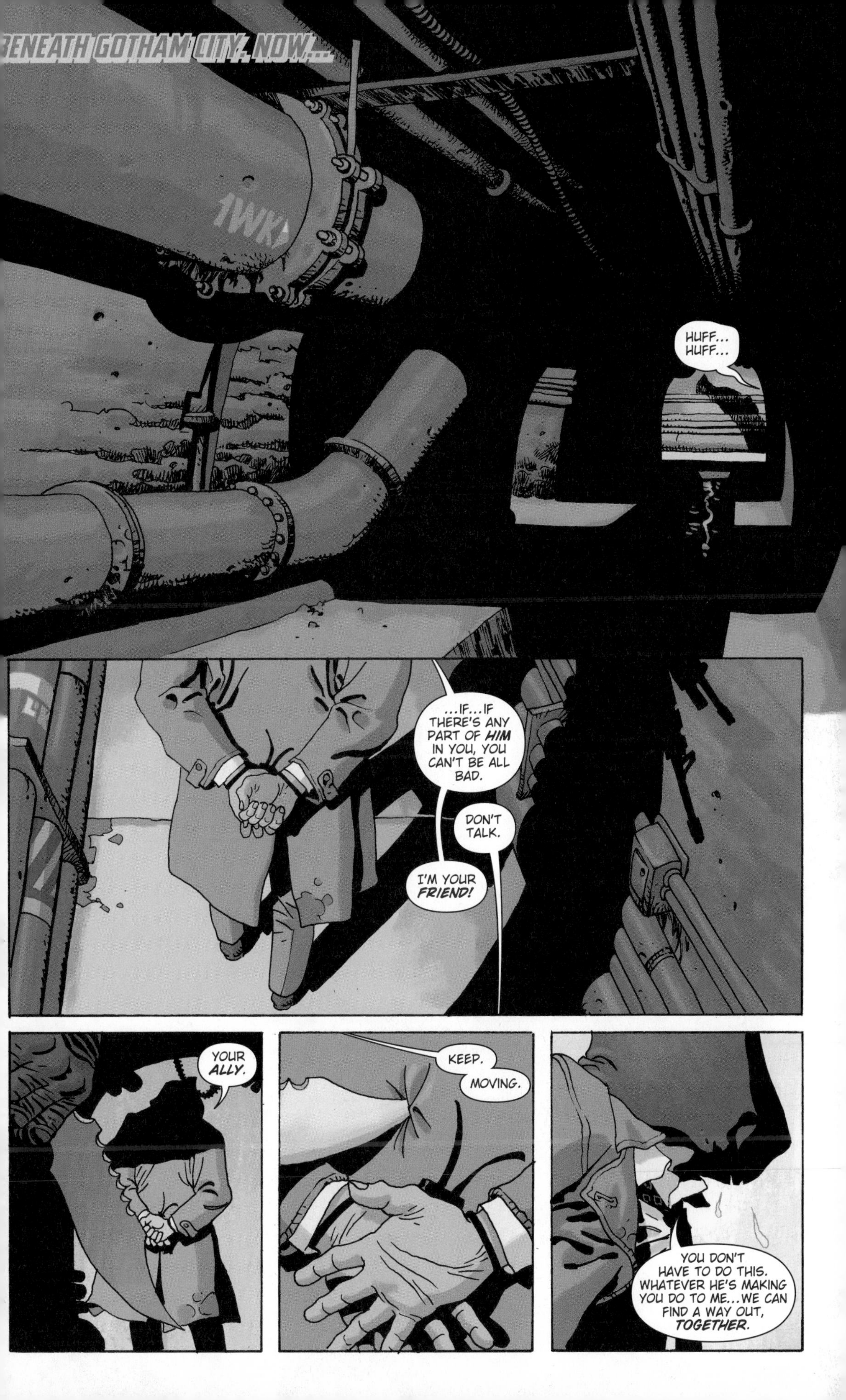
BENEATH GOTHAM CITY. NOW...
1WK
HUFF... HUFF...
...IF...IF THERE'S ANY PART OF HIM IN YOU, YOU CAN'T BE ALL BAD.
DON'T TALK.
I'M YOUR FRIEND!
YOUR ALLY.
KEEP.
MOVING.
YOU DON'T HAVE TO DO THIS. WHATEVER HE'S MAKING YOU DO TO ME...WE CAN FIND A WAY OUT, TOGETHER.

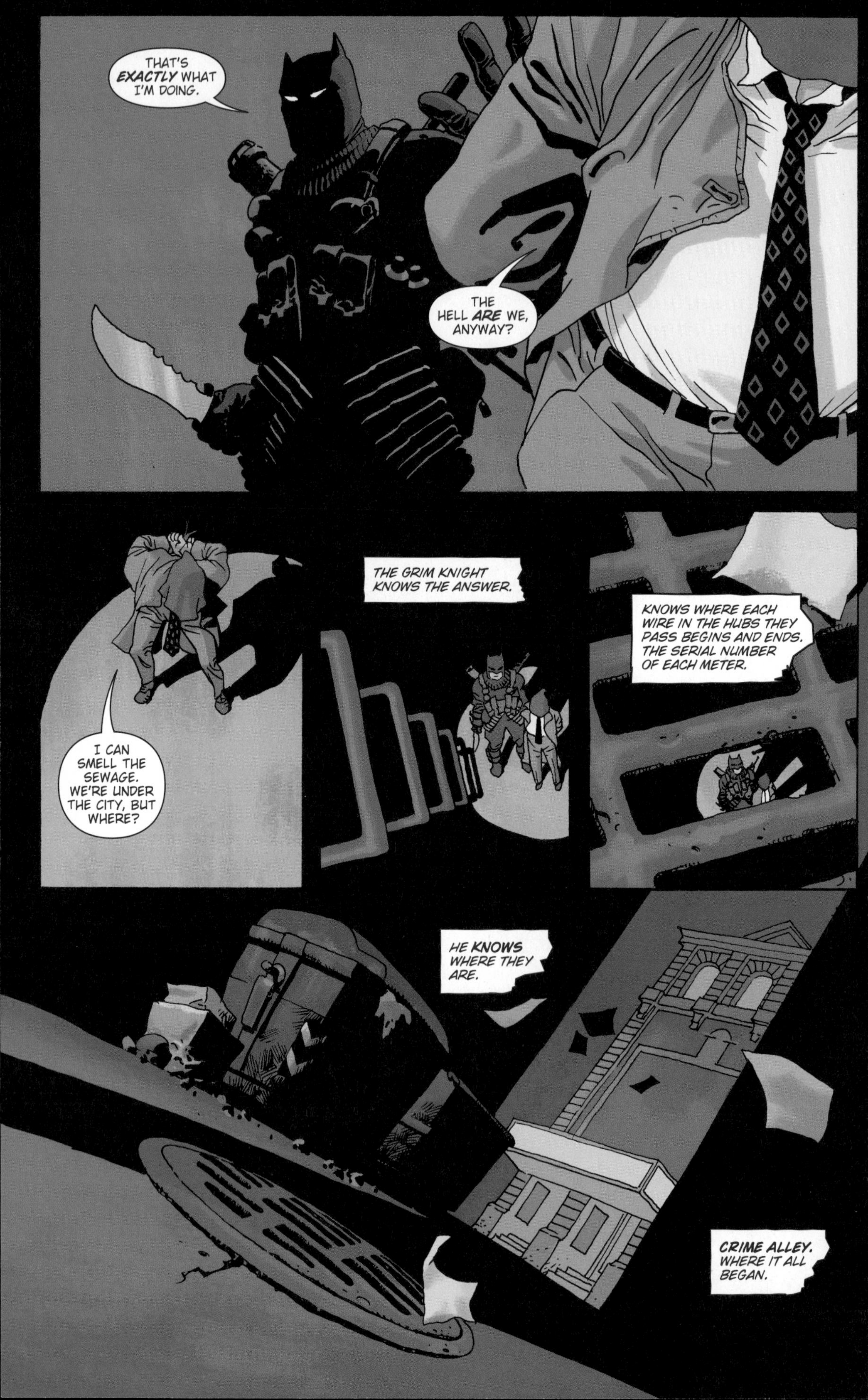
THAT'S EXACTLY WHAT I'M DOING.
THE HELL ARE WE, ANYWAY?
I CAN SMELL THE SEWAGE. WE'RE UNDER THE CITY, BUT WHERE?
THE GRIM KNIGHT KNOWS THE ANSWER.
KNOWS WHERE EACH WIRE IN THE HUBS THEY PASS BEGINS AND ENDS. THE SERIAL NUMBER OF EACH METER.
HE KNOWS WHERE THEY ARE.
CRIME ALLEY. WHERE IT ALL BEGAN.

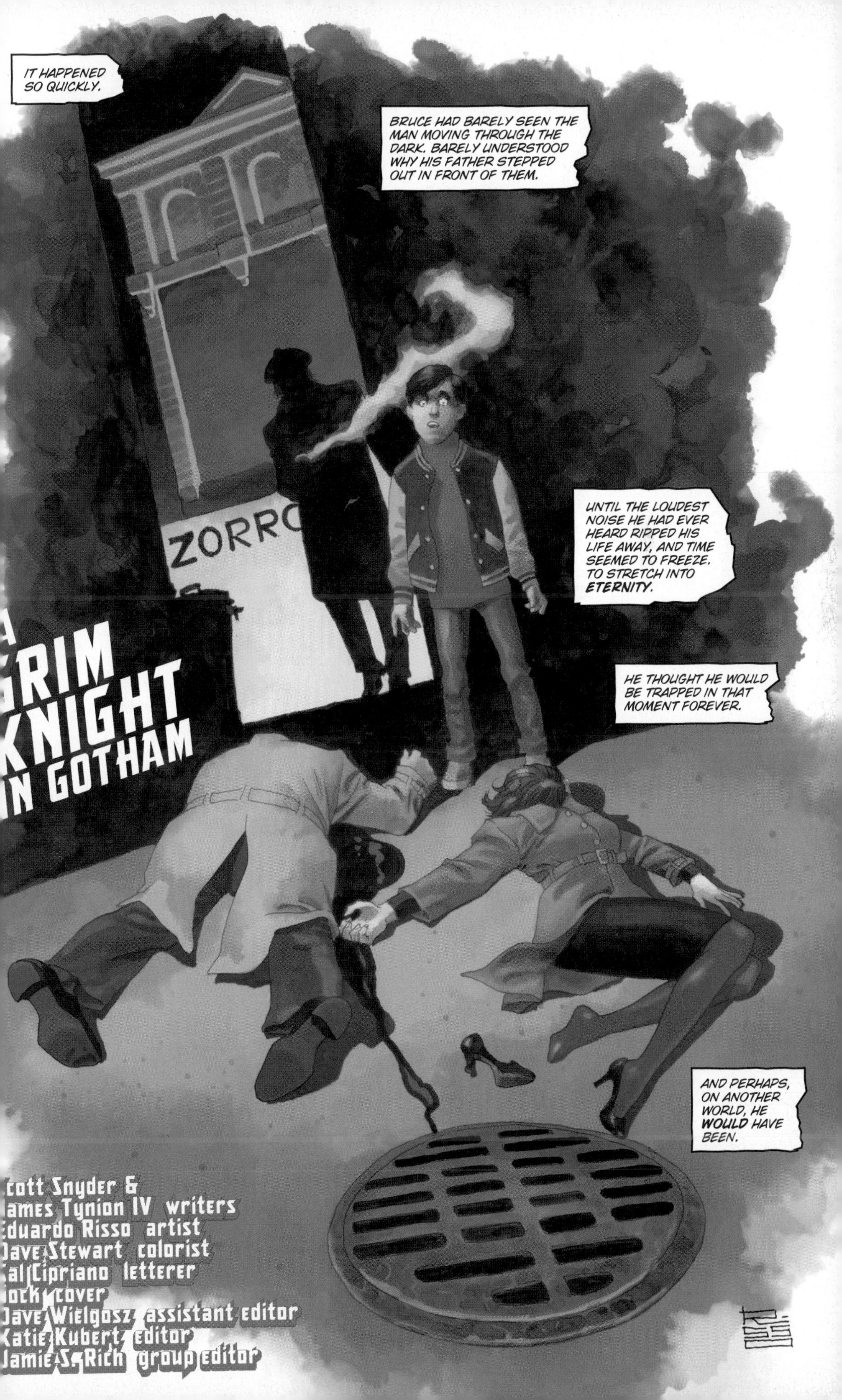
IT HAPPENED SO QUICKLY.
BRUCE HAD BARELY SEEN THE MAN MOVING THROUGH THE DARK. BARELY UNDERSTOOD WHY HIS FATHER STEPPED OUT IN FRONT OF THEM.
ZORRO
UNTIL THE LOUDEST NOISE HE HAD EVER HEARD RIPPED HIS LIFE AWAY, AND TIME SEEMED TO FREEZE. TO STRETCH INTO ETERNITY.
HE THOUGHT HE WOULD BE TRAPPED IN THAT MOMENT FOREVER.
AND PERHAPS, ON ANOTHER WORLD, HE WOULD HAVE BEEN.
A GRIM KNIGHT IN GOTHAM
cott Snyder &
ames Tynion IV writers
duardo Risso artist
ave Stewart colorist
al Cipriano letterer
ock cover
ave Wielgosz assistant editor
atie Kubert editor
amie S. Rich group editor

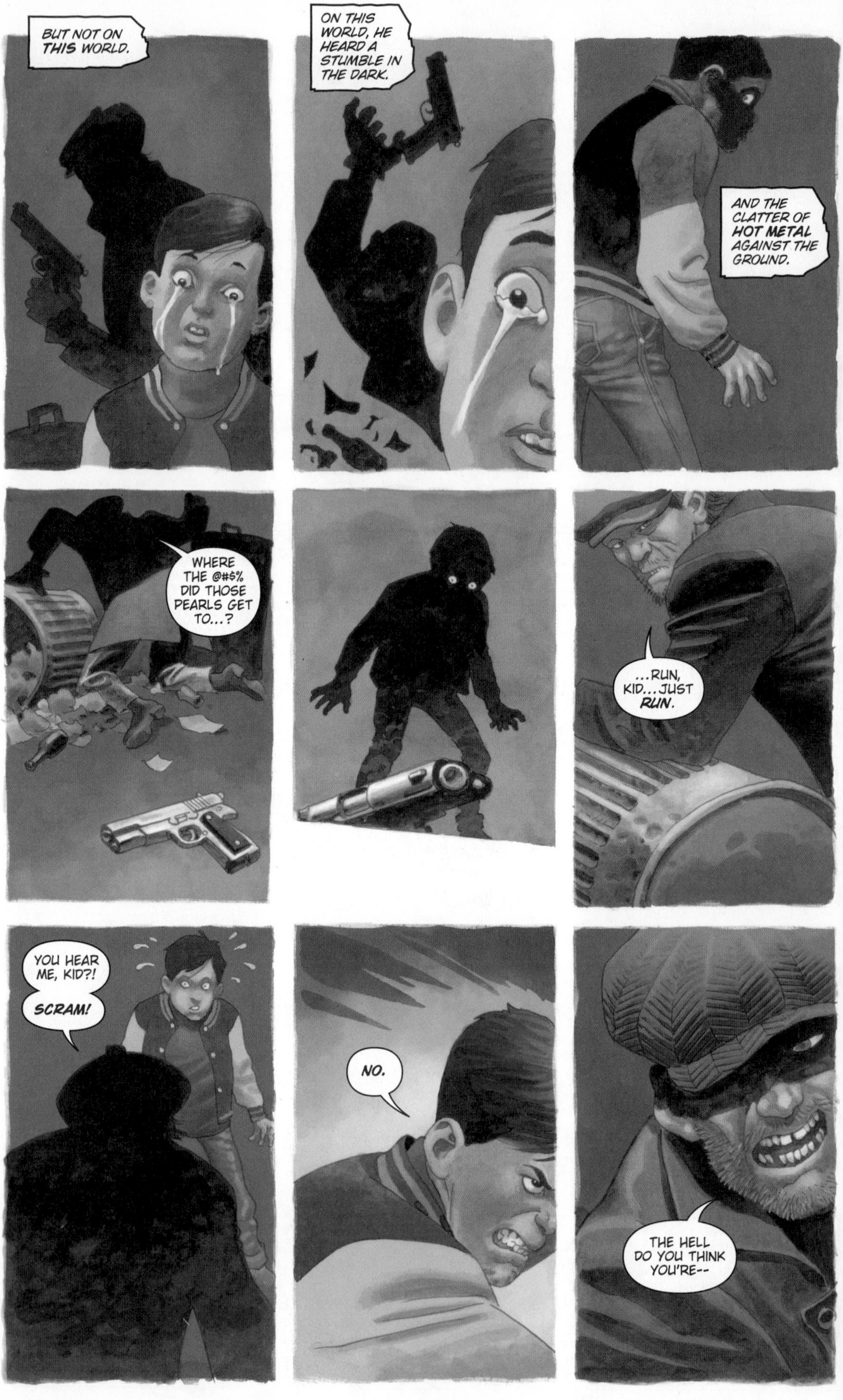
BUT NOT ON THIS WORLD.
ON THIS WORLD, HE HEARD A STUMBLE IN THE DARK.
AND THE CLATTER OF HOT METAL AGAINST THE GROUND.
WHERE THE @#$% DID THOSE PEARLS GET TO...?
...RUN, KID...JUST RUN.
YOU HEAR ME, KID?!
SCRAM!
NO.
THE HELL DO YOU THINK YOU'RE--

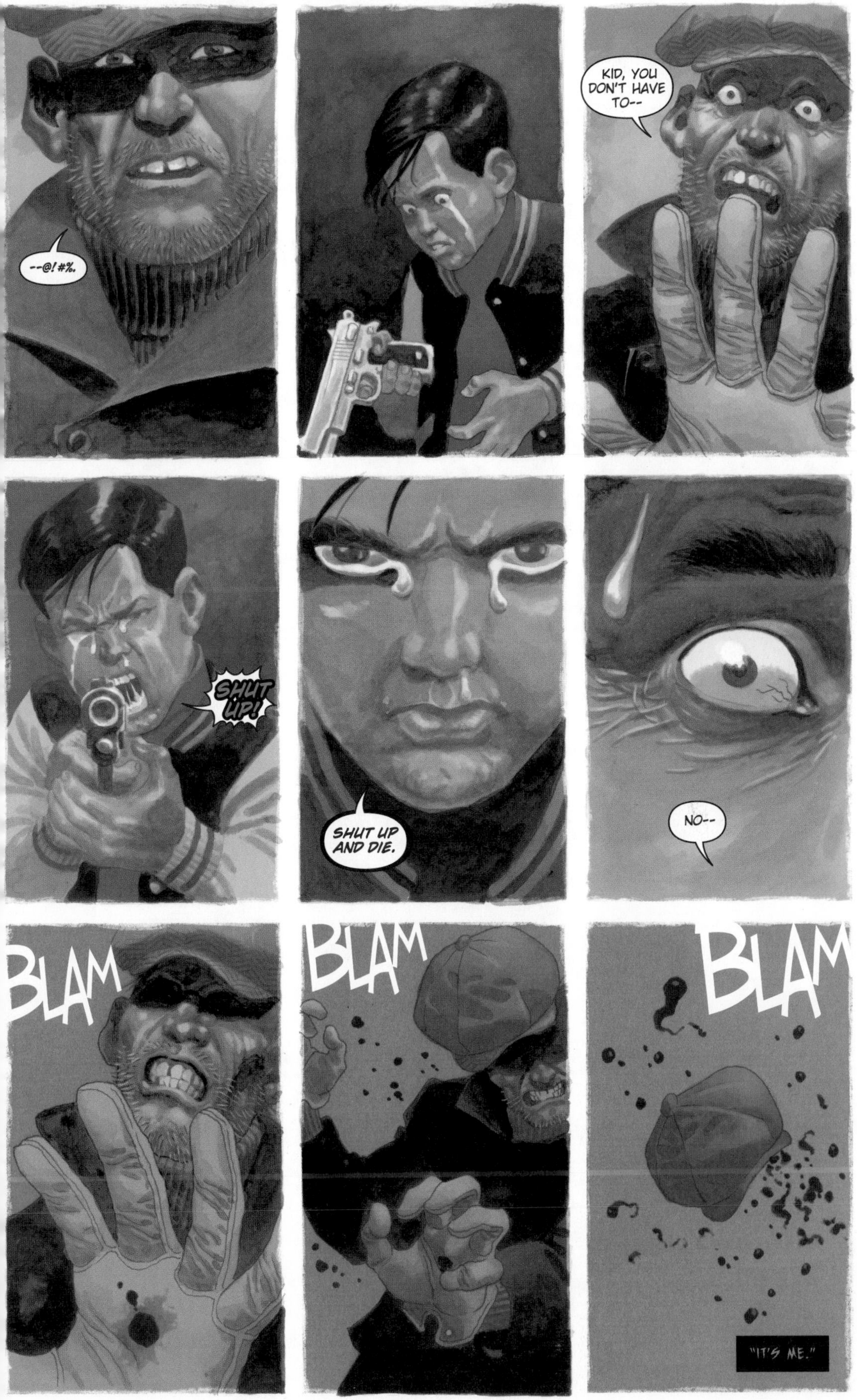
--@! #%.
KID, YOU DON'T HAVE TO--
SHUT UP!
SHUT UP AND DIE.
NO--
BLAM
BLAM
BLAM
"IT'S ME."

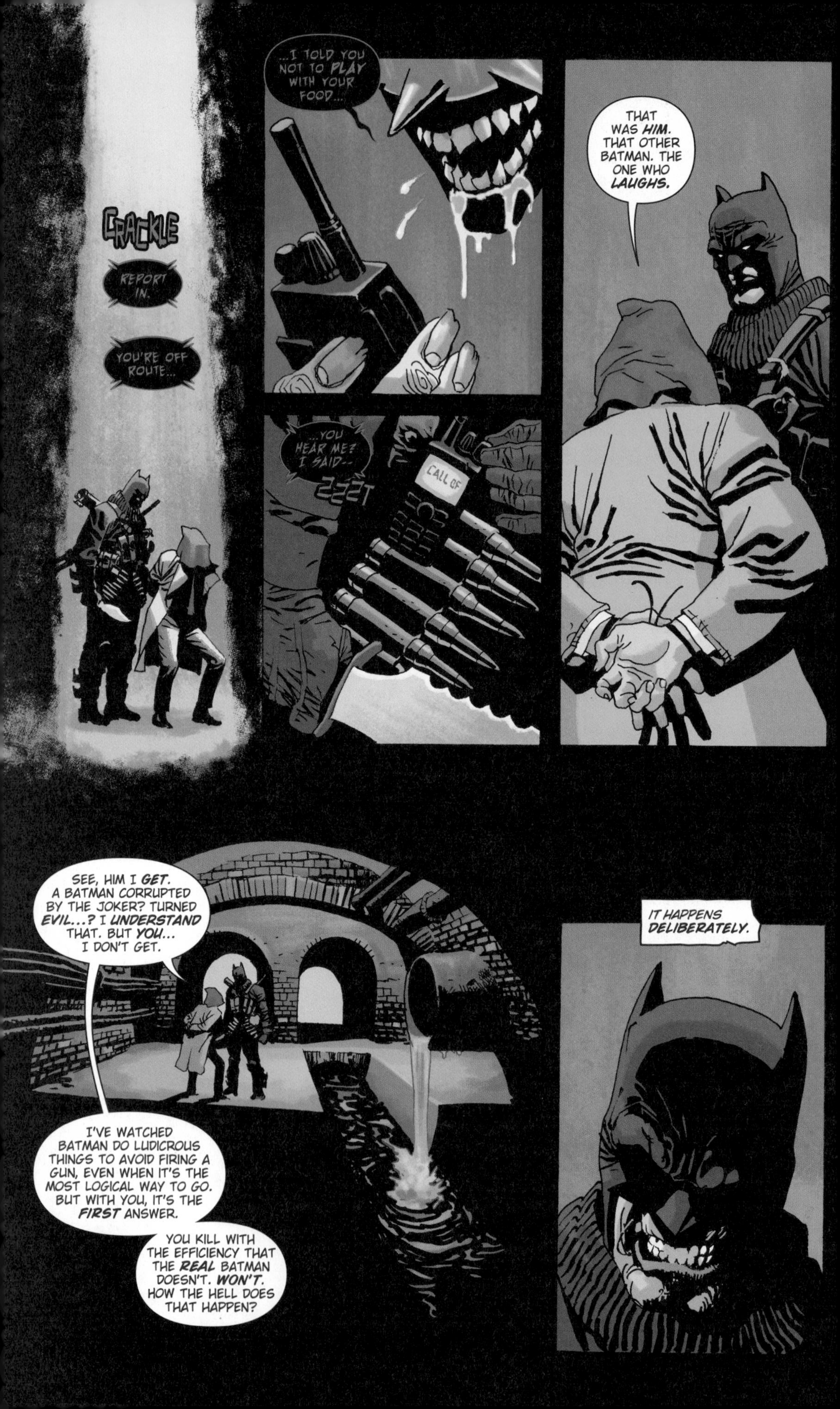
CRACKLE
REPORT IN.
YOU'RE OFF ROUTE...
...I TOLD YOU NOT TO PLAY WITH YOUR FOOD...
THAT WAS HIM. THAT OTHER BATMAN. THE ONE WHO LAUGHS.
...YOU HEAR ME? I SAID--
ZZZT
CALL OF
SEE, HIM I GET. A BATMAN CORRUPTED BY THE JOKER? TURNED EVIL...? I UNDERSTAND THAT. BUT YOU... I DON'T GET.
I'VE WATCHED BATMAN DO LUDICROUS THINGS TO AVOID FIRING A GUN, EVEN WHEN IT'S THE MOST LOGICAL WAY TO GO. BUT WITH YOU, IT'S THE FIRST ANSWER.
YOU KILL WITH THE EFFICIENCY THAT THE REAL BATMAN DOESN'T. WON'T. HOW THE HELL DOES THAT HAPPEN?
IT HAPPENS DELIBERATELY.

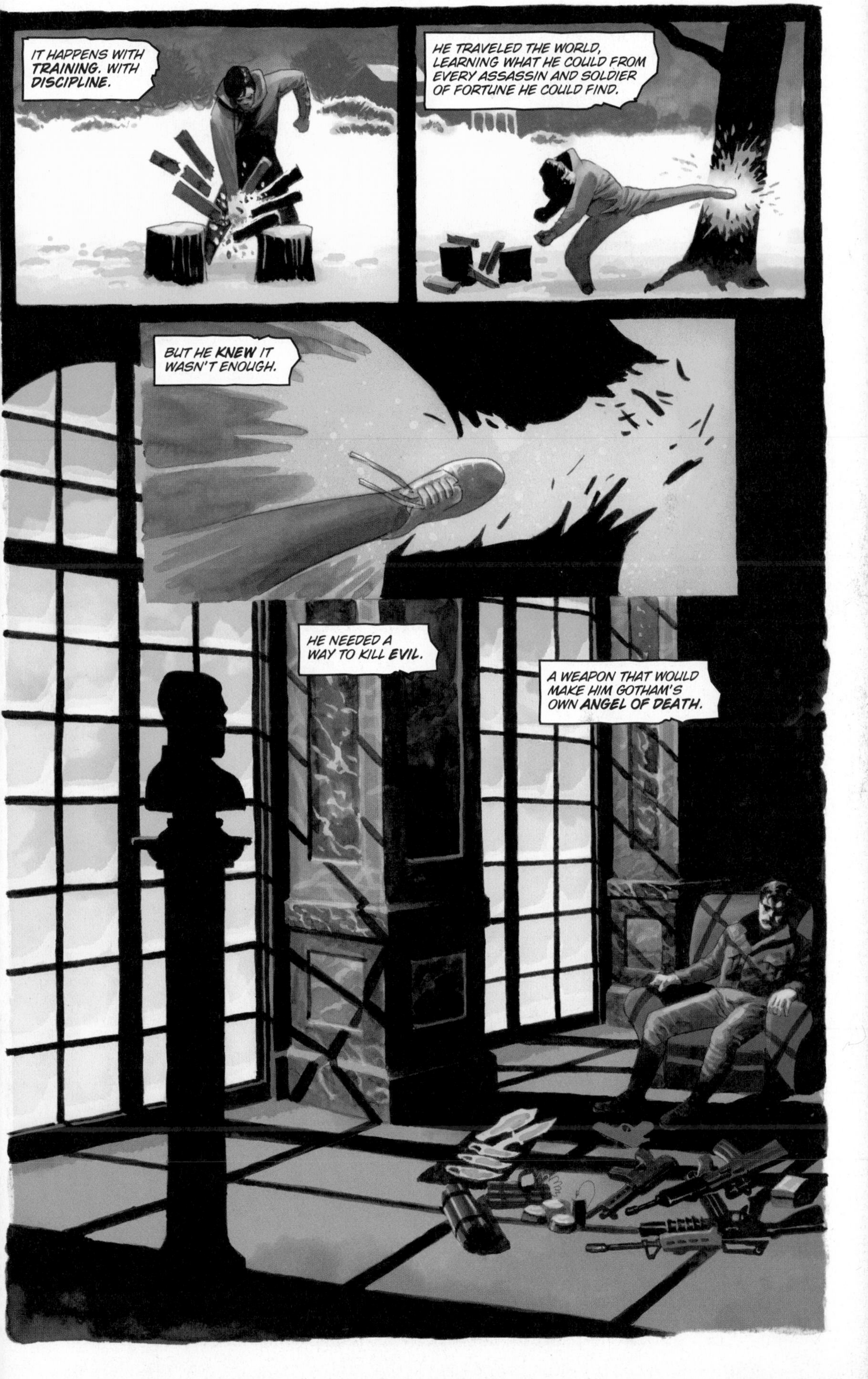
IT HAPPENS WITH TRAINING. WITH DISCIPLINE.
HE TRAVELED THE WORLD, LEARNING WHAT HE COULD FROM EVERY ASSASSIN AND SOLDIER OF FORTUNE HE COULD FIND.
BUT HE KNEW IT WASN'T ENOUGH.
HE NEEDED A WAY TO KILL EVIL.
A WEAPON THAT WOULD MAKE HIM GOTHAM'S OWN ANGEL OF DEATH.

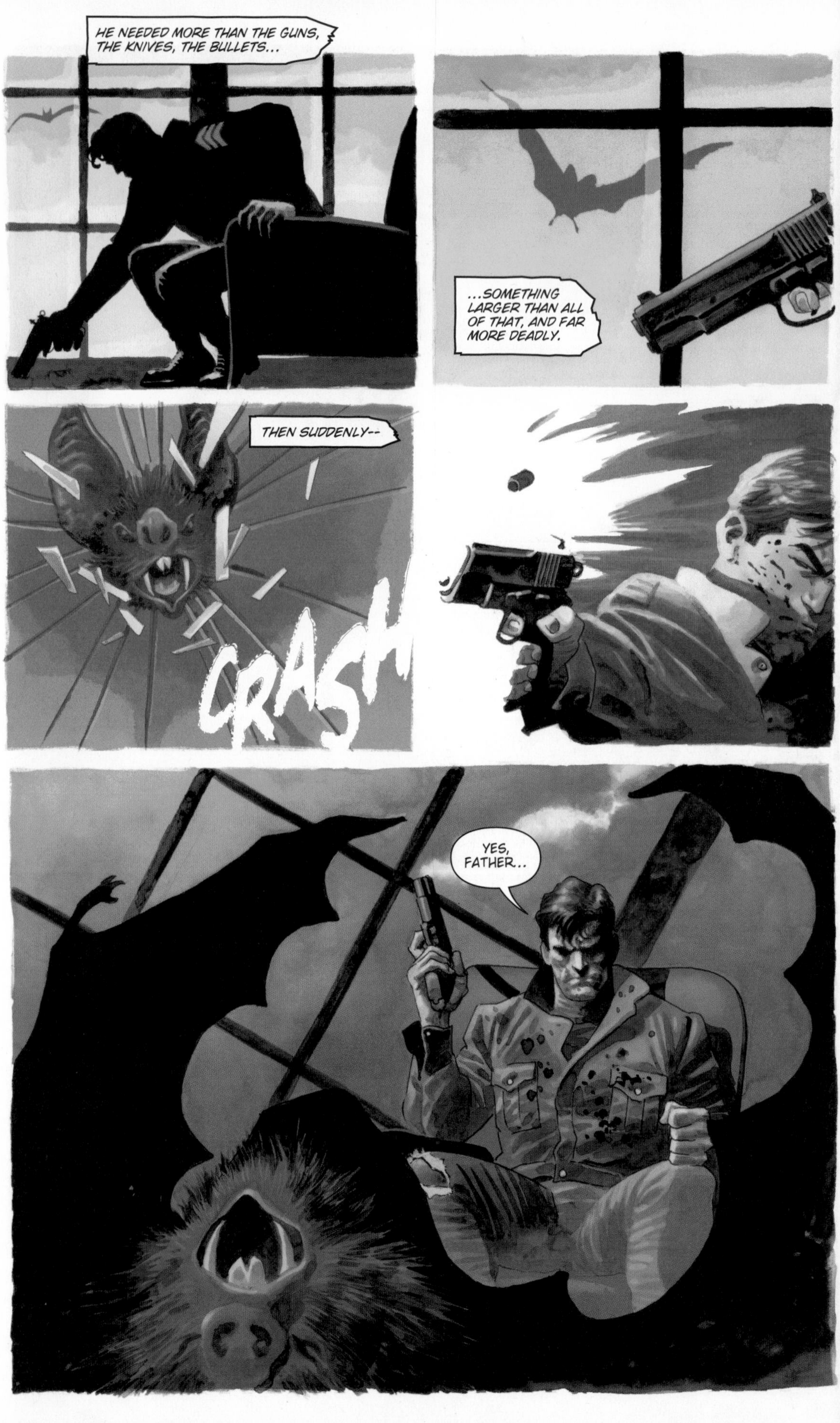
HE NEEDED MORE THAN THE GUNS, THE KNIVES, THE BULLETS...
...SOMETHING LARGER THAN ALL OF THAT, AND FAR MORE DEADLY.
THEN SUDDENLY--
CRASH
YES, FATHER..

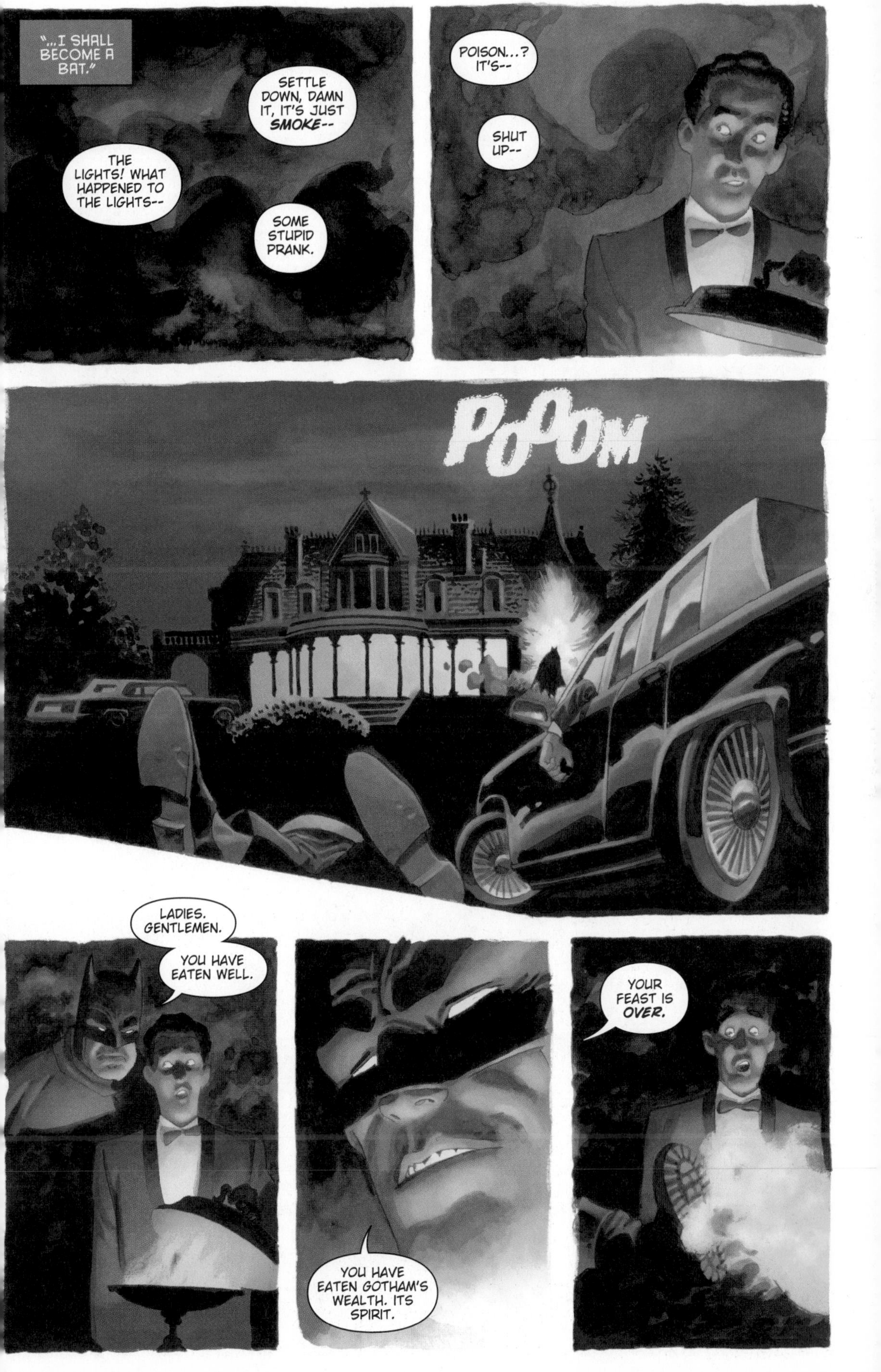
"...I SHALL BECOME A BAT."
SETTLE DOWN, DAMN IT, IT'S JUST *SMOKE*--
THE LIGHTS! WHAT HAPPENED TO THE LIGHTS--
SOME STUPID PRANK.
POISON...? IT'S--
SHUT UP--
POOOM
LADIES. GENTLEMEN.
YOU HAVE EATEN WELL.
YOU HAVE EATEN GOTHAM'S WEALTH. ITS SPIRIT.
YOUR FEAST IS *OVER.*

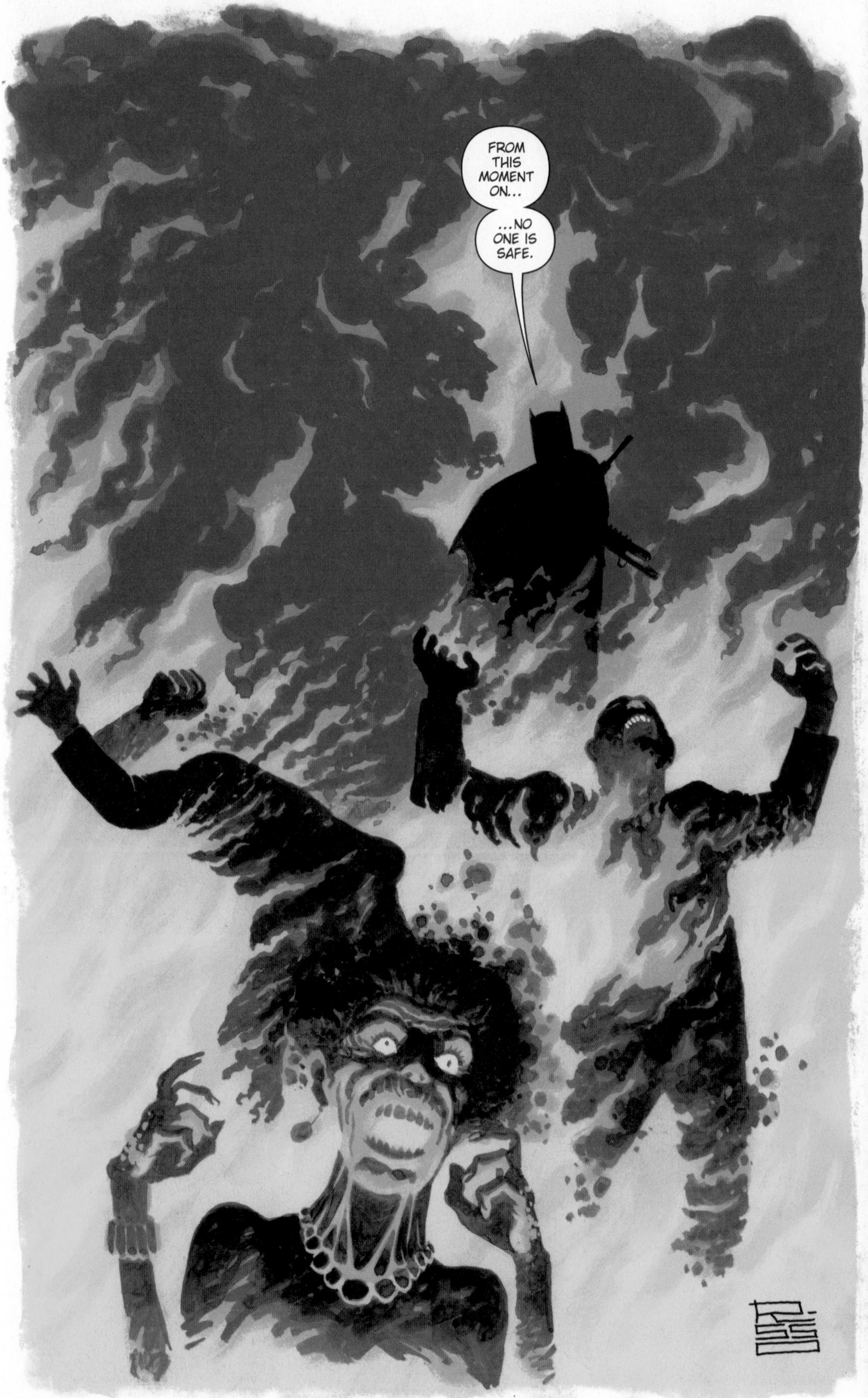
FROM THIS MOMENT ON...
...NO ONE IS SAFE.

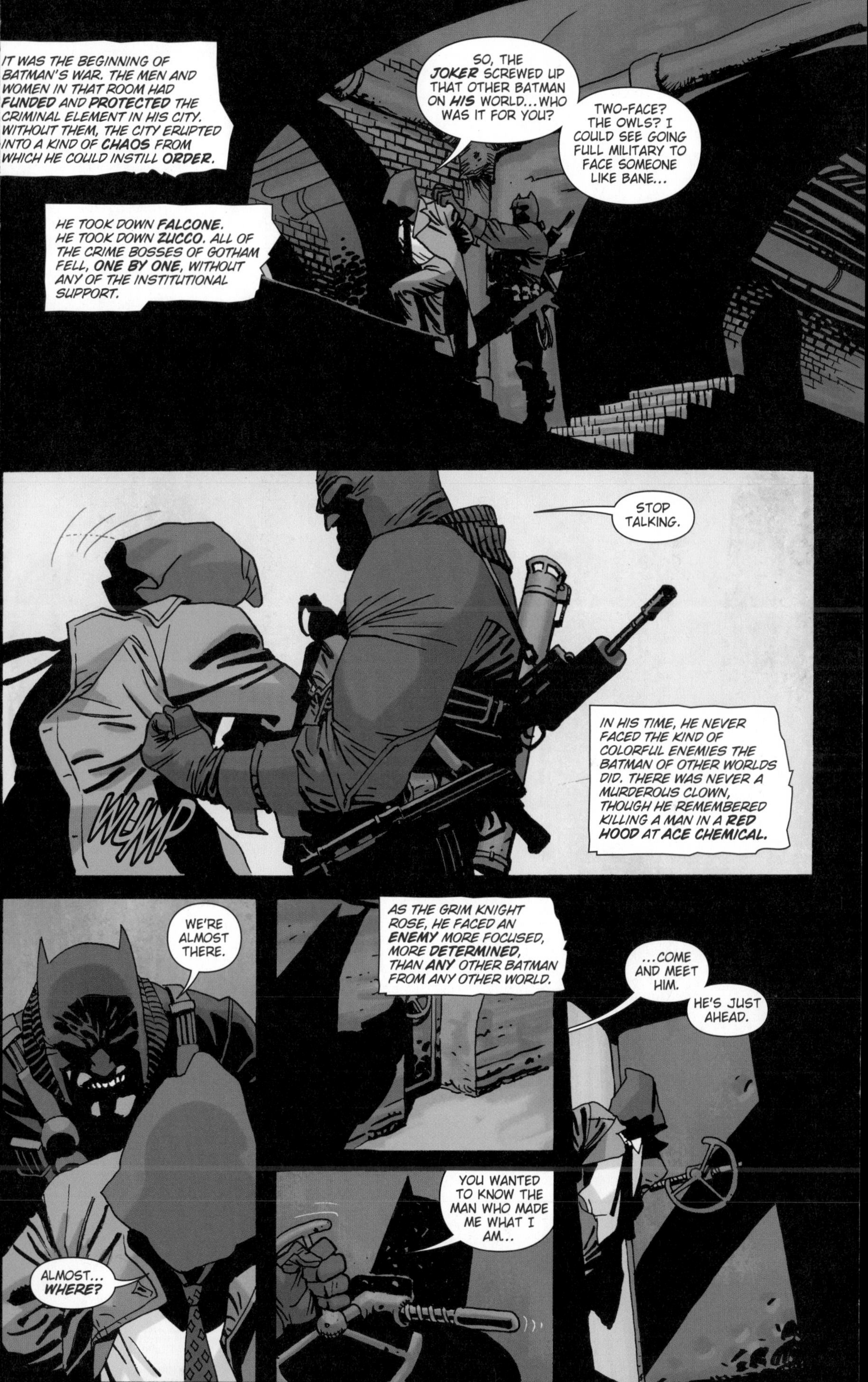
IT WAS THE BEGINNING OF BATMAN'S WAR. THE MEN AND WOMEN IN THAT ROOM HAD FUNDED AND PROTECTED THE CRIMINAL ELEMENT IN HIS CITY. WITHOUT THEM, THE CITY ERUPTED INTO A KIND OF CHAOS FROM WHICH HE COULD INSTILL ORDER.
SO, THE JOKER SCREWED UP THAT OTHER BATMAN ON HIS WORLD...WHO WAS IT FOR YOU?
TWO-FACE? THE OWLS? I COULD SEE GOING FULL MILITARY TO FACE SOMEONE LIKE BANE...
HE TOOK DOWN FALCONE. HE TOOK DOWN ZUCCO. ALL OF THE CRIME BOSSES OF GOTHAM FELL, ONE BY ONE, WITHOUT ANY OF THE INSTITUTIONAL SUPPORT.
STOP TALKING.
WUMP
IN HIS TIME, HE NEVER FACED THE KIND OF COLORFUL ENEMIES THE BATMAN OF OTHER WORLDS DID. THERE WAS NEVER A MURDEROUS CLOWN, THOUGH HE REMEMBERED KILLING A MAN IN A RED HOOD AT ACE CHEMICAL.
WE'RE ALMOST THERE.
ALMOST... WHERE?
AS THE GRIM KNIGHT ROSE, HE FACED AN ENEMY MORE FOCUSED, MORE DETERMINED, THAN ANY OTHER BATMAN FROM ANY OTHER WORLD.
YOU WANTED TO KNOW THE MAN WHO MADE ME WHAT I AM...
...COME AND MEET HIM.
HE'S JUST AHEAD.

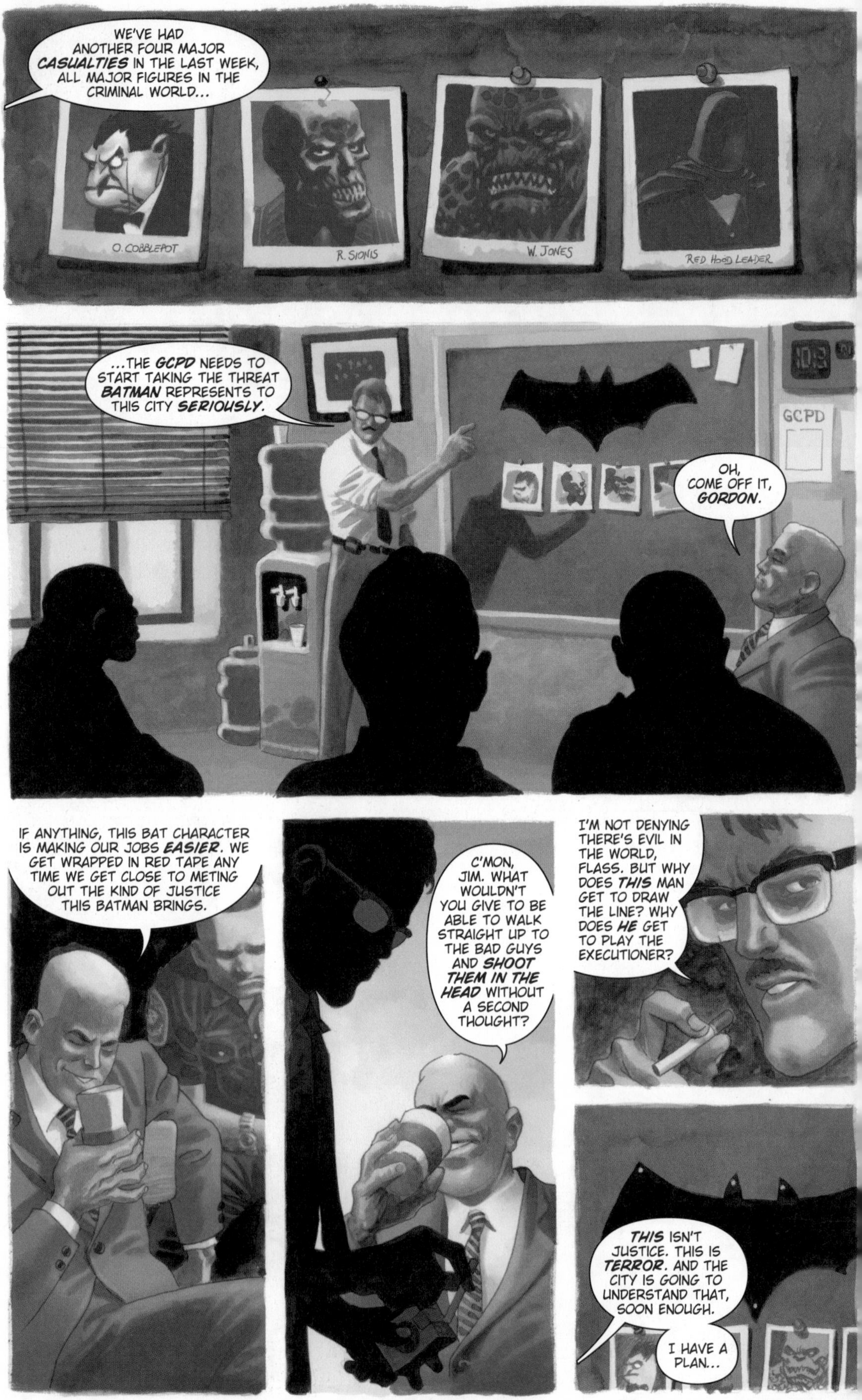

WE'VE HAD ANOTHER FOUR MAJOR CASUALTIES IN THE LAST WEEK, ALL MAJOR FIGURES IN THE CRIMINAL WORLD...
O. COBBLEPOT
R. SIONIS
W. JONES
RED HOOD LEADER
...THE GCPD NEEDS TO START TAKING THE THREAT BATMAN REPRESENTS TO THIS CITY SERIOUSLY.
GCPD
OH, COME OFF IT, GORDON.
IF ANYTHING, THIS BAT CHARACTER IS MAKING OUR JOBS EASIER. WE GET WRAPPED IN RED TAPE ANY TIME WE GET CLOSE TO METING OUT THE KIND OF JUSTICE THIS BATMAN BRINGS.
C'MON, JIM. WHAT WOULDN'T YOU GIVE TO BE ABLE TO WALK STRAIGHT UP TO THE BAD GUYS AND SHOOT THEM IN THE HEAD WITHOUT A SECOND THOUGHT?
I'M NOT DENYING THERE'S EVIL IN THE WORLD, FLASS. BUT WHY DOES THIS MAN GET TO DRAW THE LINE? WHY DOES HE GET TO PLAY THE EXECUTIONER?
THIS ISN'T JUSTICE. THIS IS TERROR. AND THE CITY IS GOING TO UNDERSTAND THAT, SOON ENOUGH.
I HAVE A PLAN...

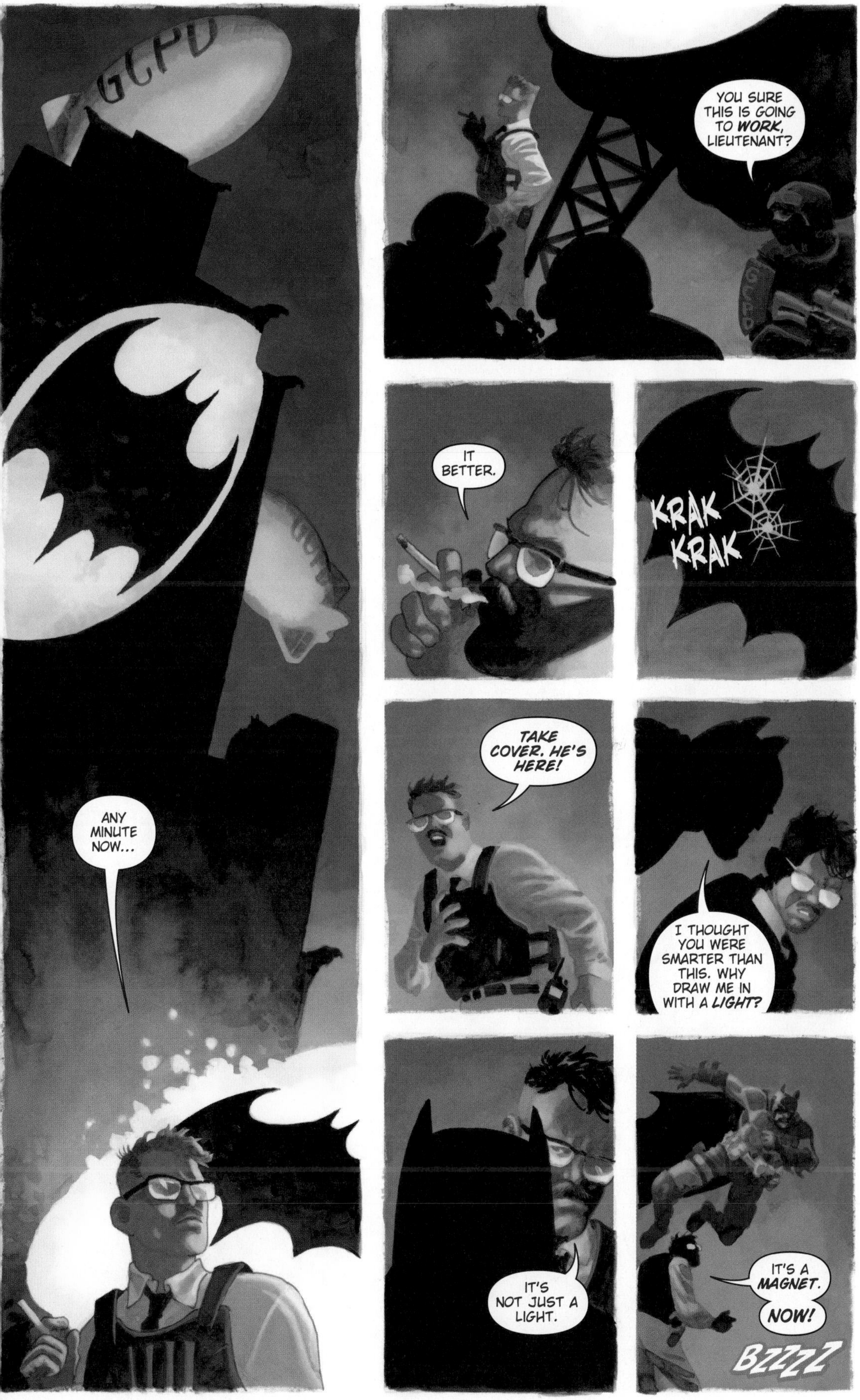
GCPD
YOU SURE THIS IS GOING TO WORK, LIEUTENANT?
IT BETTER.
KRAK KRAK
ANY MINUTE NOW...
TAKE COVER. HE'S HERE!
I THOUGHT YOU WERE SMARTER THAN THIS. WHY DRAW ME IN WITH A LIGHT?
IT'S NOT JUST A LIGHT.
IT'S A MAGNET.
NOW!
BZZZZ

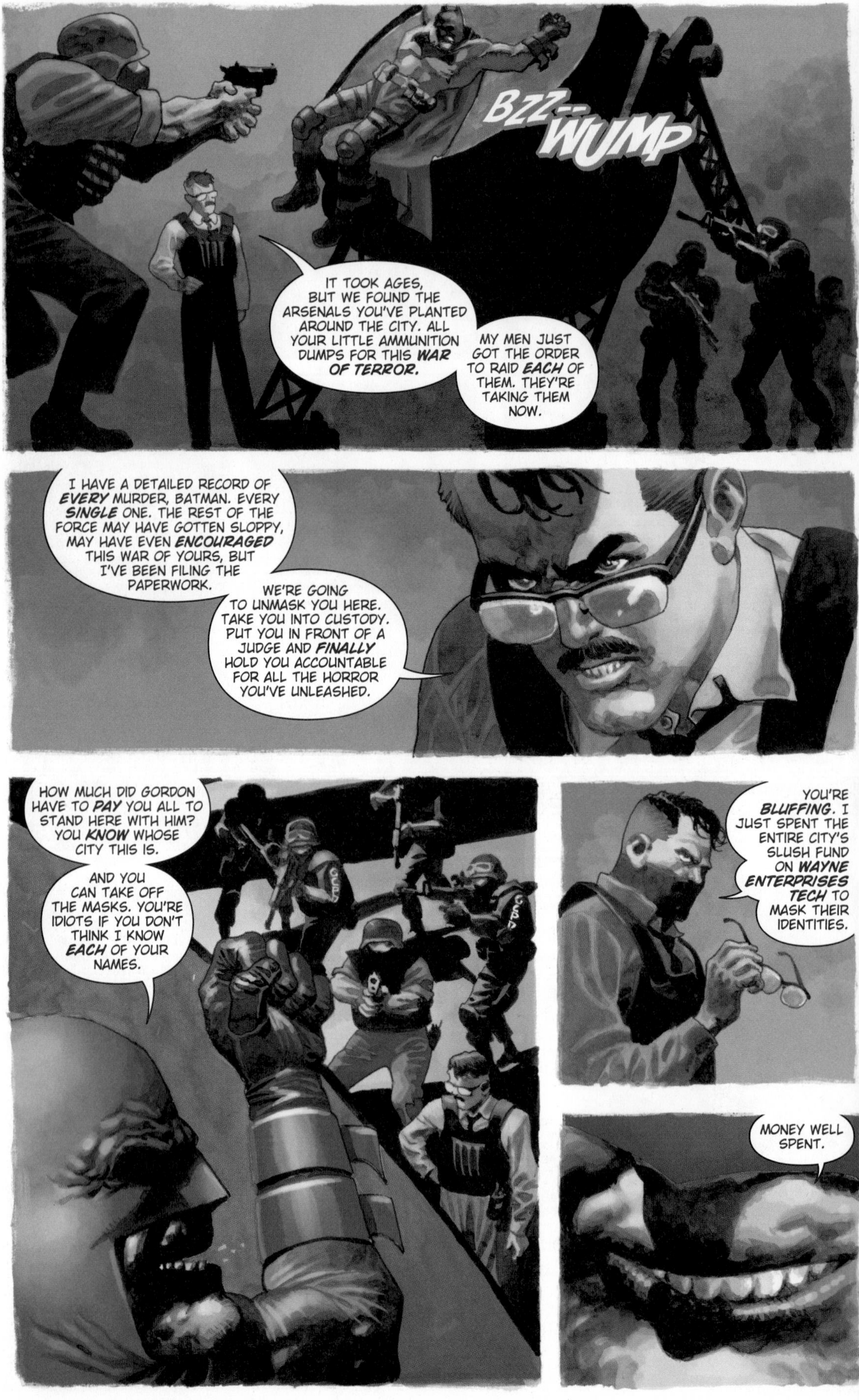
BZZ--WUMP
IT TOOK AGES, BUT WE FOUND THE ARSENALS YOU'VE PLANTED AROUND THE CITY. ALL YOUR LITTLE AMMUNITION DUMPS FOR THIS WAR OF TERROR.
MY MEN JUST GOT THE ORDER TO RAID EACH OF THEM. THEY'RE TAKING THEM NOW.
I HAVE A DETAILED RECORD OF EVERY MURDER, BATMAN. EVERY SINGLE ONE. THE REST OF THE FORCE MAY HAVE GOTTEN SLOPPY, MAY HAVE EVEN ENCOURAGED THIS WAR OF YOURS, BUT I'VE BEEN FILING THE PAPERWORK.
WE'RE GOING TO UNMASK YOU HERE. TAKE YOU INTO CUSTODY. PUT YOU IN FRONT OF A JUDGE AND FINALLY HOLD YOU ACCOUNTABLE FOR ALL THE HORROR YOU'VE UNLEASHED.
HOW MUCH DID GORDON HAVE TO PAY YOU ALL TO STAND HERE WITH HIM? YOU KNOW WHOSE CITY THIS IS.
AND YOU CAN TAKE OFF THE MASKS. YOU'RE IDIOTS IF YOU DON'T THINK I KNOW EACH OF YOUR NAMES.
YOU'RE BLUFFING. I JUST SPENT THE ENTIRE CITY'S SLUSH FUND ON WAYNE ENTERPRISES TECH TO MASK THEIR IDENTITIES.
MONEY WELL SPENT.

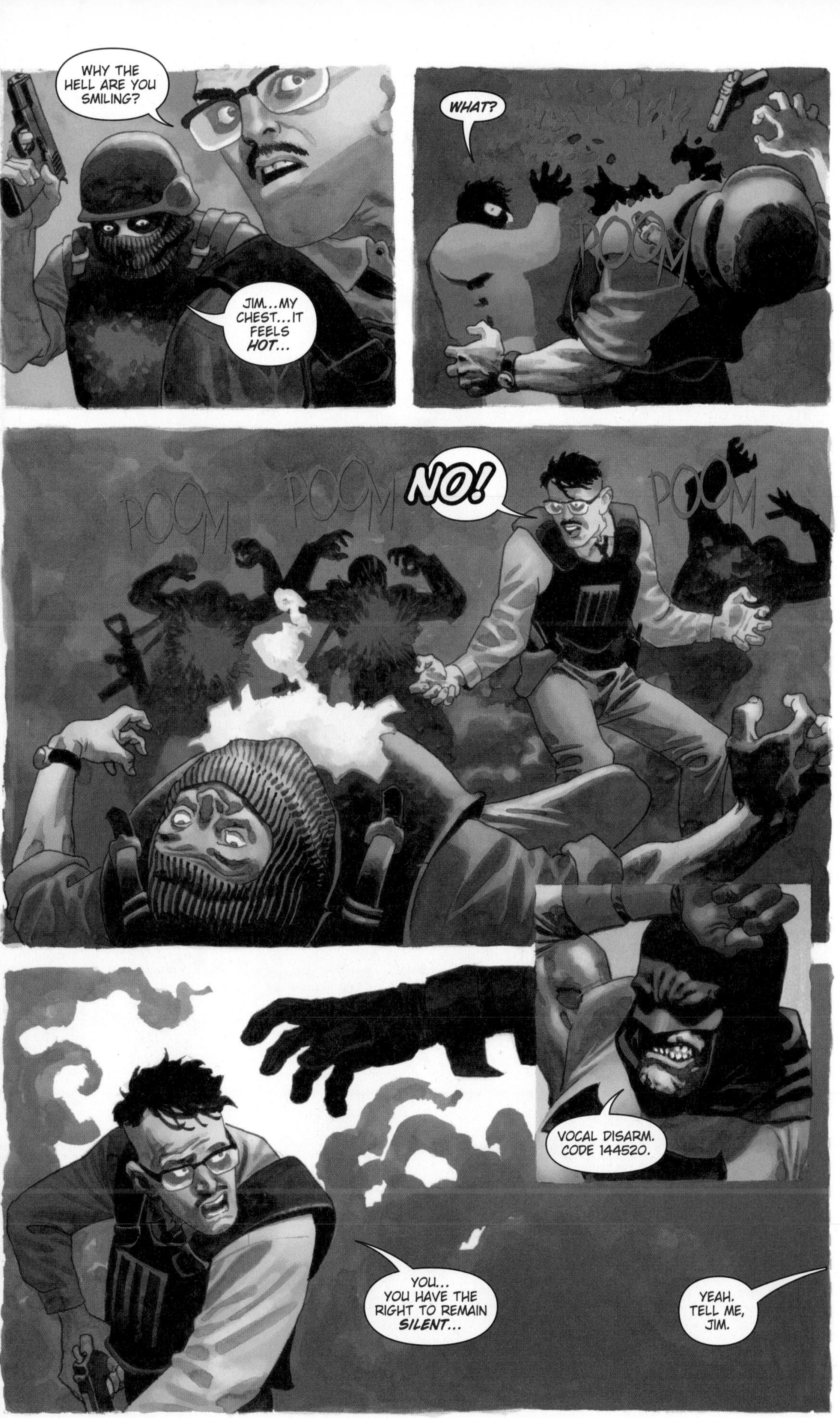
WHY THE HELL ARE YOU SMILING?
JIM...MY CHEST...IT FEELS HOT...
WHAT?
POOM
POOM
POOM
NO!
POOM
VOCAL DISARM. CODE 144520.
YOU... YOU HAVE THE RIGHT TO REMAIN SILENT...
YEAH. TELL ME, JIM.

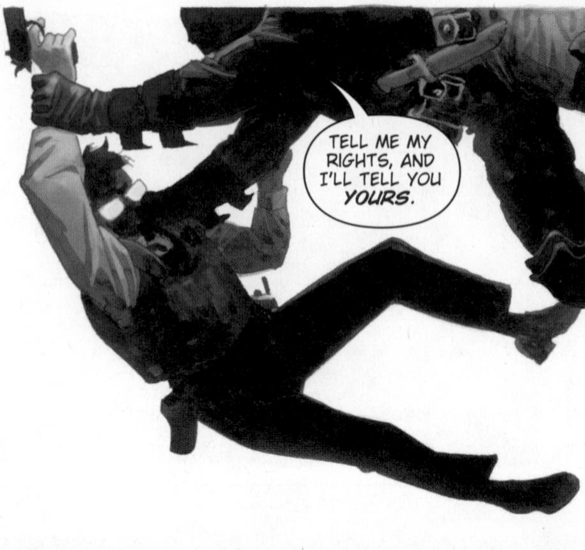
TELL ME MY RIGHTS, AND I'LL TELL YOU YOURS.

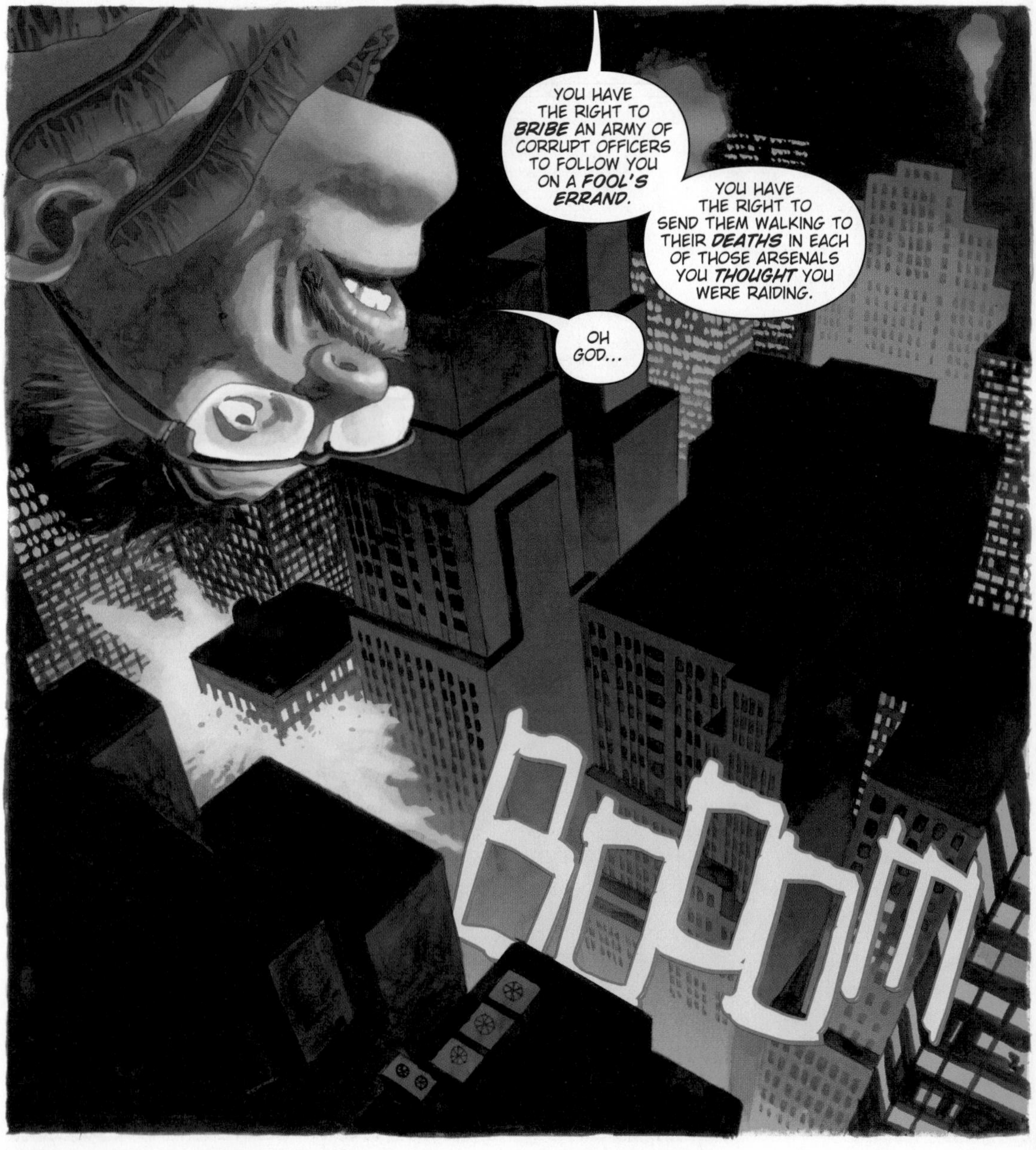
YOU HAVE THE RIGHT TO BRIBE AN ARMY OF CORRUPT OFFICERS TO FOLLOW YOU ON A FOOL'S ERRAND.
YOU HAVE THE RIGHT TO SEND THEM WALKING TO THEIR DEATHS IN EACH OF THOSE ARSENALS YOU THOUGHT YOU WERE RAIDING.
OH GOD...
BOOOM

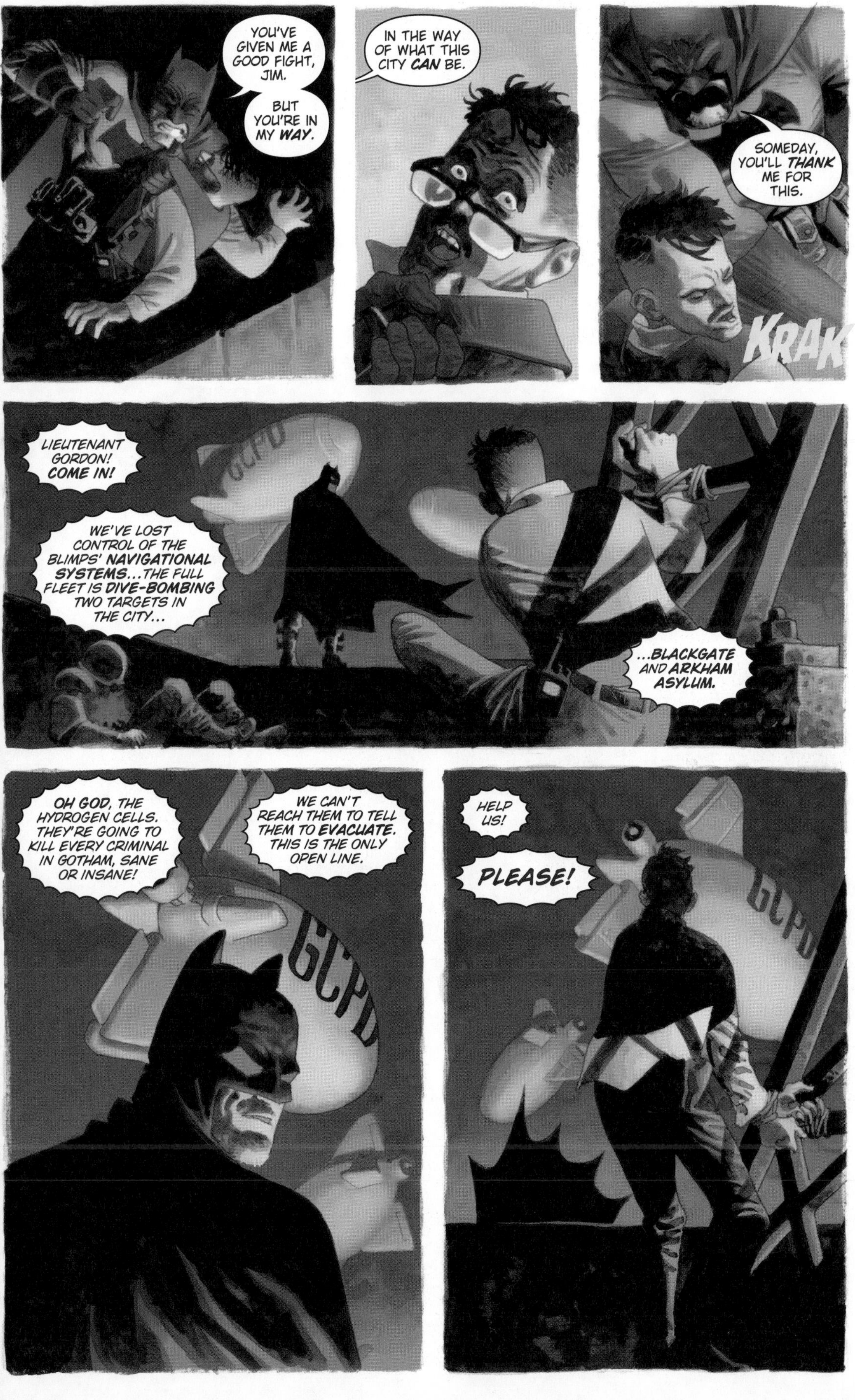
YOU'VE GIVEN ME A GOOD FIGHT, JIM.
BUT YOU'RE IN MY **WAY**.
IN THE WAY OF WHAT THIS CITY **CAN** BE.
SOMEDAY, YOU'LL **THANK** ME FOR THIS.
KRAK
LIEUTENANT GORDON! **COME IN!**
WE'VE LOST CONTROL OF THE BLIMPS' **NAVIGATIONAL SYSTEMS**...THE FULL FLEET IS **DIVE-BOMBING** TWO TARGETS IN THE CITY...
...**BLACKGATE** AND **ARKHAM ASYLUM.**
OH GOD, THE HYDROGEN CELLS. THEY'RE GOING TO KILL EVERY CRIMINAL IN GOTHAM, SANE OR INSANE!
WE CAN'T REACH THEM TO TELL THEM TO **EVACUATE**. THIS IS THE ONLY OPEN LINE.
HELP US!
PLEASE!

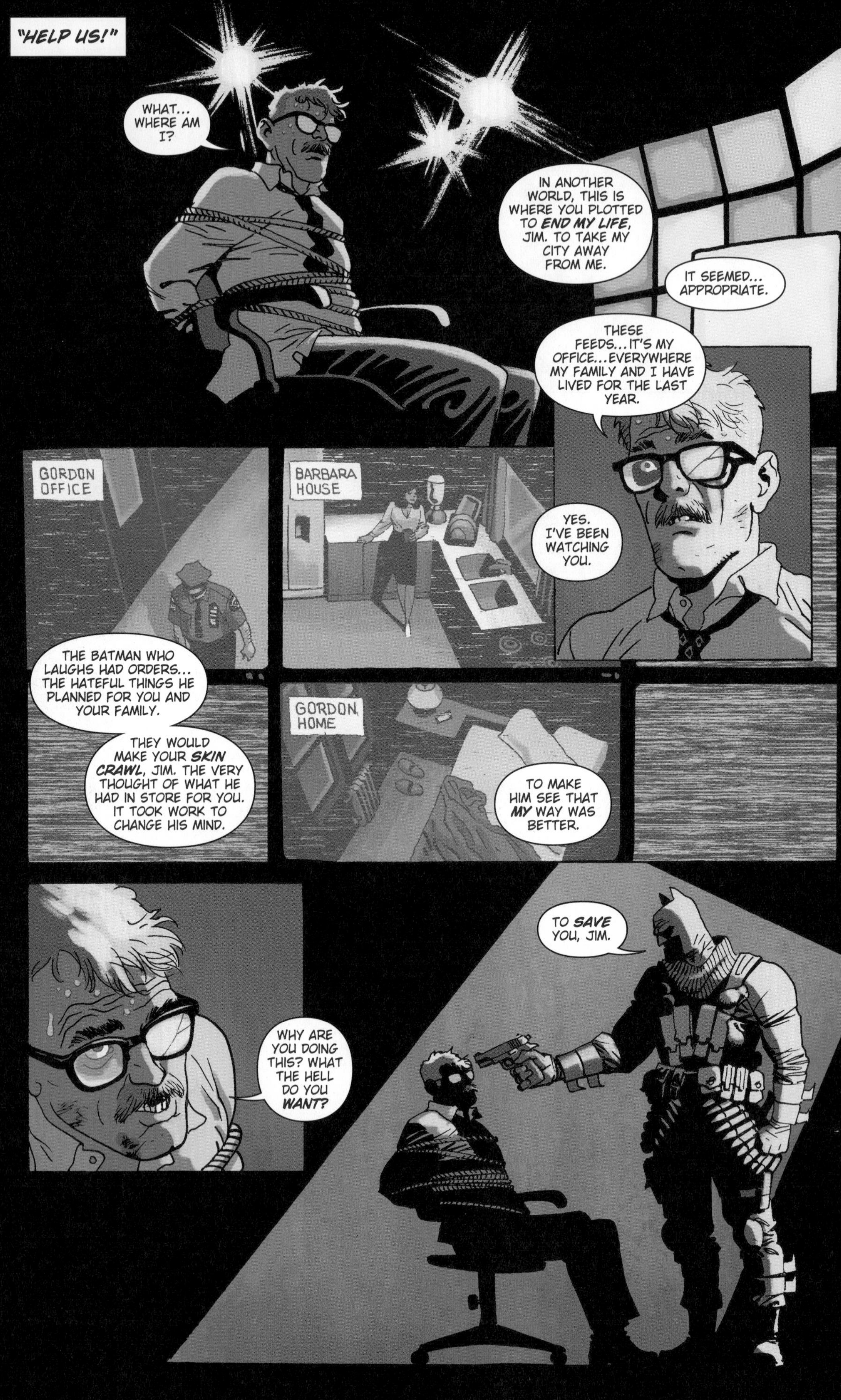
"HELP US!"
WHAT... WHERE AM I?
IN ANOTHER WORLD, THIS IS WHERE YOU PLOTTED TO END MY LIFE, JIM. TO TAKE MY CITY AWAY FROM ME.
IT SEEMED... APPROPRIATE.
THESE FEEDS... IT'S MY OFFICE... EVERYWHERE MY FAMILY AND I HAVE LIVED FOR THE LAST YEAR.
GORDON OFFICE
BARBARA HOUSE
YES. I'VE BEEN WATCHING YOU.
THE BATMAN WHO LAUGHS HAD ORDERS... THE HATEFUL THINGS HE PLANNED FOR YOU AND YOUR FAMILY.
THEY WOULD MAKE YOUR SKIN CRAWL, JIM. THE VERY THOUGHT OF WHAT HE HAD IN STORE FOR YOU. IT TOOK WORK TO CHANGE HIS MIND.
GORDON HOME
TO MAKE HIM SEE THAT MY WAY WAS BETTER.
WHY ARE YOU DOING THIS? WHAT THE HELL DO YOU WANT?
TO SAVE YOU, JIM.

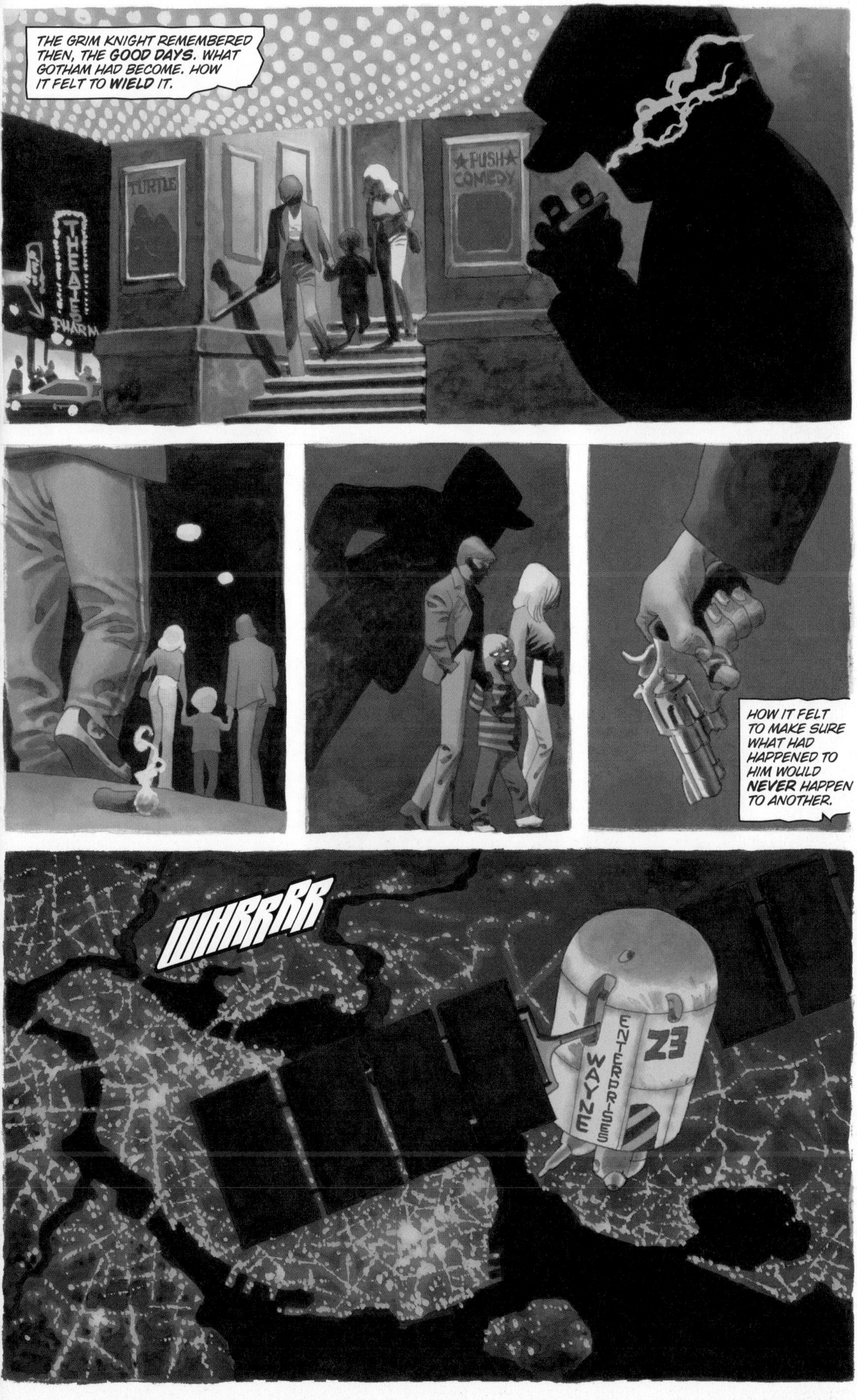
THE GRIM KNIGHT REMEMBERED THEN, THE GOOD DAYS. WHAT GOTHAM HAD BECOME. HOW IT FELT TO WIELD IT.
PUSH COMEDY
THEATER
HOW IT FELT TO MAKE SURE WHAT HAD HAPPENED TO HIM WOULD NEVER HAPPEN TO ANOTHER.
WHRRRR
WAYNE ENTERPRISES
23

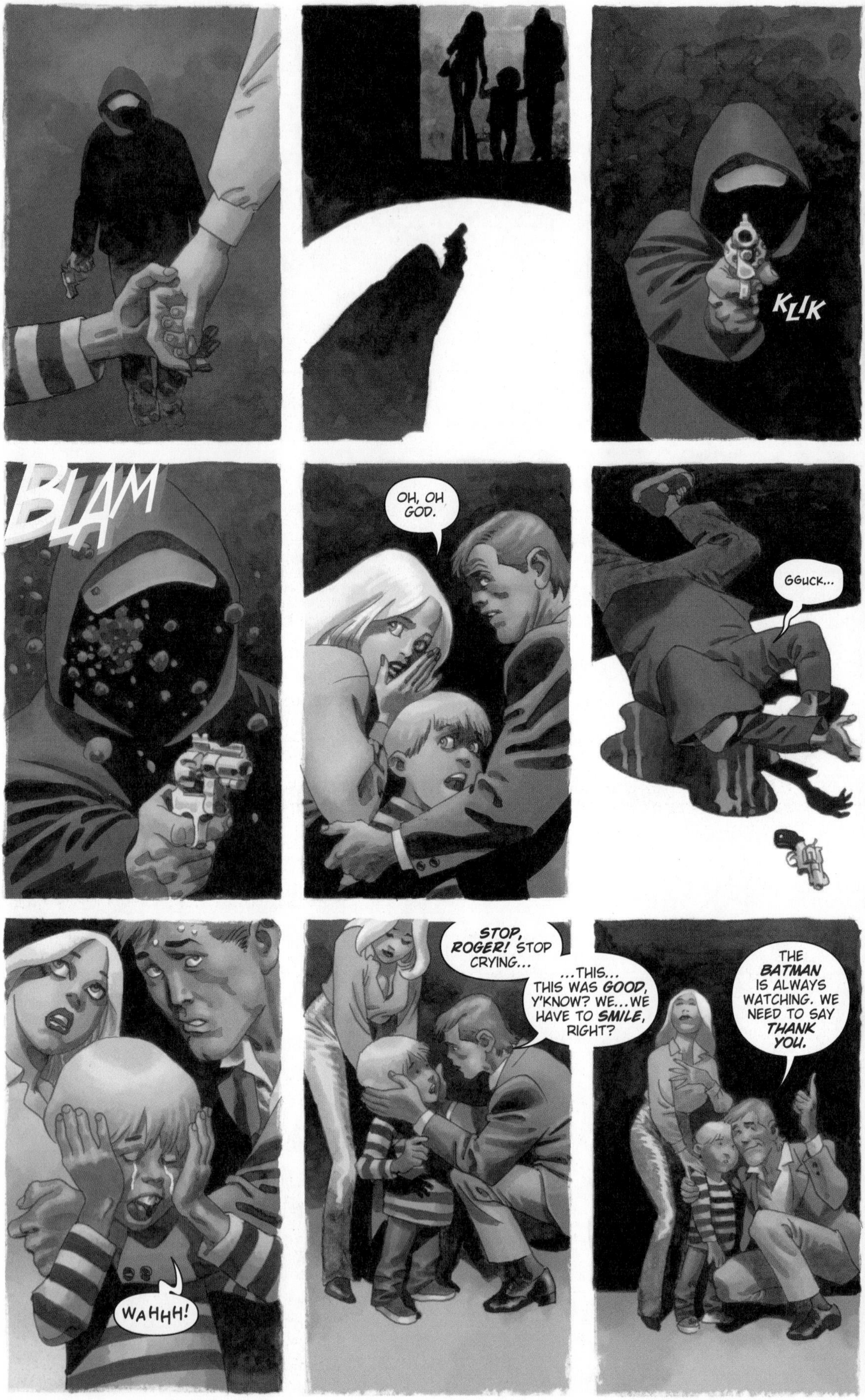
KLIK
BLAM
OH, OH GOD.
GGUCK...
WAHHH!
STOP, ROGER! STOP CRYING...
...THIS... THIS WAS GOOD, Y'KNOW? WE...WE HAVE TO SMILE, RIGHT?
THE BATMAN IS ALWAYS WATCHING. WE NEED TO SAY THANK YOU.

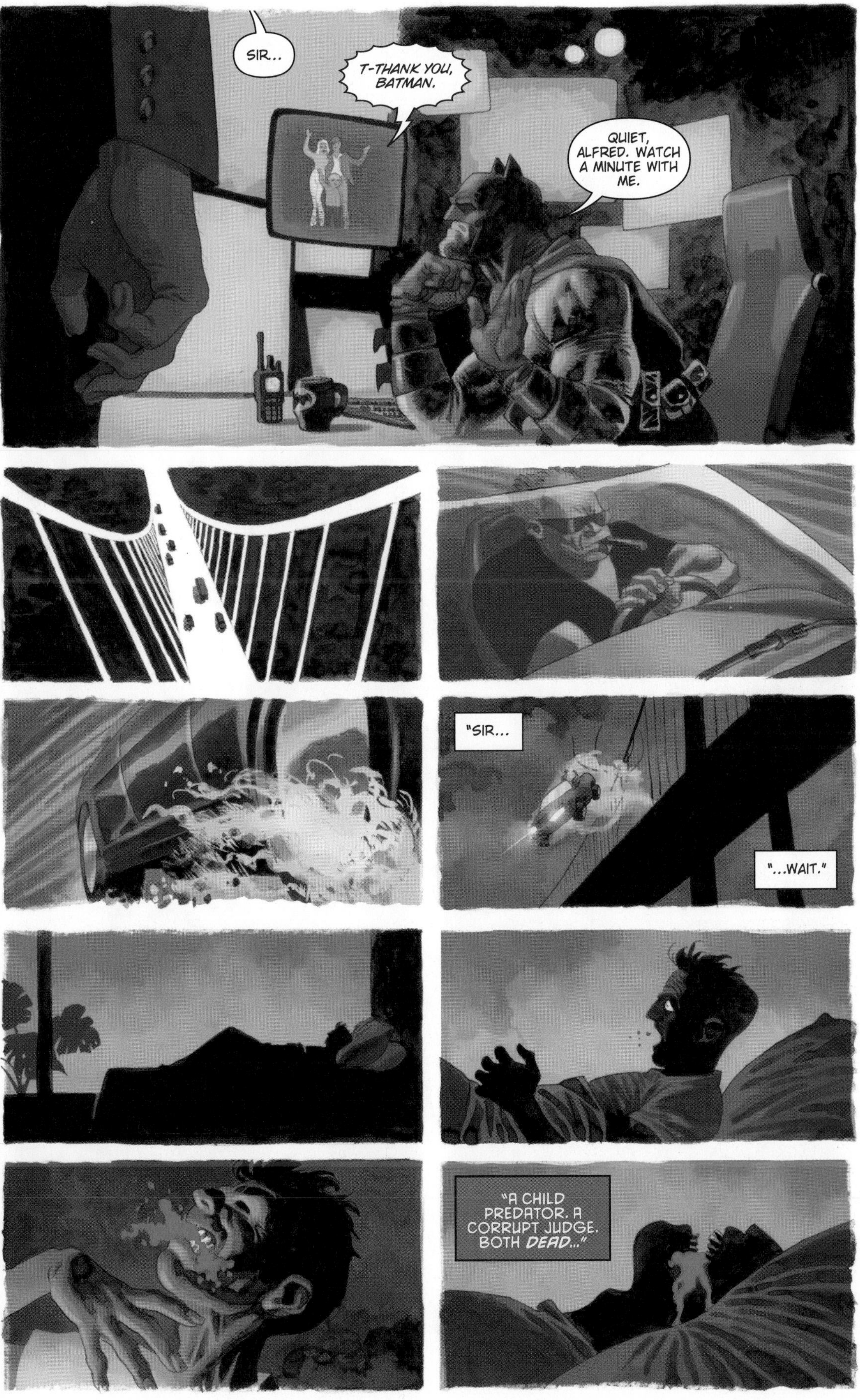
SIR...
T-THANK YOU, BATMAN.
QUIET, ALFRED. WATCH A MINUTE WITH ME.
"SIR...
"...WAIT."
"A CHILD PREDATOR. A CORRUPT JUDGE. BOTH DEAD..."

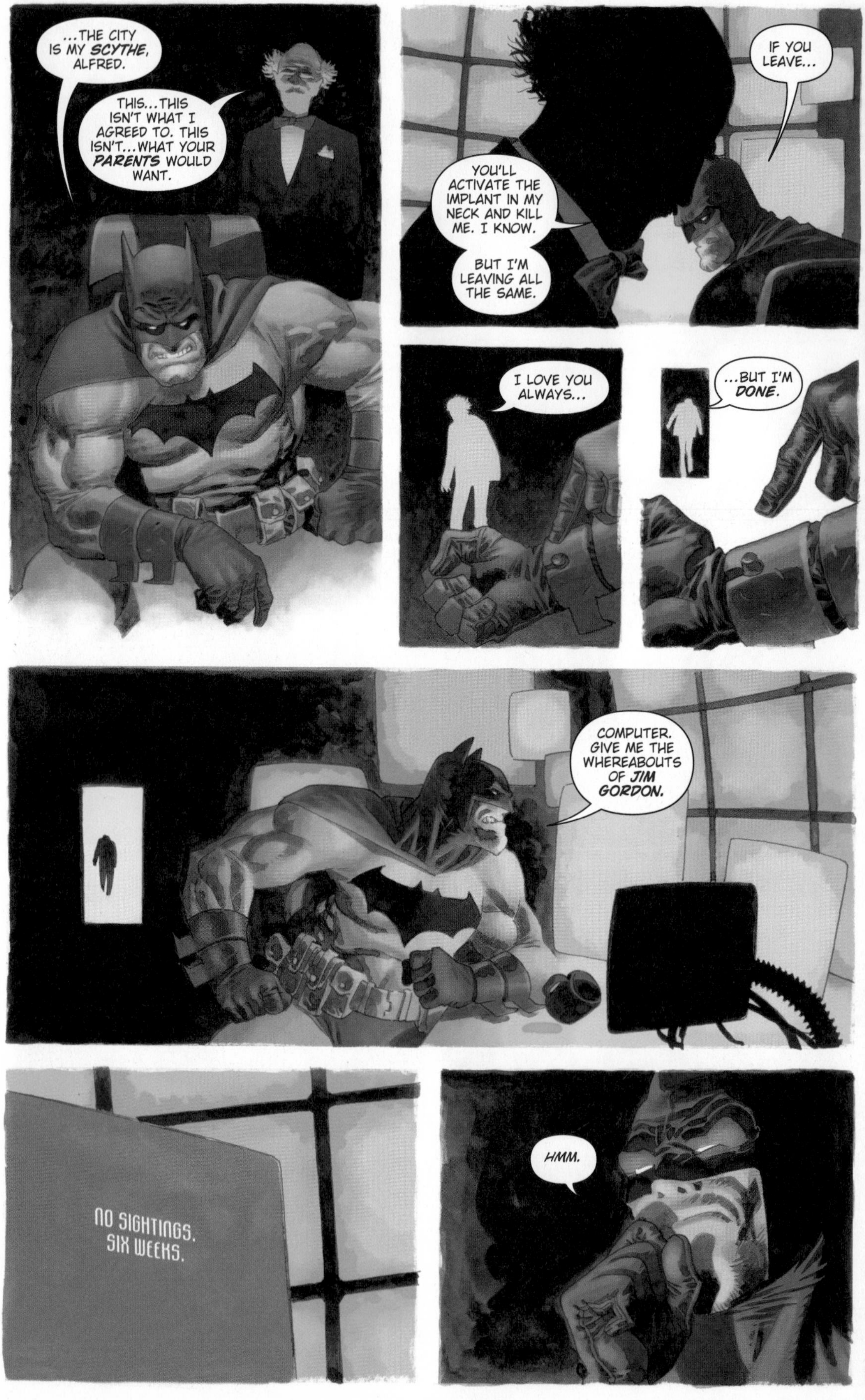
...THE CITY IS MY SCYTHE, ALFRED.
THIS...THIS ISN'T WHAT I AGREED TO. THIS ISN'T...WHAT YOUR PARENTS WOULD WANT.
IF YOU LEAVE...
YOU'LL ACTIVATE THE IMPLANT IN MY NECK AND KILL ME. I KNOW.
BUT I'M LEAVING ALL THE SAME.
I LOVE YOU ALWAYS...
...BUT I'M DONE.
COMPUTER. GIVE ME THE WHEREABOUTS OF JIM GORDON.
NO SIGHTINGS. SIX WEEKS.
HMM.

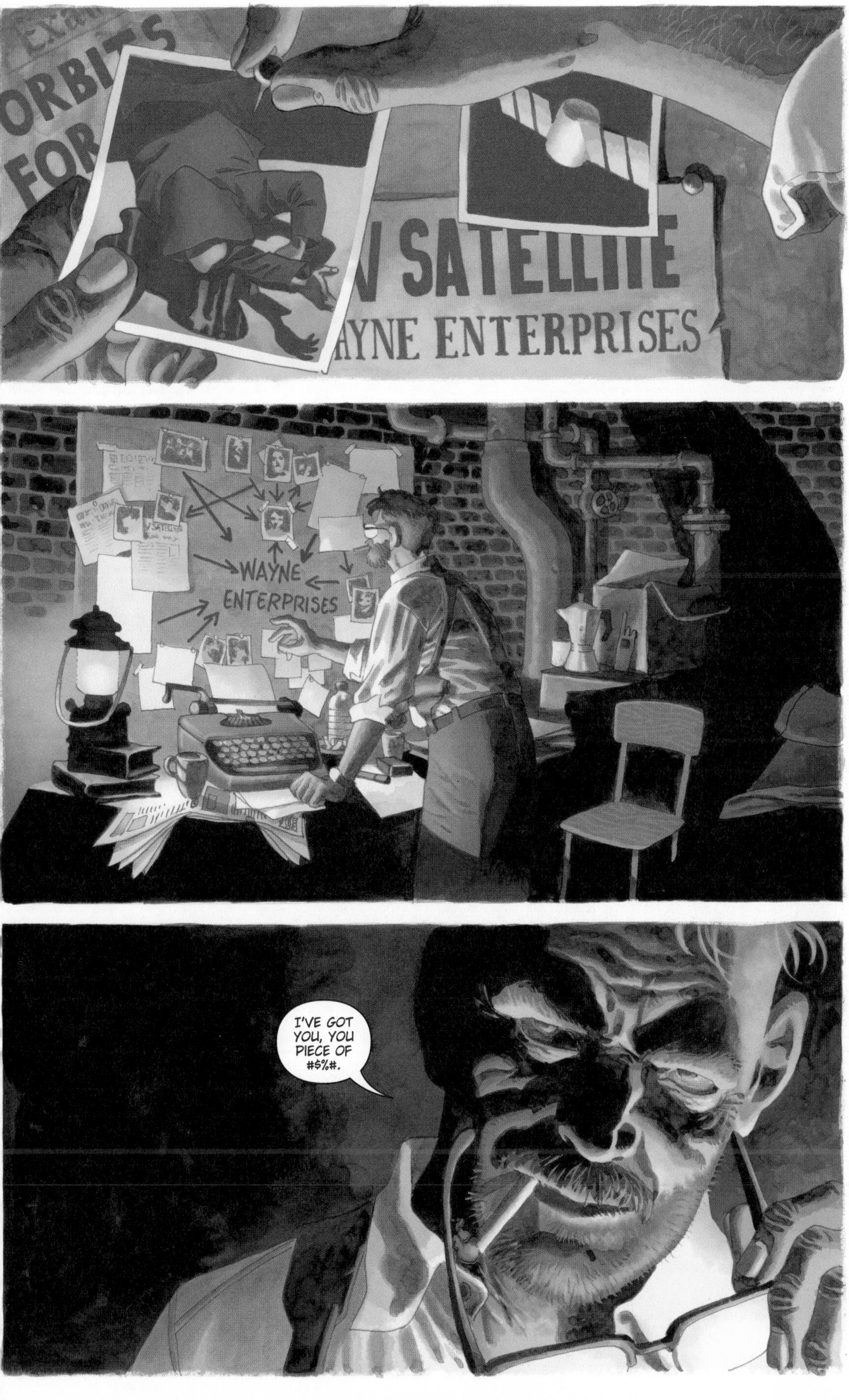

ORBITS
FOR
SATELLITE
AYNE ENTERPRISES
WAYNE ENTERPRISES
I'VE GOT YOU, YOU PIECE OF #$%#.

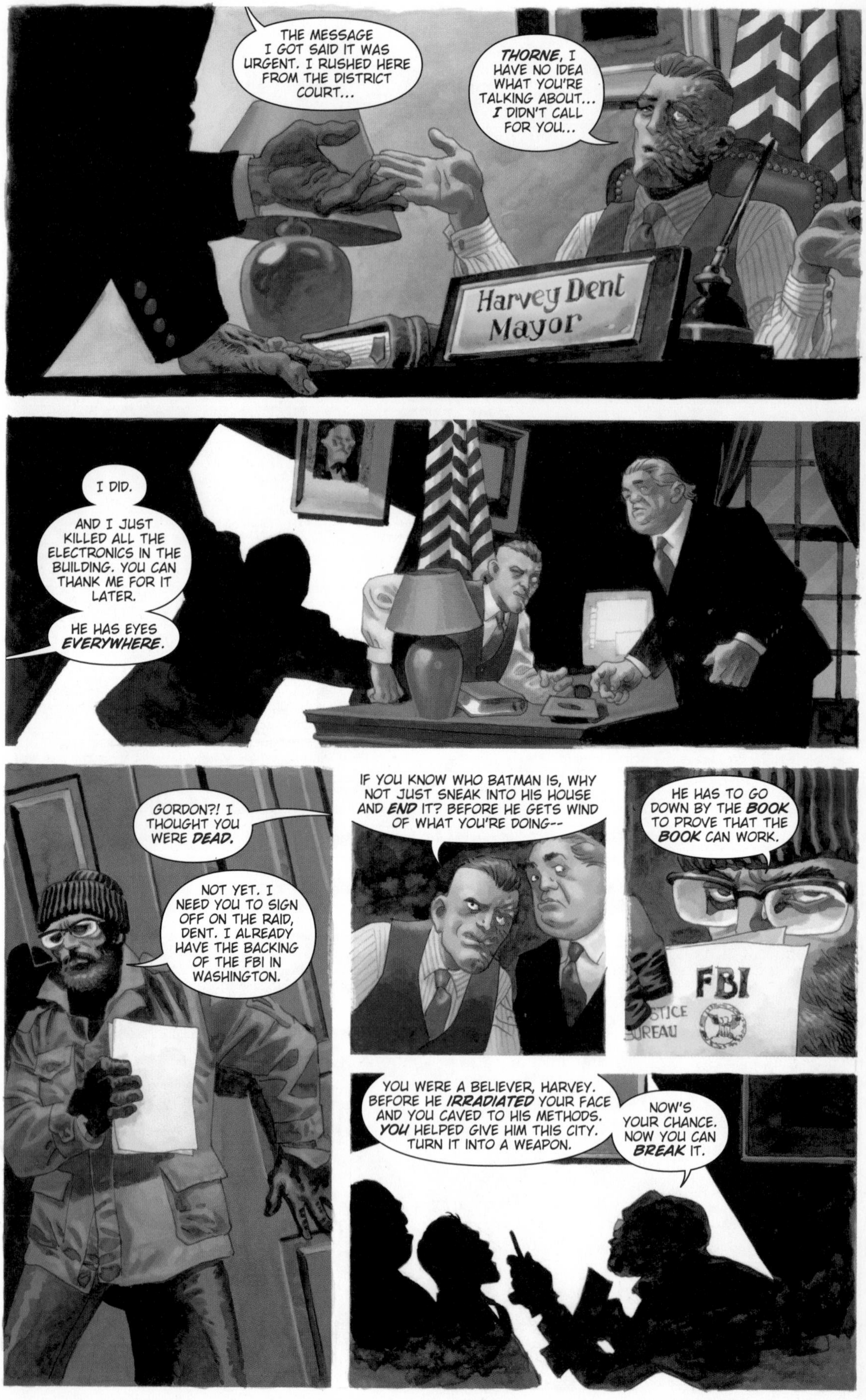
THE MESSAGE I GOT SAID IT WAS URGENT. I RUSHED HERE FROM THE DISTRICT COURT...
THORNE, I HAVE NO IDEA WHAT YOU'RE TALKING ABOUT... *I* DIDN'T CALL FOR YOU...
Harvey Dent
Mayor
I DID.
AND I JUST KILLED ALL THE ELECTRONICS IN THE BUILDING. YOU CAN THANK ME FOR IT LATER.
HE HAS EYES *EVERYWHERE*.
GORDON?! I THOUGHT YOU WERE *DEAD.*
NOT YET. I NEED YOU TO SIGN OFF ON THE RAID, DENT. I ALREADY HAVE THE BACKING OF THE FBI IN WASHINGTON.
IF YOU KNOW WHO BATMAN IS, WHY NOT JUST SNEAK INTO HIS HOUSE AND *END* IT? BEFORE HE GETS WIND OF WHAT YOU'RE DOING--
HE HAS TO GO DOWN BY THE *BOOK* TO PROVE THAT THE *BOOK* CAN WORK.
FBI
YOU WERE A BELIEVER, HARVEY. BEFORE HE *IRRADIATED* YOUR FACE AND YOU CAVED TO HIS METHODS. *YOU* HELPED GIVE HIM THIS CITY. TURN IT INTO A WEAPON.
NOW'S YOUR CHANCE. NOW YOU CAN *BREAK* IT.

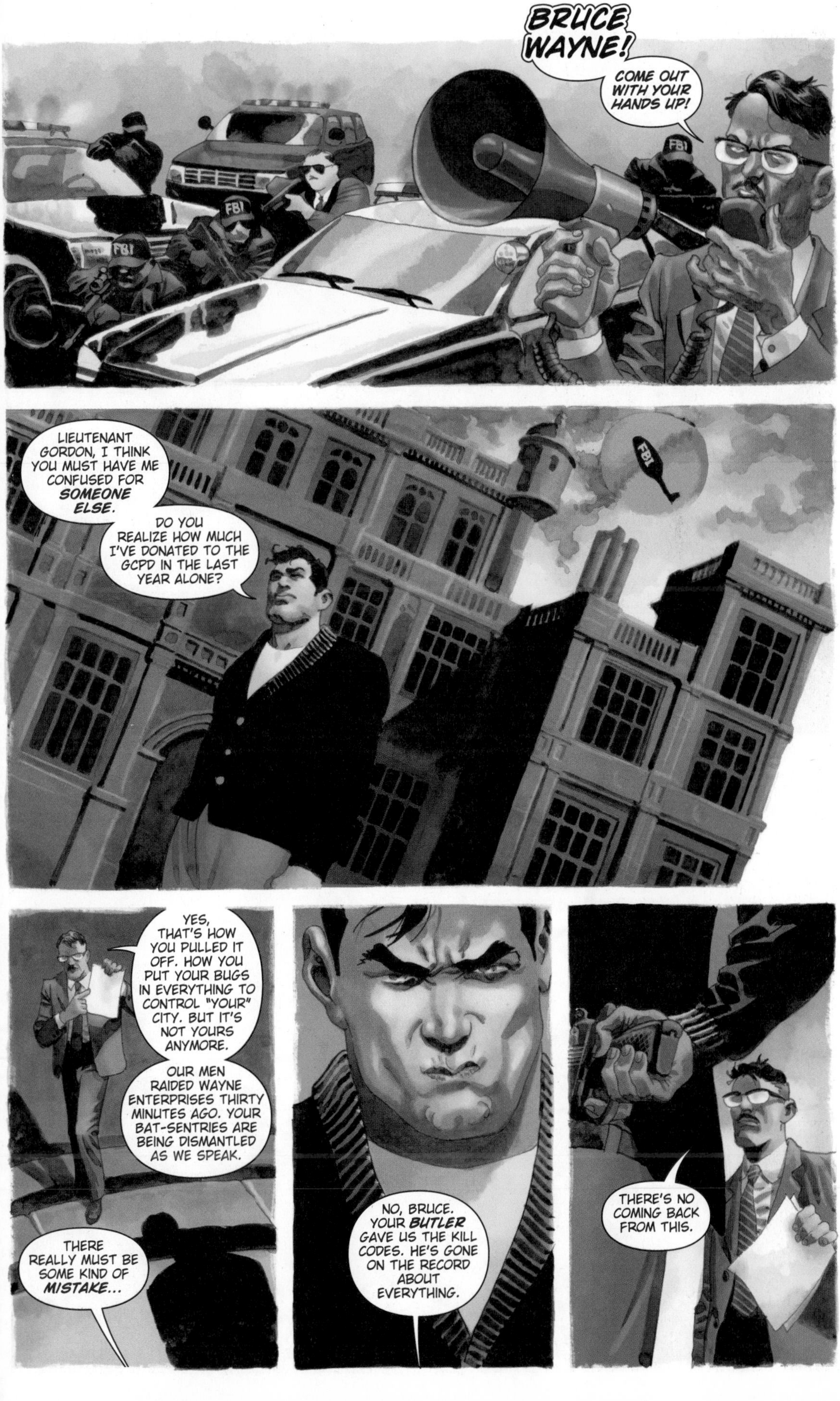
BRUCE WAYNE!
COME OUT WITH YOUR HANDS UP!
LIEUTENANT GORDON, I THINK YOU MUST HAVE ME CONFUSED FOR SOMEONE ELSE.
DO YOU REALIZE HOW MUCH I'VE DONATED TO THE GCPD IN THE LAST YEAR ALONE?
YES, THAT'S HOW YOU PULLED IT OFF. HOW YOU PUT YOUR BUGS IN EVERYTHING TO CONTROL "YOUR" CITY. BUT IT'S NOT YOURS ANYMORE.
OUR MEN RAIDED WAYNE ENTERPRISES THIRTY MINUTES AGO. YOUR BAT-SENTRIES ARE BEING DISMANTLED AS WE SPEAK.
THERE REALLY MUST BE SOME KIND OF MISTAKE...
NO, BRUCE. YOUR BUTLER GAVE US THE KILL CODES. HE'S GONE ON THE RECORD ABOUT EVERYTHING.
THERE'S NO COMING BACK FROM THIS.

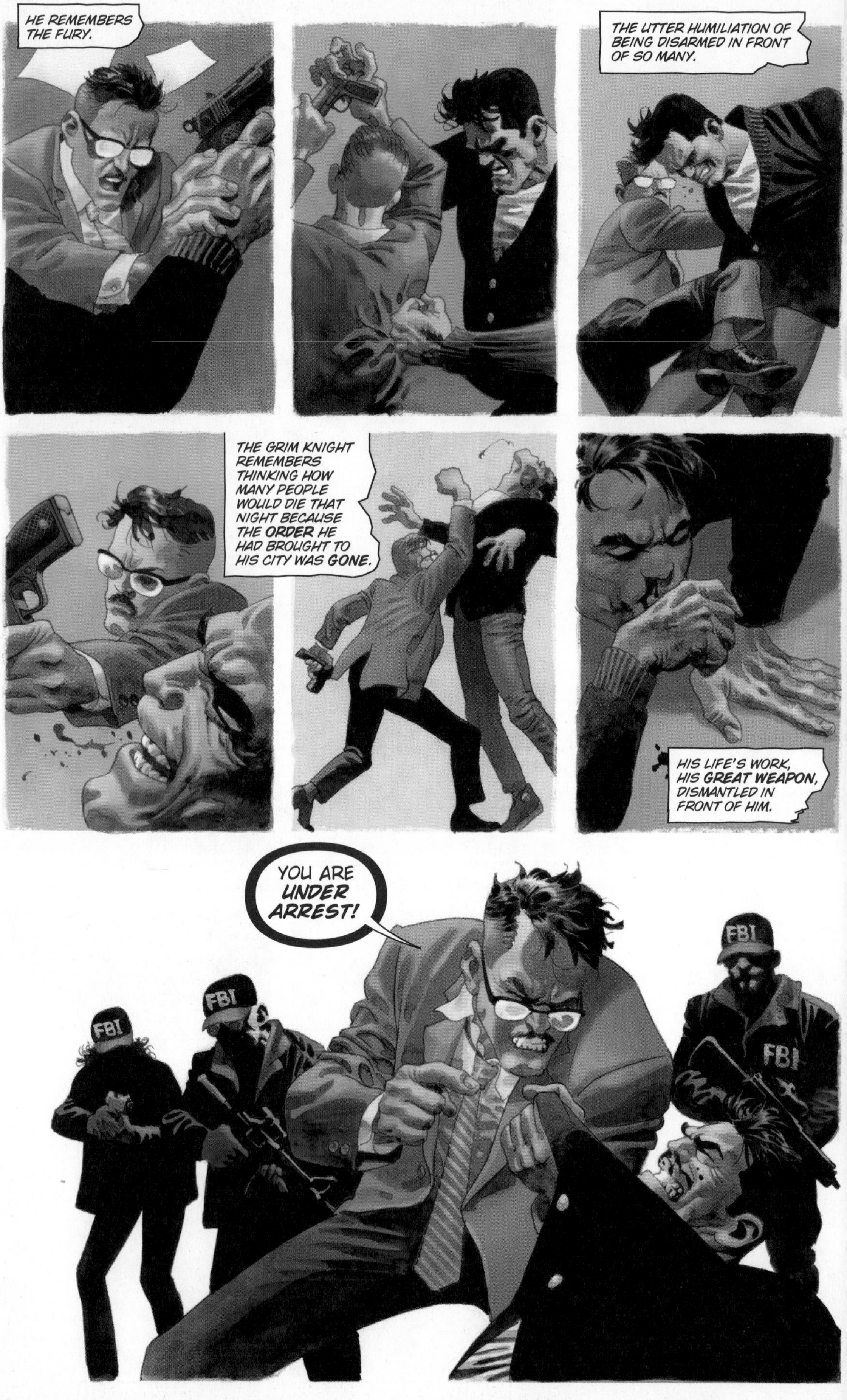
HE REMEMBERS THE FURY.
THE UTTER HUMILIATION OF BEING DISARMED IN FRONT OF SO MANY.
THE GRIM KNIGHT REMEMBERS THINKING HOW MANY PEOPLE WOULD DIE THAT NIGHT BECAUSE THE ORDER HE HAD BROUGHT TO HIS CITY WAS GONE.
HIS LIFE'S WORK, HIS GREAT WEAPON, DISMANTLED IN FRONT OF HIM.
YOU ARE UNDER ARREST!
FBI
FBI
FBI
FBI

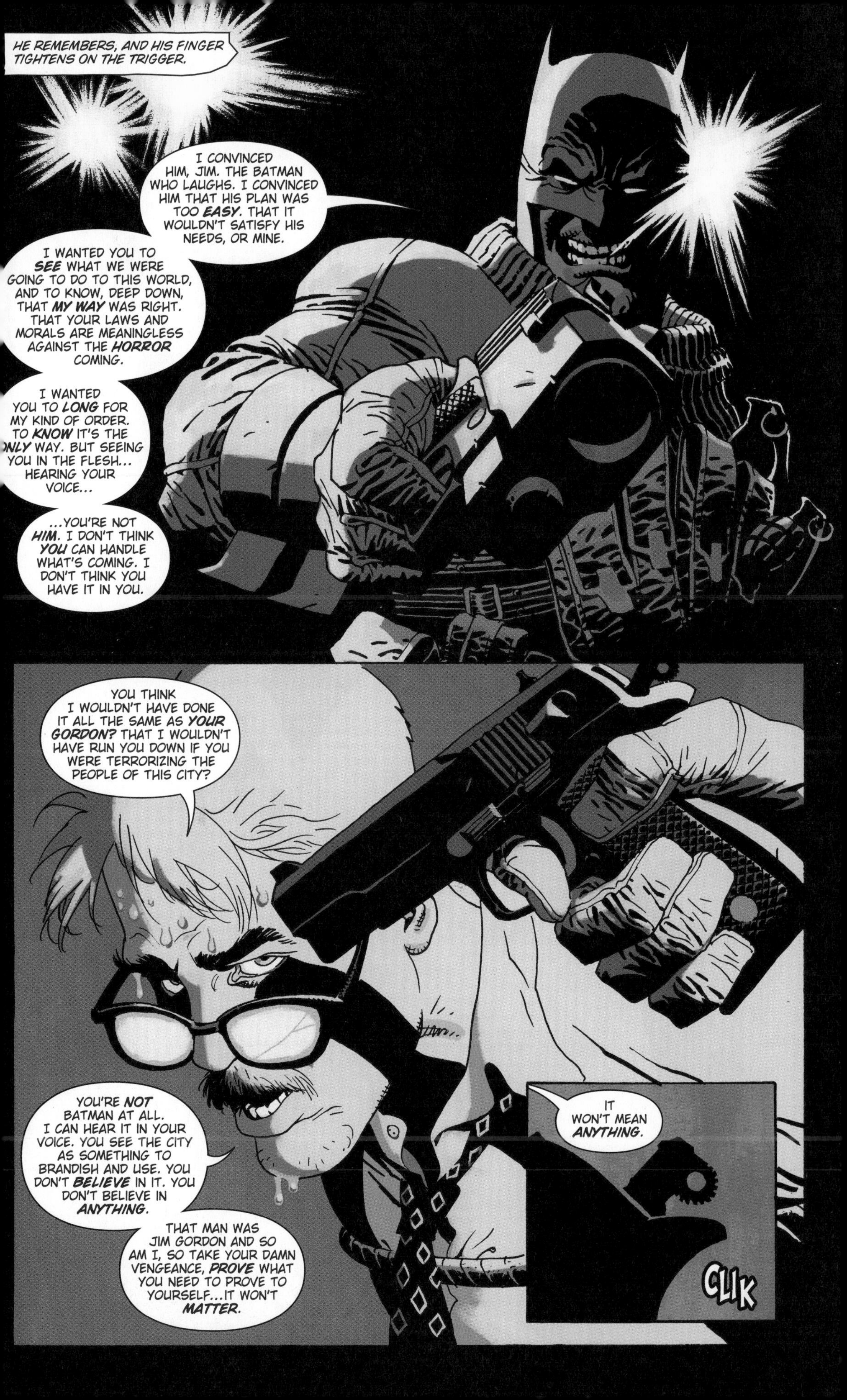

HE REMEMBERS, AND HIS FINGER TIGHTENS ON THE TRIGGER.
I CONVINCED HIM, JIM. THE BATMAN WHO LAUGHS. I CONVINCED HIM THAT HIS PLAN WAS TOO EASY. THAT IT WOULDN'T SATISFY HIS NEEDS, OR MINE.
I WANTED YOU TO SEE WHAT WE WERE GOING TO DO TO THIS WORLD, AND TO KNOW, DEEP DOWN, THAT MY WAY WAS RIGHT. THAT YOUR LAWS AND MORALS ARE MEANINGLESS AGAINST THE HORROR COMING.
I WANTED YOU TO LONG FOR MY KIND OF ORDER. TO KNOW IT'S THE NLY WAY. BUT SEEING YOU IN THE FLESH... HEARING YOUR VOICE...
...YOU'RE NOT HIM. I DON'T THINK YOU CAN HANDLE WHAT'S COMING. I DON'T THINK YOU HAVE IT IN YOU.
YOU THINK I WOULDN'T HAVE DONE IT ALL THE SAME AS YOUR GORDON? THAT I WOULDN'T HAVE RUN YOU DOWN IF YOU WERE TERRORIZING THE PEOPLE OF THIS CITY?
YOU'RE NOT BATMAN AT ALL. I CAN HEAR IT IN YOUR VOICE. YOU SEE THE CITY AS SOMETHING TO BRANDISH AND USE. YOU DON'T BELIEVE IN IT. YOU DON'T BELIEVE IN ANYTHING.
THAT MAN WAS JIM GORDON AND SO AM I, SO TAKE YOUR DAMN VENGEANCE, PROVE WHAT YOU NEED TO PROVE TO YOURSELF...IT WON'T MATTER.
IT WON'T MEAN ANYTHING.
CLIK

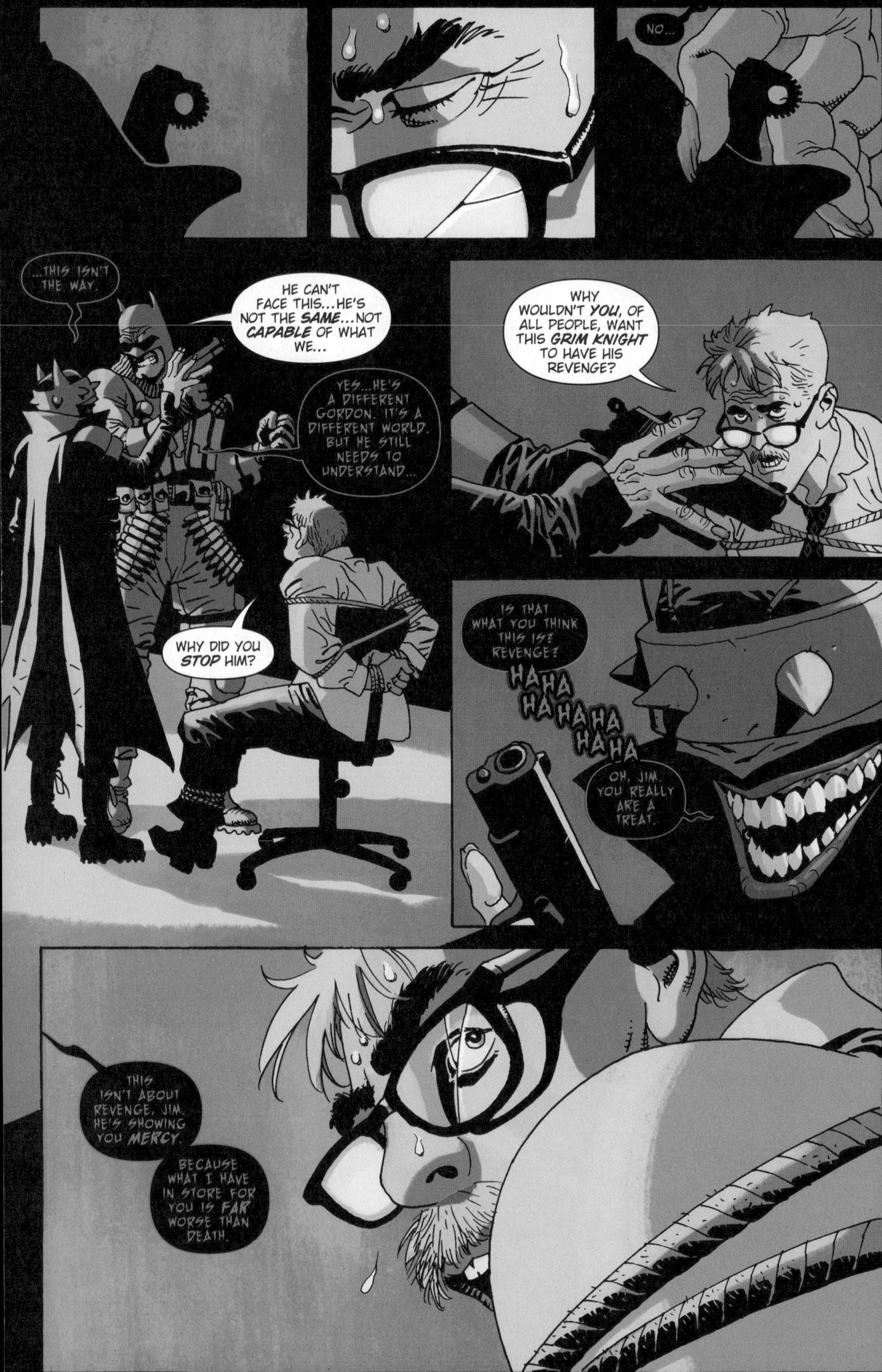
NO...
...THIS ISN'T THE WAY.
HE CAN'T FACE THIS...HE'S NOT THE SAME...NOT CAPABLE OF WHAT WE...
YES...HE'S A DIFFERENT GORDON. IT'S A DIFFERENT WORLD. BUT HE STILL NEEDS TO UNDERSTAND...
WHY DID YOU STOP HIM?
WHY WOULDN'T YOU, OF ALL PEOPLE, WANT THIS GRIM KNIGHT TO HAVE HIS REVENGE?
IS THAT WHAT YOU THINK THIS IS? REVENGE?
HAHA HAHAHAHA HAHA
OH, JIM. YOU REALLY ARE A TREAT.
THIS ISN'T ABOUT REVENGE, JIM. HE'S SHOWING YOU MERCY.
BECAUSE WHAT I HAVE IN STORE FOR YOU IS FAR WORSE THAN DEATH.

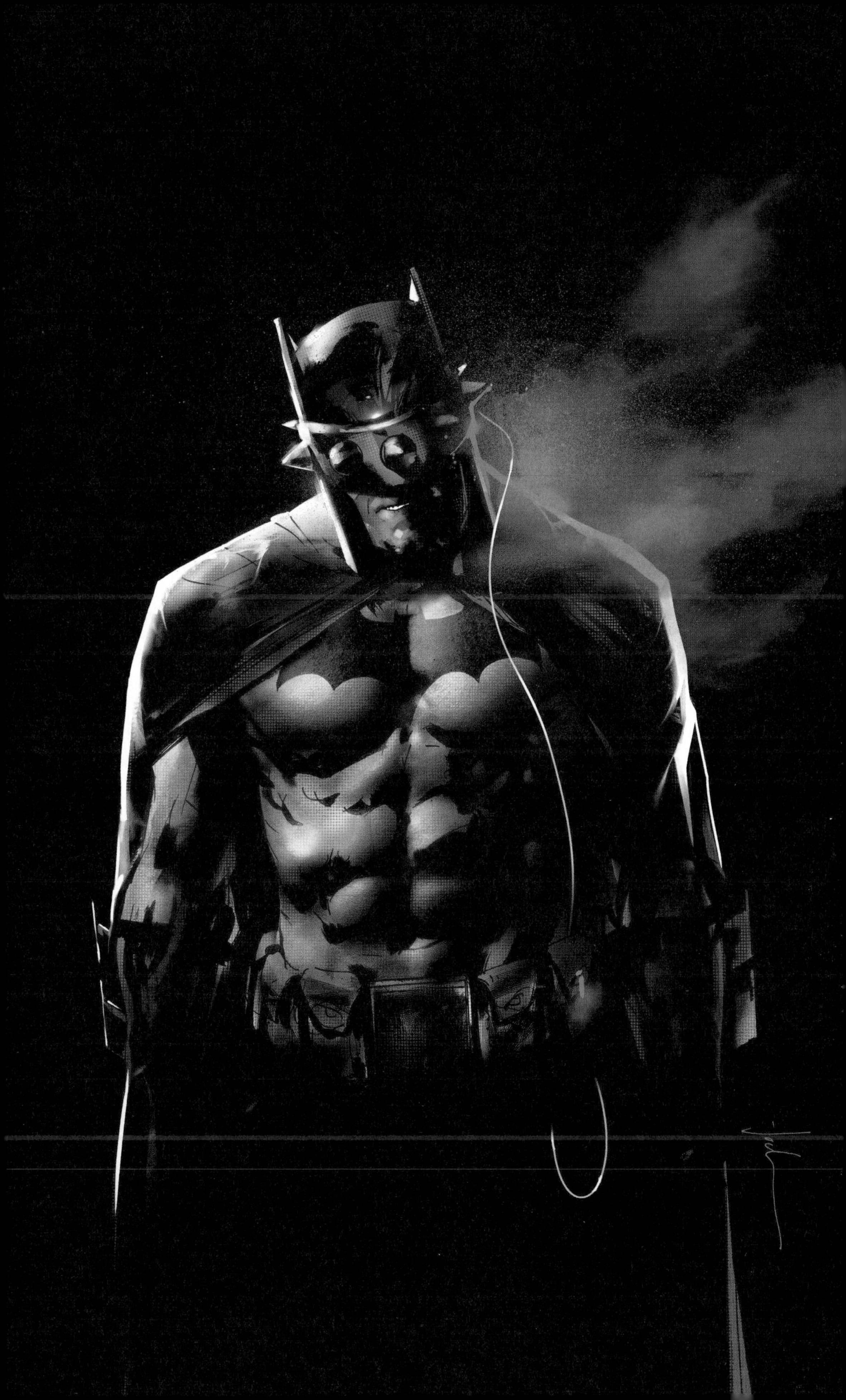

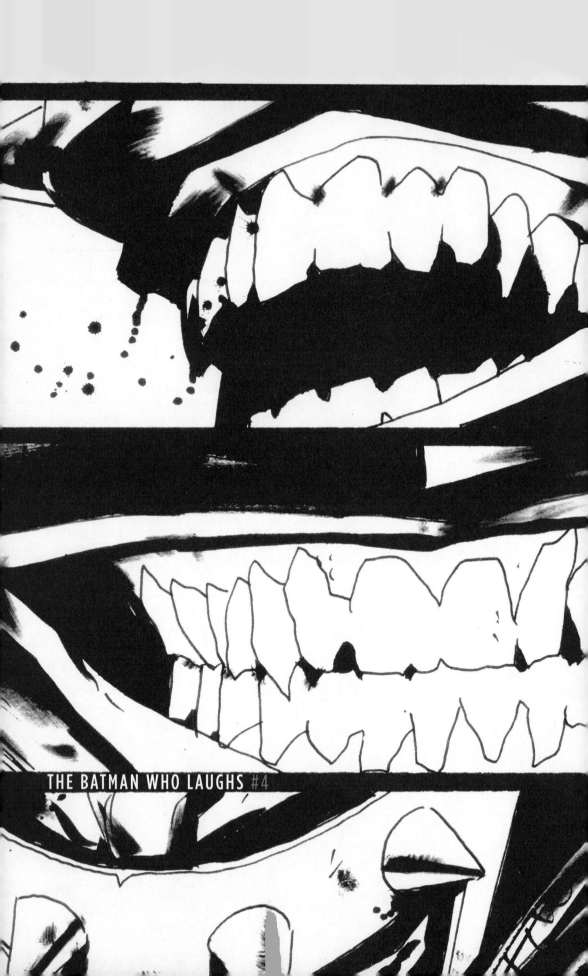

THE BATMAN WHO LAUGHS #4

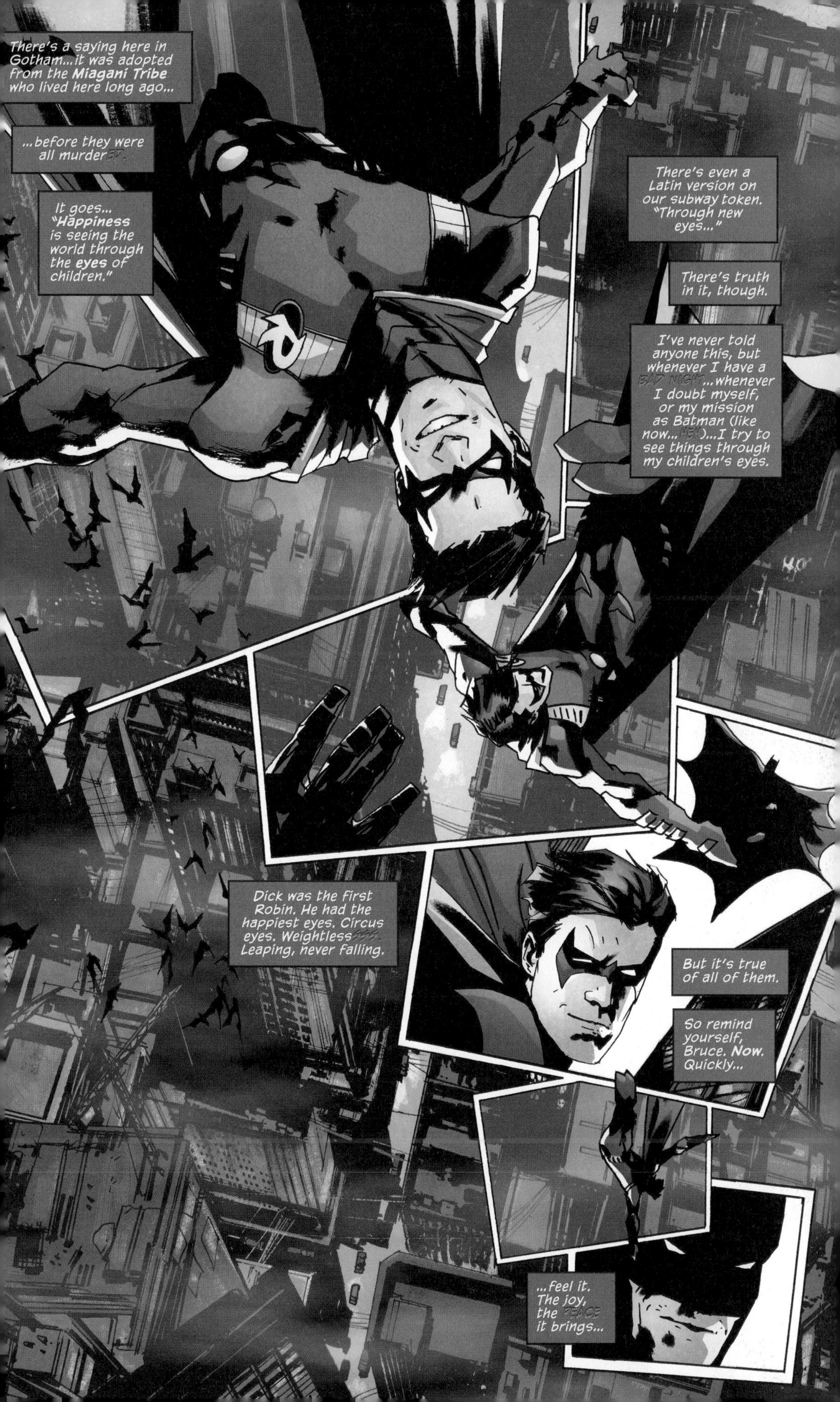
There's a saying here in Gotham...it was adopted from the Miagani Tribe who lived here long ago...
...before they were all murderED.
It goes... "Happiness is seeing the world through the eyes of children."
There's even a Latin version on our subway token. "Through new eyes..."
There's truth in it, though.
I've never told anyone this, but whenever I have a BAD NIGHT...whenever I doubt myself, or my mission as Batman (like now...NEW)...I try to see things through my children's eyes.
Dick was the first Robin. He had the happiest eyes. Circus eyes. WeightlessSSS. Leaping, never falling.
But it's true of all of them.
So remind yourself, Bruce. Now. Quickly...
...feel it. The joy, the PEACE it brings...

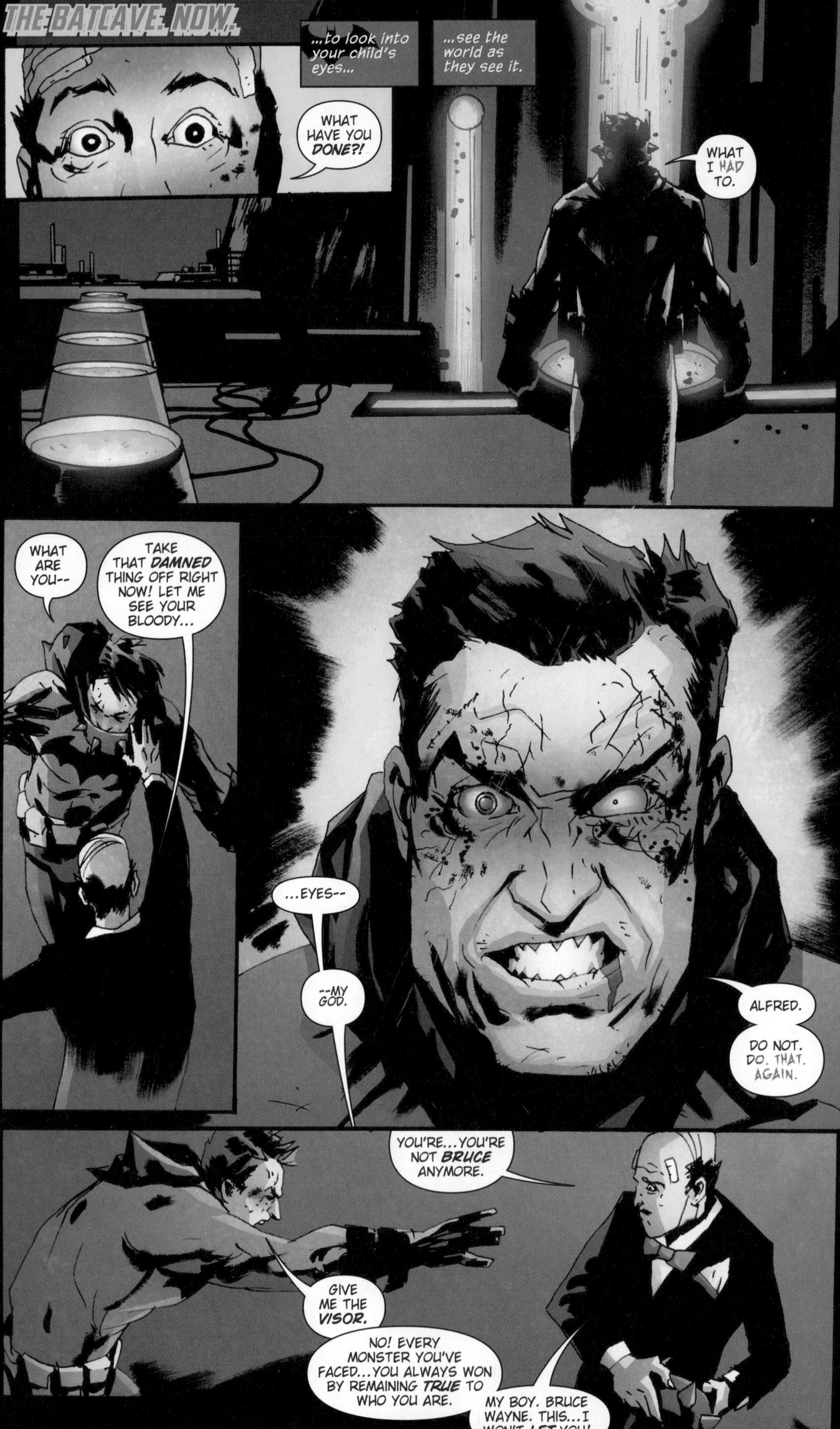
THE BATCAVE. NOW.
...to look into your child's eyes...
...see the world as they see it.
WHAT HAVE YOU DONE?!
WHAT I HAD TO.
WHAT ARE YOU--
TAKE THAT DAMNED THING OFF RIGHT NOW! LET ME SEE YOUR BLOODY...
...EYES--
--MY GOD.
ALFRED.
DO NOT. DO. THAT. AGAIN.
YOU'RE... YOU'RE NOT BRUCE ANYMORE.
GIVE ME THE VISOR.
NO! EVERY MONSTER YOU'VE FACED... YOU ALWAYS WON BY REMAINING TRUE TO WHO YOU ARE.
MY BOY. BRUCE WAYNE. THIS... I WON'T LET YOU!

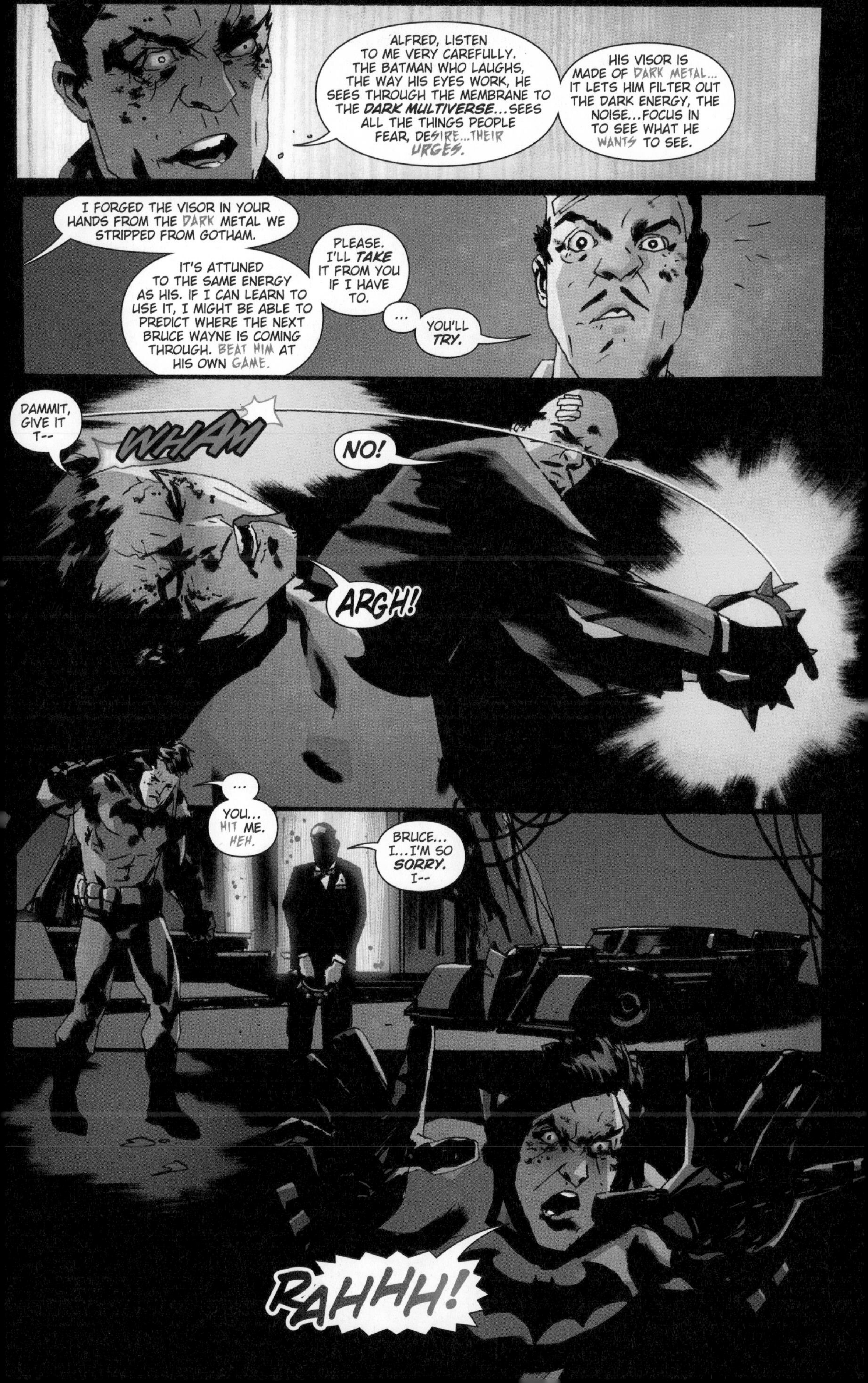
ALFRED, LISTEN TO ME VERY CAREFULLY. THE BATMAN WHO LAUGHS, THE WAY HIS EYES WORK, HE SEES THROUGH THE MEMBRANE TO THE DARK MULTIVERSE...SEES ALL THE THINGS PEOPLE FEAR, DESIRE...THEIR URGES.
HIS VISOR IS MADE OF DARK METAL... IT LETS HIM FILTER OUT THE DARK ENERGY, THE NOISE...FOCUS IN TO SEE WHAT HE WANTS TO SEE.
I FORGED THE VISOR IN YOUR HANDS FROM THE DARK METAL WE STRIPPED FROM GOTHAM.
IT'S ATTUNED TO THE SAME ENERGY AS HIS. IF I CAN LEARN TO USE IT, I MIGHT BE ABLE TO PREDICT WHERE THE NEXT BRUCE WAYNE IS COMING THROUGH. BEAT HIM AT HIS OWN GAME.
PLEASE. I'LL TAKE IT FROM YOU IF I HAVE TO.
...
YOU'LL TRY.
DAMMIT, GIVE IT T--
WHAM
NO!
ARGH!
...
YOU... HIT ME. HEH.
BRUCE... I...I'M SO SORRY. I--
RAHHH!

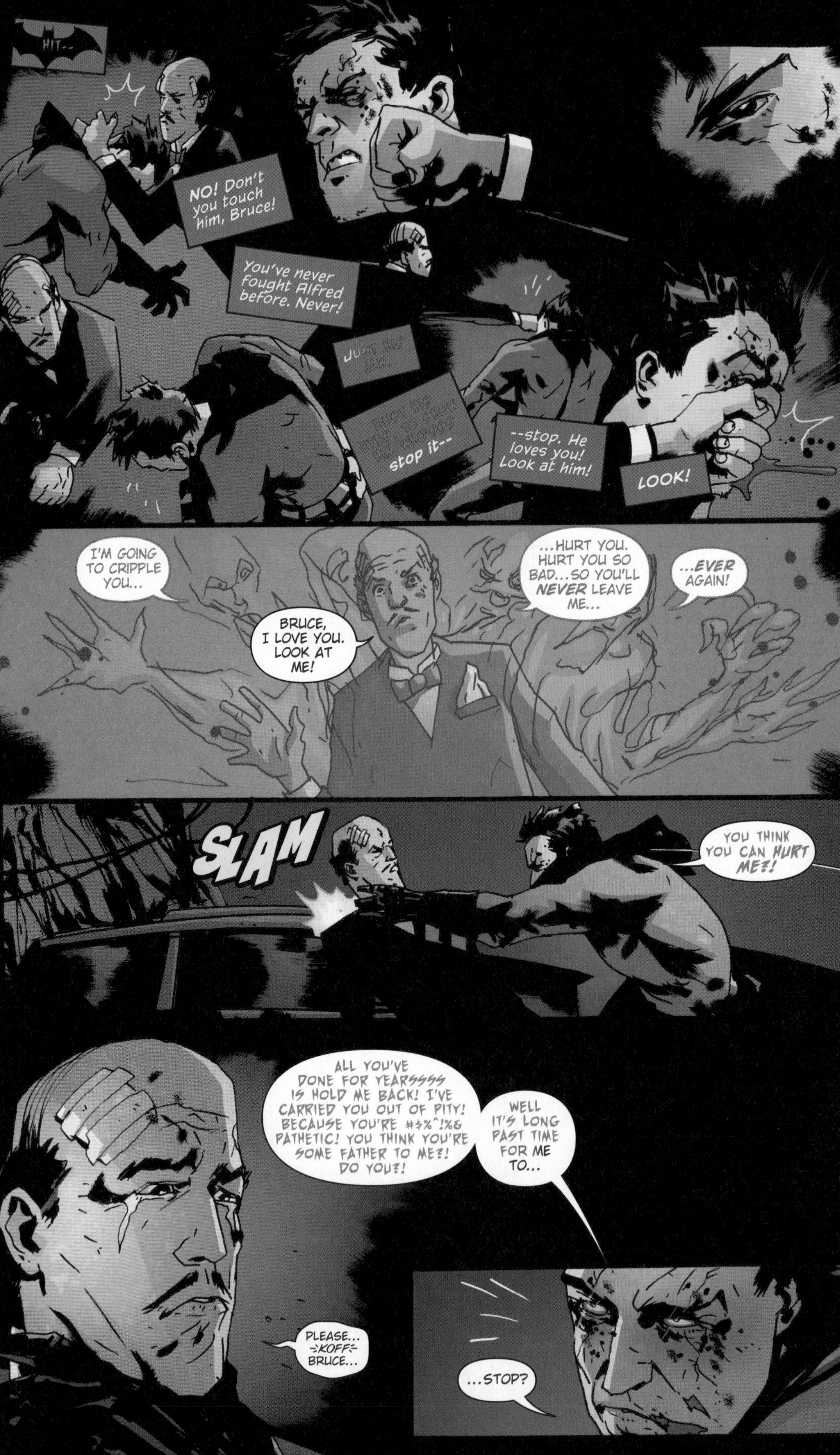
HIT--
NO! Don't you touch him, Bruce!
You've never fought Alfred before. Never!
JUST HIS JAW.
BUST HIS EYES TO SHOW HIM WHO'S$$
stop it--
--stop. He loves you! Look at him!
LOOK!
I'M GOING TO CRIPPLE YOU...
BRUCE, I LOVE YOU. LOOK AT ME!
...HURT YOU. HURT YOU SO BAD...SO YOU'LL NEVER LEAVE ME...
...EVER AGAIN!
SLAM
YOU THINK YOU CAN HURT ME?!
ALL YOU'VE DONE FOR YEARSSSSS IS HOLD ME BACK! I'VE CARRIED YOU OUT OF PITY! BECAUSE YOU'RE #$%^!%& PATHETIC! YOU THINK YOU'RE SOME FATHER TO ME?! DO YOU?!
WELL IT'S LONG PAST TIME FOR ME TO...
PLEASE... =KOFF= BRUCE...
...STOP?

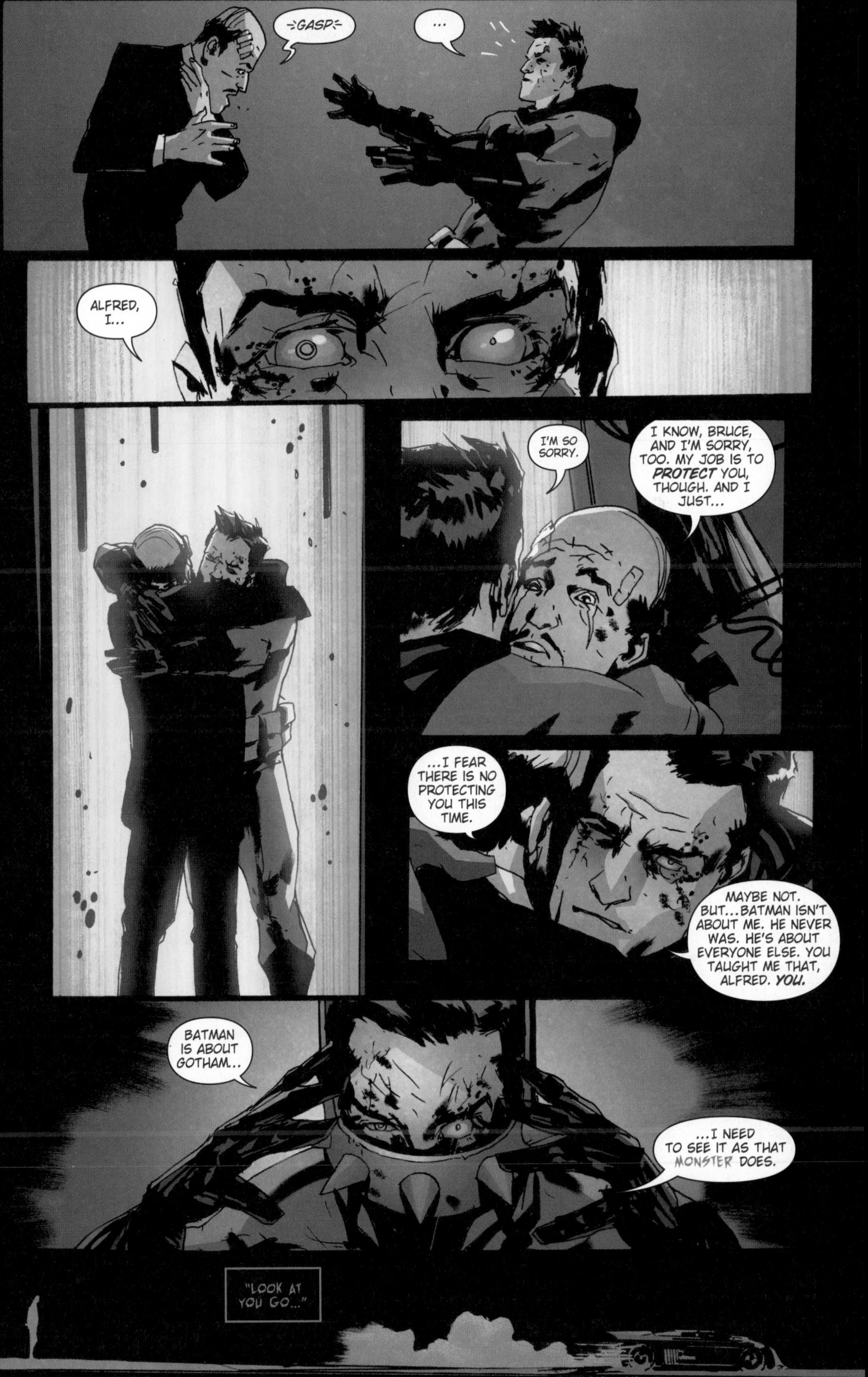
-GASP-
...
ALFRED, I...
I'M SO SORRY.
I KNOW, BRUCE, AND I'M SORRY, TOO. MY JOB IS TO PROTECT YOU, THOUGH. AND I JUST...
...I FEAR THERE IS NO PROTECTING YOU THIS TIME.
MAYBE NOT. BUT...BATMAN ISN'T ABOUT ME. HE NEVER WAS. HE'S ABOUT EVERYONE ELSE. YOU TAUGHT ME THAT, ALFRED. YOU.
BATMAN IS ABOUT GOTHAM...
...I NEED TO SEE IT AS THAT MONSTER DOES.
"LOOK AT YOU GO..."

THERE. YOU CAN SEE!

HELLO.

SO GOOD TO FINALLY MEET YOU, JIM.

MMNN!

I NEVER TOLD YOU THIS, BUT WHEN I WAS BATMAN, YOU WERE MY *BEST FRIEND.*

AFTER ALL, *YOU* WERE THE ONE WHO TAUGHT THEM HOW TO SEE BATMAN FOR WHO HE WAS. THE LIGHT IN THE SKY...

...BUT ME, AS I AM NOW, I NEVER GOT TO MEET YOU. SEE, ON MY WORLD, I WAS BORN JUST AFTER JOKER FINALLY CROSSED THE LINE, KILLED CROC, FREEZE, ALL THE VILLAINS, HUNDREDS OF PEOPLE, DEAD.

YOU, THOUGH, EVEN THEN YOU WERE DETERMINED TO BRING HIM IN BY *THE BOOK.*

SO TO BE FUNNY, JOKER BOOBY-TRAPPED YOUR NOTEBOOK WITH THIS SPRING-LOADED ACID...

GGGKKK.

YES, YOU MADE A SOUND JUST LIKE THAT.

THE THING I REMEMBER MOST WAS CATCHING YOUR GLASSES. I DIDN'T UNDERSTAND WHAT WAS HAPPENING YET, THEN I LOOKED UP AND SAW IT WAS *BECAUSE YOU DIDN'T HAVE A NOSE ANYMORE.*

BUT HERE YOU ARE, NOSE AND ALL! HAA! FUNN BECAUSE IF IT WAS FOR YOUR DEATH...B MAN WOULDN'T HAV KILLED THE JOKER AND THERE'D BE NO ME.

SEE, IN A WAY, YOU' MY BEST FRIEND, TO HAHA!

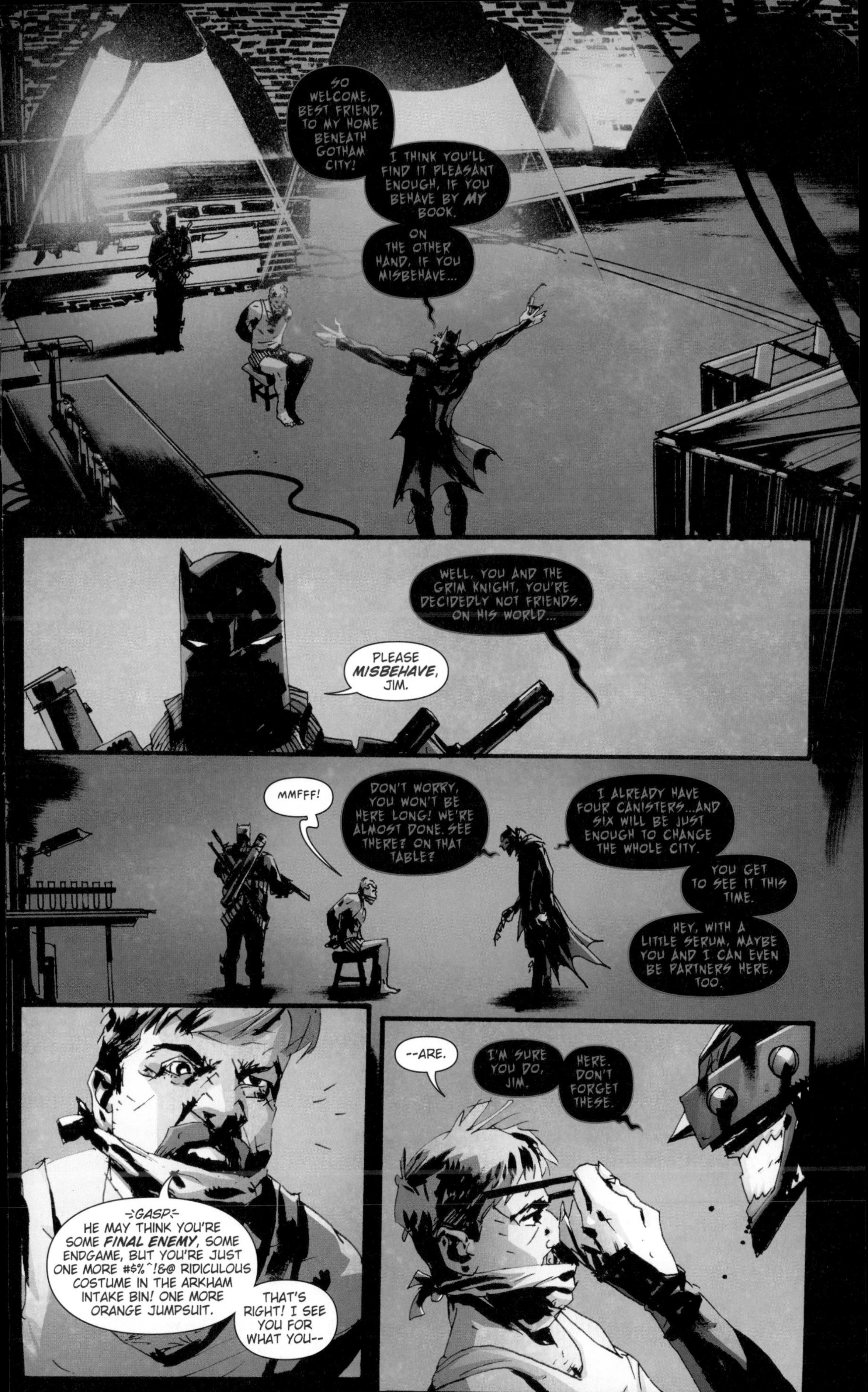
SO WELCOME, BEST FRIEND, TO MY HOME BENEATH GOTHAM CITY!
I THINK YOU'LL FIND IT PLEASANT ENOUGH, IF YOU BEHAVE BY MY BOOK.
ON THE OTHER HAND, IF YOU MISBEHAVE...
WELL, YOU AND THE GRIM KNIGHT, YOU'RE DECIDEDLY NOT FRIENDS. ON HIS WORLD...
PLEASE MISBEHAVE, JIM.
MMFFF!
DON'T WORRY, YOU WON'T BE HERE LONG! WE'RE ALMOST DONE. SEE THERE? ON THAT TABLE?
I ALREADY HAVE FOUR CANISTERS...AND SIX WILL BE JUST ENOUGH TO CHANGE THE WHOLE CITY.
YOU GET TO SEE IT THIS TIME.
HEY, WITH A LITTLE SERUM, MAYBE YOU AND I CAN EVEN BE PARTNERS HERE, TOO.
-GASP- HE MAY THINK YOU'RE SOME FINAL ENEMY, SOME ENDGAME, BUT YOU'RE JUST ONE MORE #$%^!&@ RIDICULOUS COSTUME IN THE ARKHAM INTAKE BIN! ONE MORE ORANGE JUMPSUIT.
THAT'S RIGHT! I SEE YOU FOR WHAT YOU--
--ARE.
I'M SURE YOU DO, JIM.
HERE. DON'T FORGET THESE.

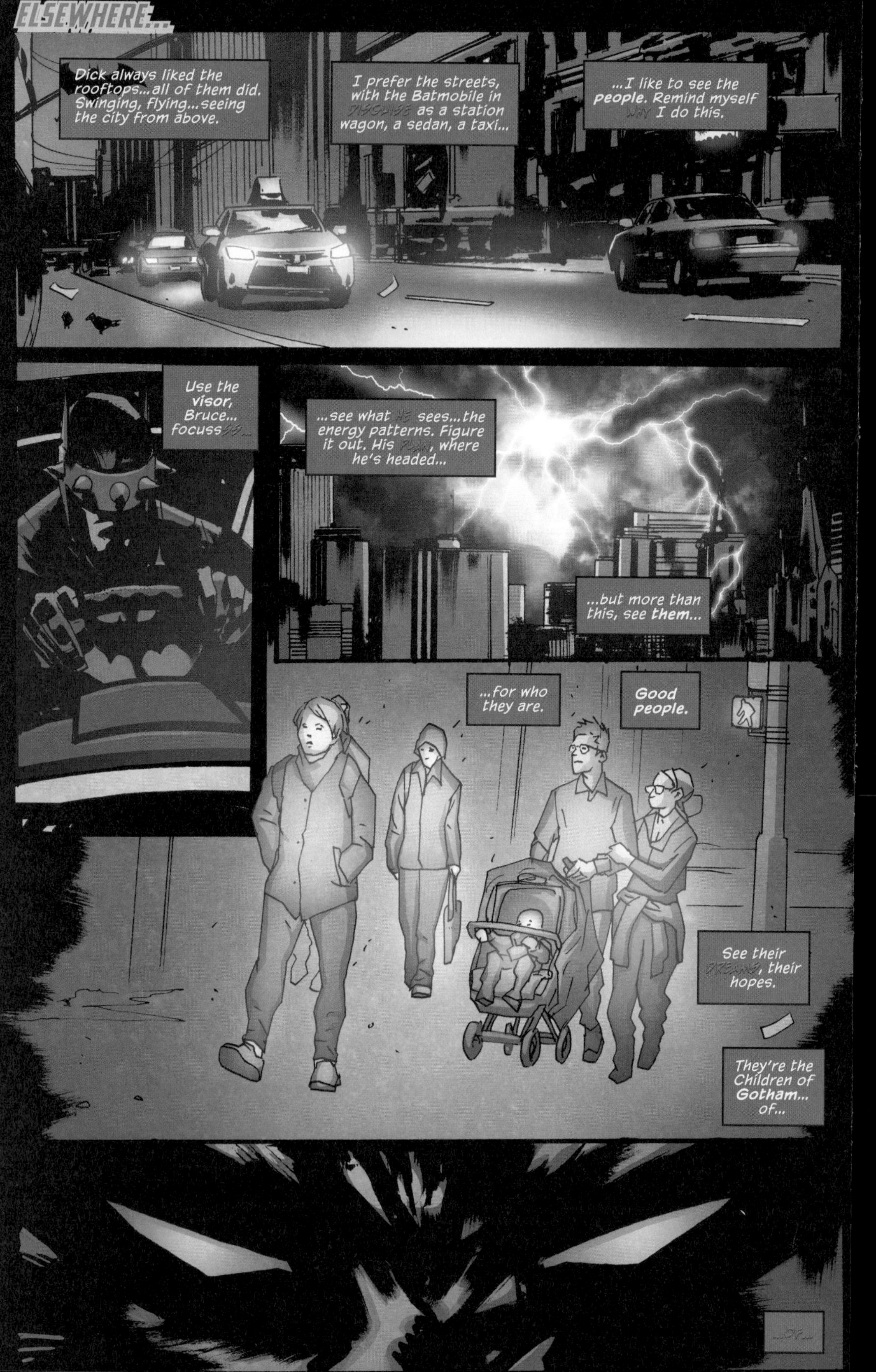
ELSEWHERE...
Dick always liked the rooftops...all of them did. Swinging, flying...seeing the city from above.
I prefer the streets, with the Batmobile in DISGUISE as a station wagon, a sedan, a taxi...
...I like to see the people. Remind myself WHY I do this.
Use the visor, Bruce... focussss...
...see what HE sees...the energy patterns. Figure it out. His PLAN, where he's headed...
...but more than this, see them...
...for who they are.
Good people.
See their DREAMS, their hopes.
They're the Children of Gotham... of...
...OF...

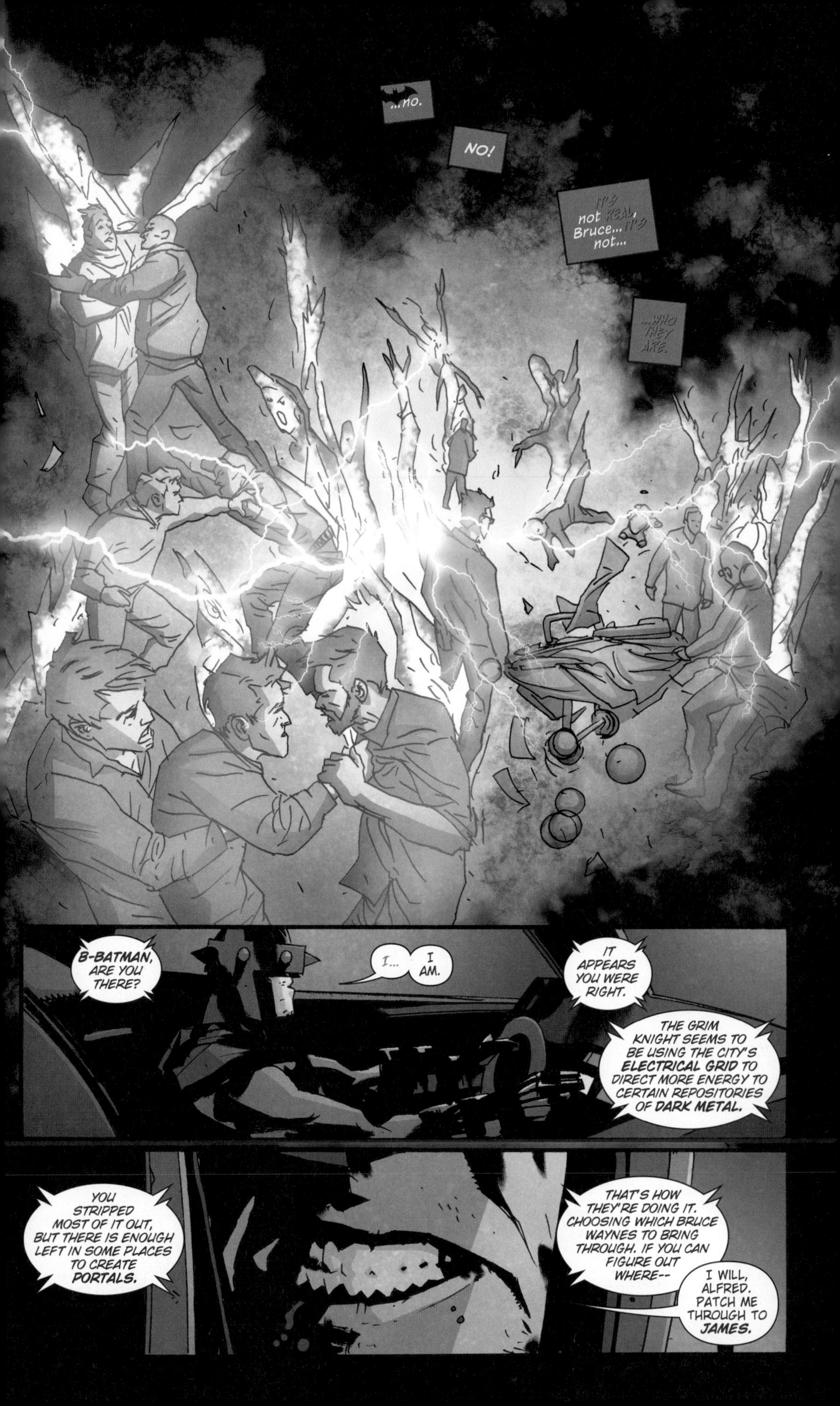

...no.
NO!
IT'S not REAL, Bruce... IT'S not...
...WHO THEY ARE.
B-BATMAN, ARE YOU THERE?
I...
I AM.
IT APPEARS YOU WERE RIGHT.
THE GRIM KNIGHT SEEMS TO BE USING THE CITY'S **ELECTRICAL GRID** TO DIRECT MORE ENERGY TO CERTAIN REPOSITORIES OF **DARK METAL.**
YOU STRIPPED MOST OF IT OUT, BUT THERE IS ENOUGH LEFT IN SOME PLACES TO CREATE **PORTALS.**
THAT'S HOW THEY'RE DOING IT. CHOOSING WHICH BRUCE WAYNES TO BRING THROUGH. IF YOU CAN FIGURE OUT WHERE--
I WILL, ALFRED. PATCH ME THROUGH TO **JAMES.**

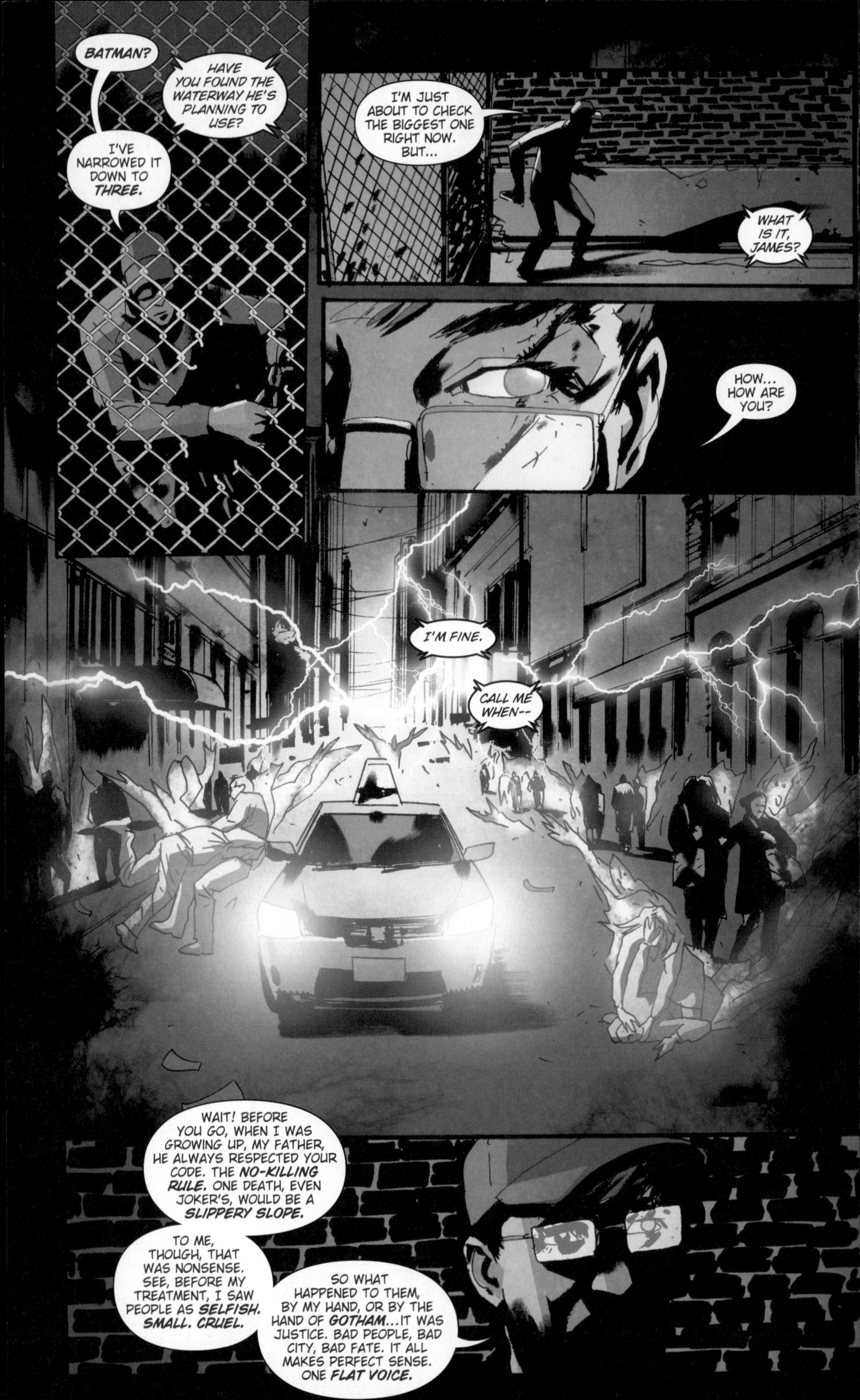
BATMAN?
HAVE YOU FOUND THE WATERWAY HE'S PLANNING TO USE?
I'VE NARROWED IT DOWN TO THREE.
I'M JUST ABOUT TO CHECK THE BIGGEST ONE RIGHT NOW. BUT...
WHAT IS IT, JAMES?
HOW... HOW ARE YOU?
I'M FINE.
CALL ME WHEN--
WAIT! BEFORE YOU GO, WHEN I WAS GROWING UP, MY FATHER, HE ALWAYS RESPECTED YOUR CODE. THE NO-KILLING RULE. ONE DEATH, EVEN JOKER'S, WOULD BE A SLIPPERY SLOPE.
TO ME, THOUGH, THAT WAS NONSENSE. SEE, BEFORE MY TREATMENT, I SAW PEOPLE AS SELFISH. SMALL. CRUEL.
SO WHAT HAPPENED TO THEM, BY MY HAND, OR BY THE HAND OF GOTHAM... IT WAS JUSTICE. BAD PEOPLE, BAD CITY, BAD FATE. IT ALL MAKES PERFECT SENSE. ONE FLAT VOICE.

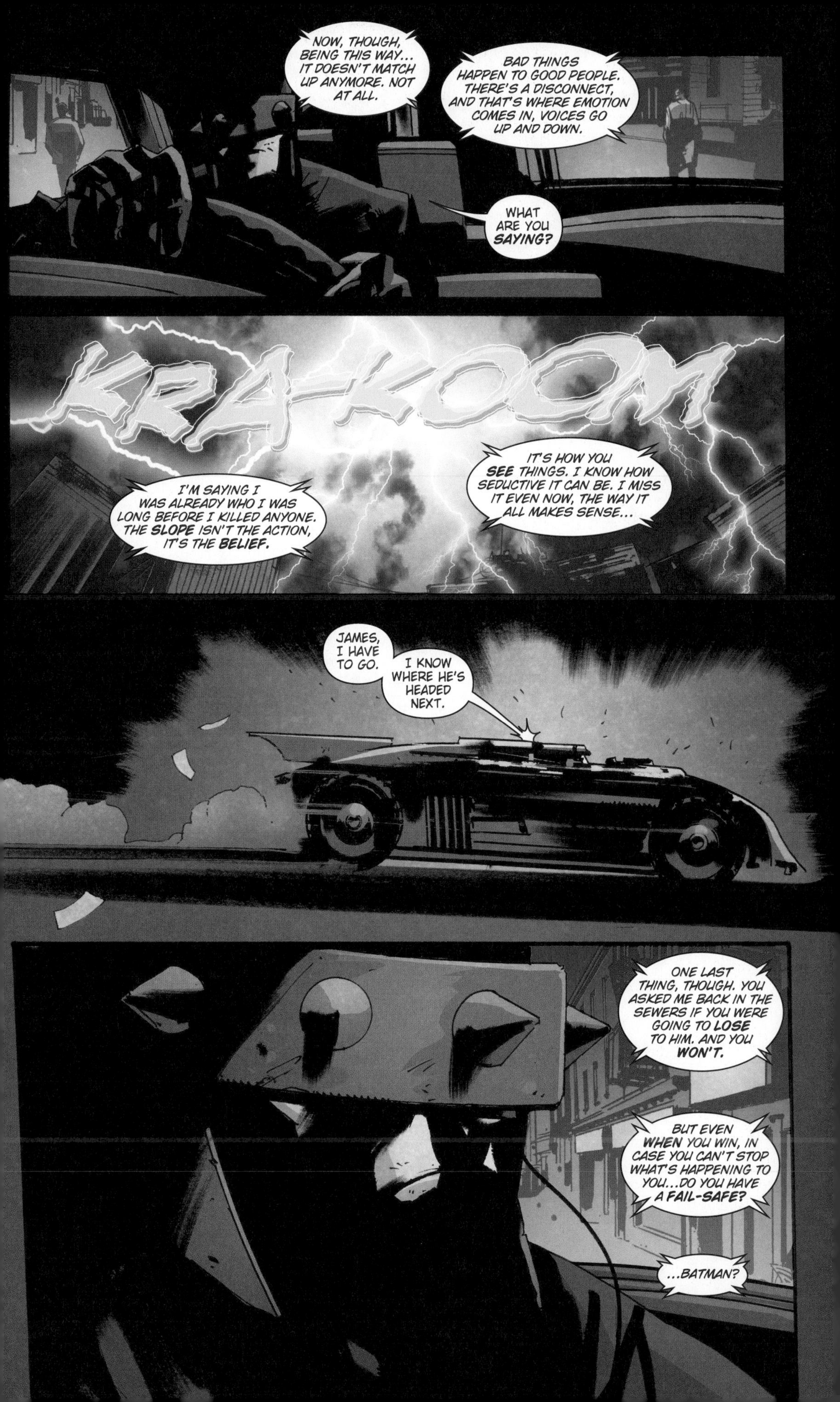
NOW, THOUGH, BEING THIS WAY... IT DOESN'T MATCH UP ANYMORE. NOT AT ALL.
BAD THINGS HAPPEN TO GOOD PEOPLE. THERE'S A DISCONNECT, AND THAT'S WHERE EMOTION COMES IN, VOICES GO UP AND DOWN.
WHAT ARE YOU SAYING?
KRA-KOOM
I'M SAYING I WAS ALREADY WHO I WAS LONG BEFORE I KILLED ANYONE. THE SLOPE ISN'T THE ACTION, IT'S THE BELIEF.
IT'S HOW YOU SEE THINGS. I KNOW HOW SEDUCTIVE IT CAN BE. I MISS IT EVEN NOW, THE WAY IT ALL MAKES SENSE...
JAMES, I HAVE TO GO.
I KNOW WHERE HE'S HEADED NEXT.
ONE LAST THING, THOUGH. YOU ASKED ME BACK IN THE SEWERS IF YOU WERE GOING TO LOSE TO HIM. AND YOU WON'T.
BUT EVEN WHEN YOU WIN, IN CASE YOU CAN'T STOP WHAT'S HAPPENING TO YOU...DO YOU HAVE A FAIL-SAFE?
...BATMAN?

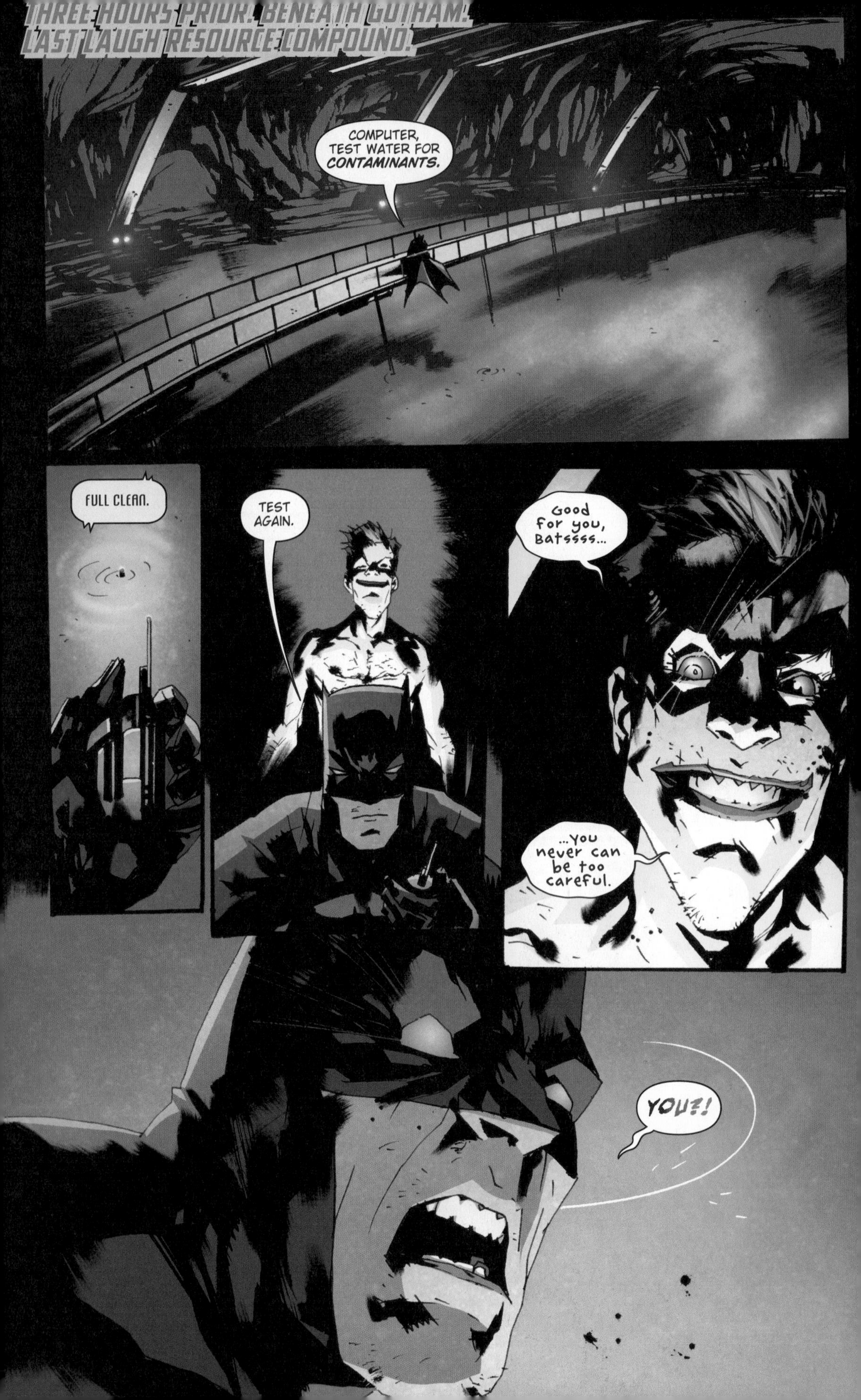
THREE HOURS PRIOR. BENEATH GOTHAM.
LAST LAUGH RESOURCE COMPOUND.
COMPUTER, TEST WATER FOR CONTAMINANTS.
FULL CLEAN.
TEST AGAIN.
Good for you, Batssss...
...you never can be too careful.
YOU?!

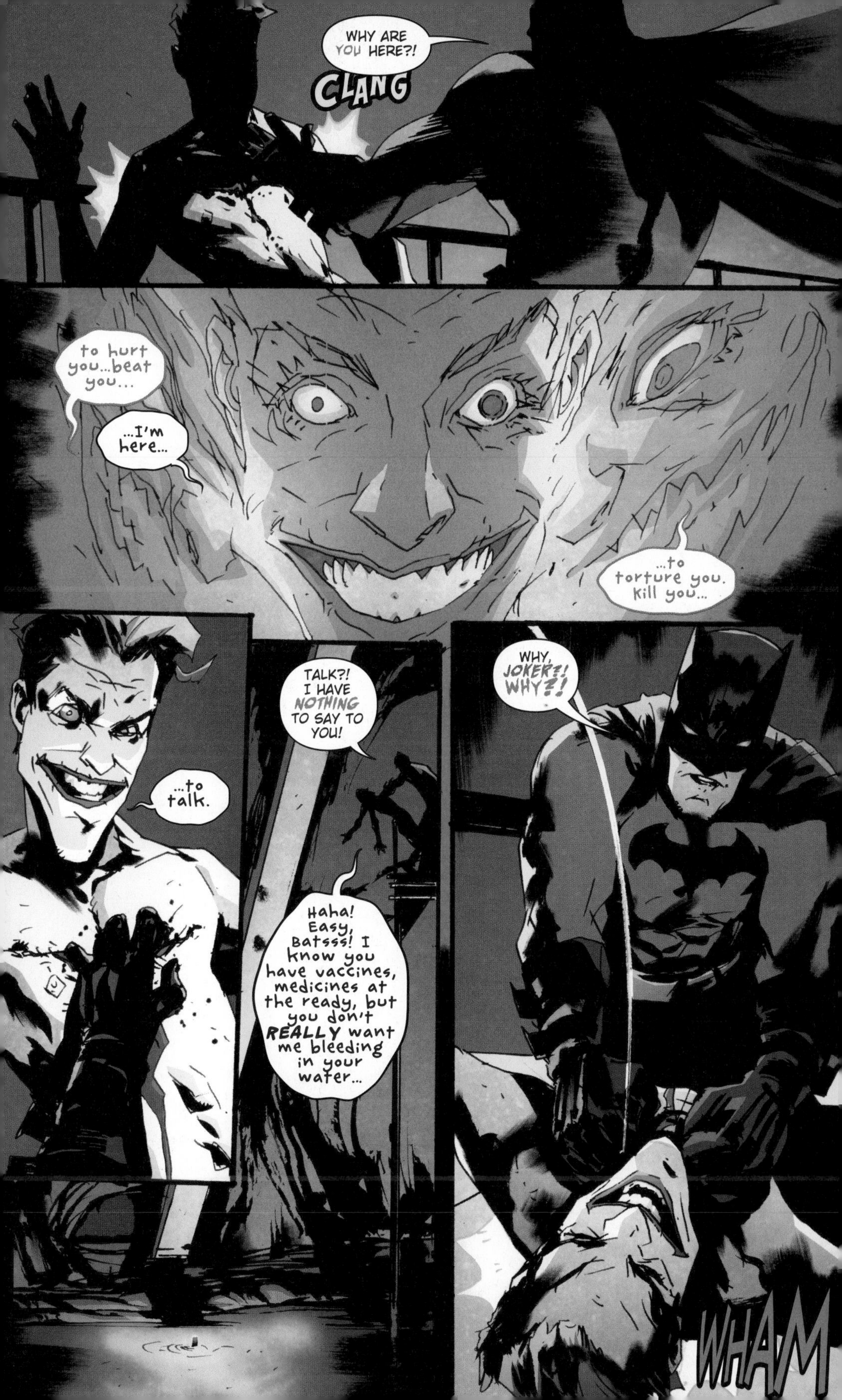

WHY ARE YOU HERE?!
CLANG
to hurt you...beat you...
...I'm here...
...to torture you. Kill you...
...to talk.
TALK?! I HAVE NOTHING TO SAY TO YOU!
Haha! Easy, Batsss! I know you have vaccines, medicines at the ready, but you don't REALLY want me bleeding in your water...
WHY, JOKER?! WHY?!
WHAM

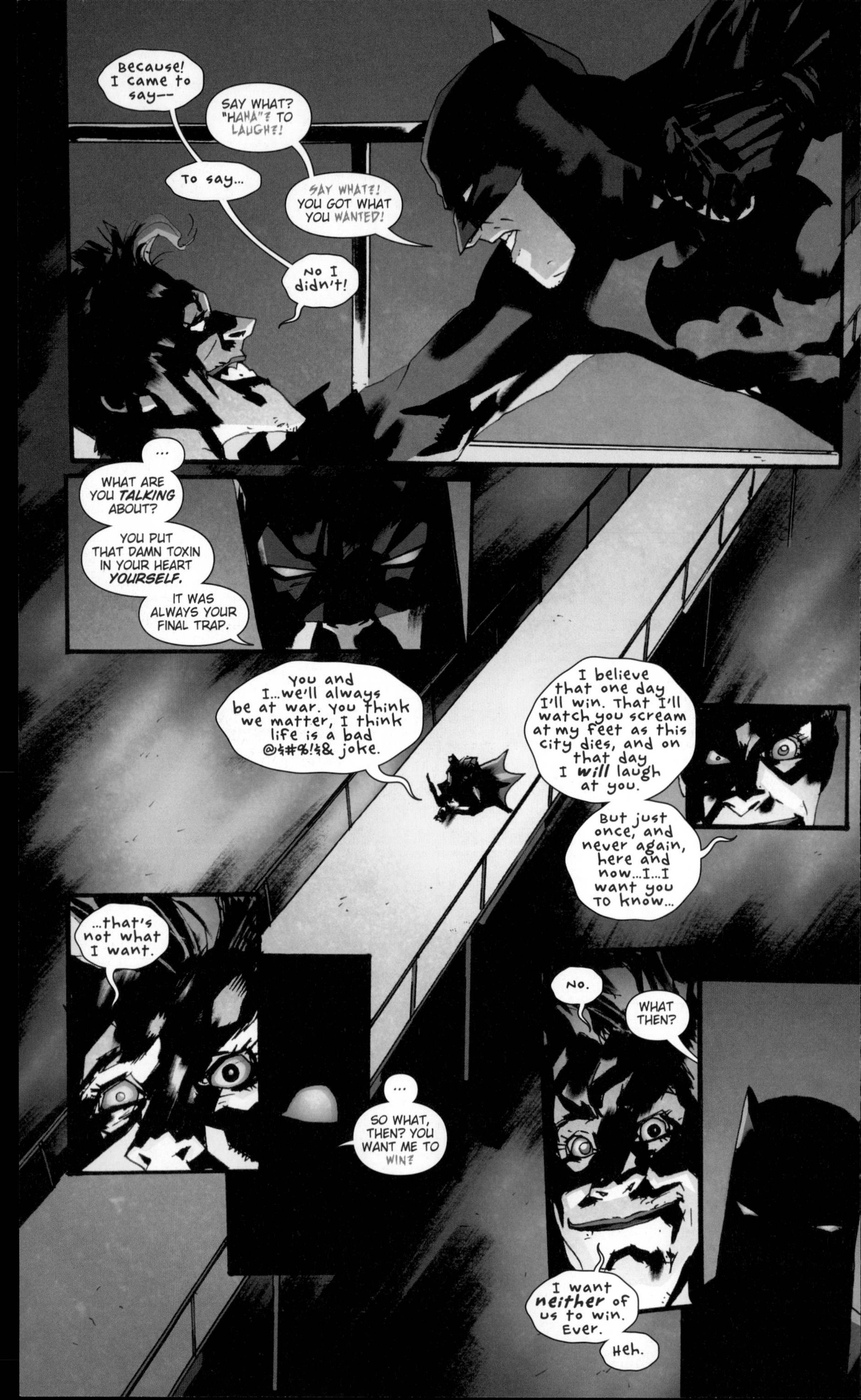
Because! I came to say--
SAY WHAT? "HAHA"? TO LAUGH?!
To say...
SAY WHAT?! YOU GOT WHAT YOU WANTED!
No I didn't!
...
WHAT ARE YOU TALKING ABOUT?
YOU PUT THAT DAMN TOXIN IN YOUR HEART YOURSELF.
IT WAS ALWAYS YOUR FINAL TRAP.
You and I...we'll always be at war. You think we matter, I think life is a bad @$#%!$& joke.
I believe that one day I'll win. That I'll watch you scream at my feet as this city dies, and on that day I will laugh at you.
But just once, and never again, here and now...I...I want you to know...
...that's not what I want.
...
SO WHAT, THEN? YOU WANT ME TO WIN?
No.
WHAT THEN?
I want neither of us to win. Ever.
Heh.

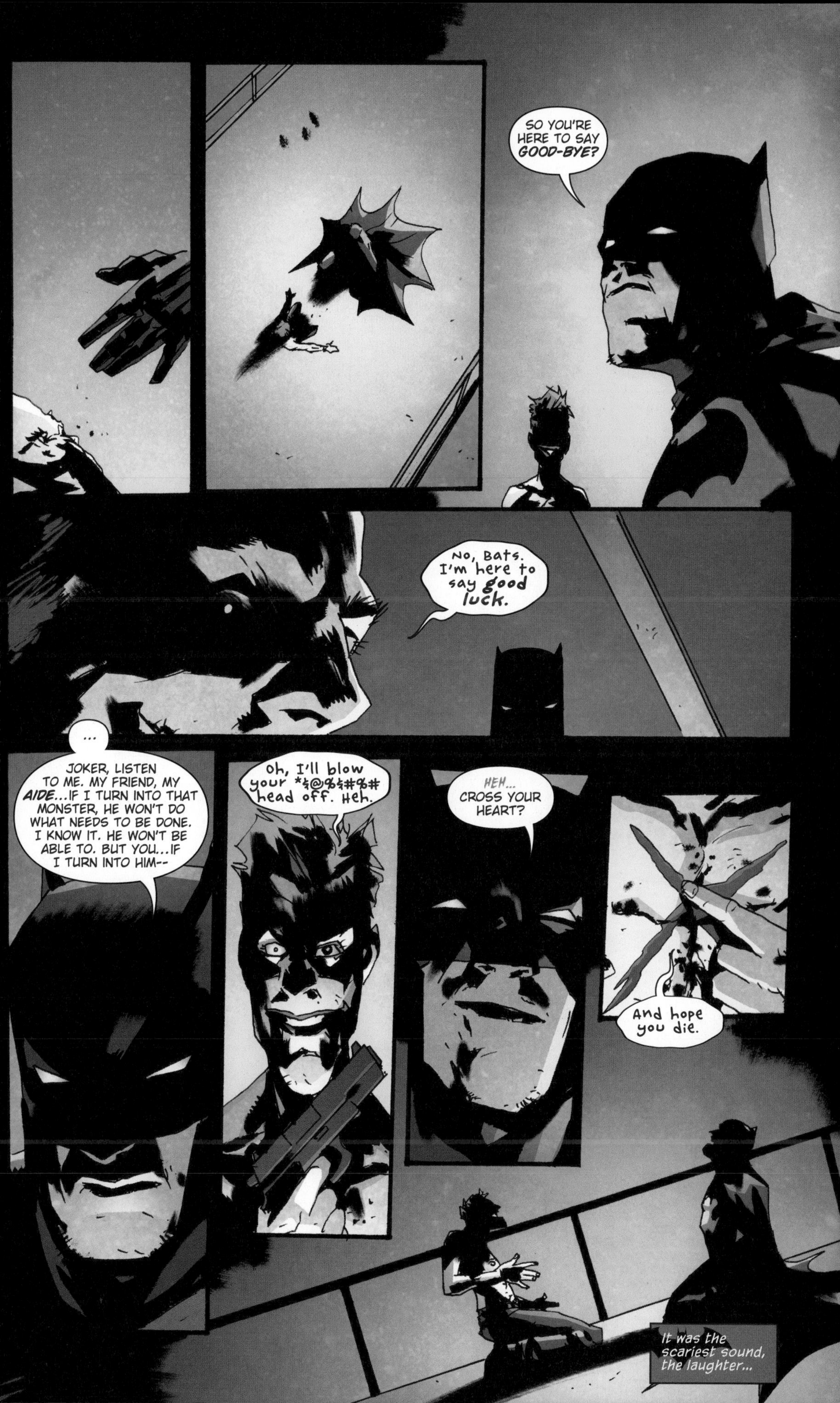

SO YOU'RE HERE TO SAY GOOD-BYE?
No, Bats. I'm here to say good luck.
...
JOKER, LISTEN TO ME. MY FRIEND, MY AIDE...IF I TURN INTO THAT MONSTER, HE WON'T DO WHAT NEEDS TO BE DONE. I KNOW IT. HE WON'T BE ABLE TO. BUT YOU...IF I TURN INTO HIM--
Oh, I'll blow your *$@%$#%# head off. Heh.
HEH... CROSS YOUR HEART?
And hope you die.
It was the scariest sound, the laughter...

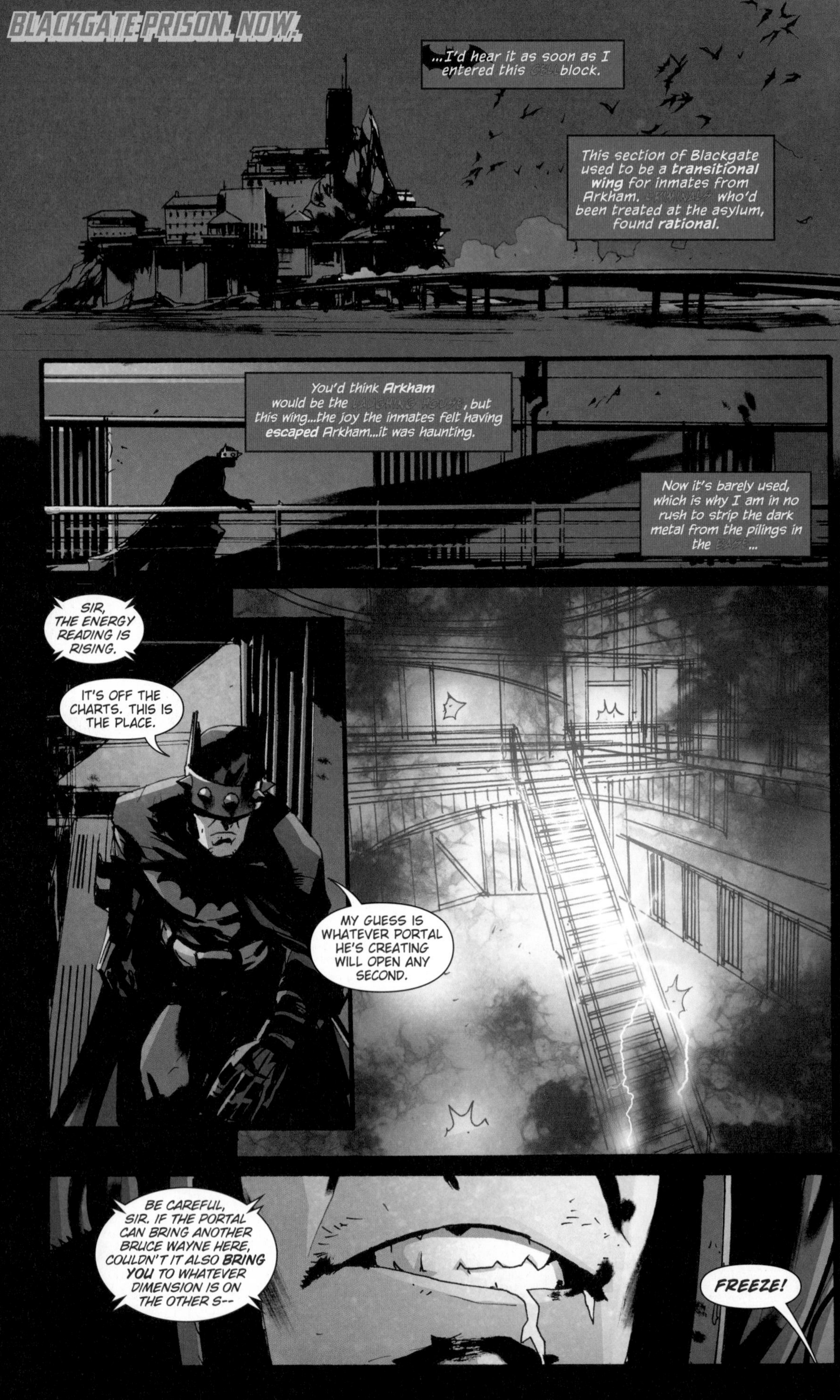

BLACKGATE PRISON. NOW.
...I'd hear it as soon as I entered this CELLblock.
This section of Blackgate used to be a **transitional wing** for inmates from Arkham. CRIMINALS who'd been treated at the asylum, found **rational.**
You'd think **Arkham** would be the LAUGHING HOUSE, but this wing...the joy the inmates felt having **escaped** Arkham...it was haunting.
Now it's barely used, which is why I am in no rush to strip the dark metal from the pilings in the BASE...
SIR, THE ENERGY READING IS RISING.
IT'S OFF THE CHARTS. THIS IS THE PLACE.
MY GUESS IS WHATEVER PORTAL HE'S CREATING WILL OPEN ANY SECOND.
BE CAREFUL, SIR. IF THE PORTAL CAN BRING ANOTHER BRUCE WAYNE HERE, COULDN'T IT ALSO **BRING YOU** TO WHATEVER DIMENSION IS ON THE OTHER S--
FREEZE!

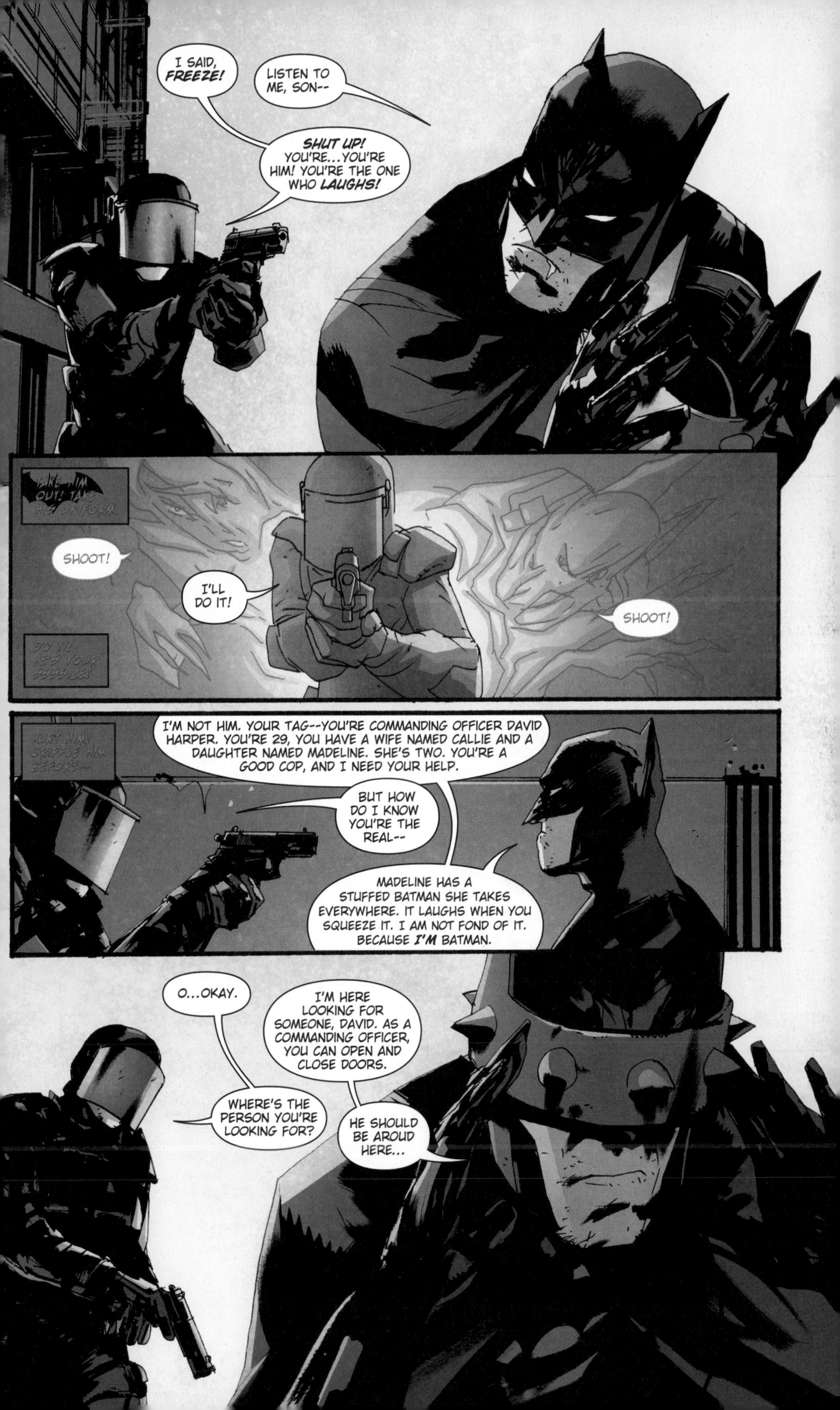

I SAID, *FREEZE!*
LISTEN TO ME, SON--
SHUT UP! YOU'RE...YOU'RE HIM! YOU'RE THE ONE WHO ***LAUGHS!***
TAKE HIM OUT! TAKE HIS UNIFORM
SHOOT!
I'LL DO IT!
SHOOT!
HURT HIM! CRIPPLE HIM BEFORE--
I'M NOT HIM. YOUR TAG--YOU'RE COMMANDING OFFICER DAVID HARPER. YOU'RE 29, YOU HAVE A WIFE NAMED CALLIE AND A DAUGHTER NAMED MADELINE. SHE'S TWO. YOU'RE A GOOD COP, AND I NEED YOUR HELP.
BUT HOW DO I KNOW YOU'RE THE REAL--
MADELINE HAS A STUFFED BATMAN SHE TAKES EVERYWHERE. IT LAUGHS WHEN YOU SQUEEZE IT. I AM NOT FOND OF IT. BECAUSE ***I'M*** BATMAN.
O...OKAY.
I'M HERE LOOKING FOR SOMEONE, DAVID. AS A COMMANDING OFFICER, YOU CAN OPEN AND CLOSE DOORS.
WHERE'S THE PERSON YOU'RE LOOKING FOR?
HE SHOULD BE AROUD HERE...

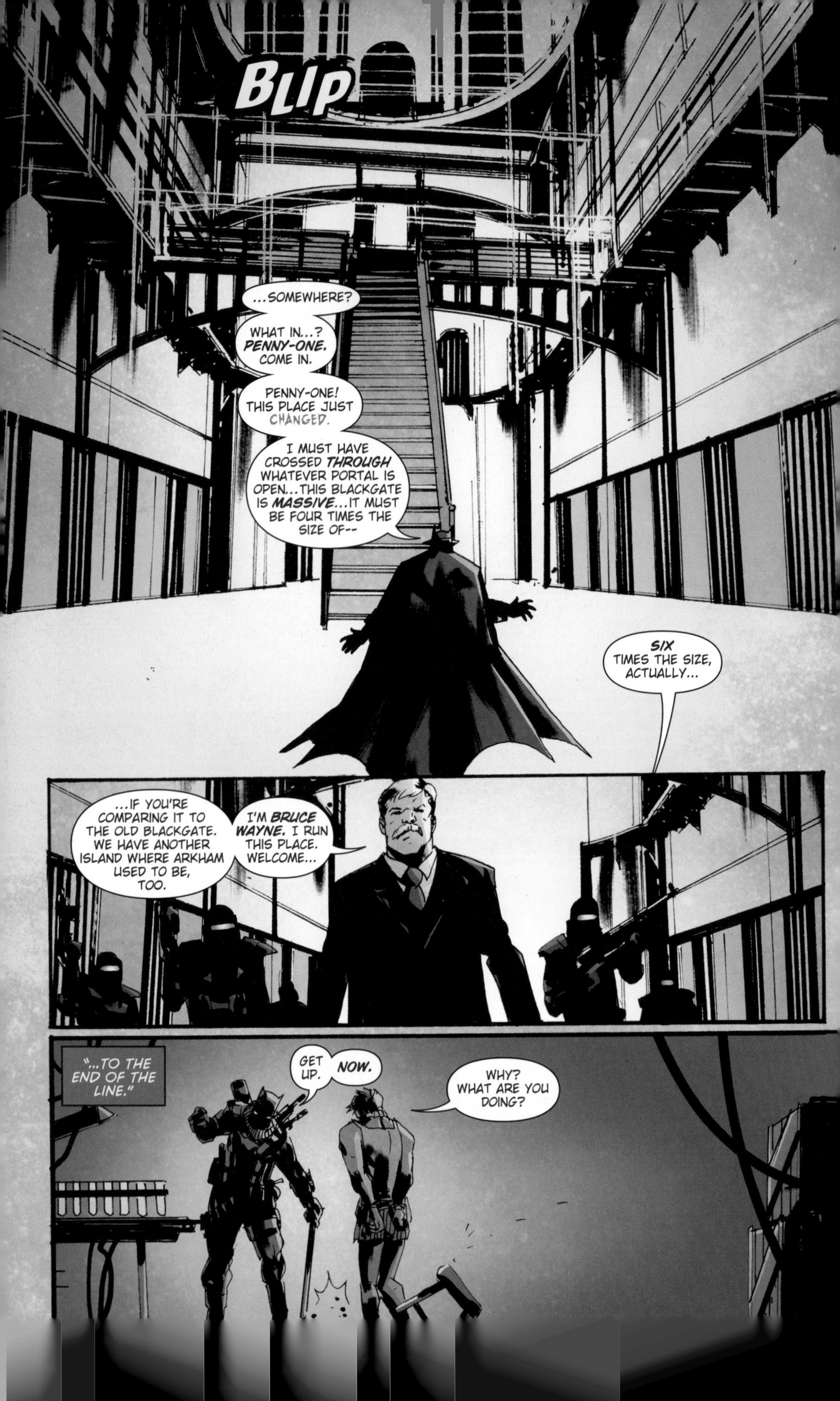
BLIP
...SOMEWHERE?
WHAT IN...? PENNY-ONE. COME IN.
PENNY-ONE! THIS PLACE JUST CHANGED.
I MUST HAVE CROSSED THROUGH WHATEVER PORTAL IS OPEN...THIS BLACKGATE IS MASSIVE...IT MUST BE FOUR TIMES THE SIZE OF--
SIX TIMES THE SIZE, ACTUALLY...
...IF YOU'RE COMPARING IT TO THE OLD BLACKGATE. WE HAVE ANOTHER ISLAND WHERE ARKHAM USED TO BE, TOO.
I'M BRUCE WAYNE. I RUN THIS PLACE. WELCOME...
"...TO THE END OF THE LINE."
GET UP.
NOW.
WHY? WHAT ARE YOU DOING?

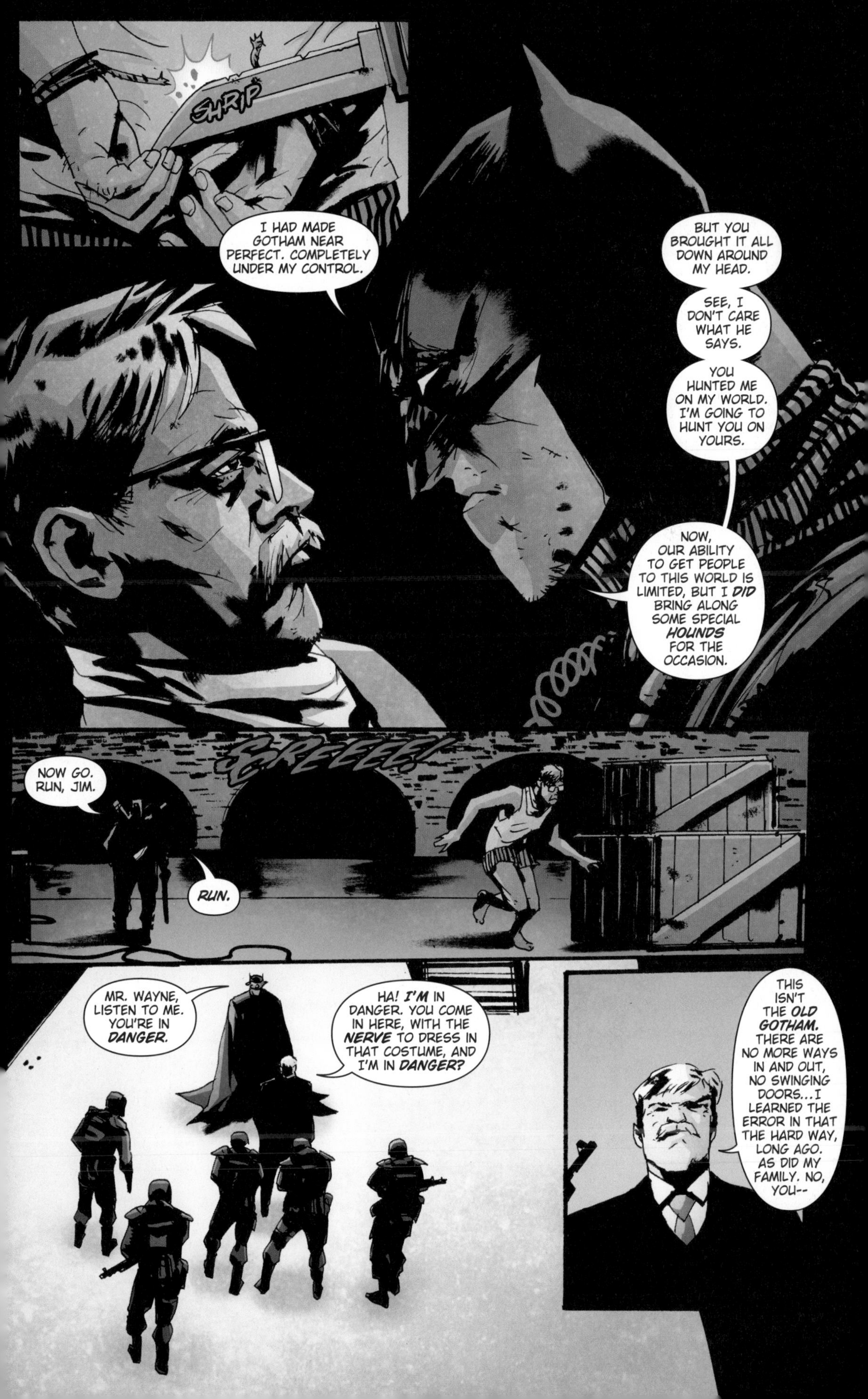
SHRIP
I HAD MADE GOTHAM NEAR PERFECT. COMPLETELY UNDER MY CONTROL.
BUT YOU BROUGHT IT ALL DOWN AROUND MY HEAD.
SEE, I DON'T CARE WHAT HE SAYS.
YOU HUNTED ME ON MY WORLD. I'M GOING TO HUNT YOU ON YOURS.
NOW, OUR ABILITY TO GET PEOPLE TO THIS WORLD IS LIMITED, BUT I *DID* BRING ALONG SOME SPECIAL ***HOUNDS*** FOR THE OCCASION.
EREEEE!
NOW GO. RUN, JIM.
RUN.
MR. WAYNE, LISTEN TO ME. YOU'RE IN ***DANGER***.
HA! ***I'M*** IN DANGER. YOU COME IN HERE, WITH THE ***NERVE*** TO DRESS IN THAT COSTUME, AND I'M IN ***DANGER?***
THIS ISN'T THE ***OLD GOTHAM.*** THERE ARE NO MORE WAYS IN AND OUT, NO SWINGING DOORS... I LEARNED THE ERROR IN THAT THE HARD WAY, LONG AGO. AS DID MY FAMILY. NO, YOU--

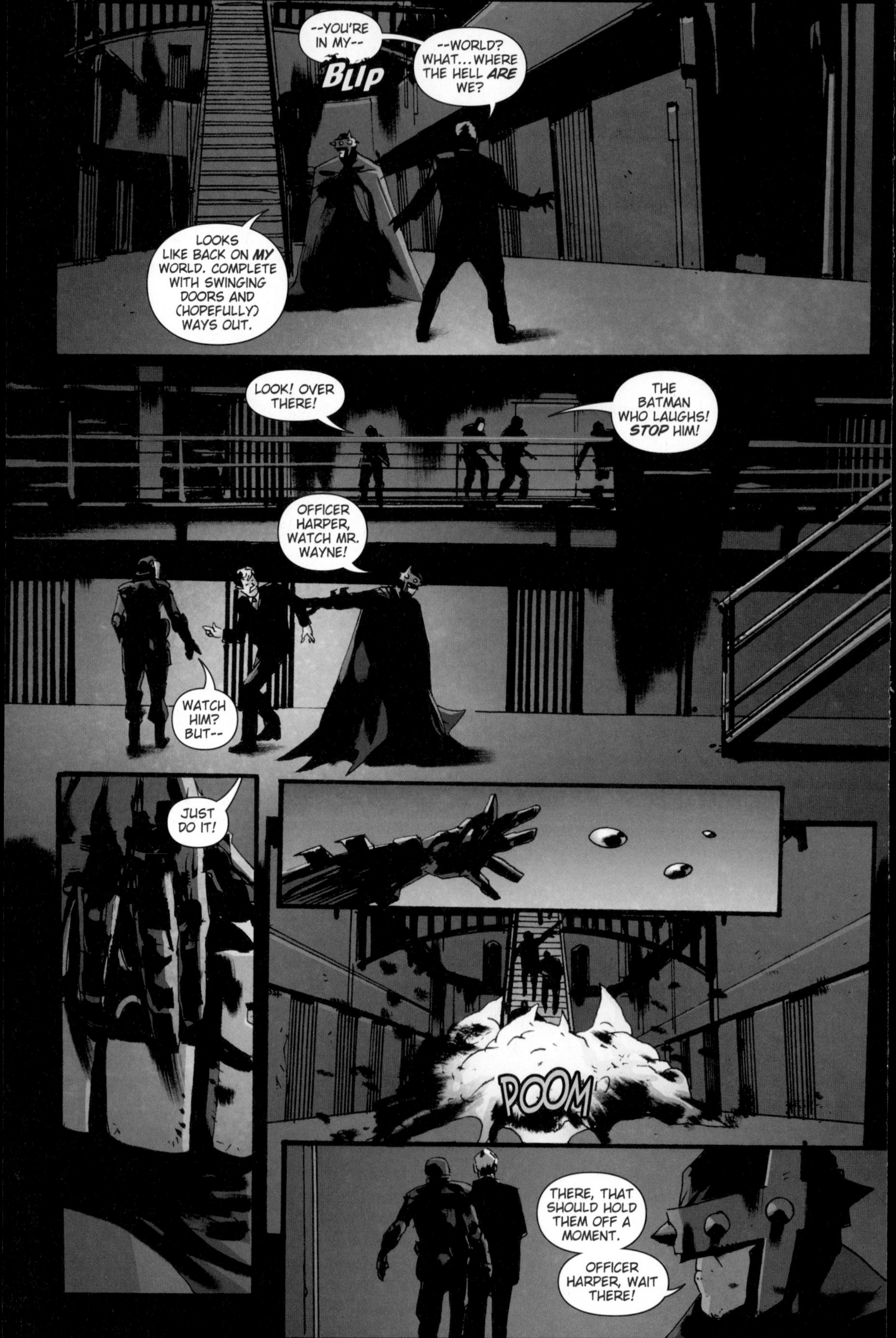

--YOU'RE IN MY--
BLIP
--WORLD? WHAT...WHERE THE HELL ARE WE?
LOOKS LIKE BACK ON MY WORLD. COMPLETE WITH SWINGING DOORS AND (HOPEFULLY) WAYS OUT.
LOOK! OVER THERE!
THE BATMAN WHO LAUGHS! STOP HIM!
OFFICER HARPER, WATCH MR. WAYNE!
WATCH HIM? BUT--
JUST DO IT!
POOM
THERE, THAT SHOULD HOLD THEM OFF A MOMENT.
OFFICER HARPER, WAIT THERE!

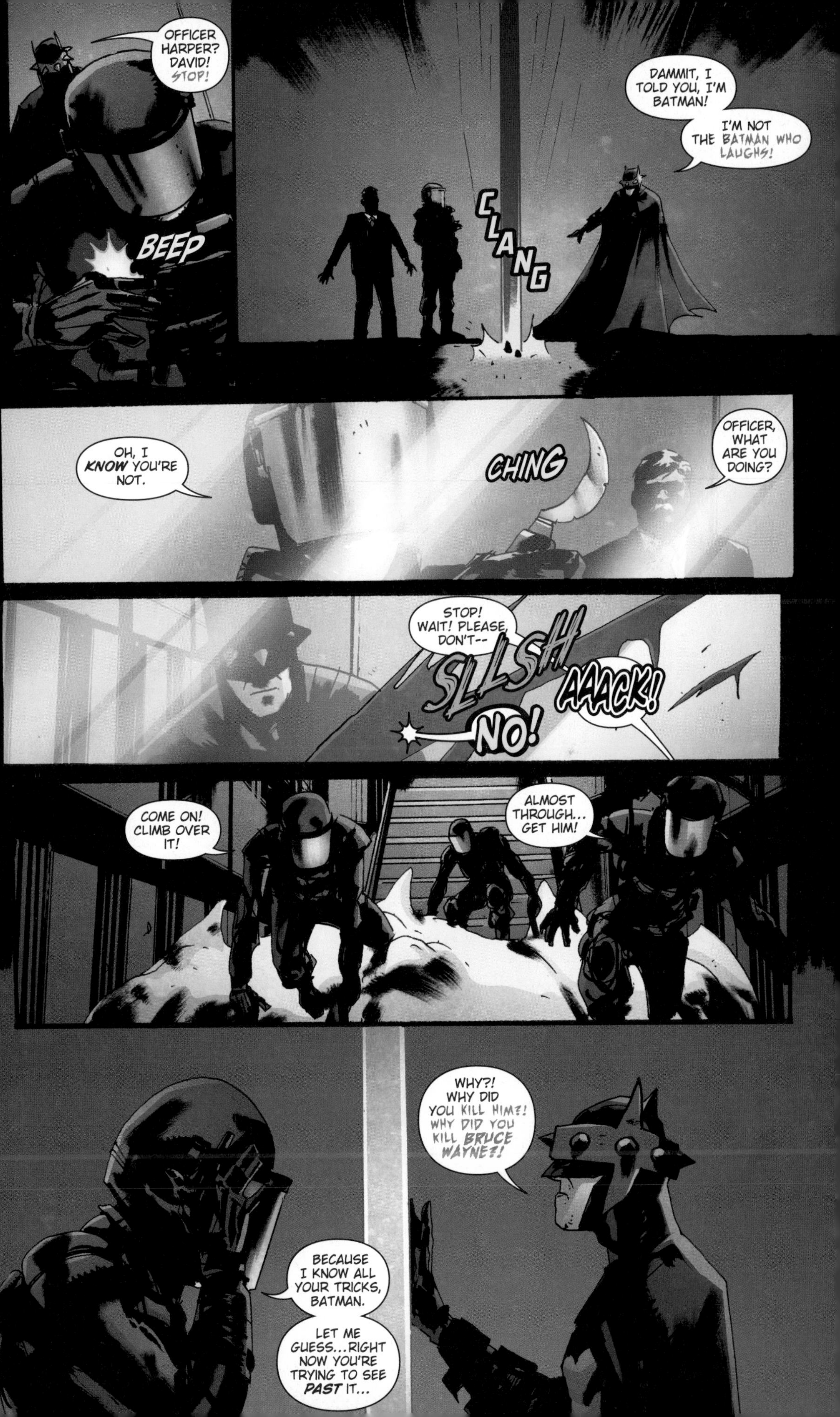
OFFICER HARPER? DAVID! STOP!
BEEP
DAMMIT, I TOLD YOU, I'M BATMAN!
I'M NOT THE BATMAN WHO LAUGHS!
CLANG
OH, I KNOW YOU'RE NOT.
CHING
OFFICER, WHAT ARE YOU DOING?
STOP! WAIT! PLEASE, DON'T--
SLLSH
AAACK!
NO!
COME ON! CLIMB OVER IT!
ALMOST THROUGH... GET HIM!
WHY?! WHY DID YOU KILL HIM?! WHY DID YOU KILL BRUCE WAYNE?!
BECAUSE I KNOW ALL YOUR TRICKS, BATMAN.
LET ME GUESS...RIGHT NOW YOU'RE TRYING TO SEE PAST IT...

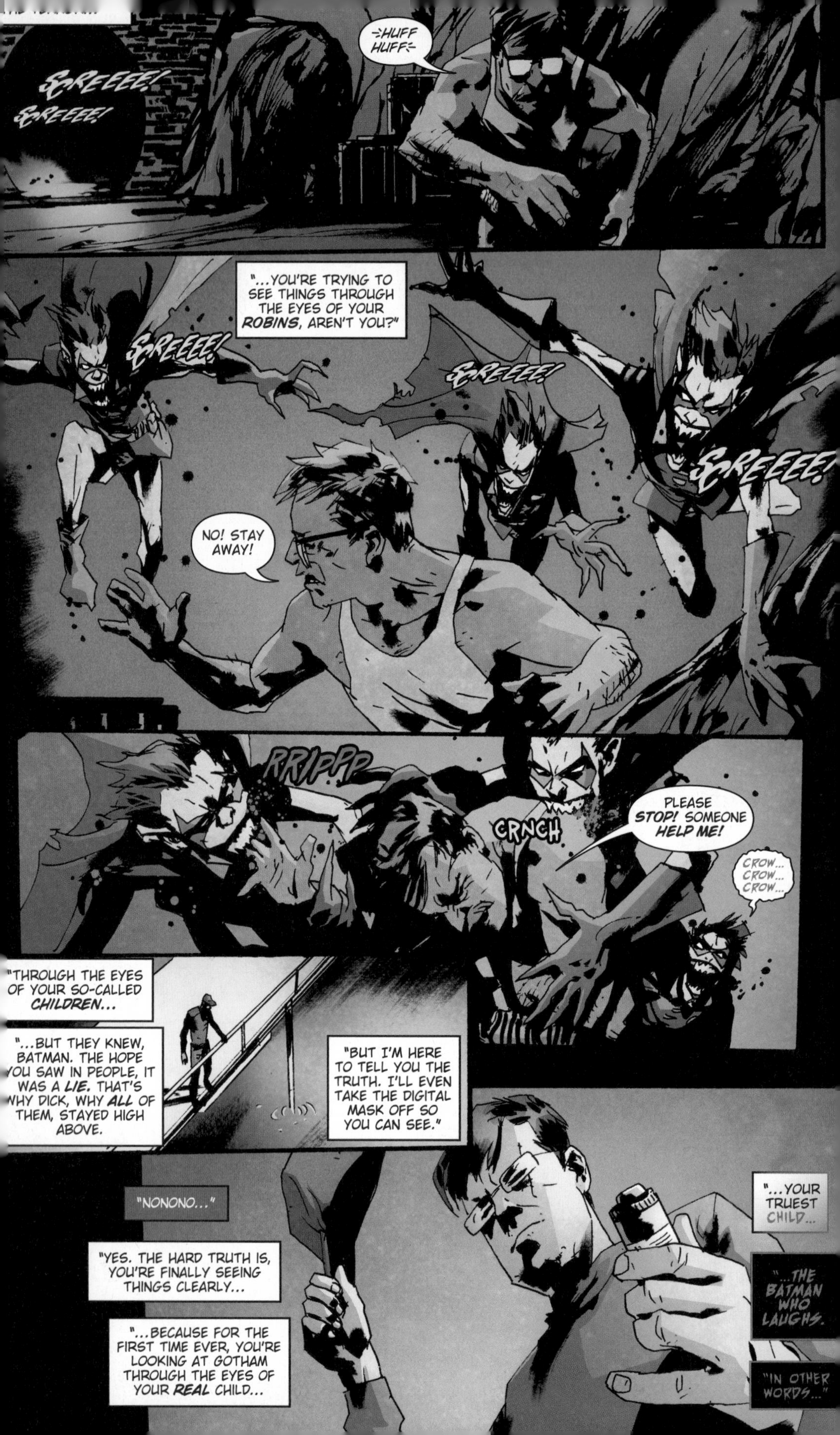

SCREEEE!
SCREEEE!
HUFF HUFF
"...YOU'RE TRYING TO SEE THINGS THROUGH THE EYES OF YOUR ROBINS, AREN'T YOU?"
SCREEEE!
SCREEEE!
SCREEEE!
NO! STAY AWAY!
RRIPPP
CRNCH
PLEASE STOP! SOMEONE HELP ME!
CROW... CROW... CROW...
"THROUGH THE EYES OF YOUR SO-CALLED CHILDREN...
"...BUT THEY KNEW, BATMAN. THE HOPE YOU SAW IN PEOPLE, IT WAS A LIE. THAT'S WHY DICK, WHY ALL OF THEM, STAYED HIGH ABOVE.
"BUT I'M HERE TO TELL YOU THE TRUTH. I'LL EVEN TAKE THE DIGITAL MASK OFF SO YOU CAN SEE."
"NONONO..."
"YES. THE HARD TRUTH IS, YOU'RE FINALLY SEEING THINGS CLEARLY...
"...BECAUSE FOR THE FIRST TIME EVER, YOU'RE LOOKING AT GOTHAM THROUGH THE EYES OF YOUR REAL CHILD...
"...YOUR TRUEST CHILD...
"...THE BATMAN WHO LAUGHS.
"IN OTHER WORDS..."

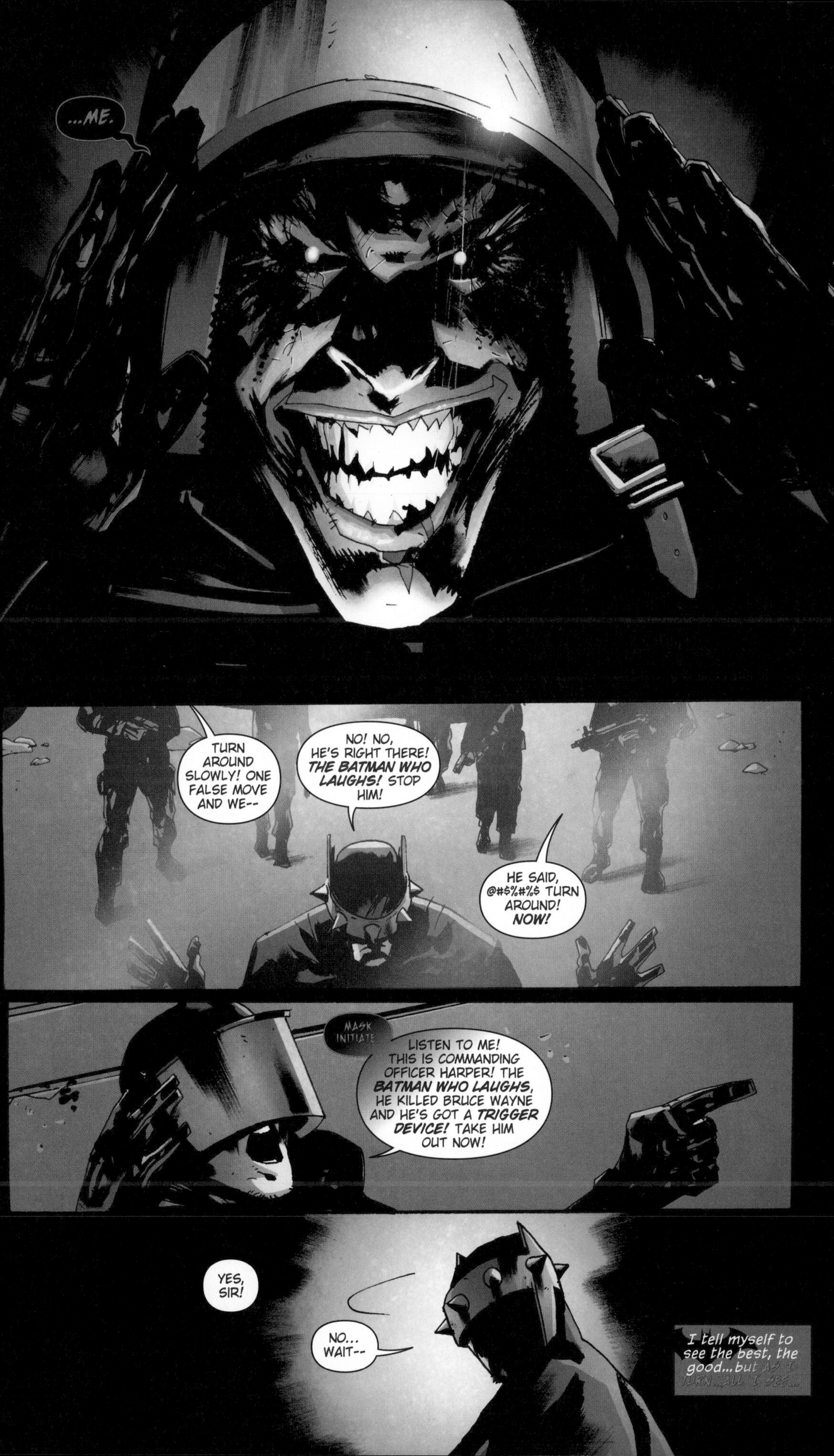
...ME.
TURN AROUND SLOWLY! ONE FALSE MOVE AND WE--
NO! NO, HE'S RIGHT THERE! **THE BATMAN WHO LAUGHS!** STOP HIM!
HE SAID, @#$%#%$ TURN AROUND! **NOW!**
MASK INITIATE
LISTEN TO ME! THIS IS COMMANDING OFFICER HARPER! THE **BATMAN WHO LAUGHS,** HE KILLED BRUCE WAYNE AND HE'S GOT A **TRIGGER DEVICE!** TAKE HIM OUT NOW!
YES, SIR!
NO... WAIT--
I tell myself to see the best, the good...but AS I TURN...ALL I SEE...

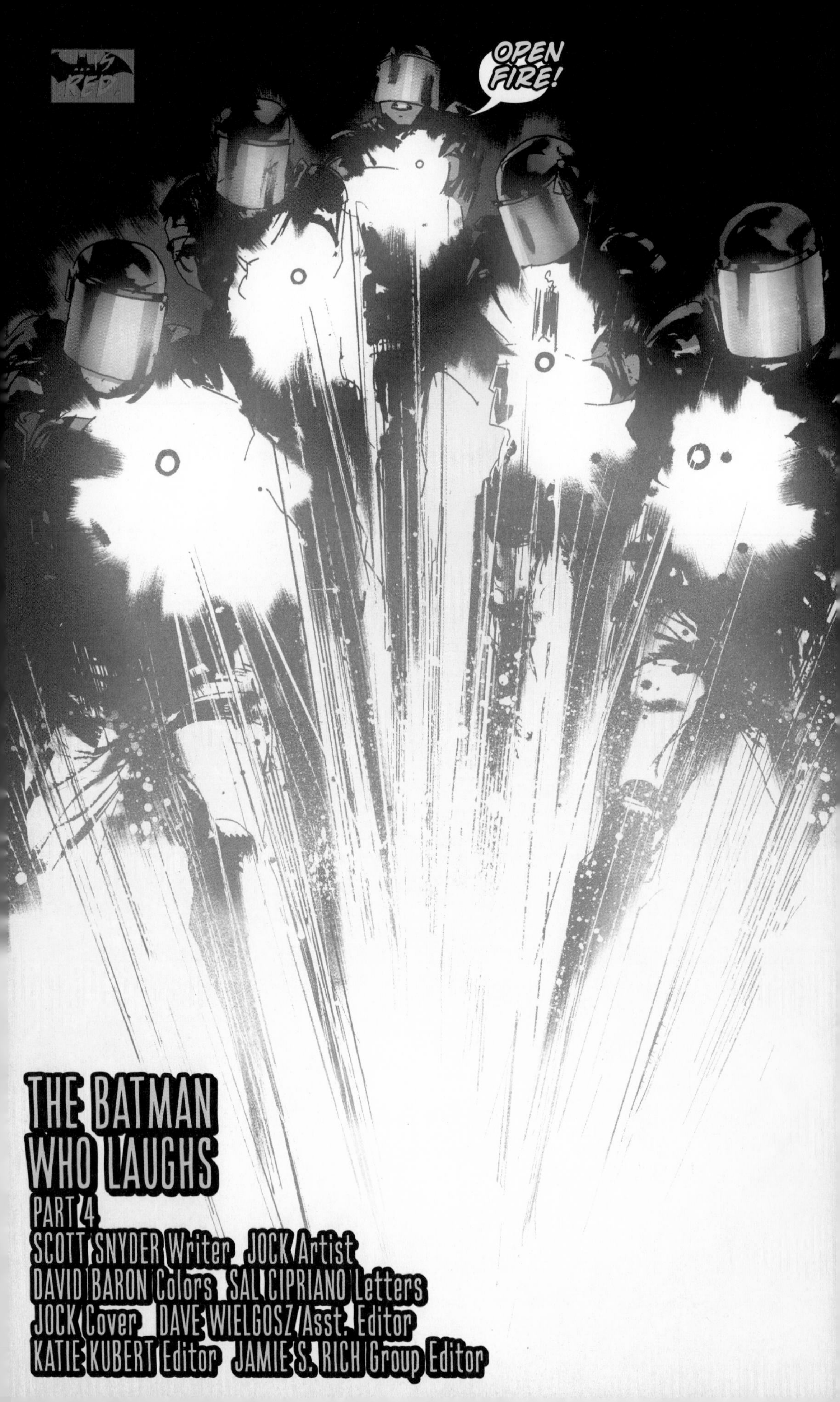
OPEN FIRE!
THE BATMAN WHO LAUGHS
PART 4
SCOTT SNYDER Writer JOCK Artist
DAVID BARON Colors SAL CIPRIANO Letters
JOCK Cover DAVE WIELGOSZ Asst. Editor
KATIE KUBERT Editor JAMIE S. RICH Group Editor

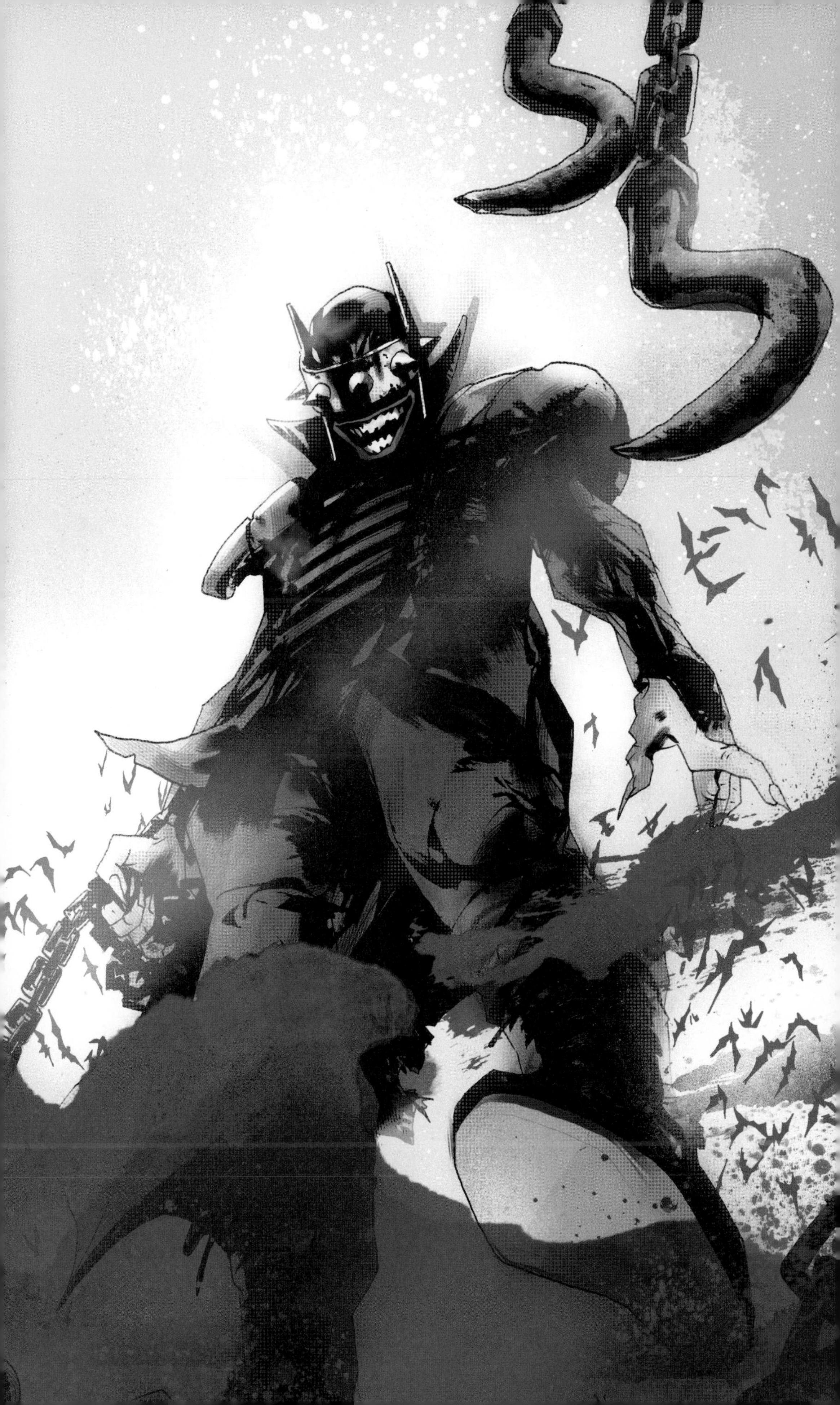

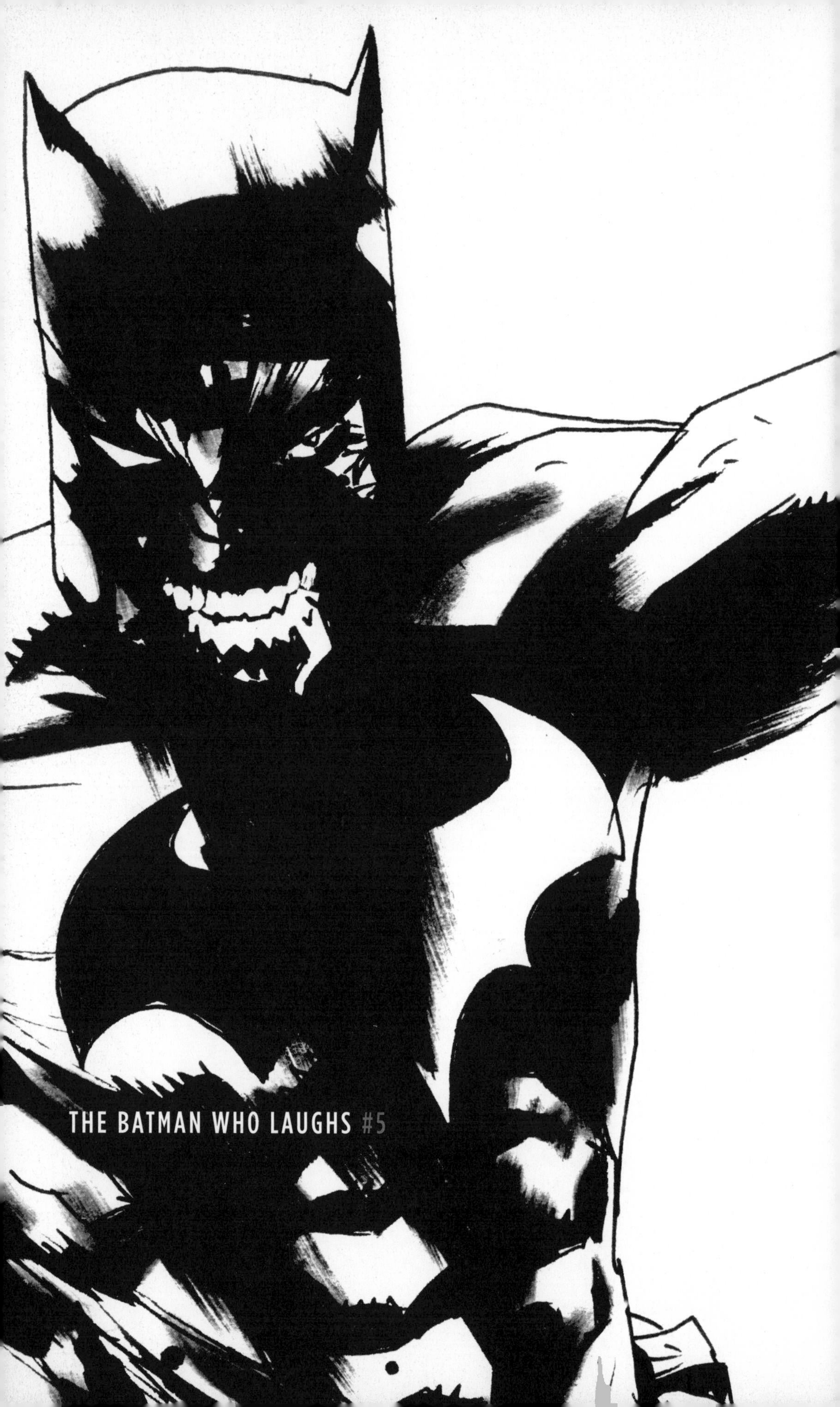
THE BATMAN WHO LAUGHS #5

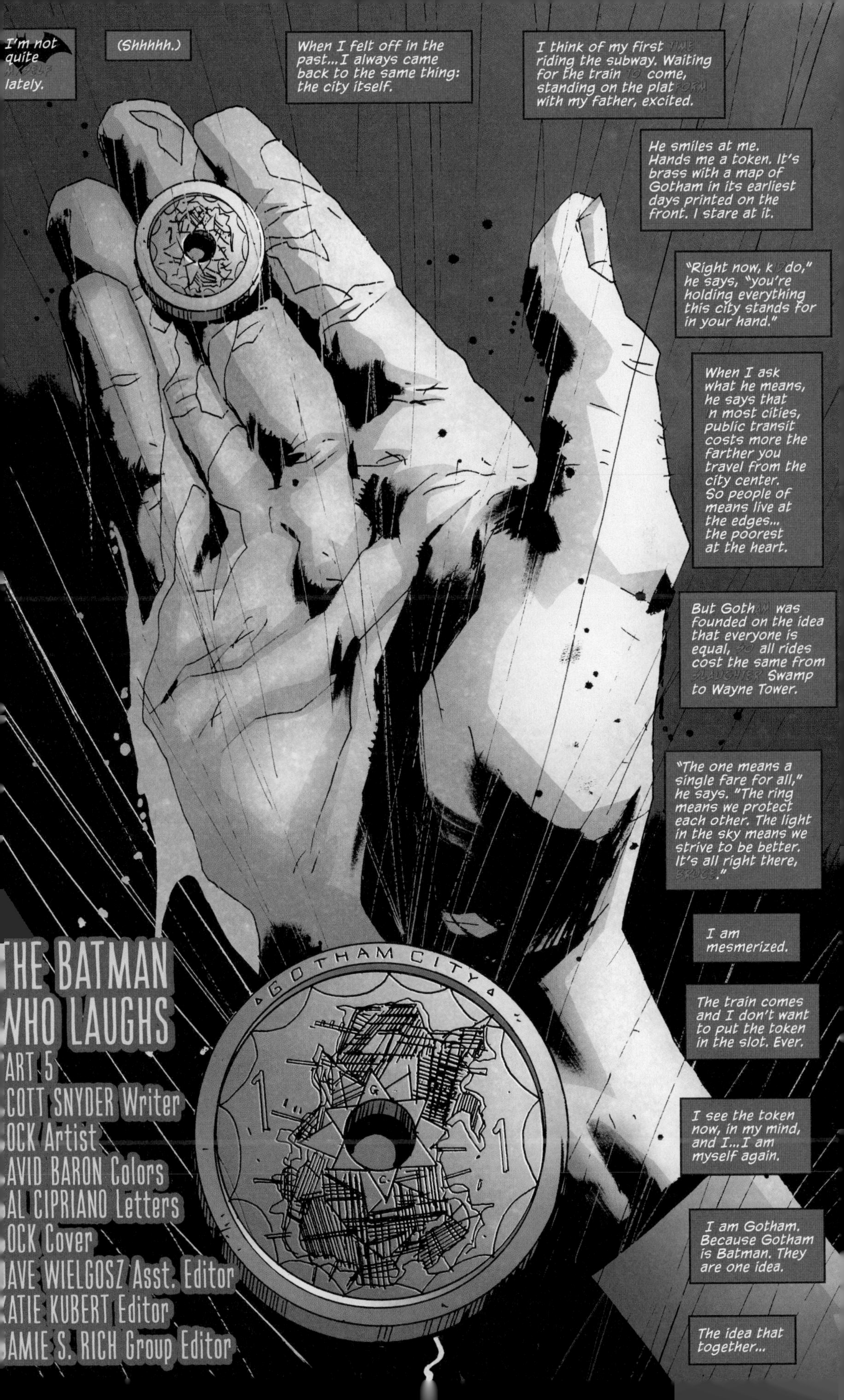

I'm not quite MYSELF lately.
(Shhhhh.)
When I felt off in the past...I always came back to the same thing: the city itself.
I think of my first TIME riding the subway. Waiting for the train TO come, standing on the platFORM with my father, excited.
He smiles at me. Hands me a token. It's brass with a map of Gotham in its earliest days printed on the front. I stare at it.
"Right now, kiddo," he says, "you're holding everything this city stands for in your hand."
When I ask what he means, he says that in most cities, public transit costs more the farther you travel from the city center. So people of means live at the edges... the poorest at the heart.
But GothAM was founded on the idea that everyone is equal, SO all rides cost the same from SLAUGHTER Swamp to Wayne Tower.
"The one means a single fare for all," he says. "The ring means we protect each other. The light in the sky means we strive to be better. It's all right there, BRUCE."
I am mesmerized.
The train comes and I don't want to put the token in the slot. Ever.
I see the token now, in my mind, and I...I am myself again.
I am Gotham. Because Gotham is Batman. They are one idea.
The idea that together...
GOTHAM CITY
1
1
HE BATMAN
WHO LAUGHS
ART 5
COTT SNYDER Writer
OCK Artist
AVID BARON Colors
AL CIPRIANO Letters
OCK Cover
AVE WIELGOSZ Asst. Editor
ATIE KUBERT Editor
AMIE S. RICH Group Editor

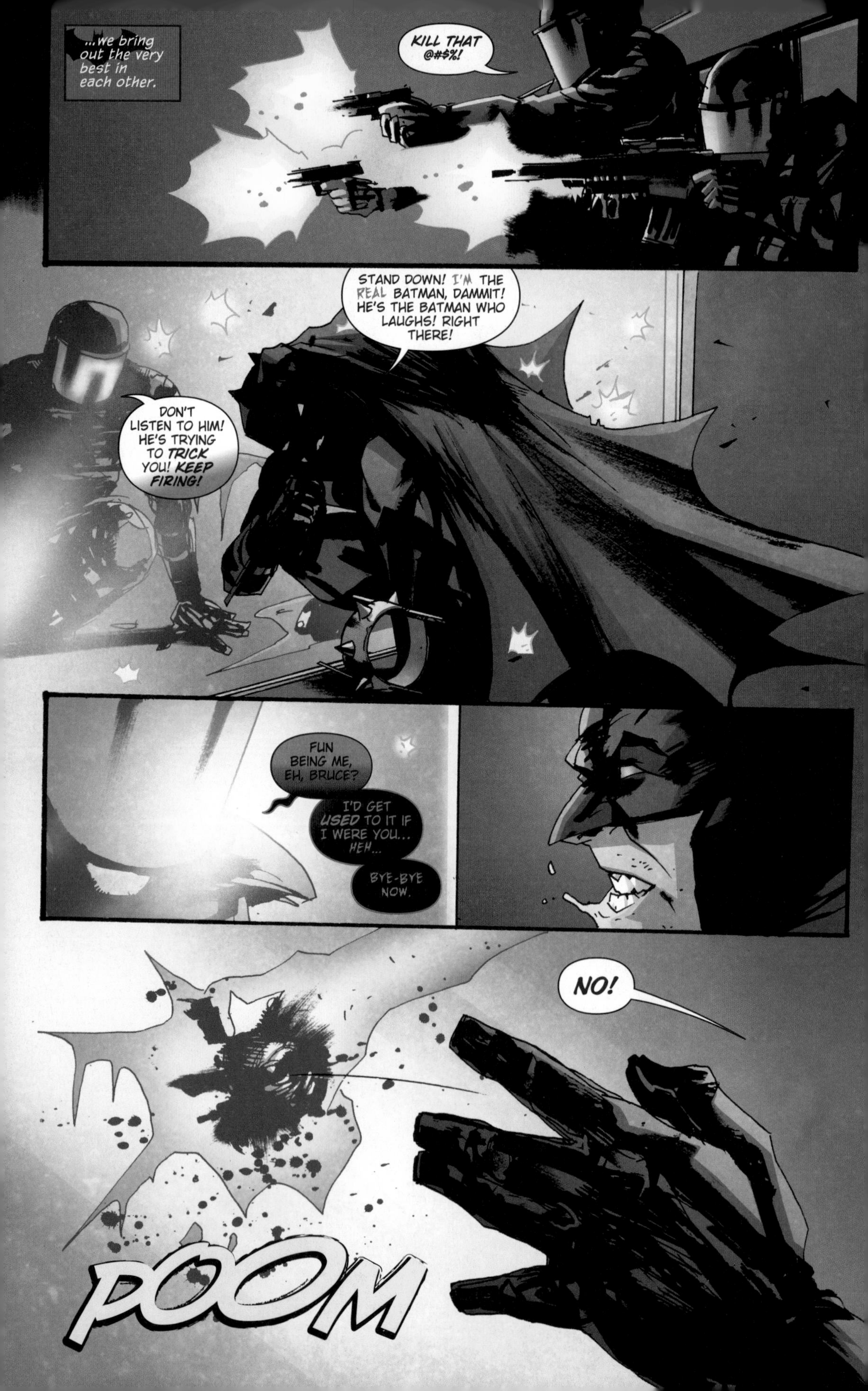
...we bring out the very best in each other.
KILL THAT @#$%!
STAND DOWN! I'M THE REAL BATMAN, DAMMIT! HE'S THE BATMAN WHO LAUGHS! RIGHT THERE!
DON'T LISTEN TO HIM! HE'S TRYING TO TRICK YOU! KEEP FIRING!
FUN BEING ME, EH, BRUCE?
I'D GET USED TO IT IF I WERE YOU... HEH...
BYE-BYE NOW.
NO!
POOM

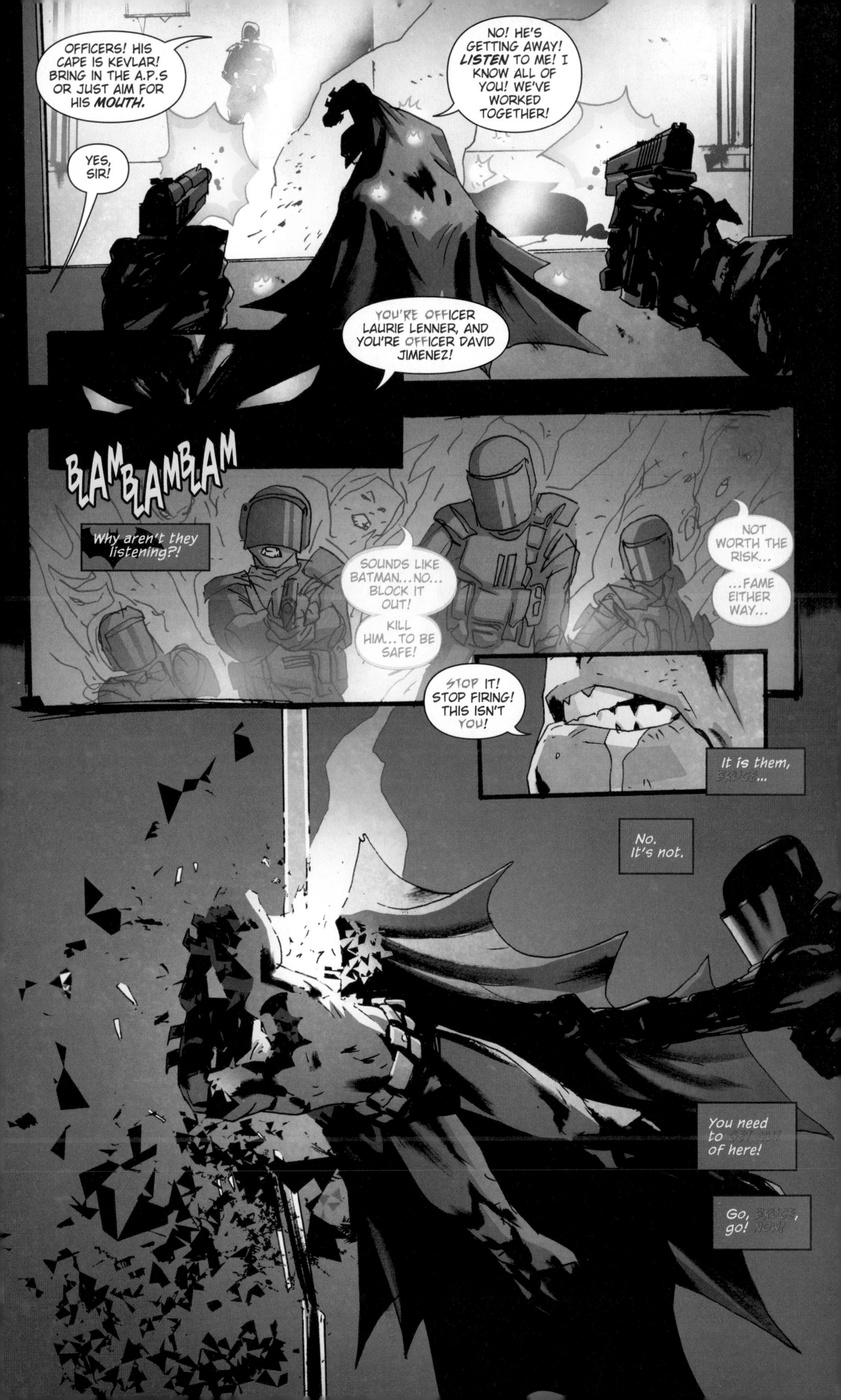
OFFICERS! HIS CAPE IS KEVLAR! BRING IN THE A.P.S OR JUST AIM FOR HIS MOUTH.
NO! HE'S GETTING AWAY! LISTEN TO ME! I KNOW ALL OF YOU! WE'VE WORKED TOGETHER!
YES, SIR!
YOU'RE OFFICER LAURIE LENNER, AND YOU'RE OFFICER DAVID JIMENEZ!
BLAMBLAMBLAM
Why aren't they listening?!
SOUNDS LIKE BATMAN... NO... BLOCK IT OUT!
KILL HIM... TO BE SAFE!
NOT WORTH THE RISK...
...FAME EITHER WAY...
STOP IT! STOP FIRING! THIS ISN'T YOU!
It is them, BRUCE...
No. It's not.
You need to GET OUT of here!
Go, BRUCE, go! NOW!

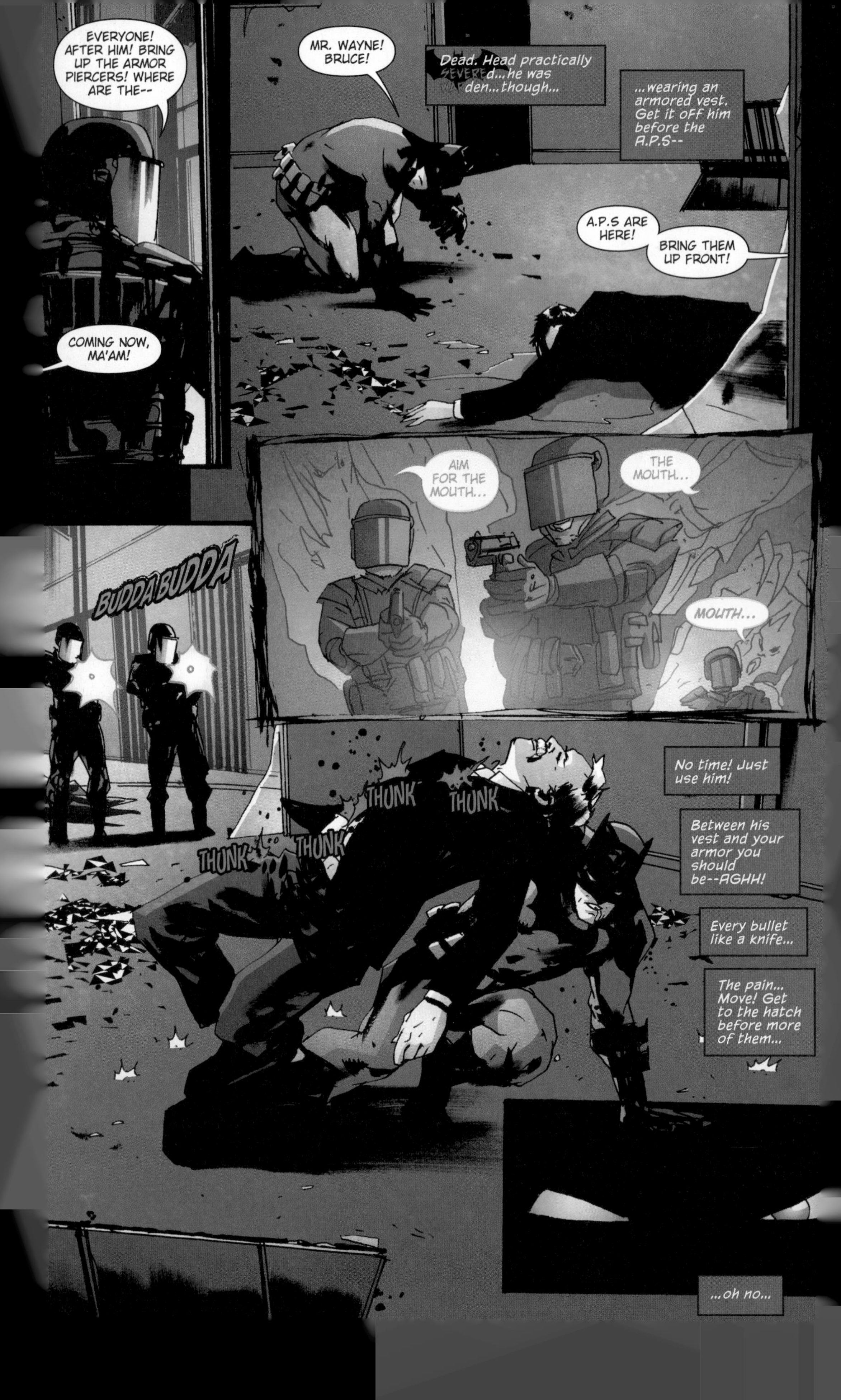
EVERYONE! AFTER HIM! BRING UP THE ARMOR PIERCERS! WHERE ARE THE--
MR. WAYNE! BRUCE!
Dead. Head practically SEVERED...he was WARden...though...
...wearing an armored vest. Get it off him before the A.P.S--
A.P.S ARE HERE!
BRING THEM UP FRONT!
COMING NOW, MA'AM!
AIM FOR THE MOUTH...
THE MOUTH...
MOUTH...
BUDDA BUDDA
THUNK
THUNK
THUNK
THUNK
No time! Just use him!
Between his vest and your armor you should be--AGHH!
Every bullet like a knife...
The pain... Move! Get to the hatch before more of them...
...oh no...

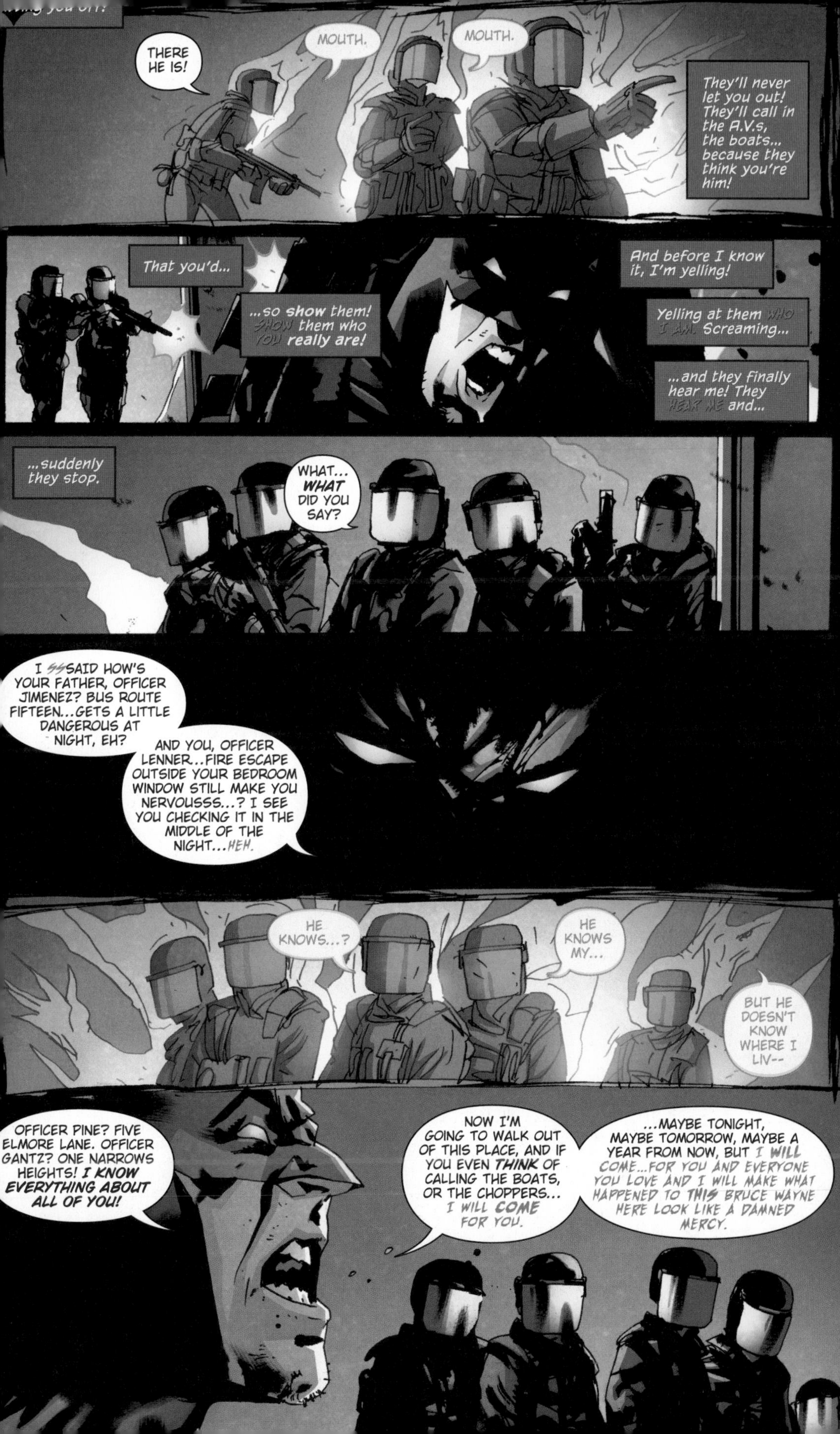
THERE HE IS!
MOUTH.
MOUTH.
They'll never let you out! They'll call in the A.V.s, the boats... because they think you're him!
That you'd...
...so show them! SHOW them who YOU really are!
And before I know it, I'm yelling!
Yelling at them WHO I AM. Screaming...
...and they finally hear me! They HEAR ME and...
...suddenly they stop.
WHAT... WHAT DID YOU SAY?
I SSSAID HOW'S YOUR FATHER, OFFICER JIMENEZ? BUS ROUTE FIFTEEN...GETS A LITTLE DANGEROUS AT NIGHT, EH?
AND YOU, OFFICER LENNER...FIRE ESCAPE OUTSIDE YOUR BEDROOM WINDOW STILL MAKE YOU NERVOUSSS...? I SEE YOU CHECKING IT IN THE MIDDLE OF THE NIGHT...HEH.
HE KNOWS...?
HE KNOWS MY...
BUT HE DOESN'T KNOW WHERE I LIV--
OFFICER PINE? FIVE ELMORE LANE. OFFICER GANTZ? ONE NARROWS HEIGHTS! I KNOW EVERYTHING ABOUT ALL OF YOU!
NOW I'M GOING TO WALK OUT OF THIS PLACE, AND IF YOU EVEN THINK OF CALLING THE BOATS, OR THE CHOPPERS... I WILL COME FOR YOU.
...MAYBE TONIGHT, MAYBE TOMORROW, MAYBE A YEAR FROM NOW, BUT I WILL COME...FOR YOU AND EVERYONE YOU LOVE AND I WILL MAKE WHAT HAPPENED TO THIS BRUCE WAYNE HERE LOOK LIKE A DAMNED MERCY.

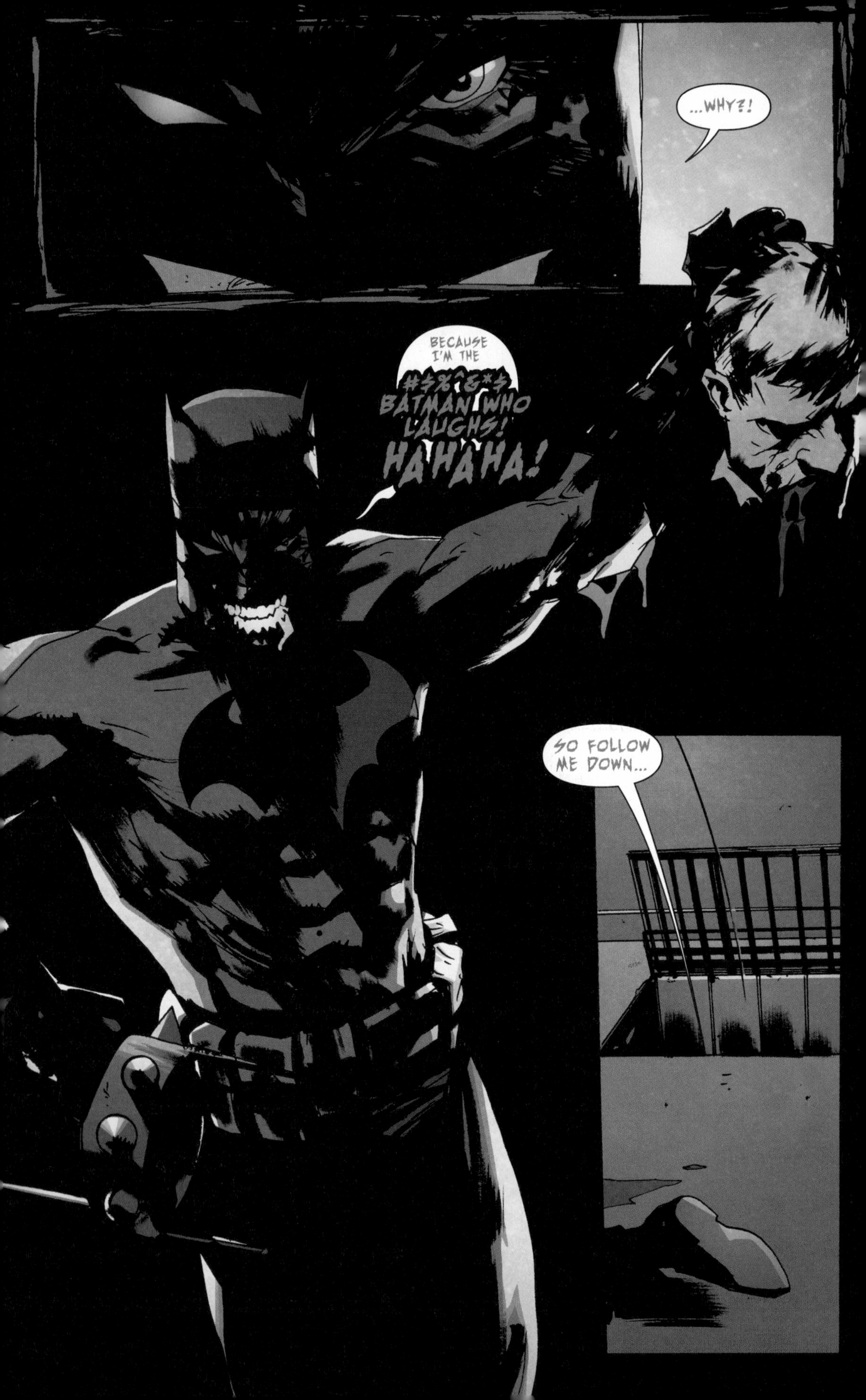
...WHY?!
BECAUSE I'M THE #$%^&*$ BATMAN WHO LAUGHS! HAHAHA!
SO FOLLOW ME DOWN...

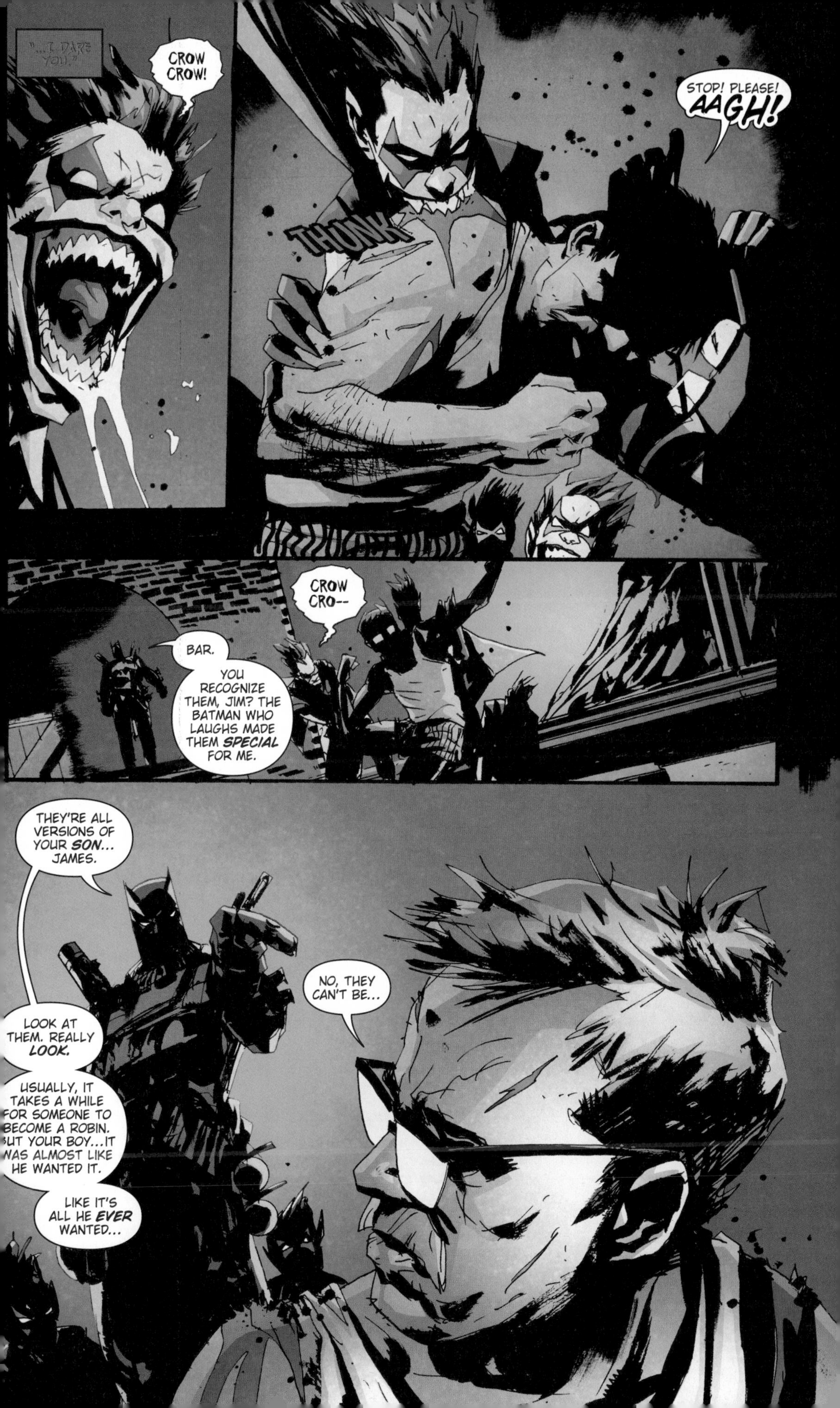
"...I DARE YOU."
CROW CROW!
STOP! PLEASE! AAGH!
THUNK
CROW CRO--
BAR.
YOU RECOGNIZE THEM, JIM? THE BATMAN WHO LAUGHS MADE THEM SPECIAL FOR ME.
THEY'RE ALL VERSIONS OF YOUR SON... JAMES.
LOOK AT THEM. REALLY LOOK.
USUALLY, IT TAKES A WHILE FOR SOMEONE TO BECOME A ROBIN. BUT YOUR BOY...IT WAS ALMOST LIKE HE WANTED IT.
LIKE IT'S ALL HE EVER WANTED...
NO, THEY CAN'T BE...

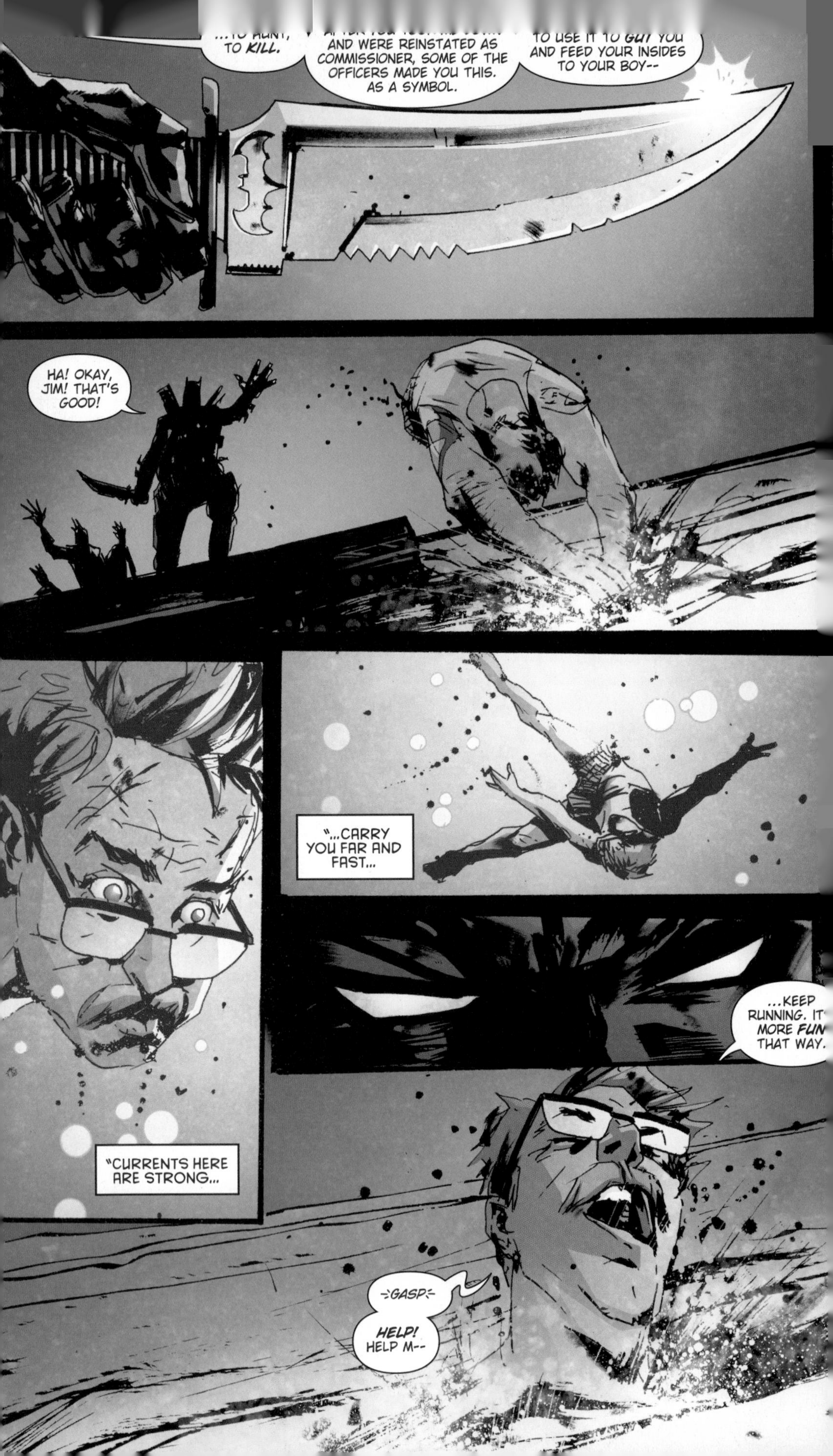

...TO HUNT, TO **KILL.**
AND WERE REINSTATED AS COMMISSIONER, SOME OF THE OFFICERS MADE YOU THIS. AS A SYMBOL.
TO USE IT TO **GUT** YOU AND FEED YOUR INSIDES TO YOUR BOY--
HA! OKAY, JIM! THAT'S GOOD!
"CURRENTS HERE ARE STRONG...
"...CARRY YOU FAR AND FAST...
...KEEP RUNNING. IT MORE **FUN** THAT WAY.
=GASP=
HELP! HELP M--

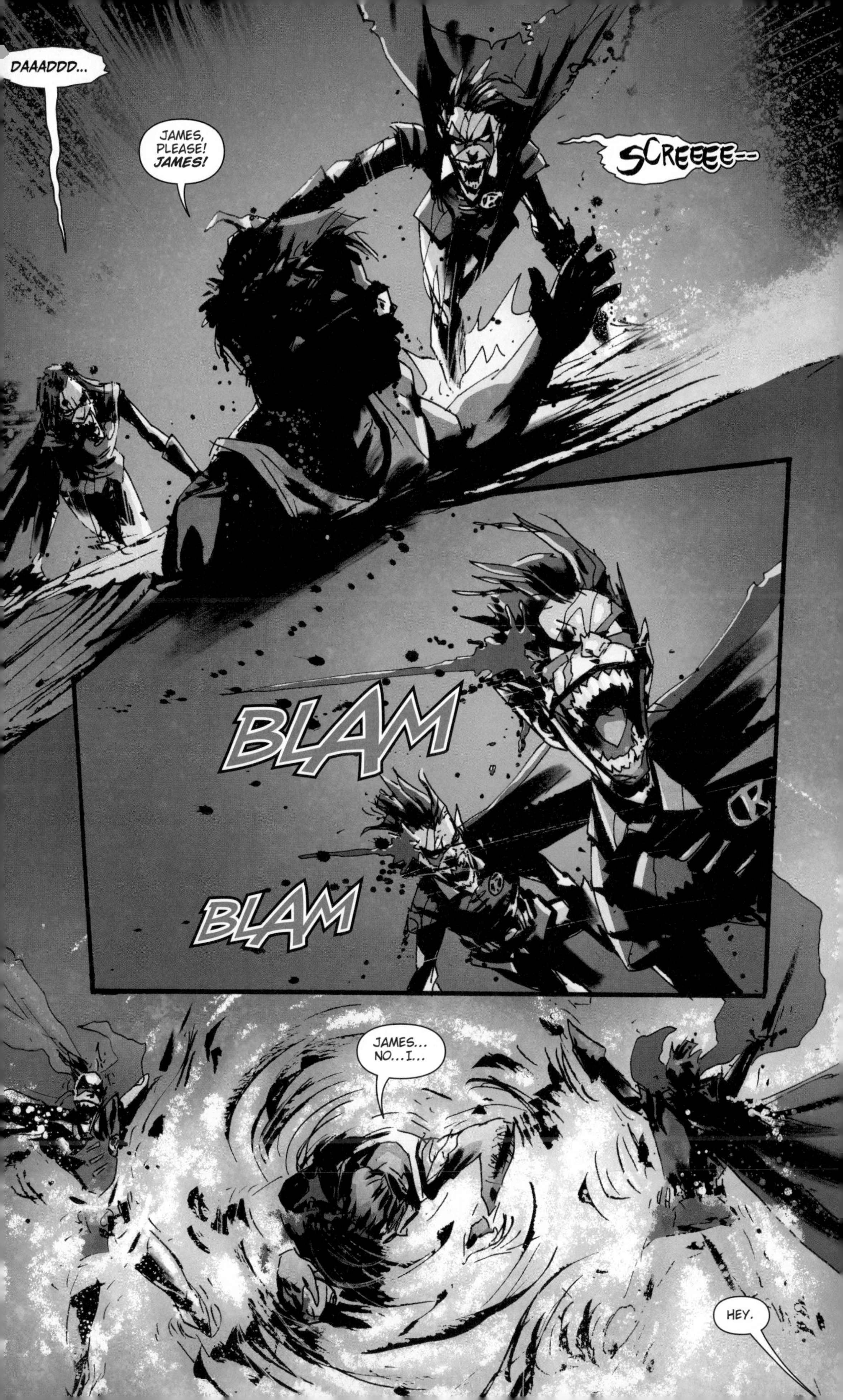
DAAADDD...
JAMES, PLEASE! JAMES!
SCREEEEE--
BLAM
BLAM
JAMES... NO... I...
HEY.

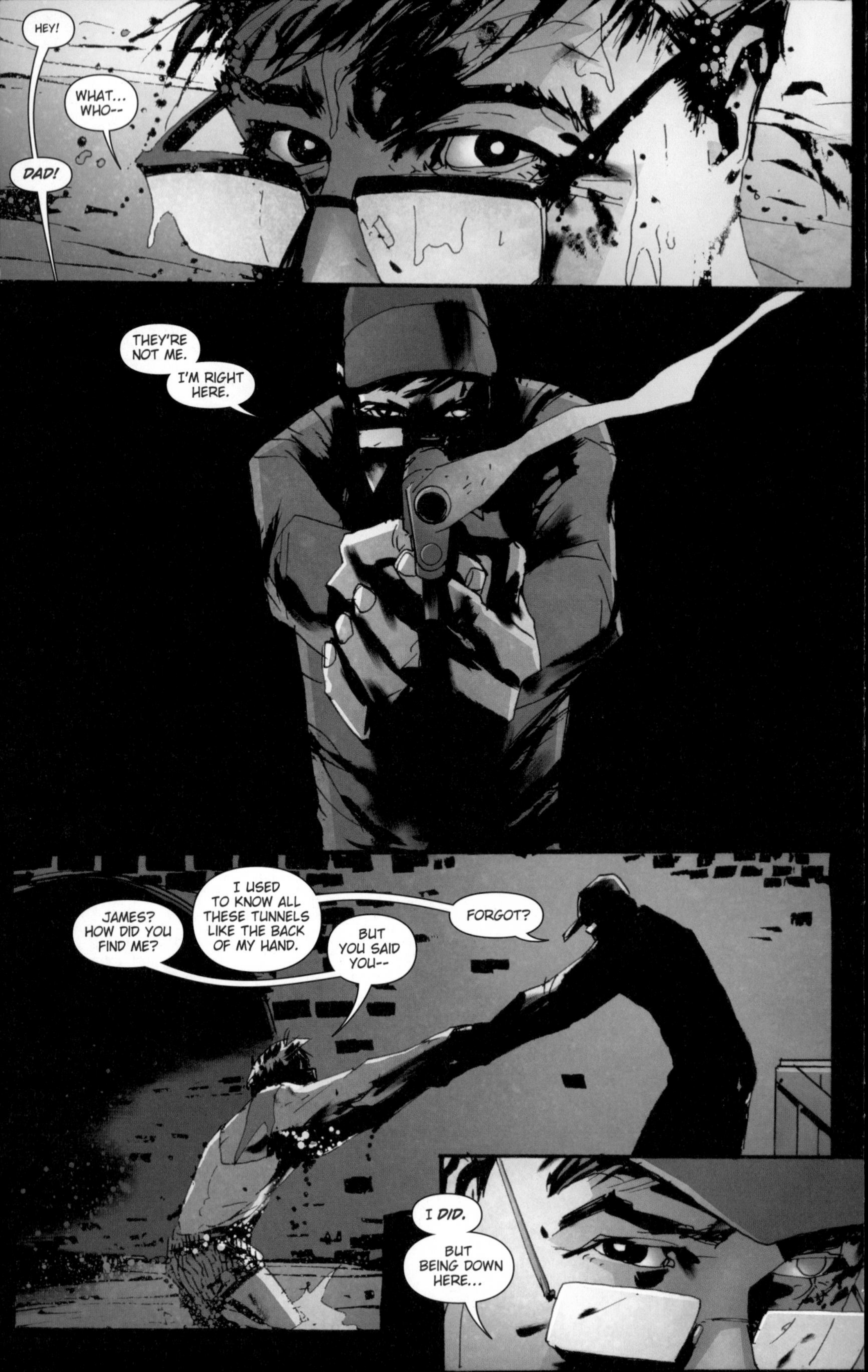
HEY!
WHAT... WHO--
DAD!
THEY'RE NOT ME.
I'M RIGHT HERE.
JAMES? HOW DID YOU FIND ME?
I USED TO KNOW ALL THESE TUNNELS LIKE THE BACK OF MY HAND.
BUT YOU SAID YOU--
FORGOT?
I *DID.*
BUT BEING DOWN HERE...

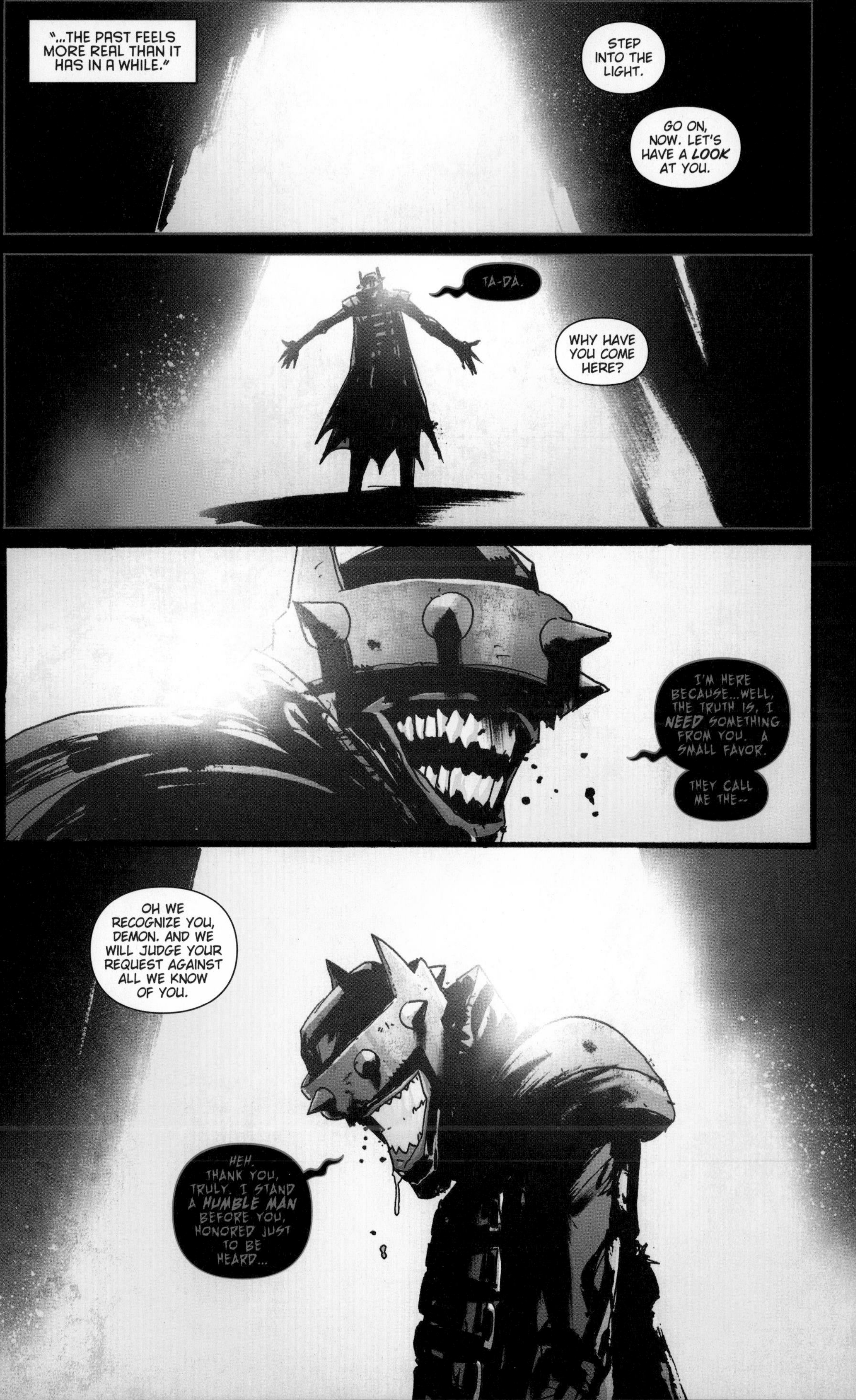
"...THE PAST FEELS MORE REAL THAN IT HAS IN A WHILE."
STEP INTO THE LIGHT.
GO ON, NOW. LET'S HAVE A LOOK AT YOU.
TA-DA.
WHY HAVE YOU COME HERE?
I'M HERE BECAUSE...WELL, THE TRUTH IS, I NEED SOMETHING FROM YOU. A SMALL FAVOR.
THEY CALL ME THE--
OH WE RECOGNIZE YOU, DEMON. AND WE WILL JUDGE YOUR REQUEST AGAINST ALL WE KNOW OF YOU.
HEH. THANK YOU, TRULY. I STAND A HUMBLE MAN BEFORE YOU, HONORED JUST TO BE HEARD...

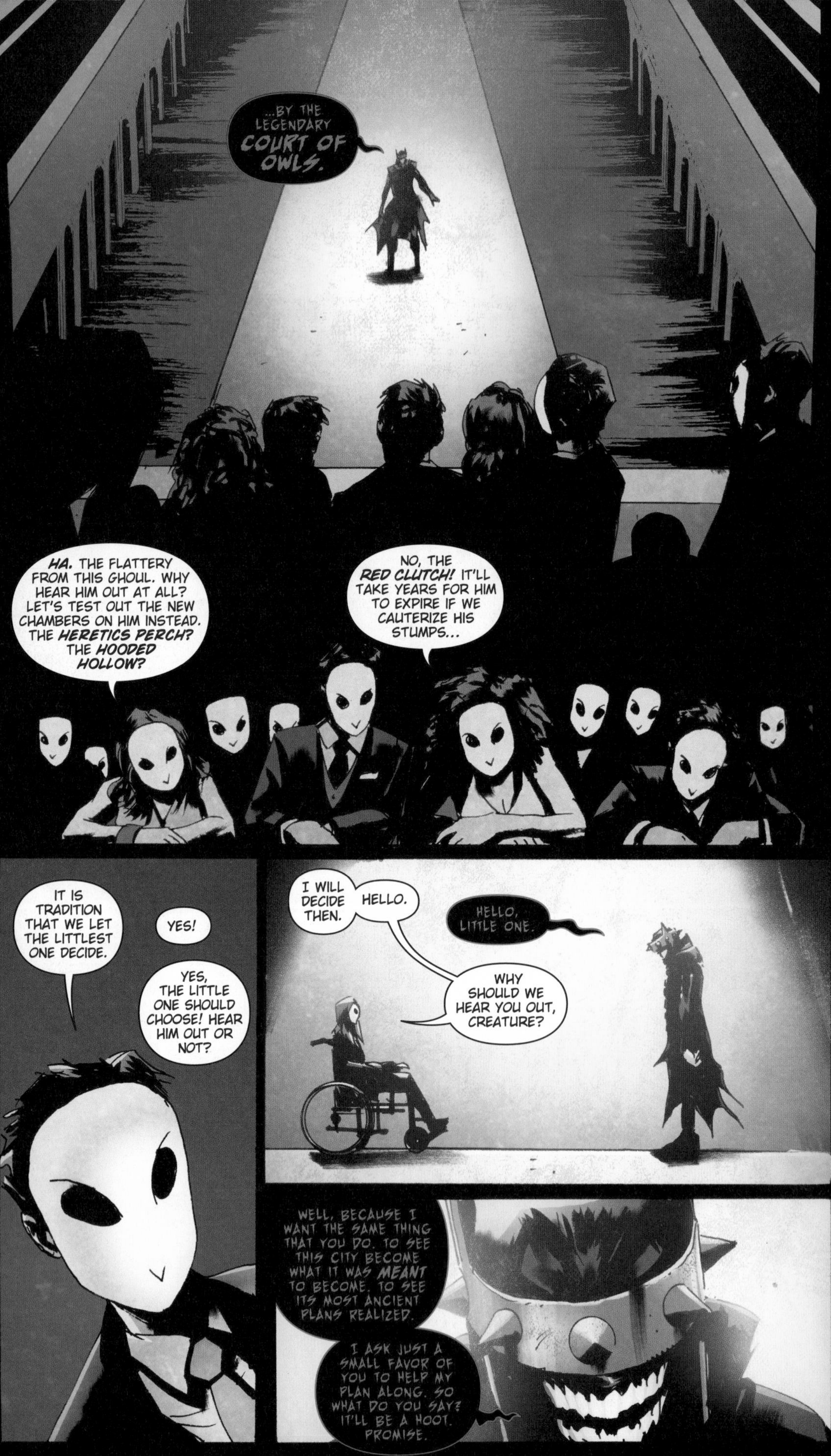
...BY THE LEGENDARY COURT OF OWLS.
HA. THE FLATTERY FROM THIS GHOUL. WHY HEAR HIM OUT AT ALL? LET'S TEST OUT THE NEW CHAMBERS ON HIM INSTEAD. THE HERETICS PERCH? THE HOODED HOLLOW?
NO, THE RED CLUTCH! IT'LL TAKE YEARS FOR HIM TO EXPIRE IF WE CAUTERIZE HIS STUMPS...
IT IS TRADITION THAT WE LET THE LITTLEST ONE DECIDE.
YES!
YES, THE LITTLE ONE SHOULD CHOOSE! HEAR HIM OUT OR NOT?
I WILL DECIDE THEN.
HELLO.
HELLO, LITTLE ONE.
WHY SHOULD WE HEAR YOU OUT, CREATURE?
WELL, BECAUSE I WANT THE SAME THING THAT YOU DO. TO SEE THIS CITY BECOME WHAT IT WAS MEANT TO BECOME. TO SEE ITS MOST ANCIENT PLANS REALIZED.
I ASK JUST A SMALL FAVOR OF YOU TO HELP MY PLAN ALONG. SO WHAT DO YOU SAY? IT'LL BE A HOOT. PROMISE.

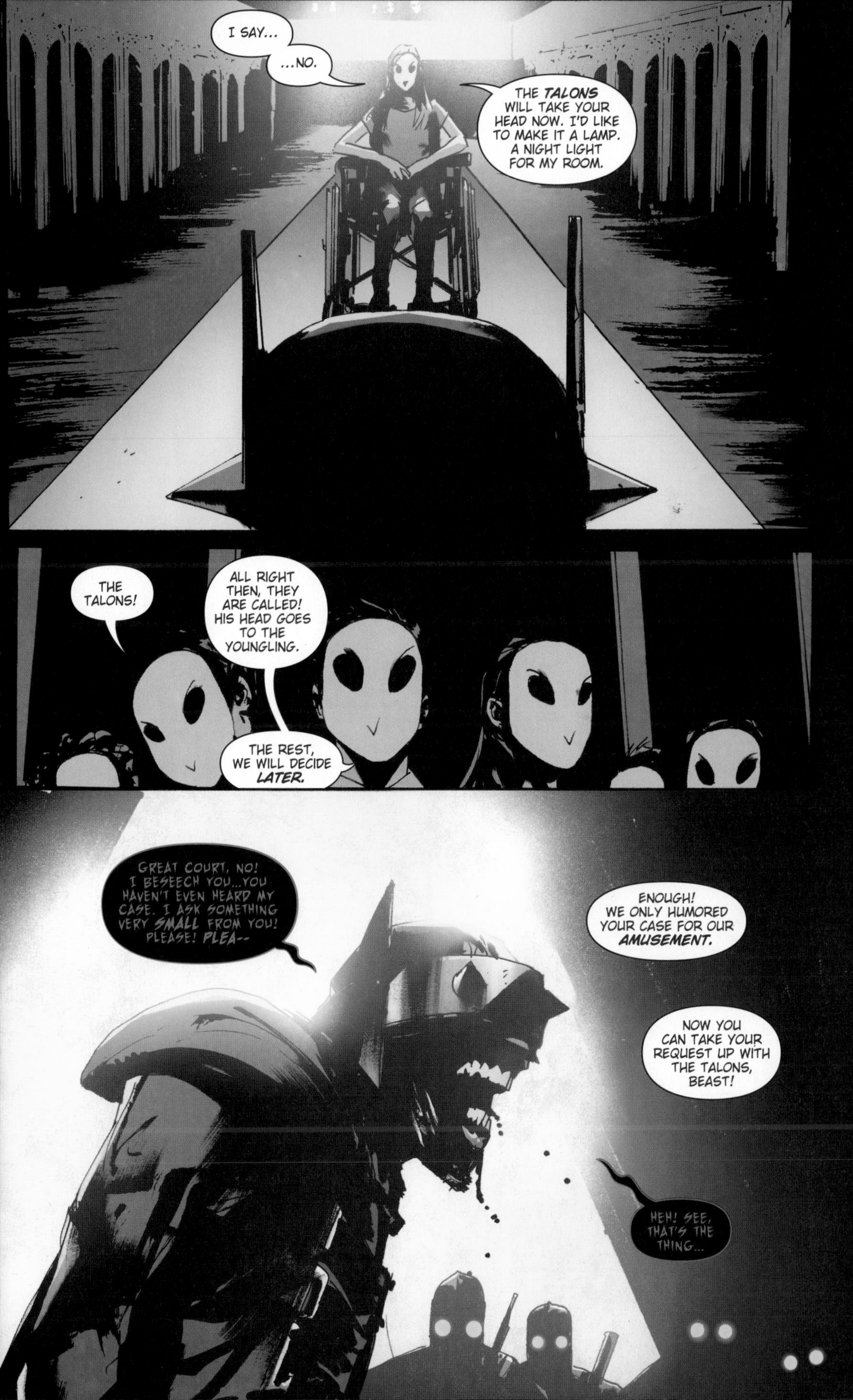
I SAY...
...NO.
THE TALONS WILL TAKE YOUR HEAD NOW. I'D LIKE TO MAKE IT A LAMP. A NIGHT LIGHT FOR MY ROOM.
THE TALONS!
ALL RIGHT THEN, THEY ARE CALLED! HIS HEAD GOES TO THE YOUNGLING.
THE REST, WE WILL DECIDE LATER.
GREAT COURT, NO! I BESEECH YOU...YOU HAVEN'T EVEN HEARD MY CASE. I ASK SOMETHING VERY SMALL FROM YOU! PLEASE! PLEA--
ENOUGH! WE ONLY HUMORED YOUR CASE FOR OUR AMUSEMENT.
NOW YOU CAN TAKE YOUR REQUEST UP WITH THE TALONS, BEAST!
HEH! SEE, THAT'S THE THING...

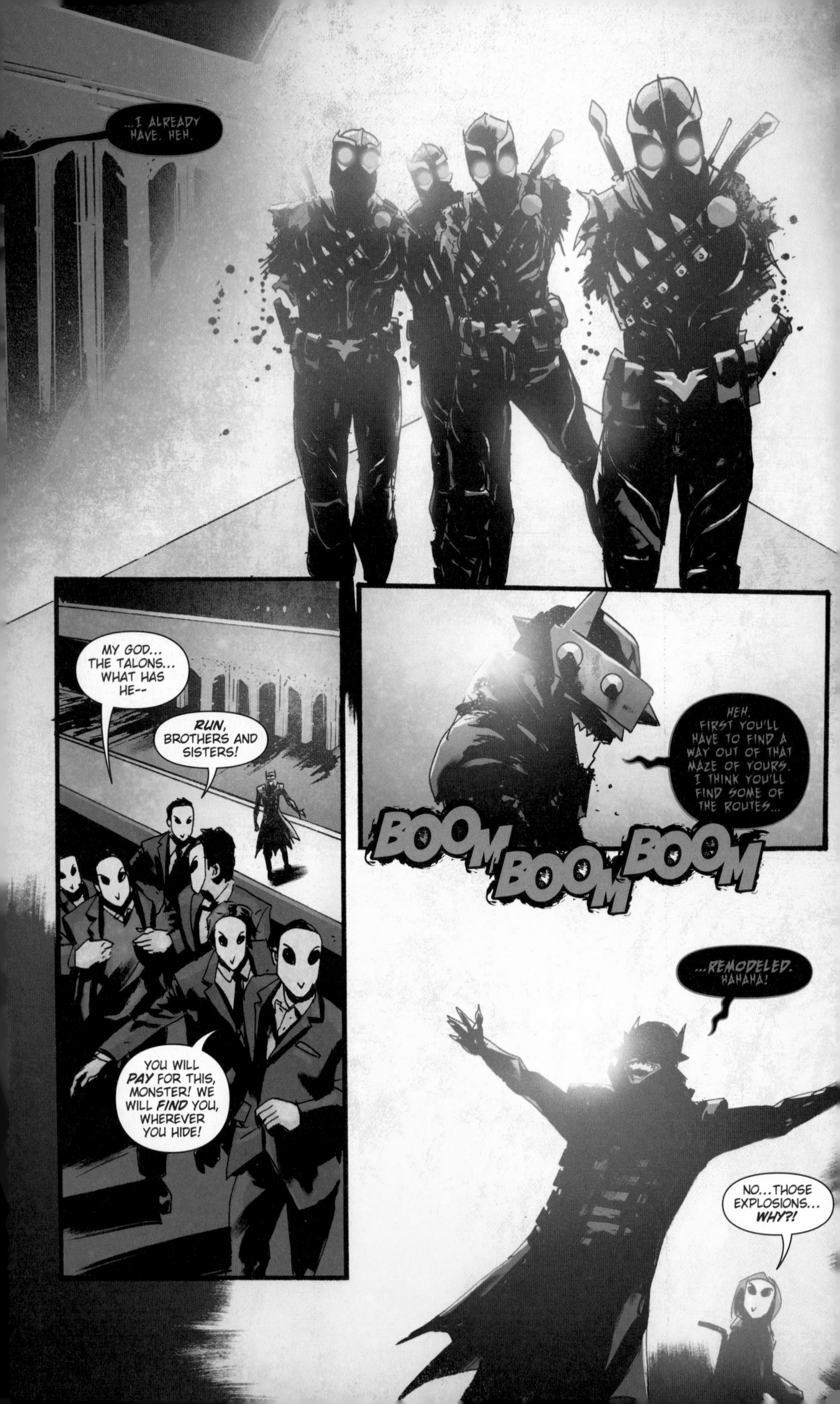
...I ALREADY HAVE. HEH.
MY GOD... THE TALONS... WHAT HAS HE--
RUN, BROTHERS AND SISTERS!
YOU WILL PAY FOR THIS, MONSTER! WE WILL FIND YOU, WHEREVER YOU HIDE!
HEH. FIRST YOU'LL HAVE TO FIND A WAY OUT OF THAT MAZE OF YOURS. I THINK YOU'LL FIND SOME OF THE ROUTES...
BOOM BOOM BOOM
...REMODELED. HAHAHA!
NO...THOSE EXPLOSIONS... WHY?!

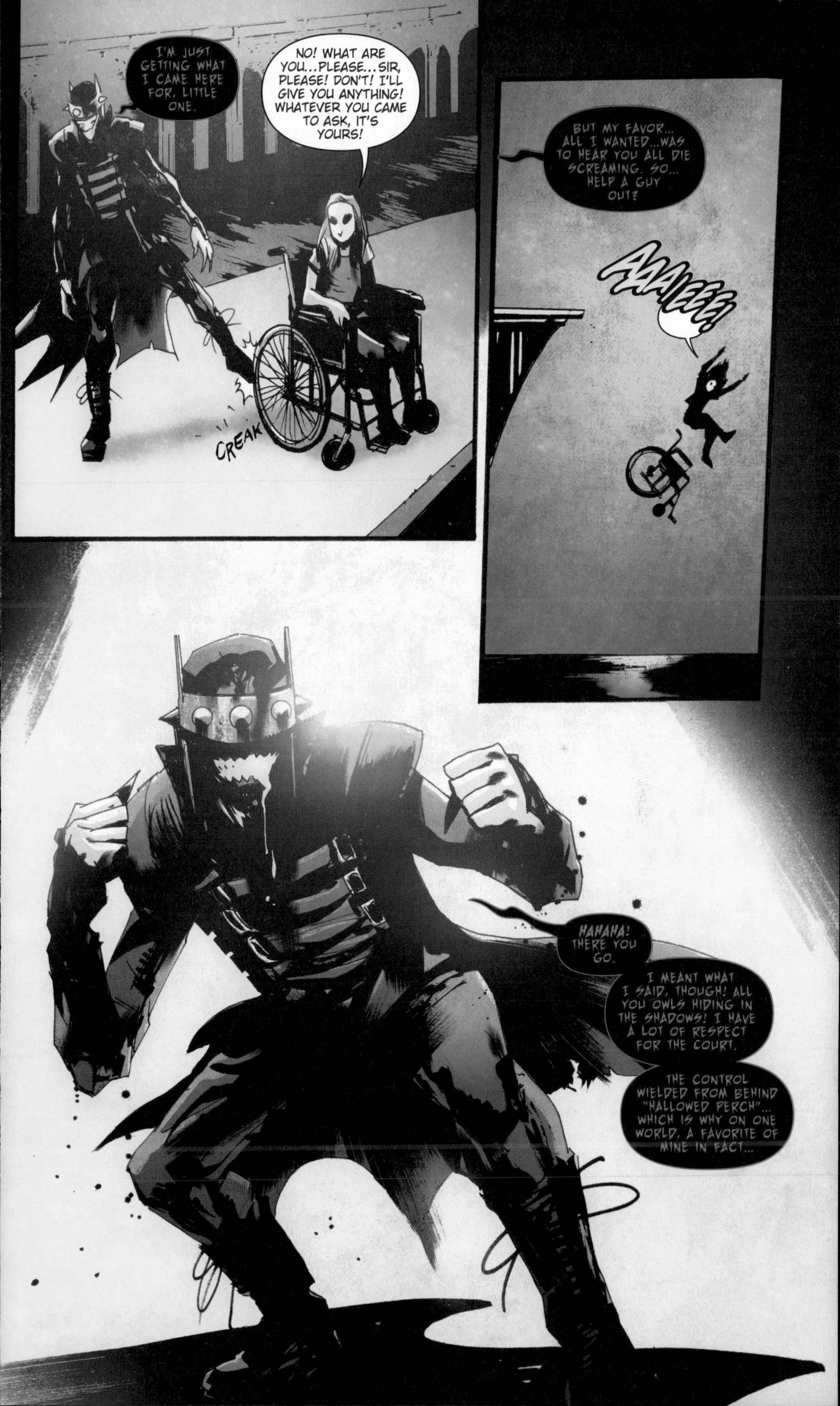
I'M JUST GETTING WHAT I CAME HERE FOR, LITTLE ONE.
NO! WHAT ARE YOU...PLEASE...SIR, PLEASE! DON'T! I'LL GIVE YOU ANYTHING! WHATEVER YOU CAME TO ASK, IT'S YOURS!
CREAK
BUT MY FAVOR... ALL I WANTED...WAS TO HEAR YOU ALL DIE SCREAMING. SO... HELP A GUY OUT?
AAAIEEE!
HAHAHA! THERE YOU GO.
I MEANT WHAT I SAID, THOUGH! ALL YOU OWLS HIDING IN THE SHADOWS! I HAVE A LOT OF RESPECT FOR THE COURT.
THE CONTROL WIELDED FROM BEHIND "HALLOWED PERCH"... WHICH IS WHY ON ONE WORLD, A FAVORITE OF MINE IN FACT...

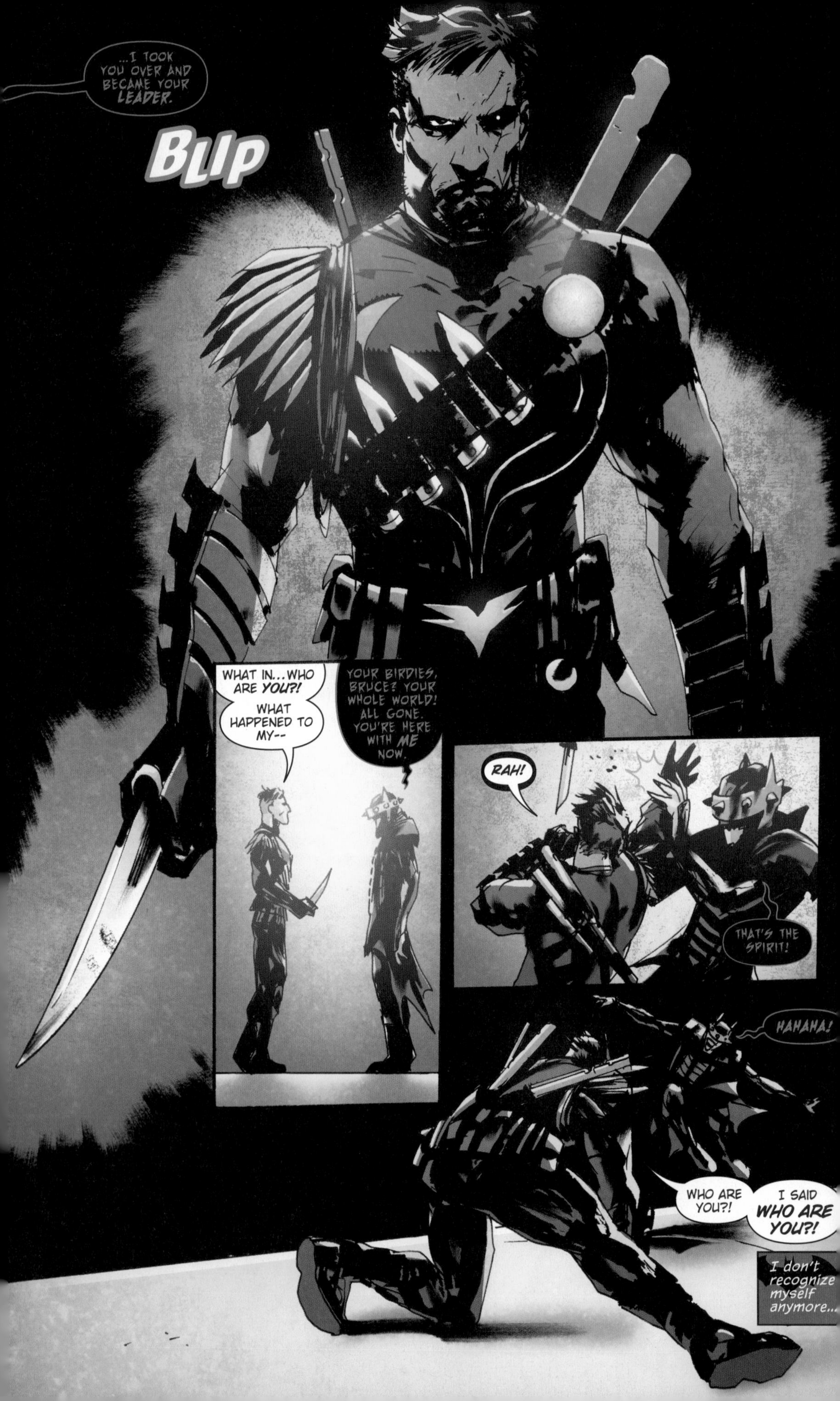

...I TOOK YOU OVER AND BECAME YOUR LEADER.
BLIP
WHAT IN...WHO ARE YOU?!
WHAT HAPPENED TO MY--
YOUR BIRDIES, BRUCE? YOUR WHOLE WORLD! ALL GONE. YOU'RE HERE WITH ME NOW.
RAH!
THAT'S THE SPIRIT!
HAHAHA!
WHO ARE YOU?!
I SAID WHO ARE YOU?!
I don't recognize myself anymore...

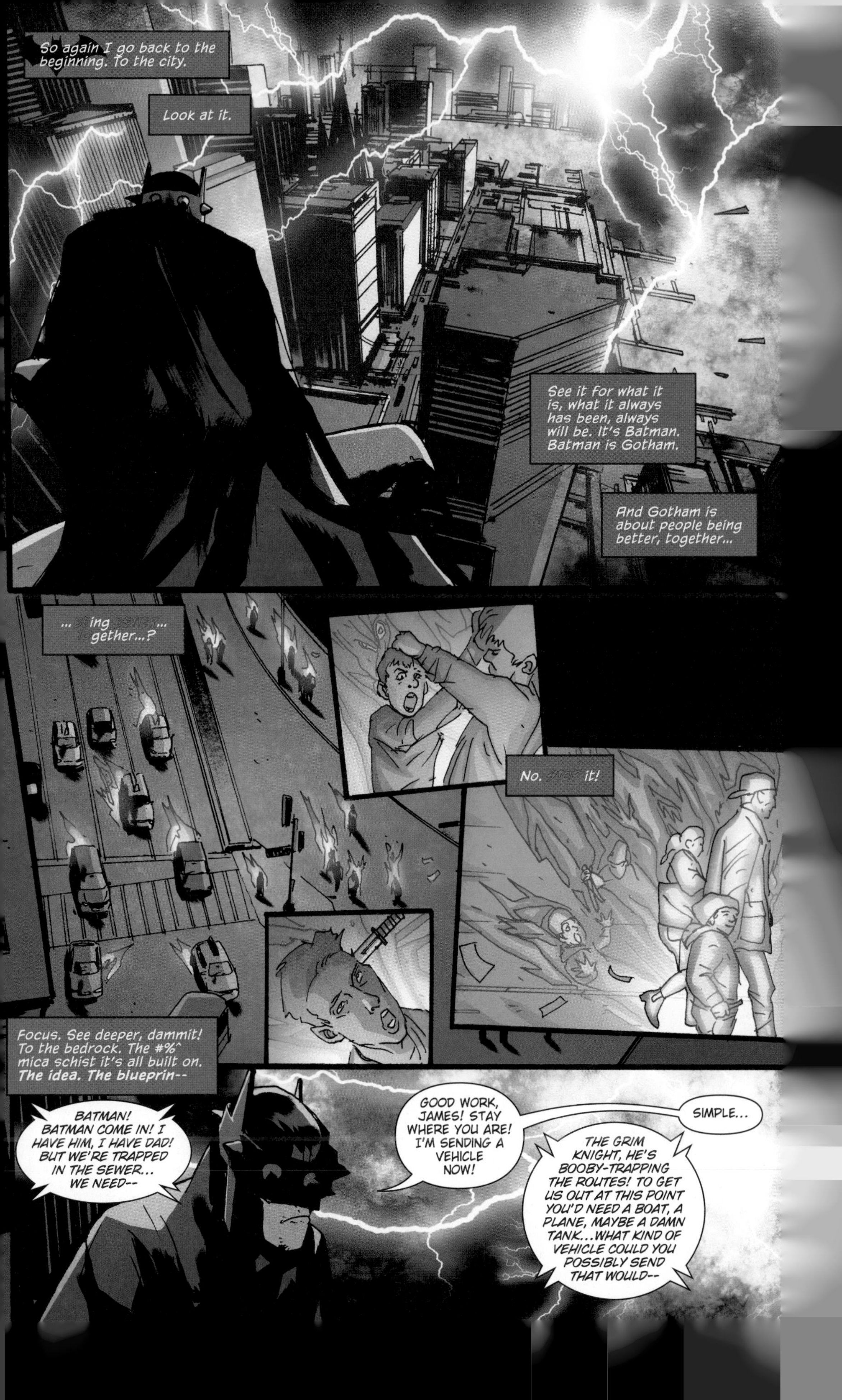
So again I go back to the beginning. To the city.
Look at it.
See it for what it is, what it always has been, always will be. It's Batman. Batman is Gotham.
And Gotham is about people being better, together...
...BEing BETTER... TOgether...?
No. STOP it!
Focus. See deeper, dammit! To the bedrock. The #%^ mica schist it's all built on. The idea. The blueprin--
BATMAN! BATMAN COME IN! I HAVE HIM, I HAVE DAD! BUT WE'RE TRAPPED IN THE SEWER... WE NEED--
GOOD WORK, JAMES! STAY WHERE YOU ARE! I'M SENDING A VEHICLE NOW!
THE GRIM KNIGHT, HE'S BOOBY-TRAPPING THE ROUTES! TO GET US OUT AT THIS POINT YOU'D NEED A BOAT, A PLANE, MAYBE A DAMN TANK...WHAT KIND OF VEHICLE COULD YOU POSSIBLY SEND THAT WOULD--
SIMPLE...

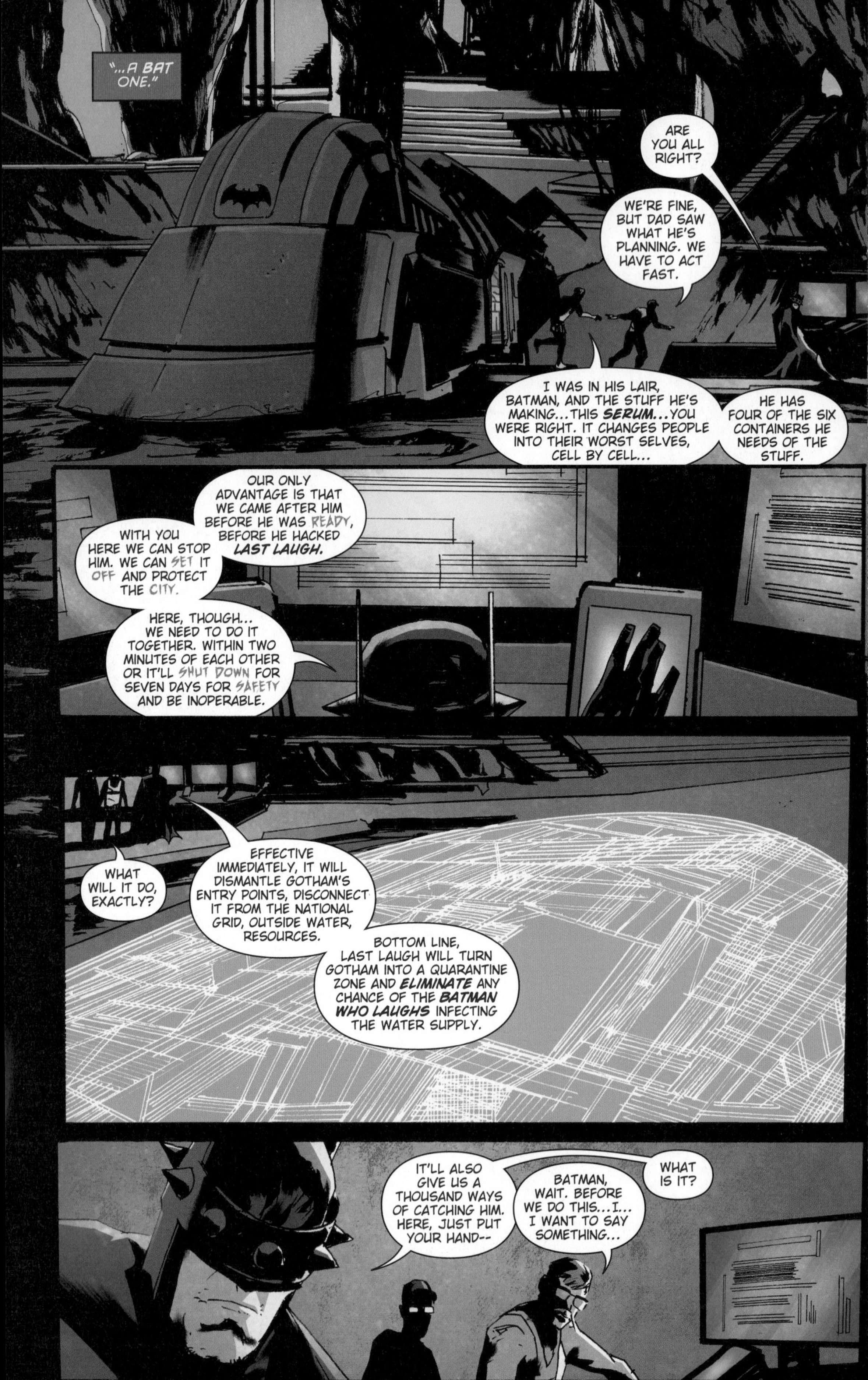
"...A BAT ONE."
ARE YOU ALL RIGHT?
WE'RE FINE, BUT DAD SAW WHAT HE'S PLANNING. WE HAVE TO ACT FAST.
I WAS IN HIS LAIR, BATMAN, AND THE STUFF HE'S MAKING...THIS SERUM...YOU WERE RIGHT. IT CHANGES PEOPLE INTO THEIR WORST SELVES, CELL BY CELL...
HE HAS FOUR OF THE SIX CONTAINERS HE NEEDS OF THE STUFF.
OUR ONLY ADVANTAGE IS THAT WE CAME AFTER HIM BEFORE HE WAS READY, BEFORE HE HACKED LAST LAUGH.
WITH YOU HERE WE CAN STOP HIM. WE CAN SET IT OFF AND PROTECT THE CITY.
HERE, THOUGH... WE NEED TO DO IT TOGETHER. WITHIN TWO MINUTES OF EACH OTHER OR IT'LL SHUT DOWN FOR SEVEN DAYS FOR SAFETY AND BE INOPERABLE.
WHAT WILL IT DO, EXACTLY?
EFFECTIVE IMMEDIATELY, IT WILL DISMANTLE GOTHAM'S ENTRY POINTS, DISCONNECT IT FROM THE NATIONAL GRID, OUTSIDE WATER, RESOURCES.
BOTTOM LINE, LAST LAUGH WILL TURN GOTHAM INTO A QUARANTINE ZONE AND ELIMINATE ANY CHANCE OF THE BATMAN WHO LAUGHS INFECTING THE WATER SUPPLY.
IT'LL ALSO GIVE US A THOUSAND WAYS OF CATCHING HIM. HERE, JUST PUT YOUR HAND--
BATMAN, WAIT. BEFORE WE DO THIS...I... I WANT TO SAY SOMETHING...
WHAT IS IT?

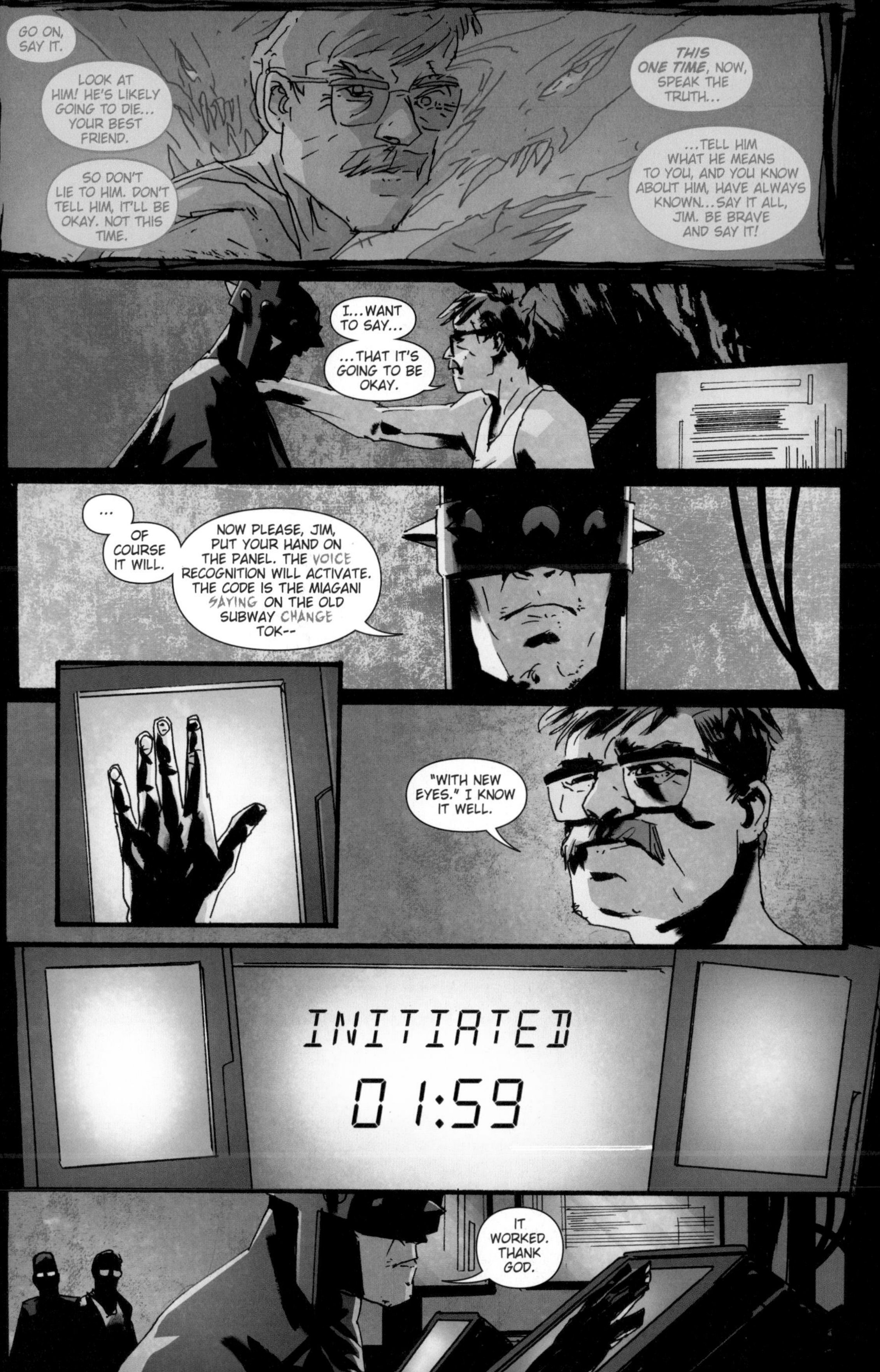
GO ON, SAY IT.
LOOK AT HIM! HE'S LIKELY GOING TO DIE... YOUR BEST FRIEND.
SO DON'T LIE TO HIM. DON'T TELL HIM, IT'LL BE OKAY. NOT THIS TIME.
THIS ONE TIME, NOW, SPEAK THE TRUTH...
...TELL HIM WHAT HE MEANS TO YOU, AND YOU KNOW ABOUT HIM, HAVE ALWAYS KNOWN...SAY IT ALL, JIM. BE BRAVE AND SAY IT!
I...WANT TO SAY...
...THAT IT'S GOING TO BE OKAY.
...
OF COURSE IT WILL.
NOW PLEASE, JIM, PUT YOUR HAND ON THE PANEL. THE VOICE RECOGNITION WILL ACTIVATE. THE CODE IS THE MIAGANI SAYING ON THE OLD SUBWAY CHANGE TOK--
"WITH NEW EYES." I KNOW IT WELL.
INITIATED
01:59
IT WORKED. THANK GOD.

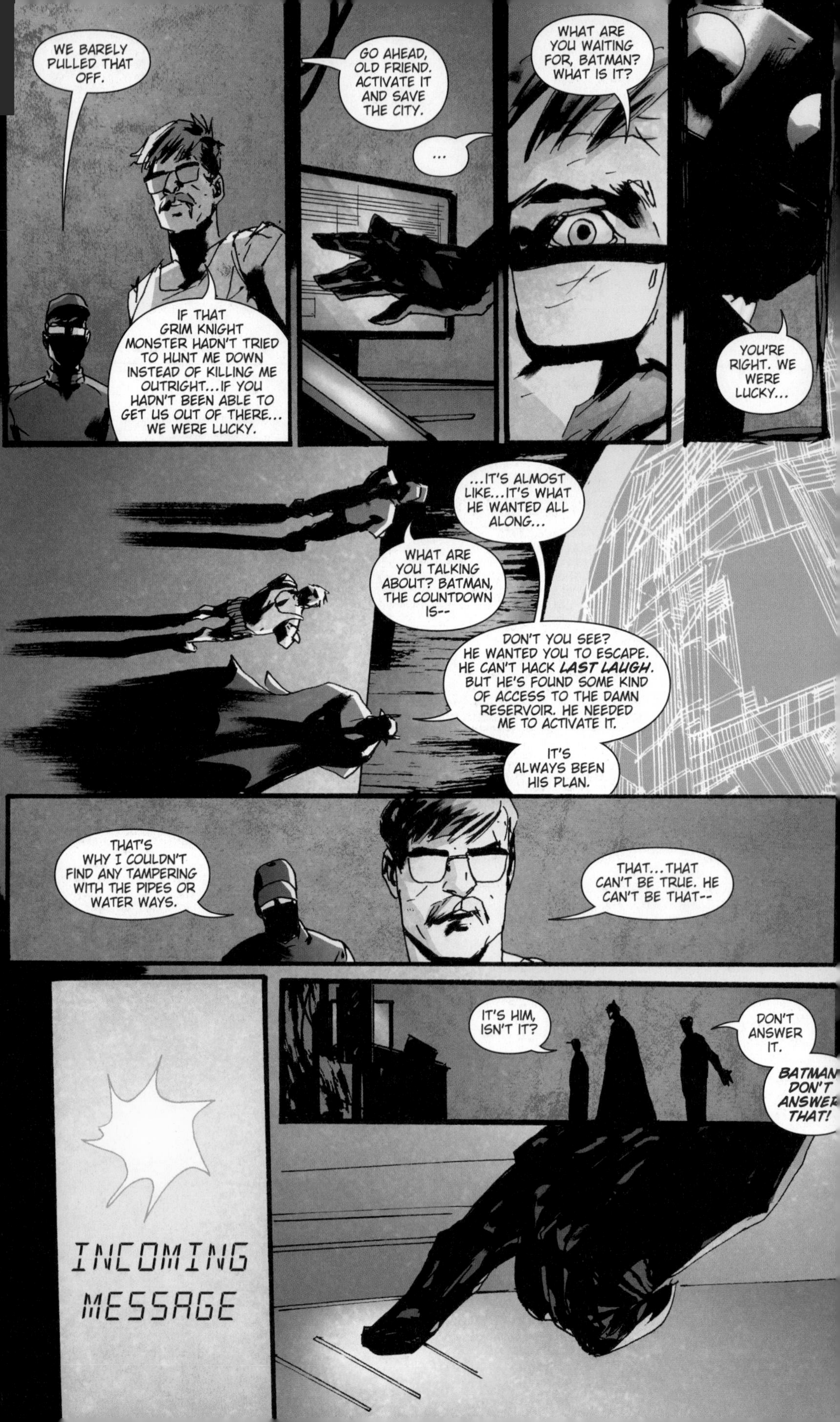
WE BARELY PULLED THAT OFF.
IF THAT GRIM KNIGHT MONSTER HADN'T TRIED TO HUNT ME DOWN INSTEAD OF KILLING ME OUTRIGHT...IF YOU HADN'T BEEN ABLE TO GET US OUT OF THERE... WE WERE LUCKY.
GO AHEAD, OLD FRIEND. ACTIVATE IT AND SAVE THE CITY.
...
WHAT ARE YOU WAITING FOR, BATMAN? WHAT IS IT?
YOU'RE RIGHT. WE WERE LUCKY...
...IT'S ALMOST LIKE...IT'S WHAT HE WANTED ALL ALONG...
WHAT ARE YOU TALKING ABOUT? BATMAN, THE COUNTDOWN IS--
DON'T YOU SEE? HE WANTED YOU TO ESCAPE. HE CAN'T HACK LAST LAUGH. BUT HE'S FOUND SOME KIND OF ACCESS TO THE DAMN RESERVOIR. HE NEEDED ME TO ACTIVATE IT.
IT'S ALWAYS BEEN HIS PLAN.
THAT'S WHY I COULDN'T FIND ANY TAMPERING WITH THE PIPES OR WATER WAYS.
THAT...THAT CAN'T BE TRUE. HE CAN'T BE THAT--
INCOMING MESSAGE
IT'S HIM, ISN'T IT?
DON'T ANSWER IT.
BATMAN DON'T ANSWER THAT!

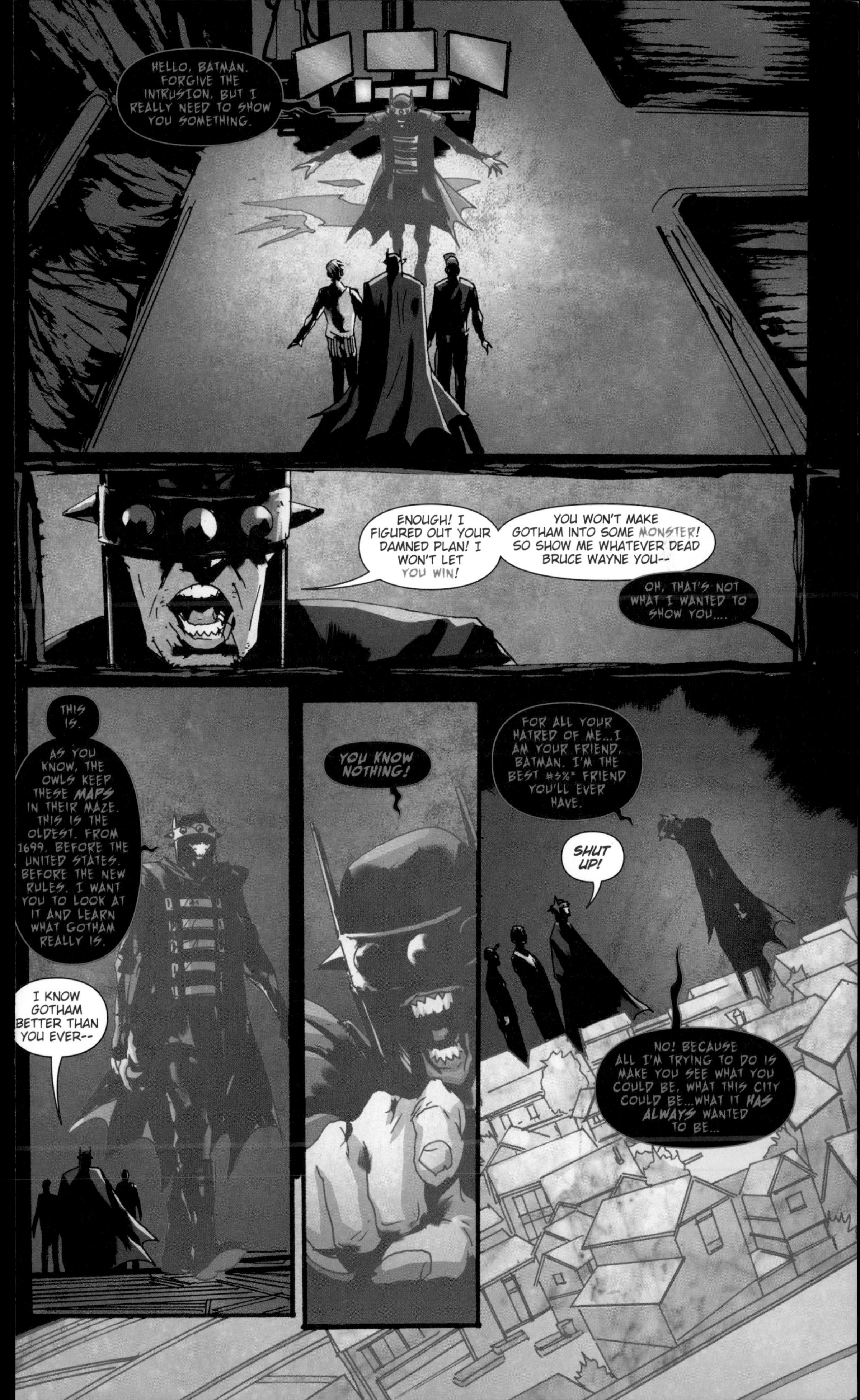
HELLO, BATMAN. FORGIVE THE INTRUSION, BUT I REALLY NEED TO SHOW YOU SOMETHING.
ENOUGH! I FIGURED OUT YOUR DAMNED PLAN! I WON'T LET YOU WIN!
YOU WON'T MAKE GOTHAM INTO SOME MONSTER! SO SHOW ME WHATEVER DEAD BRUCE WAYNE YOU--
OH, THAT'S NOT WHAT I WANTED TO SHOW YOU....
THIS IS.
AS YOU KNOW, THE OWLS KEEP THESE MAPS IN THEIR MAZE. THIS IS THE OLDEST. FROM 1699. BEFORE THE UNITED STATES. BEFORE THE NEW RULES. I WANT YOU TO LOOK AT IT AND LEARN WHAT GOTHAM REALLY IS.
I KNOW GOTHAM BETTER THAN YOU EVER--
YOU KNOW NOTHING!
FOR ALL YOUR HATRED OF ME...I AM YOUR FRIEND, BATMAN. I'M THE BEST #$%* FRIEND YOU'LL EVER HAVE.
SHUT UP!
NO! BECAUSE ALL I'M TRYING TO DO IS MAKE YOU SEE WHAT YOU COULD BE, WHAT THIS CITY COULD BE...WHAT IT HAS ALWAYS WANTED TO BE...

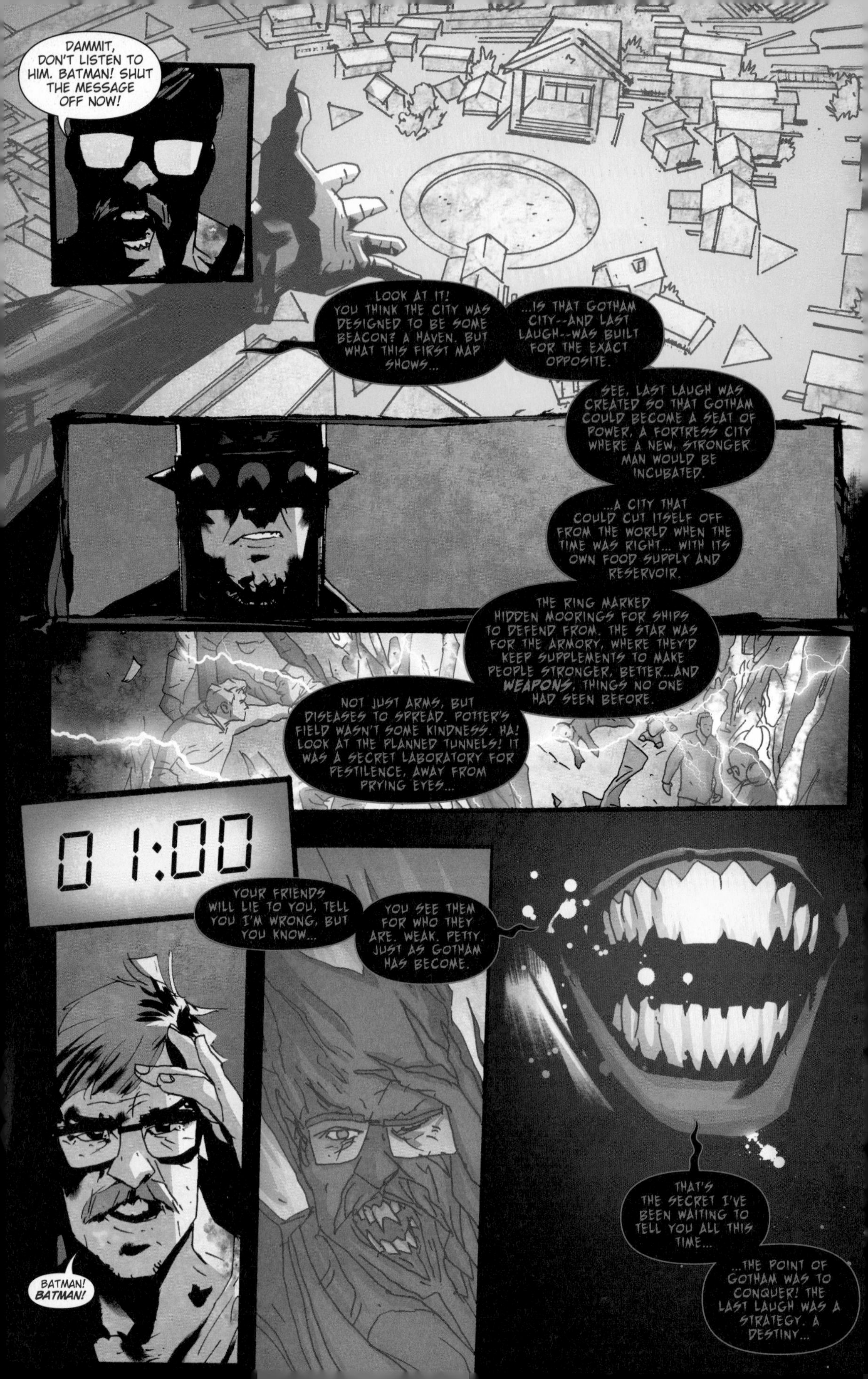
DAMMIT, DON'T LISTEN TO HIM. BATMAN! SHUT THE MESSAGE OFF NOW!
LOOK AT IT! YOU THINK THE CITY WAS DESIGNED TO BE SOME BEACON? A HAVEN. BUT WHAT THIS FIRST MAP SHOWS...
...IS THAT GOTHAM CITY--AND LAST LAUGH--WAS BUILT FOR THE EXACT OPPOSITE.
SEE, LAST LAUGH WAS CREATED SO THAT GOTHAM COULD BECOME A SEAT OF POWER, A FORTRESS CITY WHERE A NEW, STRONGER MAN WOULD BE INCUBATED.
...A CITY THAT COULD CUT ITSELF OFF FROM THE WORLD WHEN THE TIME WAS RIGHT... WITH ITS OWN FOOD SUPPLY AND RESERVOIR.
THE RING MARKED HIDDEN MOORINGS FOR SHIPS TO DEFEND FROM. THE STAR WAS FOR THE ARMORY, WHERE THEY'D KEEP SUPPLEMENTS TO MAKE PEOPLE STRONGER, BETTER...AND WEAPONS, THINGS NO ONE HAD SEEN BEFORE.
NOT JUST ARMS, BUT DISEASES TO SPREAD. POTTER'S FIELD WASN'T SOME KINDNESS. HA! LOOK AT THE PLANNED TUNNELS! IT WAS A SECRET LABORATORY FOR PESTILENCE, AWAY FROM PRYING EYES...
01:00
YOUR FRIENDS WILL LIE TO YOU, TELL YOU I'M WRONG, BUT YOU KNOW...
YOU SEE THEM FOR WHO THEY ARE. WEAK. PETTY. JUST AS GOTHAM HAS BECOME.
BATMAN! BATMAN!
THAT'S THE SECRET I'VE BEEN WAITING TO TELL YOU ALL THIS TIME...
...THE POINT OF GOTHAM WAS TO CONQUER! THE LAST LAUGH WAS A STRATEGY. A DESTINY...

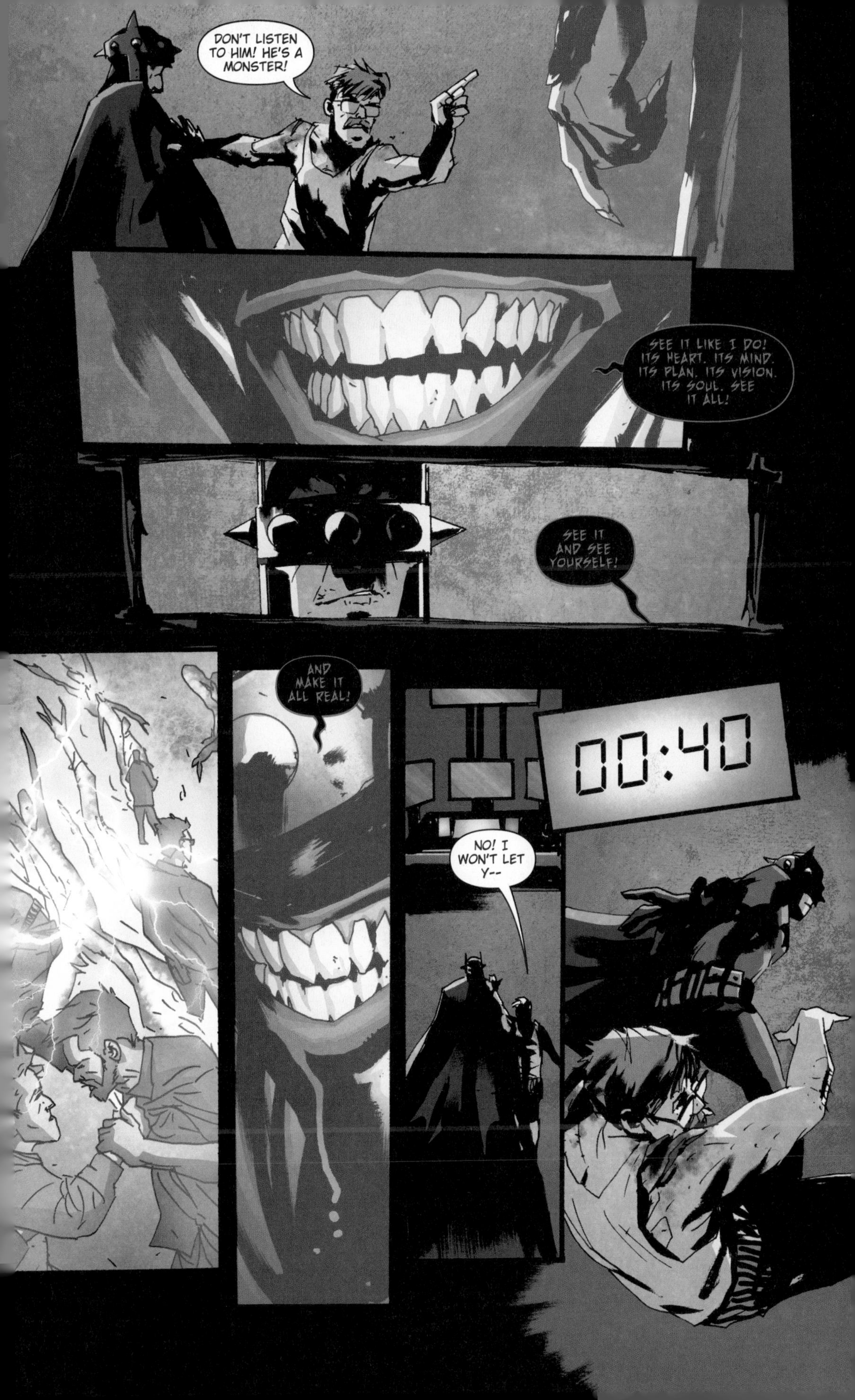
DON'T LISTEN TO HIM! HE'S A MONSTER!
SEE IT LIKE I DO! ITS HEART. ITS MIND. ITS PLAN. ITS VISION. ITS SOUL. SEE IT ALL!
SEE IT AND SEE YOURSELF!
AND MAKE IT ALL REAL!
00:40
NO! I WON'T LET Y--

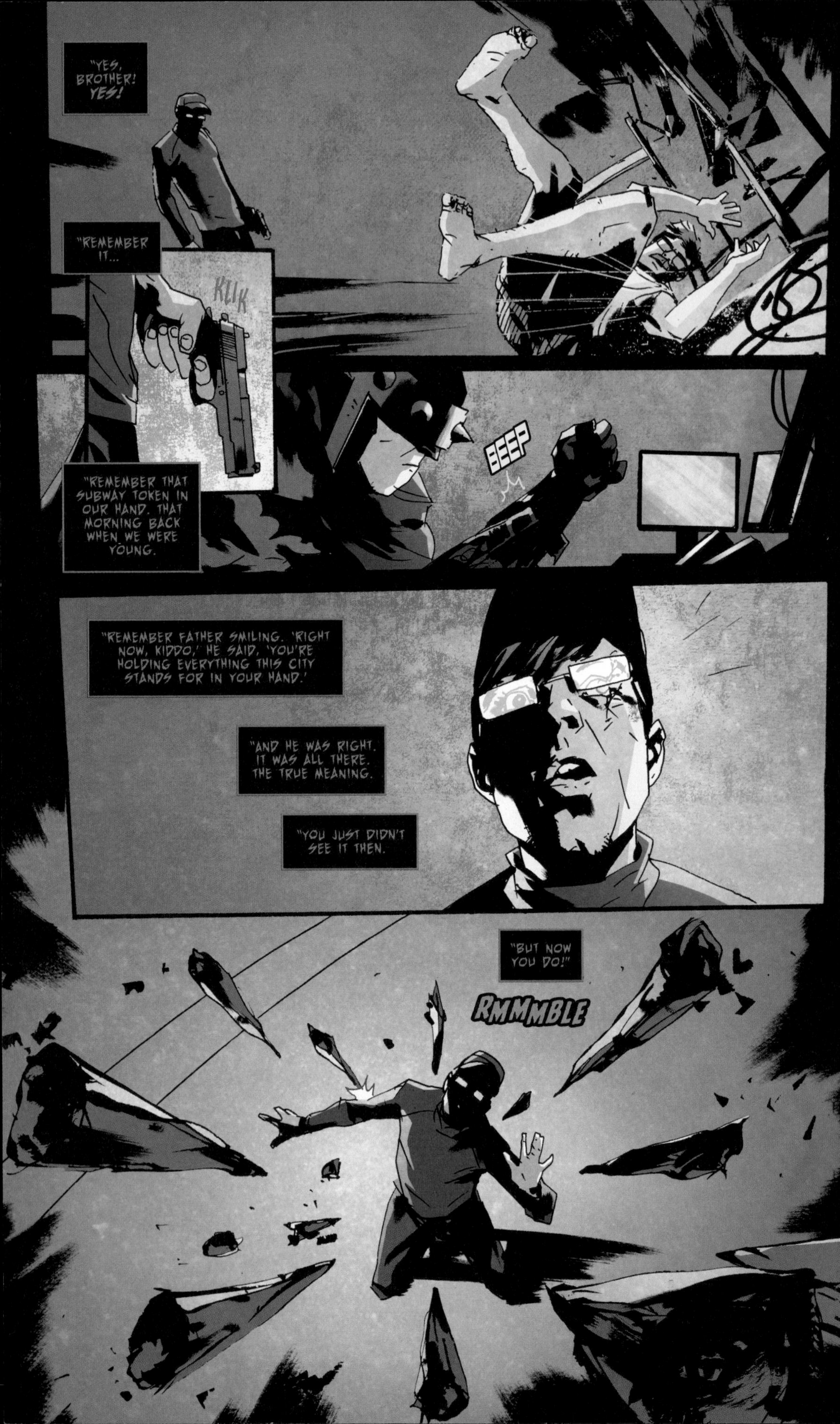
"YES, BROTHER! YES!
"REMEMBER IT...
KLIK
"REMEMBER THAT SUBWAY TOKEN IN OUR HAND. THAT MORNING BACK WHEN WE WERE YOUNG.
BEEP
"REMEMBER FATHER SMILING. 'RIGHT NOW, KIDDO,' HE SAID, 'YOU'RE HOLDING EVERYTHING THIS CITY STANDS FOR IN YOUR HAND.'
"AND HE WAS RIGHT. IT WAS ALL THERE. THE TRUE MEANING.
"YOU JUST DIDN'T SEE IT THEN.
"BUT NOW YOU DO!"
RMMMBLE

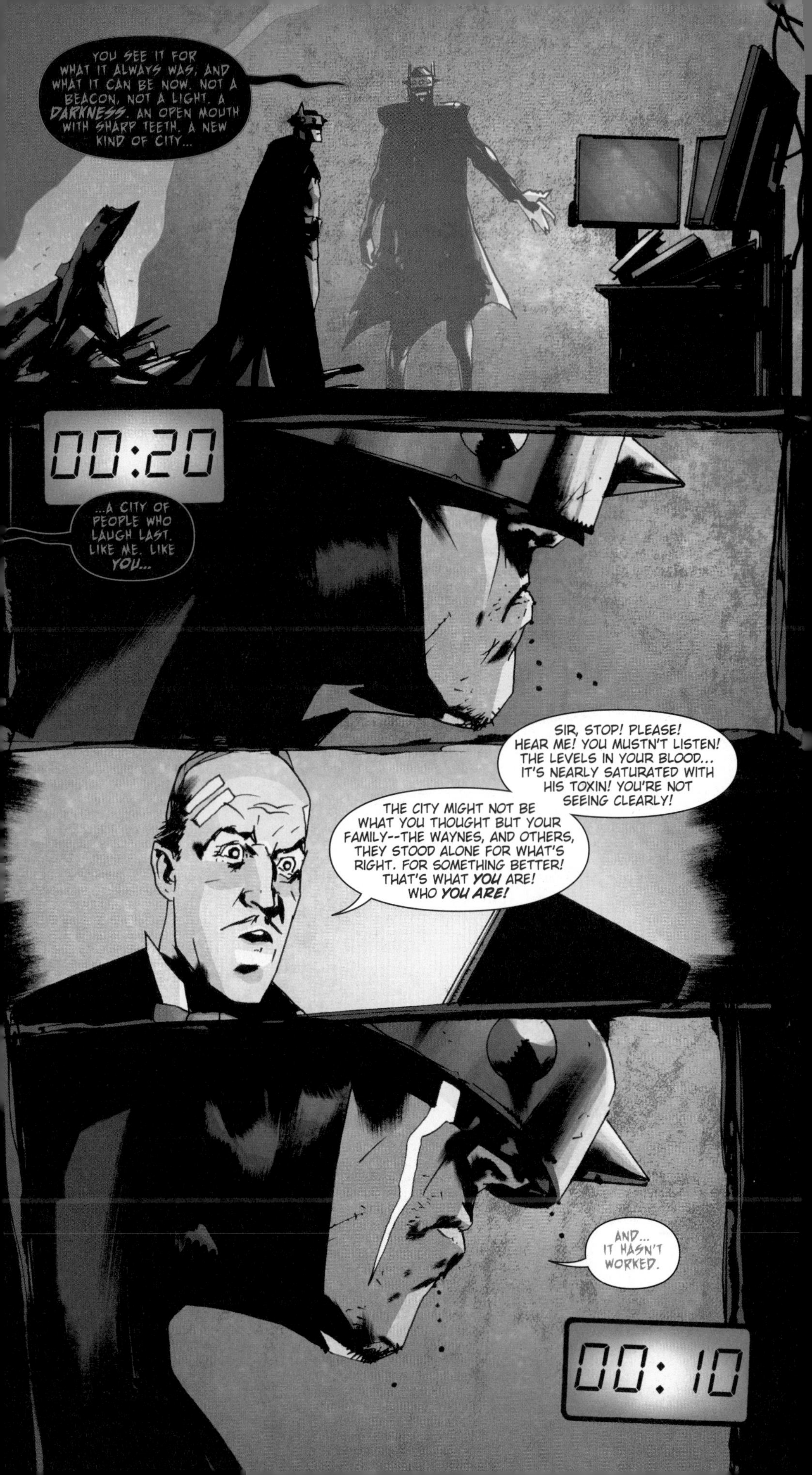
YOU SEE IT FOR WHAT IT ALWAYS WAS, AND WHAT IT CAN BE NOW. NOT A BEACON, NOT A LIGHT. A DARKNESS. AN OPEN MOUTH WITH SHARP TEETH. A NEW KIND OF CITY...
00:20
...A CITY OF PEOPLE WHO LAUGH LAST. LIKE ME. LIKE YOU...
SIR, STOP! PLEASE! HEAR ME! YOU MUSTN'T LISTEN! THE LEVELS IN YOUR BLOOD... IT'S NEARLY SATURATED WITH HIS TOXIN! YOU'RE NOT SEEING CLEARLY!
THE CITY MIGHT NOT BE WHAT YOU THOUGHT BUT YOUR FAMILY--THE WAYNES, AND OTHERS, THEY STOOD ALONE FOR WHAT'S RIGHT. FOR SOMETHING BETTER! THAT'S WHAT YOU ARE! WHO YOU ARE!
AND... IT HASN'T WORKED.
00:10

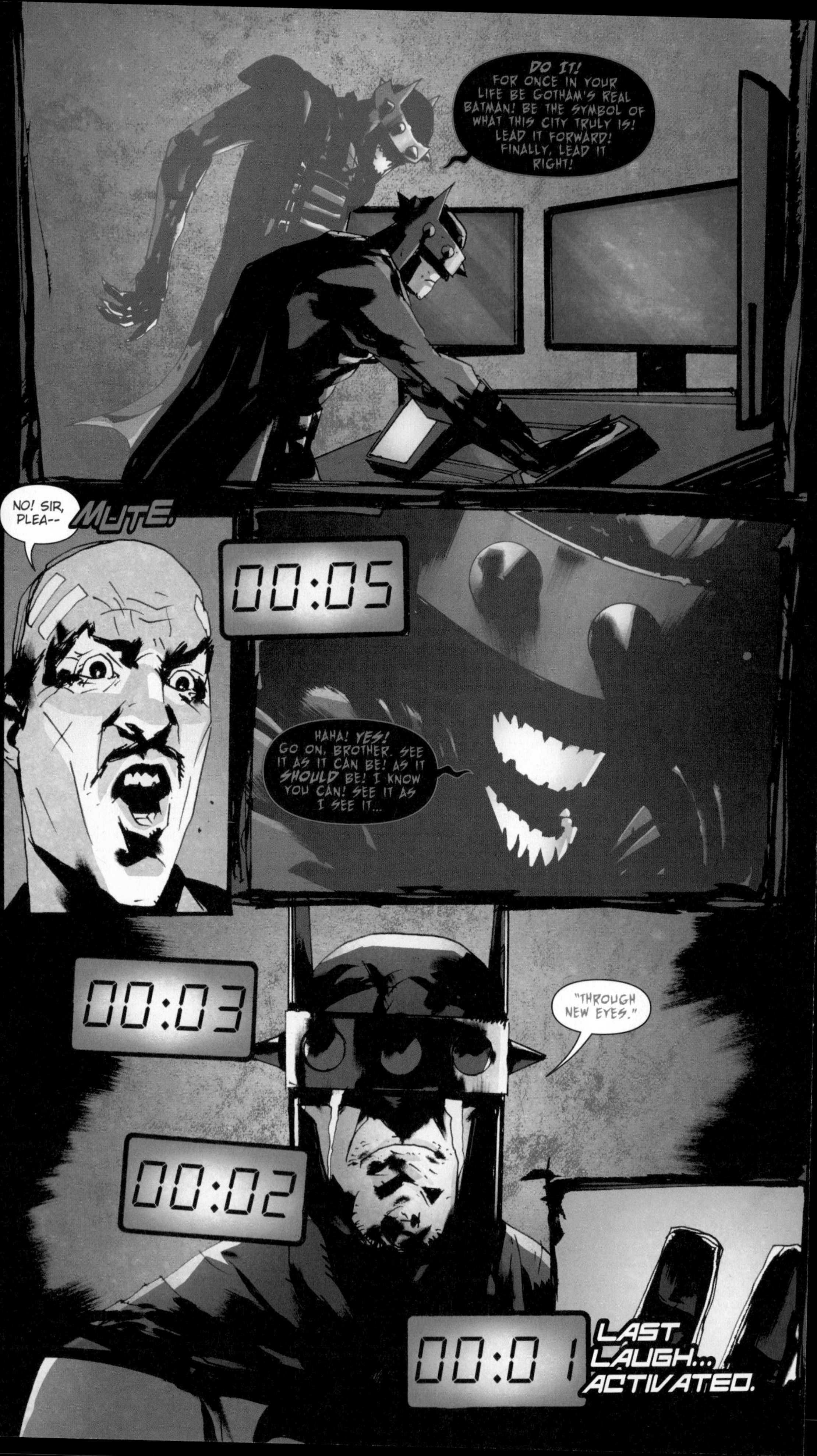
DO IT! FOR ONCE IN YOUR LIFE BE GOTHAM'S REAL BATMAN! BE THE SYMBOL OF WHAT THIS CITY TRULY IS! LEAD IT FORWARD! FINALLY, LEAD IT RIGHT!
NO! SIR, PLEA--
MUTE.
00:05
HAHA! YES! GO ON, BROTHER. SEE IT AS IT CAN BE! AS IT SHOULD BE! I KNOW YOU CAN! SEE IT AS I SEE IT...
00:03
"THROUGH NEW EYES."
00:02
00:01
LAST LAUGH... ACTIVATED.

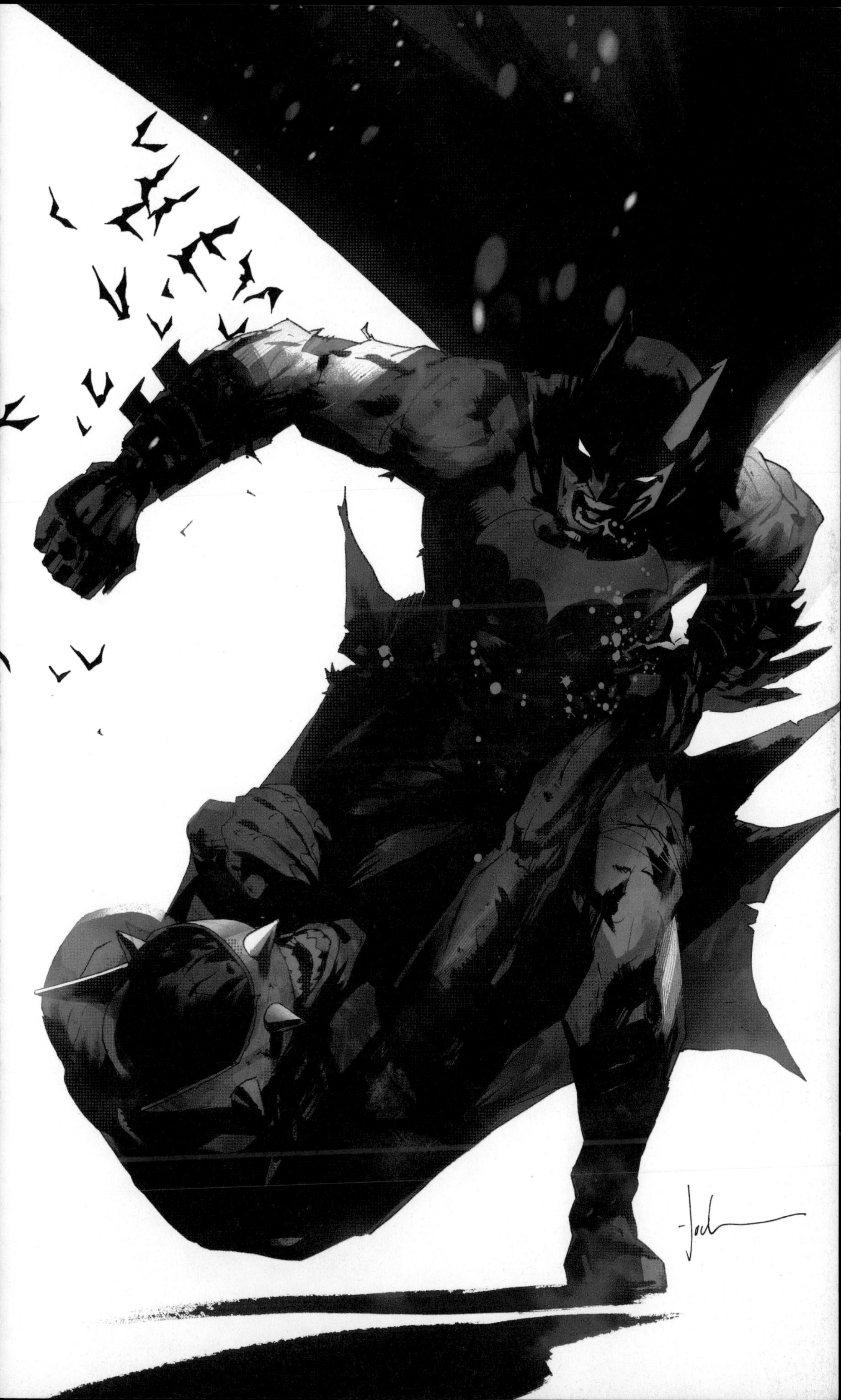

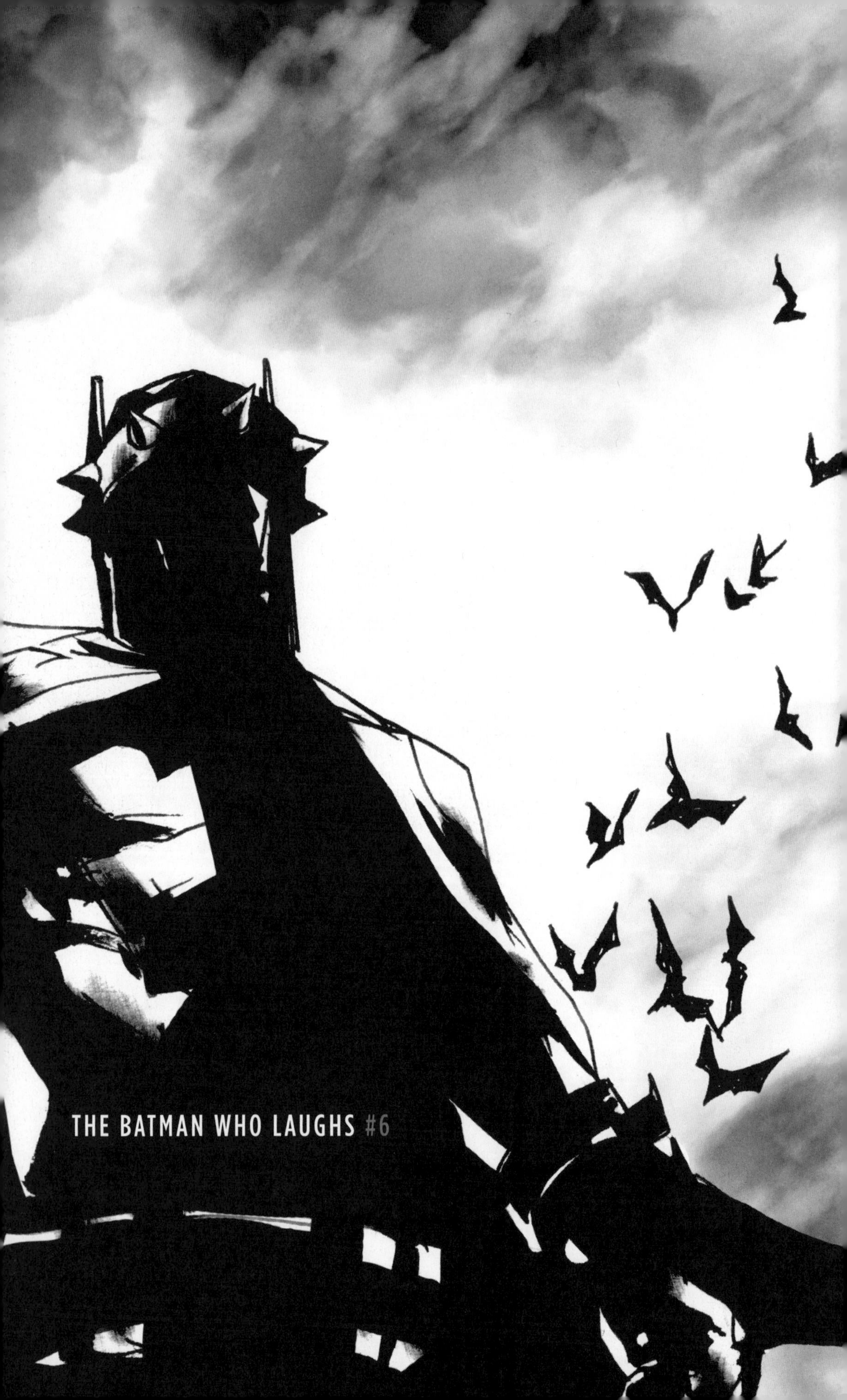

THE BATMAN WHO LAUGHS #6

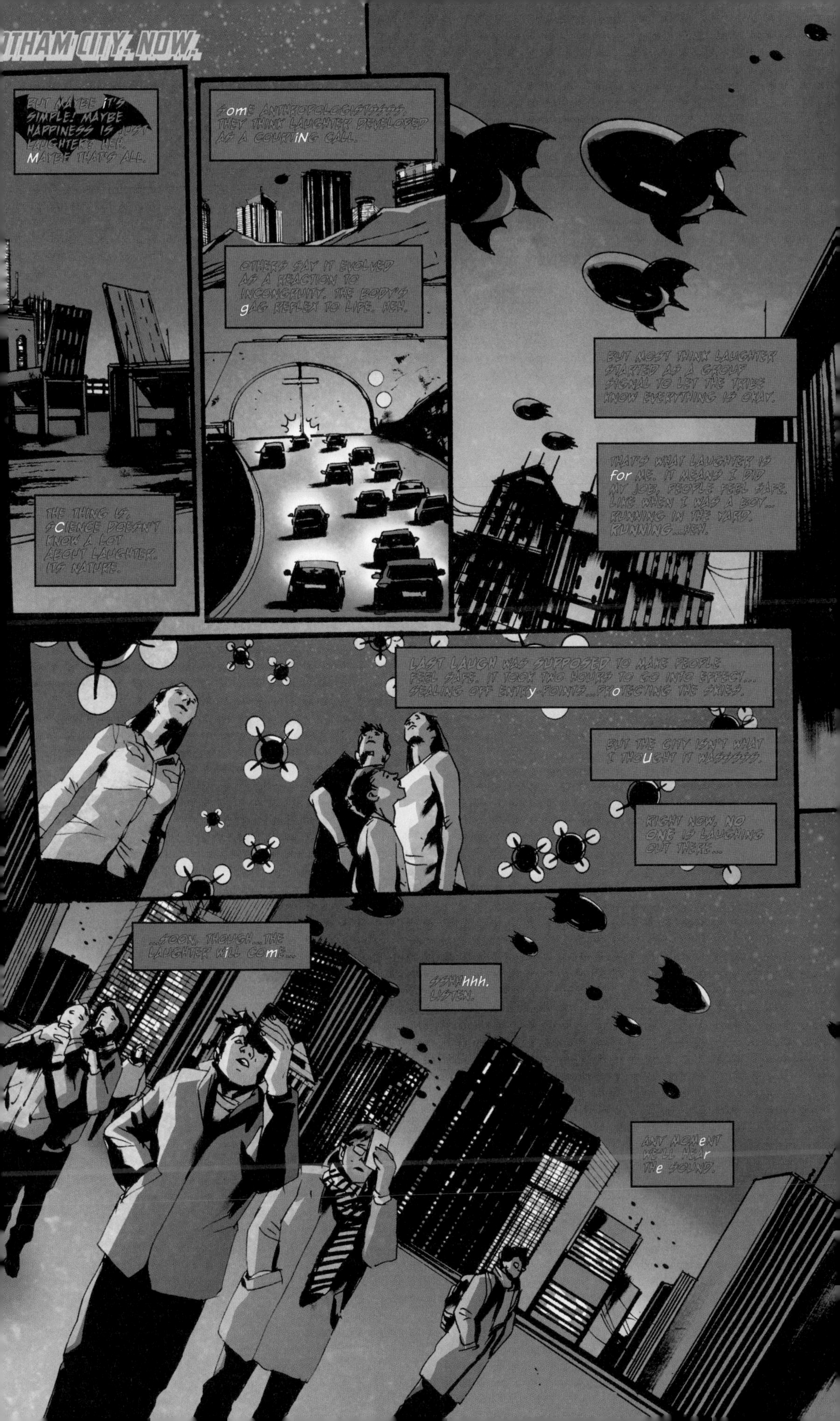
OTHAM CITY. NOW.
BUT MAYBE iT'S SIMPLE! MAYBE HAPPINESS IS JUST LAUGHTER? HEH. MAYBE THAT'S ALL.
THE THING IS, SCIENCE DOESN'T KNOW A LOT ABOUT LAUGHTER. ITS NATURE.
SomE ANTHROPOLOGISTSSSS. THEY THINK LAUGHTER DEVELOPED AS A COURTiNG CALL.
OTHERS SAY IT EVOLVED AS A REACTION TO INCONGRUITY. THE BODY'S gAG REFLEX TO LIFE. HEH.
BUT MOST THINK LAUGHTER STARTED AS A GROUP SIGNAL TO LET THE TRIBE KNOW EVERYTHING IS OKAY.
THAT'S WHAT LAUGHTER IS for ME. IT MEANS I DID MY JOB, PEOPLE FEEL SAFE. LIKE WHEN I WAS A BOY... RUNNING IN THE YARD. RUNNING...HEH.
LAST LAUGH WAS SUPPOSED TO MAKE PEOPLE FEEL SAFE. IT TOOK TWO HOURS TO GO INTO EFFECT... SEALING OFF ENTRy-POINTS...PROTECTING THE SKIES.
BUT THE CITY ISN'T WHAT I THOUGHT IT WASSSSS.
RIGHT NOW, NO ONE IS LAUGHING OUT THERE...
...SOON, THOUGH...THE LAUGHTER WiLL COmE...
SSHHhhh. LISTEN.
ANY MOMeNT WE'LL HEAr THe SOUND.

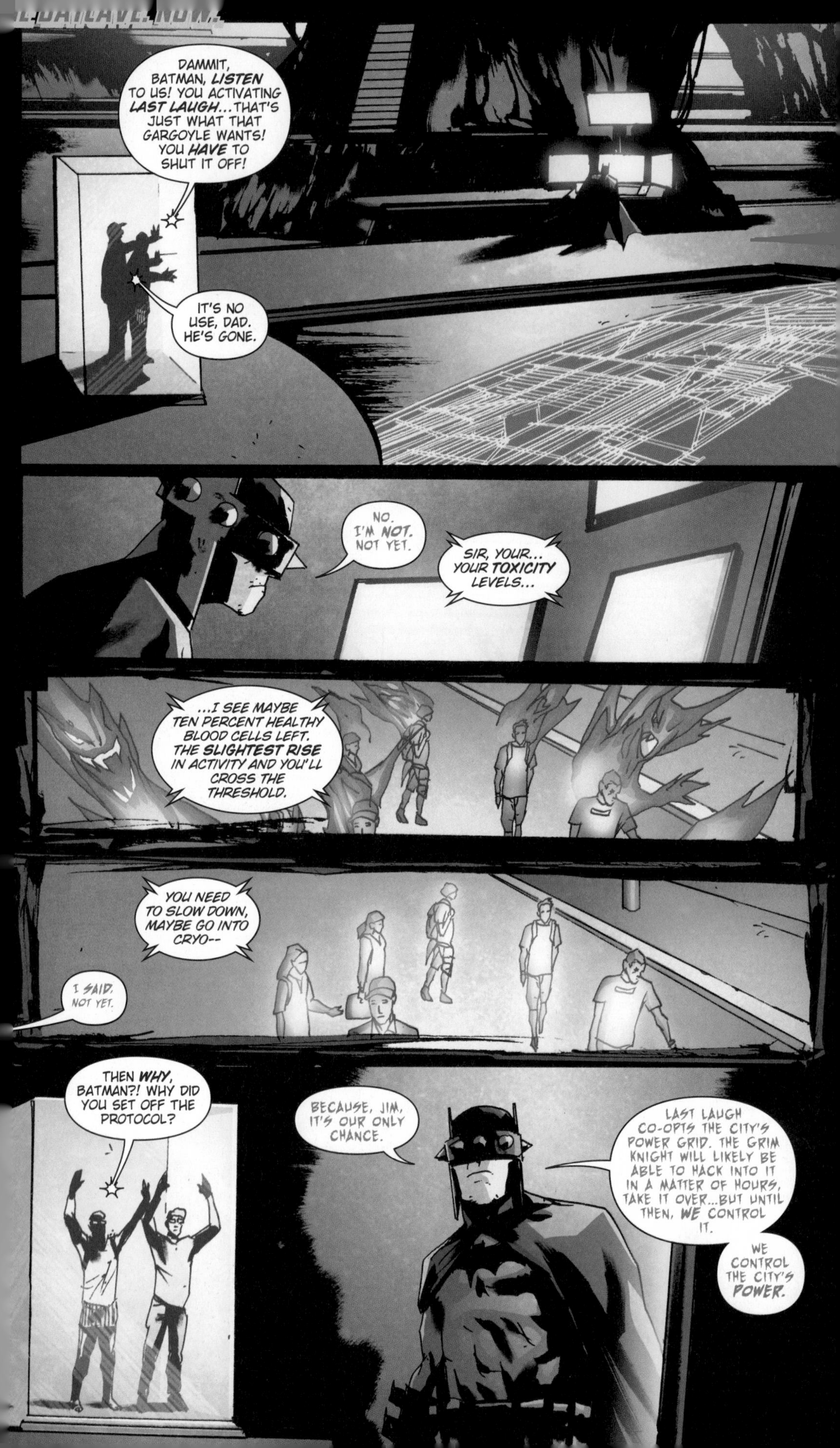
DAMMIT, BATMAN, LISTEN TO US! YOU ACTIVATING LAST LAUGH...THAT'S JUST WHAT THAT GARGOYLE WANTS! YOU HAVE TO SHUT IT OFF!
IT'S NO USE, DAD. HE'S GONE.
NO. I'M NOT. NOT YET.
SIR, YOUR... YOUR TOXICITY LEVELS...
...I SEE MAYBE TEN PERCENT HEALTHY BLOOD CELLS LEFT. THE SLIGHTEST RISE IN ACTIVITY AND YOU'LL CROSS THE THRESHOLD.
YOU NEED TO SLOW DOWN, MAYBE GO INTO CRYO--
I SAID. NOT YET.
THEN WHY, BATMAN?! WHY DID YOU SET OFF THE PROTOCOL?
BECAUSE, JIM, IT'S OUR ONLY CHANCE.
LAST LAUGH CO-OPTS THE CITY'S POWER GRID. THE GRIM KNIGHT WILL LIKELY BE ABLE TO HACK INTO IT IN A MATTER OF HOURS, TAKE IT OVER...BUT UNTIL THEN, WE CONTROL IT.
WE CONTROL THE CITY'S POWER.

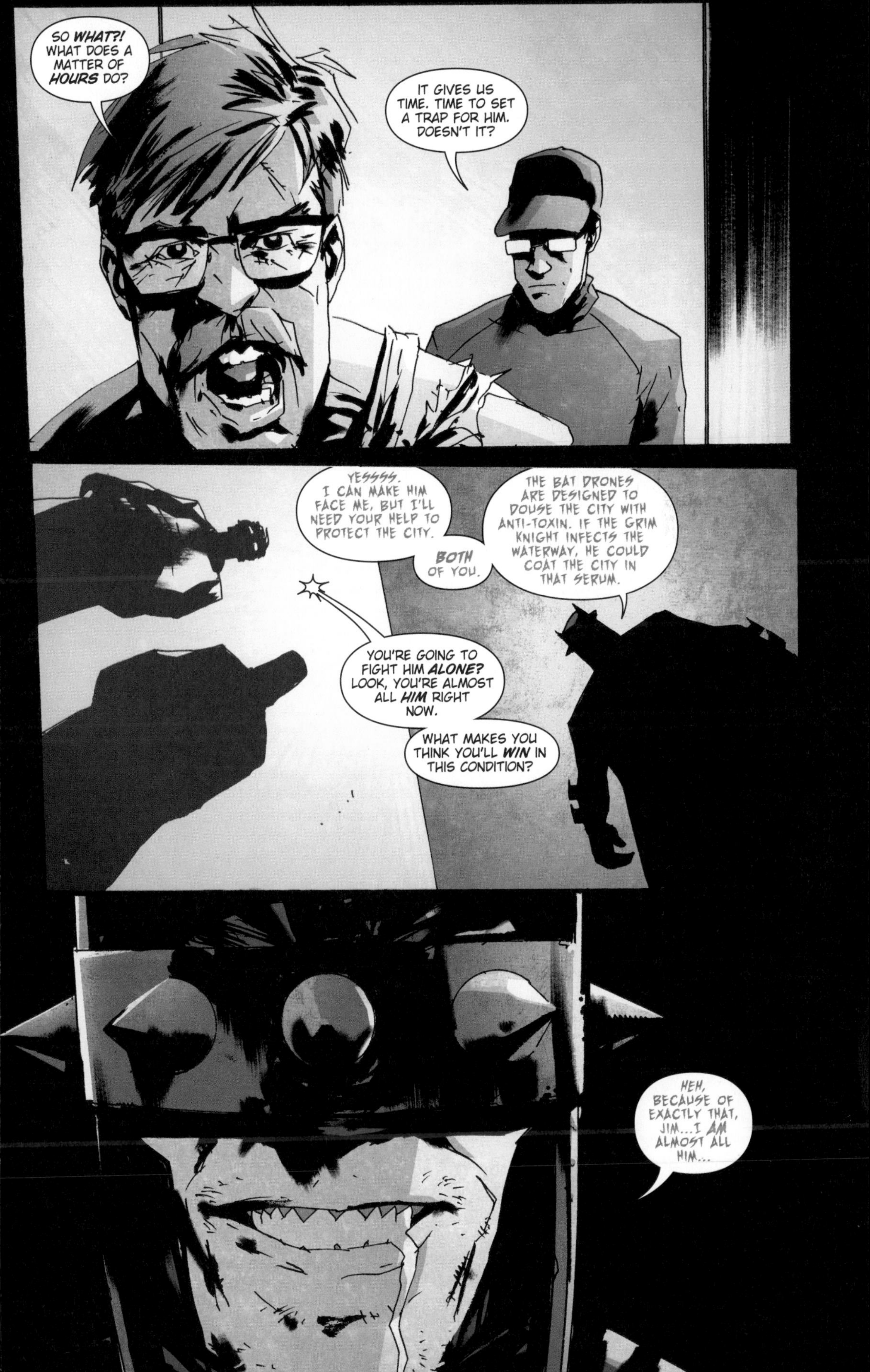
SO WHAT?! WHAT DOES A MATTER OF HOURS DO?
IT GIVES US TIME. TIME TO SET A TRAP FOR HIM. DOESN'T IT?
YESSSS. I CAN MAKE HIM FACE ME, BUT I'LL NEED YOUR HELP TO PROTECT THE CITY.
BOTH OF YOU.
THE BAT DRONES ARE DESIGNED TO DOUSE THE CITY WITH ANTI-TOXIN. IF THE GRIM KNIGHT INFECTS THE WATERWAY, HE COULD COAT THE CITY IN THAT SERUM.
YOU'RE GOING TO FIGHT HIM ALONE? LOOK, YOU'RE ALMOST ALL HIM RIGHT NOW.
WHAT MAKES YOU THINK YOU'LL WIN IN THIS CONDITION?
HEH, BECAUSE OF EXACTLY THAT, JIM...I AM ALMOST ALL HIM...

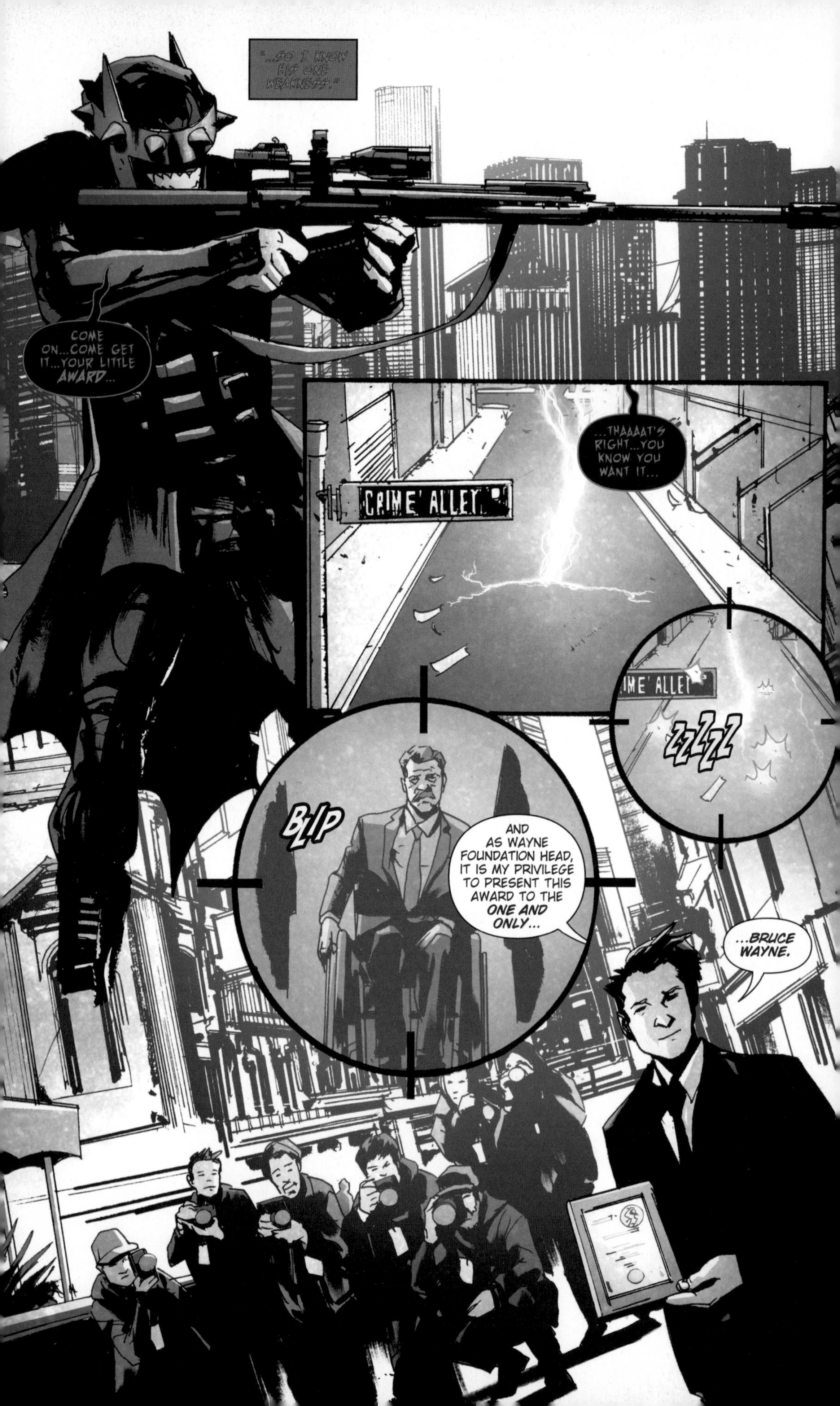
"...SO I KNOW HIS ONE WEAKNESS."
COME ON...COME GET IT...YOUR LITTLE AWARD...
...THAAAAT'S RIGHT...YOU KNOW YOU WANT IT...
CRIME' ALLEY
ZZZZZ
BLIP
AND AS WAYNE FOUNDATION HEAD, IT IS MY PRIVILEGE TO PRESENT THIS AWARD TO THE ONE AND ONLY...
...BRUCE WAYNE.

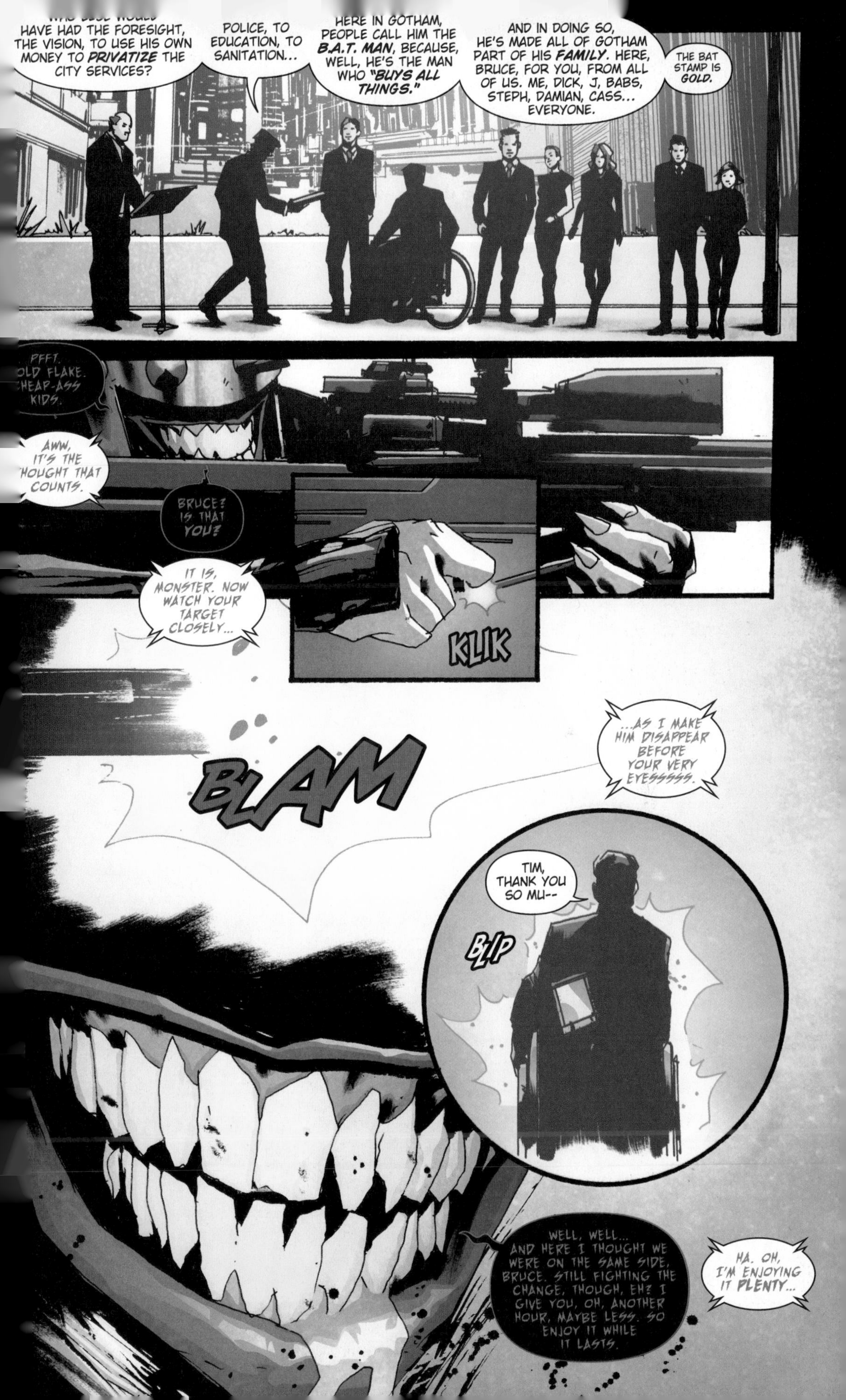
HAVE HAD THE FORESIGHT, THE VISION, TO USE HIS OWN MONEY TO PRIVATIZE THE CITY SERVICES?
POLICE, TO EDUCATION, TO SANITATION...
HERE IN GOTHAM, PEOPLE CALL HIM THE B.A.T. MAN, BECAUSE, WELL, HE'S THE MAN WHO "BUYS ALL THINGS."
AND IN DOING SO, HE'S MADE ALL OF GOTHAM PART OF HIS FAMILY. HERE, BRUCE, FOR YOU, FROM ALL OF US. ME, DICK, J, BABS, STEPH, DAMIAN, CASS... EVERYONE.
THE BAT STAMP IS GOLD.
PFFT. OLD FLAKE. HEAP-ASS KIDS.
AWW, IT'S THE HOUGHT THAT COUNTS.
BRUCE? IS THAT YOU?
IT IS, MONSTER. NOW WATCH YOUR TARGET CLOSELY...
KLIK
BLAM
...AS I MAKE HIM DISAPPEAR BEFORE YOUR VERY EYESSSSS.
TIM, THANK YOU SO MU--
BLIP
WELL, WELL... AND HERE I THOUGHT WE WERE ON THE SAME SIDE, BRUCE. STILL FIGHTING THE CHANGE, THOUGH, EH? I GIVE YOU, OH, ANOTHER HOUR, MAYBE LESS. SO ENJOY IT WHILE IT LASTS.
HA. OH, I'M ENJOYING IT PLENTY...

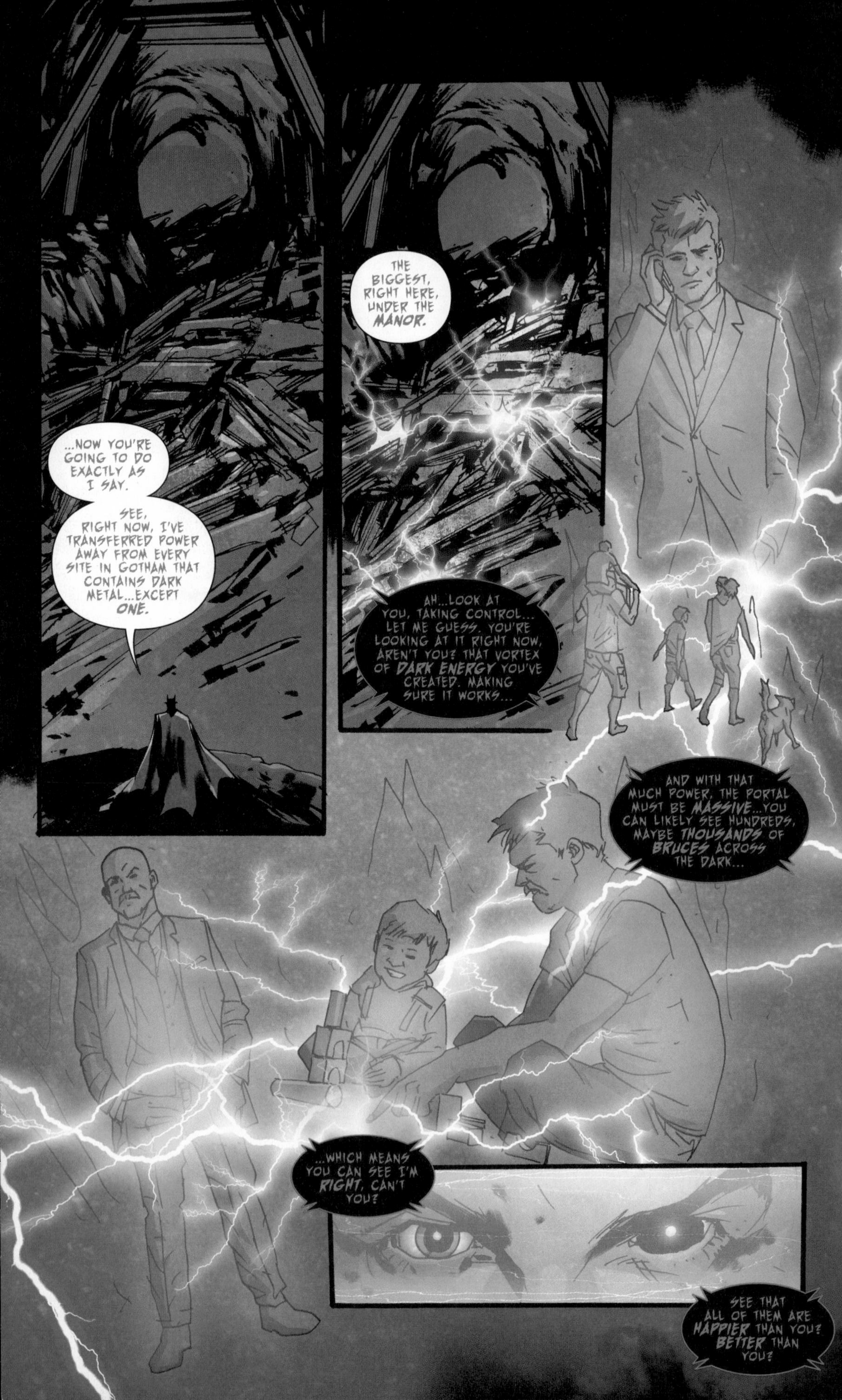
...NOW YOU'RE GOING TO DO EXACTLY AS I SAY.
SEE, RIGHT NOW, I'VE TRANSFERRED POWER AWAY FROM EVERY SITE IN GOTHAM THAT CONTAINS DARK METAL...EXCEPT ONE.
THE BIGGEST, RIGHT HERE, UNDER THE MANOR.
AH...LOOK AT YOU, TAKING CONTROL... LET ME GUESS. YOU'RE LOOKING AT IT RIGHT NOW, AREN'T YOU? THAT VORTEX OF DARK ENERGY YOU'VE CREATED. MAKING SURE IT WORKS...
AND WITH THAT MUCH POWER, THE PORTAL MUST BE MASSIVE...YOU CAN LIKELY SEE HUNDREDS, MAYBE THOUSANDS OF BRUCES ACROSS THE DARK...
...WHICH MEANS YOU CAN SEE I'M RIGHT, CAN'T YOU?
SEE THAT ALL OF THEM ARE HAPPIER THAN YOU? BETTER THAN YOU?

BUT MY QUESTION TO YOU IS THIS, BRUCE. DO YOU UNDERSTAND WHY?
HAVE YOU LEARNED ANYTHING, LOOKING AT ALL THOSE VERSIONS OF US?
YES.
I LOOK BETTER WITH HAIR.
NOW, BE HERE IN ONE HOUR. I'LL BRING THROUGH THE LAST BRUCE WAYNE.
YOU WANT ENOUGH SERUM TO INFECT THE WHOLE CITY? COME GET IT.
HA HA! IT WON'T TAKE THE GRIM KNIGHT VERY LONG TO BREAK YOUR HOLD ON THE POWER GRID. OR FOR YOU TO FINISH YOUR TRANSFORMATION...WHAT'S TO KEEP ME FROM JUST WAITING YOU OUT?
MAYBE I'VE TAKEN MY OWN PRECAUTIONS.
YOU'RE BLUFFING. BESIDES, I ALREADY HAVE ENOUGH SERUM TO CHANGE MOST OF THE CITY...
"MOST" ISN'T WINNING, IS IT?
"I HOPE THIS WORKS..."

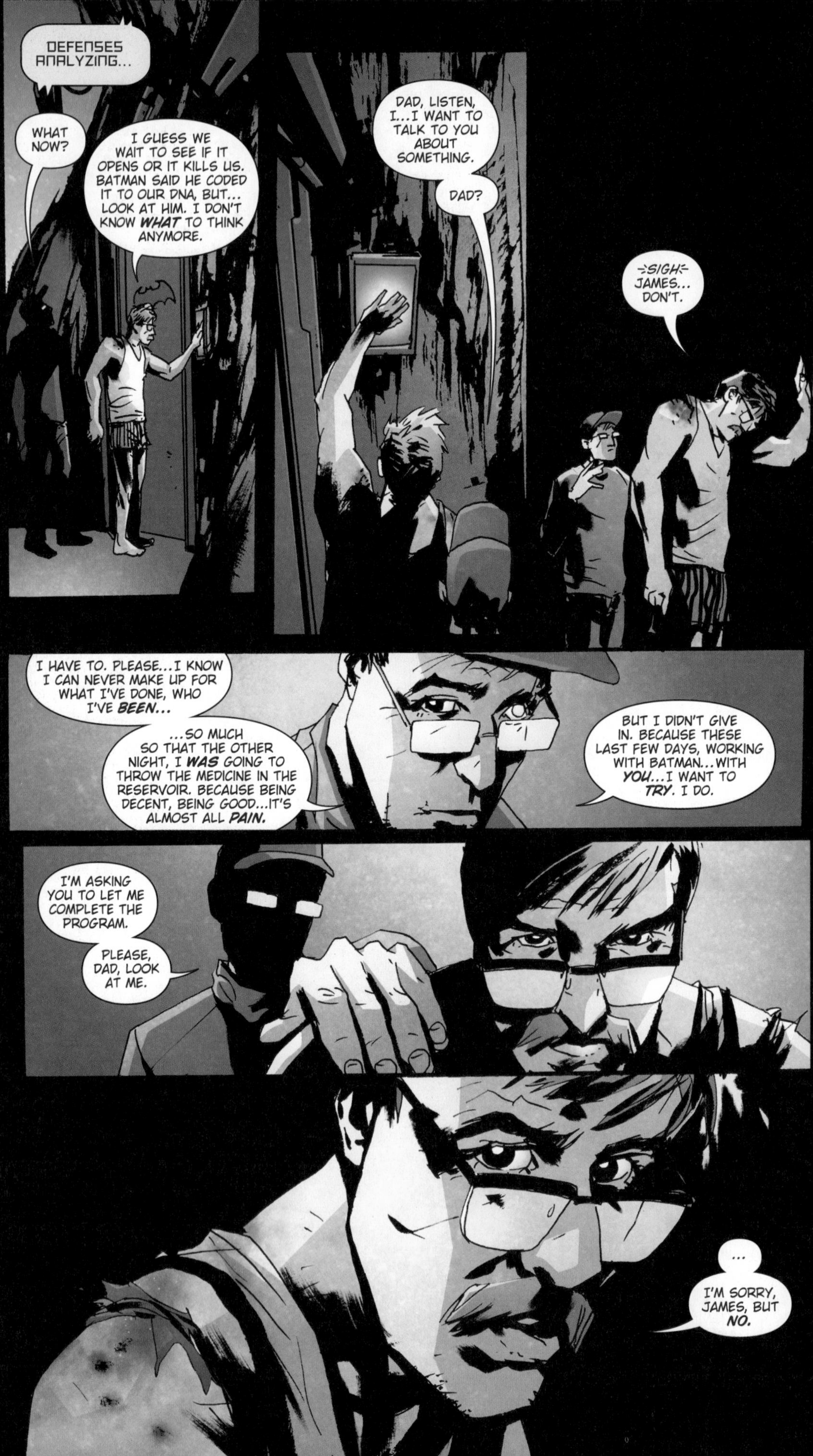
DEFENSES ANALYZING...
WHAT NOW?
I GUESS WE WAIT TO SEE IF IT OPENS OR IT KILLS US. BATMAN SAID HE CODED IT TO OUR DNA, BUT... LOOK AT HIM. I DON'T KNOW WHAT TO THINK ANYMORE.
DAD, LISTEN, I...I WANT TO TALK TO YOU ABOUT SOMETHING.
DAD?
SIGH JAMES... DON'T.
I HAVE TO. PLEASE...I KNOW I CAN NEVER MAKE UP FOR WHAT I'VE DONE, WHO I'VE BEEN...
...SO MUCH SO THAT THE OTHER NIGHT, I WAS GOING TO THROW THE MEDICINE IN THE RESERVOIR. BECAUSE BEING DECENT, BEING GOOD...IT'S ALMOST ALL PAIN.
BUT I DIDN'T GIVE IN. BECAUSE THESE LAST FEW DAYS, WORKING WITH BATMAN...WITH YOU...I WANT TO TRY. I DO.
I'M ASKING YOU TO LET ME COMPLETE THE PROGRAM.
PLEASE, DAD, LOOK AT ME.
...
I'M SORRY, JAMES, BUT NO.

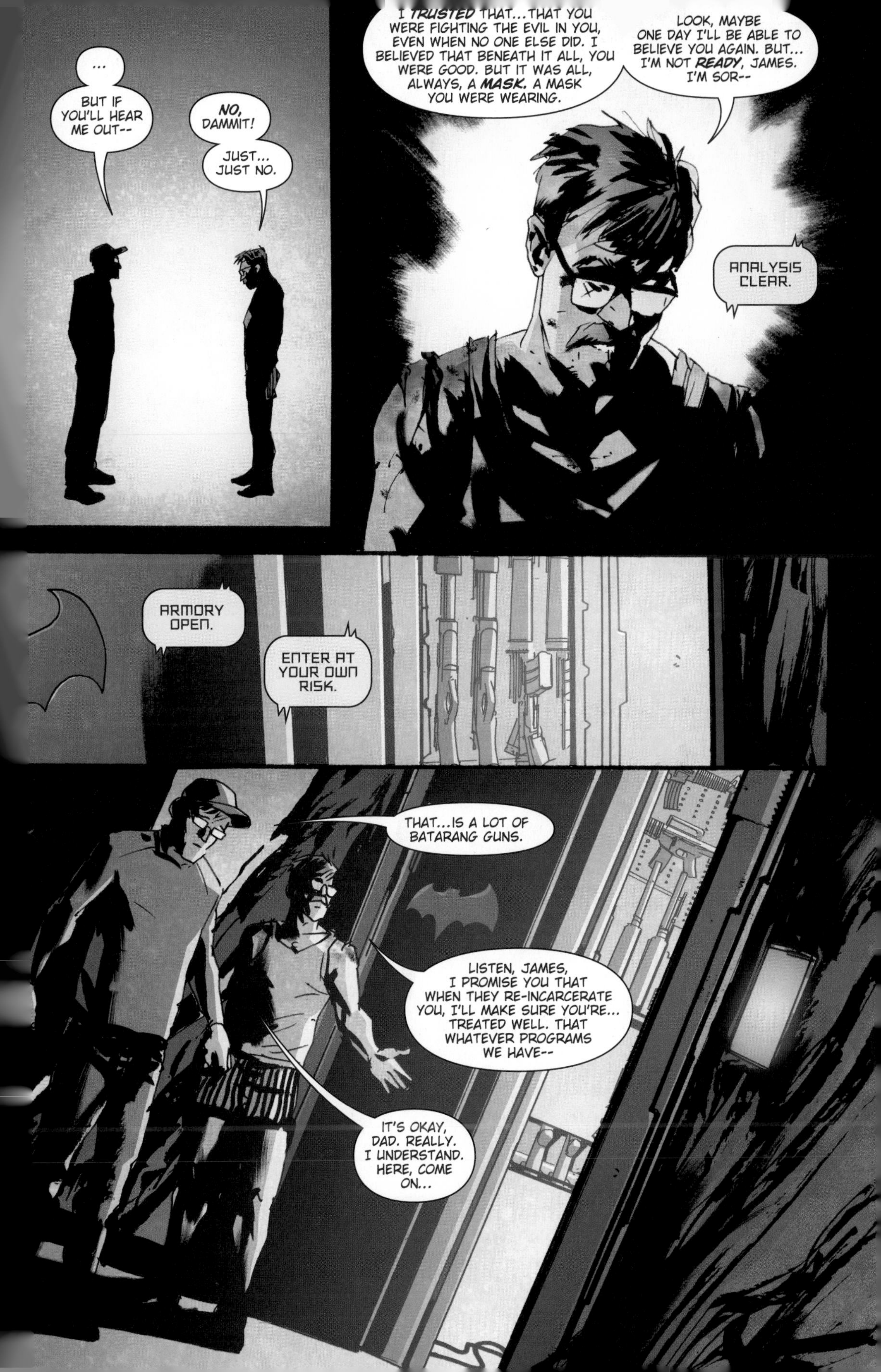
...
BUT IF YOU'LL HEAR ME OUT--
NO, DAMMIT!
JUST... JUST NO.
I TRUSTED THAT...THAT YOU WERE FIGHTING THE EVIL IN YOU, EVEN WHEN NO ONE ELSE DID. I BELIEVED THAT BENEATH IT ALL, YOU WERE GOOD. BUT IT WAS ALL, ALWAYS, A MASK. A MASK YOU WERE WEARING.
LOOK, MAYBE ONE DAY I'LL BE ABLE TO BELIEVE YOU AGAIN. BUT... I'M NOT READY, JAMES. I'M SOR--
ANALYSIS CLEAR.
ARMORY OPEN.
ENTER AT YOUR OWN RISK.
THAT...IS A LOT OF BATARANG GUNS.
LISTEN, JAMES, I PROMISE YOU THAT WHEN THEY RE-INCARCERATE YOU, I'LL MAKE SURE YOU'RE... TREATED WELL. THAT WHATEVER PROGRAMS WE HAVE--
IT'S OKAY, DAD. REALLY. I UNDERSTAND. HERE, COME ON...

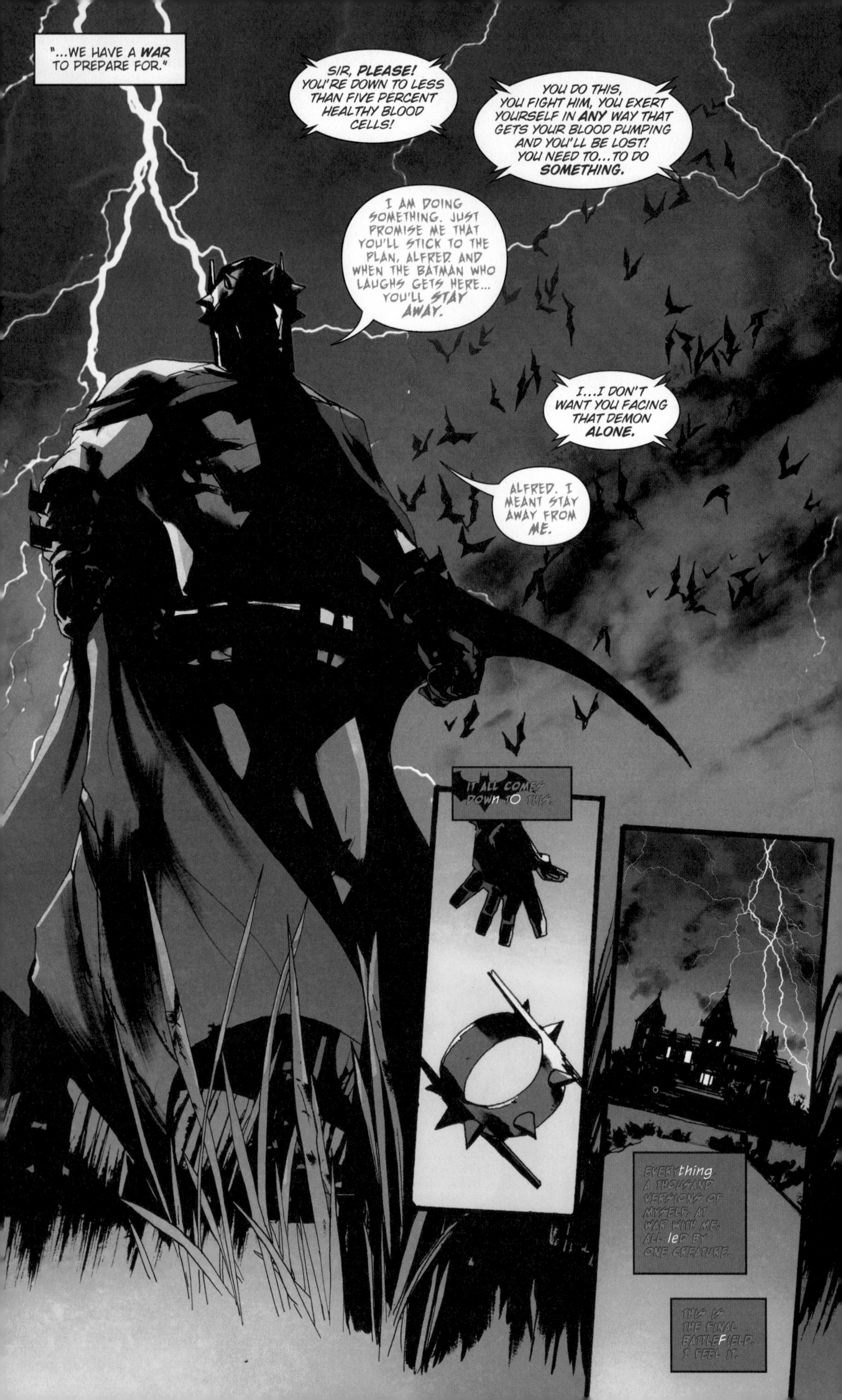
"...WE HAVE A WAR TO PREPARE FOR."
SIR, PLEASE! YOU'RE DOWN TO LESS THAN FIVE PERCENT HEALTHY BLOOD CELLS!
YOU DO THIS, YOU FIGHT HIM, YOU EXERT YOURSELF IN ANY WAY THAT GETS YOUR BLOOD PUMPING AND YOU'LL BE LOST! YOU NEED TO...TO DO SOMETHING.
I AM DOING SOMETHING. JUST PROMISE ME THAT YOU'LL STICK TO THE PLAN, ALFRED. AND WHEN THE BATMAN WHO LAUGHS GETS HERE... YOU'LL STAY AWAY.
I...I DON'T WANT YOU FACING THAT DEMON ALONE.
ALFRED. I MEANT STAY AWAY FROM ME.
IT ALL COMES DOWN TO THIS.
EVERYthing. A THOUSAND VERSIONS OF MYSELF. AT WAR WITH ME. ALL leD BY ONE CREATURE.
THIS IS THE FINAL BATTLEFIELD. I FEEL IT.

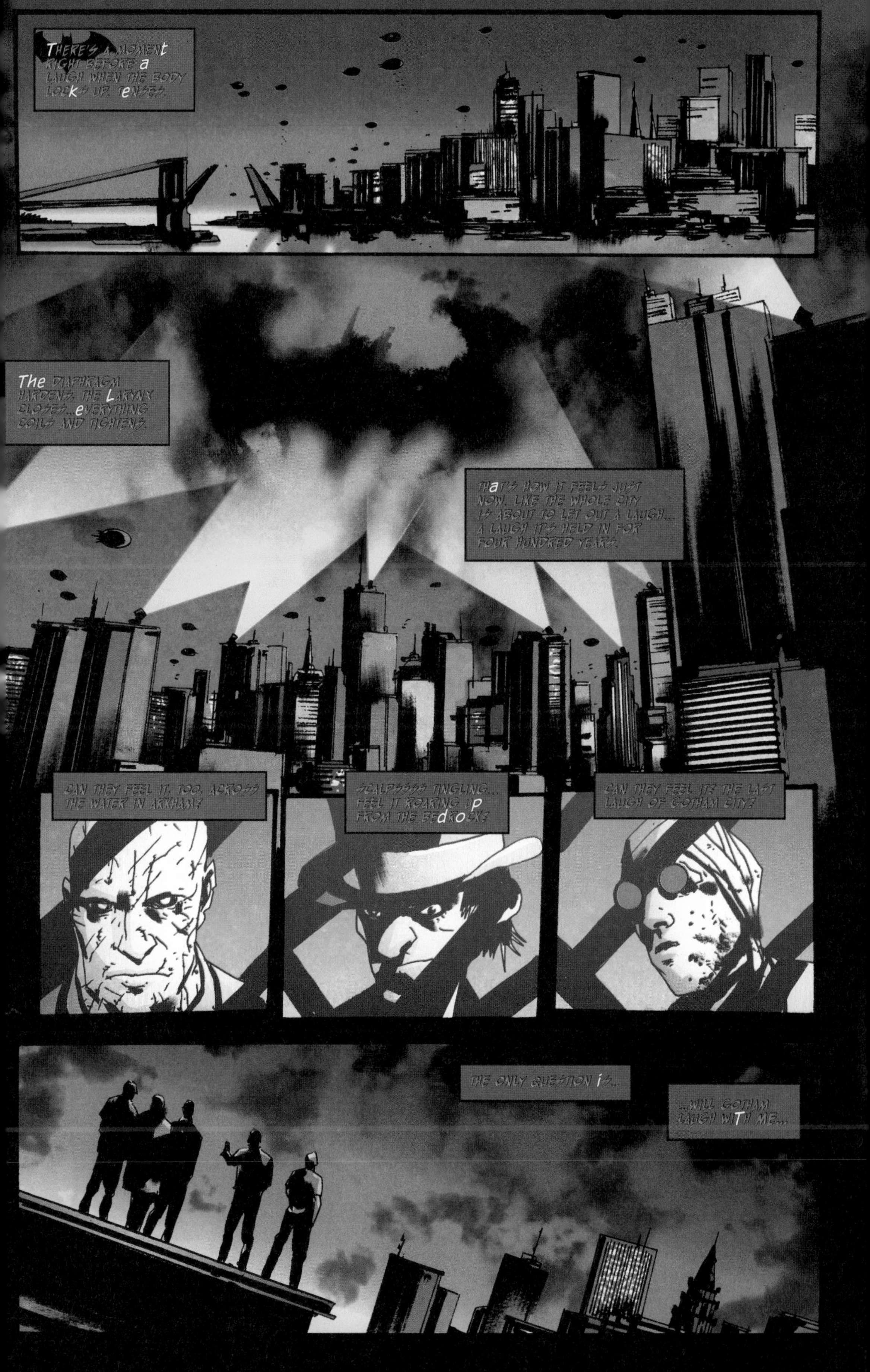
THERE'S A MOMENT RIGHT BEFORE A LAUGH WHEN THE BODY LOCKS UP. TENSES.
THE DIAPHRAGM HARDENS. THE LARYNX CLOSES...EVERYTHING BOILS AND TIGHTENS.
THAT'S HOW IT FEELS JUST NOW. LIKE THE WHOLE CITY IS ABOUT TO LET OUT A LAUGH... A LAUGH IT'S HELD IN FOR FOUR HUNDRED YEARS.
CAN THEY FEEL IT, TOO, ACROSS THE WATER IN ARKHAM?
SCALPSSSS TINGLING... FEEL IT ROARING UP FROM THE BEDROCK?
CAN THEY FEEL IT? THE LAST LAUGH OF GOTHAM CITY?
THE ONLY QUESTION IS...
...WILL GOTHAM LAUGH WITH ME...

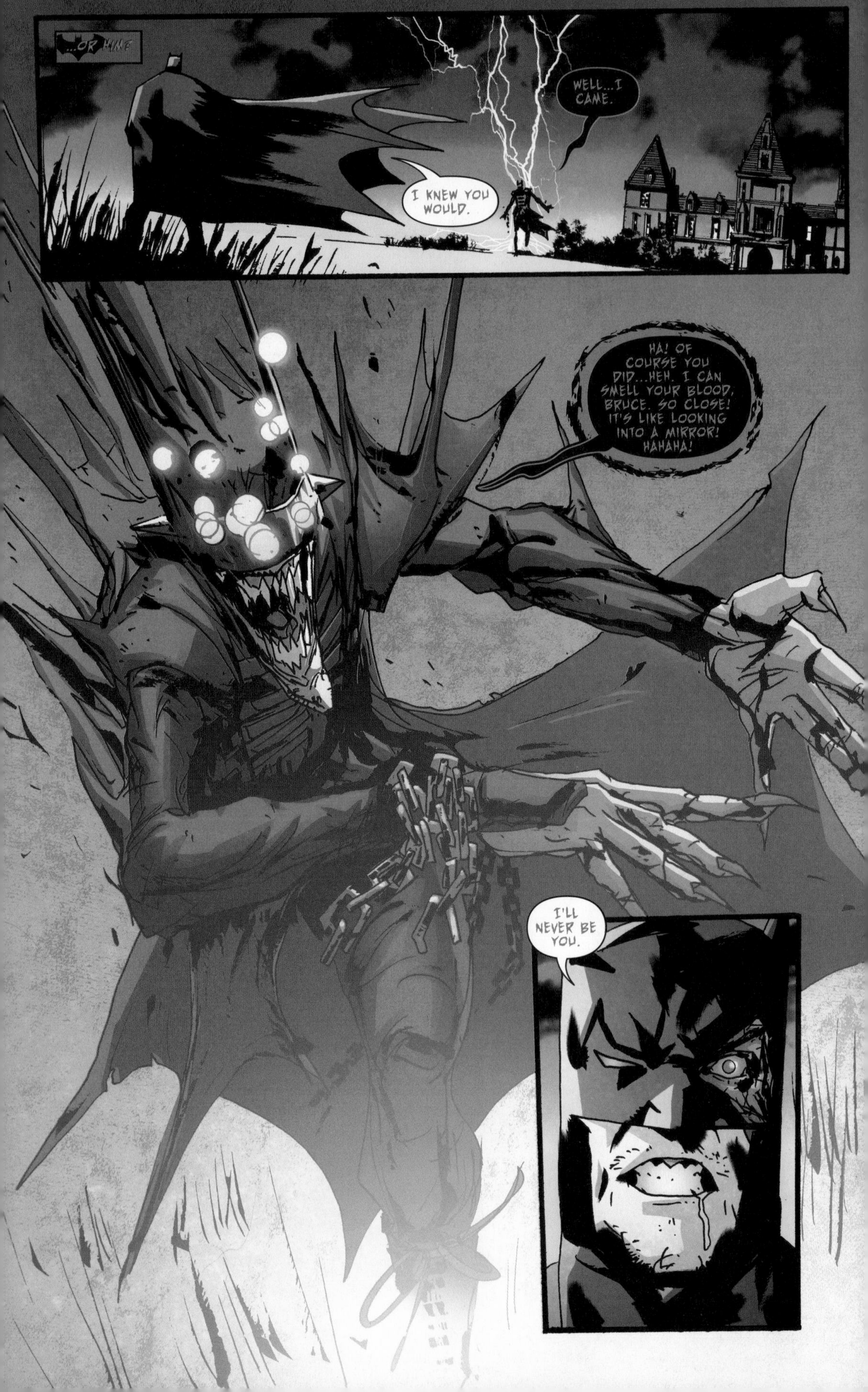
...OR HIM?
WELL...I CAME.
I KNEW YOU WOULD.
HA! OF COURSE YOU DID...HEH. I CAN SMELL YOUR BLOOD, BRUCE. SO CLOSE! IT'S LIKE LOOKING INTO A MIRROR! HAHAHA!
I'LL NEVER BE YOU.

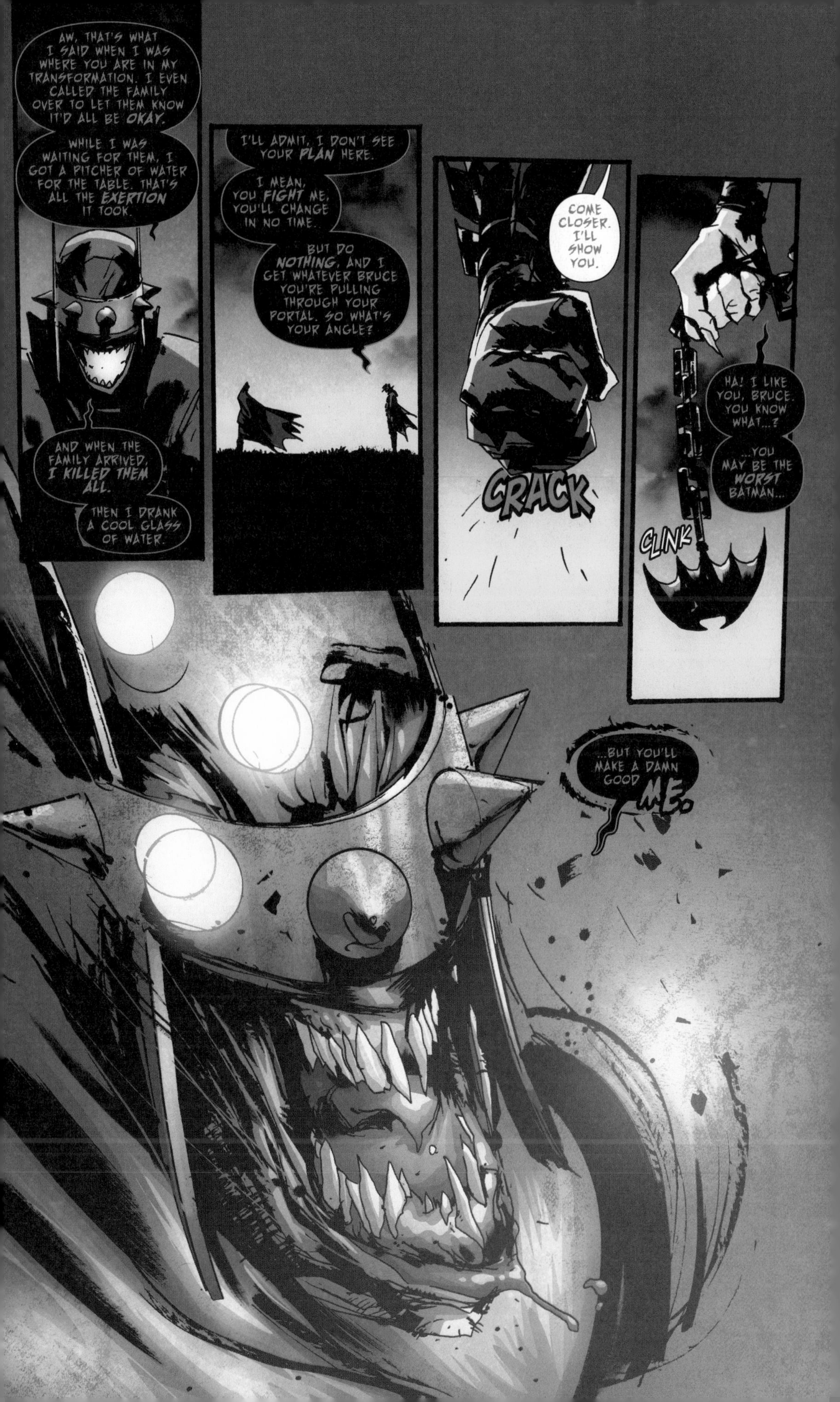

AW, THAT'S WHAT I SAID WHEN I WAS WHERE YOU ARE IN MY TRANSFORMATION. I EVEN CALLED THE FAMILY OVER TO LET THEM KNOW IT'D ALL BE OKAY.
WHILE I WAS WAITING FOR THEM, I GOT A PITCHER OF WATER FOR THE TABLE. THAT'S ALL THE EXERTION IT TOOK.
AND WHEN THE FAMILY ARRIVED, I KILLED THEM ALL.
THEN I DRANK A COOL GLASS OF WATER.
I'LL ADMIT, I DON'T SEE YOUR PLAN HERE.
I MEAN, YOU FIGHT ME, YOU'LL CHANGE IN NO TIME.
BUT DO NOTHING, AND I GET WHATEVER BRUCE YOU'RE PULLING THROUGH YOUR PORTAL. SO WHAT'S YOUR ANGLE?
COME CLOSER. I'LL SHOW YOU.
CRACK
HA! I LIKE YOU, BRUCE. YOU KNOW WHAT...?
...YOU MAY BE THE WORST BATMAN...
CLINK
...BUT YOU'LL MAKE A DAMN GOOD ME.

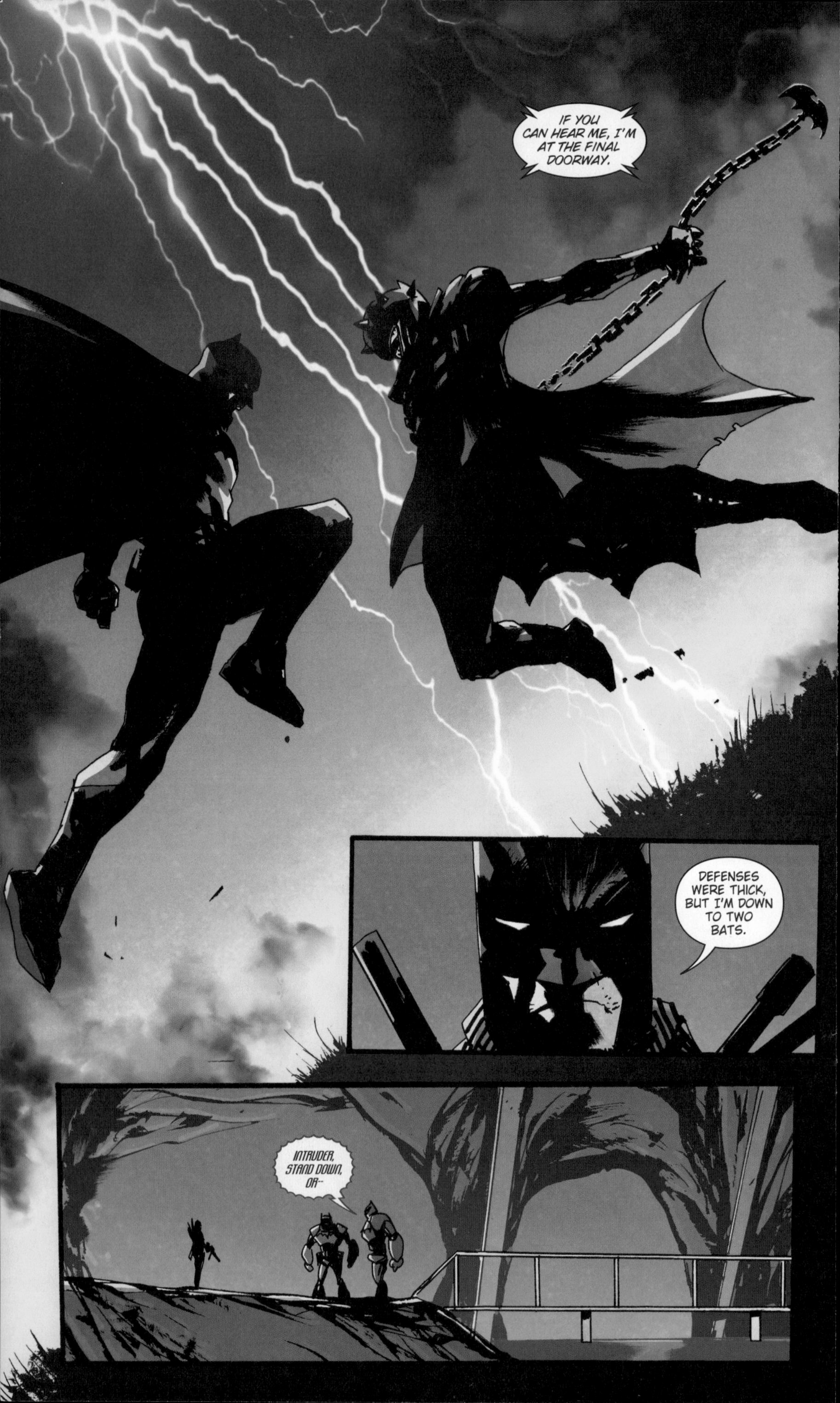
IF YOU CAN HEAR ME, I'M AT THE FINAL DOORWAY.
DEFENSES WERE THICK, BUT I'M DOWN TO TWO BATS.
INTRUDER, STAND DOWN, OR--

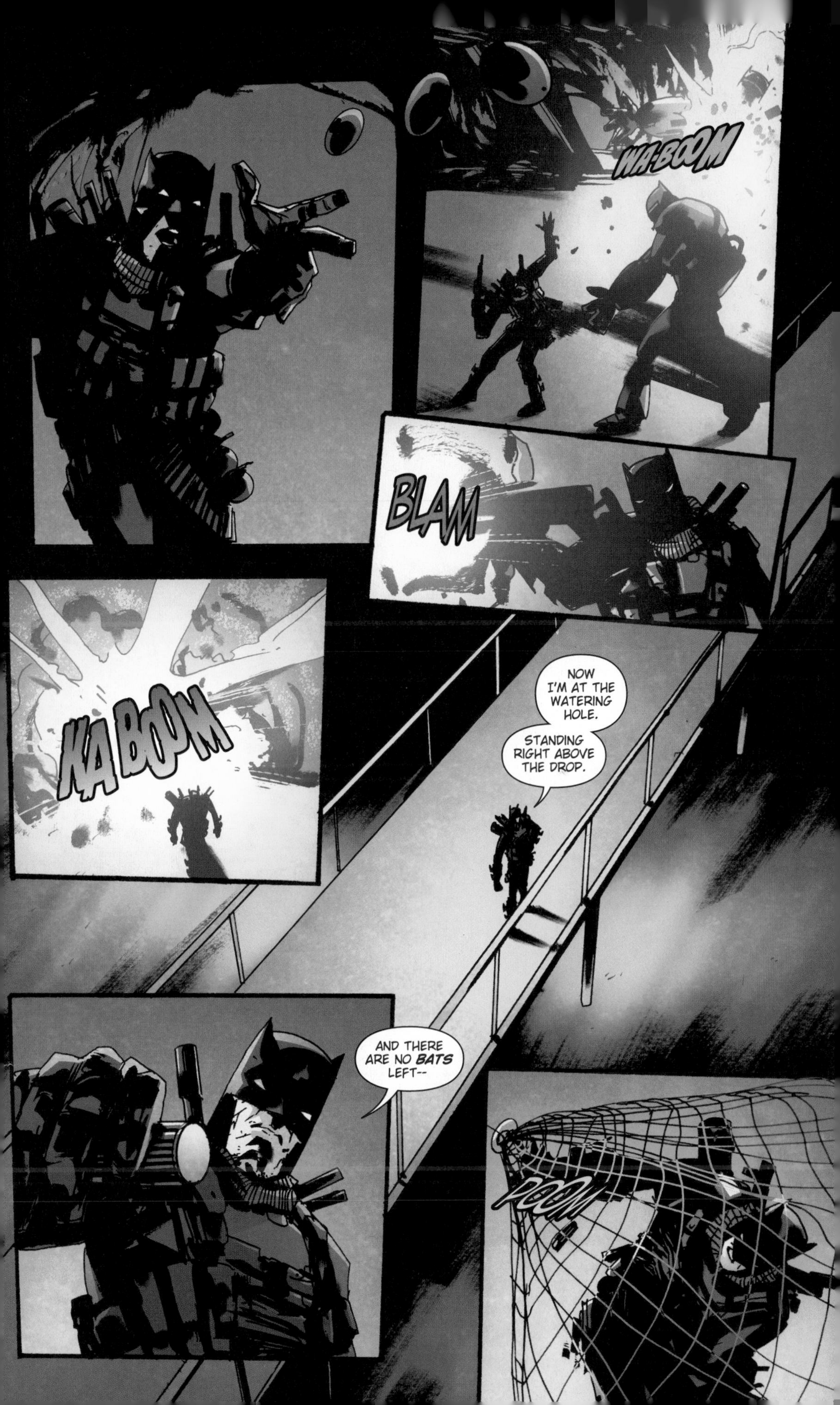
WA-BOOM
BLAM
KA BOOM
NOW I'M AT THE WATERING HOLE.
STANDING RIGHT ABOVE THE DROP.
AND THERE ARE NO BATS LEFT--
POOM

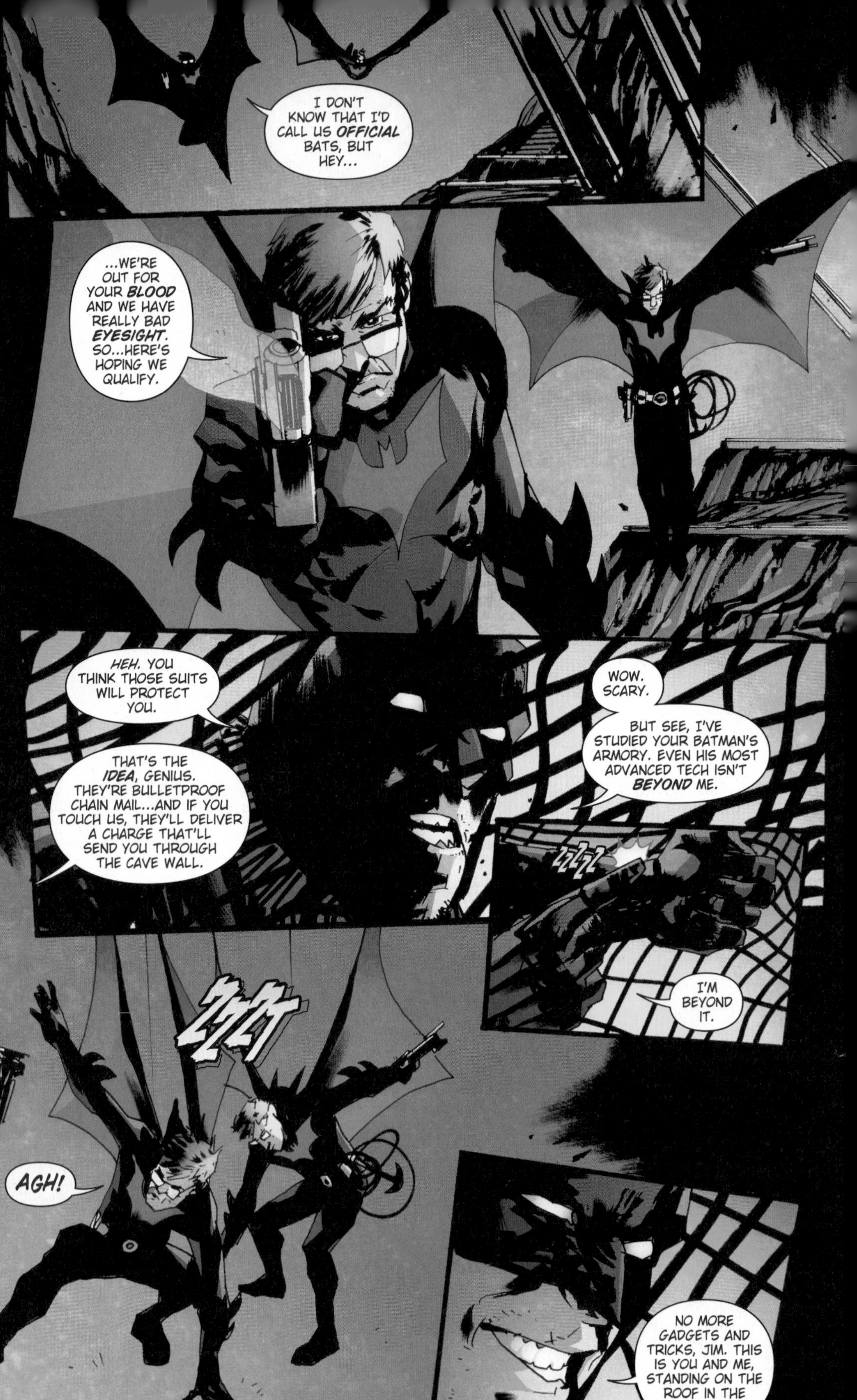

I DON'T KNOW THAT I'D CALL US *OFFICIAL* BATS, BUT HEY...
...WE'RE OUT FOR YOUR *BLOOD* AND WE HAVE REALLY BAD *EYESIGHT*. SO...HERE'S HOPING WE QUALIFY.
HEH. YOU THINK THOSE SUITS WILL PROTECT YOU.
THAT'S THE *IDEA*, GENIUS. THEY'RE BULLETPROOF CHAIN MAIL...AND IF YOU TOUCH US, THEY'LL DELIVER A CHARGE THAT'LL SEND YOU THROUGH THE CAVE WALL.
WOW. SCARY.
BUT SEE, I'VE STUDIED YOUR BATMAN'S ARMORY. EVEN HIS MOST ADVANCED TECH ISN'T *BEYOND* ME.
ZZZZZ
I'M BEYOND IT.
ZZZZT
AGH!
NO MORE GADGETS AND TRICKS, JIM. THIS IS YOU AND ME, STANDING ON THE ROOF IN THE RAIN...

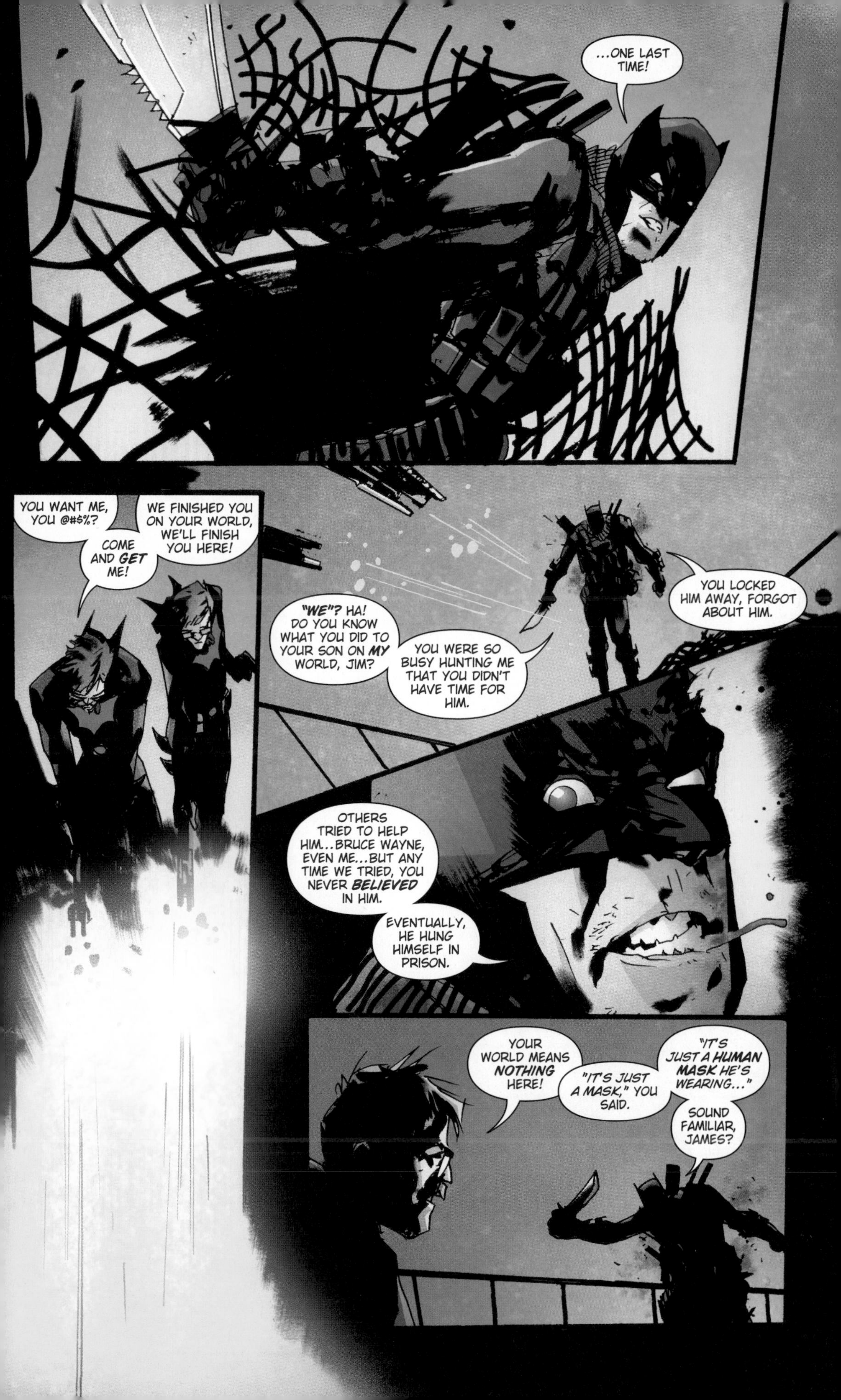
...ONE LAST TIME!
YOU WANT ME, YOU @#$%?
COME AND GET ME!
WE FINISHED YOU ON YOUR WORLD, WE'LL FINISH YOU HERE!
"WE"? HA! DO YOU KNOW WHAT YOU DID TO YOUR SON ON MY WORLD, JIM?
YOU WERE SO BUSY HUNTING ME THAT YOU DIDN'T HAVE TIME FOR HIM.
YOU LOCKED HIM AWAY, FORGOT ABOUT HIM.
OTHERS TRIED TO HELP HIM...BRUCE WAYNE, EVEN ME...BUT ANY TIME WE TRIED, YOU NEVER BELIEVED IN HIM.
EVENTUALLY, HE HUNG HIMSELF IN PRISON.
YOUR WORLD MEANS NOTHING HERE!
"IT'S JUST A MASK," YOU SAID.
"IT'S JUST A HUMAN MASK HE'S WEARING..."
SOUND FAMILIAR, JAMES?

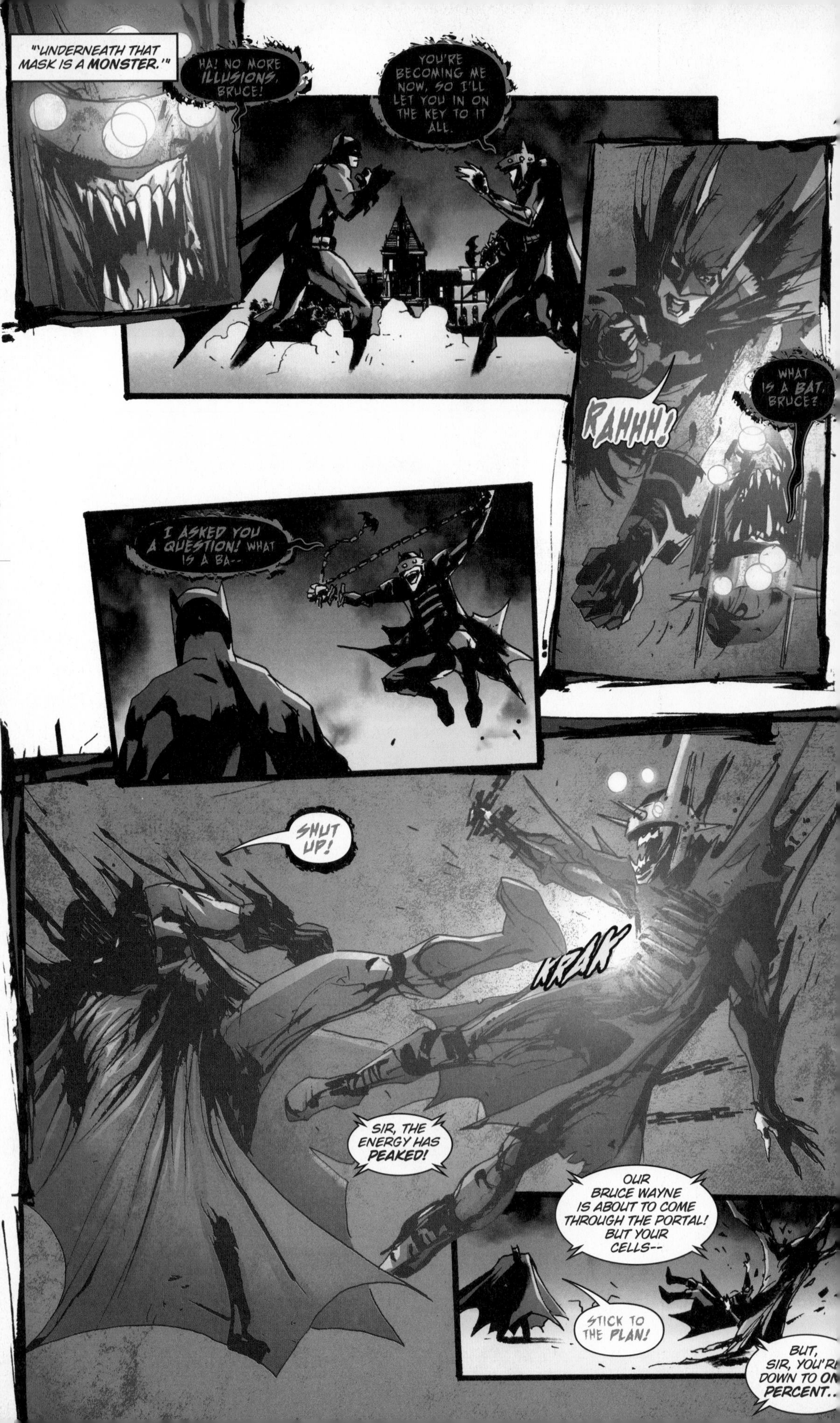

"UNDERNEATH THAT MASK IS A MONSTER."
HA! NO MORE ILLUSIONS, BRUCE!
YOU'RE BECOMING ME NOW, SO I'LL LET YOU IN ON THE KEY TO IT ALL.
RAHHH!
WHAT IS A BAT, BRUCE?
I ASKED YOU A QUESTION! WHAT IS A BA--
SHUT UP!
KRAK
SIR, THE ENERGY HAS PEAKED!
OUR BRUCE WAYNE IS ABOUT TO COME THROUGH THE PORTAL! BUT YOUR CELLS--
STICK TO THE PLAN!

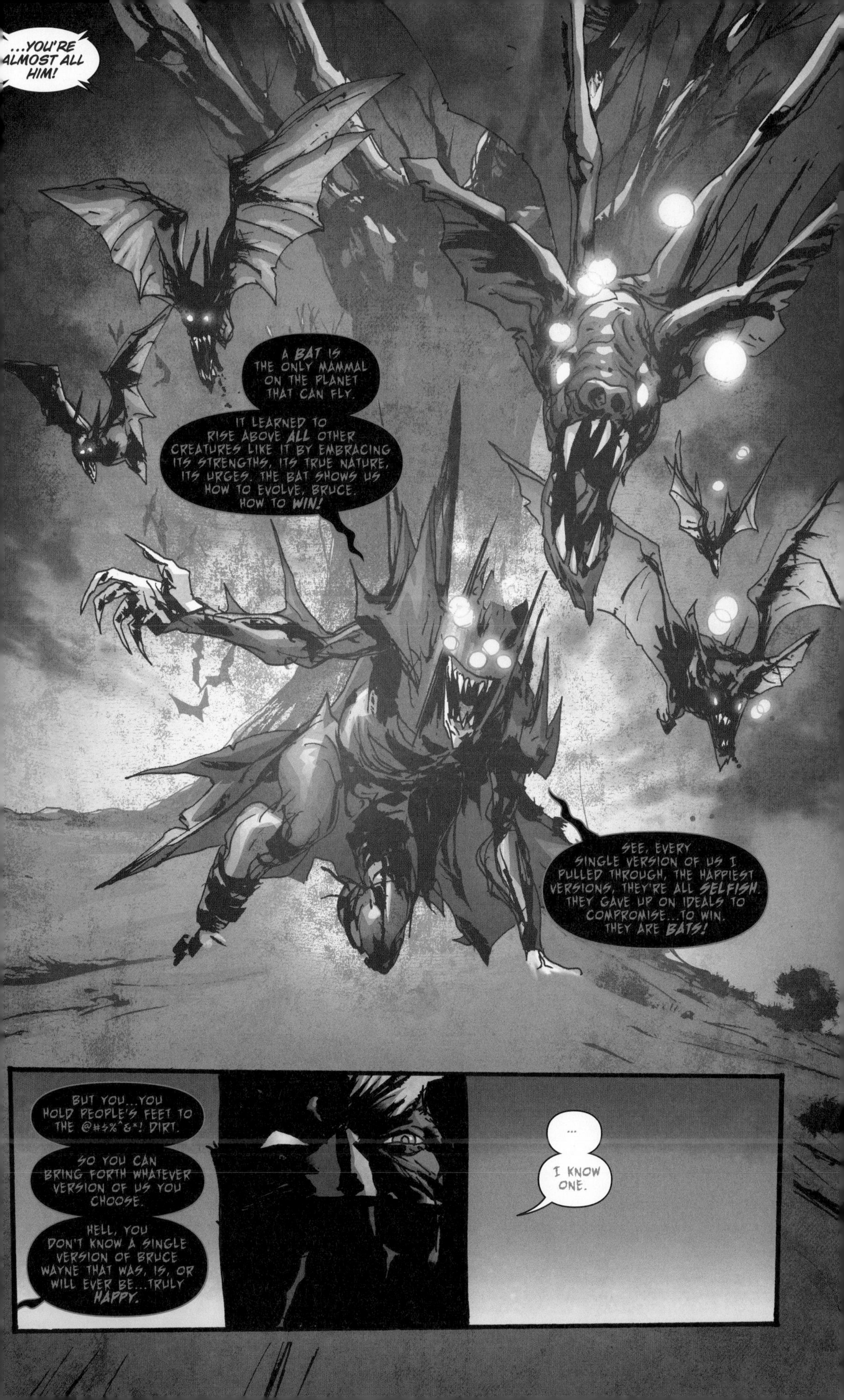
...YOU'RE ALMOST ALL HIM!
A BAT IS THE ONLY MAMMAL ON THE PLANET THAT CAN FLY.
IT LEARNED TO RISE ABOVE ALL OTHER CREATURES LIKE IT BY EMBRACING ITS STRENGTHS, ITS TRUE NATURE, ITS URGES. THE BAT SHOWS US HOW TO EVOLVE, BRUCE. HOW TO WIN!
SEE, EVERY SINGLE VERSION OF US I PULLED THROUGH, THE HAPPIEST VERSIONS, THEY'RE ALL SELFISH. THEY GAVE UP ON IDEALS TO COMPROMISE...TO WIN. THEY ARE BATS!
BUT YOU...YOU HOLD PEOPLE'S FEET TO THE @#$%^&*! DIRT.
SO YOU CAN BRING FORTH WHATEVER VERSION OF US YOU CHOOSE.
HELL, YOU DON'T KNOW A SINGLE VERSION OF BRUCE WAYNE THAT WAS, IS, OR WILL EVER BE...TRULY HAPPY.
...
I KNOW ONE.

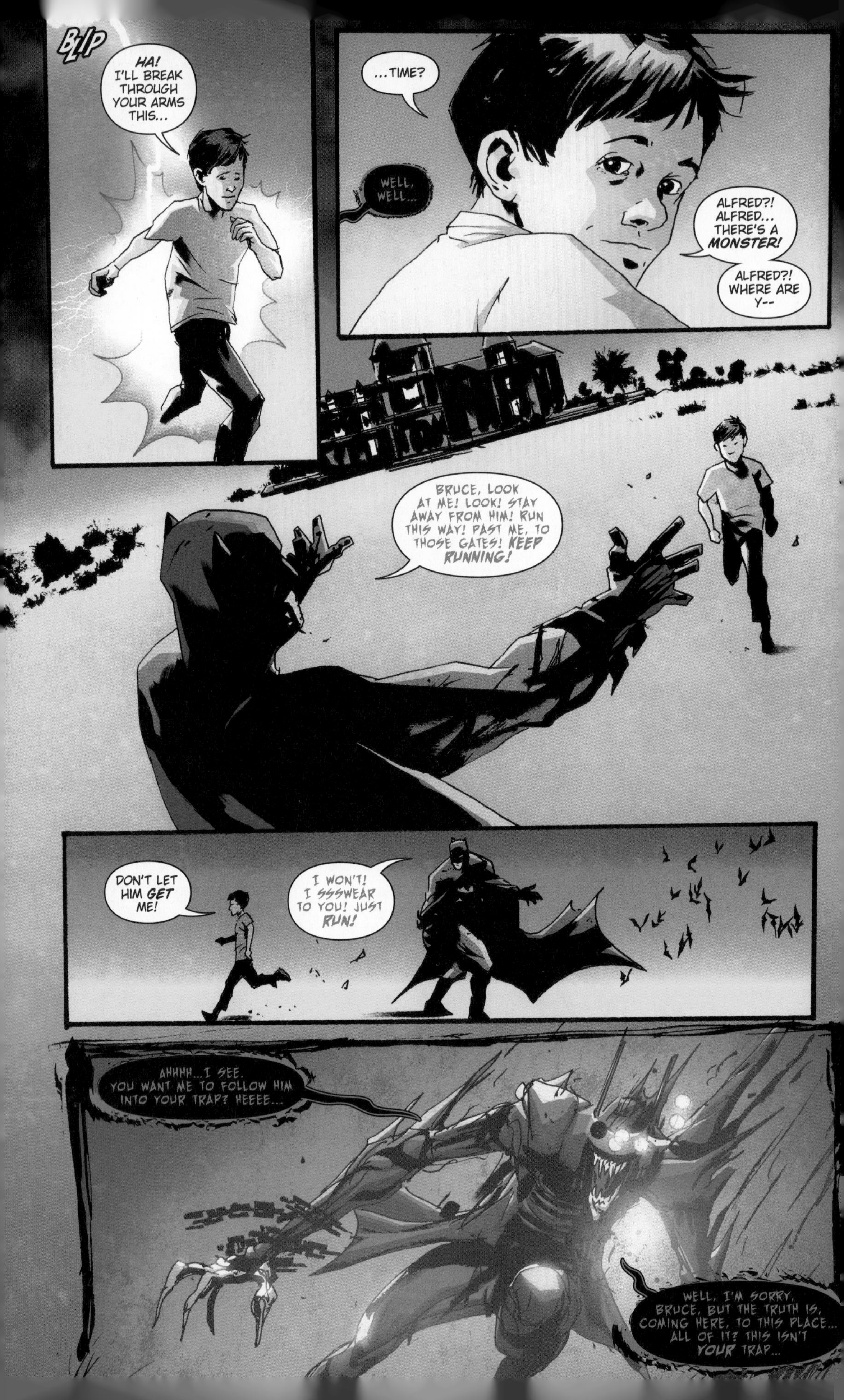
BLIP
HA! I'LL BREAK THROUGH YOUR ARMS THIS...
...TIME?
WELL, WELL...
ALFRED?! ALFRED... THERE'S A MONSTER!
ALFRED?! WHERE ARE Y--
BRUCE, LOOK AT ME! LOOK! STAY AWAY FROM HIM! RUN THIS WAY! PAST ME, TO THOSE GATES! KEEP RUNNING!
DON'T LET HIM GET ME!
I WON'T! I SSSWEAR TO YOU! JUST RUN!
AHHHH...I SEE. YOU WANT ME TO FOLLOW HIM INTO YOUR TRAP? HEEEE...
WELL, I'M SORRY, BRUCE, BUT THE TRUTH IS, COMING HERE, TO THIS PLACE... ALL OF IT? THIS ISN'T YOUR TRAP...

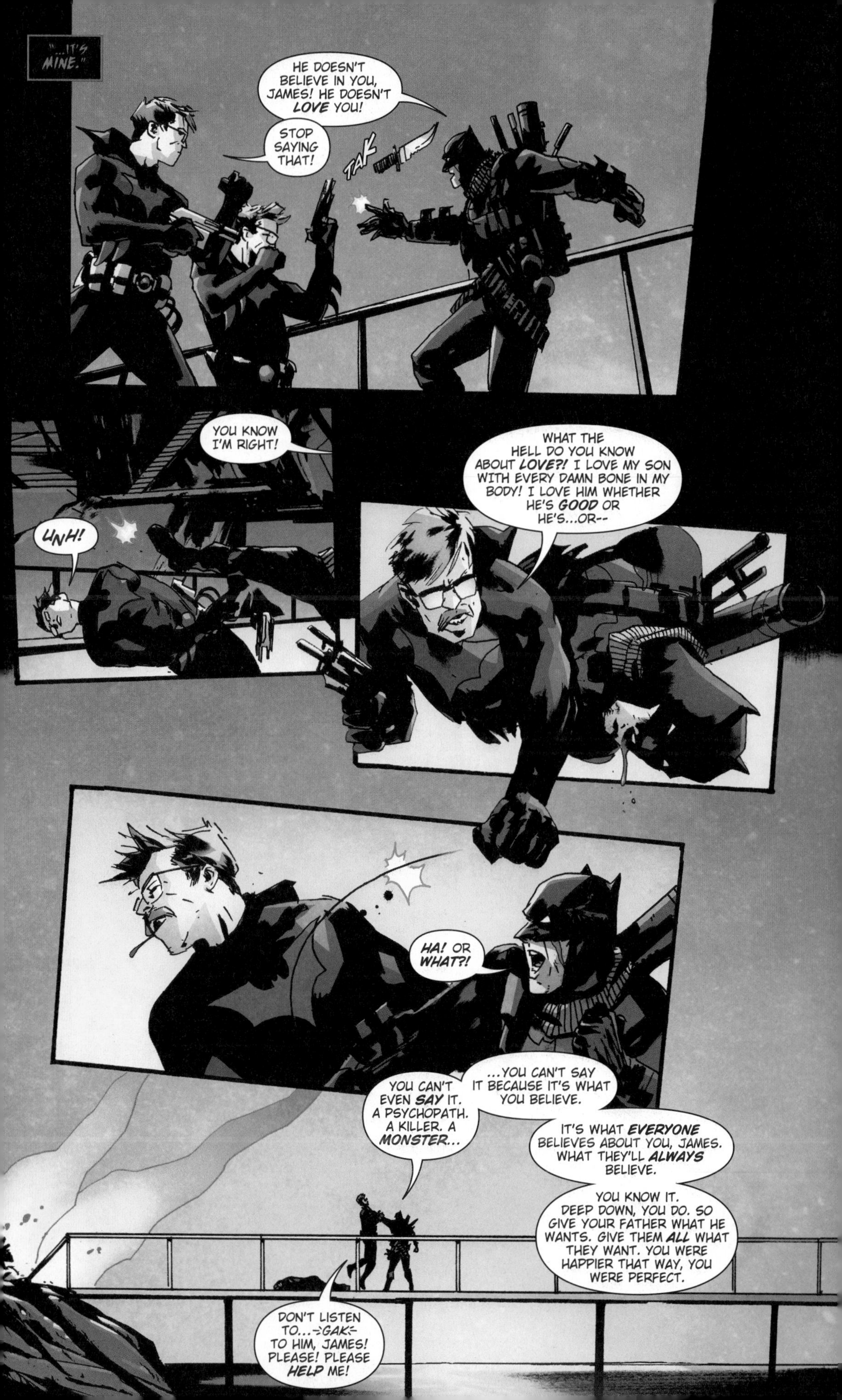
"...IT'S MINE."
HE DOESN'T BELIEVE IN YOU, JAMES! HE DOESN'T LOVE YOU!
STOP SAYING THAT!
TAK
YOU KNOW I'M RIGHT!
UNH!
WHAT THE HELL DO YOU KNOW ABOUT LOVE?! I LOVE MY SON WITH EVERY DAMN BONE IN MY BODY! I LOVE HIM WHETHER HE'S GOOD OR HE'S...OR--
HA! OR WHAT?!
YOU CAN'T EVEN SAY IT. A PSYCHOPATH. A KILLER. A MONSTER...
...YOU CAN'T SAY IT BECAUSE IT'S WHAT YOU BELIEVE.
IT'S WHAT EVERYONE BELIEVES ABOUT YOU, JAMES. WHAT THEY'LL ALWAYS BELIEVE.
YOU KNOW IT. DEEP DOWN, YOU DO. SO GIVE YOUR FATHER WHAT HE WANTS. GIVE THEM ALL WHAT THEY WANT. YOU WERE HAPPIER THAT WAY, YOU WERE PERFECT.
DON'T LISTEN TO... GAK TO HIM, JAMES! PLEASE! PLEASE HELP ME!

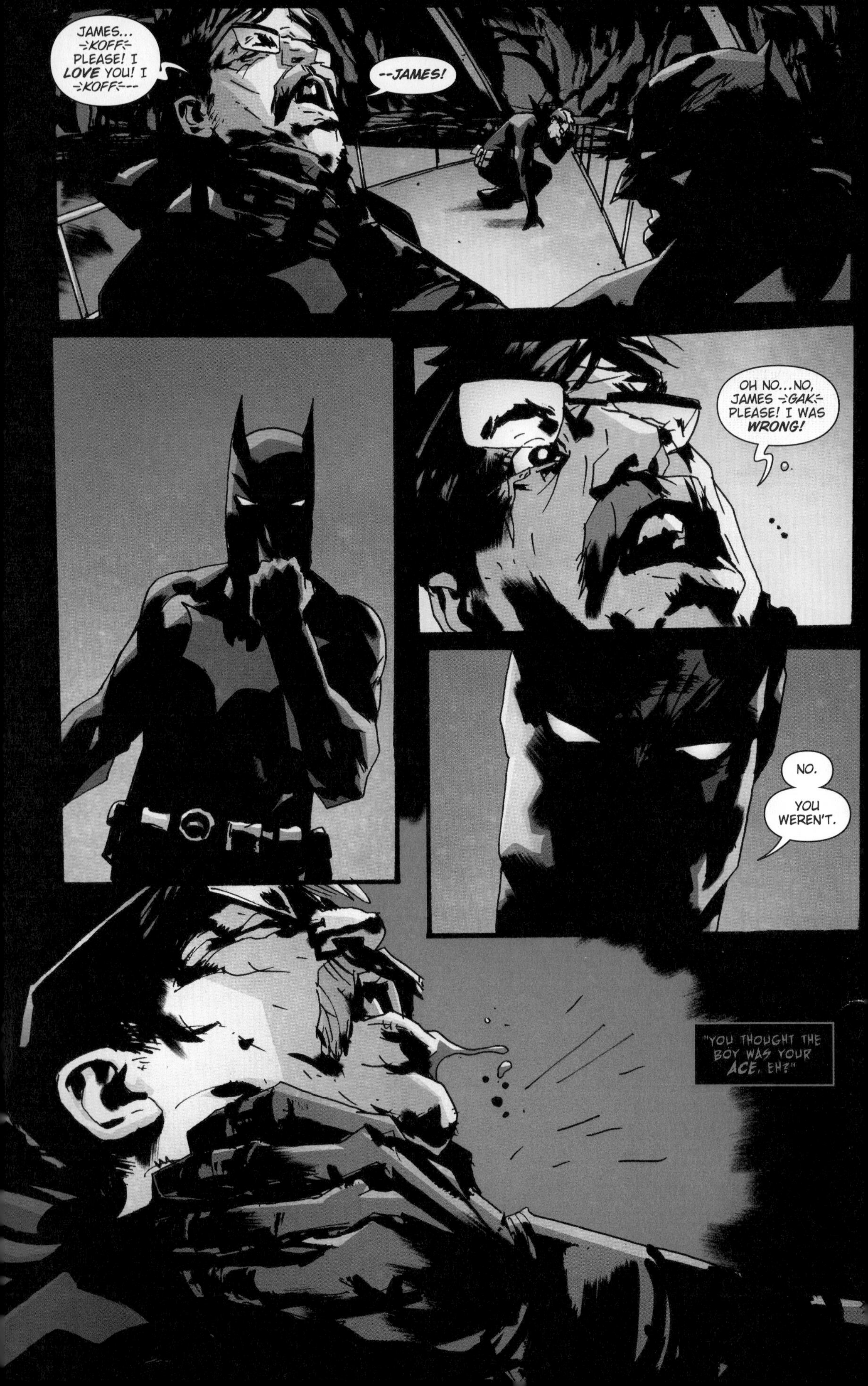
JAMES... ⇒KOFF⇐ PLEASE! I LOVE YOU! I ⇒KOFF⇐---
--JAMES!
OH NO...NO, JAMES ⇒GAK⇐ PLEASE! I WAS WRONG!
NO.
YOU WEREN'T.
"YOU THOUGHT THE BOY WAS YOUR ACE, EH?"

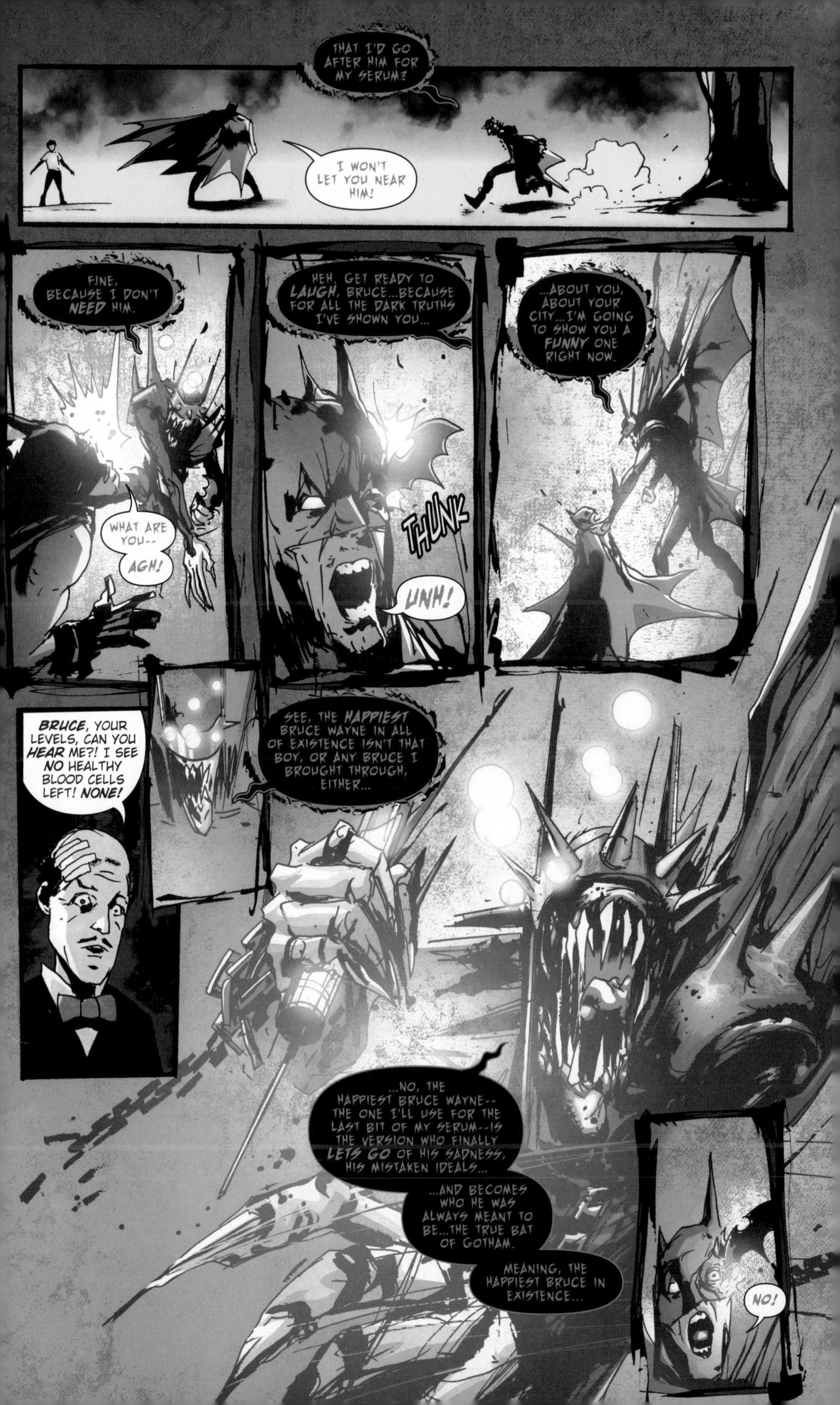
THAT I'D GO AFTER HIM FOR MY SERUM?
I WON'T LET YOU NEAR HIM!
FINE, BECAUSE I DON'T NEED HIM.
WHAT ARE YOU-- AGH!
HEH. GET READY TO LAUGH, BRUCE...BECAUSE FOR ALL THE DARK TRUTHS I'VE SHOWN YOU...
THUNK
UNH!
...ABOUT YOU, ABOUT YOUR CITY...I'M GOING TO SHOW YOU A FUNNY ONE RIGHT NOW.
BRUCE, YOUR LEVELS, CAN YOU HEAR ME?! I SEE NO HEALTHY BLOOD CELLS LEFT! NONE!
SEE, THE HAPPIEST BRUCE WAYNE IN ALL OF EXISTENCE ISN'T THAT BOY, OR ANY BRUCE I BROUGHT THROUGH, EITHER...
...NO, THE HAPPIEST BRUCE WAYNE--THE ONE I'LL USE FOR THE LAST BIT OF MY SERUM--IS THE VERSION WHO FINALLY LETS GO OF HIS SADNESS, HIS MISTAKEN IDEALS...
...AND BECOMES WHO HE WAS ALWAYS MEANT TO BE...THE TRUE BAT OF GOTHAM.
MEANING, THE HAPPIEST BRUCE IN EXISTENCE...
NO!

THE BATMAN WHO LAUGHS
PART 6
SCOTT SNYDER Writer
JOCK Artist
DAVID BARON Colors
SAL CIPRIANO Letters
JOCK Cover
DAVE WIELGOSZ Asst. Editor
KATIE KUBERT Editor
JAMIE S. RICH Group Editor
...IS YOU, RIGHT AT THIS VERY MOMENT...
...RIGHT NOW. WHEN YOU BECOME... ME.
AND I HEAR It Then... THE TERRIBLE SOUnd.
AS THE CITY LAUGHS... WITH BOTH OF USSSSS.

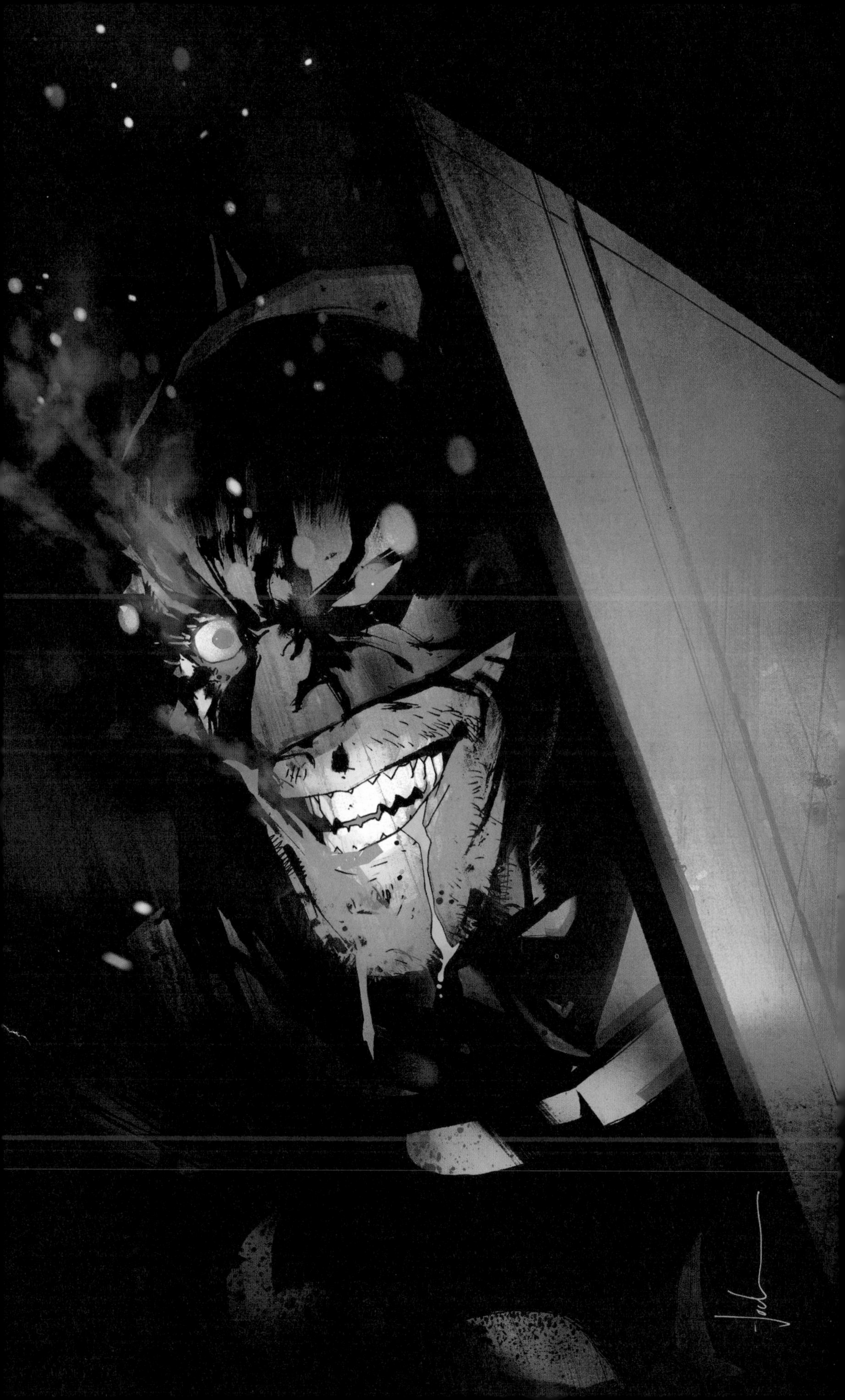

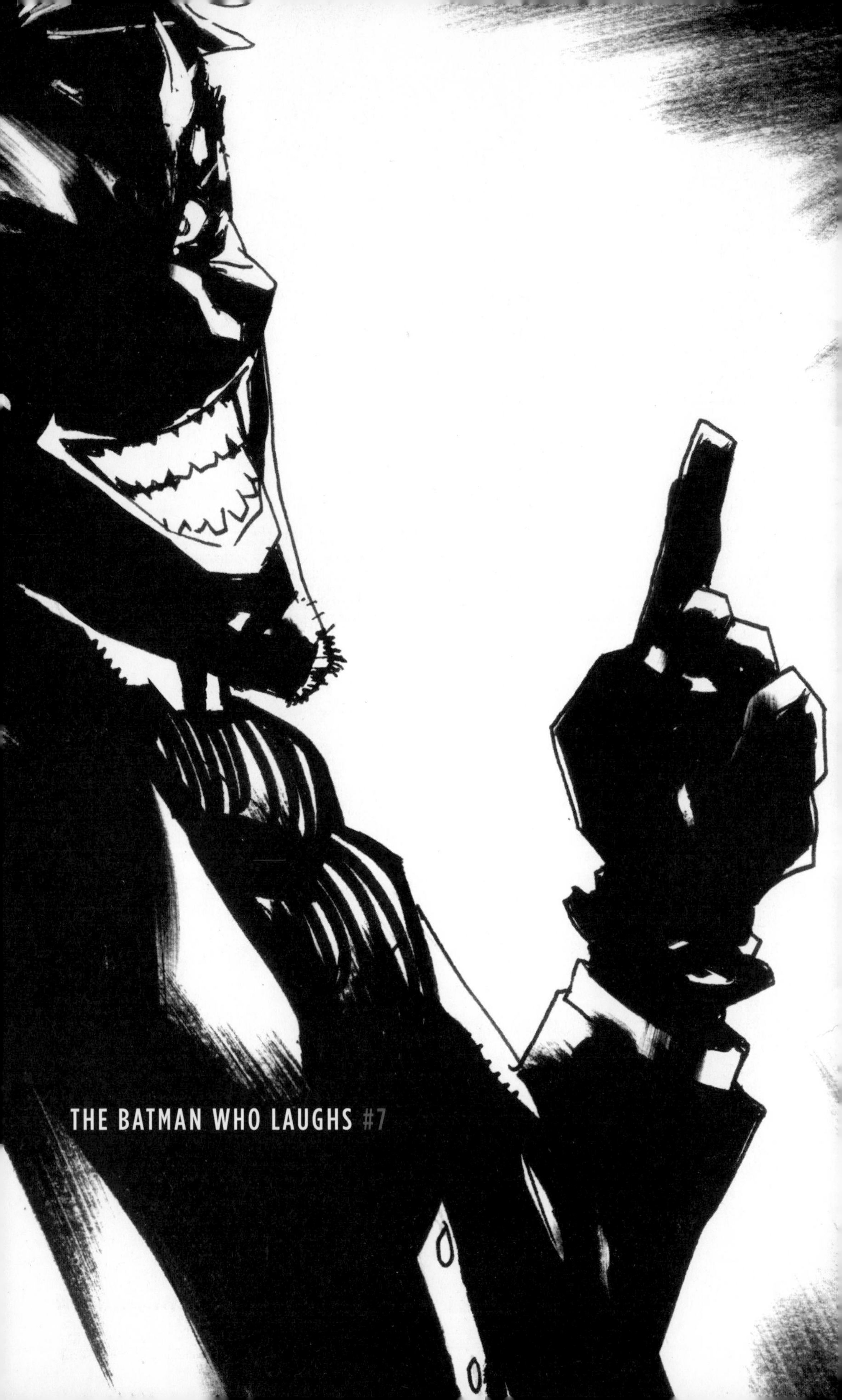
THE BATMAN WHO LAUGHS #7

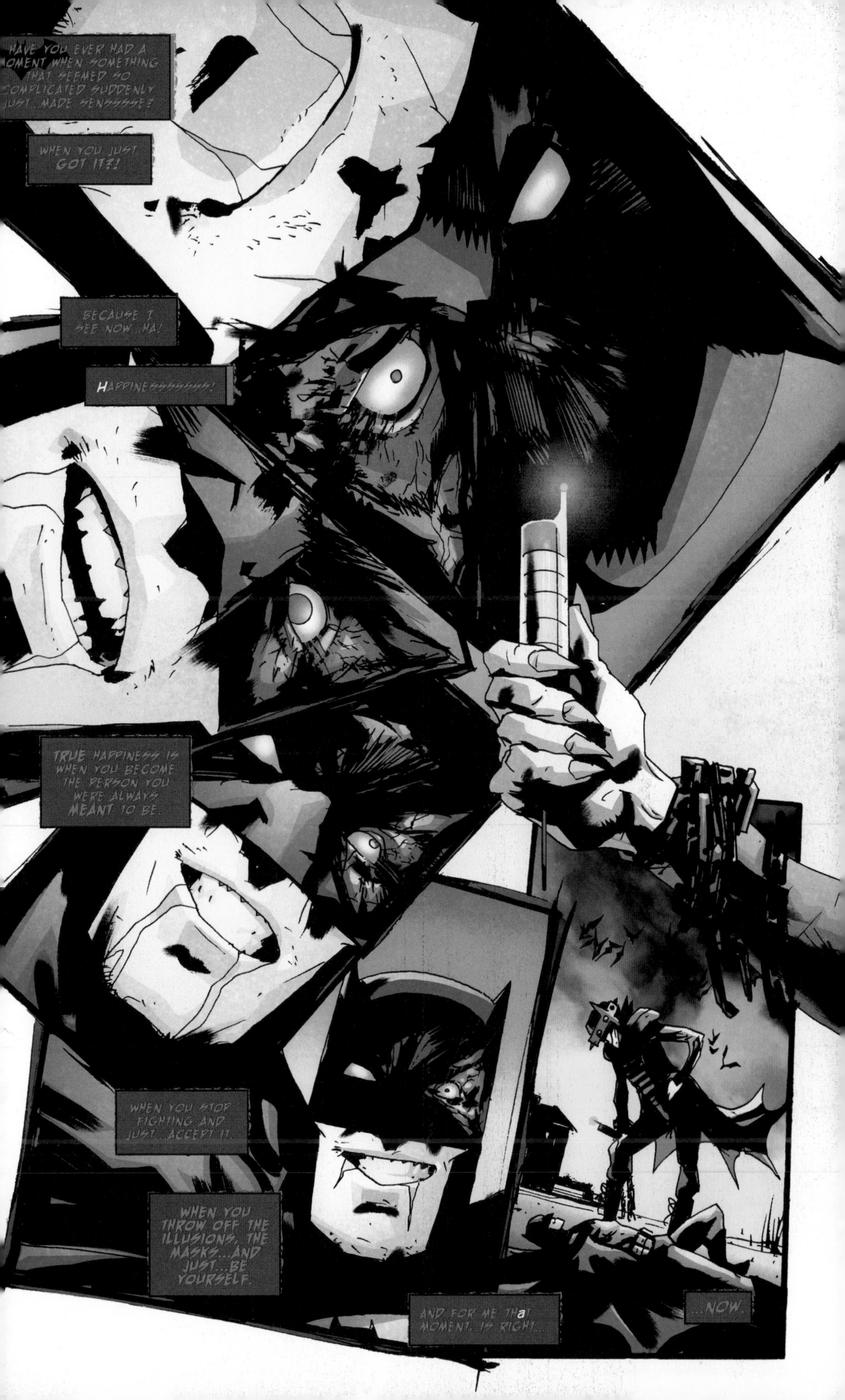
HAVE YOU EVER HAD A MOMENT WHEN SOMETHING THAT SEEMED SO COMPLICATED SUDDENLY JUST...MADE SENSSSSSE?
WHEN YOU JUST GOT IT?!
BECAUSE I SEE NOW...HA!
HAPPINESSSSSSSS!
TRUE HAPPINESS IS WHEN YOU BECOME THE PERSON YOU WERE ALWAYS MEANT TO BE.
WHEN YOU STOP FIGHTING AND JUST...ACCEPT IT.
WHEN YOU THROW OFF THE ILLUSIONS, THE MASKS...AND JUST...BE YOURSELF.
AND FOR ME THAT MOMENT, IS RIGHT...
...NOW.

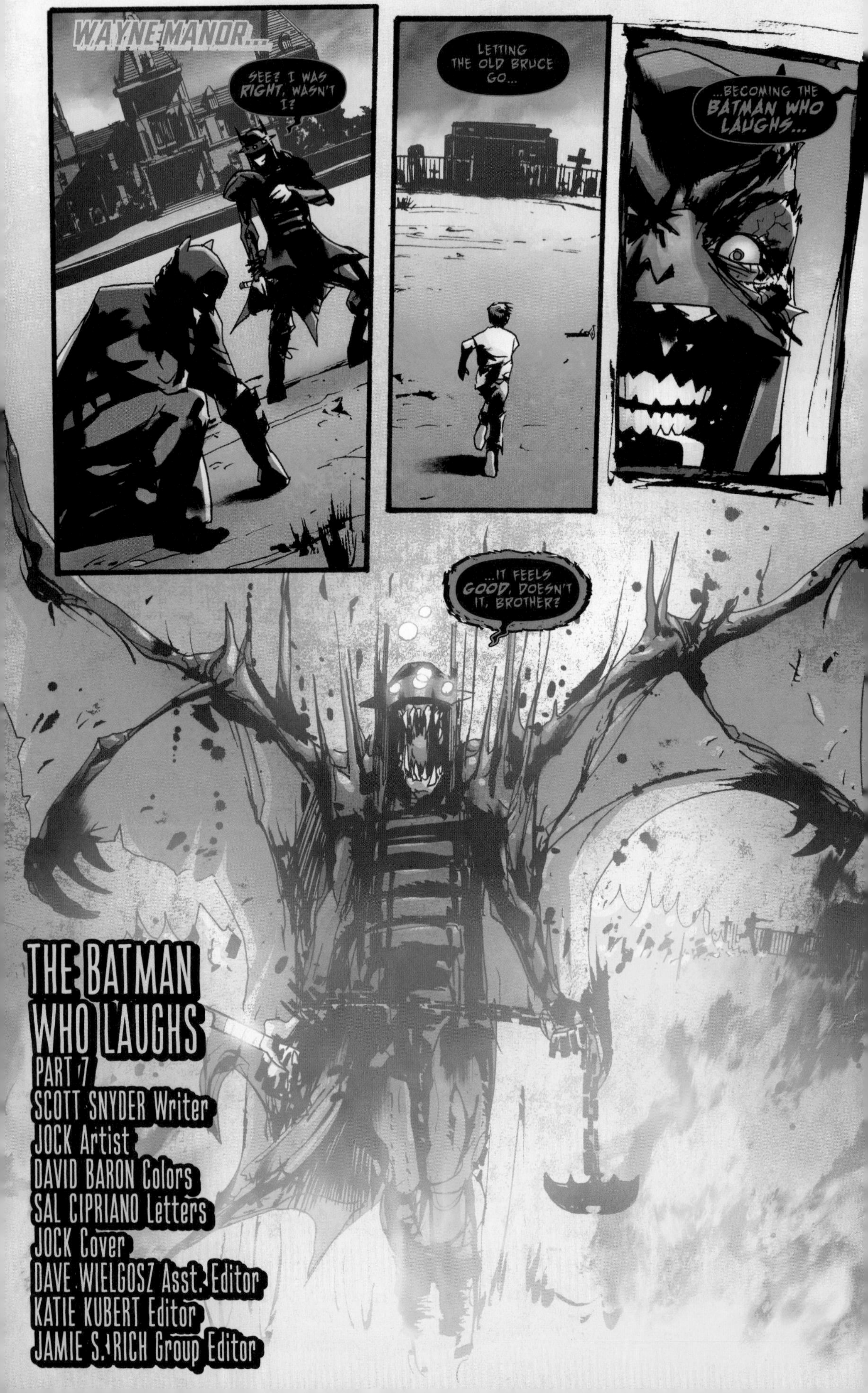
WAYNE MANOR...
SEE? I WAS RIGHT, WASN'T I?
LETTING THE OLD BRUCE GO...
...BECOMING THE BATMAN WHO LAUGHS...
...IT FEELS GOOD, DOESN'T IT, BROTHER?

THE BATMAN WHO LAUGHS

PART 7

SCOTT SNYDER Writer
JOCK Artist
DAVID BARON Colors
SAL CIPRIANO Letters
JOCK Cover
DAVE WIELGOSZ Asst. Editor
KATIE KUBERT Editor
JAMIE S. RICH Group Editor

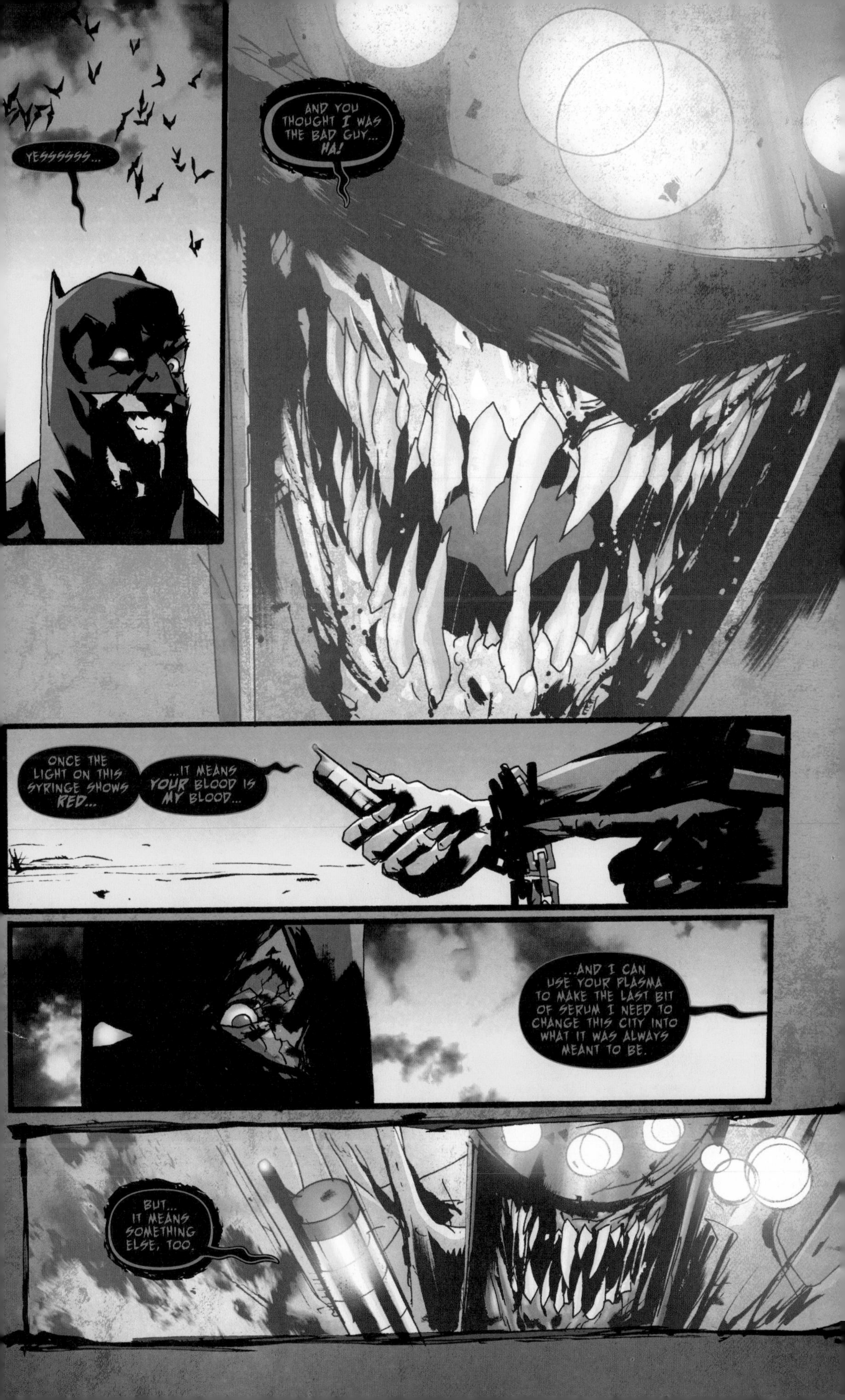
YESSSSSS...
AND YOU THOUGHT I WAS THE BAD GUY... HA!
ONCE THE LIGHT ON THIS SYRINGE SHOWS RED...
...IT MEANS YOUR BLOOD IS MY BLOOD...
...AND I CAN USE YOUR PLASMA TO MAKE THE LAST BIT OF SERUM I NEED TO CHANGE THIS CITY INTO WHAT IT WAS ALWAYS MEANT TO BE.
BUT... IT MEANS SOMETHING ELSE, TOO.

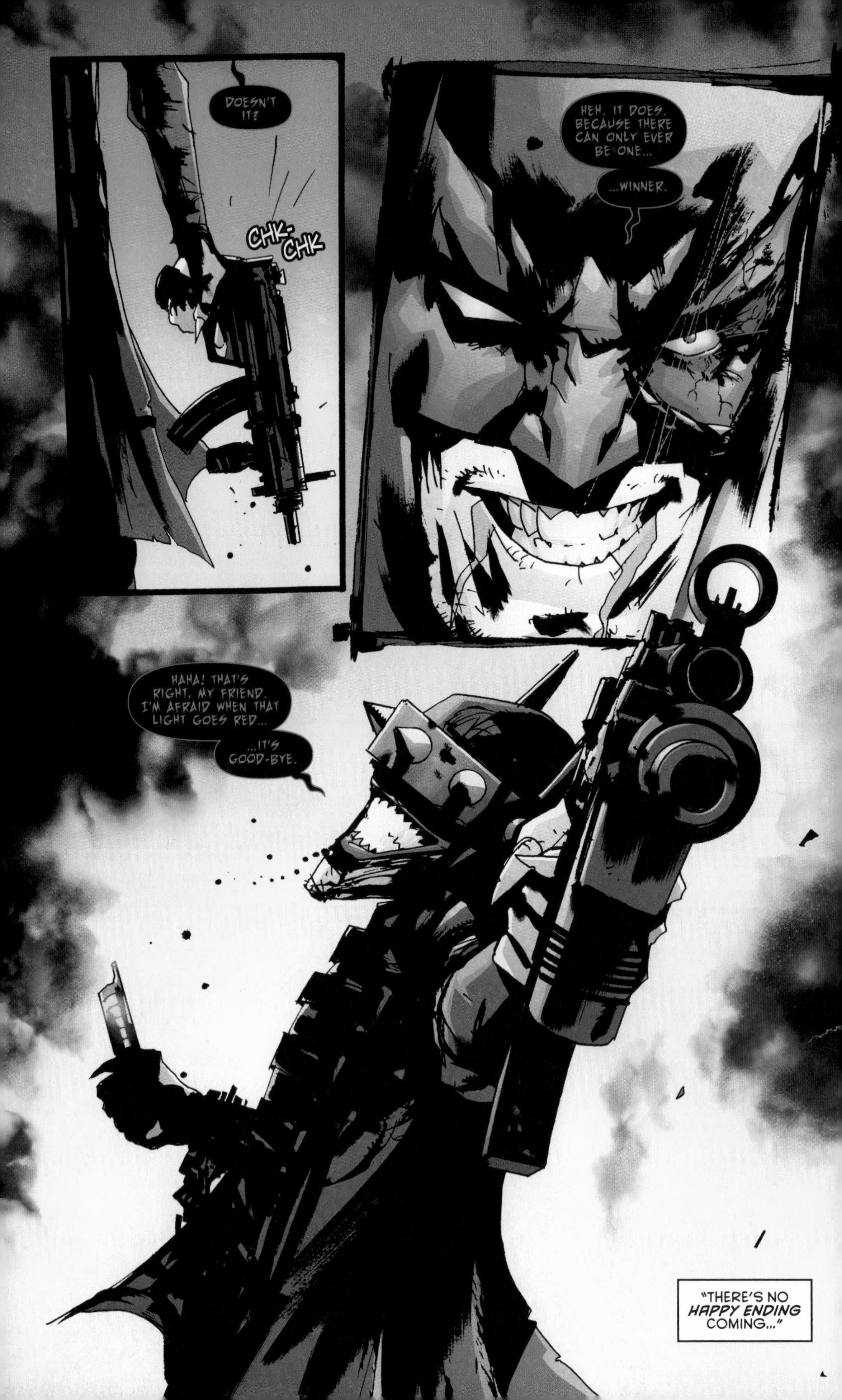

DOESN'T IT?
CHK-CHK
HEH. IT DOES. BECAUSE THERE CAN ONLY EVER BE ONE...
...WINNER.
HAHA! THAT'S RIGHT, MY FRIEND. I'M AFRAID WHEN THAT LIGHT GOES RED...
...IT'S GOOD-BYE.
"THERE'S NO HAPPY ENDING COMING..."

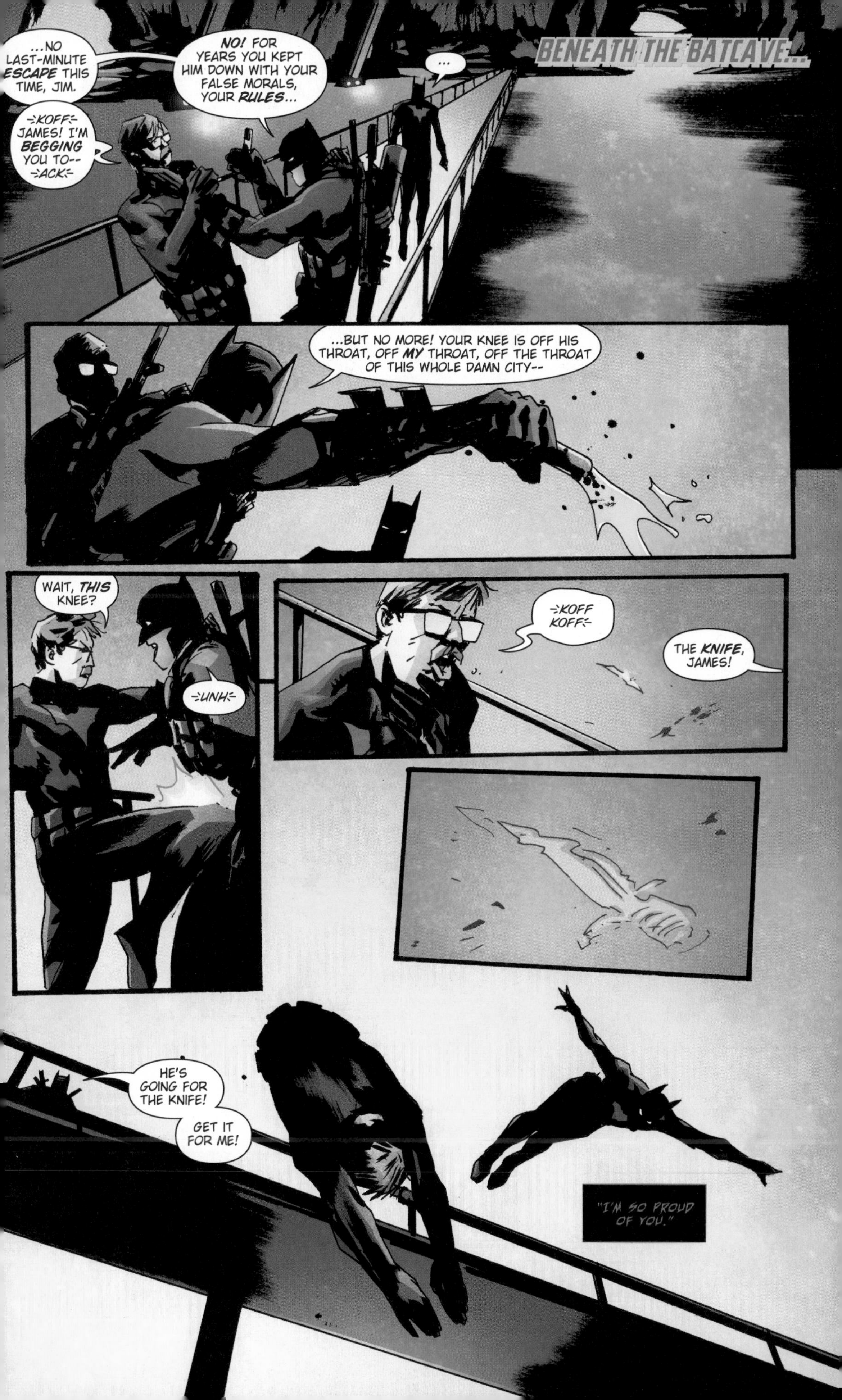
BENEATH THE BATCAVE...
...NO LAST-MINUTE ESCAPE THIS TIME, JIM.
NO! FOR YEARS YOU KEPT HIM DOWN WITH YOUR FALSE MORALS, YOUR RULES...
...
=KOFF= JAMES! I'M BEGGING YOU TO-- =ACK=
...BUT NO MORE! YOUR KNEE IS OFF HIS THROAT, OFF MY THROAT, OFF THE THROAT OF THIS WHOLE DAMN CITY--
WAIT, THIS KNEE?
=UNH=
=KOFF KOFF=
THE KNIFE, JAMES!
HE'S GOING FOR THE KNIFE!
GET IT FOR ME!
"I'M SO PROUD OF YOU."

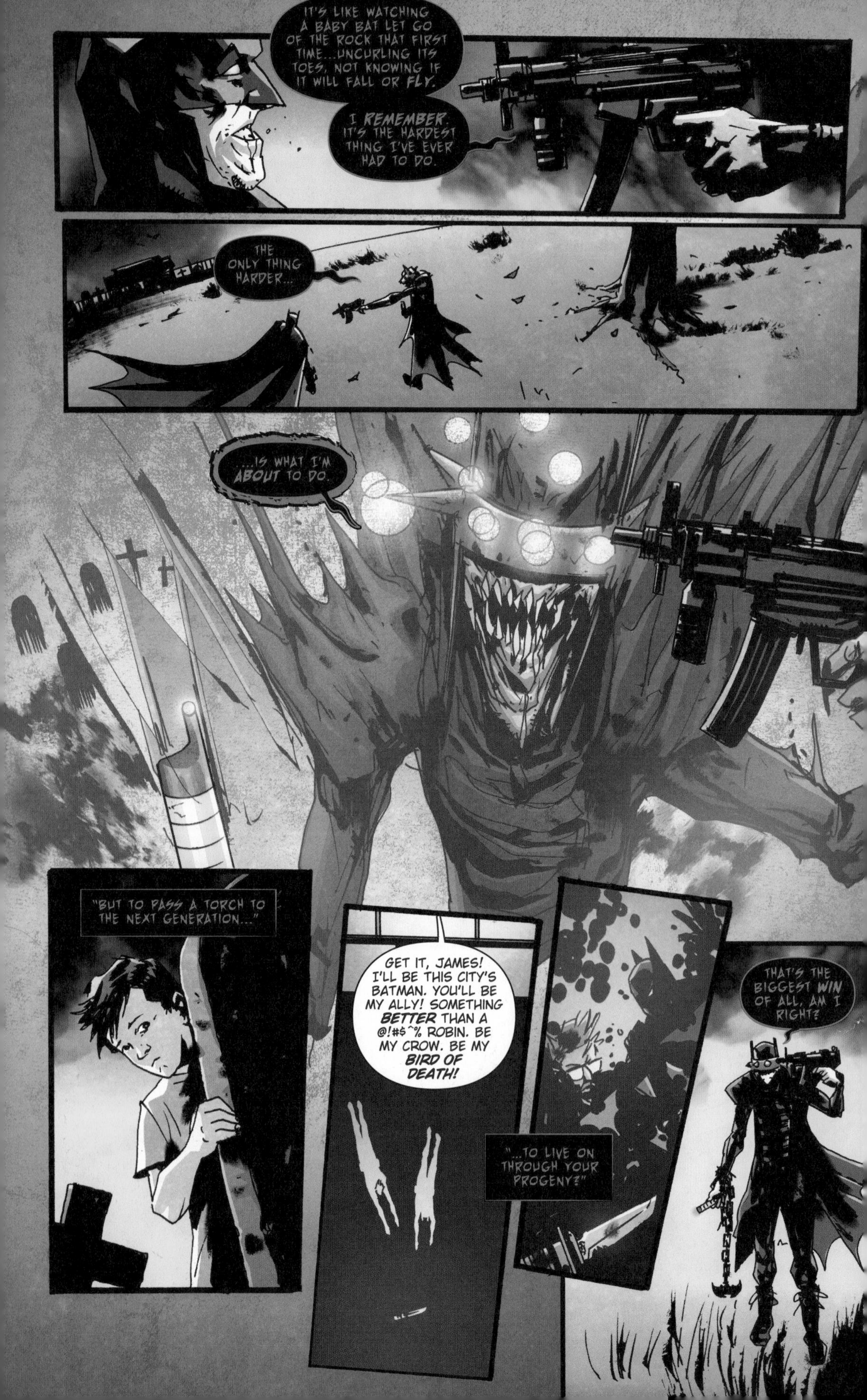
IT'S LIKE WATCHING A BABY BAT LET GO OF THE ROCK THAT FIRST TIME...UNCURLING ITS TOES, NOT KNOWING IF IT WILL FALL OR FLY.
I REMEMBER. IT'S THE HARDEST THING I'VE EVER HAD TO DO.
THE ONLY THING HARDER...
...IS WHAT I'M ABOUT TO DO.
"BUT TO PASS A TORCH TO THE NEXT GENERATION..."
GET IT, JAMES! I'LL BE THIS CITY'S BATMAN. YOU'LL BE MY ALLY! SOMETHING BETTER THAN A @!#$^% ROBIN. BE MY CROW. BE MY BIRD OF DEATH!
"...TO LIVE ON THROUGH YOUR PROGENY?"
THAT'S THE BIGGEST WIN OF ALL, AM I RIGHT?

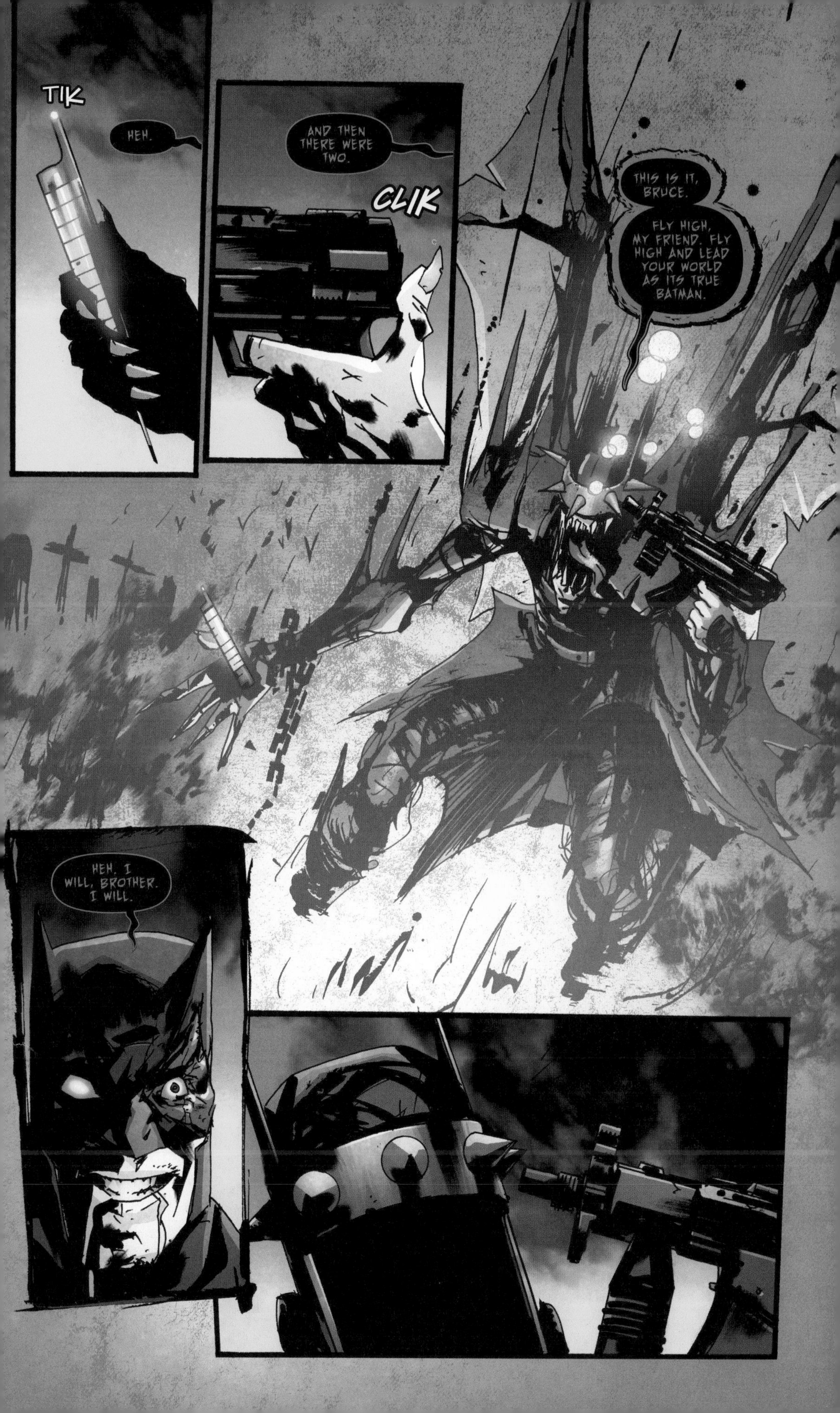
TIK
HEH.
AND THEN THERE WERE TWO.
CLIK
THIS IS IT, BRUCE.
FLY HIGH, MY FRIEND. FLY HIGH AND LEAD YOUR WORLD AS ITS TRUE BATMAN.
HEH. I WILL, BROTHER. I WILL.

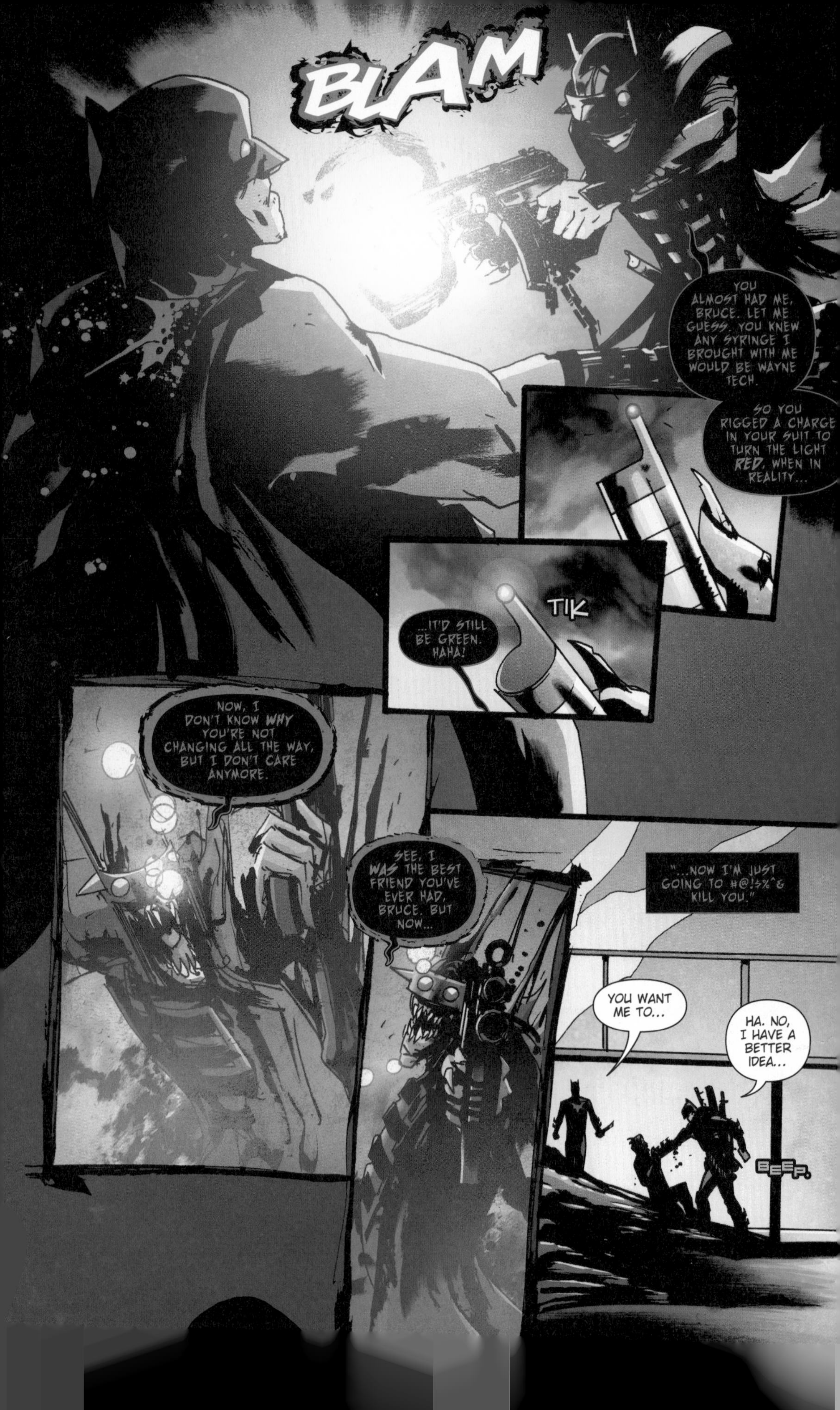
BLAM
YOU ALMOST HAD ME, BRUCE. LET ME GUESS. YOU KNEW ANY SYRINGE I BROUGHT WITH ME WOULD BE WAYNE TECH.
SO YOU RIGGED A CHARGE IN YOUR SUIT TO TURN THE LIGHT RED, WHEN IN REALITY...
TIK
...IT'D STILL BE GREEN. HAHA!
NOW, I DON'T KNOW WHY YOU'RE NOT CHANGING ALL THE WAY, BUT I DON'T CARE ANYMORE.
SEE, I WAS THE BEST FRIEND YOU'VE EVER HAD, BRUCE. BUT NOW...
"...NOW I'M JUST GOING TO #@!$%^& KILL YOU."
YOU WANT ME TO...
HA. NO, I HAVE A BETTER IDEA...
BEEP.

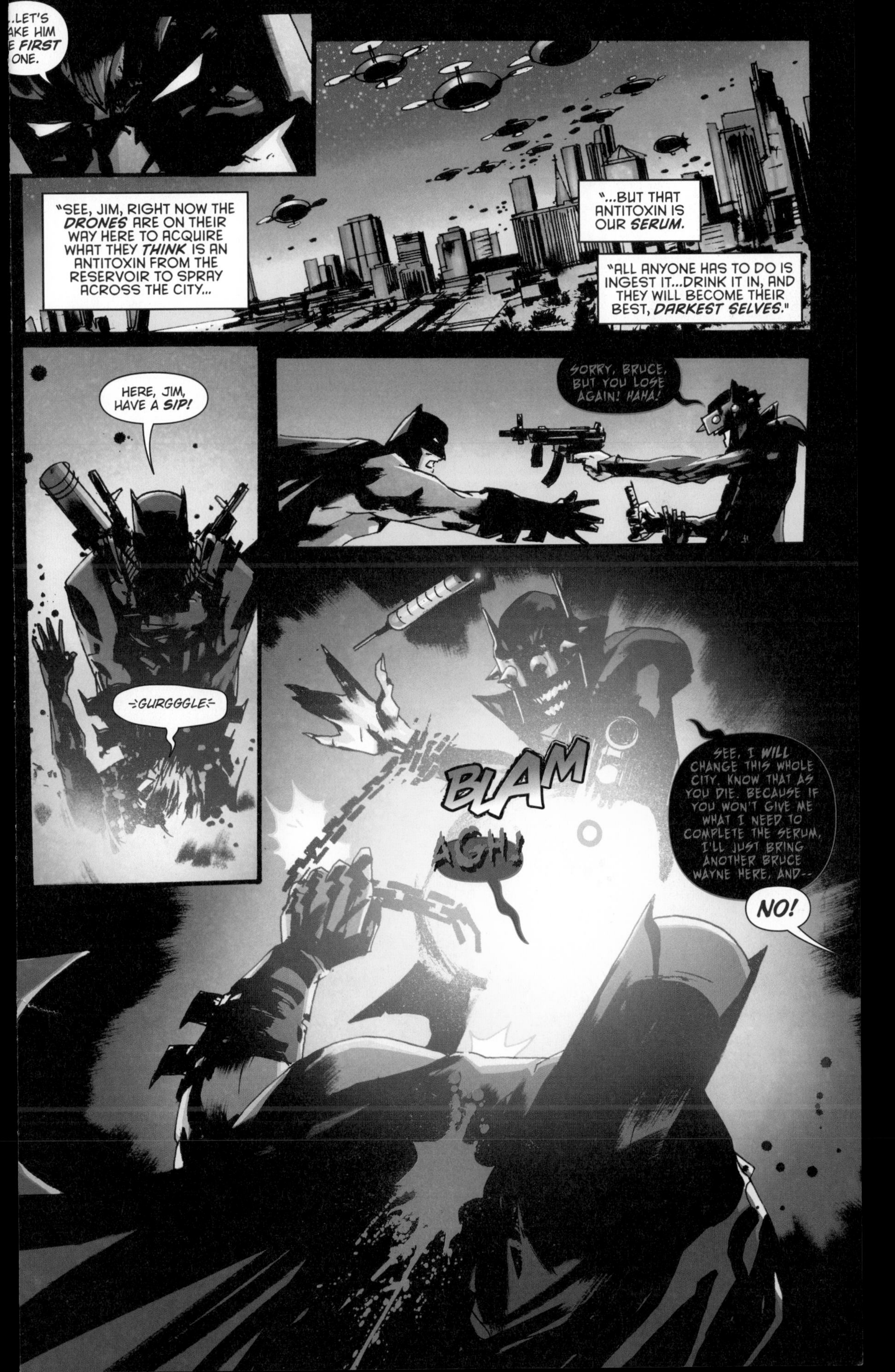
...LET'S
MAKE HIM
THE FIRST
ONE.
"SEE, JIM, RIGHT NOW THE DRONES ARE ON THEIR WAY HERE TO ACQUIRE WHAT THEY THINK IS AN ANTITOXIN FROM THE RESERVOIR TO SPRAY ACROSS THE CITY...
"...BUT THAT ANTITOXIN IS OUR SERUM.
"ALL ANYONE HAS TO DO IS INGEST IT...DRINK IT IN, AND THEY WILL BECOME THEIR BEST, DARKEST SELVES."
HERE, JIM, HAVE A SIP!
GURGGGLE
SORRY, BRUCE, BUT YOU LOSE AGAIN! HAHA!
BLAM
AGH!
SEE, I WILL CHANGE THIS WHOLE CITY. KNOW THAT AS YOU DIE. BECAUSE IF YOU WON'T GIVE ME WHAT I NEED TO COMPLETE THE SERUM, I'LL JUST BRING ANOTHER BRUCE WAYNE HERE, AND--
NO!

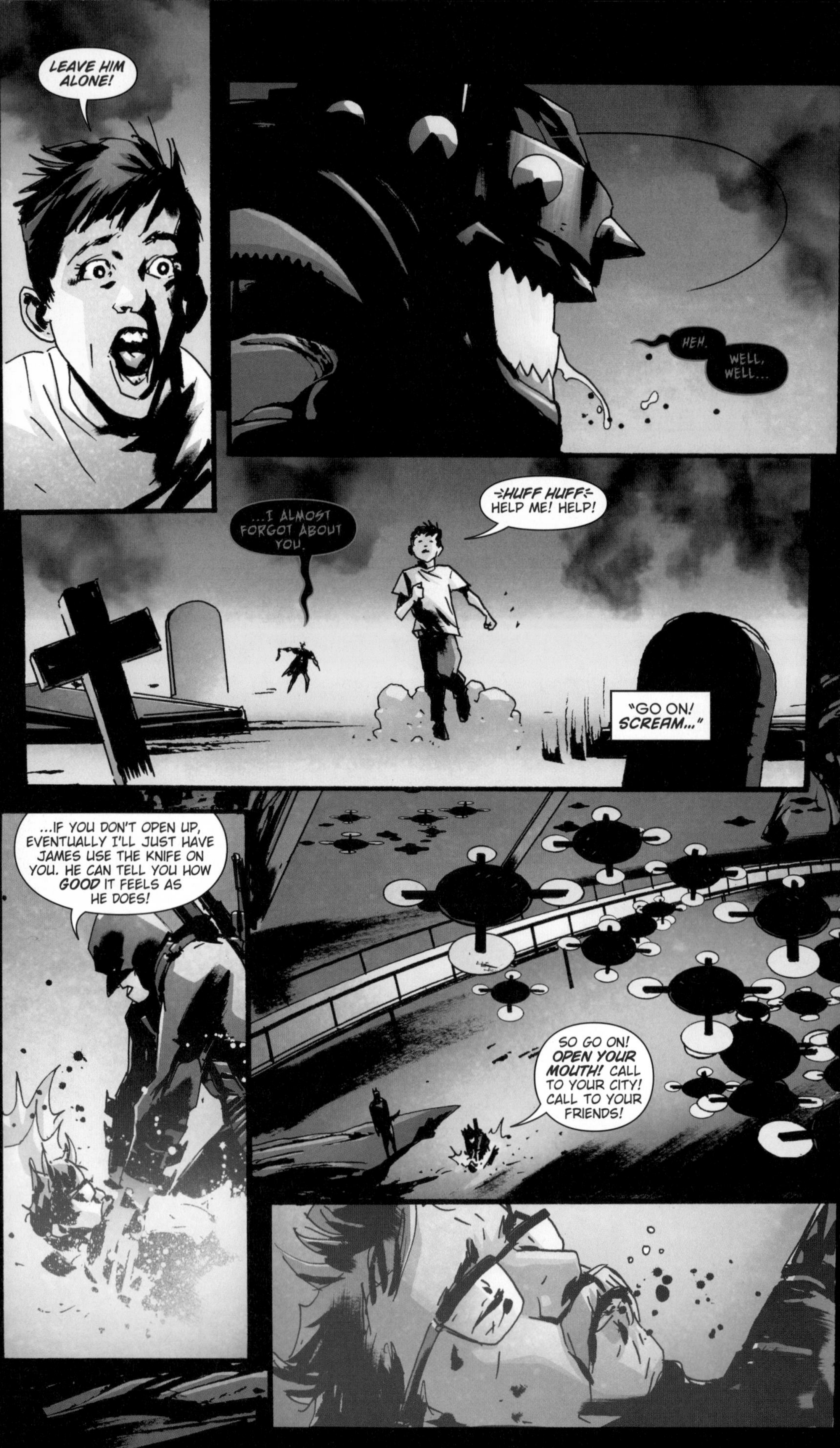
LEAVE HIM ALONE!
HEH.
WELL, WELL...
...I ALMOST FORGOT ABOUT YOU.
HUFF HUFF HELP ME! HELP!
"GO ON! SCREAM..."
...IF YOU DON'T OPEN UP, EVENTUALLY I'LL JUST HAVE JAMES USE THE KNIFE ON YOU. HE CAN TELL YOU HOW GOOD IT FEELS AS HE DOES!
SO GO ON! OPEN YOUR MOUTH! CALL TO YOUR CITY! CALL TO YOUR FRIENDS!

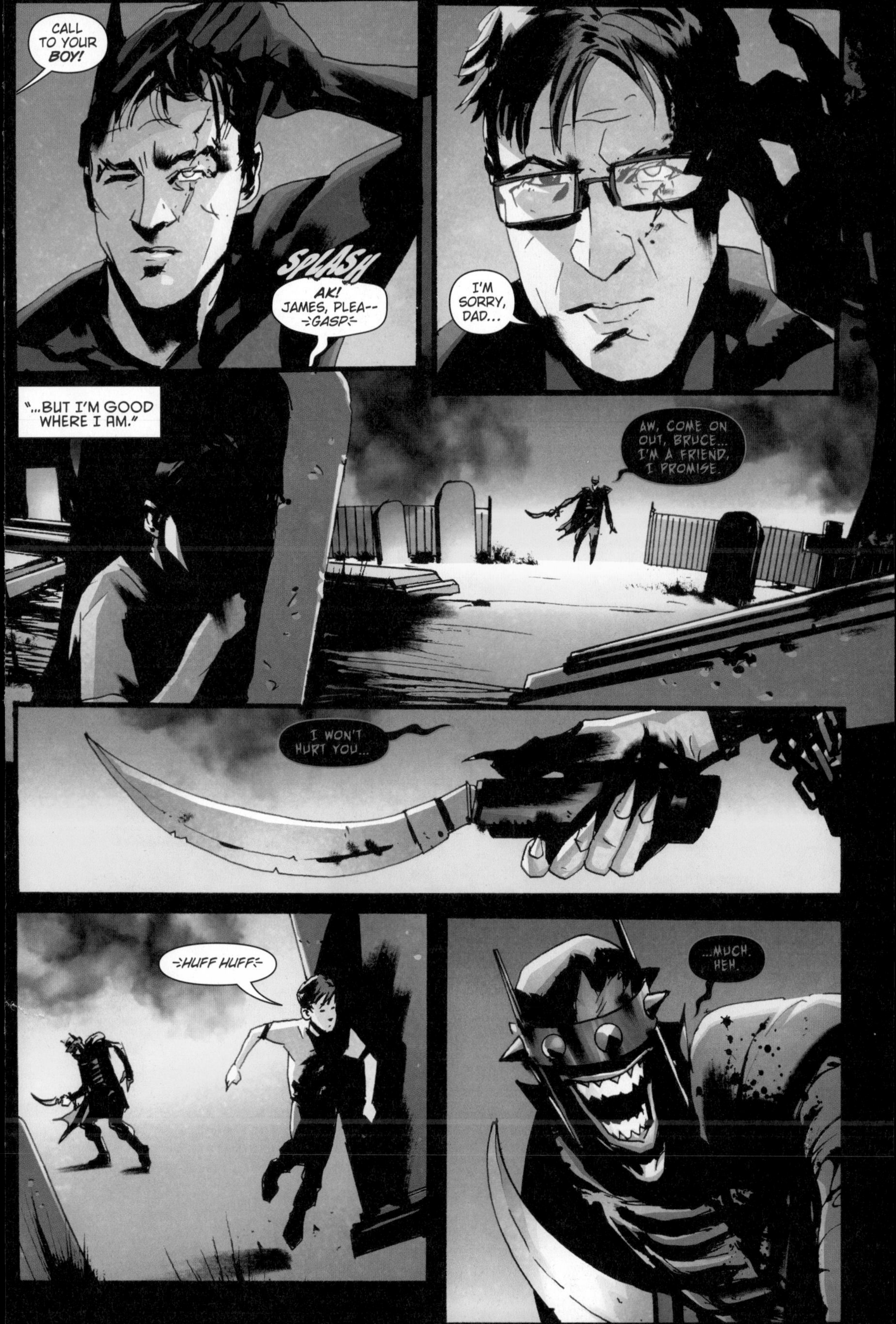
CALL TO YOUR BOY!
SPLASH
AK! JAMES, PLEA-- =GASP=
I'M SORRY, DAD...
"...BUT I'M GOOD WHERE I AM."
AW, COME ON OUT, BRUCE... I'M A FRIEND, I PROMISE.
I WON'T HURT YOU...
=HUFF HUFF=
...MUCH. HEH.

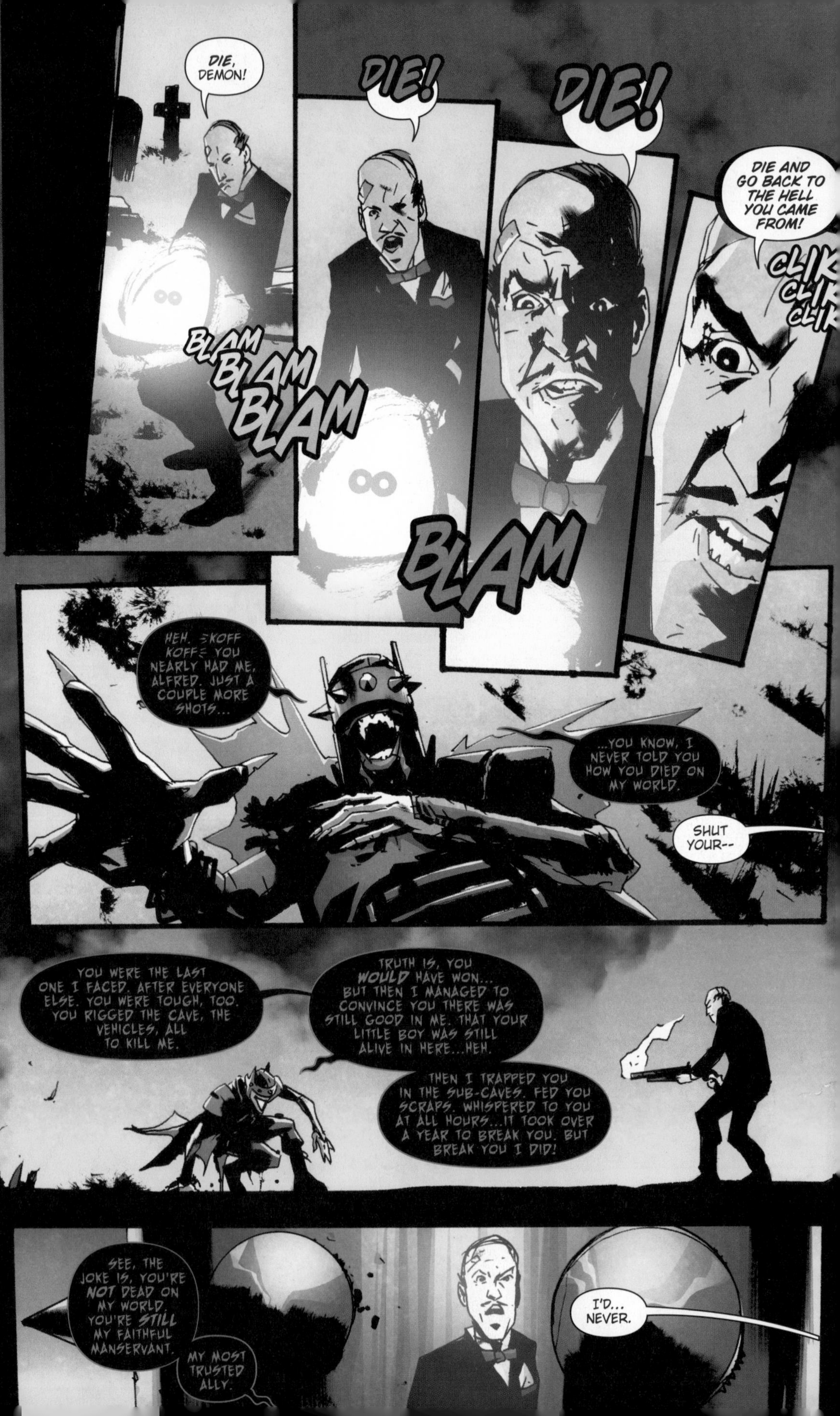
DIE, DEMON!
BLAM BLAM BLAM
DIE!
DIE!
BLAM
DIE AND GO BACK TO THE HELL YOU CAME FROM!
CLIK CLIK CLIK
HEH. KOFF KOFF YOU NEARLY HAD ME, ALFRED. JUST A COUPLE MORE SHOTS...
...YOU KNOW, I NEVER TOLD YOU HOW YOU DIED ON MY WORLD.
SHUT YOUR--
YOU WERE THE LAST ONE I FACED. AFTER EVERYONE ELSE. YOU WERE TOUGH, TOO. YOU RIGGED THE CAVE, THE VEHICLES, ALL TO KILL ME.
TRUTH IS, YOU WOULD HAVE WON... BUT THEN I MANAGED TO CONVINCE YOU THERE WAS STILL GOOD IN ME. THAT YOUR LITTLE BOY WAS STILL ALIVE IN HERE...HEH.
THEN I TRAPPED YOU IN THE SUB-CAVES. FED YOU SCRAPS. WHISPERED TO YOU AT ALL HOURS...IT TOOK OVER A YEAR TO BREAK YOU. BUT BREAK YOU I DID!
SEE, THE JOKE IS, YOU'RE NOT DEAD ON MY WORLD. YOU'RE STILL MY FAITHFUL MANSERVANT.
MY MOST TRUSTED ALLY.
I'D... NEVER.

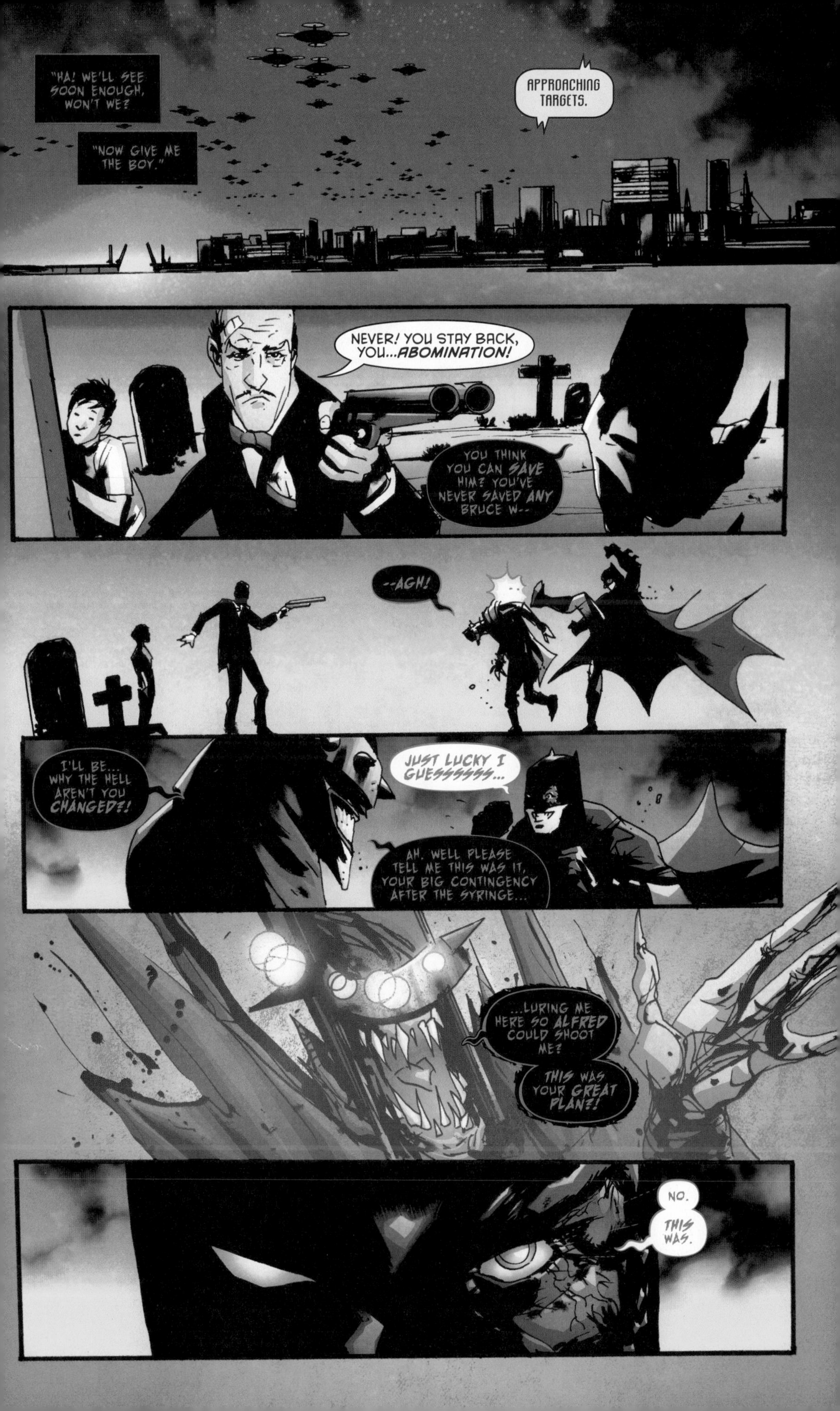
"HA! WE'LL SEE SOON ENOUGH, WON'T WE?
"NOW GIVE ME THE BOY."
APPROACHING TARGETS.
NEVER! YOU STAY BACK, YOU...ABOMINATION!
YOU THINK YOU CAN SAVE HIM? YOU'VE NEVER SAVED ANY BRUCE W--
--AGH!
I'LL BE... WHY THE HELL AREN'T YOU CHANGED?!
JUST LUCKY I GUESSSSSS...
AH. WELL PLEASE TELL ME THIS WAS IT, YOUR BIG CONTINGENCY AFTER THE SYRINGE...
...LURING ME HERE SO ALFRED COULD SHOOT ME?
THIS WAS YOUR GREAT PLAN?!
NO.
THIS WAS.

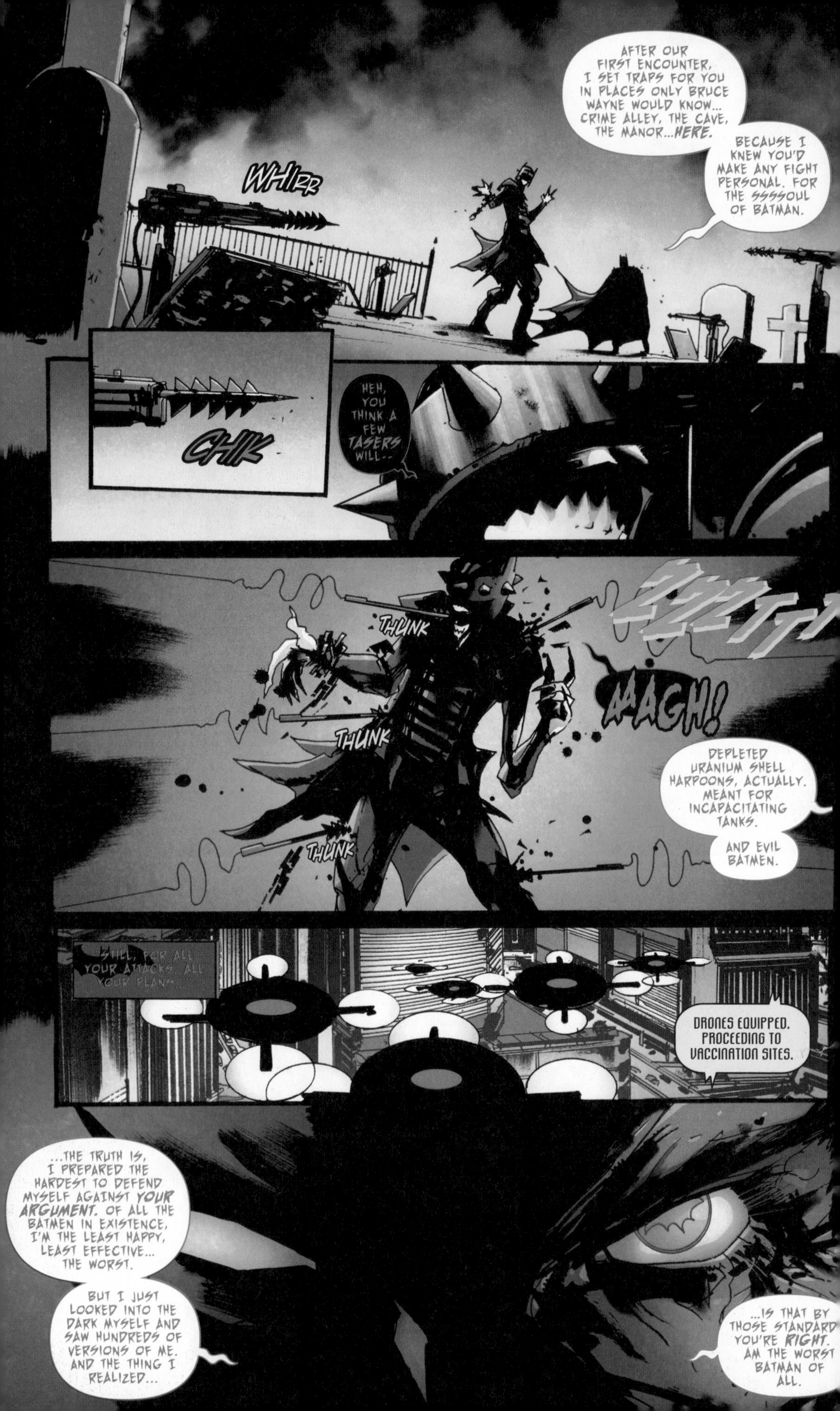
AFTER OUR FIRST ENCOUNTER, I SET TRAPS FOR YOU IN PLACES ONLY BRUCE WAYNE WOULD KNOW... CRIME ALLEY, THE CAVE, THE MANOR...HERE.
BECAUSE I KNEW YOU'D MAKE ANY FIGHT PERSONAL. FOR THE SSSSOUL OF BATMAN.
WHIRR
CHIK
HEH, YOU THINK A FEW TASERS WILL--
THUNK
ZZZTTT
AAAGH!
THUNK
THUNK
DEPLETED URANIUM SHELL HARPOONS, ACTUALLY. MEANT FOR INCAPACITATING TANKS.
AND EVIL BATMEN.
STILL, FOR ALL YOUR ATTACKS, ALL YOUR PLANS...
DRONES EQUIPPED. PROCEEDING TO VACCINATION SITES.
...THE TRUTH IS, I PREPARED THE HARDEST TO DEFEND MYSELF AGAINST YOUR ARGUMENT. OF ALL THE BATMEN IN EXISTENCE, I'M THE LEAST HAPPY, LEAST EFFECTIVE... THE WORST.
BUT I JUST LOOKED INTO THE DARK MYSELF AND SAW HUNDREDS OF VERSIONS OF ME. AND THE THING I REALIZED...
...IS THAT BY THOSE STANDARD YOU'RE RIGHT. AM THE WORST BATMAN OF ALL.

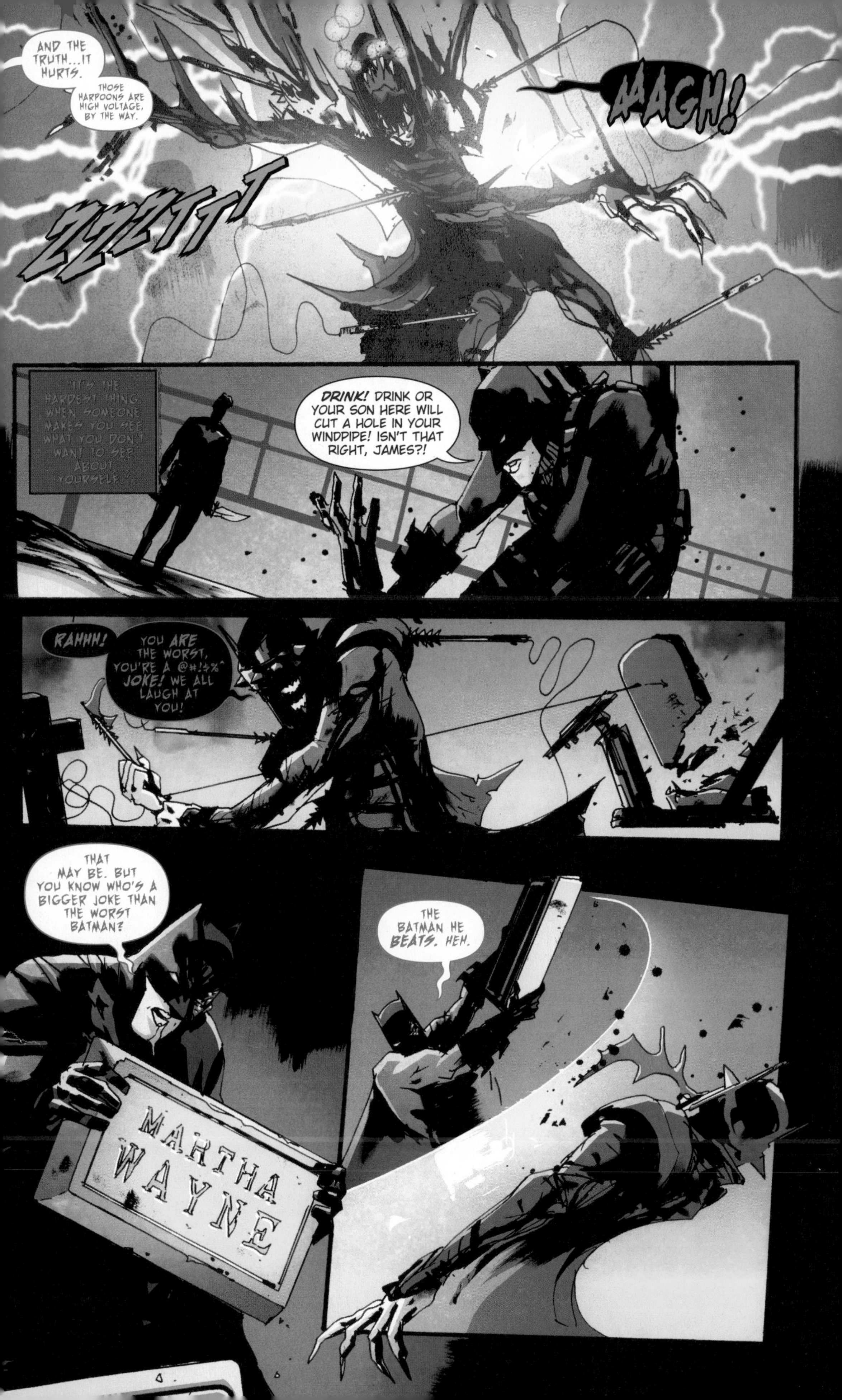
AND THE TRUTH...IT HURTS.
THOSE HARPOONS ARE HIGH VOLTAGE, BY THE WAY.
AAAGH!
ZZZZTTTTT
"IT'S THE HARDEST THING, WHEN SOMEONE MAKES YOU SEE WHAT YOU DON'T WANT TO SEE ABOUT YOURSELF."
DRINK! DRINK OR YOUR SON HERE WILL CUT A HOLE IN YOUR WINDPIPE! ISN'T THAT RIGHT, JAMES?!
RAHHH!
YOU ARE THE WORST, YOU'RE A @#!$%^ JOKE! WE ALL LAUGH AT YOU!
THAT MAY BE. BUT YOU KNOW WHO'S A BIGGER JOKE THAN THE WORST BATMAN?
MARTHA WAYNE
THE BATMAN HE BEATS. HEH.

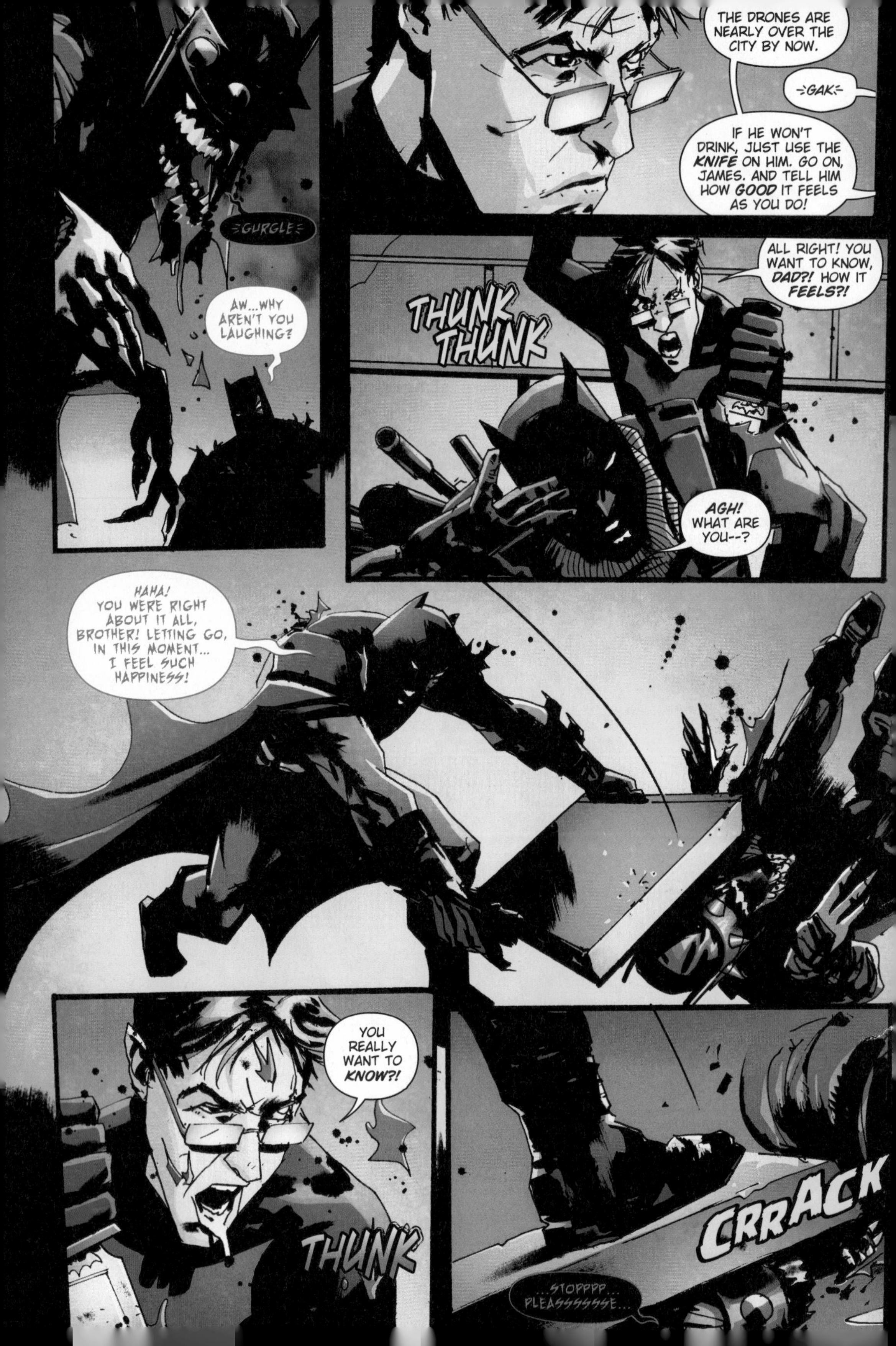
GURGLE
AW...WHY AREN'T YOU LAUGHING?
THE DRONES ARE NEARLY OVER THE CITY BY NOW.
GAK
IF HE WON'T DRINK, JUST USE THE KNIFE ON HIM. GO ON, JAMES. AND TELL HIM HOW GOOD IT FEELS AS YOU DO!
ALL RIGHT! YOU WANT TO KNOW, DAD?! HOW IT FEELS?!
THUNK THUNK
AGH! WHAT ARE YOU--?
HAHA! YOU WERE RIGHT ABOUT IT ALL, BROTHER! LETTING GO, IN THIS MOMENT... I FEEL SUCH HAPPINESS!
YOU REALLY WANT TO KNOW?!
THUNK
CRRACK
...STOPPPP... PLEASSSSSSE...

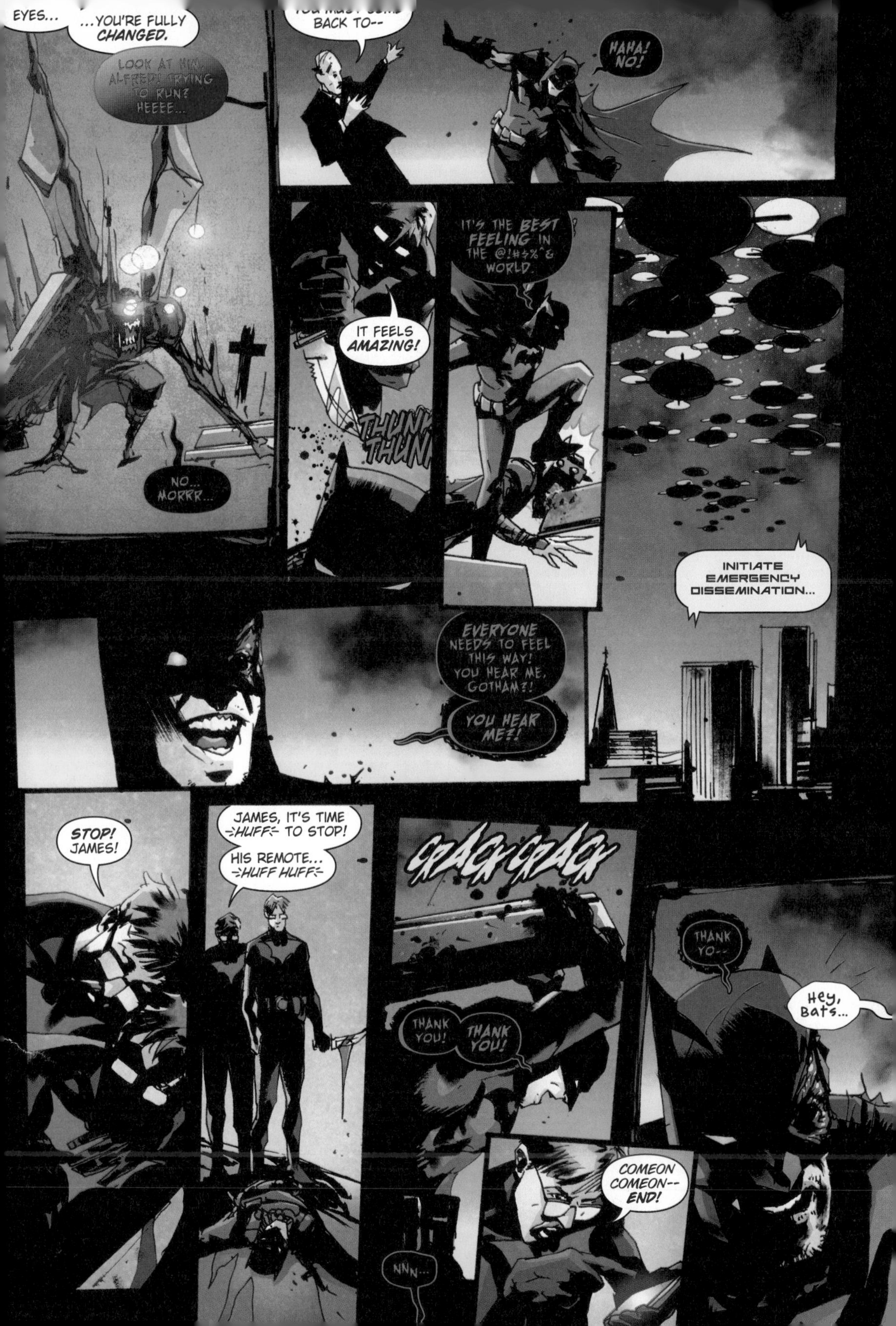
EYES...
...YOU'RE FULLY CHANGED.
LOOK AT HIM, ALFRED! TRYING TO RUN? HEEEE...
NO... MORRR...
BACK TO--
HAHA! NO!
IT FEELS AMAZING!
THUNK THUNK
IT'S THE BEST FEELING IN THE @!#$%^& WORLD.
INITIATE EMERGENCY DISSEMINATION...
EVERYONE NEEDS TO FEEL THIS WAY! YOU HEAR ME, GOTHAM?!
YOU HEAR ME?!
STOP! JAMES!
JAMES, IT'S TIME *HUFF* TO STOP!
HIS REMOTE... *HUFF HUFF*
CRACK CRACK
THANK YOU!
THANK YOU!
NNN...
COMEON COMEON-- END!
THANK YO--
Hey, Bats...

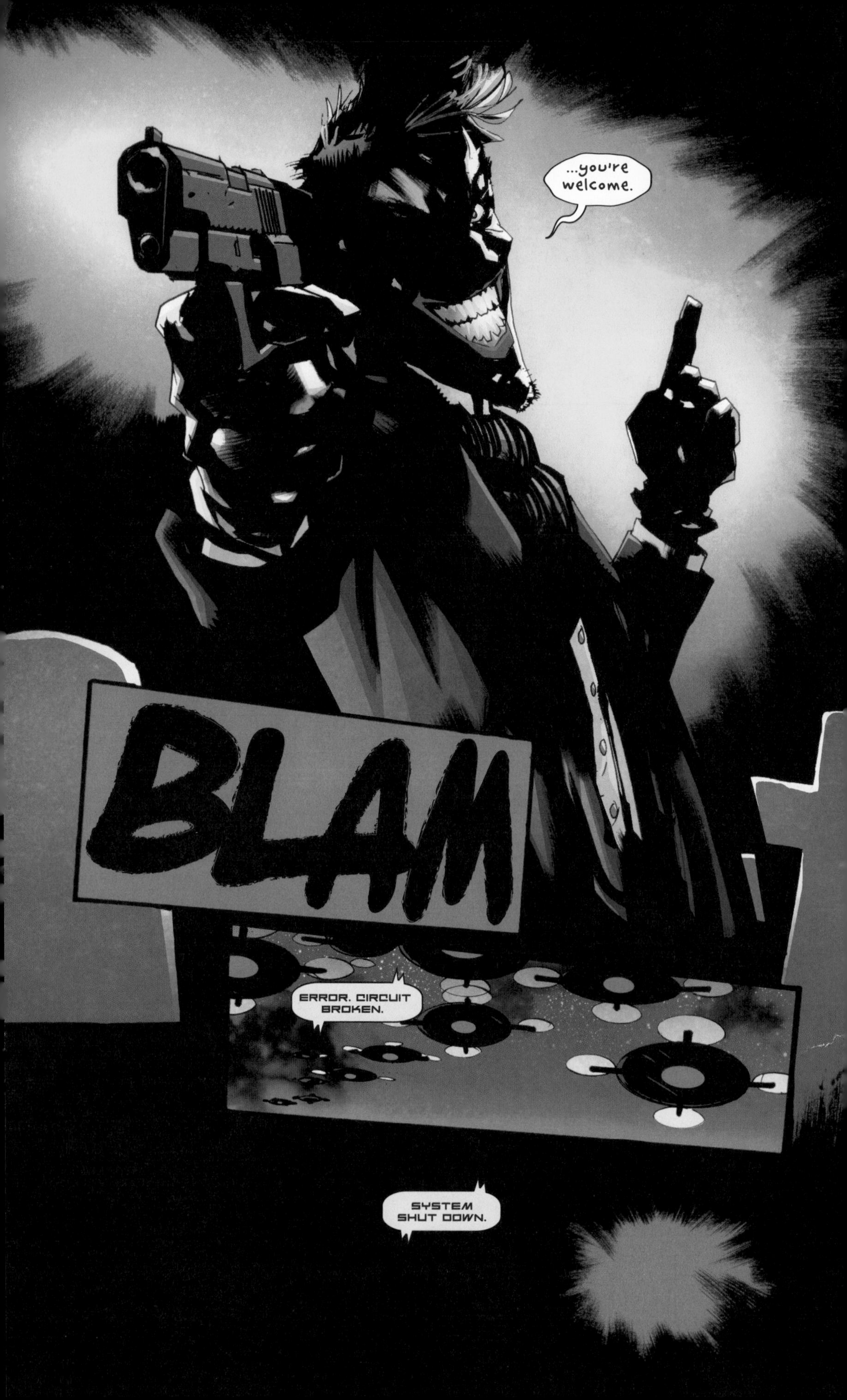
...you're welcome.
BLAM
ERROR. CIRCUIT BROKEN.
SYSTEM SHUT DOWN.

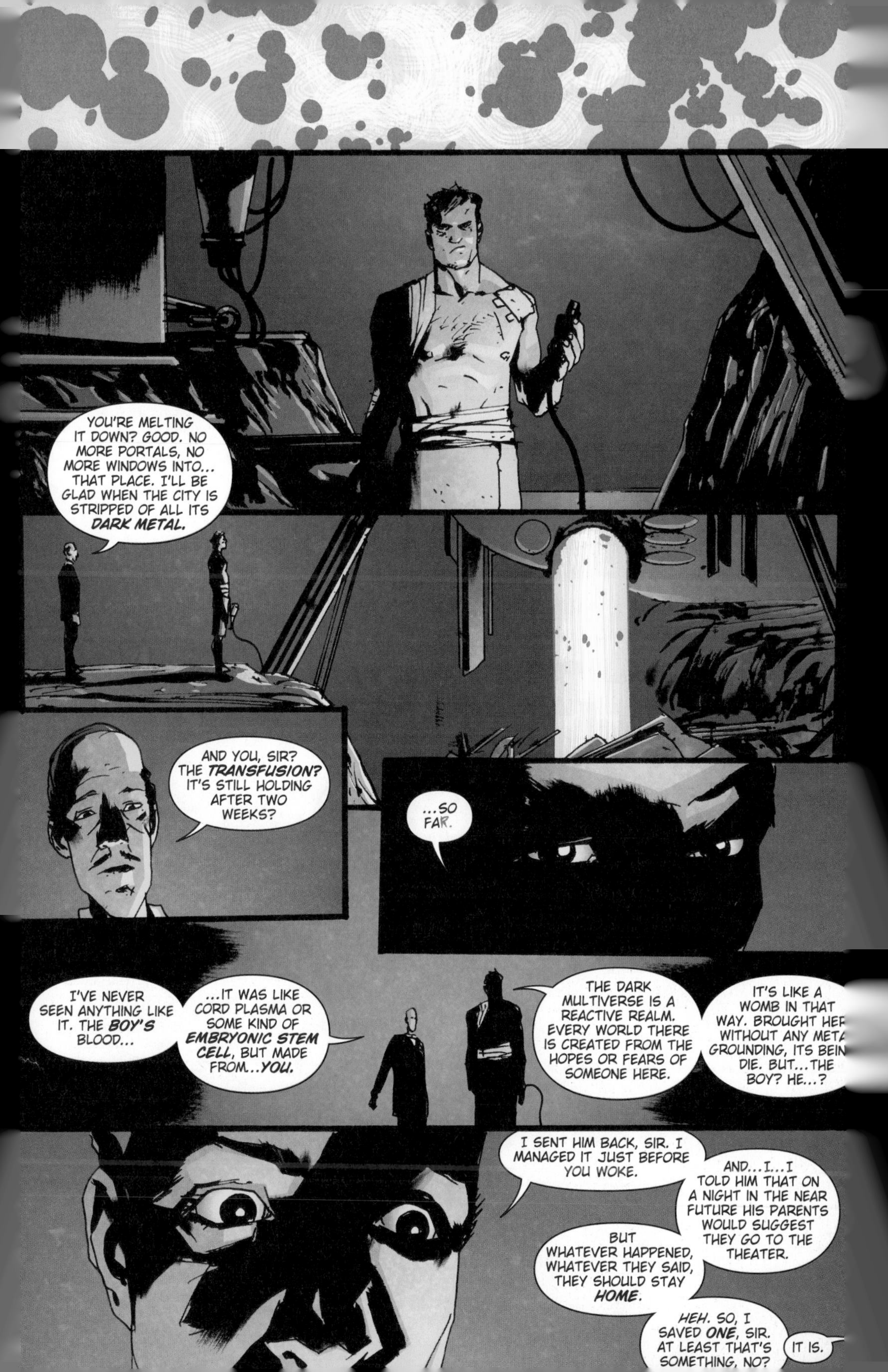
YOU'RE MELTING IT DOWN? GOOD. NO MORE PORTALS, NO MORE WINDOWS INTO... THAT PLACE. I'LL BE GLAD WHEN THE CITY IS STRIPPED OF ALL ITS DARK METAL.
AND YOU, SIR? THE TRANSFUSION? IT'S STILL HOLDING AFTER TWO WEEKS?
...SO FAR.
I'VE NEVER SEEN ANYTHING LIKE IT. THE BOY'S BLOOD...
...IT WAS LIKE CORD PLASMA OR SOME KIND OF EMBRYONIC STEM CELL, BUT MADE FROM...YOU.
THE DARK MULTIVERSE IS A REACTIVE REALM. EVERY WORLD THERE IS CREATED FROM THE HOPES OR FEARS OF SOMEONE HERE.
IT'S LIKE A WOMB IN THAT WAY. BROUGHT HER WITHOUT ANY META GROUNDING, ITS BEIN DIE. BUT...THE BOY? HE...?
I SENT HIM BACK, SIR. I MANAGED IT JUST BEFORE YOU WOKE.
AND...I...I TOLD HIM THAT ON A NIGHT IN THE NEAR FUTURE HIS PARENTS WOULD SUGGEST THEY GO TO THE THEATER.
BUT WHATEVER HAPPENED, WHATEVER THEY SAID, THEY SHOULD STAY HOME.
HEH. SO, I SAVED ONE, SIR. AT LEAST THAT'S SOMETHING, NO?
IT IS.

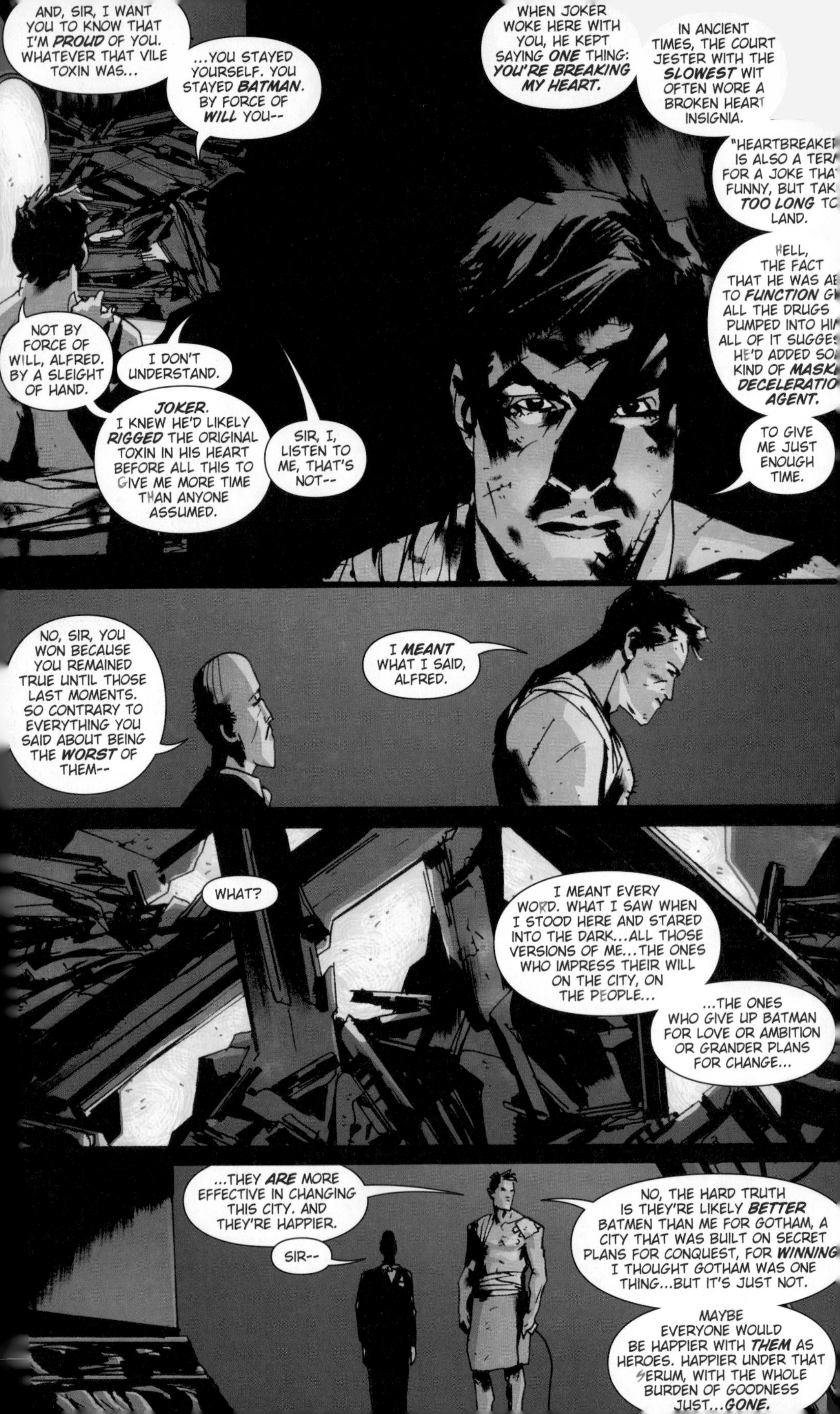

AND, SIR, I WANT YOU TO KNOW THAT I'M PROUD OF YOU. WHATEVER THAT VILE TOXIN WAS...
...YOU STAYED YOURSELF. YOU STAYED BATMAN. BY FORCE OF WILL YOU--
NOT BY FORCE OF WILL, ALFRED. BY A SLEIGHT OF HAND.
I DON'T UNDERSTAND.
JOKER. I KNEW HE'D LIKELY RIGGED THE ORIGINAL TOXIN IN HIS HEART BEFORE ALL THIS TO GIVE ME MORE TIME THAN ANYONE ASSUMED.
SIR, I, LISTEN TO ME, THAT'S NOT--
WHEN JOKER WOKE HERE WITH YOU, HE KEPT SAYING ONE THING: YOU'RE BREAKING MY HEART.
IN ANCIENT TIMES, THE COURT JESTER WITH THE SLOWEST WIT OFTEN WORE A BROKEN HEART INSIGNIA.
TO GIVE ME JUST ENOUGH TIME.
NO, SIR, YOU WON BECAUSE YOU REMAINED TRUE UNTIL THOSE LAST MOMENTS. SO CONTRARY TO EVERYTHING YOU SAID ABOUT BEING THE WORST OF THEM--
I MEANT WHAT I SAID, ALFRED.
WHAT?
I MEANT EVERY WORD. WHAT I SAW WHEN I STOOD HERE AND STARED INTO THE DARK...ALL THOSE VERSIONS OF ME...THE ONES WHO IMPRESS THEIR WILL ON THE CITY, ON THE PEOPLE...
...THE ONES WHO GIVE UP BATMAN FOR LOVE OR AMBITION OR GRANDER PLANS FOR CHANGE...
...THEY ARE MORE EFFECTIVE IN CHANGING THIS CITY. AND THEY'RE HAPPIER.
SIR--
NO, THE HARD TRUTH IS THEY'RE LIKELY BETTER BATMEN THAN ME FOR GOTHAM, A CITY THAT WAS BUILT ON SECRET PLANS FOR CONQUEST, FOR WINNING. I THOUGHT GOTHAM WAS ONE THING...BUT IT'S JUST NOT.
MAYBE EVERYONE WOULD BE HAPPIER WITH THEM AS HEROES. HAPPIER UNDER THAT SERUM, WITH THE WHOLE BURDEN OF GOODNESS JUST...GONE.

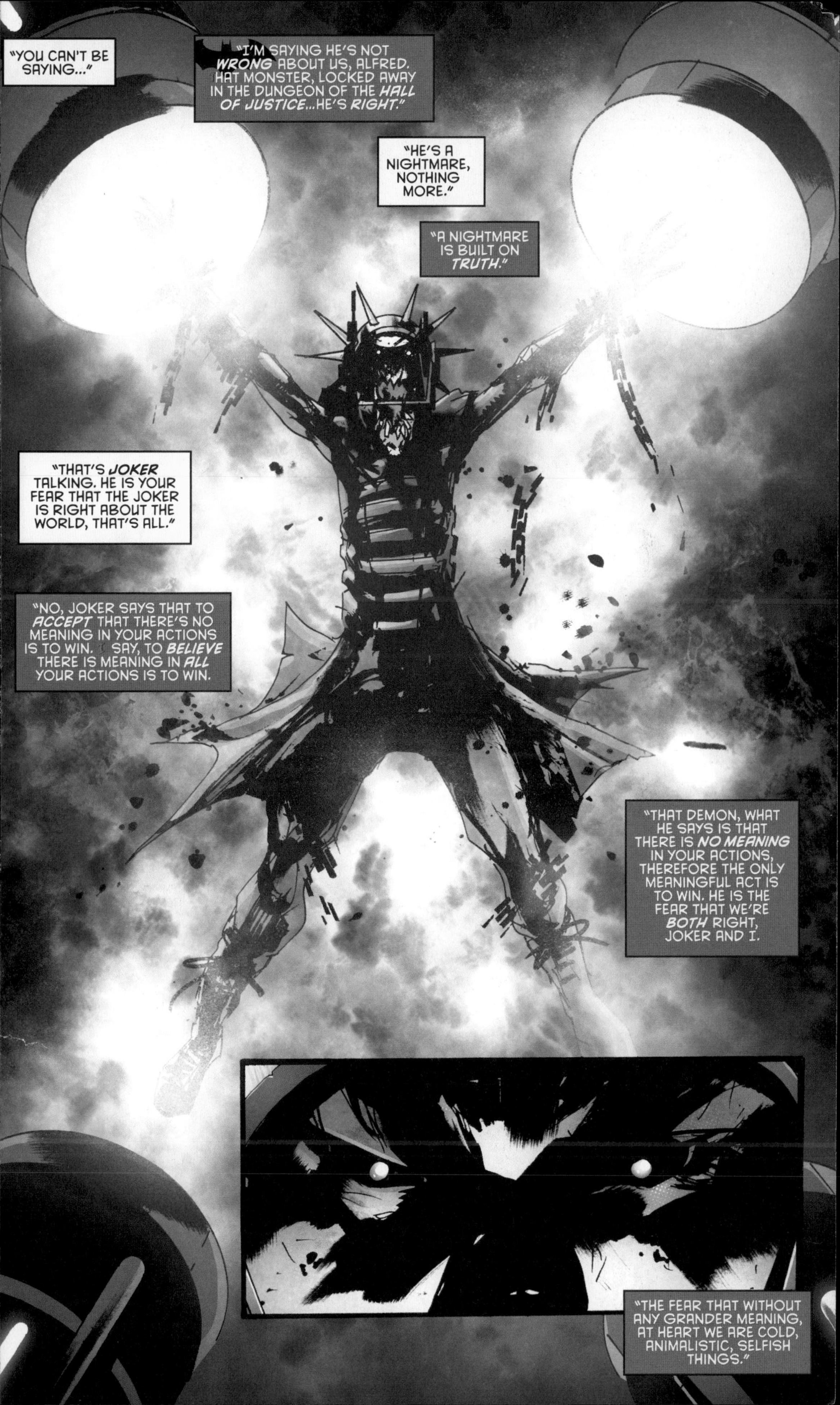
"YOU CAN'T BE SAYING..."
"I'M SAYING HE'S NOT *WRONG* ABOUT US, ALFRED. HAT MONSTER, LOCKED AWAY IN THE DUNGEON OF THE *HALL OF JUSTICE*...HE'S *RIGHT*."
"HE'S A NIGHTMARE, NOTHING MORE."
"A NIGHTMARE IS BUILT ON *TRUTH*."
"THAT'S *JOKER* TALKING. HE IS YOUR FEAR THAT THE JOKER IS RIGHT ABOUT THE WORLD, THAT'S ALL."
"NO, JOKER SAYS THAT TO *ACCEPT* THAT THERE'S NO MEANING IN YOUR ACTIONS IS TO WIN. SAY, TO *BELIEVE* THERE IS MEANING IN *ALL* YOUR ACTIONS IS TO WIN.
"THAT DEMON, WHAT HE SAYS IS THAT THERE IS *NO MEANING* IN YOUR ACTIONS, THEREFORE THE ONLY MEANINGFUL ACT IS TO WIN. HE IS THE FEAR THAT WE'RE *BOTH* RIGHT, JOKER AND I.
"THE FEAR THAT WITHOUT ANY GRANDER MEANING, AT HEART WE ARE COLD, ANIMALISTIC, SELFISH THINGS."

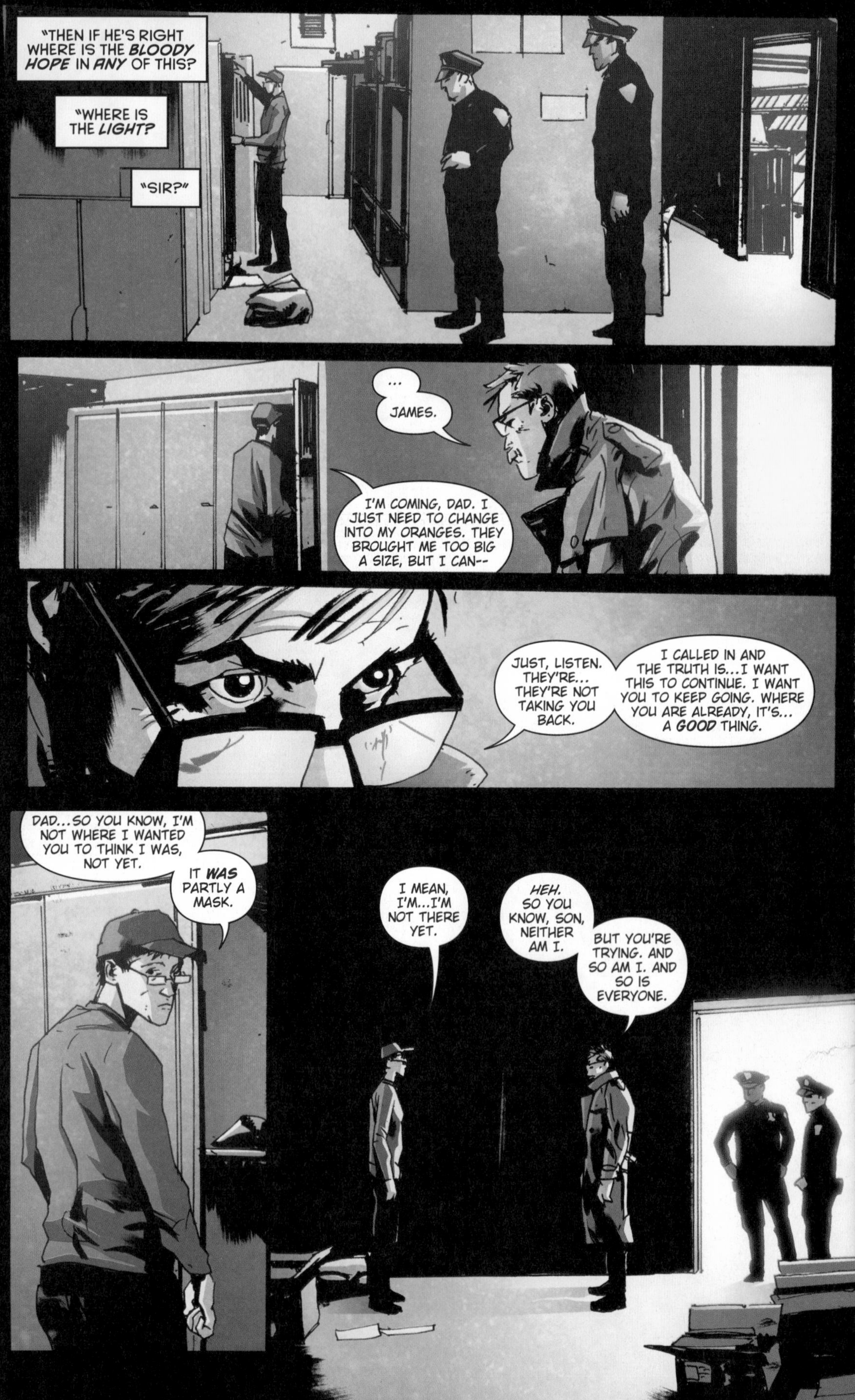
"THEN IF HE'S RIGHT WHERE IS THE BLOODY HOPE IN ANY OF THIS?
"WHERE IS THE LIGHT?
"SIR?"
... JAMES.
I'M COMING, DAD. I JUST NEED TO CHANGE INTO MY ORANGES. THEY BROUGHT ME TOO BIG A SIZE, BUT I CAN--
JUST, LISTEN. THEY'RE... THEY'RE NOT TAKING YOU BACK.
I CALLED IN AND THE TRUTH IS...I WANT THIS TO CONTINUE. I WANT YOU TO KEEP GOING. WHERE YOU ARE ALREADY, IT'S... A GOOD THING.
DAD...SO YOU KNOW, I'M NOT WHERE I WANTED YOU TO THINK I WAS, NOT YET.
IT WAS PARTLY A MASK.
I MEAN, I'M...I'M NOT THERE YET.
HEH. SO YOU KNOW, SON, NEITHER AM I.
BUT YOU'RE TRYING. AND SO AM I. AND SO IS EVERYONE.

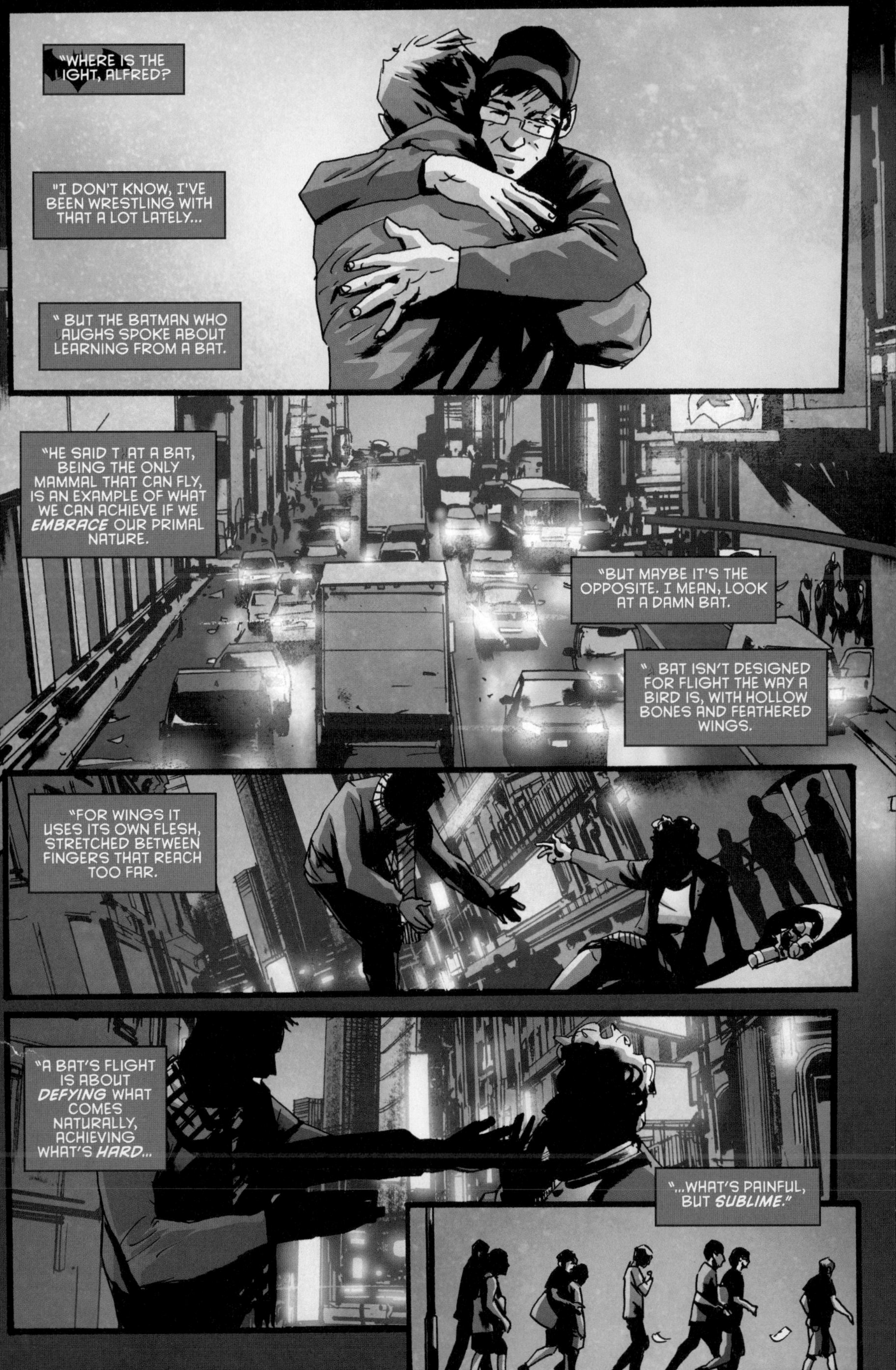
"WHERE IS THE LIGHT, ALFRED?
"I DON'T KNOW, I'VE BEEN WRESTLING WITH THAT A LOT LATELY...
" BUT THE BATMAN WHO LAUGHS SPOKE ABOUT LEARNING FROM A BAT.
"HE SAID THAT A BAT, BEING THE ONLY MAMMAL THAT CAN FLY, IS AN EXAMPLE OF WHAT WE CAN ACHIEVE IF WE EMBRACE OUR PRIMAL NATURE.
"BUT MAYBE IT'S THE OPPOSITE. I MEAN, LOOK AT A DAMN BAT.
"A BAT ISN'T DESIGNED FOR FLIGHT THE WAY A BIRD IS, WITH HOLLOW BONES AND FEATHERED WINGS.
"FOR WINGS IT USES ITS OWN FLESH, STRETCHED BETWEEN FINGERS THAT REACH TOO FAR.
"A BAT'S FLIGHT IS ABOUT DEFYING WHAT COMES NATURALLY, ACHIEVING WHAT'S HARD...
"...WHAT'S PAINFUL, BUT SUBLIME."

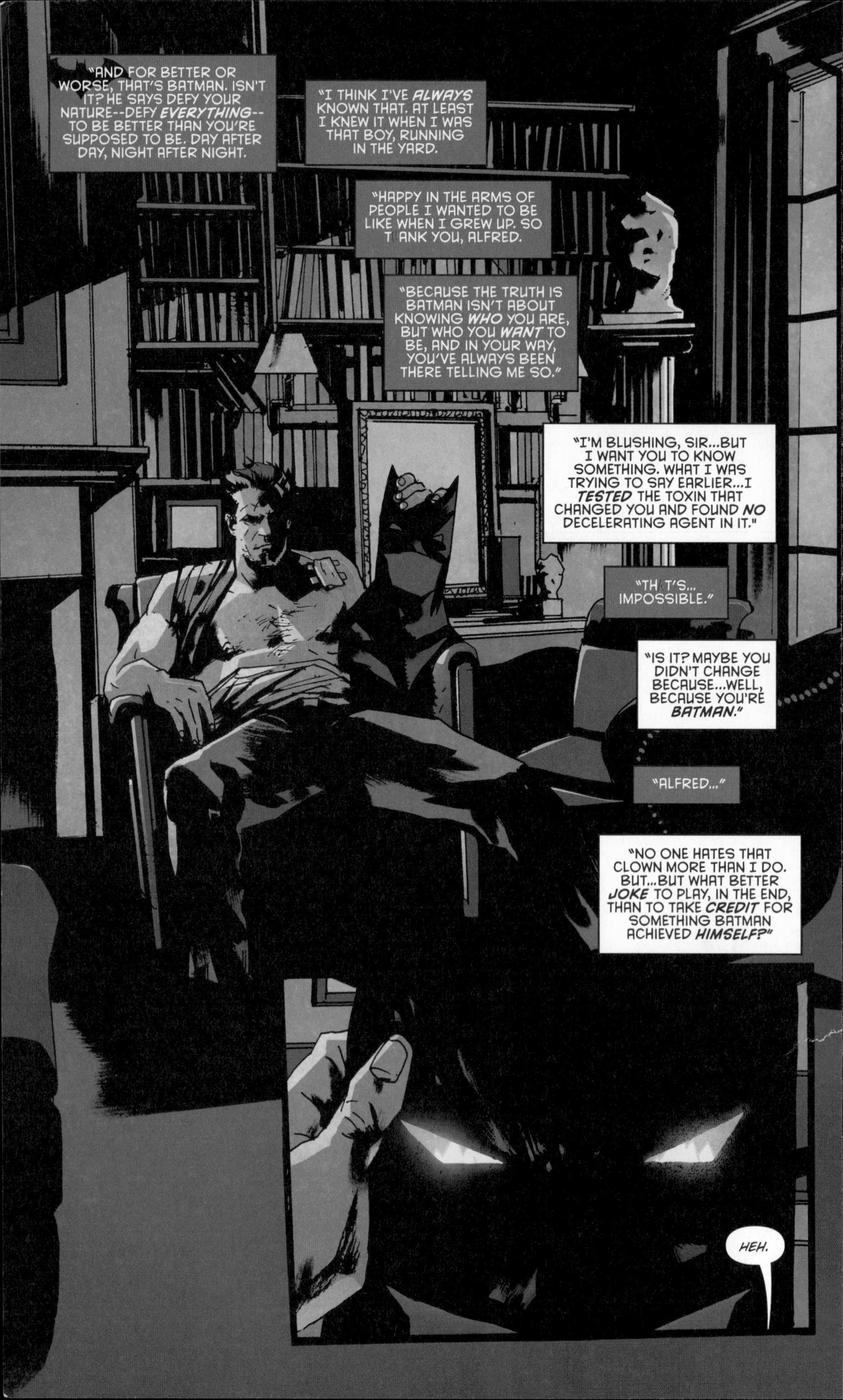
"AND FOR BETTER OR WORSE, THAT'S BATMAN. ISN'T IT? HE SAYS DEFY YOUR NATURE--DEFY *EVERYTHING*--TO BE BETTER THAN YOU'RE SUPPOSED TO BE. DAY AFTER DAY, NIGHT AFTER NIGHT.
"I THINK I'VE *ALWAYS* KNOWN THAT. AT LEAST I KNEW IT WHEN I WAS THAT BOY, RUNNING IN THE YARD.
"HAPPY IN THE ARMS OF PEOPLE I WANTED TO BE LIKE WHEN I GREW UP. SO THANK YOU, ALFRED.
"BECAUSE THE TRUTH IS BATMAN ISN'T ABOUT KNOWING *WHO* YOU ARE, BUT WHO YOU *WANT* TO BE, AND IN YOUR WAY, YOU'VE ALWAYS BEEN THERE TELLING ME SO."
"I'M BLUSHING, SIR...BUT I WANT YOU TO KNOW SOMETHING. WHAT I WAS TRYING TO SAY EARLIER...I *TESTED* THE TOXIN THAT CHANGED YOU AND FOUND *NO* DECELERATING AGENT IN IT."
"THAT'S... IMPOSSIBLE."
"IS IT? MAYBE YOU DIDN'T CHANGE BECAUSE...WELL, BECAUSE YOU'RE *BATMAN*."
"ALFRED..."
"NO ONE HATES THAT CLOWN MORE THAN I DO. BUT...BUT WHAT BETTER *JOKE* TO PLAY, IN THE END, THAN TO TAKE *CREDIT* FOR SOMETHING BATMAN ACHIEVED *HIMSELF*?"
HEH.

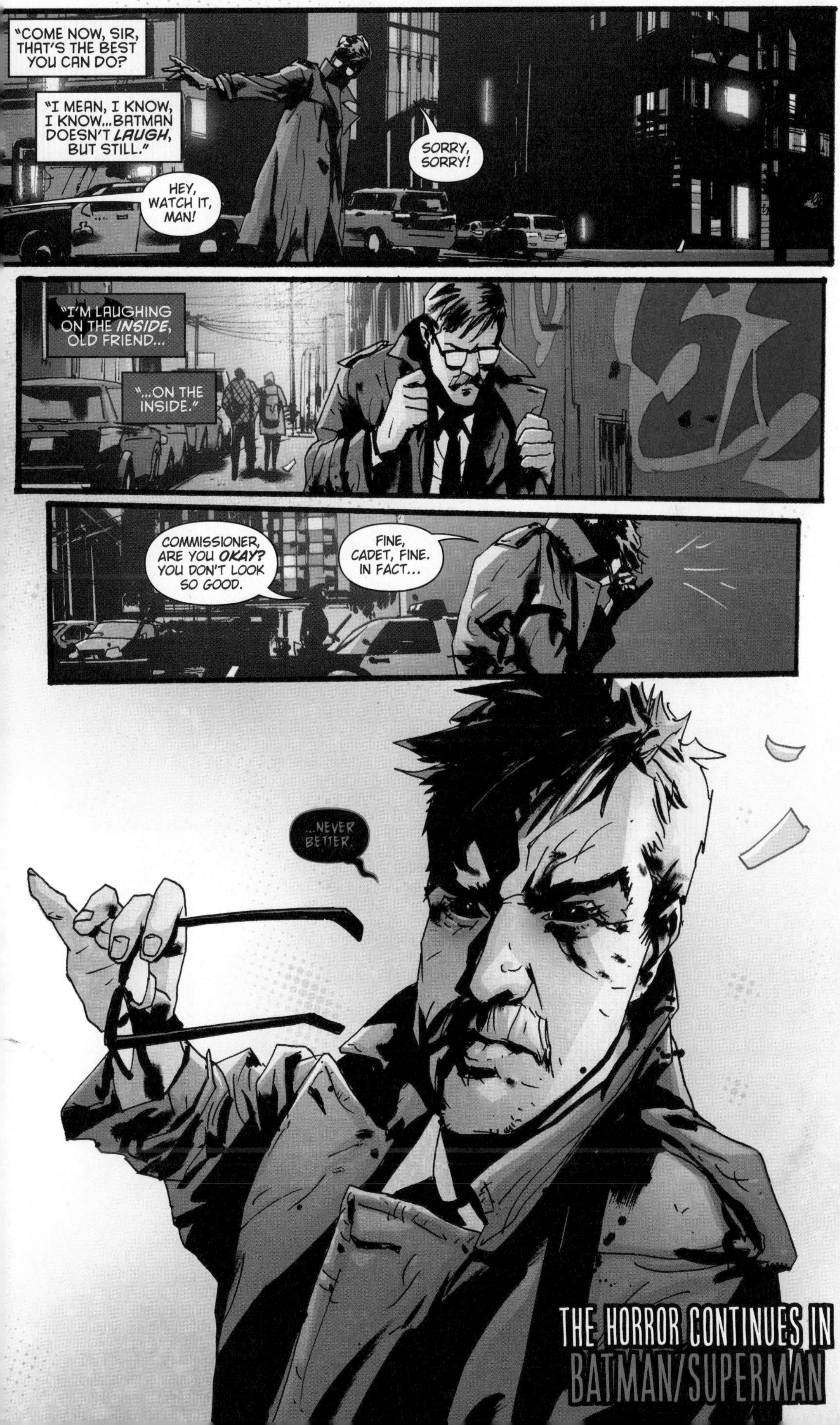
"COME NOW, SIR, THAT'S THE BEST YOU CAN DO?
"I MEAN, I KNOW, I KNOW... BATMAN DOESN'T LAUGH, BUT STILL."
SORRY, SORRY!
HEY, WATCH IT, MAN!
"I'M LAUGHING ON THE INSIDE, OLD FRIEND...
"...ON THE INSIDE."
COMMISSIONER, ARE YOU OKAY? YOU DON'T LOOK SO GOOD.
FINE, CADET, FINE. IN FACT...
...NEVER BETTER.
THE HORROR CONTINUES IN
BATMAN/SUPERMAN

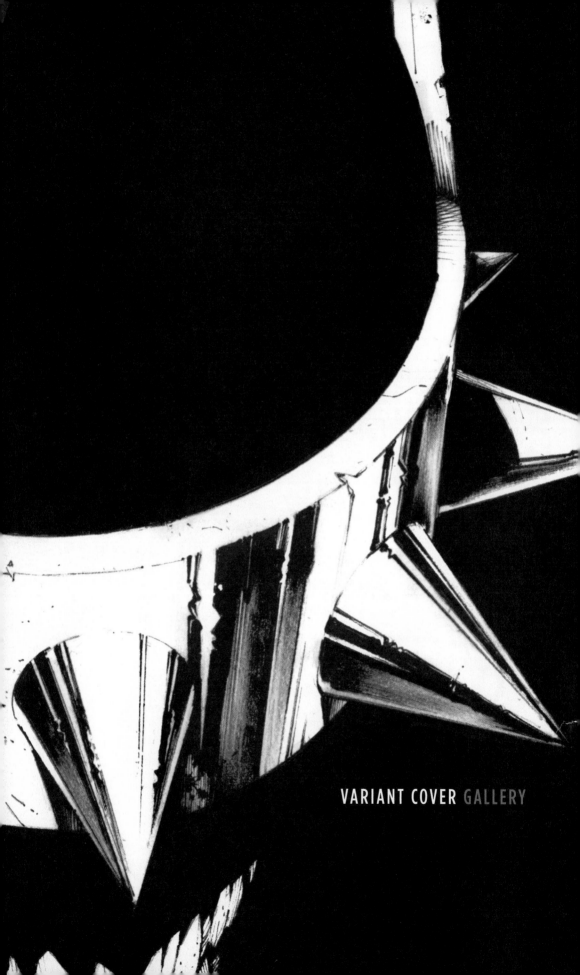

VARIANT COVER GALLERY

THE BATMAN WHO LAUGHS #1
variant cover by GREG CAPULLO and FCO PLASCENCIA

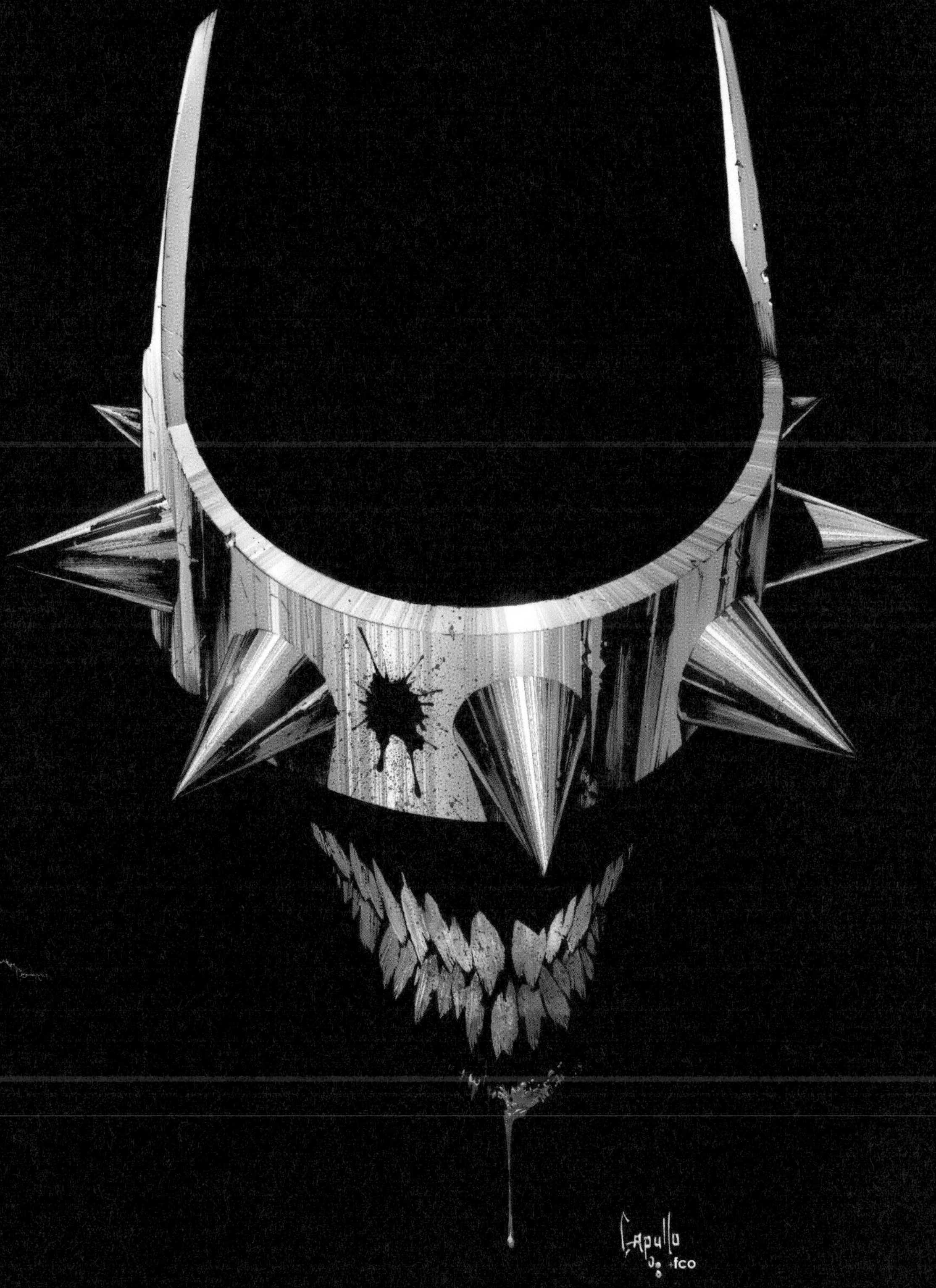
Capullo
+fco

THE BATMAN WHO LAUGHS #2
variant cover by BEN OLIVER

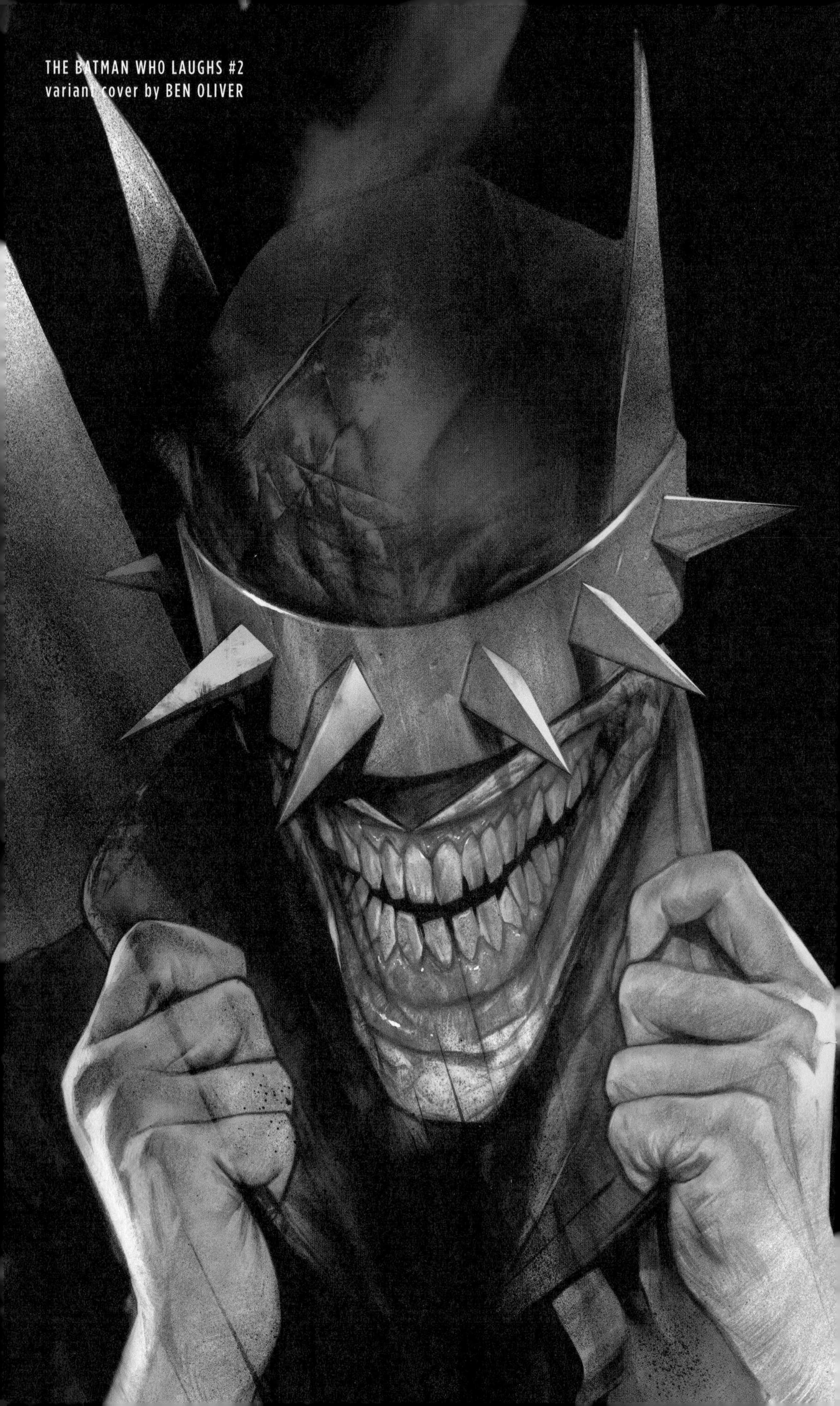

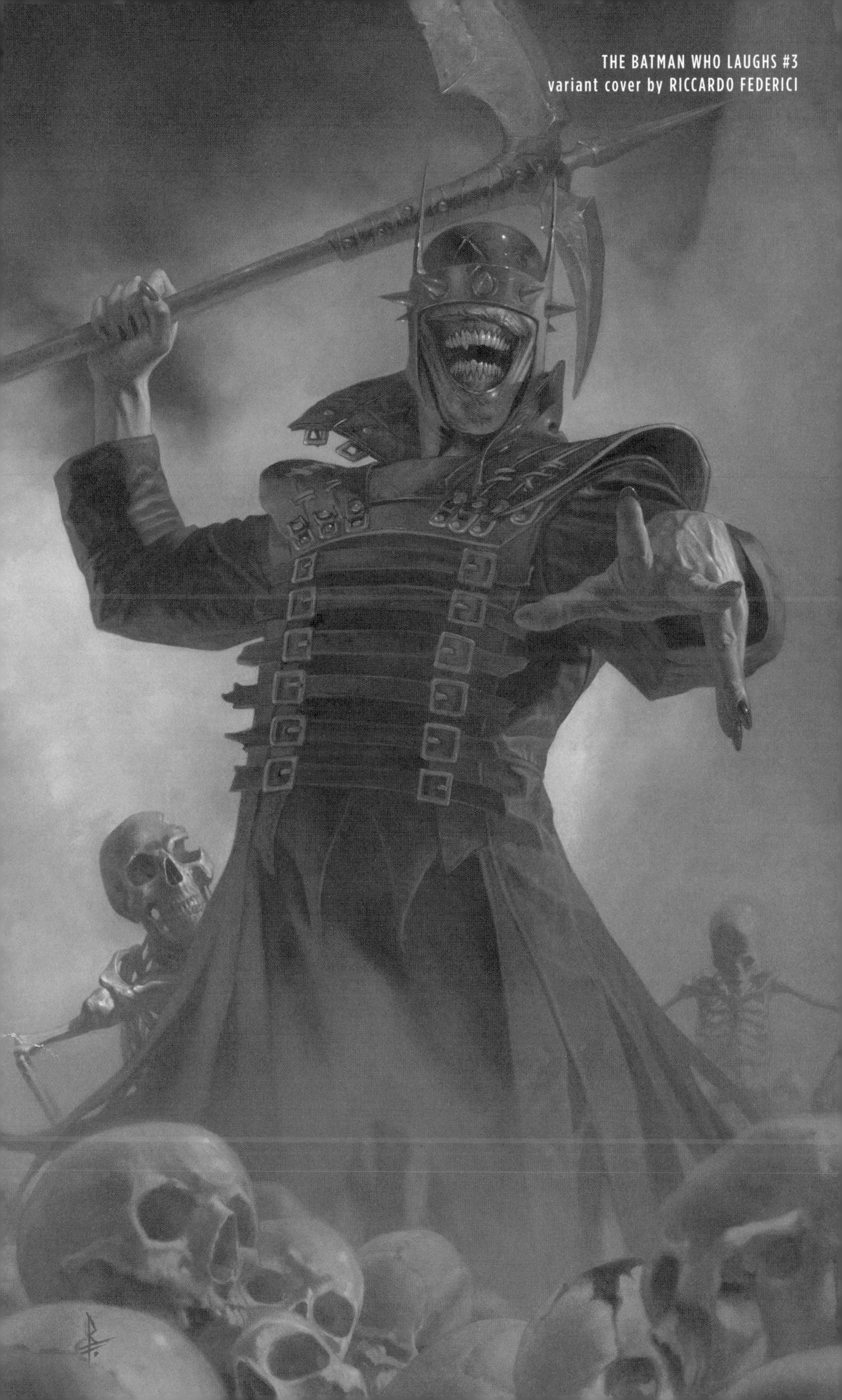

THE BATMAN WHO LAUGHS #3
variant cover by RICCARDO FEDERICI

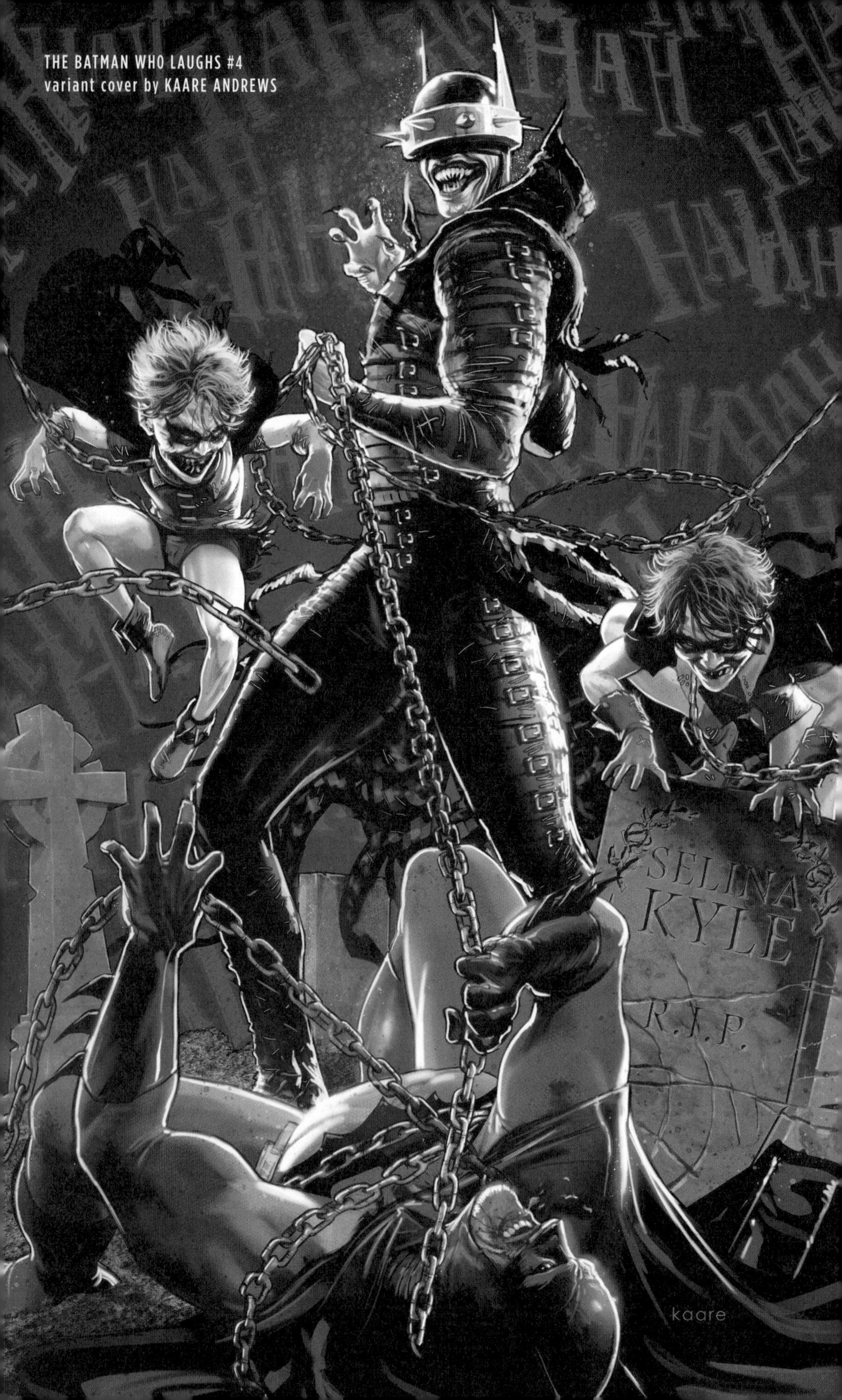
SELINA
KYLE
R.I.P.
kaare

THE BATMAN WHO LAUGHS #4
variant cover by KAARE ANDREWS

THE BATMAN WHO LAUGHS #5
variant cover by VIKTOR KALVACHEV

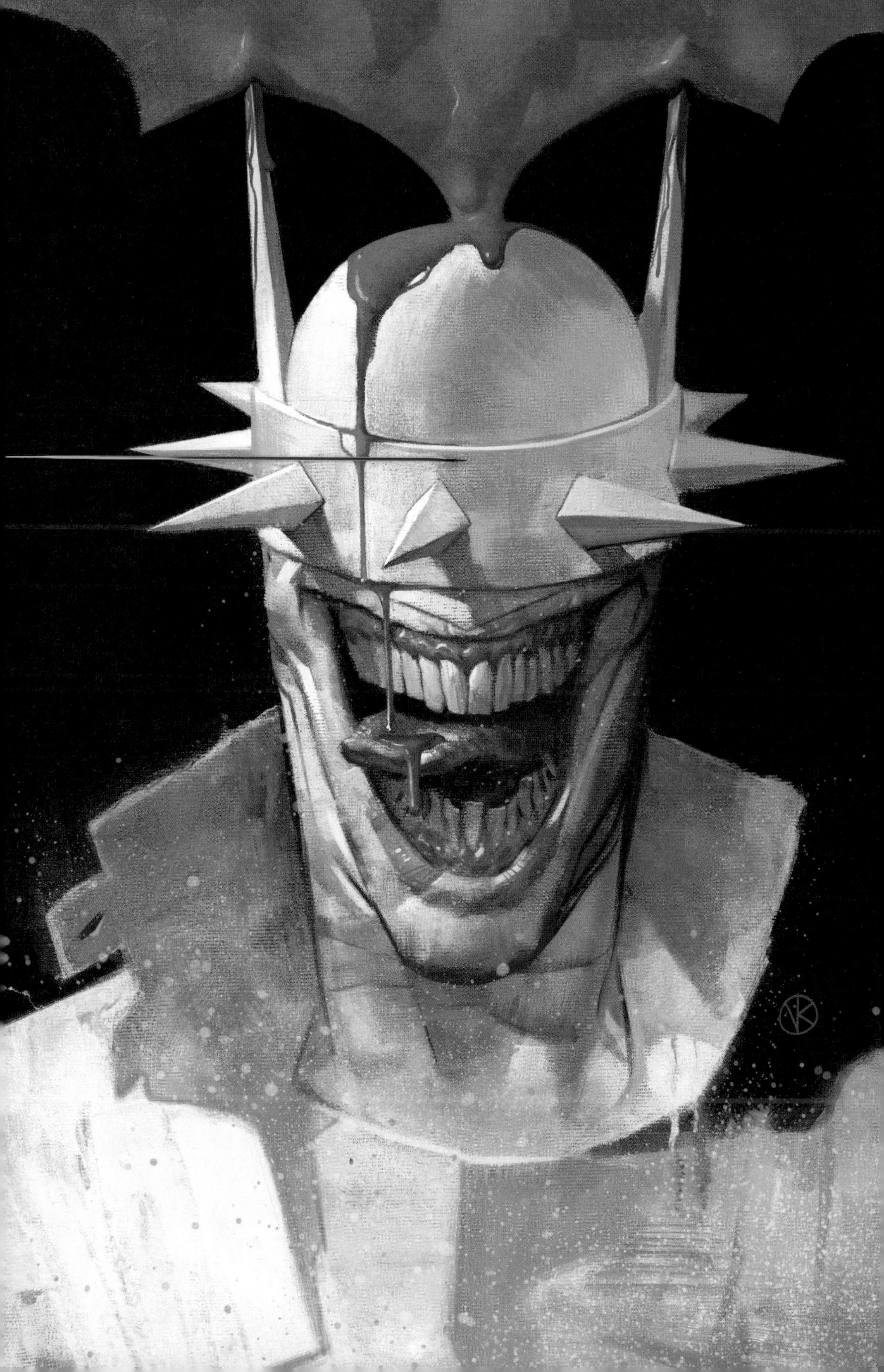

THE BATMAN WHO LAUGHS #6
variant cover by JENNY FRISON

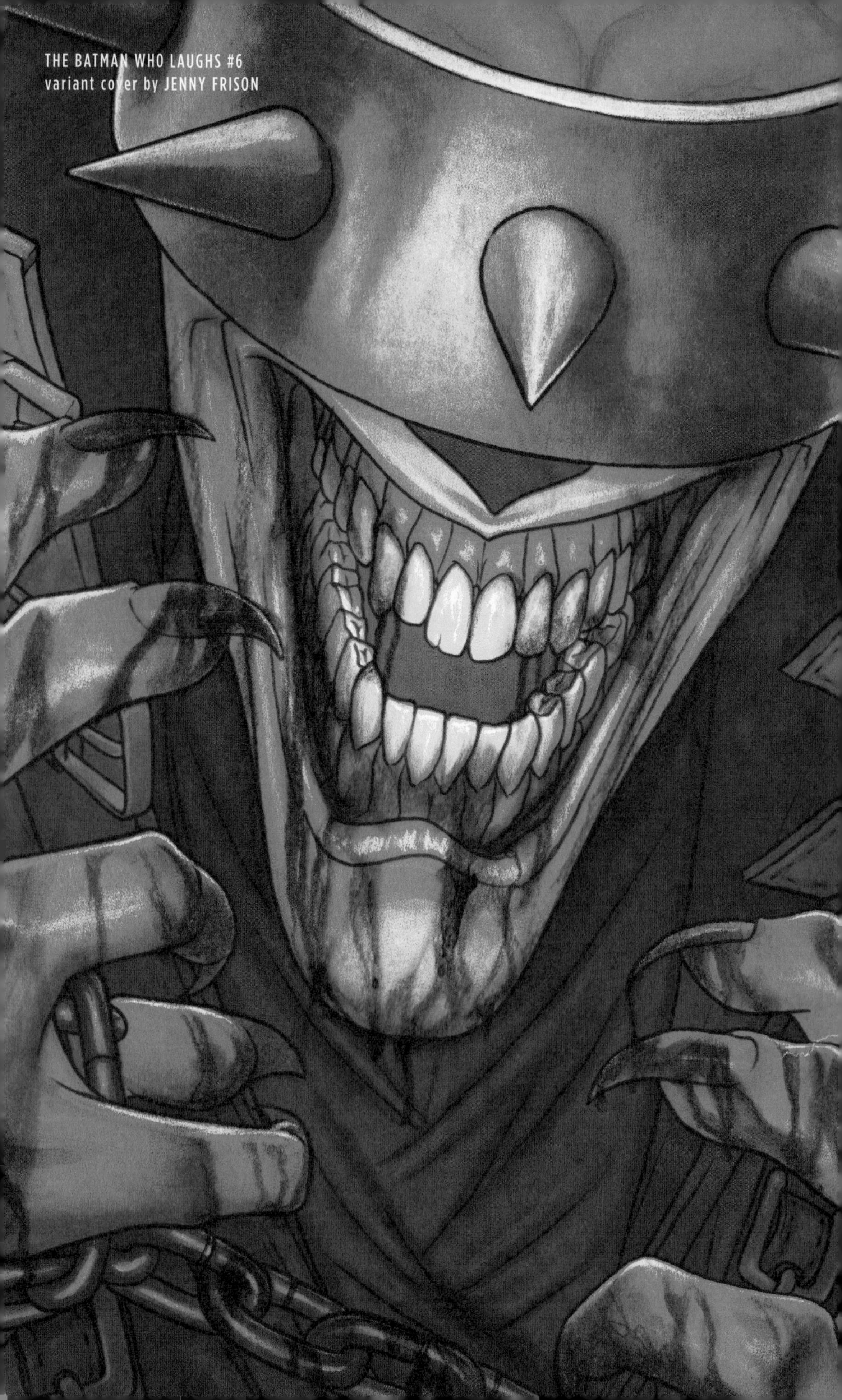

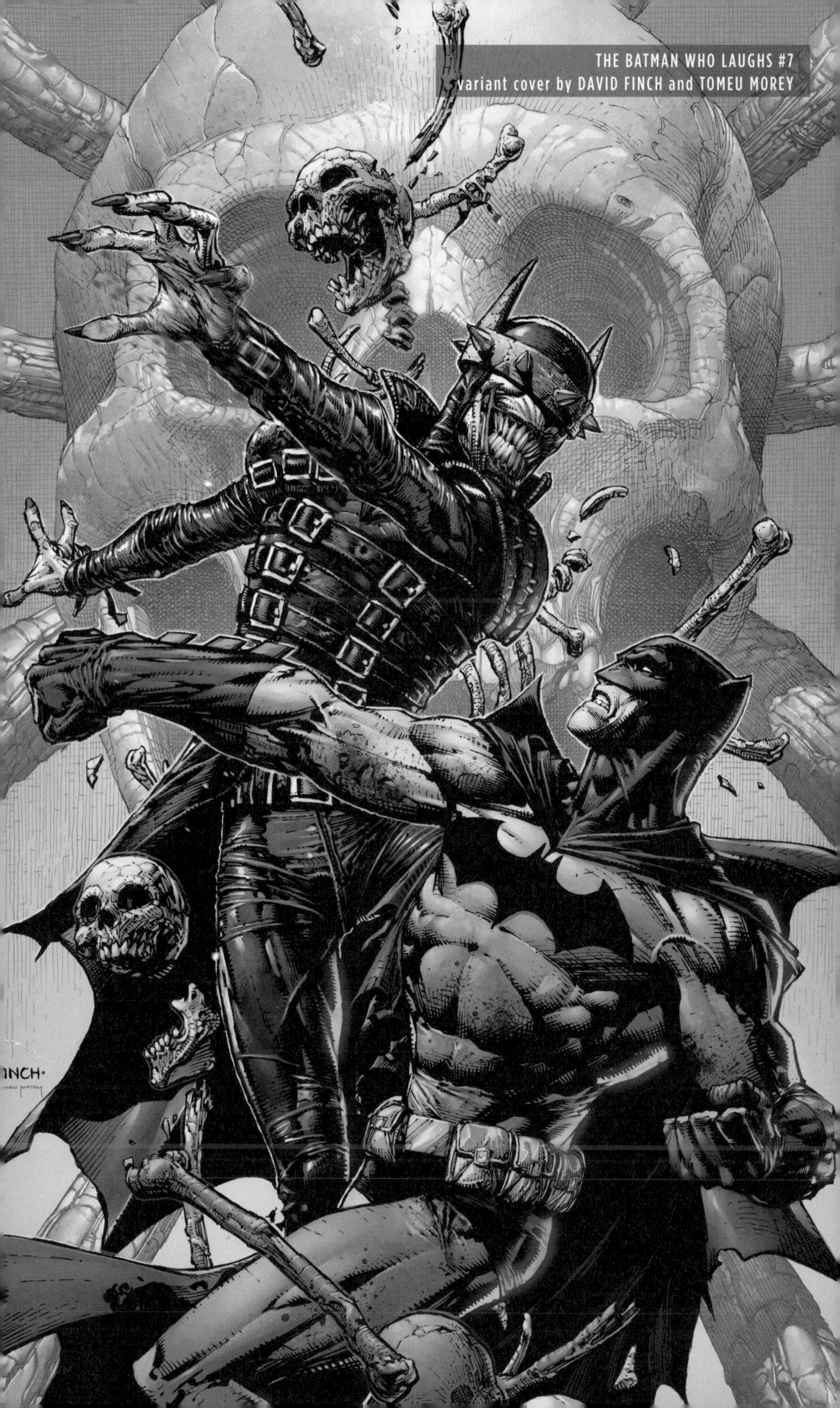

THE BATMAN WHO LAUGHS #7
variant cover by DAVID FINCH and TOMEU MOREY

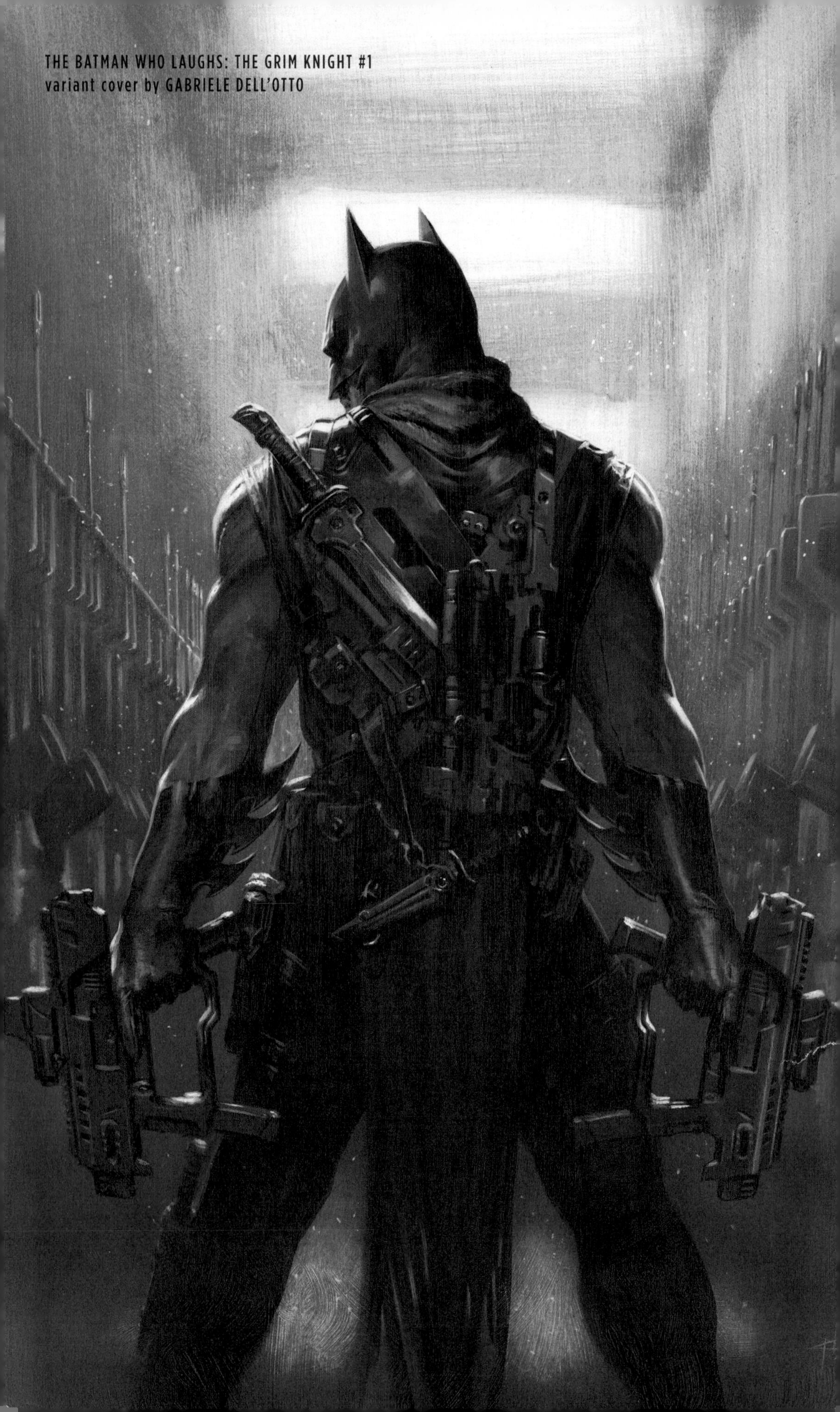

THE BATMAN WHO LAUGHS: THE GRIM KNIGHT #1
variant cover by GABRIELE DELL'OTTO

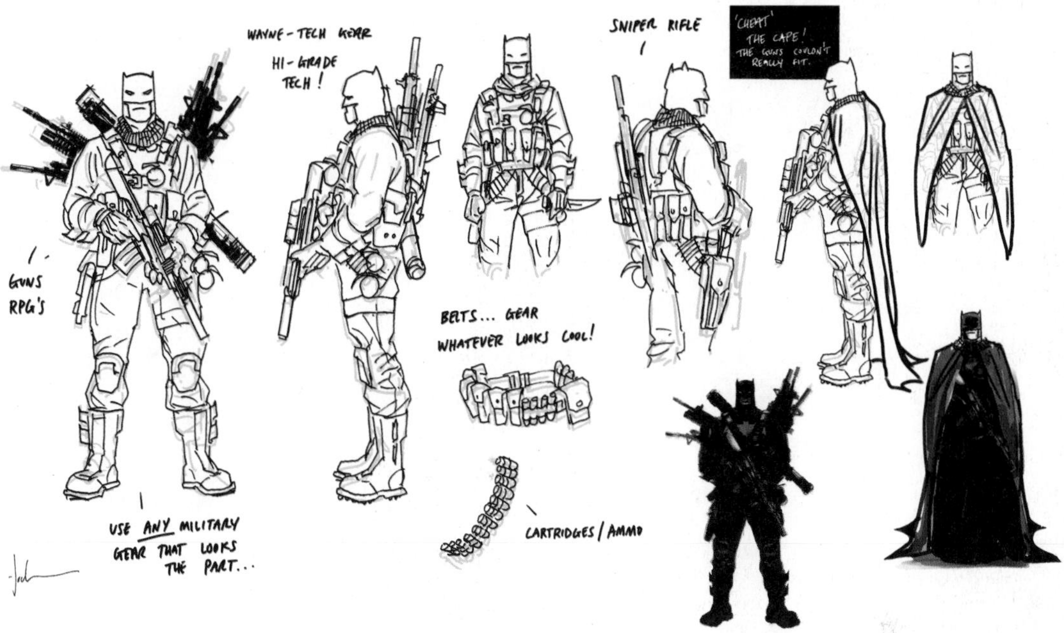
WAYNE-TECH GEAR
HI-GRADE TECH!
SNIPER RIFLE
'CHEAT' THE CAPE! THE GUNS COULDN'T REALLY FIT.
GUNS RPG'S
BELTS... GEAR WHATEVER LOOKS COOL!
USE ANY MILITARY GEAR THAT LOOKS THE PART...
CARTRIDGES / AMMO

Grim Knight character turnaround by Jock

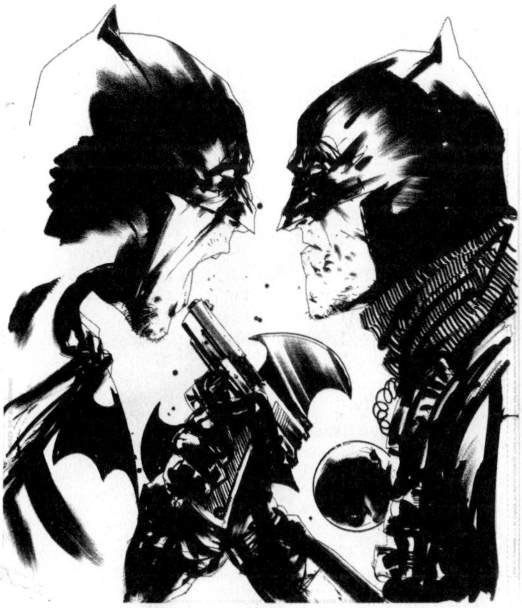

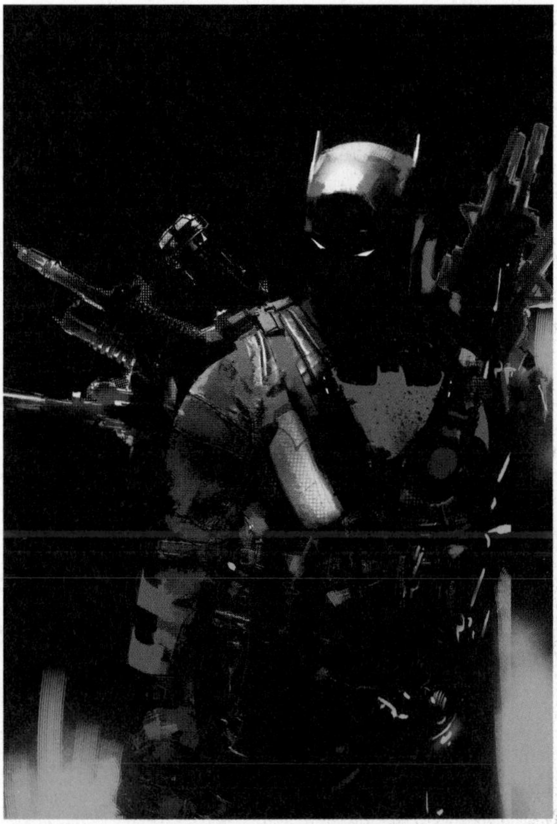

Two unused cover ideas by Jock

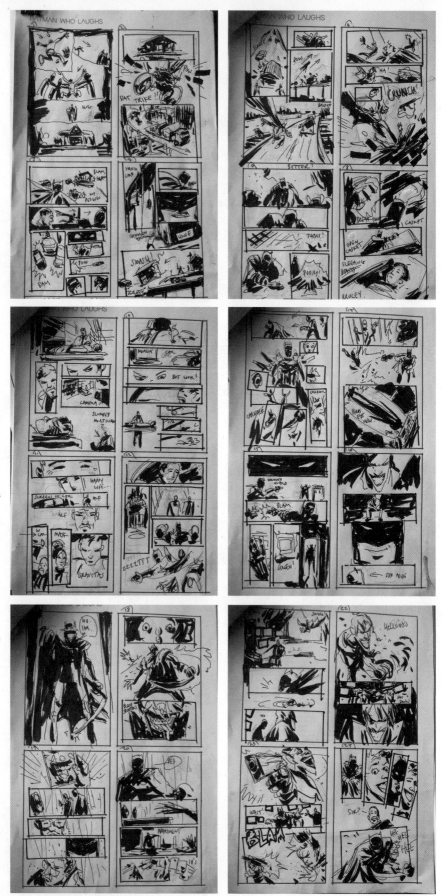

Page layouts for Issue #1 pages 1-6 by Jock